GUARDI
OF THE G

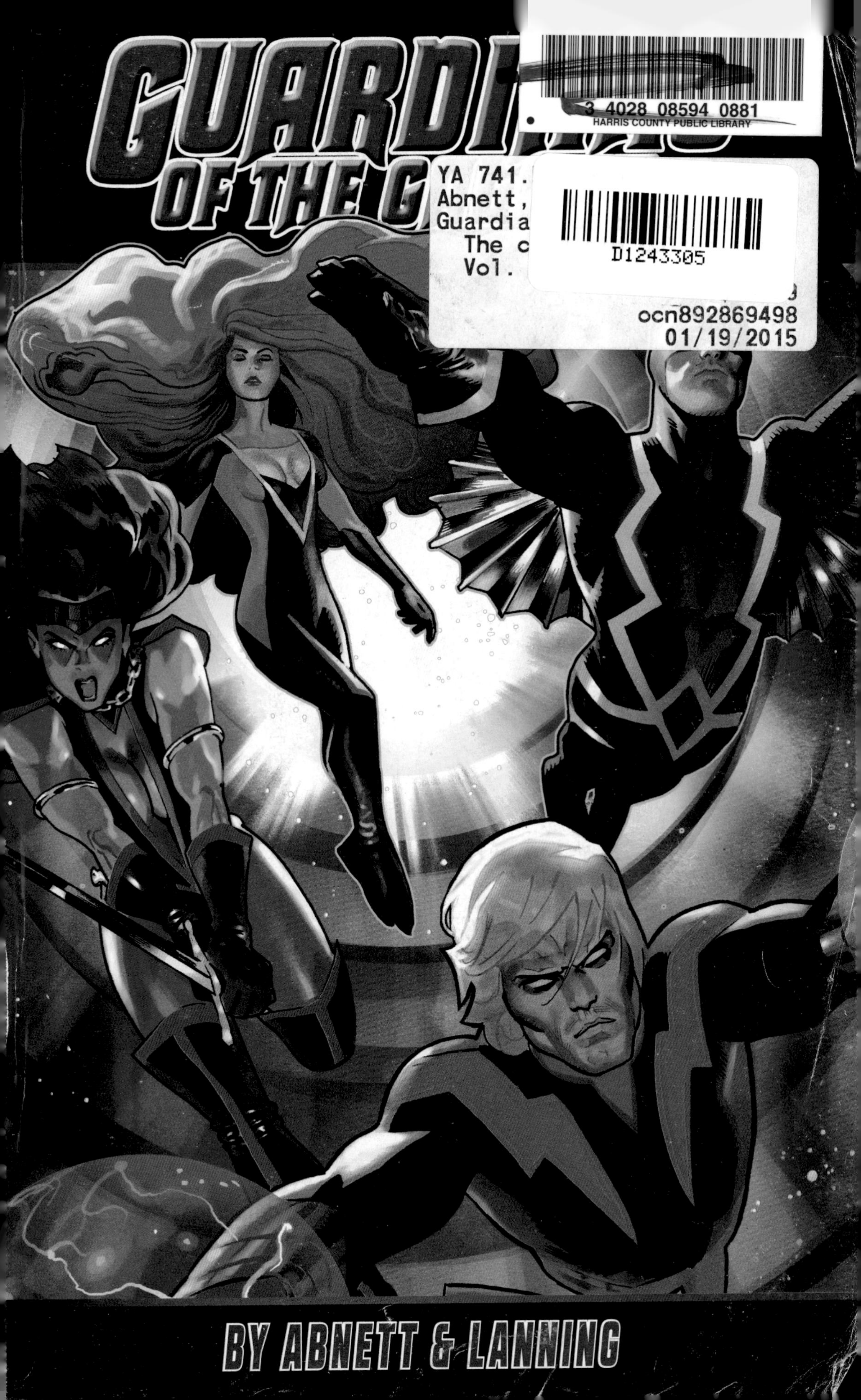

BY ABNETT & LANNING

GUARDIANS OF THE GALAXY

WRITERS

DAN ABNETT & ANDY LANNING

PENCILERS

BRAD WALKER (#13-15, #17, #20-22 & #25)
& WES CRAIG (#16, #18-19 & #23-24)

INKERS

VICTOR OLAZABA (#13-15, #17 & #20-21), WES CRAIG (#16 & #18-19),
ANDREW HENNESSY (#21-22 & #25) & SERGE LAPOINTE (#23-24)
with LIVESAY (#15) & SCOTT HANNA (#17)

COLORISTS

WIL QUINTANA (#13, #20-22 & #25), JAY DAVID RAMOS (#14-15 & #17) &
NATHAN FAIRBAIRN (#16, #18-19 & #23-24)

LETTERERS

VC'S JOE CARAMAGNA with CHRIS ELIOPOULOS (#15)

COVER ART

SALVADOR LARROCA & FRANK D'ARMATA (#13-15), PASQUAL FERRY
& FRANK D'ARMATA (#16 & #18), DANIEL ACUÑA (#17), ALEX GARNER
(#19-20 & #22-25) and DAVE WILKINS (#21)

ASSISTANT EDITORS

MICHAEL HORWITZ & RACHEL PINNELAS

EDITOR

BILL ROSEMANN

COLLECTION EDITOR: Mark D. Beazley • DIGITAL TRAFFIC COORDINATOR: Joe Hochstein
ASSOCIATE MANAGING EDITOR: Alex Starbuck • EDITOR, SPECIAL PROJECTS: Jennifer Grünwald
SENIOR EDITOR, SPECIAL PROJECTS: Jeff Youngquist • LAYOUT: Jeph York
SVP PRINT, SALES & MARKETING: David Gabriel • EDITOR IN CHIEF: Axel Alonso
CHIEF CREATIVE OFFICER: Joe Quesada • PUBLISHER: Dan Buckley • EXECUTIVE PRODUCER: Alan Fine

GUARDIANS OF THE GALAXY BY ABNETT & LANNING: THE COMPLETE COLLECTION VOL. 2. Contains material originally published in magazine form as GUARDIANS OF THE GALAXY #13-25. First printing 2014. ISBN# 978-0-7851-9063-9. Published by MARVEL WORLDWIDE, INC., a subsidiary of MARVEL ENTERTAINMENT, LLC. OFFICE OF PUBLICATION: 135 West 50th Street, New York, NY 10020. **Printed in the U.S.A.** ALAN FINE, EVP - Office of the President, Marvel Worldwide, Inc. and EVP & CMO Marvel Characters B.V.; DAN BUCKLEY, Publisher & President - Print, Animation & Digital Divisions; JOE QUESADA, Chief Creative Officer; TOM BREVOORT, SVP of Publishing; DAVID BOGART, SVP of Operations & Procurement, Publishing; C.B. CEBULSKI, SVP of Creator & Content Development; DAVID GABRIEL, SVP Print, Sales & Marketing; JIM O'KEEFE, VP of Operations & Logistics; DAN CARR, Executive Director of Publishing Technology; SUSAN CRESPI, Editorial Operations Manager; ALEX MORALES, Publishing Operations Manager; STAN LEE, Chairman Emeritus. For information regarding advertising in Marvel Comics or on Marvel.com, please contact Niza Disla, Director of Marvel Partnerships, at ndisla@marvel.com. For Marvel subscription inquiries, please call 800-217-9158.

IN THE WAKE OF TWO CATASTROPHIC ANNIHILATION EVENTS, THE UNIVERSE IS IN A FRAGILE AND WEAKENED STATE. WITH THE FABRIC OF SPACE ITSELF DAMAGED, ANOMALOUS FISSURES ARE BEGINNING TO APPEAR, FISSURES THAT COULD CRACK AND SPREAD, COLLAPSING REALITY AND LETTING IN THINGS THAT SHOULD NOT EXIST IN OUR DIMENSION.

GUIDED BY THE MYSTICAL INSIGHT OF THE NEWLY RETURNED ADAM WARLOCK, THE GUN-SLINGING STAR-LORD HAS FORGED A PROACTIVE TEAM OF PROVEN COSMIC CHAMPIONS READY TO PROTECT THE VULNERABLE UNIVERSE AND PREVENT ANY LARGE-SCALE DISASTERS FROM EVER HAPPENING AGAIN. TOGETHER, STAR-LORD, WARLOCK, GAMORA, DRAX, MANTIS AND ROCKET RACCOON ARE THE GUARDIANS OF THE GALAXY!

WITH PORTENTS WARNING OF AN APPROACHING CALAMITY, STAR-LORD RE-FORMED HIS RECENTLY FRACTURED TEAM IN TIME TO FACE IT. NEW ADDITIONS INCLUDE EARTHMAN AND FORMER VIGILANTE JACK FLAG, THE RESURRECTED MOONDRAGON, AND MARTYR, PHYLA-VELL'S NEW MORBID ALTER EGO. THE TEAM APPEARS TO BE BACK AT FULL STRENGTH.

HOWEVER, THE OPENING SHOTS OF THE WAR OF KINGS — A MASSIVE CONFLICT BETWEEN THE SHI'AR IMPERIUM AND THE KREE STELLAR EMPIRE — HAVE ALREADY BEEN FIRED, AND THE GUARDIANS OF THE GALAXY MAY FIND THEMSELVES IN DEEP TROUBLE SOONER THAN THEY IMAGINE...

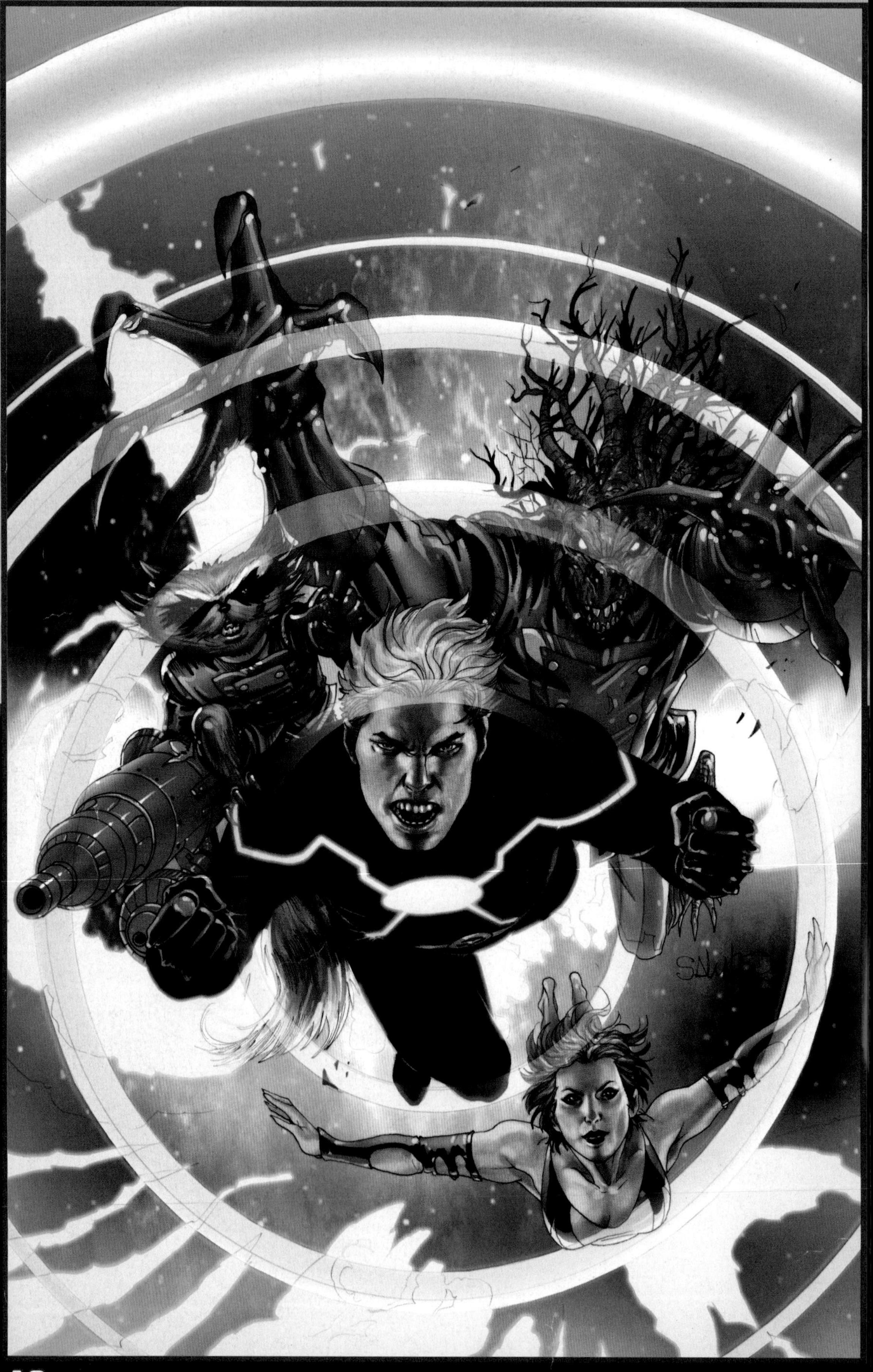

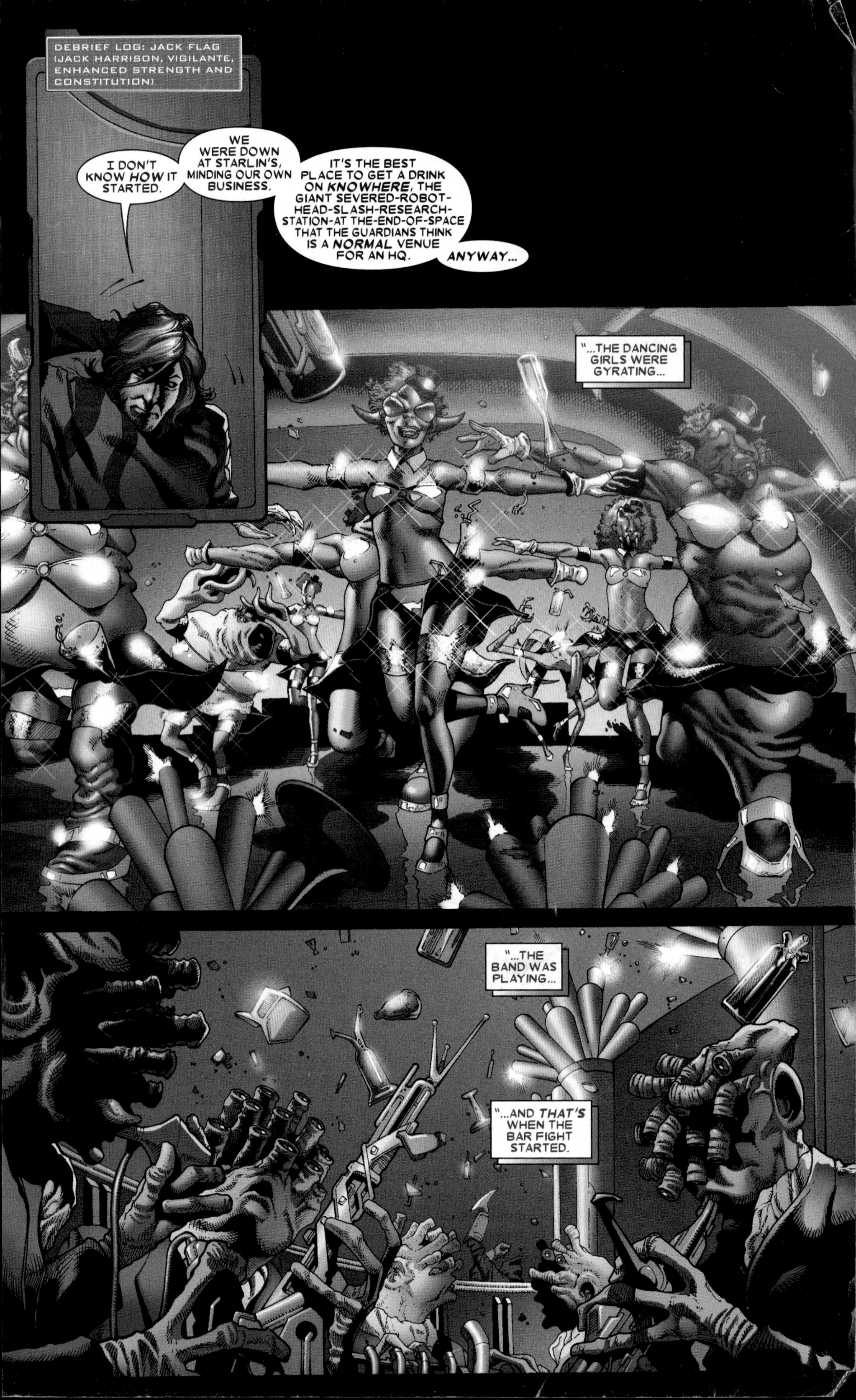

DEBRIEF LOG: JACK FLAG (JACK HARRISON, VIGILANTE, ENHANCED STRENGTH AND CONSTITUTION)
I DON'T KNOW *HOW* IT STARTED.
WE WERE DOWN AT STARLIN'S, MINDING OUR OWN BUSINESS.
IT'S THE BEST PLACE TO GET A DRINK ON *KNOWHERE*, THE GIANT SEVERED-ROBOT-HEAD-SLASH-RESEARCH-STATION-AT-THE-END-OF-SPACE THAT THE GUARDIANS THINK IS A *NORMAL* VENUE FOR AN HQ.
ANYWAY...
"...THE DANCING GIRLS WERE GYRATING...
"...THE BAND WAS PLAYING...
"...AND *THAT'S* WHEN THE BAR FIGHT STARTED.

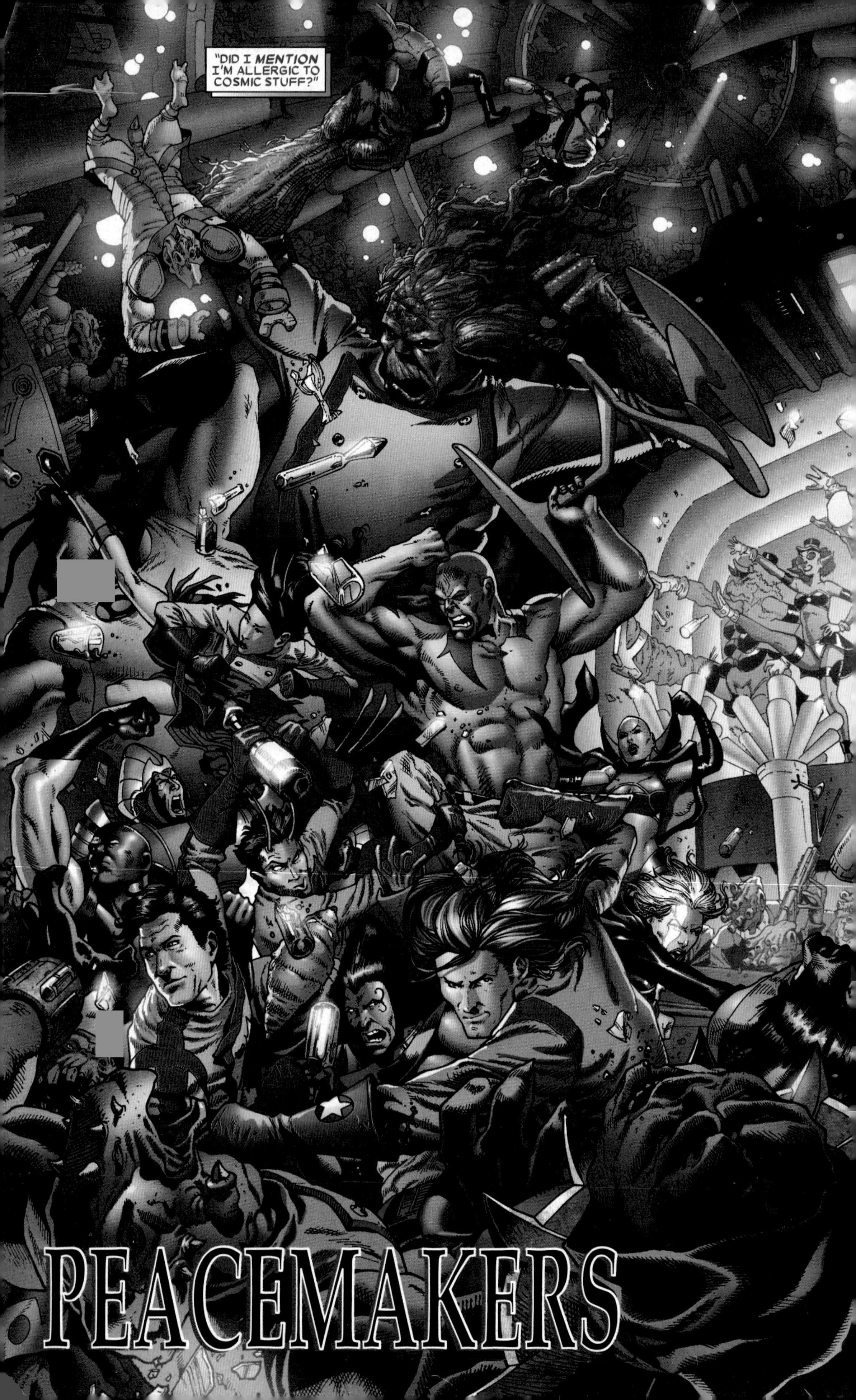
"DID I *MENTION* I'M ALLERGIC TO COSMIC STUFF?"
PEACEMAKERS

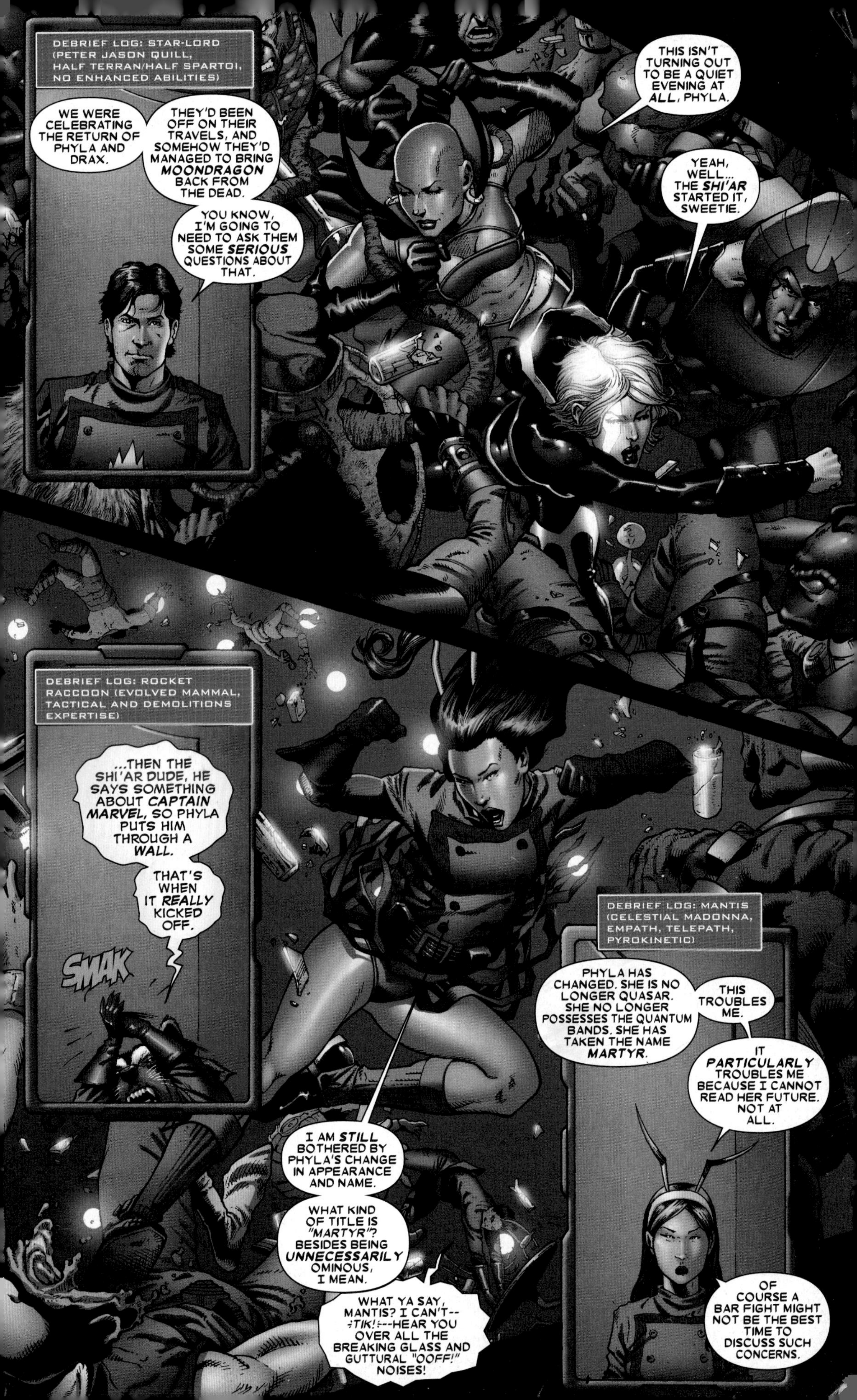
DEBRIEF LOG: STAR-LORD (PETER JASON QUILL, HALF TERRAN/HALF SPARTOI, NO ENHANCED ABILITIES)
WE WERE CELEBRATING THE RETURN OF PHYLA AND DRAX.
THEY'D BEEN OFF ON THEIR TRAVELS, AND SOMEHOW THEY'D MANAGED TO BRING MOONDRAGON BACK FROM THE DEAD.
YOU KNOW, I'M GOING TO NEED TO ASK THEM SOME SERIOUS QUESTIONS ABOUT THAT.
THIS ISN'T TURNING OUT TO BE A QUIET EVENING AT ALL, PHYLA.
YEAH, WELL... THE SHI'AR STARTED IT, SWEETIE.
DEBRIEF LOG: ROCKET RACCOON (EVOLVED MAMMAL, TACTICAL AND DEMOLITIONS EXPERTISE)
...THEN THE SHI'AR DUDE, HE SAYS SOMETHING ABOUT CAPTAIN MARVEL, SO PHYLA PUTS HIM THROUGH A WALL.
THAT'S WHEN IT REALLY KICKED OFF.
SMAK
DEBRIEF LOG: MANTIS (CELESTIAL MADONNA, EMPATH, TELEPATH, PYROKINETIC)
PHYLA HAS CHANGED. SHE IS NO LONGER QUASAR. SHE NO LONGER POSSESSES THE QUANTUM BANDS. SHE HAS TAKEN THE NAME MARTYR.
THIS TROUBLES ME.
IT PARTICULARLY TROUBLES ME BECAUSE I CANNOT READ HER FUTURE. NOT AT ALL.
I AM STILL BOTHERED BY PHYLA'S CHANGE IN APPEARANCE AND NAME.
WHAT KIND OF TITLE IS "MARTYR"? BESIDES BEING UNNECESSARILY OMINOUS, I MEAN.
WHAT YA SAY, MANTIS? I CAN'T-- -TIK!- --HEAR YOU OVER ALL THE BREAKING GLASS AND GUTTURAL "OOFF!" NOISES!
OF COURSE A BAR FIGHT MIGHT NOT BE THE BEST TIME TO DISCUSS SUCH CONCERNS.

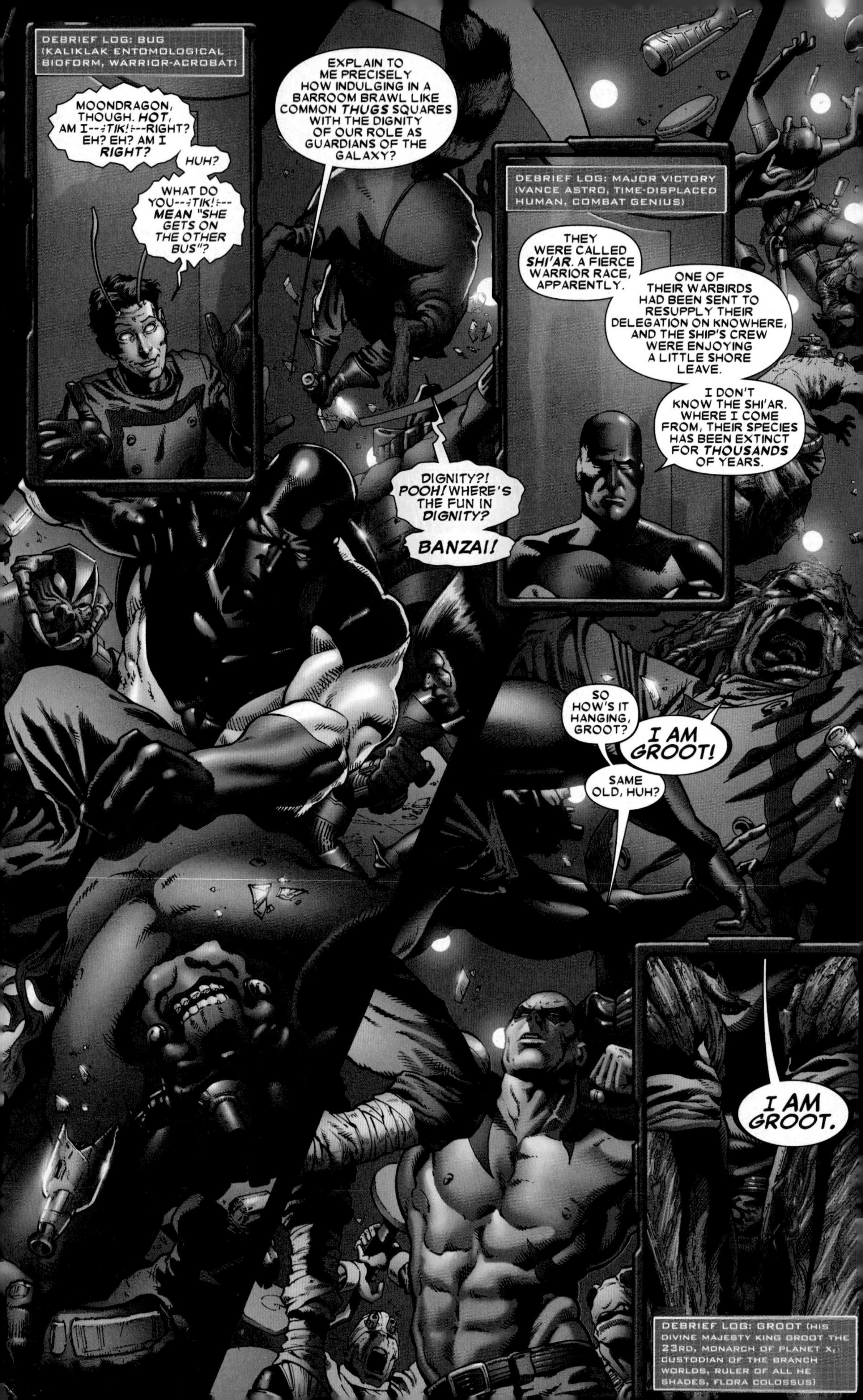

DEBRIEF LOG: BUG (KALIKLAK ENTOMOLOGICAL BIOFORM, WARRIOR-ACROBAT)
MOONDRAGON, THOUGH. HOT, AM I--¡TIK!--RIGHT? EH? EH? AM I RIGHT?
HUH?
WHAT DO YOU--¡TIK!--MEAN "SHE GETS ON THE OTHER BUS"?
EXPLAIN TO ME PRECISELY HOW INDULGING IN A BARROOM BRAWL LIKE COMMON THUGS SQUARES WITH THE DIGNITY OF OUR ROLE AS GUARDIANS OF THE GALAXY?
DIGNITY?! POOH! WHERE'S THE FUN IN DIGNITY?
BANZAI!
DEBRIEF LOG: MAJOR VICTORY (VANCE ASTRO, TIME-DISPLACED HUMAN, COMBAT GENIUS)
THEY WERE CALLED SHI'AR. A FIERCE WARRIOR RACE, APPARENTLY.
ONE OF THEIR WARBIRDS HAD BEEN SENT TO RESUPPLY THEIR DELEGATION ON KNOWHERE, AND THE SHIP'S CREW WERE ENJOYING A LITTLE SHORE LEAVE.
I DON'T KNOW THE SHI'AR. WHERE I COME FROM, THEIR SPECIES HAS BEEN EXTINCT FOR THOUSANDS OF YEARS.
SO HOW'S IT HANGING, GROOT?
I AM GROOT!
SAME OLD, HUH?
I AM GROOT.
DEBRIEF LOG: GROOT (HIS DIVINE MAJESTY KING GROOT THE 23RD, MONARCH OF PLANET X, CUSTODIAN OF THE BRANCH WORLDS, RULER OF ALL HE SHADES, FLORA COLOSSUS)

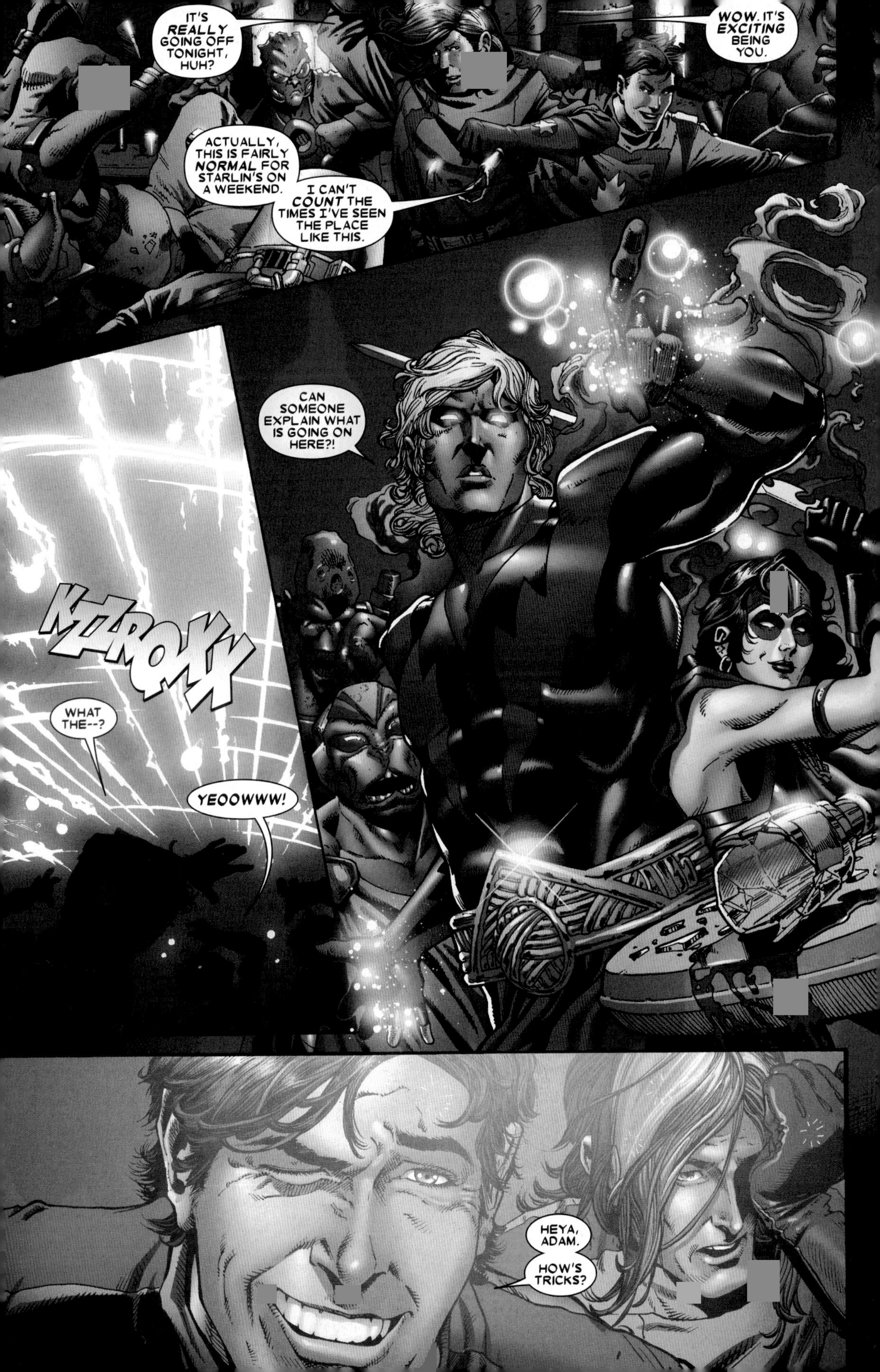
IT'S REALLY GOING OFF TONIGHT, HUH?
WOW. IT'S EXCITING BEING YOU.
ACTUALLY, THIS IS FAIRLY NORMAL FOR STARLIN'S ON A WEEKEND.
I CAN'T COUNT THE TIMES I'VE SEEN THE PLACE LIKE THIS.
CAN SOMEONE EXPLAIN WHAT IS GOING ON HERE?!
KZZROKK
WHAT THE--?
YEOOWWW!
HEYA, ADAM.
HOW'S TRICKS?

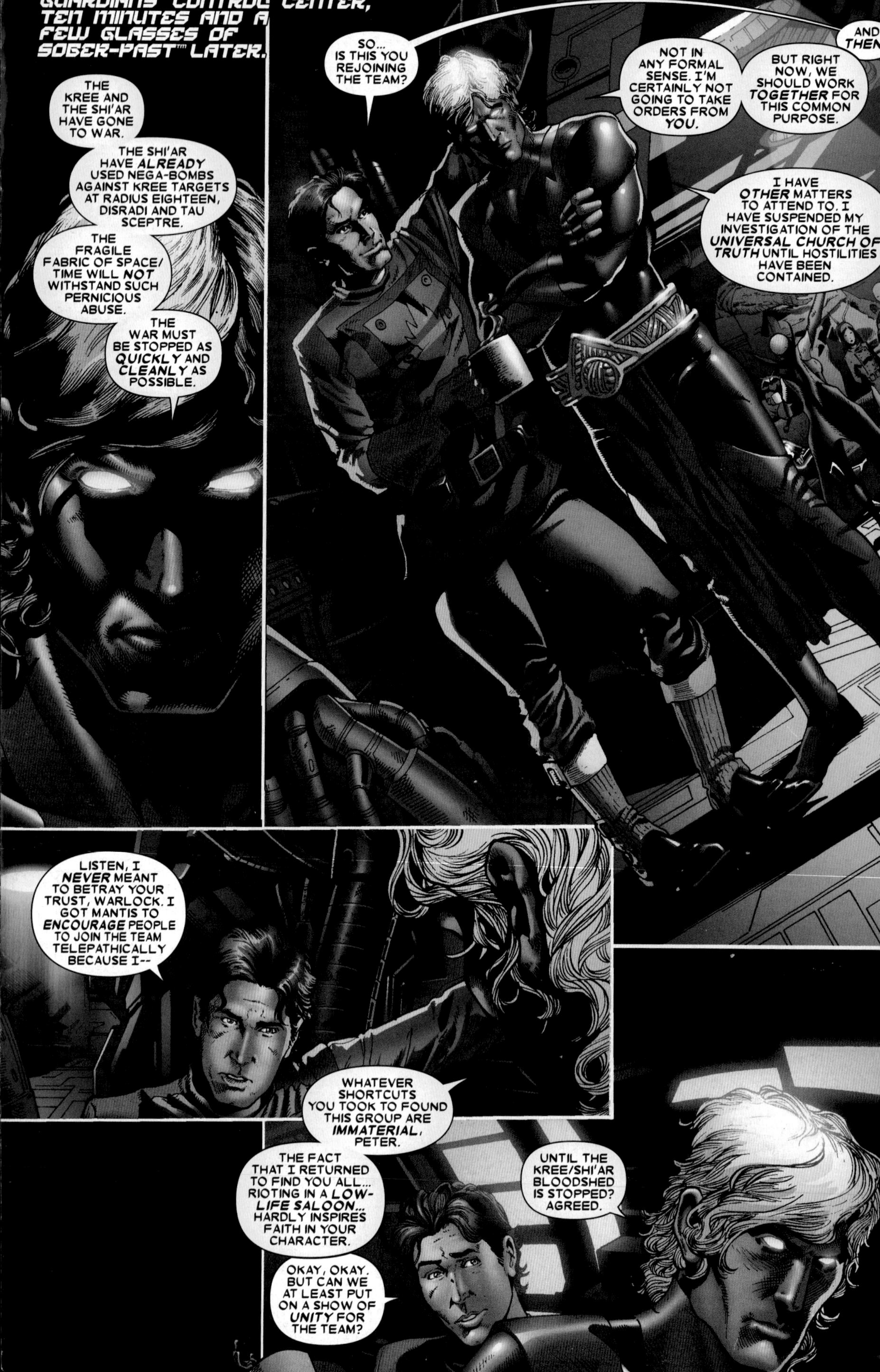
GUARDIANS' CONTROL CENTER, TEN MINUTES AND A FEW GLASSES OF SOBER-PAST™ LATER.
THE KREE AND THE SHI'AR HAVE GONE TO WAR.
THE SHI'AR HAVE ALREADY USED NEGA-BOMBS AGAINST KREE TARGETS AT RADIUS EIGHTEEN, DISRADI AND TAU SCEPTRE.
THE FRAGILE FABRIC OF SPACE/TIME WILL NOT WITHSTAND SUCH PERNICIOUS ABUSE.
THE WAR MUST BE STOPPED AS QUICKLY AND CLEANLY AS POSSIBLE.
SO... IS THIS YOU REJOINING THE TEAM?
NOT IN ANY FORMAL SENSE. I'M CERTAINLY NOT GOING TO TAKE ORDERS FROM YOU.
BUT RIGHT NOW, WE SHOULD WORK TOGETHER FOR THIS COMMON PURPOSE.
AND THEN
I HAVE OTHER MATTERS TO ATTEND TO. I HAVE SUSPENDED MY INVESTIGATION OF THE UNIVERSAL CHURCH OF TRUTH UNTIL HOSTILITIES HAVE BEEN CONTAINED.
LISTEN, I NEVER MEANT TO BETRAY YOUR TRUST, WARLOCK. I GOT MANTIS TO ENCOURAGE PEOPLE TO JOIN THE TEAM TELEPATHICALLY BECAUSE I--
WHATEVER SHORTCUTS YOU TOOK TO FOUND THIS GROUP ARE IMMATERIAL, PETER.
THE FACT THAT I RETURNED TO FIND YOU ALL... RIOTING IN A LOW-LIFE SALOON... HARDLY INSPIRES FAITH IN YOUR CHARACTER.
OKAY, OKAY. BUT CAN WE AT LEAST PUT ON A SHOW OF UNITY FOR THE TEAM?
UNTIL THE KREE/SHI'AR BLOODSHED IS STOPPED? AGREED.

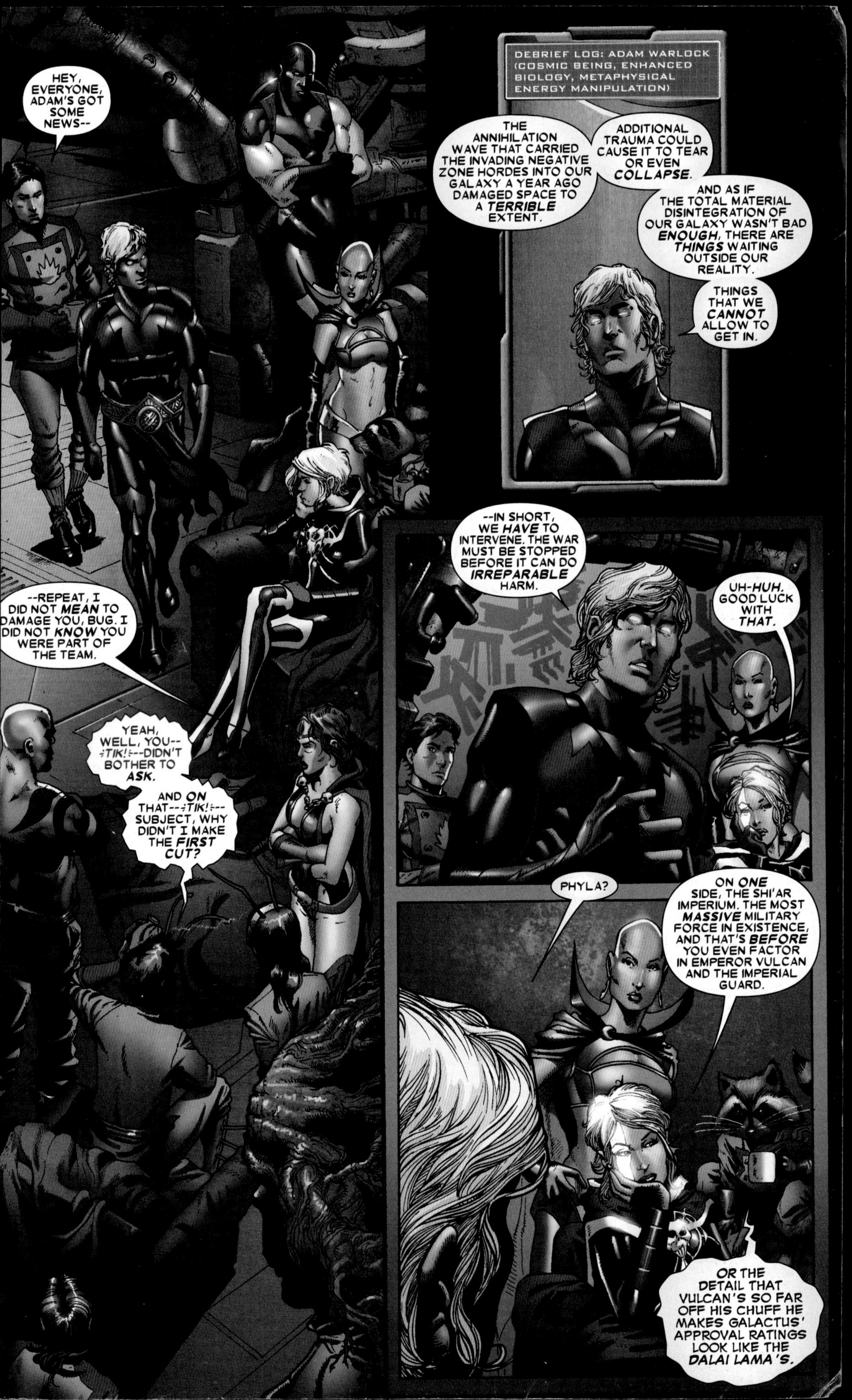
HEY, EVERYONE, ADAM'S GOT SOME NEWS--
DEBRIEF LOG: ADAM WARLOCK (COSMIC BEING, ENHANCED BIOLOGY, METAPHYSICAL ENERGY MANIPULATION)
THE ANNIHILATION WAVE THAT CARRIED THE INVADING NEGATIVE ZONE HORDES INTO OUR GALAXY A YEAR AGO DAMAGED SPACE TO A TERRIBLE EXTENT.
ADDITIONAL TRAUMA COULD CAUSE IT TO TEAR OR EVEN COLLAPSE.
AND AS IF THE TOTAL MATERIAL DISINTEGRATION OF OUR GALAXY WASN'T BAD ENOUGH, THERE ARE THINGS WAITING OUTSIDE OUR REALITY.
THINGS THAT WE CANNOT ALLOW TO GET IN.
--REPEAT, I DID NOT MEAN TO DAMAGE YOU, BUG. I DID NOT KNOW YOU WERE PART OF THE TEAM.
YEAH, WELL, YOU-- ÷TIK!÷--DIDN'T BOTHER TO ASK.
AND ON THAT--÷TIK!÷-- SUBJECT, WHY DIDN'T I MAKE THE FIRST CUT?
--IN SHORT, WE HAVE TO INTERVENE. THE WAR MUST BE STOPPED BEFORE IT CAN DO IRREPARABLE HARM.
UH-HUH. GOOD LUCK WITH THAT.
PHYLA?
ON ONE SIDE, THE SHI'AR IMPERIUM. THE MOST MASSIVE MILITARY FORCE IN EXISTENCE, AND THAT'S BEFORE YOU EVEN FACTOR IN EMPEROR VULCAN AND THE IMPERIAL GUARD.
OR THE DETAIL THAT VULCAN'S SO FAR OFF HIS CHUFF HE MAKES GALACTUS' APPROVAL RATINGS LOOK LIKE THE DALAI LAMA'S.

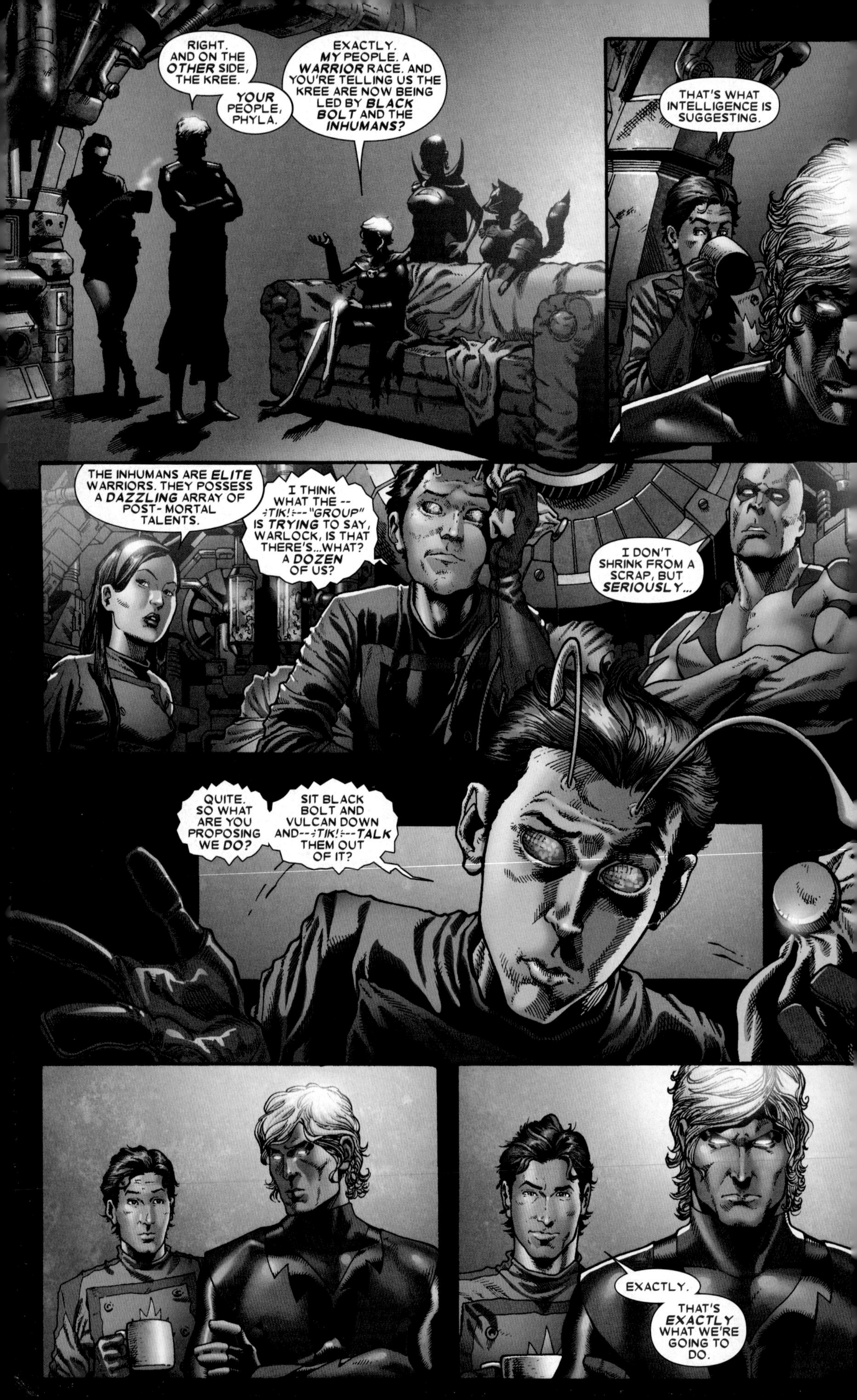
RIGHT. AND ON THE OTHER SIDE, THE KREE.
YOUR PEOPLE, PHYLA.
EXACTLY. MY PEOPLE. A WARRIOR RACE. AND YOU'RE TELLING US THE KREE ARE NOW BEING LED BY BLACK BOLT AND THE INHUMANS?
THAT'S WHAT INTELLIGENCE IS SUGGESTING.
THE INHUMANS ARE ELITE WARRIORS. THEY POSSESS A DAZZLING ARRAY OF POST-MORTAL TALENTS.
I THINK WHAT THE -- TIK! -- "GROUP" IS TRYING TO SAY, WARLOCK, IS THAT THERE'S...WHAT? A DOZEN OF US?
I DON'T SHRINK FROM A SCRAP, BUT SERIOUSLY...
QUITE. SO WHAT ARE YOU PROPOSING WE DO?
SIT BLACK BOLT AND VULCAN DOWN AND-- TIK! --TALK THEM OUT OF IT?
EXACTLY.
THAT'S EXACTLY WHAT WE'RE GOING TO DO.

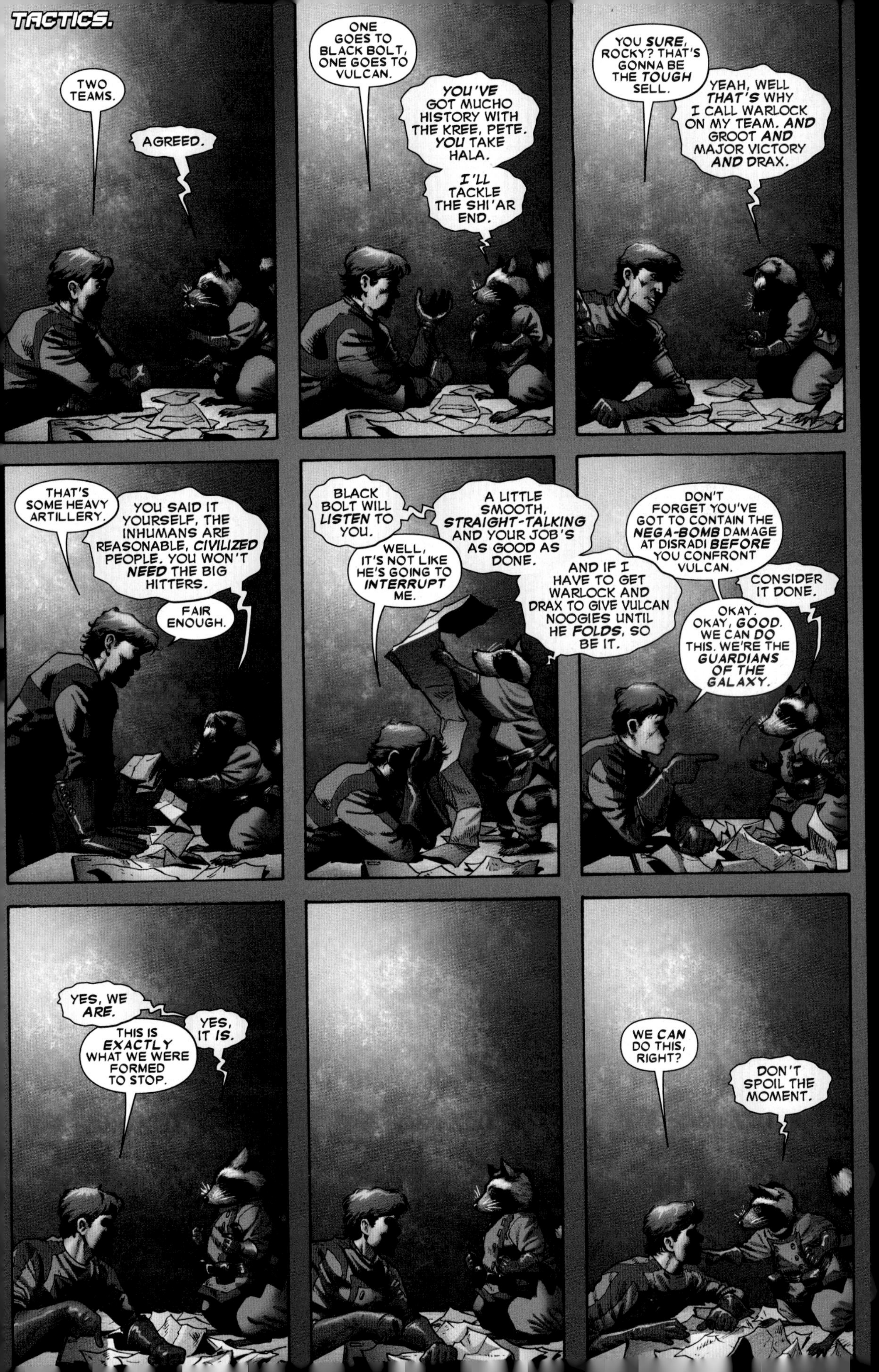
TACTICS.
TWO TEAMS.
AGREED.
ONE GOES TO BLACK BOLT, ONE GOES TO VULCAN.
YOU'VE GOT MUCHO HISTORY WITH THE KREE, PETE. YOU TAKE HALA.
I'LL TACKLE THE SHI'AR END.
YOU SURE, ROCKY? THAT'S GONNA BE THE TOUGH SELL.
YEAH, WELL THAT'S WHY I CALL WARLOCK ON MY TEAM. AND GROOT AND MAJOR VICTORY AND DRAX.
THAT'S SOME HEAVY ARTILLERY.
YOU SAID IT YOURSELF, THE INHUMANS ARE REASONABLE, CIVILIZED PEOPLE. YOU WON'T NEED THE BIG HITTERS.
FAIR ENOUGH.
BLACK BOLT WILL LISTEN TO YOU.
A LITTLE SMOOTH, STRAIGHT-TALKING AND YOUR JOB'S AS GOOD AS DONE.
WELL, IT'S NOT LIKE HE'S GOING TO INTERRUPT ME.
AND IF I HAVE TO GET WARLOCK AND DRAX TO GIVE VULCAN NOOGIES UNTIL HE FOLDS, SO BE IT.
DON'T FORGET YOU'VE GOT TO CONTAIN THE NEGA-BOMB DAMAGE AT DISRADI BEFORE YOU CONFRONT VULCAN.
CONSIDER IT DONE.
OKAY. OKAY, GOOD. WE CAN DO THIS. WE'RE THE GUARDIANS OF THE GALAXY.
YES, WE ARE.
YES, IT IS.
THIS IS EXACTLY WHAT WE WERE FORMED TO STOP.
WE CAN DO THIS, RIGHT?
DON'T SPOIL THE MOMENT.

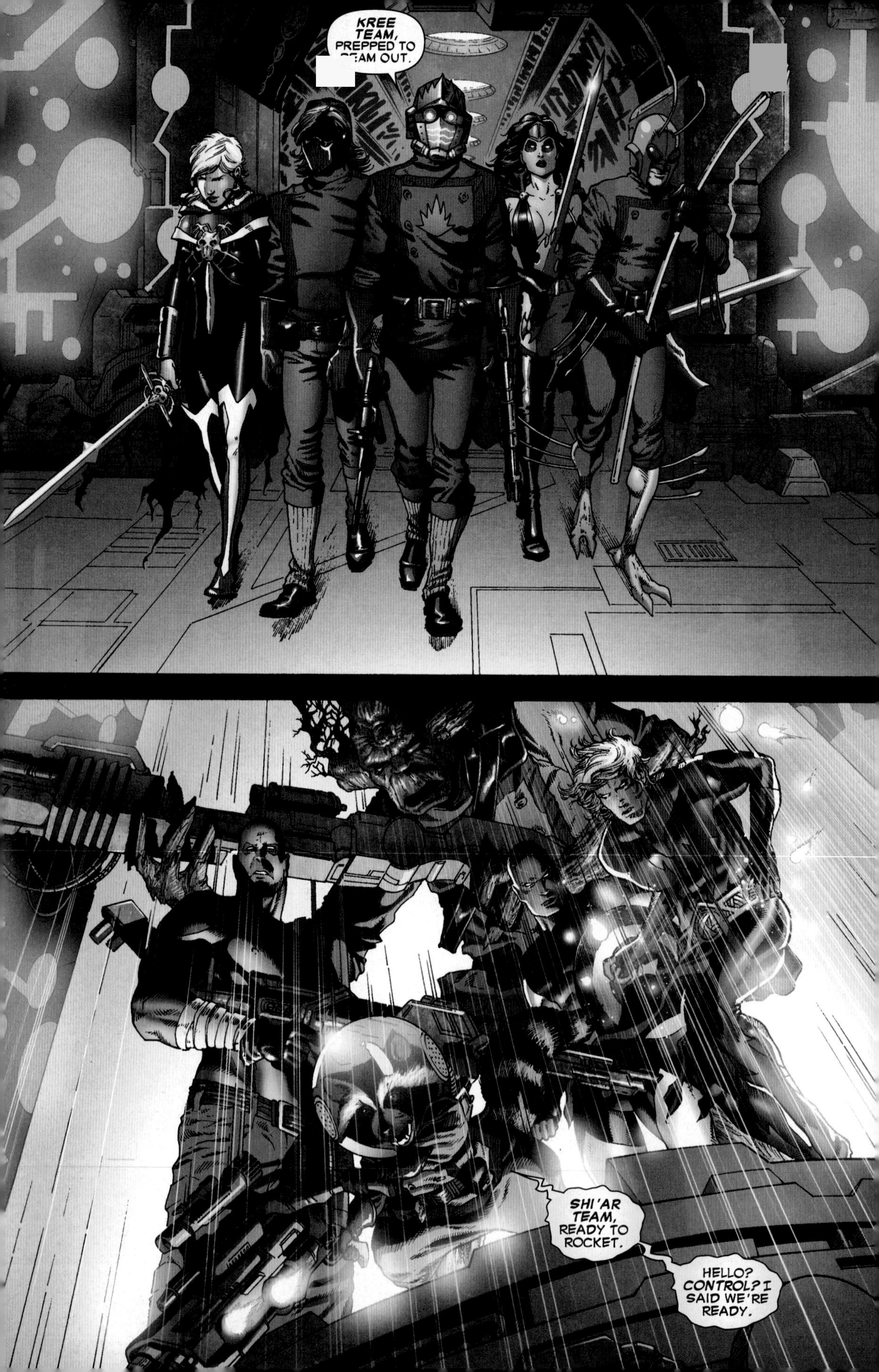
KREE TEAM, PREPPED TO BEAM OUT.
SHI'AR TEAM, READY TO ROCKET.
HELLO? CONTROL? I SAID WE'RE READY.

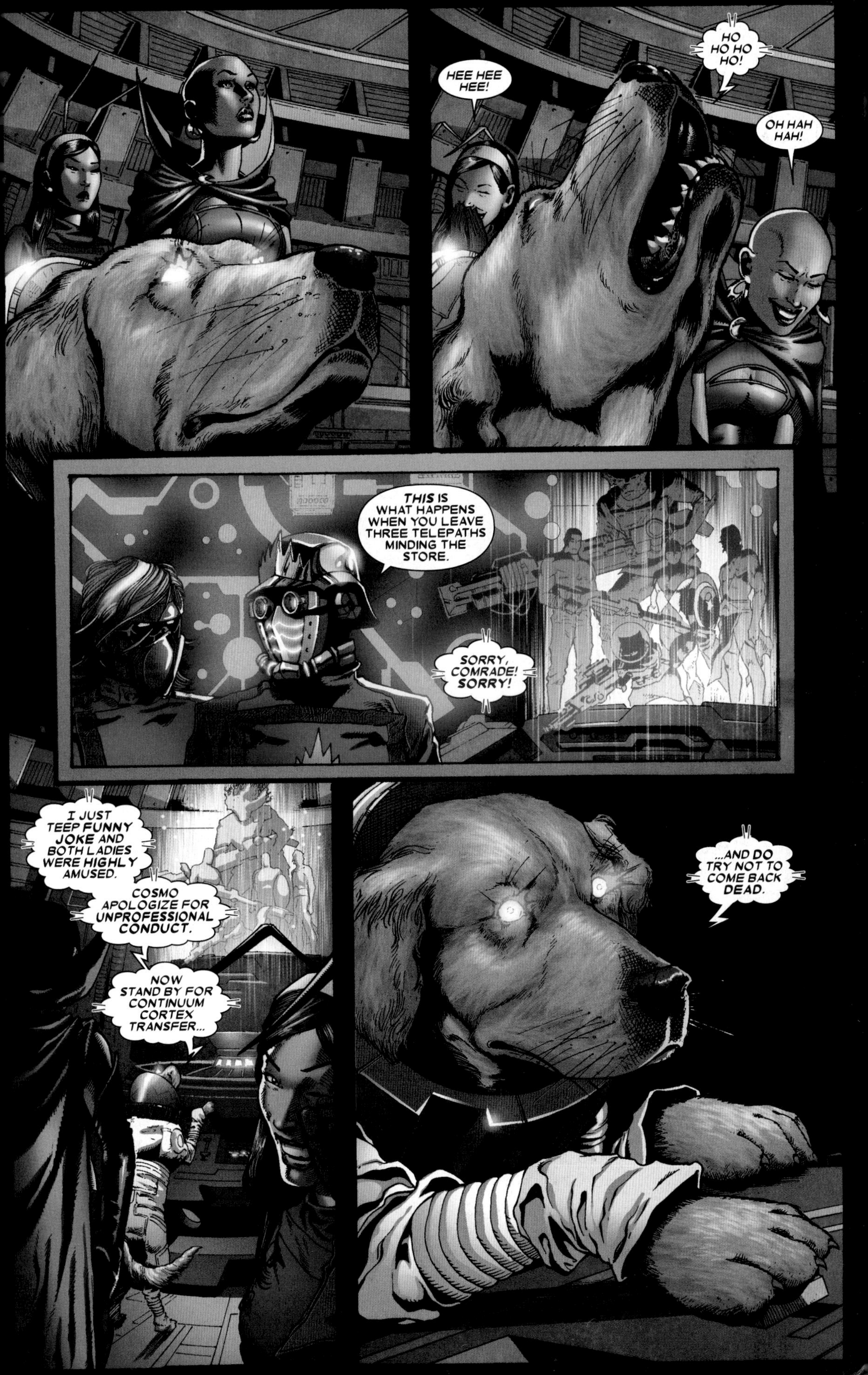
HEE HEE HEE!
HO HO HO HO!
OH HAH HAH!
THIS IS WHAT HAPPENS WHEN YOU LEAVE THREE TELEPATHS MINDING THE STORE.
SORRY, COMRADE! SORRY!
I JUST TEEP FUNNY JOKE AND BOTH LADIES WERE HIGHLY AMUSED.
COSMO APOLOGIZE FOR UNPROFESSIONAL CONDUCT.
NOW STAND BY FOR CONTINUUM CORTEX TRANSFER...
...AND DO TRY NOT TO COME BACK DEAD.

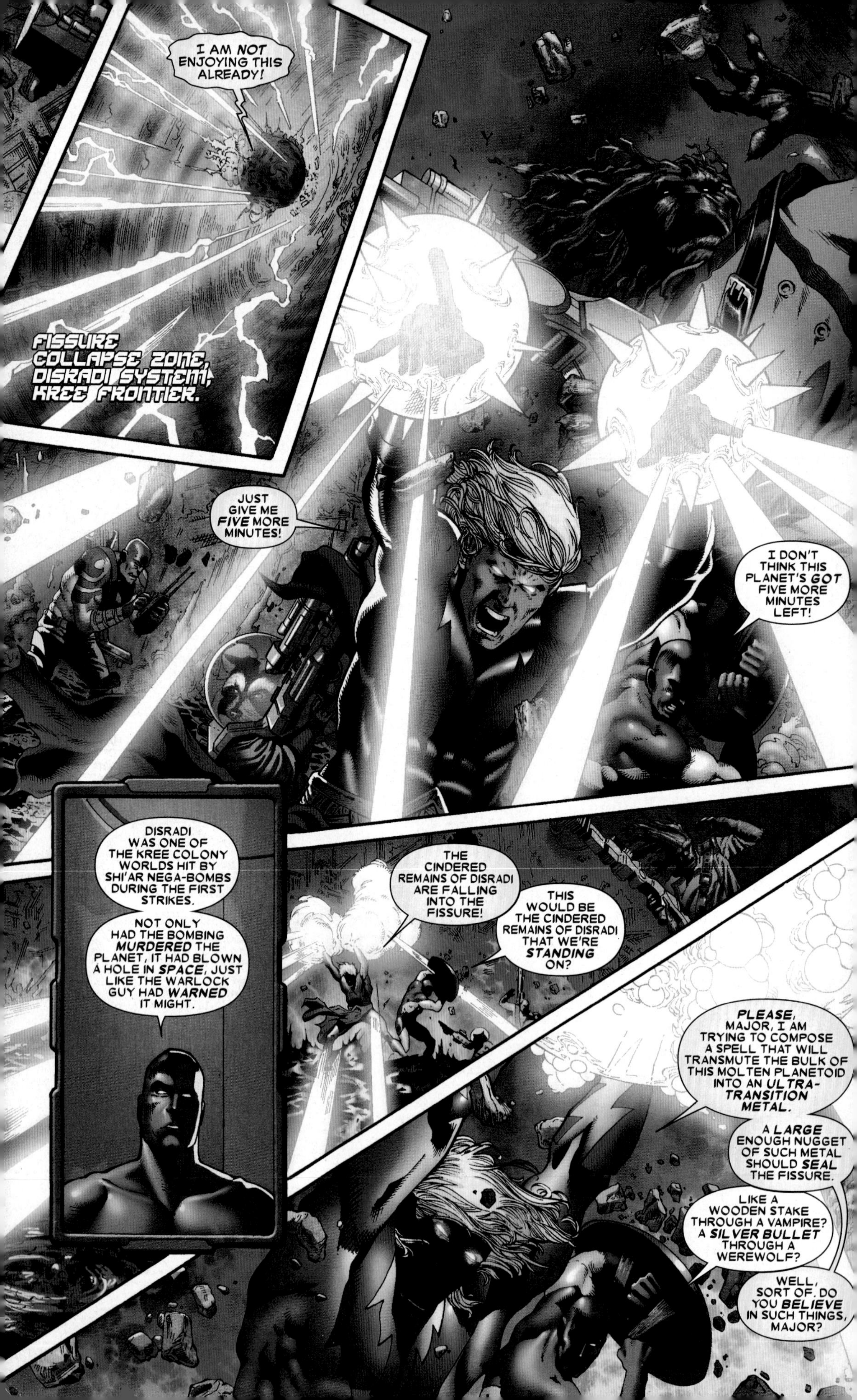
I AM NOT ENJOYING THIS ALREADY!
FISSURE COLLAPSE ZONE, DISRADI SYSTEM, KREE FRONTIER.
JUST GIVE ME FIVE MORE MINUTES!
I DON'T THINK THIS PLANET'S GOT FIVE MORE MINUTES LEFT!
DISRADI WAS ONE OF THE KREE COLONY WORLDS HIT BY SHI'AR NEGA-BOMBS DURING THE FIRST STRIKES.
NOT ONLY HAD THE BOMBING MURDERED THE PLANET, IT HAD BLOWN A HOLE IN SPACE, JUST LIKE THE WARLOCK GUY HAD WARNED IT MIGHT.
THE CINDERED REMAINS OF DISRADI ARE FALLING INTO THE FISSURE!
THIS WOULD BE THE CINDERED REMAINS OF DISRADI THAT WE'RE STANDING ON?
PLEASE, MAJOR, I AM TRYING TO COMPOSE A SPELL THAT WILL TRANSMUTE THE BULK OF THIS MOLTEN PLANETOID INTO AN ULTRA-TRANSITION METAL.
A LARGE ENOUGH NUGGET OF SUCH METAL SHOULD SEAL THE FISSURE.
LIKE A WOODEN STAKE THROUGH A VAMPIRE? A SILVER BULLET THROUGH A WEREWOLF?
WELL, SORT OF. DO YOU BELIEVE IN SUCH THINGS, MAJOR?

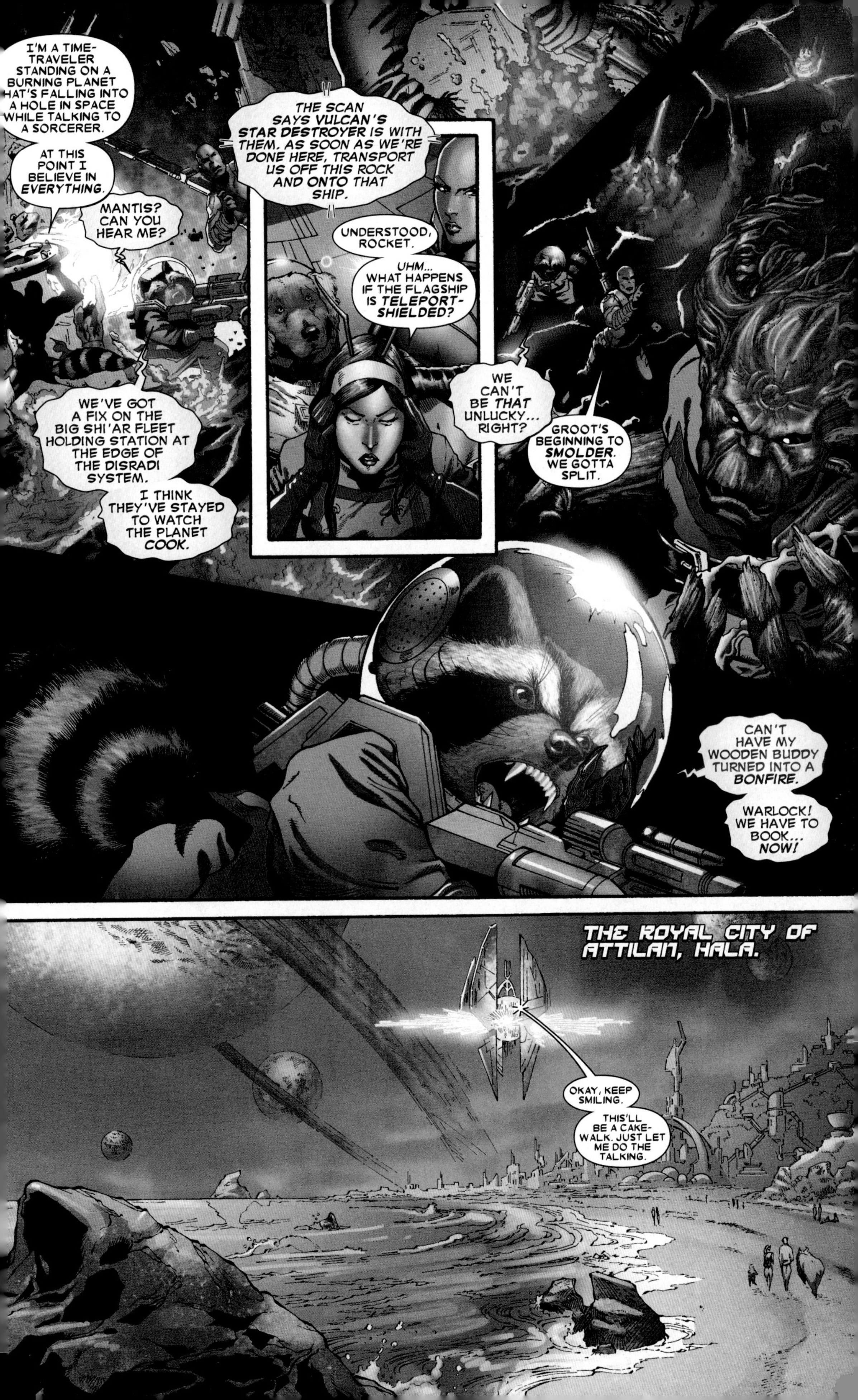
I'M A TIME-TRAVELER STANDING ON A BURNING PLANET HAT'S FALLING INTO A HOLE IN SPACE WHILE TALKING TO A SORCERER.
AT THIS POINT I BELIEVE IN EVERYTHING.
MANTIS? CAN YOU HEAR ME?
WE'VE GOT A FIX ON THE BIG SHI'AR FLEET HOLDING STATION AT THE EDGE OF THE DISRADI SYSTEM.
I THINK THEY'VE STAYED TO WATCH THE PLANET COOK.
THE SCAN SAYS VULCAN'S STAR DESTROYER IS WITH THEM. AS SOON AS WE'RE DONE HERE, TRANSPORT US OFF THIS ROCK AND ONTO THAT SHIP.
UNDERSTOOD, ROCKET.
UHM... WHAT HAPPENS IF THE FLAGSHIP IS TELEPORT-SHIELDED?
WE CAN'T BE THAT UNLUCKY... RIGHT?
GROOT'S BEGINNING TO SMOLDER. WE GOTTA SPLIT.
CAN'T HAVE MY WOODEN BUDDY TURNED INTO A BONFIRE.
WARLOCK! WE HAVE TO BOOK... NOW!
THE ROYAL CITY OF ATTILAN, HALA.
OKAY, KEEP SMILING.
THIS'LL BE A CAKE-WALK. JUST LET ME DO THE TALKING.

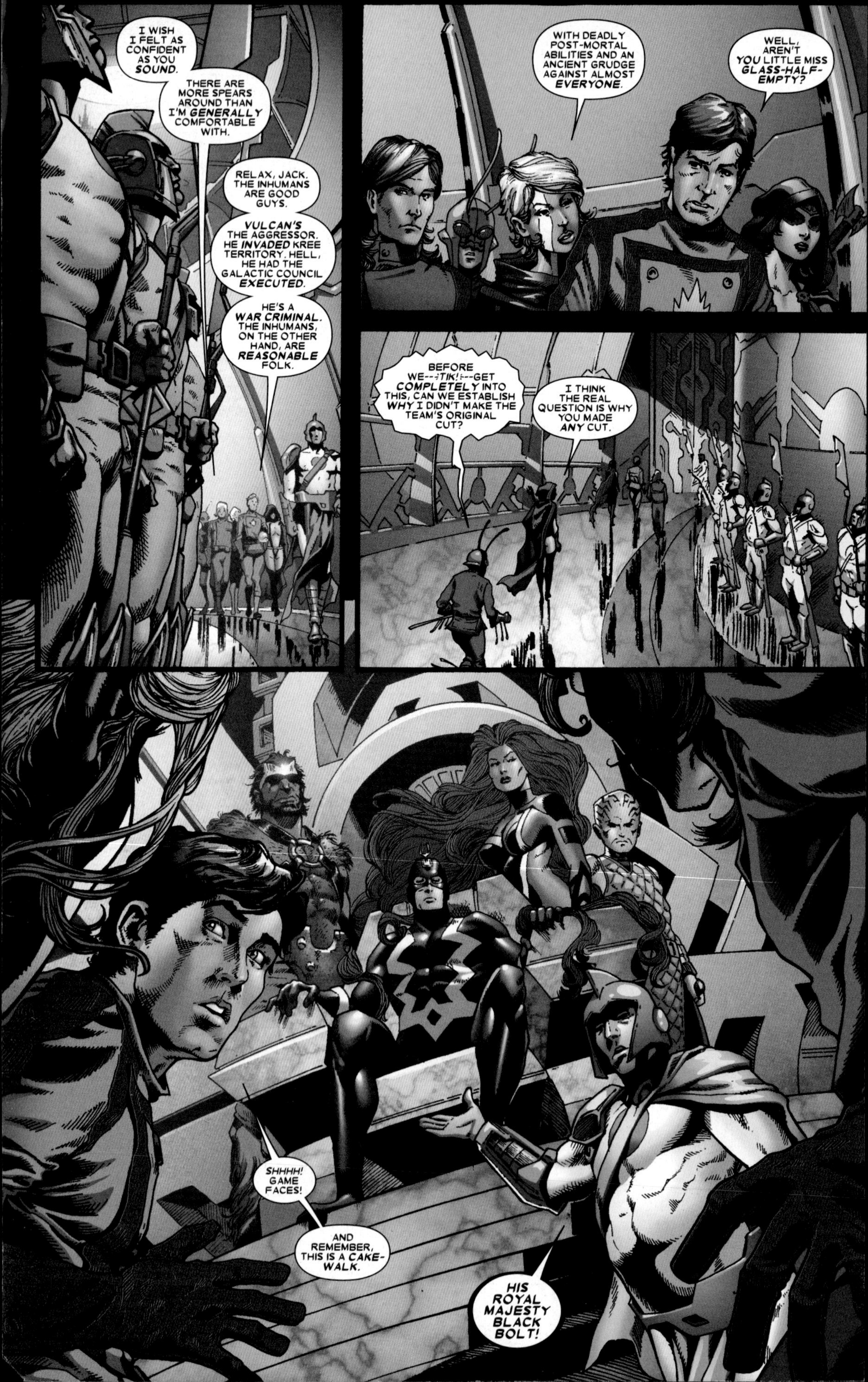
I WISH I FELT AS CONFIDENT AS YOU SOUND.
THERE ARE MORE SPEARS AROUND THAN I'M GENERALLY COMFORTABLE WITH.
RELAX, JACK. THE INHUMANS ARE GOOD GUYS.
VULCAN'S THE AGGRESSOR. HE INVADED KREE TERRITORY. HELL, HE HAD THE GALACTIC COUNCIL EXECUTED.
HE'S A WAR CRIMINAL. THE INHUMANS, ON THE OTHER HAND, ARE REASONABLE FOLK.
WITH DEADLY POST-MORTAL ABILITIES AND AN ANCIENT GRUDGE AGAINST ALMOST EVERYONE.
WELL, AREN'T YOU LITTLE MISS GLASS-HALF-EMPTY?
BEFORE WE--TIK!--GET COMPLETELY INTO THIS, CAN WE ESTABLISH WHY I DIDN'T MAKE THE TEAM'S ORIGINAL CUT?
I THINK THE REAL QUESTION IS WHY YOU MADE ANY CUT.
SHHHH! GAME FACES!
AND REMEMBER, THIS IS A CAKE-WALK.
HIS ROYAL MAJESTY BLACK BOLT!

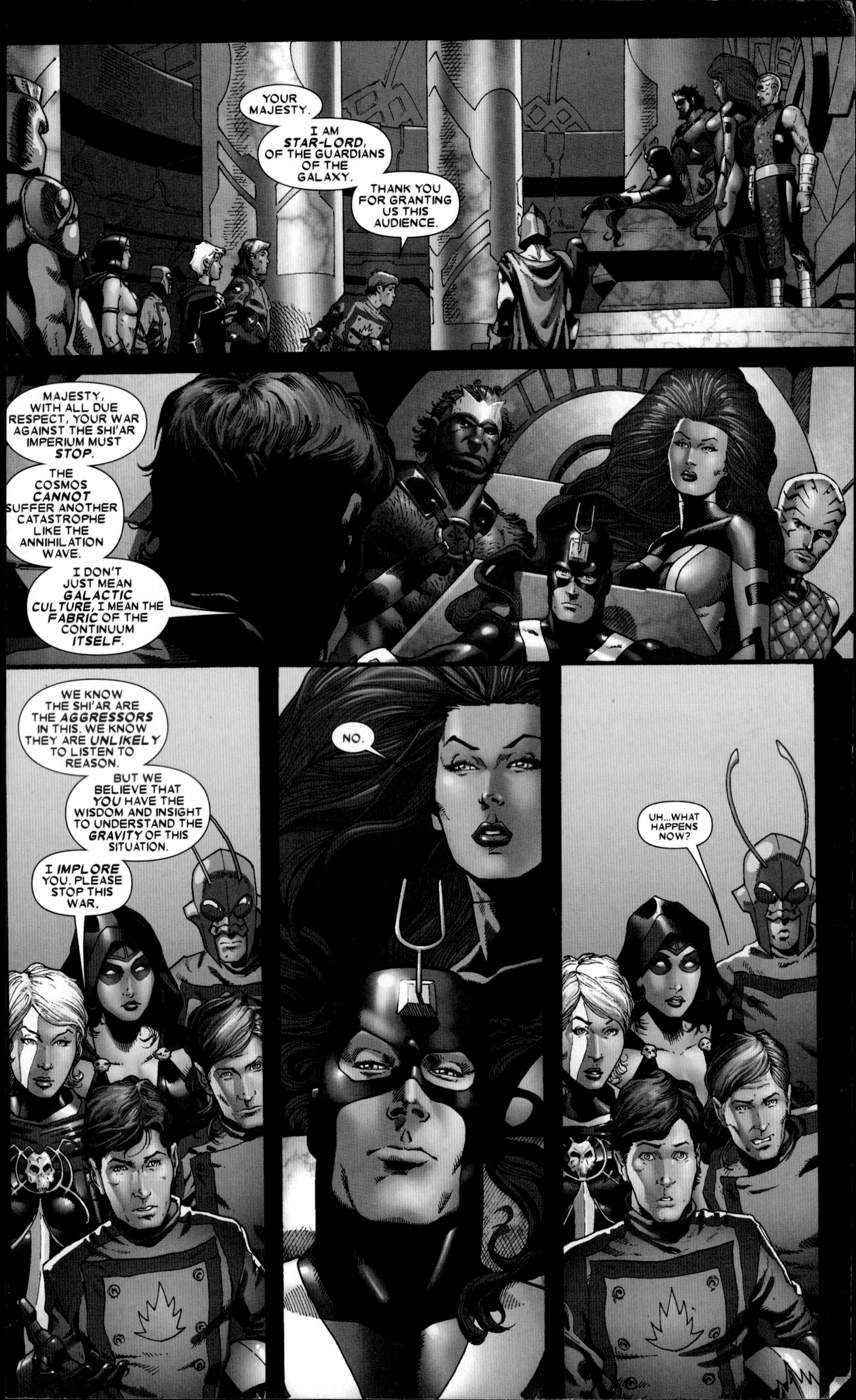
YOUR MAJESTY.
I AM STAR-LORD, OF THE GUARDIANS OF THE GALAXY.
THANK YOU FOR GRANTING US THIS AUDIENCE.
MAJESTY, WITH ALL DUE RESPECT, YOUR WAR AGAINST THE SHI'AR IMPERIUM MUST STOP.
THE COSMOS CANNOT SUFFER ANOTHER CATASTROPHE LIKE THE ANNIHILATION WAVE.
I DON'T JUST MEAN GALACTIC CULTURE, I MEAN THE FABRIC OF THE CONTINUUM ITSELF.
WE KNOW THE SHI'AR ARE THE AGGRESSORS IN THIS. WE KNOW THEY ARE UNLIKELY TO LISTEN TO REASON.
BUT WE BELIEVE THAT YOU HAVE THE WISDOM AND INSIGHT TO UNDERSTAND THE GRAVITY OF THIS SITUATION.
I IMPLORE YOU. PLEASE STOP THIS WAR.
NO.
UH...WHAT HAPPENS NOW?

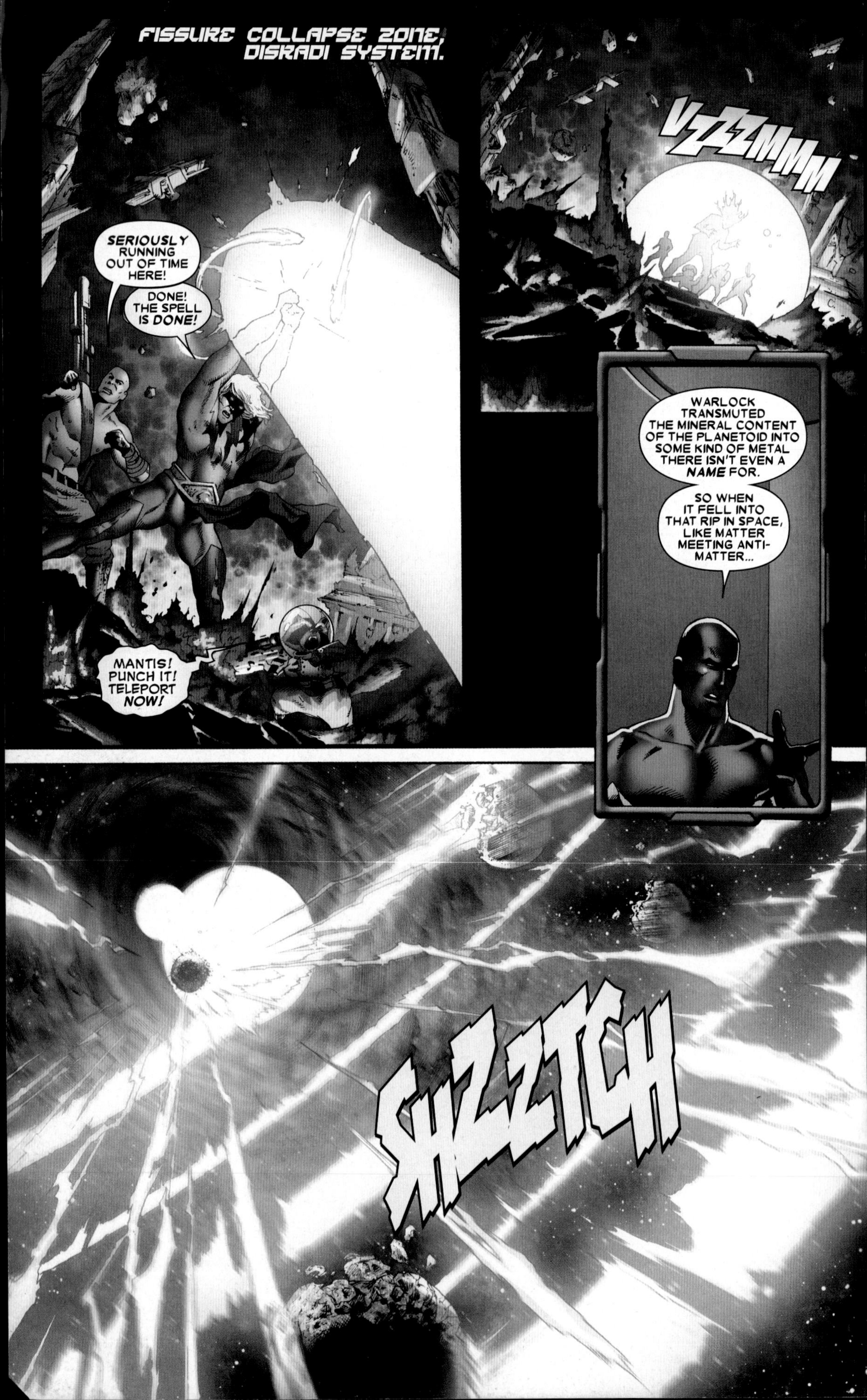
FISSURE COLLAPSE ZONE, DISKADI SYSTEM.
SERIOUSLY RUNNING OUT OF TIME HERE!
DONE! THE SPELL IS DONE!
MANTIS! PUNCH IT! TELEPORT NOW!
VZZZMMMM
WARLOCK TRANSMUTED THE MINERAL CONTENT OF THE PLANETOID INTO SOME KIND OF METAL THERE ISN'T EVEN A NAME FOR.
SO WHEN IT FELL INTO THAT RIP IN SPACE, LIKE MATTER MEETING ANTI-MATTER...
SHZZTCH

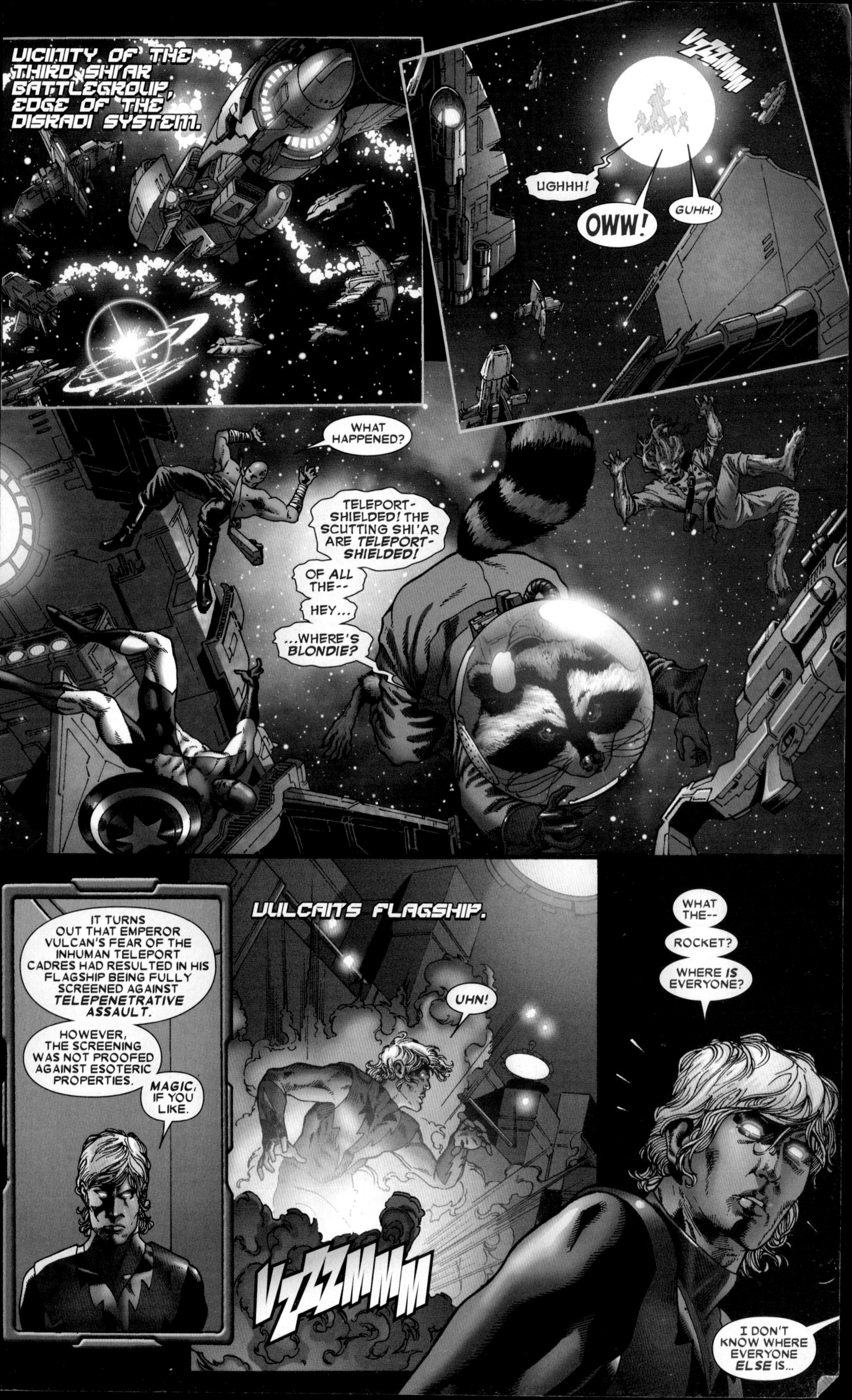
VICINITY OF THE THIRD SHI'AR BATTLEGROUP, EDGE OF THE DISRADI SYSTEM.
VZZMMM
UGHHH!
OWW!
GUHH!
WHAT HAPPENED?
TELEPORT-SHIELDED! THE SCUTTING SHI'AR ARE TELEPORT-SHIELDED!
OF ALL THE--
HEY...
...WHERE'S BLONDIE?
IT TURNS OUT THAT EMPEROR VULCAN'S FEAR OF THE INHUMAN TELEPORT CADRES HAD RESULTED IN HIS FLAGSHIP BEING FULLY SCREENED AGAINST TELEPENETRATIVE ASSAULT.
HOWEVER, THE SCREENING WAS NOT PROOFED AGAINST ESOTERIC PROPERTIES.
MAGIC, IF YOU LIKE.
VULCAN'S FLAGSHIP.
UHN!
VZZMMMM
WHAT THE--
ROCKET?
WHERE IS EVERYONE?
I DON'T KNOW WHERE EVERYONE ELSE IS...

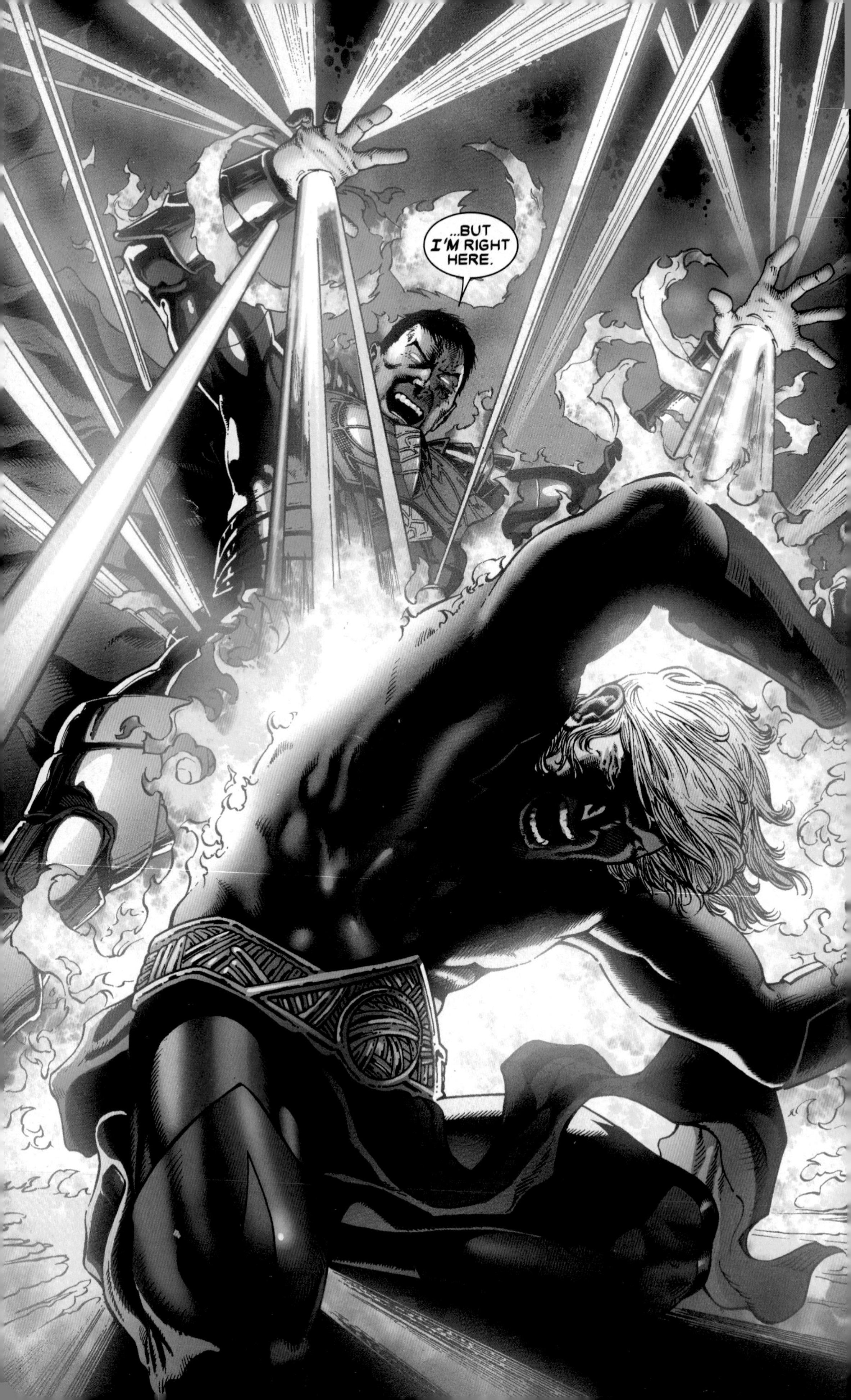
...BUT I'M RIGHT HERE.

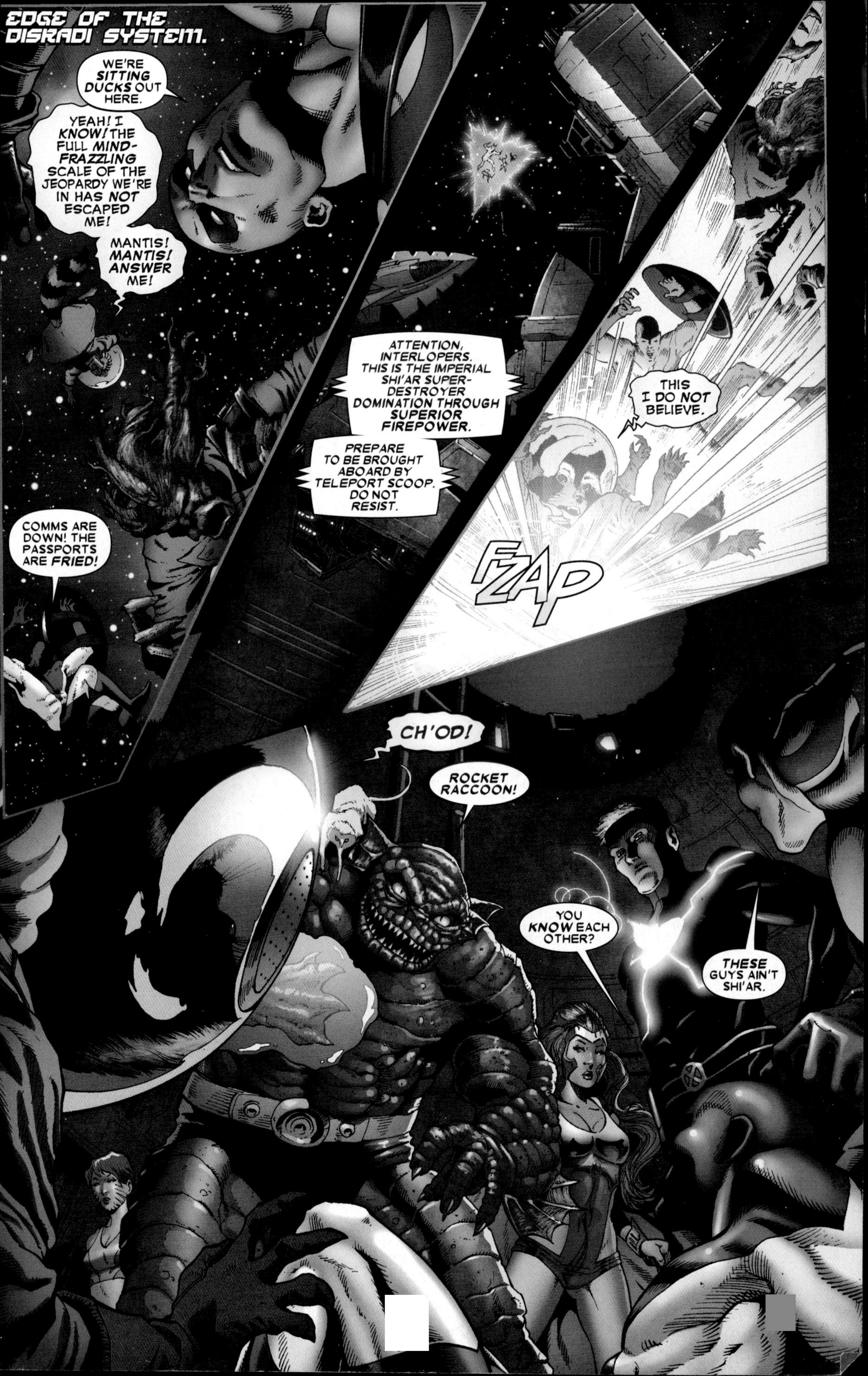
EDGE OF THE DISKADI SYSTEM.
WE'RE SITTING DUCKS OUT HERE.
YEAH! I KNOW! THE FULL MIND-FRAZZLING SCALE OF THE JEOPARDY WE'RE IN HAS NOT ESCAPED ME!
MANTIS! MANTIS! ANSWER ME!
COMMS ARE DOWN! THE PASSPORTS ARE FRIED!
ATTENTION, INTERLOPERS. THIS IS THE IMPERIAL SHI'AR SUPER-DESTROYER DOMINATION THROUGH SUPERIOR FIREPOWER.
PREPARE TO BE BROUGHT ABOARD BY TELEPORT SCOOP. DO NOT RESIST.
THIS I DO NOT BELIEVE.
FZZAP
CH'OD!
ROCKET RACCOON!
YOU KNOW EACH OTHER?
THESE GUYS AIN'T SHI'AR.

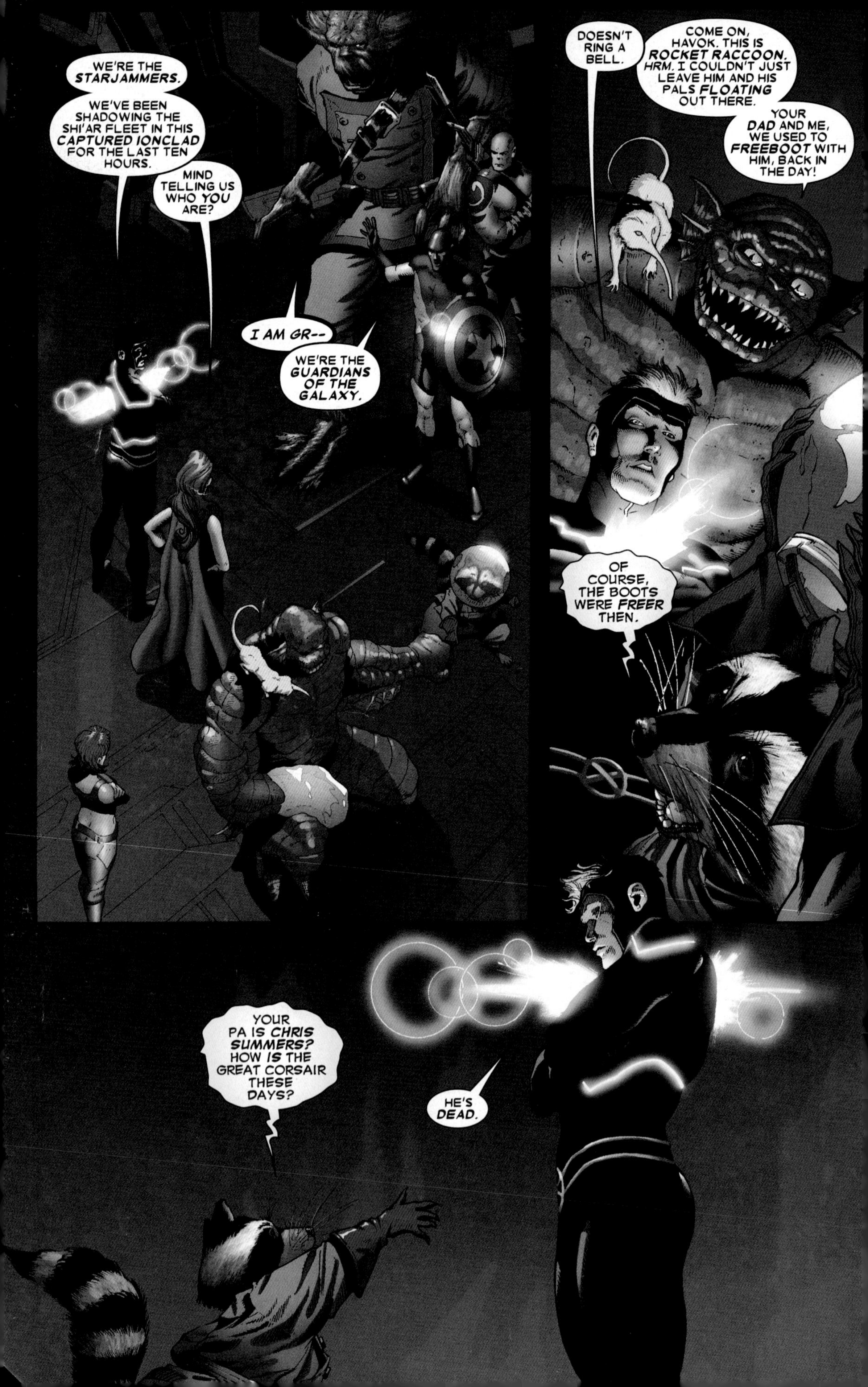
WE'RE THE STARJAMMERS.
WE'VE BEEN SHADOWING THE SHI'AR FLEET IN THIS CAPTURED IONCLAD FOR THE LAST TEN HOURS.
MIND TELLING US WHO YOU ARE?
I AM GR--
WE'RE THE GUARDIANS OF THE GALAXY.
DOESN'T RING A BELL.
COME ON, HAVOK. THIS IS ROCKET RACCOON. HRM. I COULDN'T JUST LEAVE HIM AND HIS PALS FLOATING OUT THERE.
YOUR DAD AND ME, WE USED TO FREEBOOT WITH HIM, BACK IN THE DAY!
OF COURSE, THE BOOTS WERE FREER THEN.
YOUR PA IS CHRIS SUMMERS? HOW IS THE GREAT CORSAIR THESE DAYS?
HE'S DEAD.

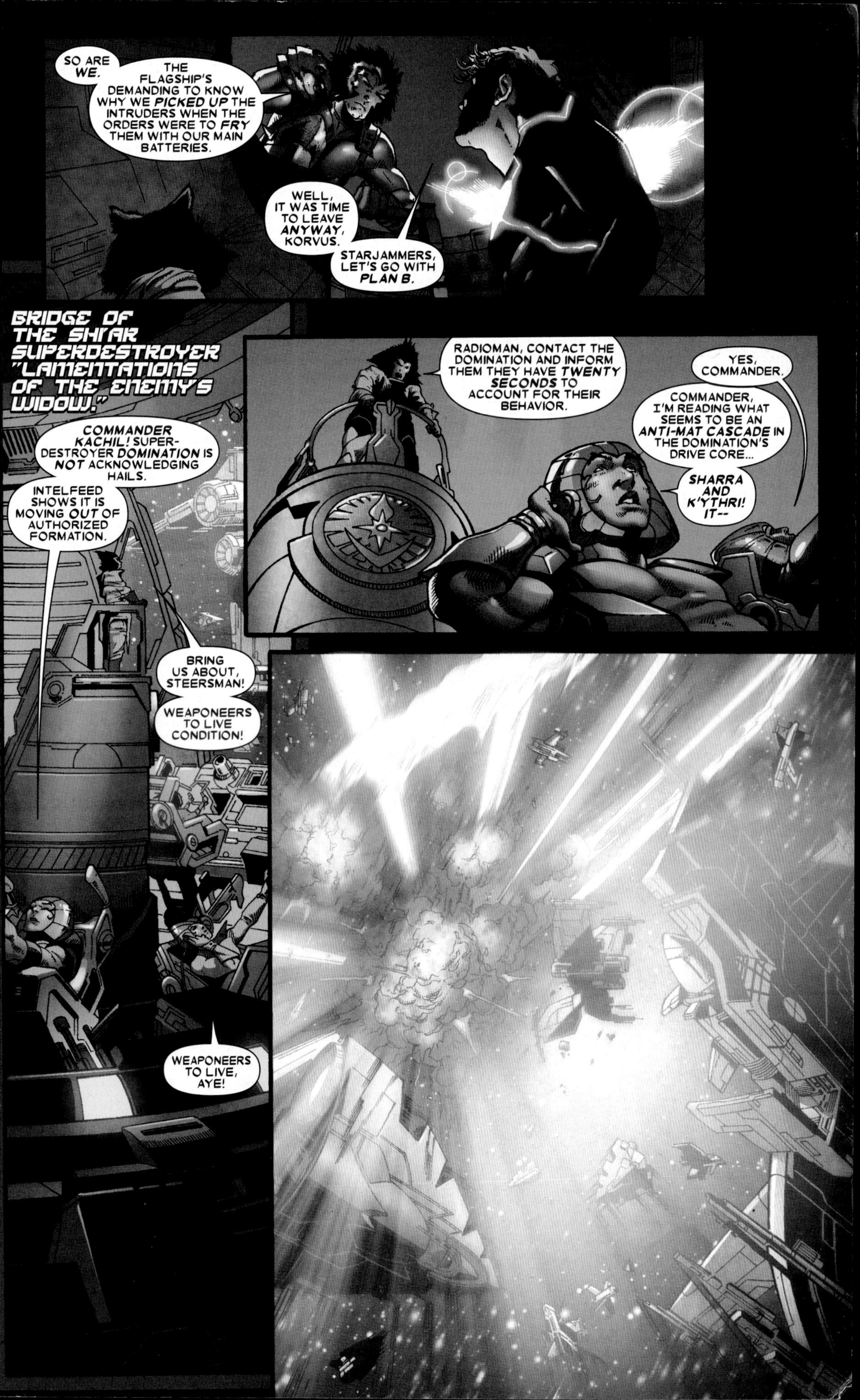
SO ARE WE.
THE FLAGSHIP'S DEMANDING TO KNOW WHY WE PICKED UP THE INTRUDERS WHEN THE ORDERS WERE TO FRY THEM WITH OUR MAIN BATTERIES.
WELL, IT WAS TIME TO LEAVE ANYWAY, KORVUS.
STARJAMMERS, LET'S GO WITH PLAN B.
BRIDGE OF THE SHI'AR SUPERDESTROYER "LAMENTATIONS OF THE ENEMY'S WIDOW."
COMMANDER KACHIL! SUPER-DESTROYER DOMINATION IS NOT ACKNOWLEDGING HAILS.
INTELFEED SHOWS IT IS MOVING OUT OF AUTHORIZED FORMATION.
RADIOMAN, CONTACT THE DOMINATION AND INFORM THEM THEY HAVE TWENTY SECONDS TO ACCOUNT FOR THEIR BEHAVIOR.
YES, COMMANDER.
COMMANDER, I'M READING WHAT SEEMS TO BE AN ANTI-MAT CASCADE IN THE DOMINATION'S DRIVE CORE...
SHARRA AND K'YTHRI! IT--
BRING US ABOUT, STEERSMAN!
WEAPONEERS TO LIVE CONDITION!
WEAPONEERS TO LIVE, AYE!

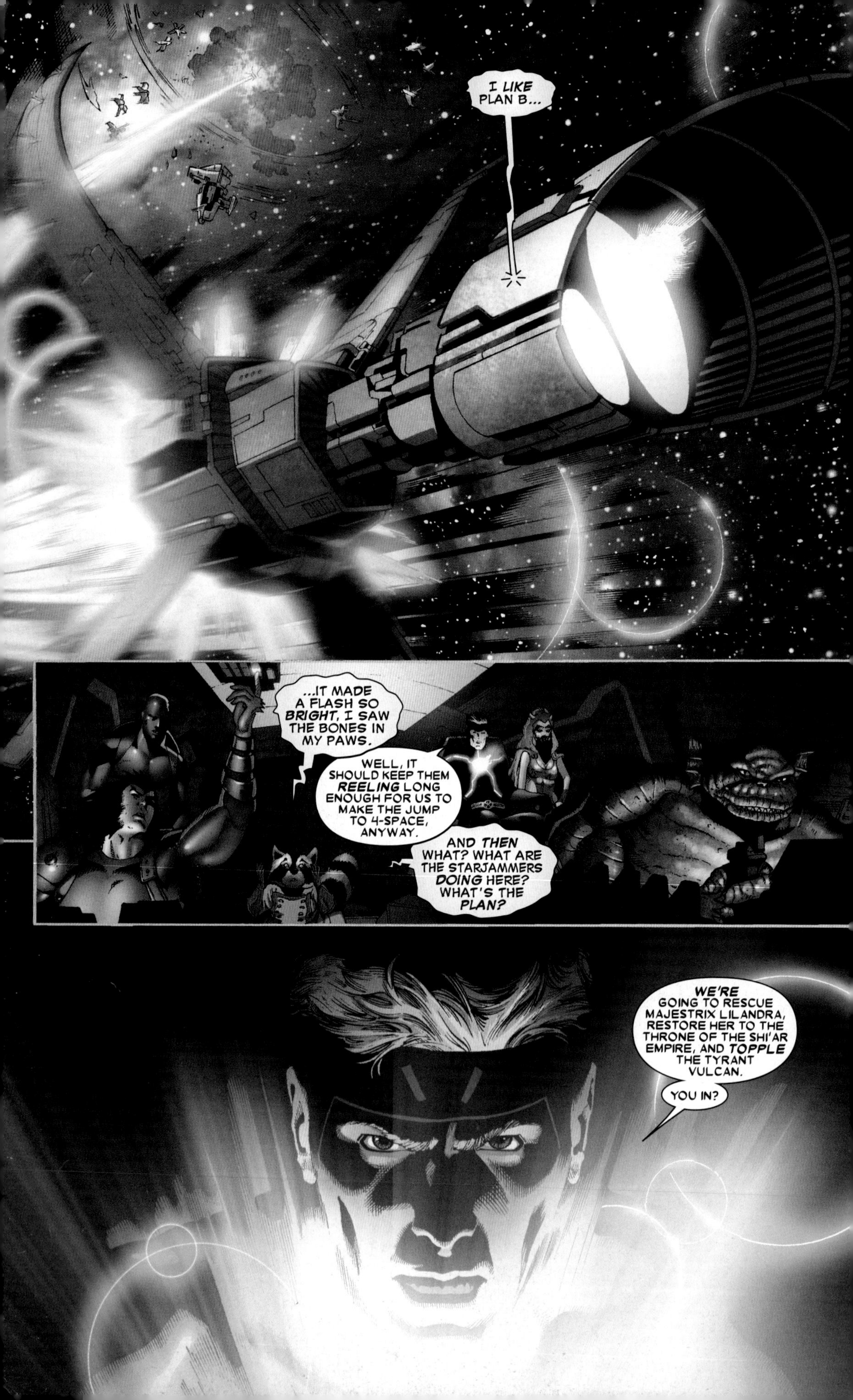
I LIKE PLAN B...
...IT MADE A FLASH SO BRIGHT, I SAW THE BONES IN MY PAWS.
WELL, IT SHOULD KEEP THEM REELING LONG ENOUGH FOR US TO MAKE THE JUMP TO 4-SPACE, ANYWAY.
AND THEN WHAT? WHAT ARE THE STARJAMMERS DOING HERE? WHAT'S THE PLAN?
WE'RE GOING TO RESCUE MAJESTRIX LILANDRA, RESTORE HER TO THE THRONE OF THE SHI'AR EMPIRE, AND TOPPLE THE TYRANT VULCAN.
YOU IN?

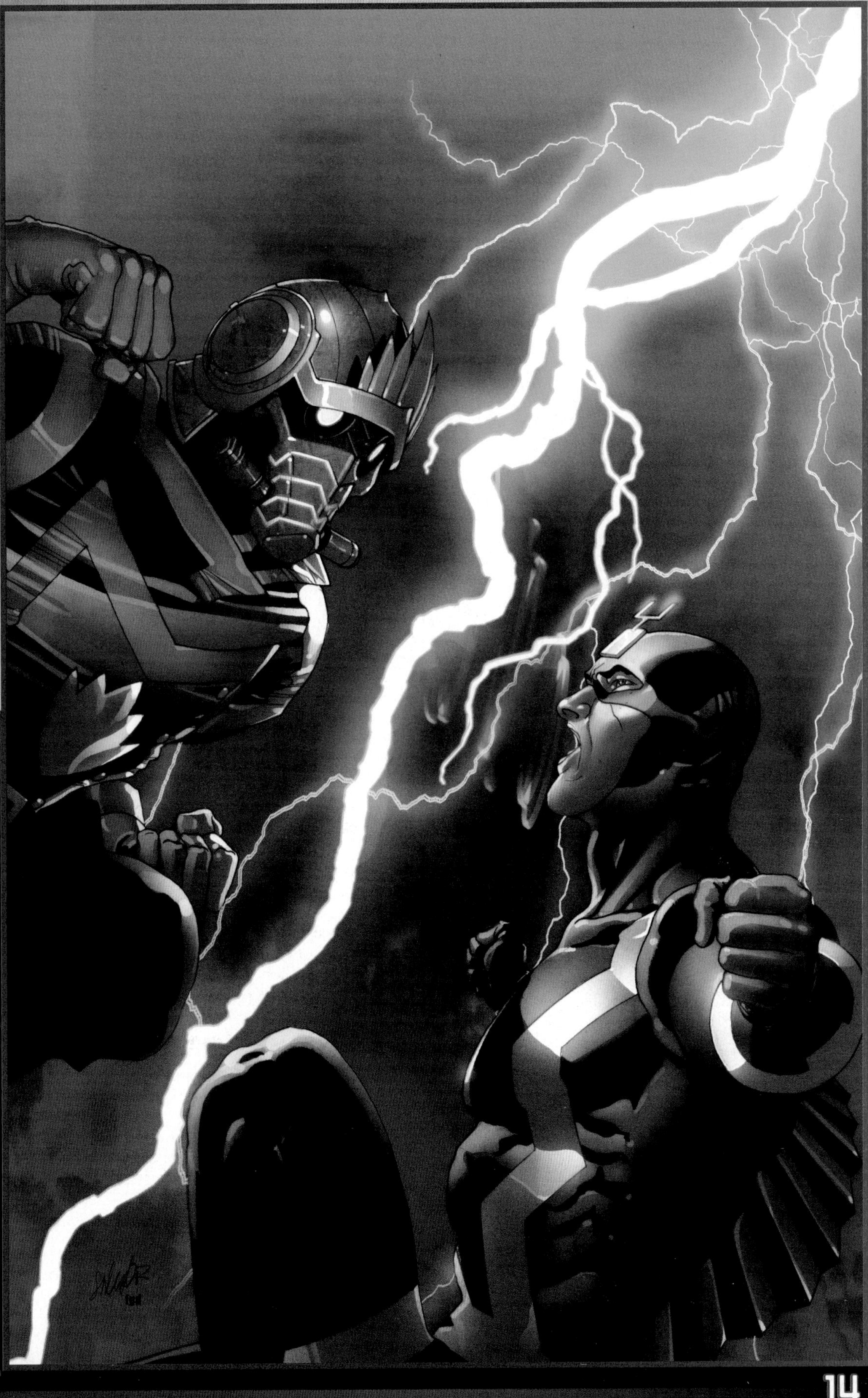

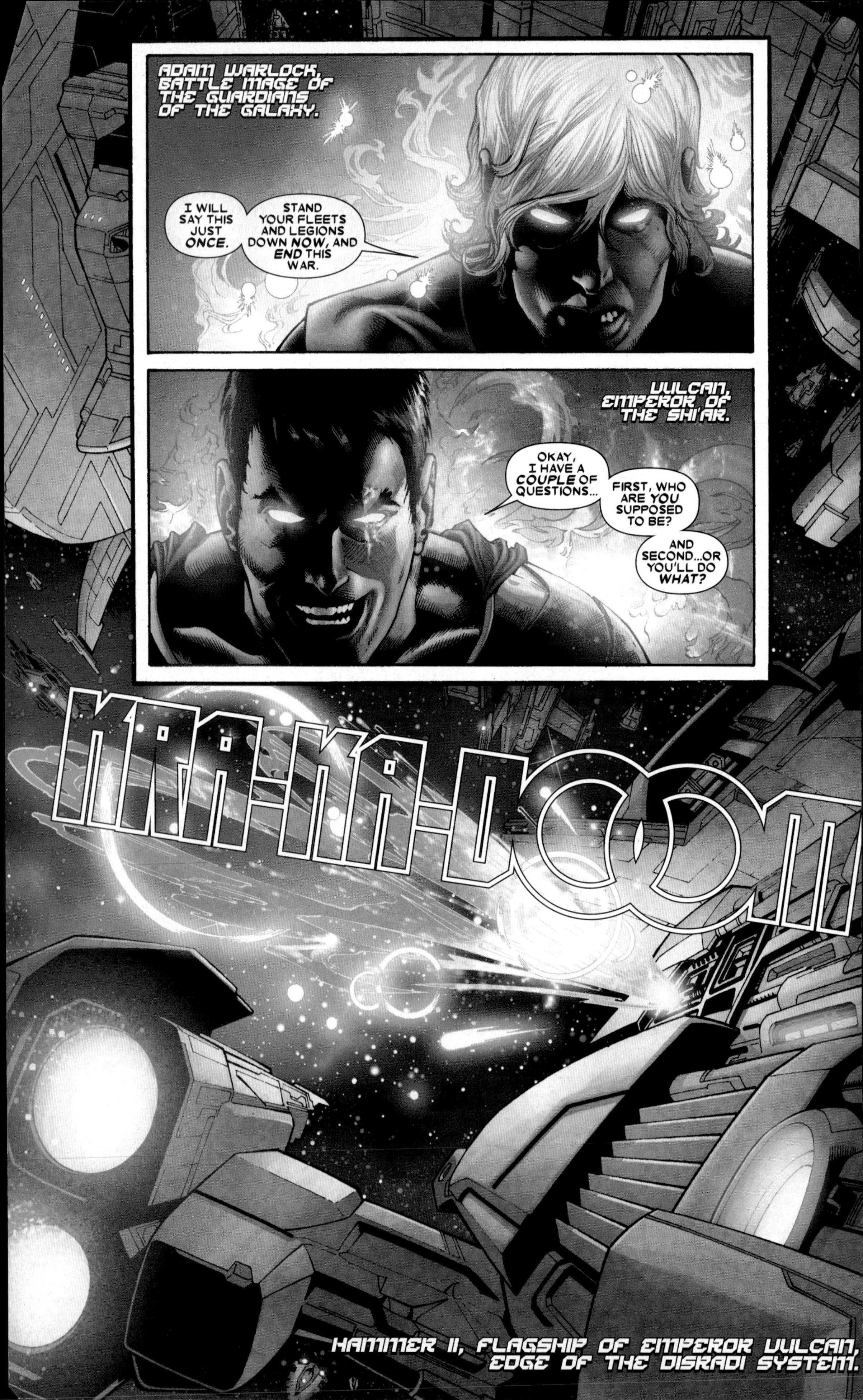
ADAM WARLOCK, BATTLE MAGE OF THE GUARDIANS OF THE GALAXY.
I WILL SAY THIS JUST ONCE.
STAND YOUR FLEETS AND LEGIONS DOWN NOW, AND END THIS WAR.
VULCAN, EMPEROR OF THE SHI'AR.
OKAY, I HAVE A COUPLE OF QUESTIONS...
FIRST, WHO ARE YOU SUPPOSED TO BE?
AND SECOND...OR YOU'LL DO WHAT?
KRA-KA-DOOM
HAMMER II, FLAGSHIP OF EMPEROR VULCAN, EDGE OF THE DISRADI SYSTEM.

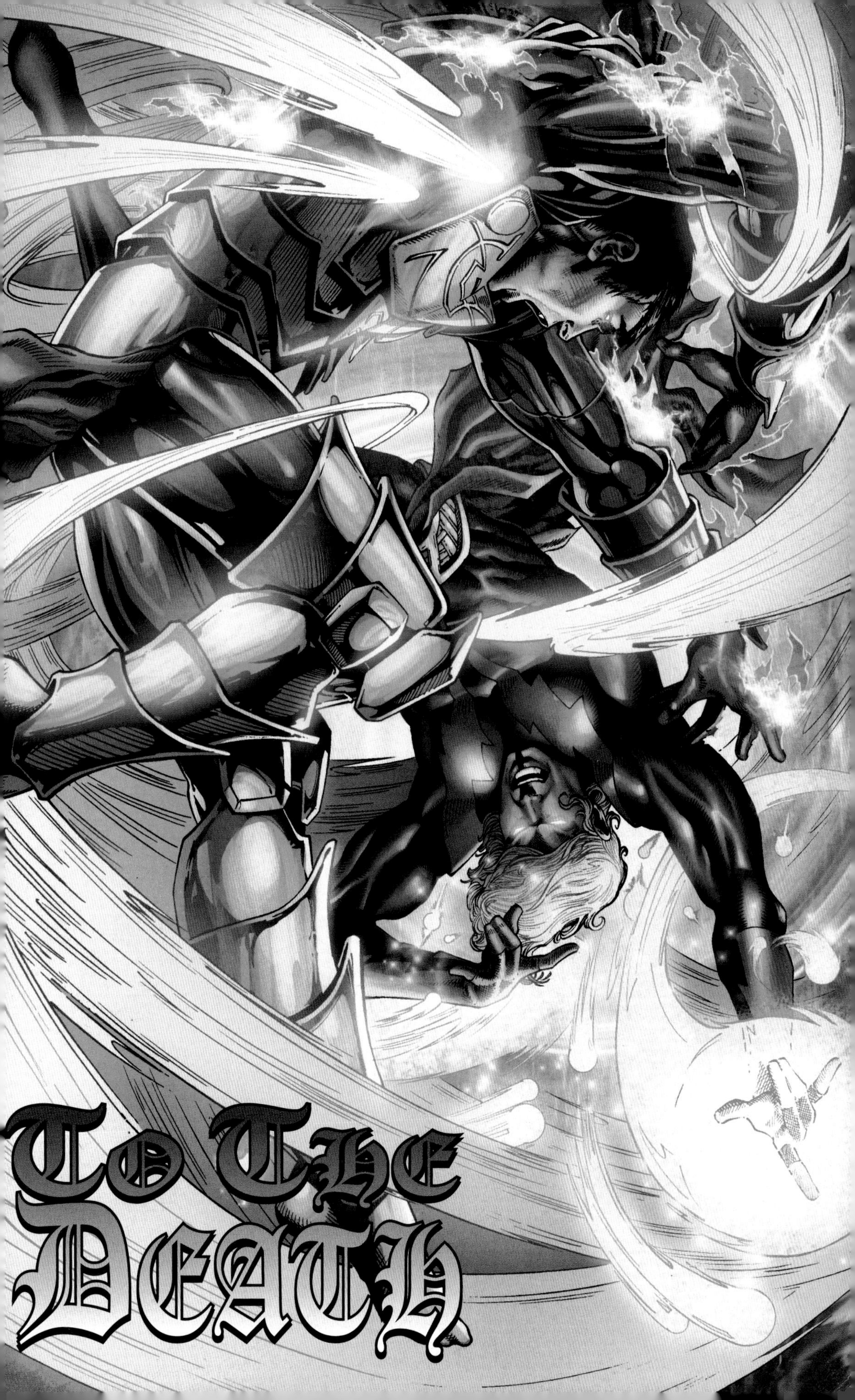
TO THE
DEATH

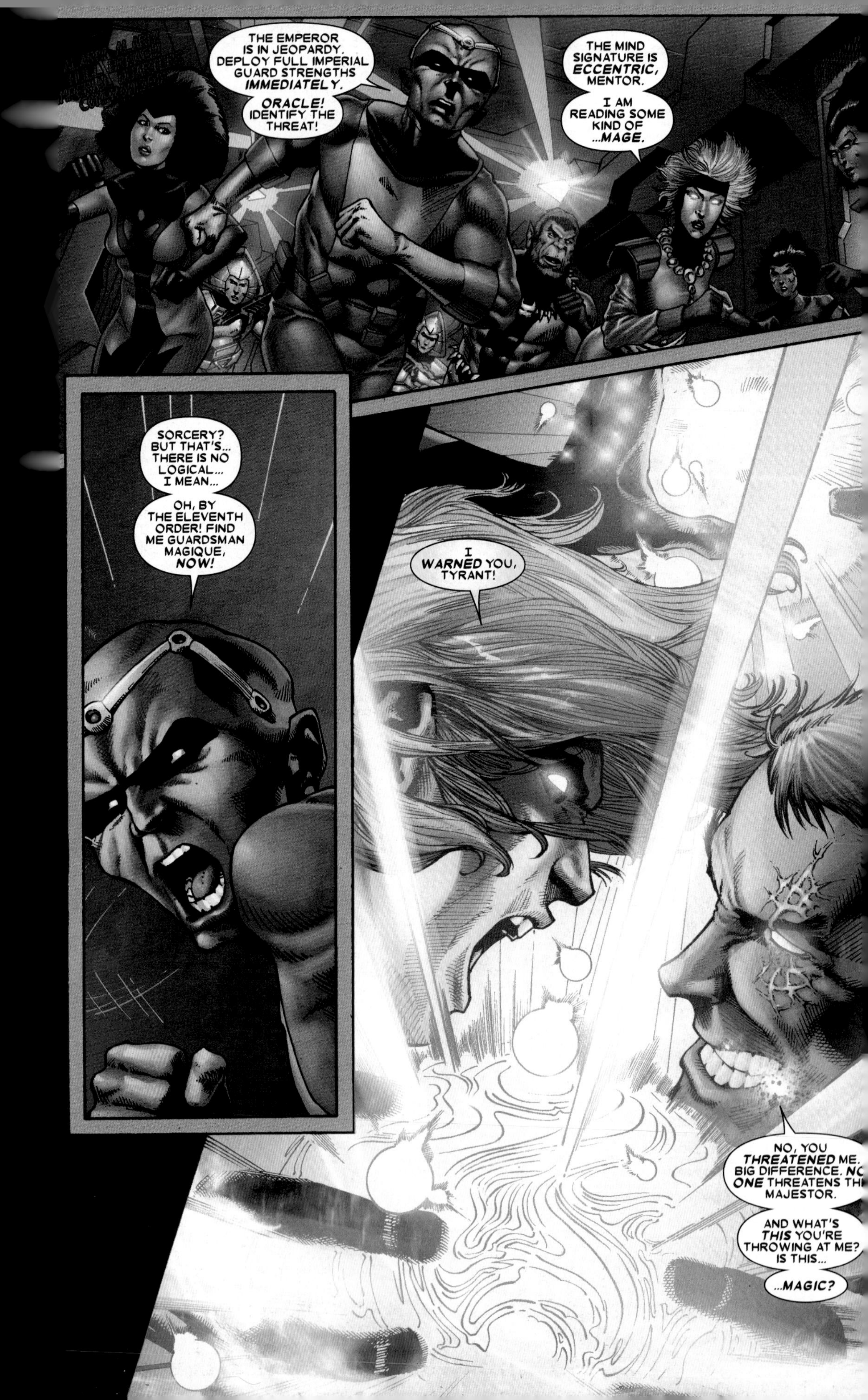
THE EMPEROR IS IN JEOPARDY. DEPLOY FULL IMPERIAL GUARD STRENGTHS IMMEDIATELY.
ORACLE! IDENTIFY THE THREAT!
THE MIND SIGNATURE IS ECCENTRIC, MENTOR.
I AM READING SOME KIND OF ...MAGE.
SORCERY? BUT THAT'S... THERE IS NO LOGICAL... I MEAN...
OH, BY THE ELEVENTH ORDER! FIND ME GUARDSMAN MAGIQUE, NOW!
I WARNED YOU, TYRANT!
NO, YOU THREATENED ME. BIG DIFFERENCE. N ONE THREATENS TH MAJESTOR.
AND WHAT'S THIS YOU'RE THROWING AT ME? IS THIS...
...MAGIC?

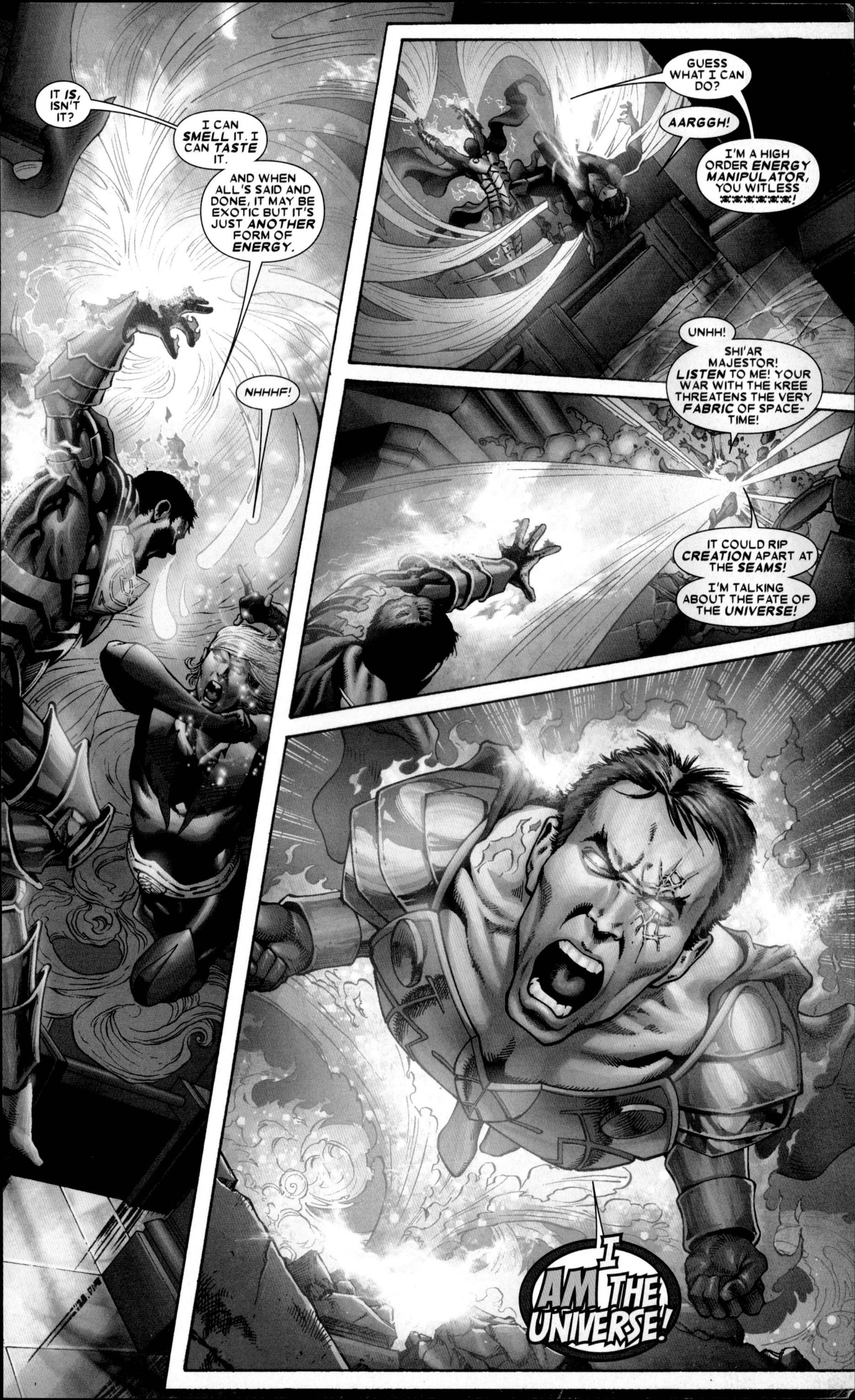
IT IS, ISN'T IT?
I CAN SMELL IT. I CAN TASTE IT.
AND WHEN ALL'S SAID AND DONE, IT MAY BE EXOTIC BUT IT'S JUST ANOTHER FORM OF ENERGY.
NHHHF!
GUESS WHAT I CAN DO?
AARGGH!
I'M A HIGH ORDER ENERGY MANIPULATOR, YOU WITLESS
UNHH!
SHI'AR MAJESTOR! LISTEN TO ME! YOUR WAR WITH THE KREE THREATENS THE VERY FABRIC OF SPACE-TIME!
IT COULD RIP CREATION APART AT THE SEAMS!
I'M TALKING ABOUT THE FATE OF THE UNIVERSE!
I AM THE UNIVERSE!

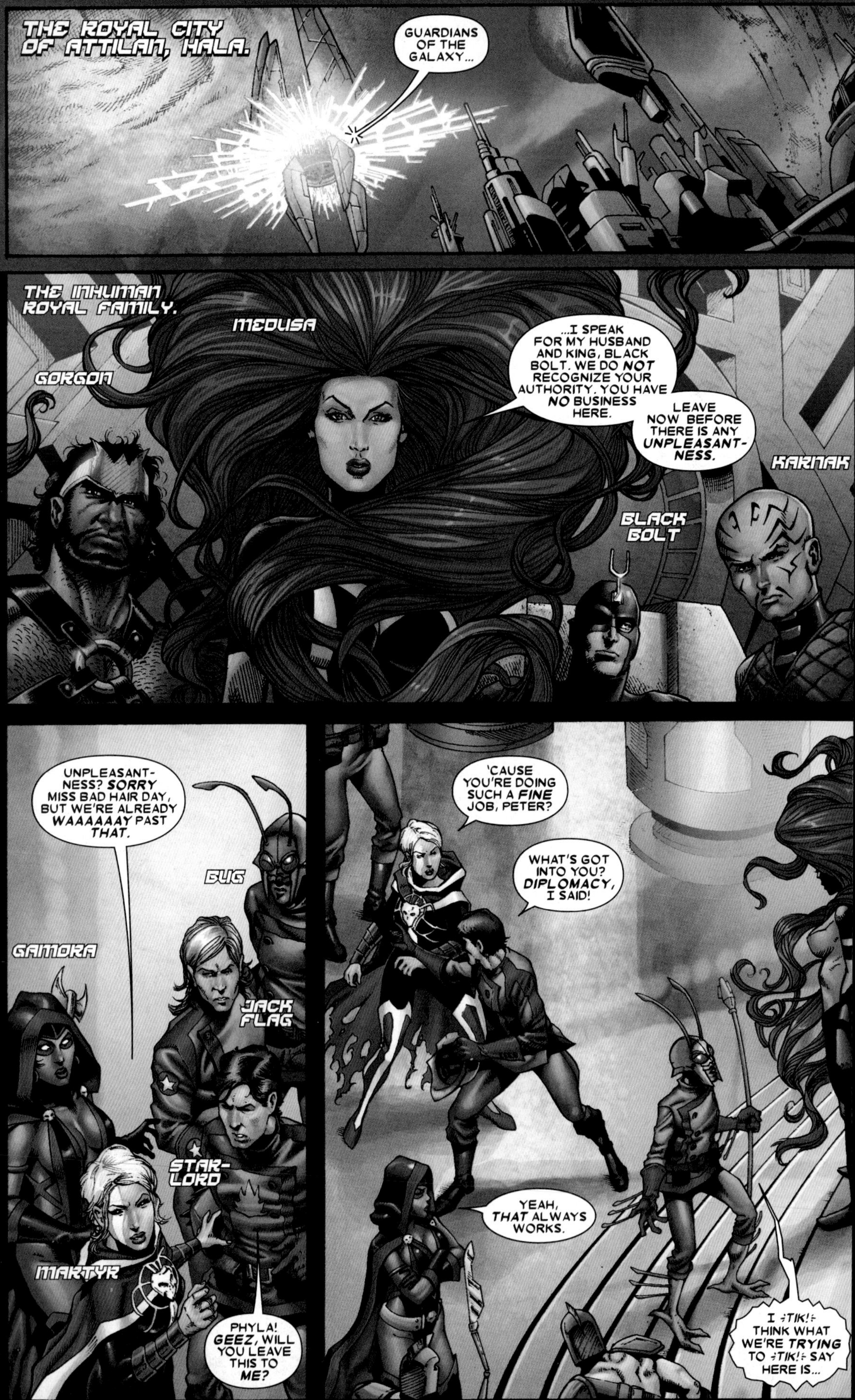
THE ROYAL CITY OF ATTILAN, HALA.
GUARDIANS OF THE GALAXY...
THE INHUMAN ROYAL FAMILY.
MEDUSA
GORGON
...I SPEAK FOR MY HUSBAND AND KING, BLACK BOLT. WE DO NOT RECOGNIZE YOUR AUTHORITY. YOU HAVE NO BUSINESS HERE.
LEAVE NOW BEFORE THERE IS ANY UNPLEASANT-NESS.
KARNAK
BLACK BOLT
UNPLEASANT-NESS? SORRY MISS BAD HAIR DAY, BUT WE'RE ALREADY WAAAAAAY PAST THAT.
BUG
GAMORA
JACK FLAG
STAR-LORD
MARTYR
PHYLA! GEEZ, WILL YOU LEAVE THIS TO ME?
'CAUSE YOU'RE DOING SUCH A FINE JOB, PETER?
WHAT'S GOT INTO YOU? DIPLOMACY, I SAID!
YEAH, THAT ALWAYS WORKS.
I ‡TIK!‡ THINK WHAT WE'RE TRYING TO ‡TIK!‡ SAY HERE IS...

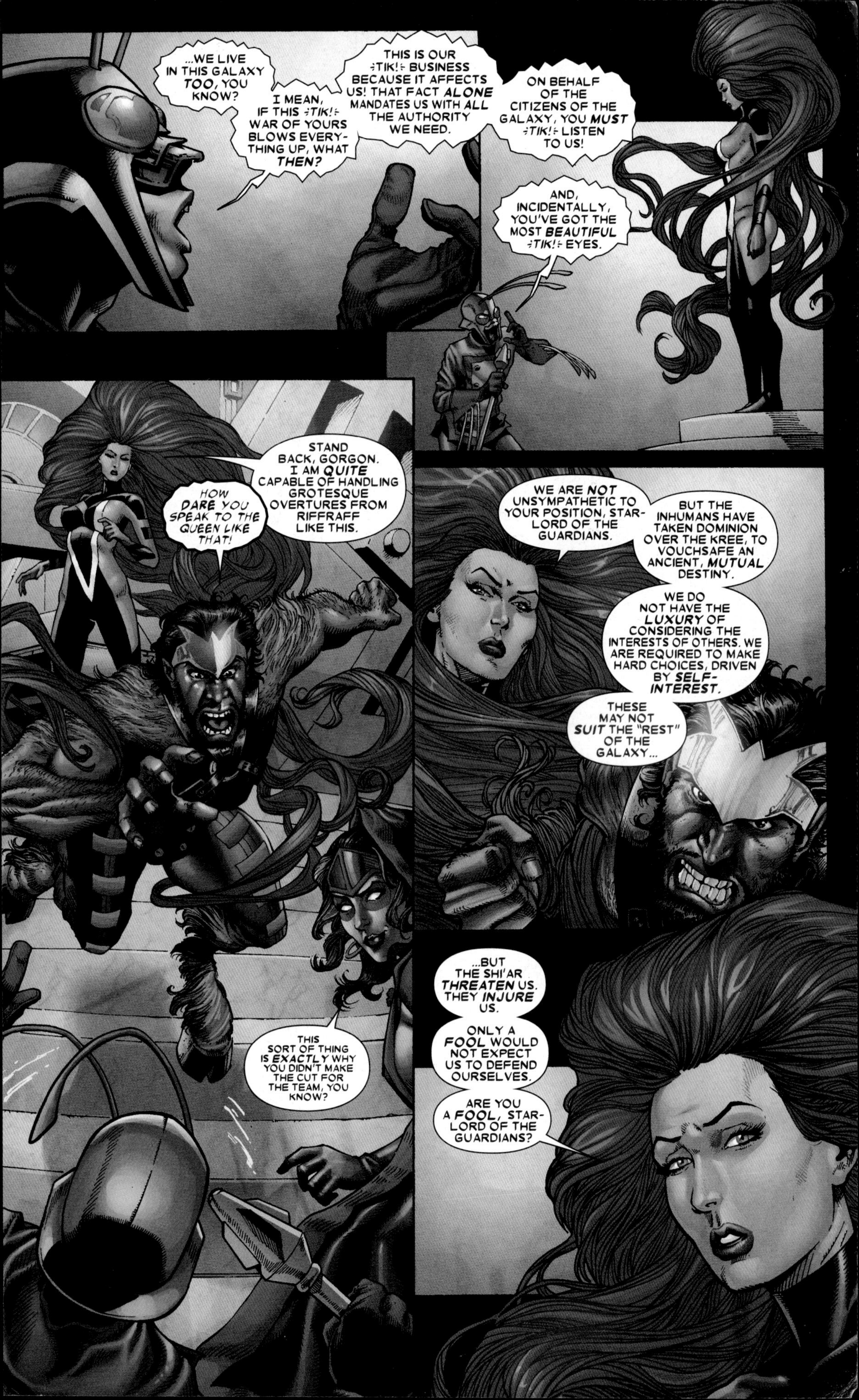
...WE LIVE IN THIS GALAXY TOO, YOU KNOW?
I MEAN, IF THIS ⫶TIK!⫶ WAR OF YOURS BLOWS EVERYTHING UP, WHAT THEN?
THIS IS OUR ⫶TIK!⫶ BUSINESS BECAUSE IT AFFECTS US! THAT FACT ALONE MANDATES US WITH ALL THE AUTHORITY WE NEED.
ON BEHALF OF THE CITIZENS OF THE GALAXY, YOU MUST ⫶TIK!⫶ LISTEN TO US!
AND, INCIDENTALLY, YOU'VE GOT THE MOST BEAUTIFUL ⫶TIK!⫶ EYES.
STAND BACK, GORGON. I AM QUITE CAPABLE OF HANDLING GROTESQUE OVERTURES FROM RIFFRAFF LIKE THIS.
HOW DARE YOU SPEAK TO THE QUEEN LIKE THAT!
THIS SORT OF THING IS EXACTLY WHY YOU DIDN'T MAKE THE CUT FOR THE TEAM, YOU KNOW?
WE ARE NOT UNSYMPATHETIC TO YOUR POSITION, STAR-LORD OF THE GUARDIANS.
BUT THE INHUMANS HAVE TAKEN DOMINION OVER THE KREE, TO VOUCHSAFE AN ANCIENT, MUTUAL DESTINY.
WE DO NOT HAVE THE LUXURY OF CONSIDERING THE INTERESTS OF OTHERS. WE ARE REQUIRED TO MAKE HARD CHOICES, DRIVEN BY SELF-INTEREST.
THESE MAY NOT SUIT THE "REST" OF THE GALAXY...
...BUT THE SHI'AR THREATEN US. THEY INJURE US.
ONLY A FOOL WOULD NOT EXPECT US TO DEFEND OURSELVES.
ARE YOU A FOOL, STAR-LORD OF THE GUARDIANS?

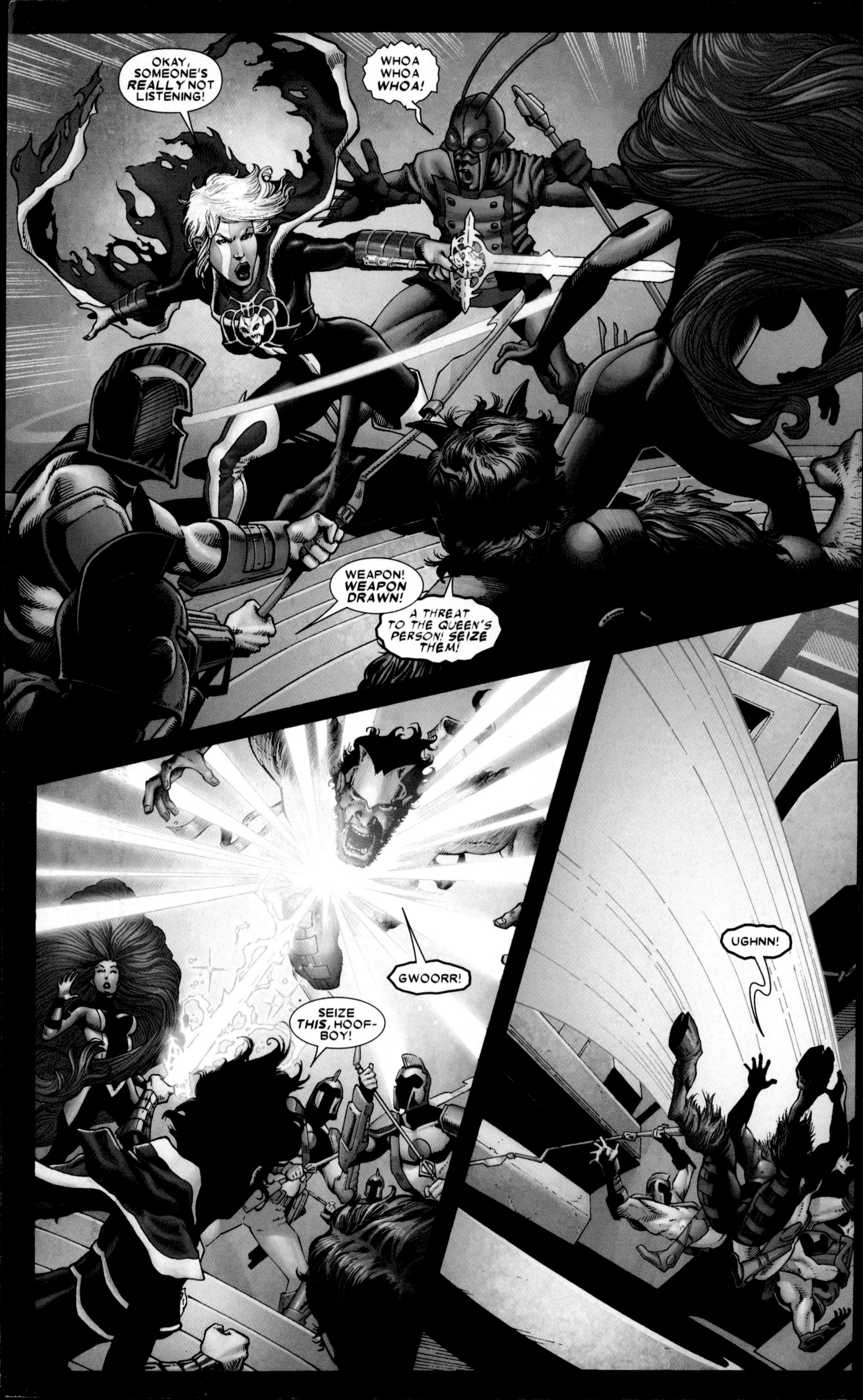
OKAY, SOMEONE'S REALLY NOT LISTENING!
WHOA WHOA WHOA!
WEAPON! WEAPON DRAWN!
A THREAT TO THE QUEEN'S PERSON! SEIZE THEM!
GWOORR!
SEIZE THIS, HOOF-BOY!
UGHNN!

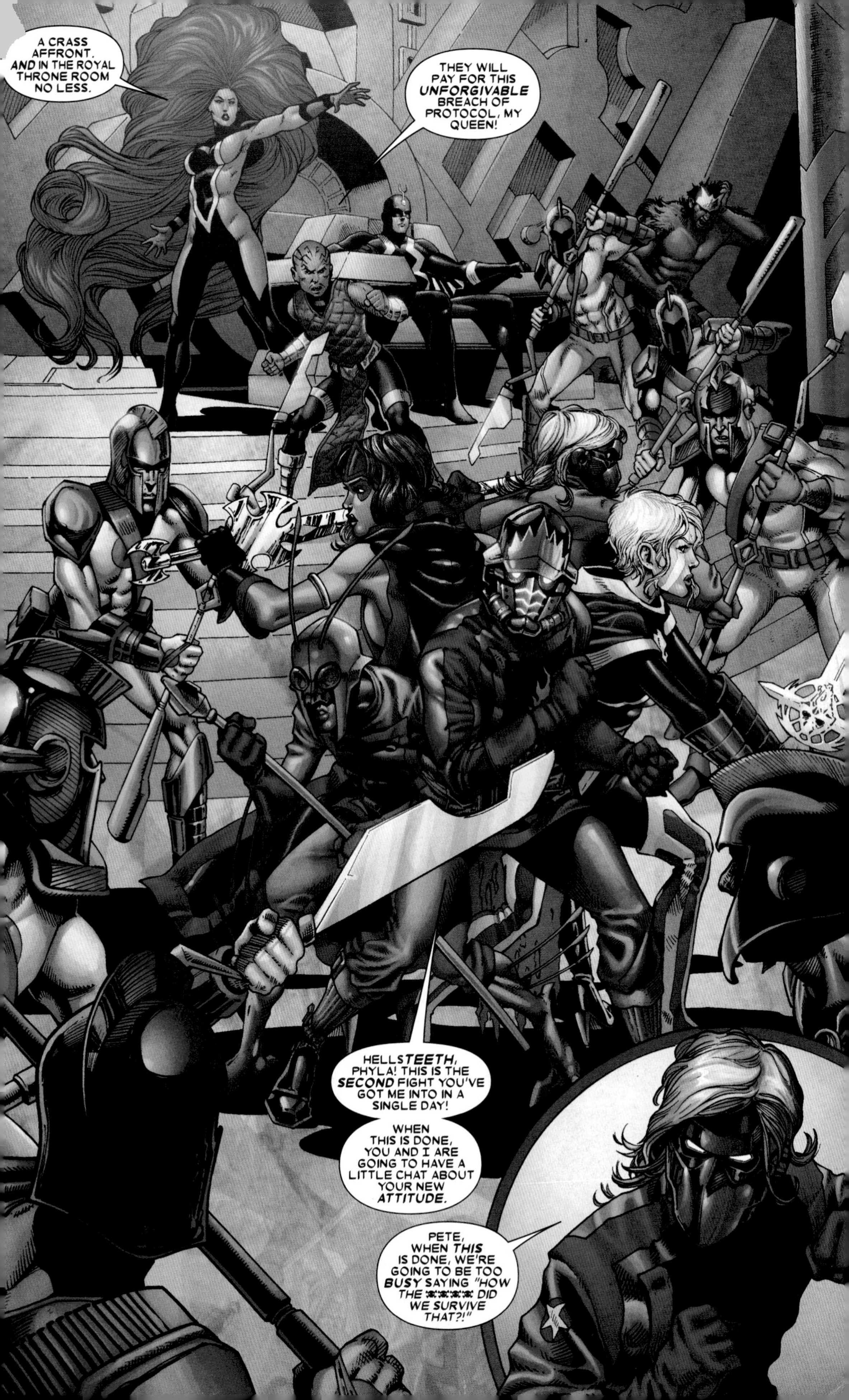
A CRASS AFFRONT. AND IN THE ROYAL THRONE ROOM NO LESS.
THEY WILL PAY FOR THIS UNFORGIVABLE BREACH OF PROTOCOL, MY QUEEN!
HELLSTEETH, PHYLA! THIS IS THE SECOND FIGHT YOU'VE GOT ME INTO IN A SINGLE DAY!
WHEN THIS IS DONE, YOU AND I ARE GOING TO HAVE A LITTLE CHAT ABOUT YOUR NEW ATTITUDE.
PETE, WHEN THIS IS DONE, WE'RE GOING TO BE TOO BUSY SAYING "HOW THE ✱✱✱✱ DID WE SURVIVE THAT?!"

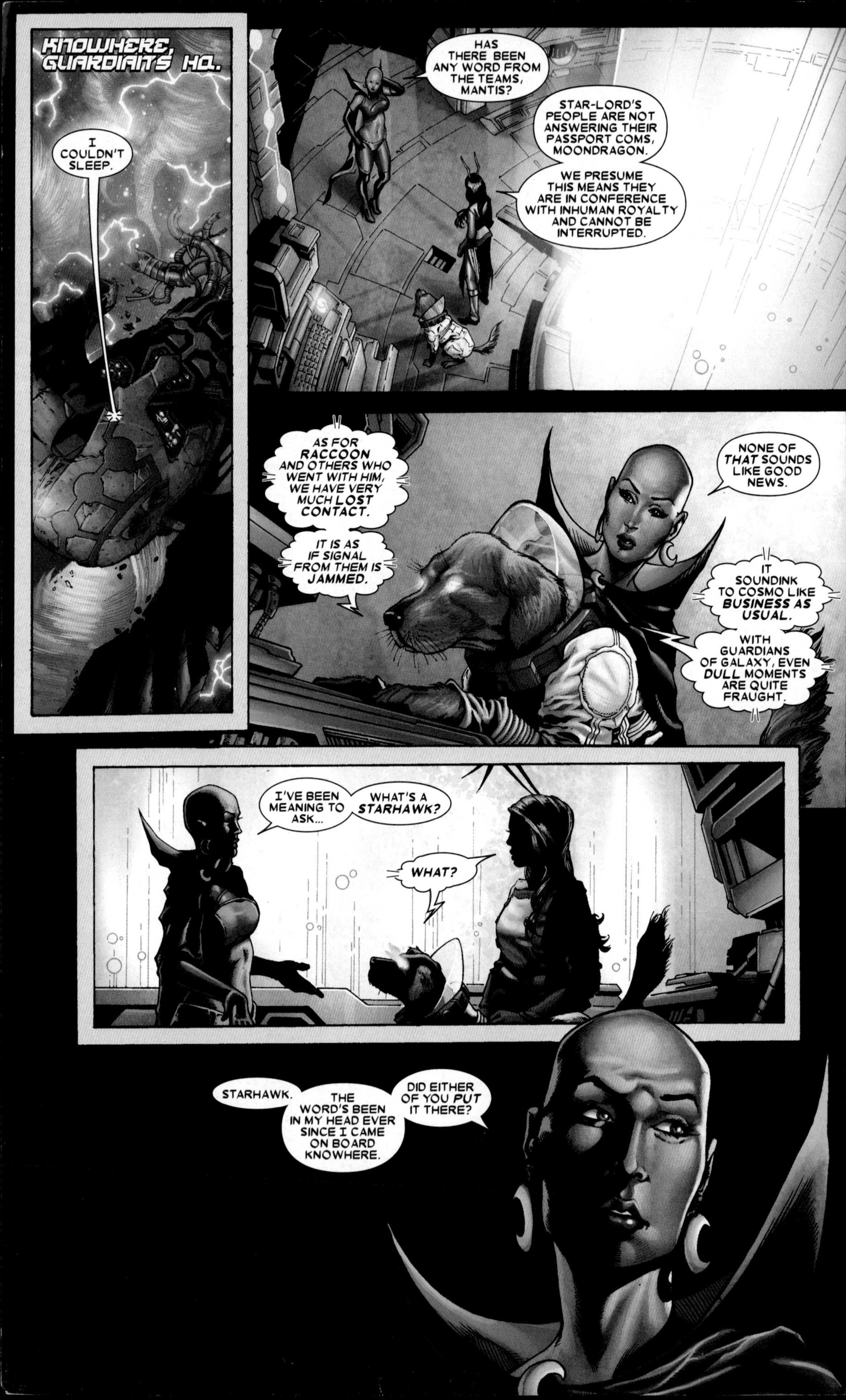
KNOWHERE, GUARDIANS' HQ.
I COULDN'T SLEEP.
HAS THERE BEEN ANY WORD FROM THE TEAMS, MANTIS?
STAR-LORD'S PEOPLE ARE NOT ANSWERING THEIR PASSPORT COMS, MOONDRAGON.
WE PRESUME THIS MEANS THEY ARE IN CONFERENCE WITH INHUMAN ROYALTY AND CANNOT BE INTERRUPTED.
AS FOR RACCOON AND OTHERS WHO WENT WITH HIM, WE HAVE VERY MUCH LOST CONTACT.
IT IS AS IF SIGNAL FROM THEM IS JAMMED.
NONE OF THAT SOUNDS LIKE GOOD NEWS.
IT SOUNDINK TO COSMO LIKE BUSINESS AS USUAL.
WITH GUARDIANS OF GALAXY, EVEN DULL MOMENTS ARE QUITE FRAUGHT.
I'VE BEEN MEANING TO ASK...
WHAT'S A STARHAWK?
WHAT?
STARHAWK.
THE WORD'S BEEN IN MY HEAD EVER SINCE I CAME ON BOARD KNOWHERE.
DID EITHER OF YOU PUT IT THERE?

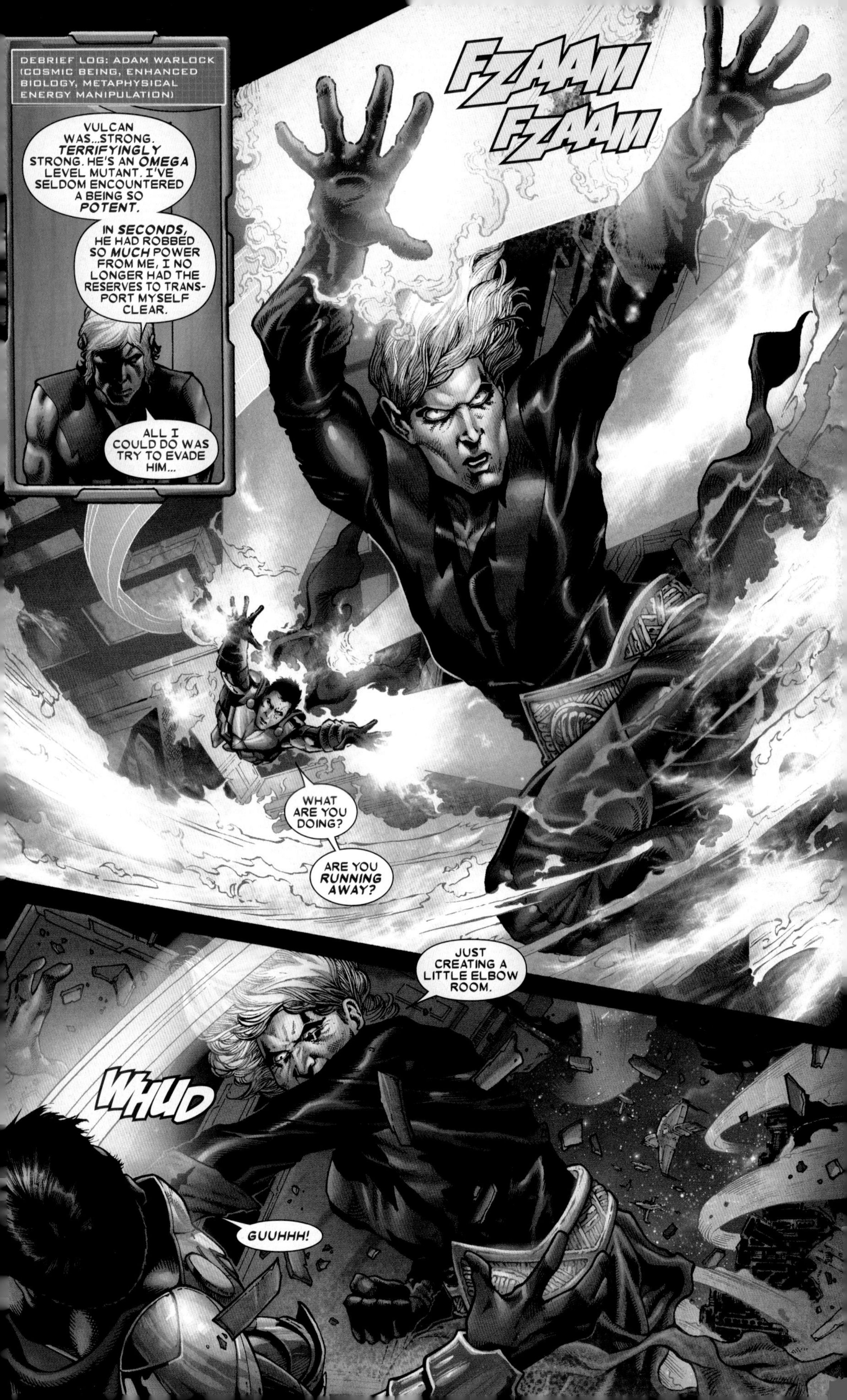
DEBRIEF LOG: ADAM WARLOCK (COSMIC BEING, ENHANCED BIOLOGY, METAPHYSICAL ENERGY MANIPULATION)
VULCAN WAS...STRONG. TERRIFYINGLY STRONG. HE'S AN OMEGA LEVEL MUTANT. I'VE SELDOM ENCOUNTERED A BEING SO POTENT.
IN SECONDS, HE HAD ROBBED SO MUCH POWER FROM ME, I NO LONGER HAD THE RESERVES TO TRANS-PORT MYSELF CLEAR.
ALL I COULD DO WAS TRY TO EVADE HIM...
FZAAM FZAAM
WHAT ARE YOU DOING?
ARE YOU RUNNING AWAY?
JUST CREATING A LITTLE ELBOW ROOM.
WHUD
GUUHHH!

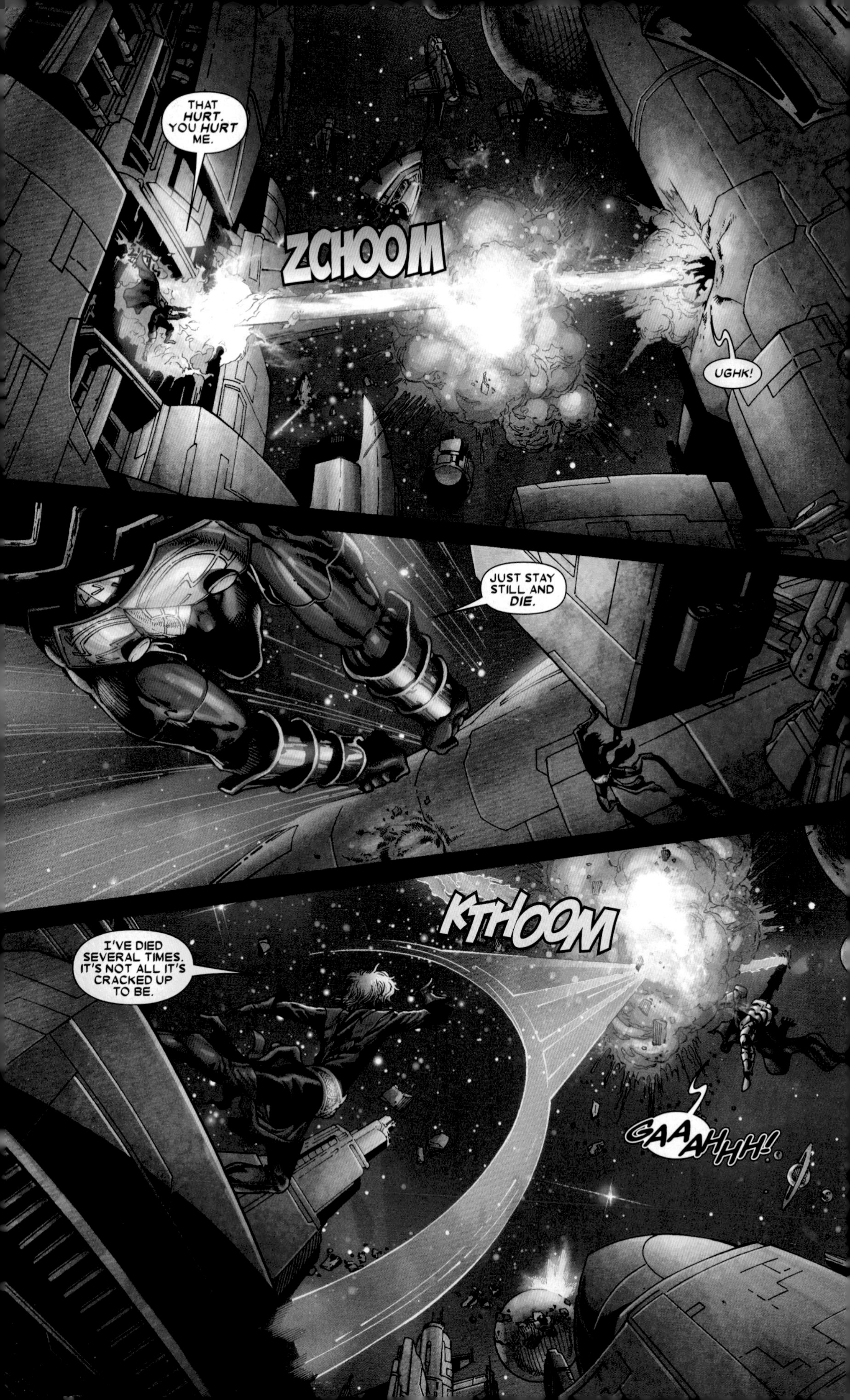
THAT HURT. YOU HURT ME.
ZCHOOM
UGHK!
JUST STAY STILL AND DIE.
I'VE DIED SEVERAL TIMES. IT'S NOT ALL IT'S CRACKED UP TO BE.
KTHOOM
GAAAHHH!

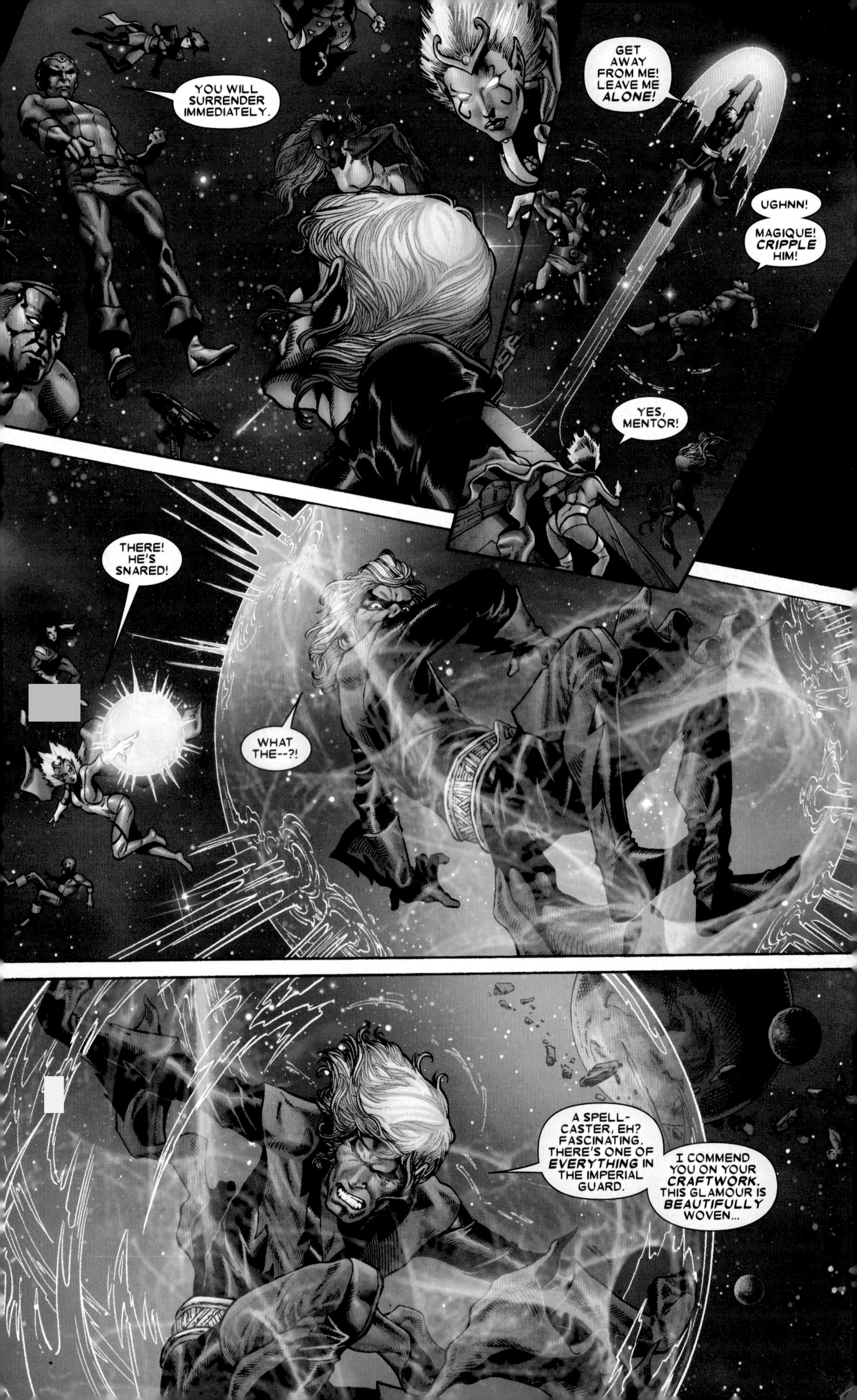
YOU WILL SURRENDER IMMEDIATELY.
GET AWAY FROM ME! LEAVE ME ALONE!
UGHNN!
MAGIQUE! CRIPPLE HIM!
YES, MENTOR!
THERE! HE'S SNARED!
WHAT THE--?!
A SPELL-CASTER, EH? FASCINATING. THERE'S ONE OF EVERYTHING IN THE IMPERIAL GUARD.
I COMMEND YOU ON YOUR CRAFTWORK. THIS GLAMOUR IS BEAUTIFULLY WOVEN...

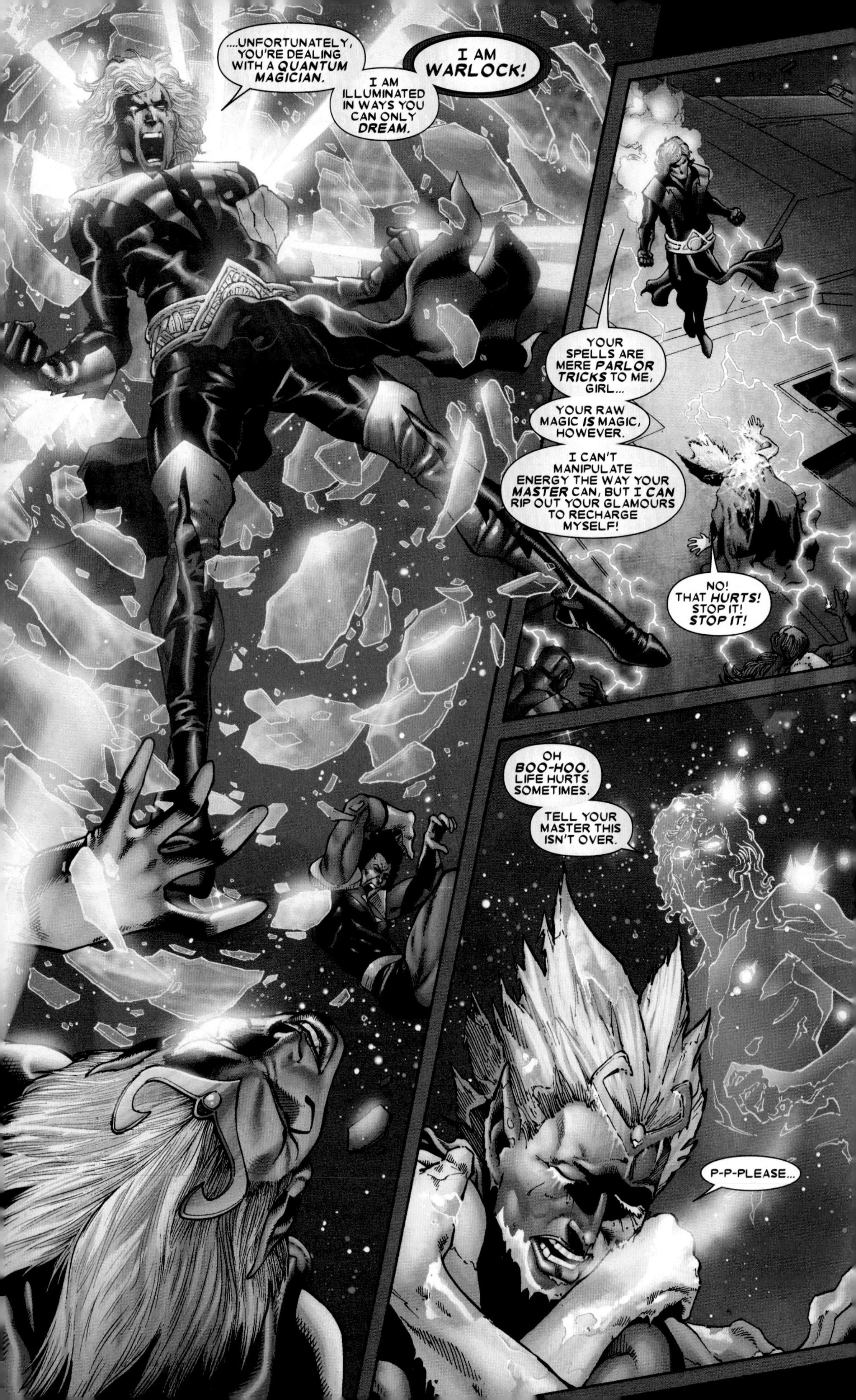
...UNFORTUNATELY, YOU'RE DEALING WITH A QUANTUM MAGICIAN.
I AM ILLUMINATED IN WAYS YOU CAN ONLY DREAM.
I AM WARLOCK!
YOUR SPELLS ARE MERE PARLOR TRICKS TO ME, GIRL...
YOUR RAW MAGIC IS MAGIC, HOWEVER.
I CAN'T MANIPULATE ENERGY THE WAY YOUR MASTER CAN, BUT I CAN RIP OUT YOUR GLAMOURS TO RECHARGE MYSELF!
NO! THAT HURTS! STOP IT! STOP IT!
OH BOO-HOO. LIFE HURTS SOMETIMES.
TELL YOUR MASTER THIS ISN'T OVER.
P-P-PLEASE...

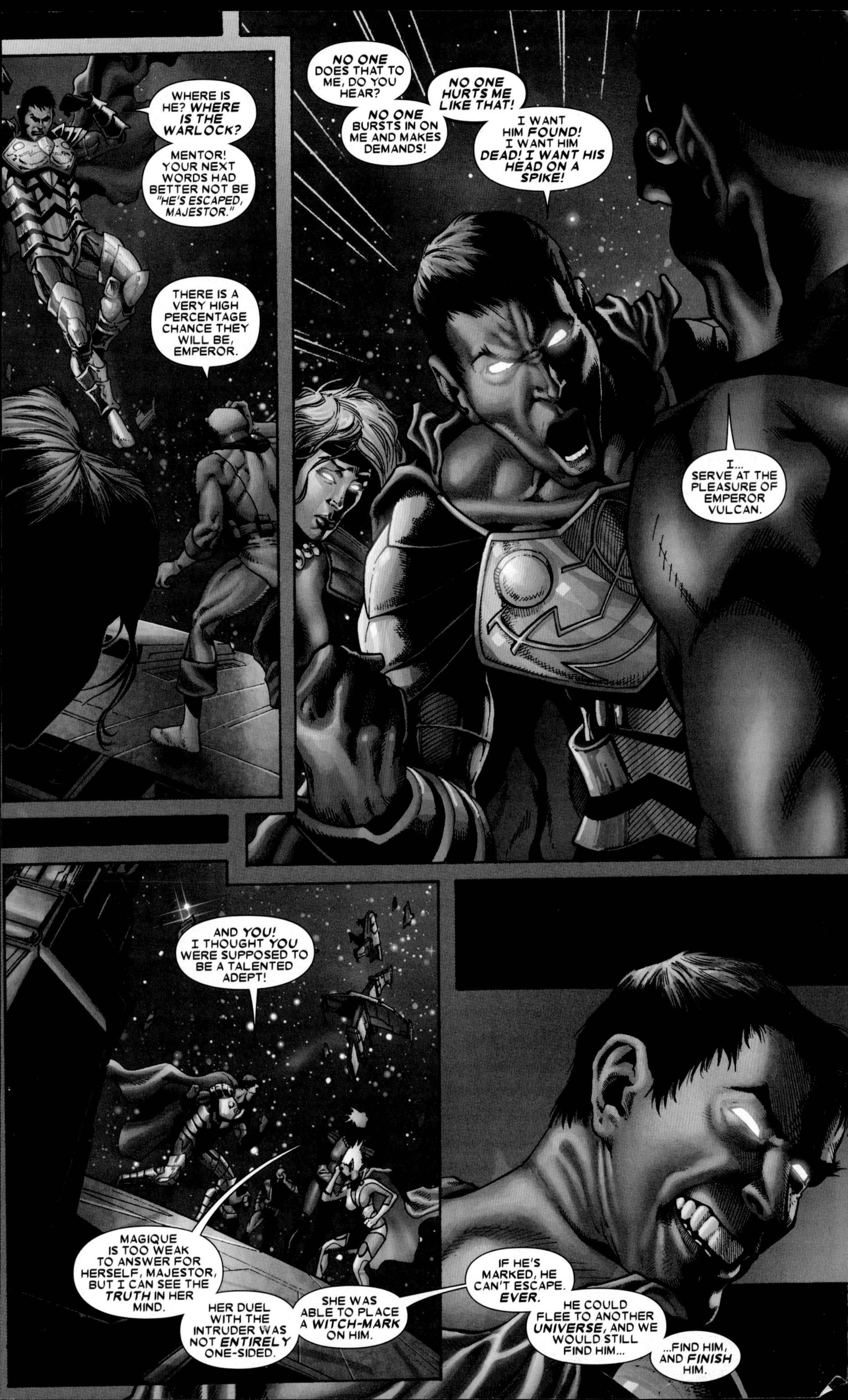
WHERE IS HE? *WHERE IS THE WARLOCK?*
MENTOR! YOUR NEXT WORDS HAD BETTER NOT BE *"HE'S ESCAPED, MAJESTOR."*
THERE IS A VERY HIGH PERCENTAGE CHANCE THEY WILL BE, EMPEROR.
NO ONE DOES THAT TO ME, DO YOU HEAR?
NO ONE BURSTS IN ON ME AND MAKES DEMANDS!
NO ONE HURTS ME LIKE THAT!
I WANT HIM *FOUND!* I WANT HIM *DEAD! I WANT HIS HEAD ON A SPIKE!*
I... SERVE AT THE PLEASURE OF EMPEROR VULCAN.
AND *YOU!* I THOUGHT *YOU* WERE SUPPOSED TO BE A TALENTED ADEPT!
MAGIQUE IS TOO WEAK TO ANSWER FOR HERSELF, MAJESTOR, BUT I CAN SEE THE *TRUTH* IN HER MIND.
HER DUEL WITH THE INTRUDER WAS NOT *ENTIRELY* ONE-SIDED.
SHE WAS ABLE TO PLACE A *WITCH-MARK* ON HIM.
IF HE'S MARKED, HE CAN'T ESCAPE. *EVER.*
HE COULD FLEE TO ANOTHER *UNIVERSE*, AND WE WOULD STILL FIND HIM...
...FIND HIM, AND *FINISH* HIM.

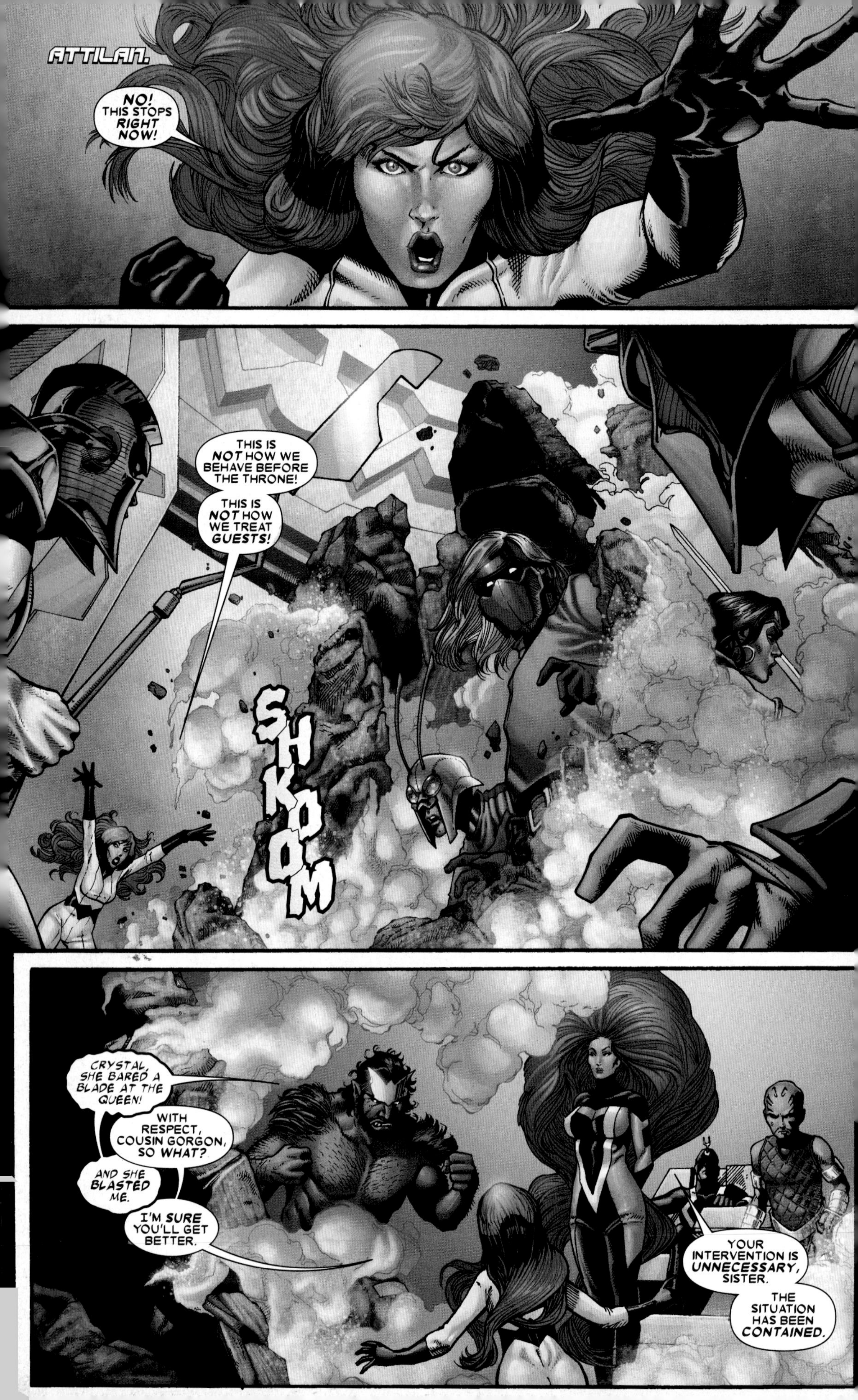
ATTILAN.
NO! THIS STOPS RIGHT NOW!
THIS IS NOT HOW WE BEHAVE BEFORE THE THRONE!
THIS IS NOT HOW WE TREAT GUESTS!
SHKOOM
CRYSTAL, SHE BARED A BLADE AT THE QUEEN!
WITH RESPECT, COUSIN GORGON, SO WHAT?
AND SHE BLASTED ME.
I'M SURE YOU'LL GET BETTER.
YOUR INTERVENTION IS UNNECESSARY, SISTER.
THE SITUATION HAS BEEN CONTAINED.

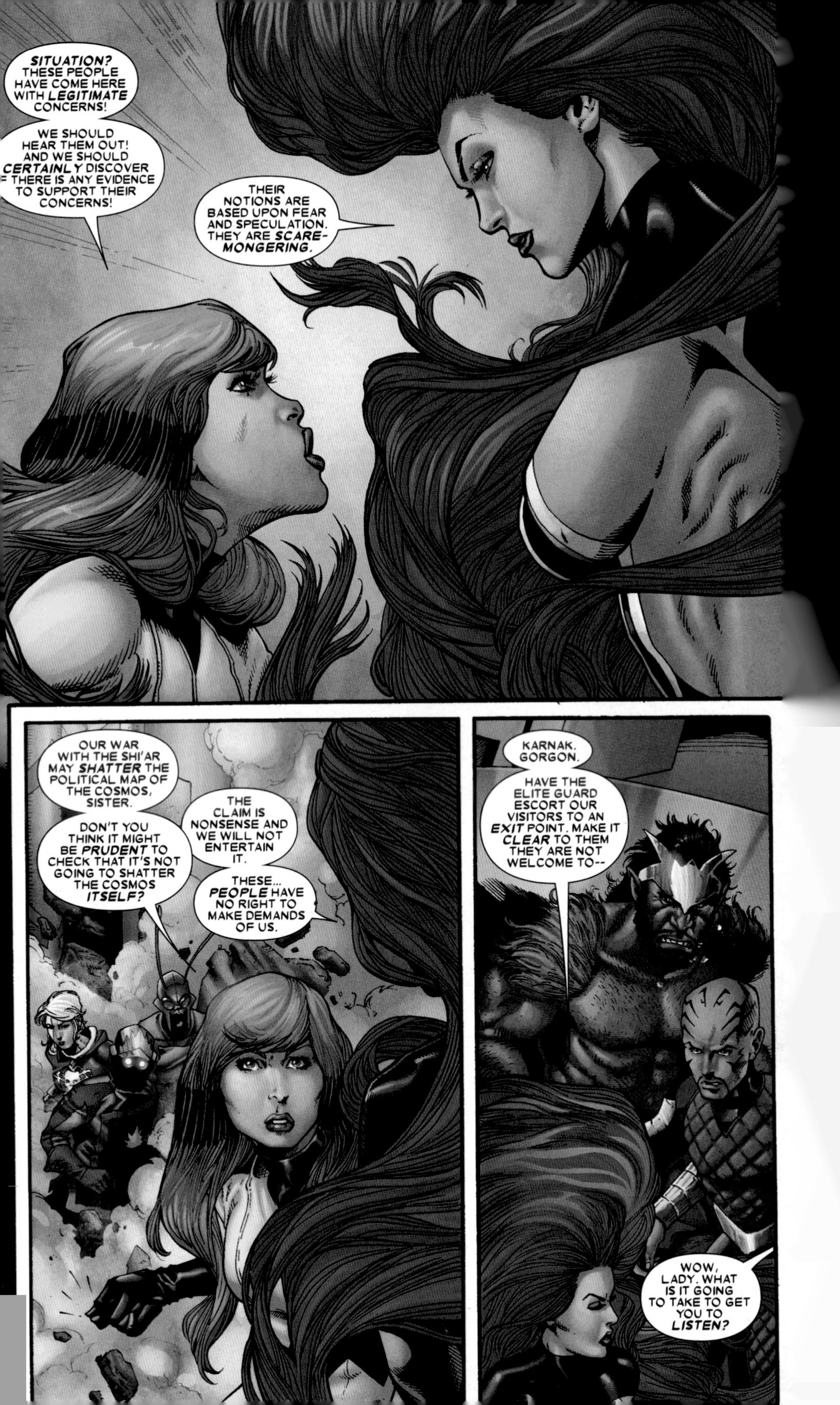
SITUATION? THESE PEOPLE HAVE COME HERE WITH LEGITIMATE CONCERNS!
WE SHOULD HEAR THEM OUT! AND WE SHOULD CERTAINLY DISCOVER IF THERE IS ANY EVIDENCE TO SUPPORT THEIR CONCERNS!
THEIR NOTIONS ARE BASED UPON FEAR AND SPECULATION. THEY ARE SCARE-MONGERING.
OUR WAR WITH THE SHI'AR MAY SHATTER THE POLITICAL MAP OF THE COSMOS, SISTER.
DON'T YOU THINK IT MIGHT BE PRUDENT TO CHECK THAT IT'S NOT GOING TO SHATTER THE COSMOS ITSELF?
THE CLAIM IS NONSENSE AND WE WILL NOT ENTERTAIN IT.
THESE... PEOPLE HAVE NO RIGHT TO MAKE DEMANDS OF US.
KARNAK. GORGON.
HAVE THE ELITE GUARD ESCORT OUR VISITORS TO AN EXIT POINT. MAKE IT CLEAR TO THEM THEY ARE NOT WELCOME TO--
WOW, LADY. WHAT IS IT GOING TO TAKE TO GET YOU TO LISTEN?

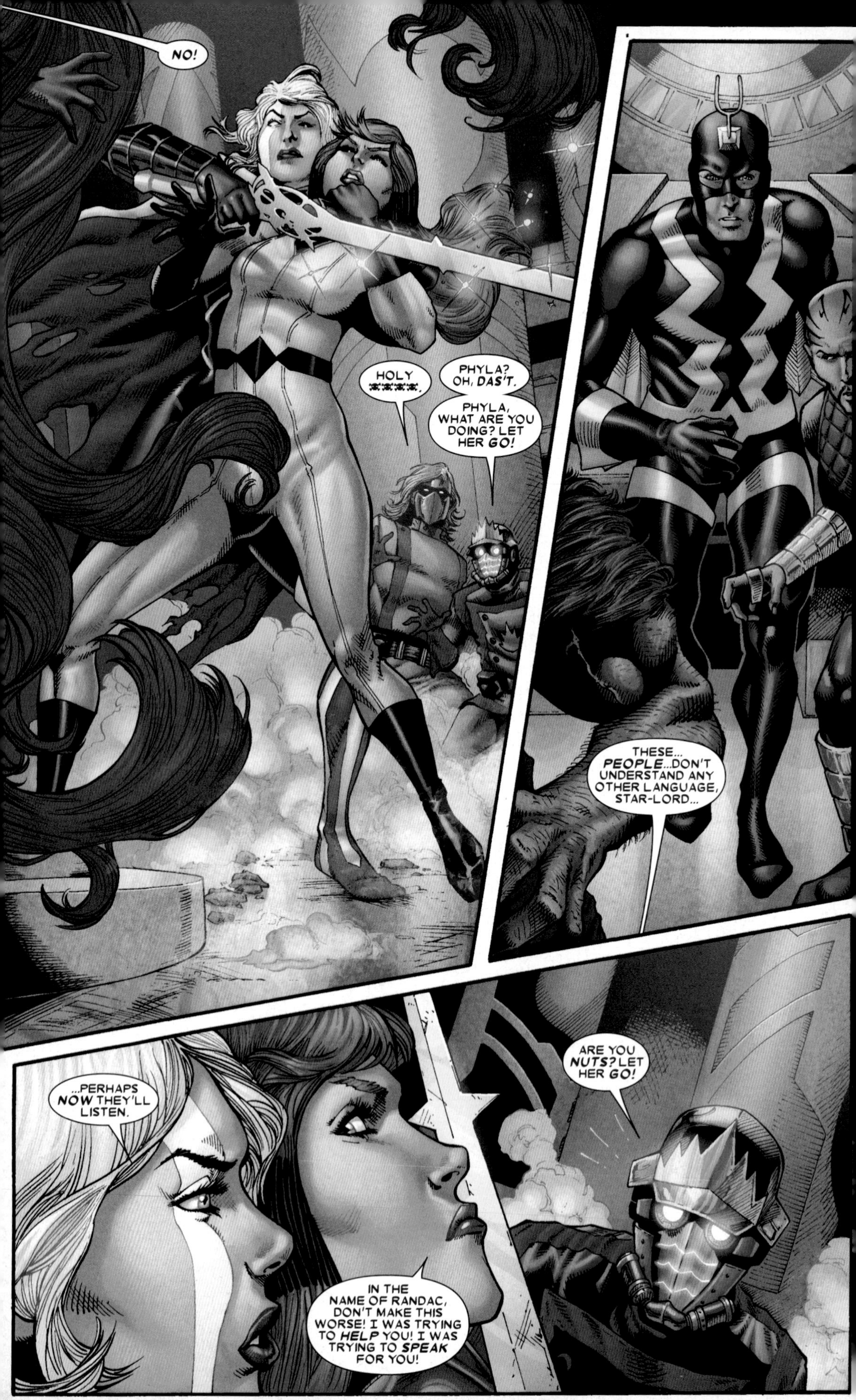
NO!
HOLY
PHYLA? OH, DAS'T.
PHYLA, WHAT ARE YOU DOING? LET HER GO!
THESE... PEOPLE...DON'T UNDERSTAND ANY OTHER LANGUAGE, STAR-LORD...
...PERHAPS NOW THEY'LL LISTEN.
ARE YOU NUTS? LET HER GO!
IN THE NAME OF RANDAC, DON'T MAKE THIS WORSE! I WAS TRYING TO HELP YOU! I WAS TRYING TO SPEAK FOR YOU!

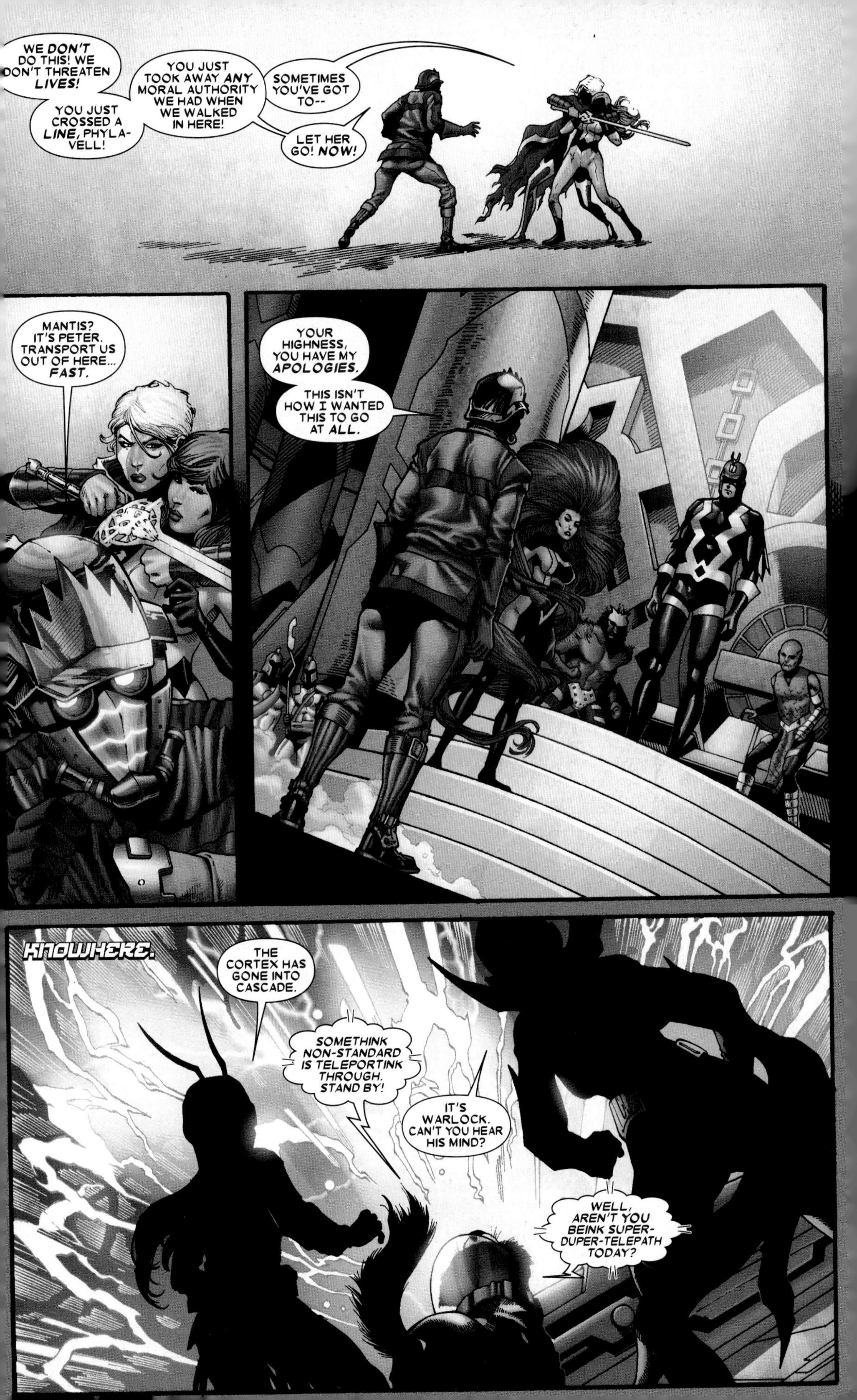

WE DON'T DO THIS! WE DON'T THREATEN LIVES!
YOU JUST CROSSED A LINE, PHYLA-VELL!
YOU JUST TOOK AWAY ANY MORAL AUTHORITY WE HAD WHEN WE WALKED IN HERE!
SOMETIMES YOU'VE GOT TO--
LET HER GO! NOW!
MANTIS? IT'S PETER. TRANSPORT US OUT OF HERE... FAST.
YOUR HIGHNESS, YOU HAVE MY APOLOGIES.
THIS ISN'T HOW I WANTED THIS TO GO AT ALL.
KNOWHERE.
THE CORTEX HAS GONE INTO CASCADE.
SOMETHINK NON-STANDARD IS TELEPORTINK THROUGH. STAND BY!
IT'S WARLOCK. CAN'T YOU HEAR HIS MIND?
WELL, AREN'T YOU BEINK SUPER-DUPER-TELEPATH TODAY?

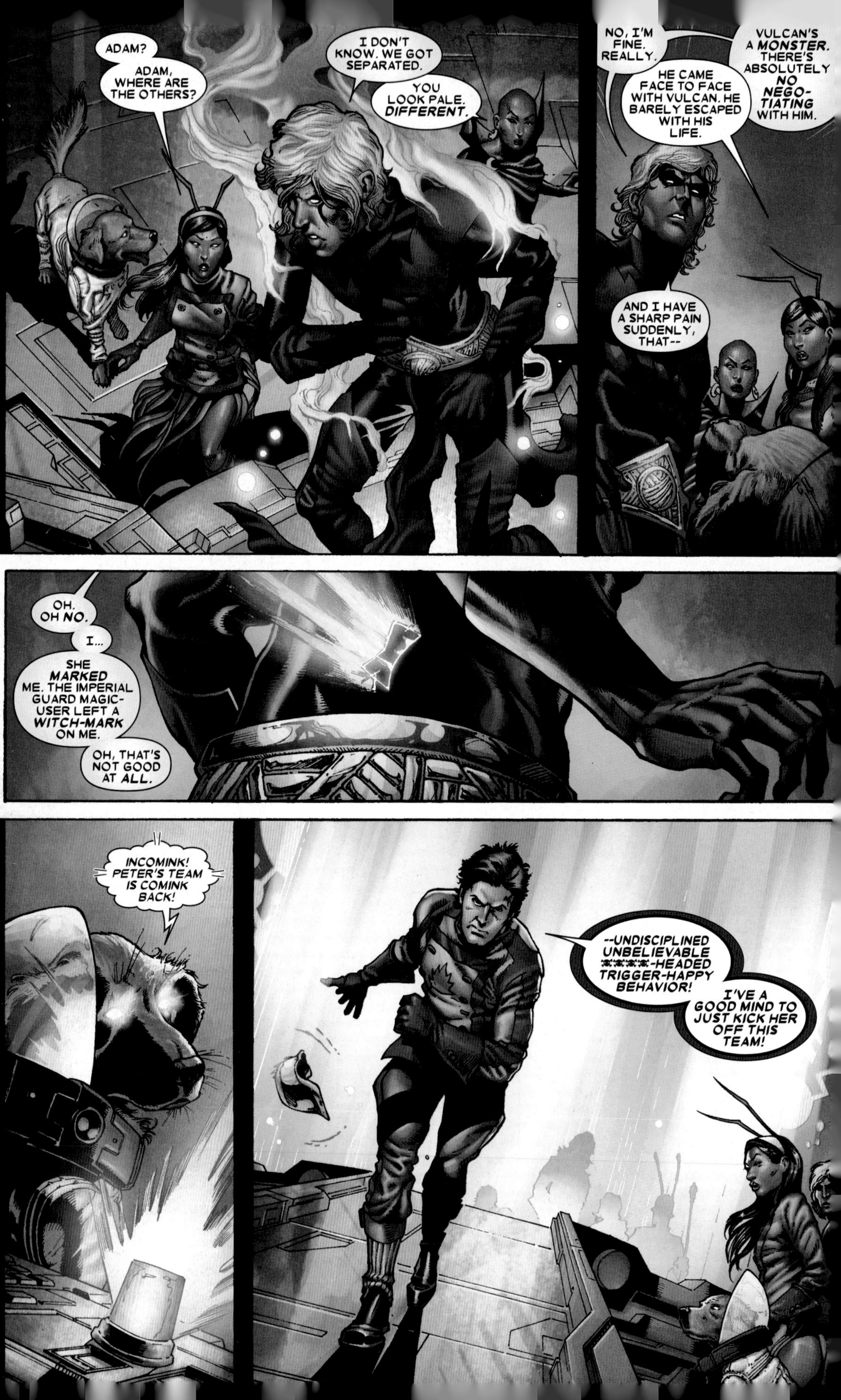
ADAM?
ADAM, WHERE ARE THE OTHERS?
I DON'T KNOW. WE GOT SEPARATED.
YOU LOOK PALE. DIFFERENT.
NO, I'M FINE. REALLY.
HE CAME FACE TO FACE WITH VULCAN. HE BARELY ESCAPED WITH HIS LIFE.
VULCAN'S A MONSTER. THERE'S ABSOLUTELY NO NEGO-TIATING WITH HIM.
AND I HAVE A SHARP PAIN SUDDENLY, THAT--
OH. OH NO.
I...
SHE MARKED ME. THE IMPERIAL GUARD MAGIC-USER LEFT A WITCH-MARK ON ME.
OH, THAT'S NOT GOOD AT ALL.
INCOMINK! PETER'S TEAM IS COMINK BACK!
--UNDISCIPLINED UNBELIEVABLE ☠☠☠-HEADED TRIGGER-HAPPY BEHAVIOR!
I'VE A GOOD MIND TO JUST KICK HER OFF THIS TEAM!

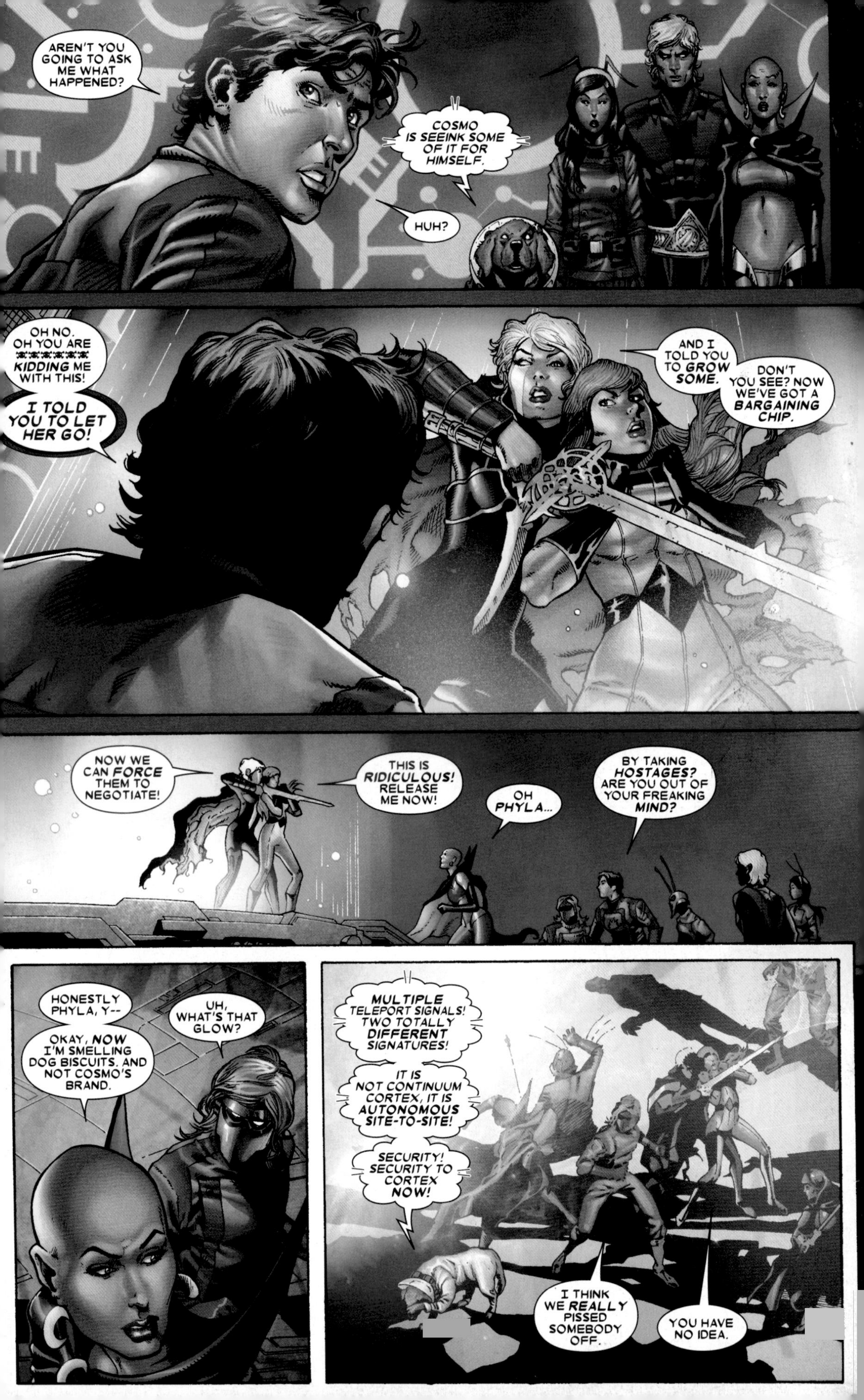
ARE'T YOU GOING TO ASK ME WHAT HAPPENED?
COSMO IS SEEINK SOME OF IT FOR HIMSELF.
HUH?
OH NO. OH YOU ARE KIDDING ME WITH THIS!
I TOLD YOU TO LET HER GO!
AND I TOLD YOU TO GROW SOME.
DON'T YOU SEE? NOW WE'VE GOT A BARGAINING CHIP.
NOW WE CAN FORCE THEM TO NEGOTIATE!
THIS IS RIDICULOUS! RELEASE ME NOW!
OH PHYLA...
BY TAKING HOSTAGES? ARE YOU OUT OF YOUR FREAKING MIND?
HONESTLY PHYLA, Y--
UH, WHAT'S THAT GLOW?
OKAY, NOW I'M SMELLING DOG BISCUITS. AND NOT COSMO'S BRAND.
MULTIPLE TELEPORT SIGNALS! TWO TOTALLY DIFFERENT SIGNATURES!
IT IS NOT CONTINUUM CORTEX, IT IS AUTONOMOUS SITE-TO-SITE!
SECURITY! SECURITY TO CORTEX NOW!
I THINK WE REALLY PISSED SOMEBODY OFF.
YOU HAVE NO IDEA.

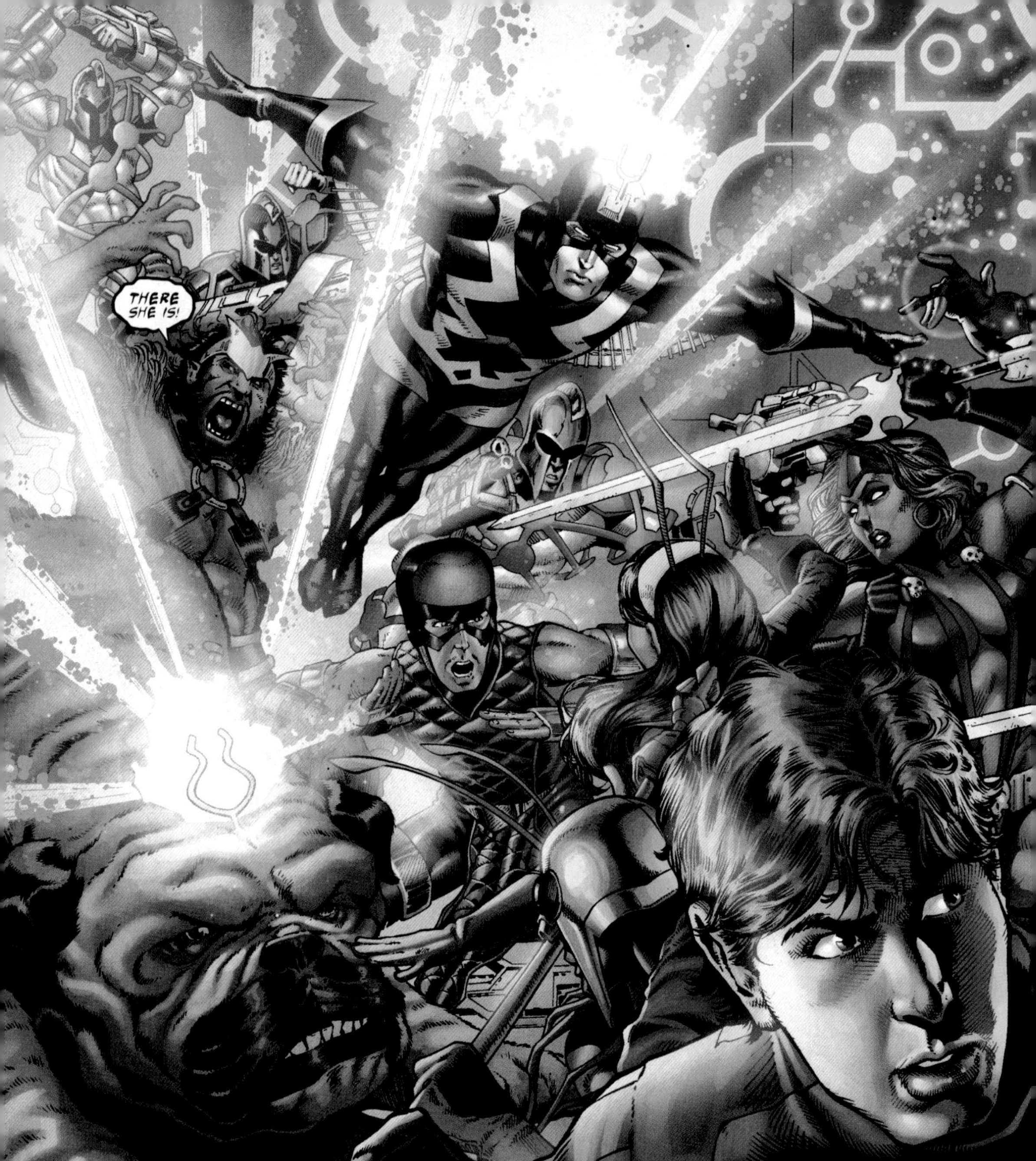
THERE SHE IS!

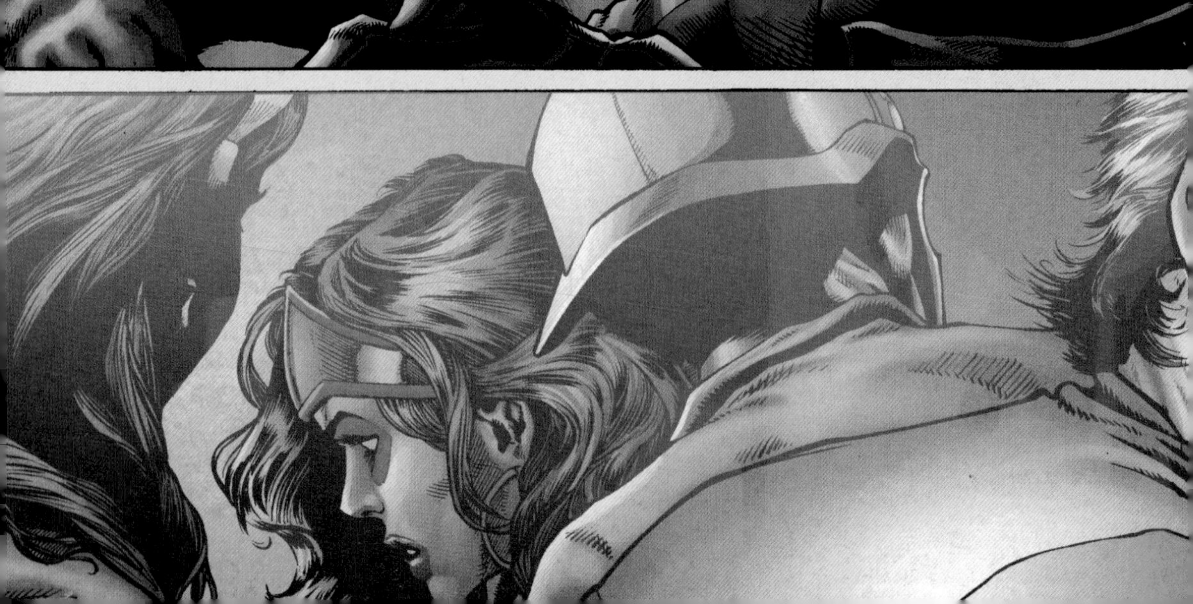

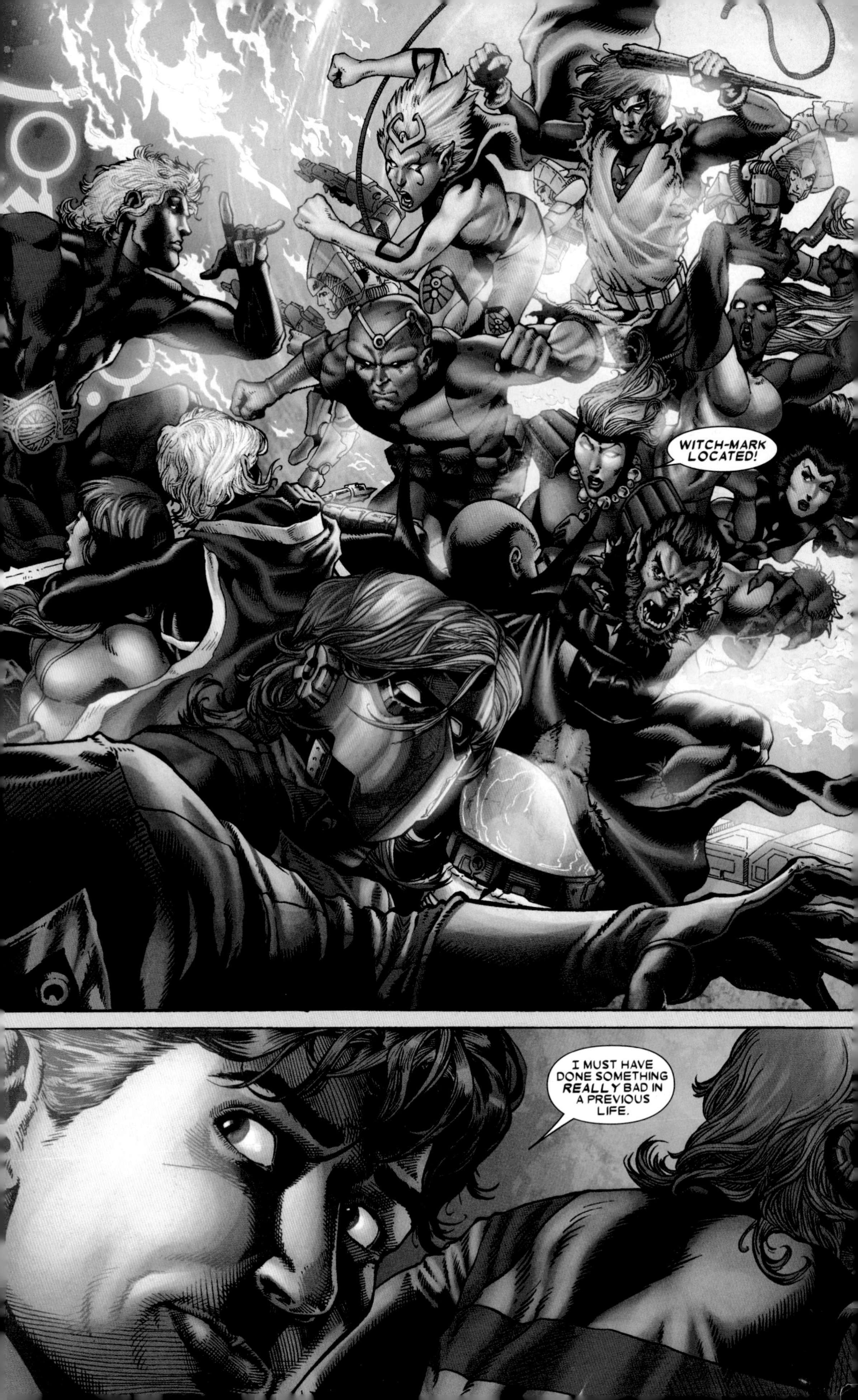
WITCH-MARK LOCATED!
I MUST HAVE DONE SOMETHING REALLY BAD IN A PREVIOUS LIFE.

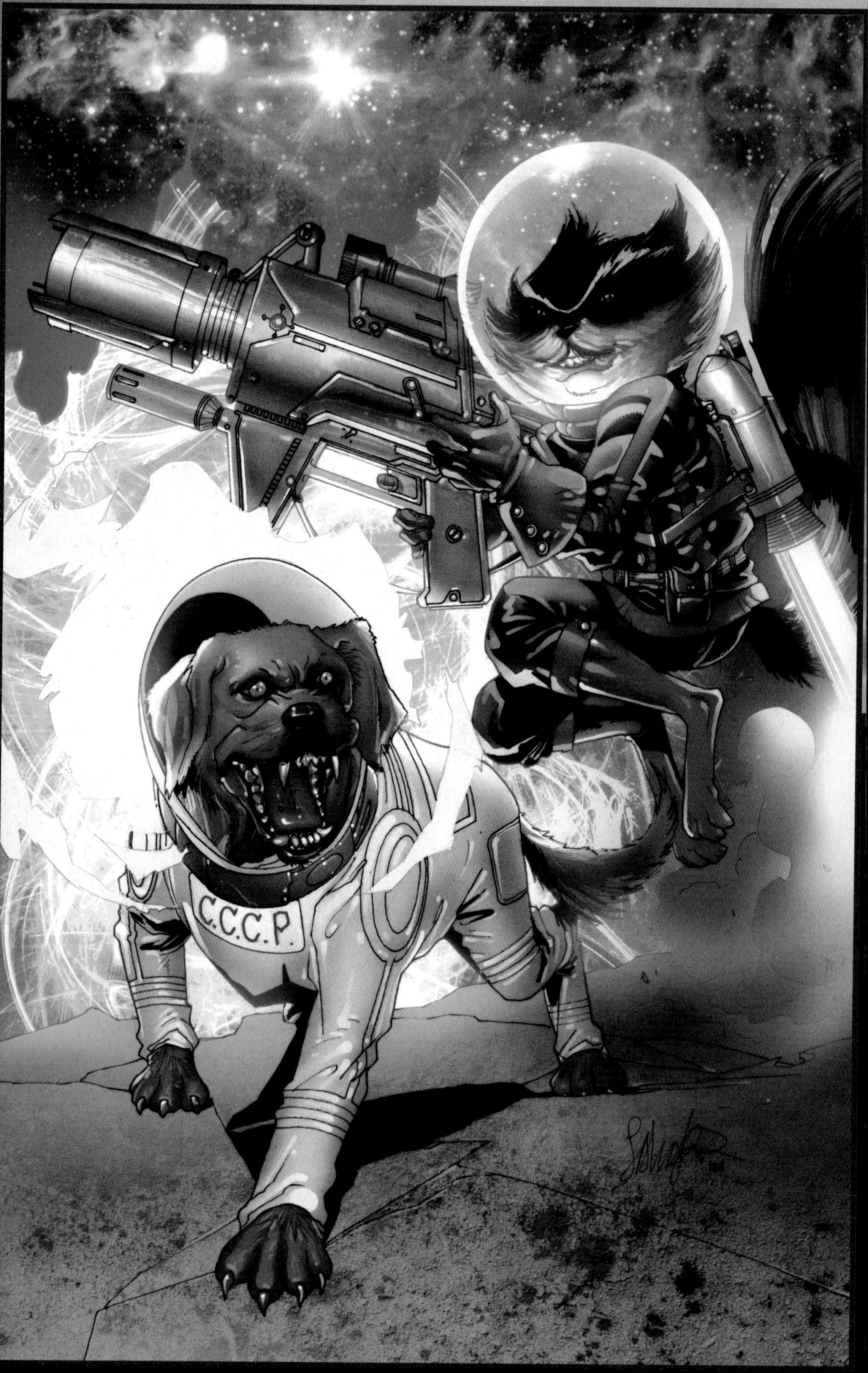
C.C.C.P.

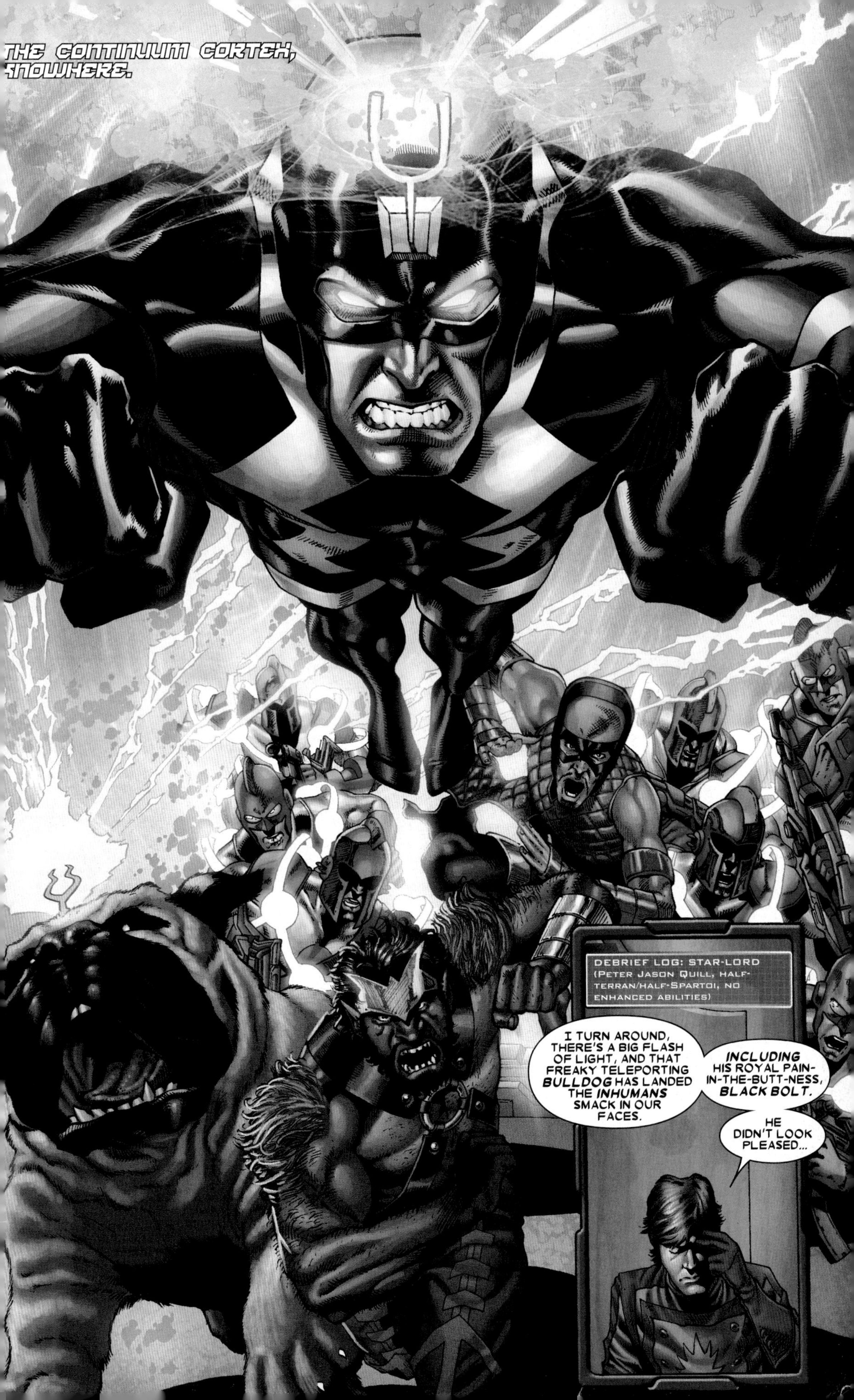
THE CONTINUUM CORTEX, KNOWHERE.
DEBRIEF LOG: STAR-LORD (PETER JASON QUILL, HALF-TERRAN/HALF-SPARTOI, NO ENHANCED ABILITIES)
I TURN AROUND, THERE'S A BIG FLASH OF LIGHT, AND THAT FREAKY TELEPORTING BULLDOG HAS LANDED THE INHUMANS SMACK IN OUR FACES.
INCLUDING HIS ROYAL PAIN-IN-THE-BUTT-NESS, BLACK BOLT.
HE DIDN'T LOOK PLEASED...

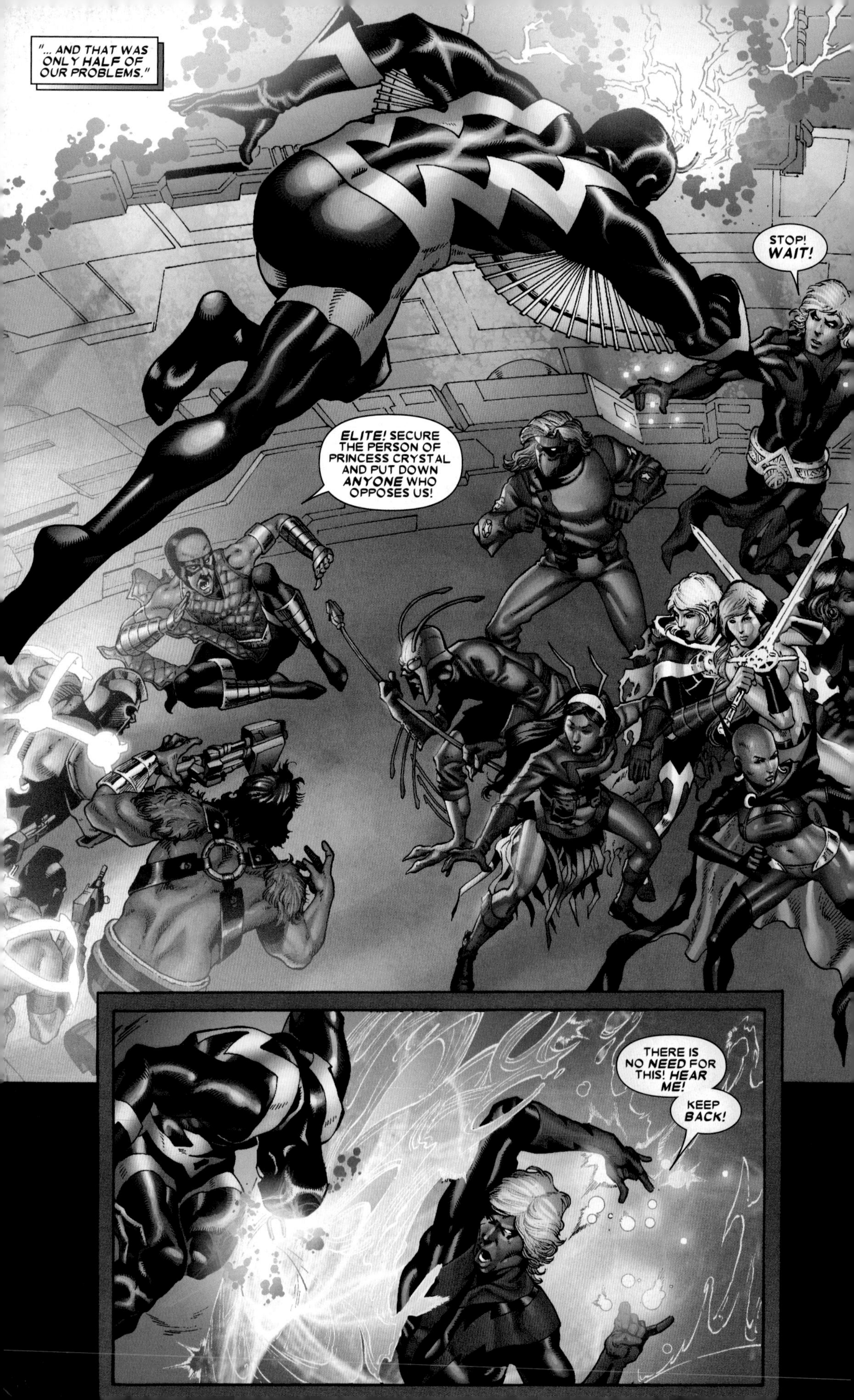
"... AND THAT WAS ONLY HALF OF OUR PROBLEMS."
STOP! WAIT!
ELITE! SECURE THE PERSON OF PRINCESS CRYSTAL AND PUT DOWN ANYONE WHO OPPOSES US!
THERE IS NO NEED FOR THIS! HEAR ME!
KEEP BACK!

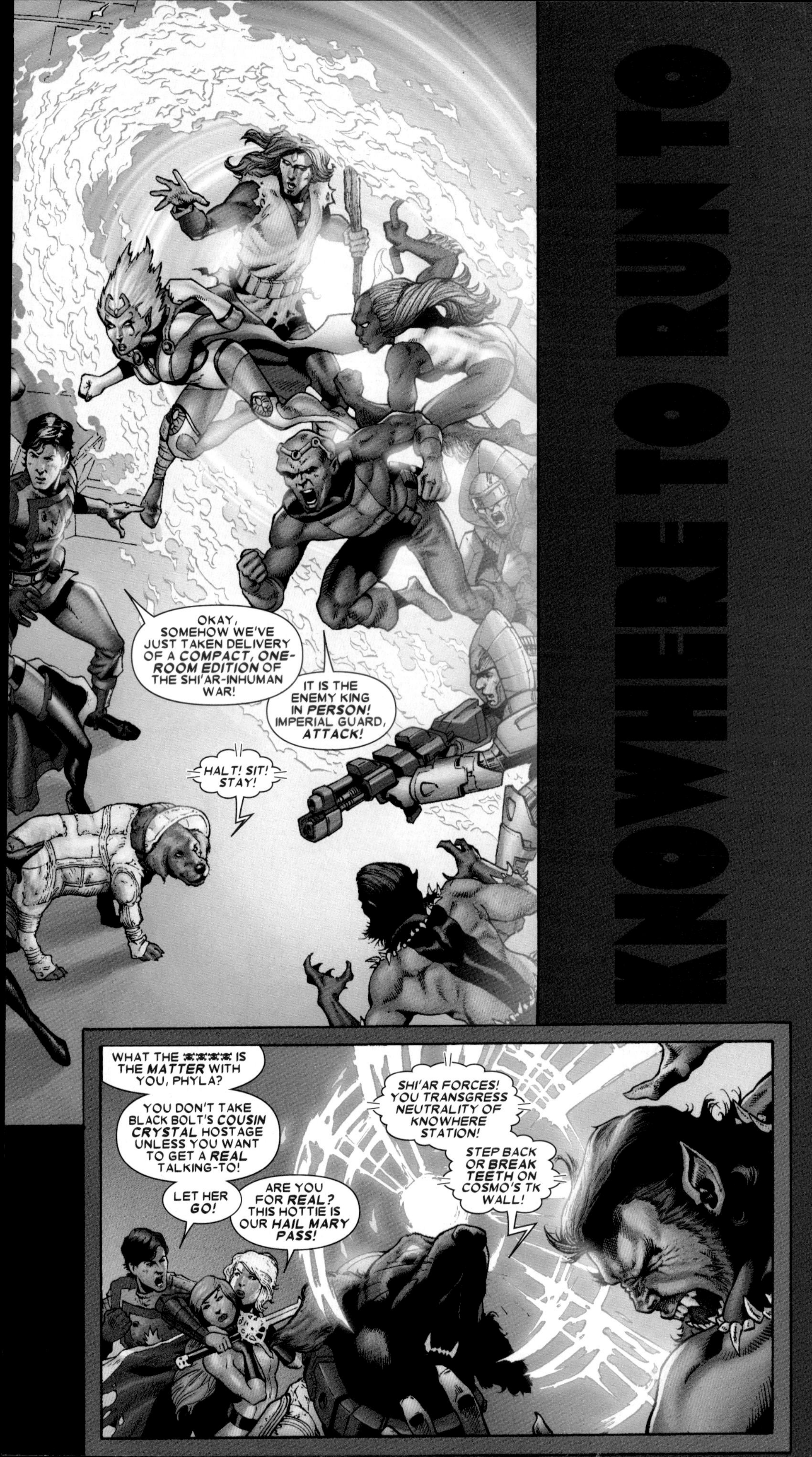
KNOWHERE TO RUN TO
OKAY, SOMEHOW WE'VE JUST TAKEN DELIVERY OF A COMPACT, ONE-ROOM EDITION OF THE SHI'AR-INHUMAN WAR!
IT IS THE ENEMY KING IN PERSON! IMPERIAL GUARD, ATTACK!
HALT! SIT! STAY!
WHAT THE ☠✲☠✲ IS THE MATTER WITH YOU, PHYLA?
YOU DON'T TAKE BLACK BOLT'S COUSIN CRYSTAL HOSTAGE UNLESS YOU WANT TO GET A REAL TALKING-TO!
LET HER GO!
ARE YOU FOR REAL? THIS HOTTIE IS OUR HAIL MARY PASS!
SHI'AR FORCES! YOU TRANSGRESS NEUTRALITY OF KNOWHERE STATION!
STEP BACK OR BREAK TEETH ON COSMO'S TK WALL!

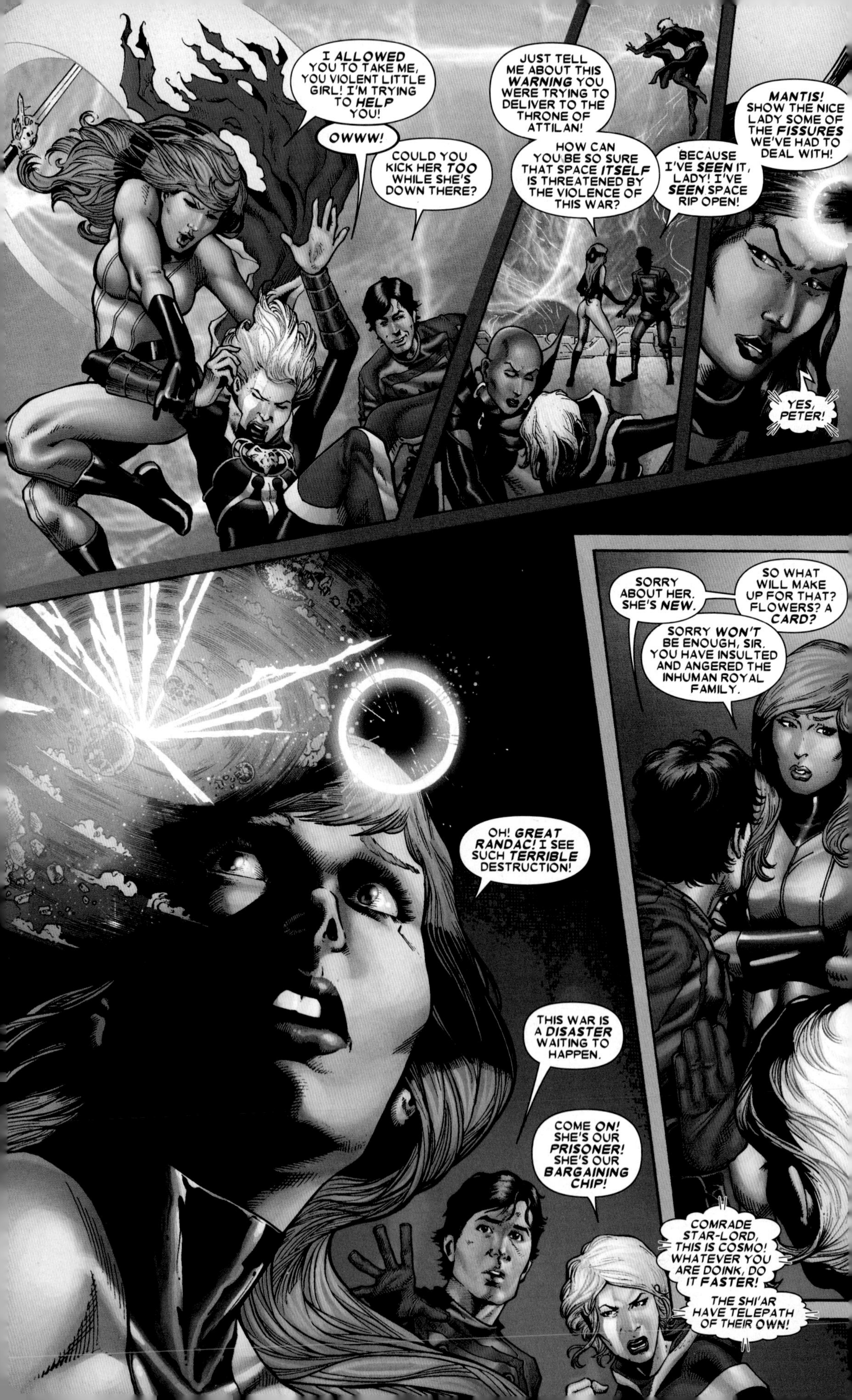
I ALLOWED YOU TO TAKE ME, YOU VIOLENT LITTLE GIRL! I'M TRYING TO HELP YOU!
OWWW!
COULD YOU KICK HER TOO WHILE SHE'S DOWN THERE?
JUST TELL ME ABOUT THIS WARNING YOU WERE TRYING TO DELIVER TO THE THRONE OF ATTILAN!
HOW CAN YOU BE SO SURE THAT SPACE ITSELF IS THREATENED BY THE VIOLENCE OF THIS WAR?
BECAUSE I'VE SEEN IT, LADY! I'VE SEEN SPACE RIP OPEN!
MANTIS! SHOW THE NICE LADY SOME OF THE FISSURES WE'VE HAD TO DEAL WITH!
YES, PETER!
OH! GREAT RANDAC! I SEE SUCH TERRIBLE DESTRUCTION!
THIS WAR IS A DISASTER WAITING TO HAPPEN.
SORRY ABOUT HER. SHE'S NEW.
SO WHAT WILL MAKE UP FOR THAT? FLOWERS? A CARD?
SORRY WON'T BE ENOUGH, SIR. YOU HAVE INSULTED AND ANGERED THE INHUMAN ROYAL FAMILY.
COME ON! SHE'S OUR PRISONER! SHE'S OUR BARGAINING CHIP!
COMRADE STAR-LORD, THIS IS COSMO! WHATEVER YOU ARE DOINK, DO IT FASTER!
THE SHI'AR HAVE TELEPATH OF THEIR OWN!

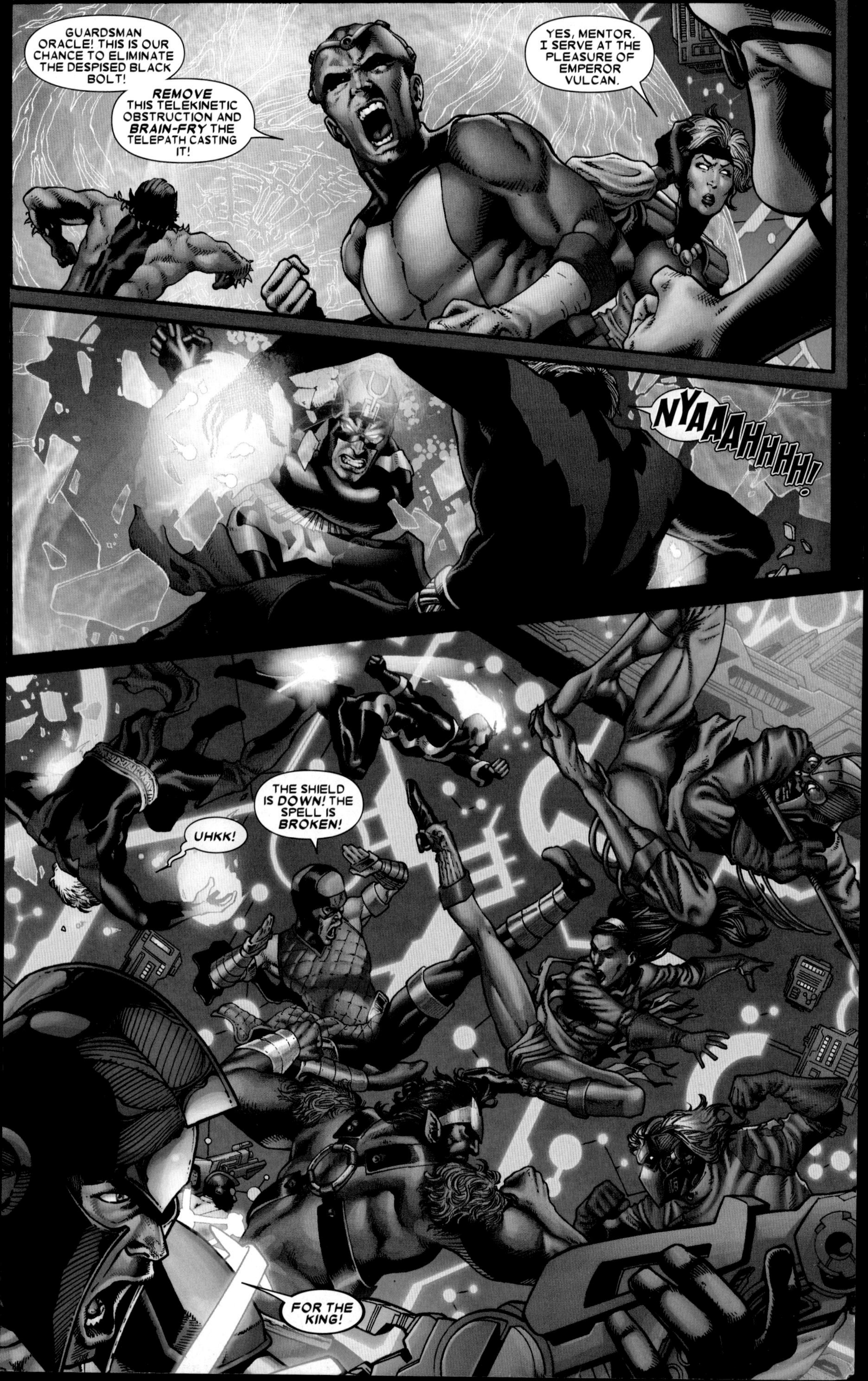
GUARDSMAN ORACLE! THIS IS OUR CHANCE TO ELIMINATE THE DESPISED BLACK BOLT!
REMOVE THIS TELEKINETIC OBSTRUCTION AND BRAIN-FRY THE TELEPATH CASTING IT!
YES, MENTOR. I SERVE AT THE PLEASURE OF EMPEROR VULCAN.
NYAAAHHHH!
UHKK!
THE SHIELD IS DOWN! THE SPELL IS BROKEN!
FOR THE KING!

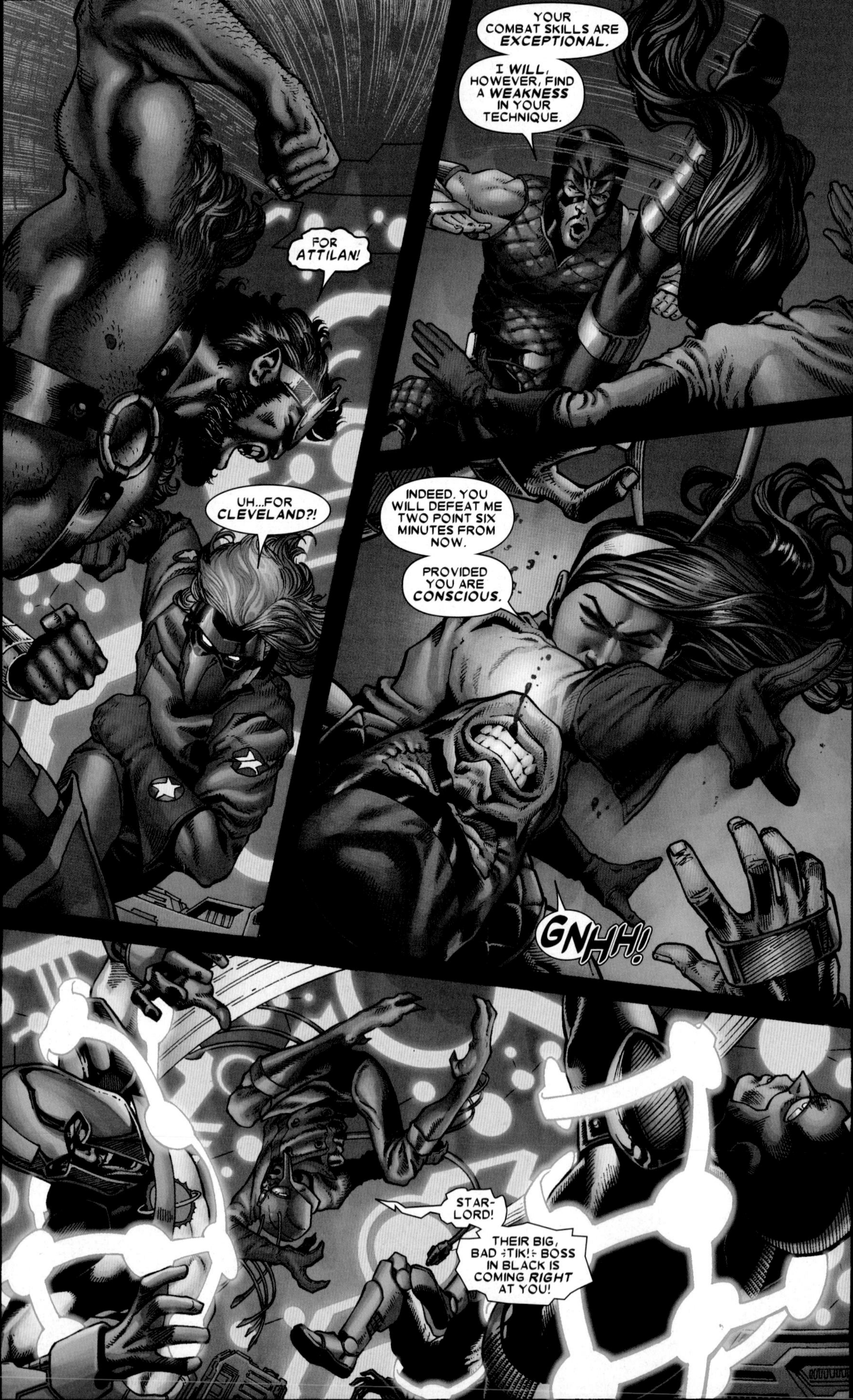
FOR ATTILAN!
UH...FOR CLEVELAND?!
YOUR COMBAT SKILLS ARE EXCEPTIONAL.
I WILL, HOWEVER, FIND A WEAKNESS IN YOUR TECHNIQUE.
INDEED. YOU WILL DEFEAT ME TWO POINT SIX MINUTES FROM NOW.
PROVIDED YOU ARE CONSCIOUS.
GNHH!
STAR-LORD!
THEIR BIG, BAD ÷TIK!÷ BOSS IN BLACK IS COMING RIGHT AT YOU!

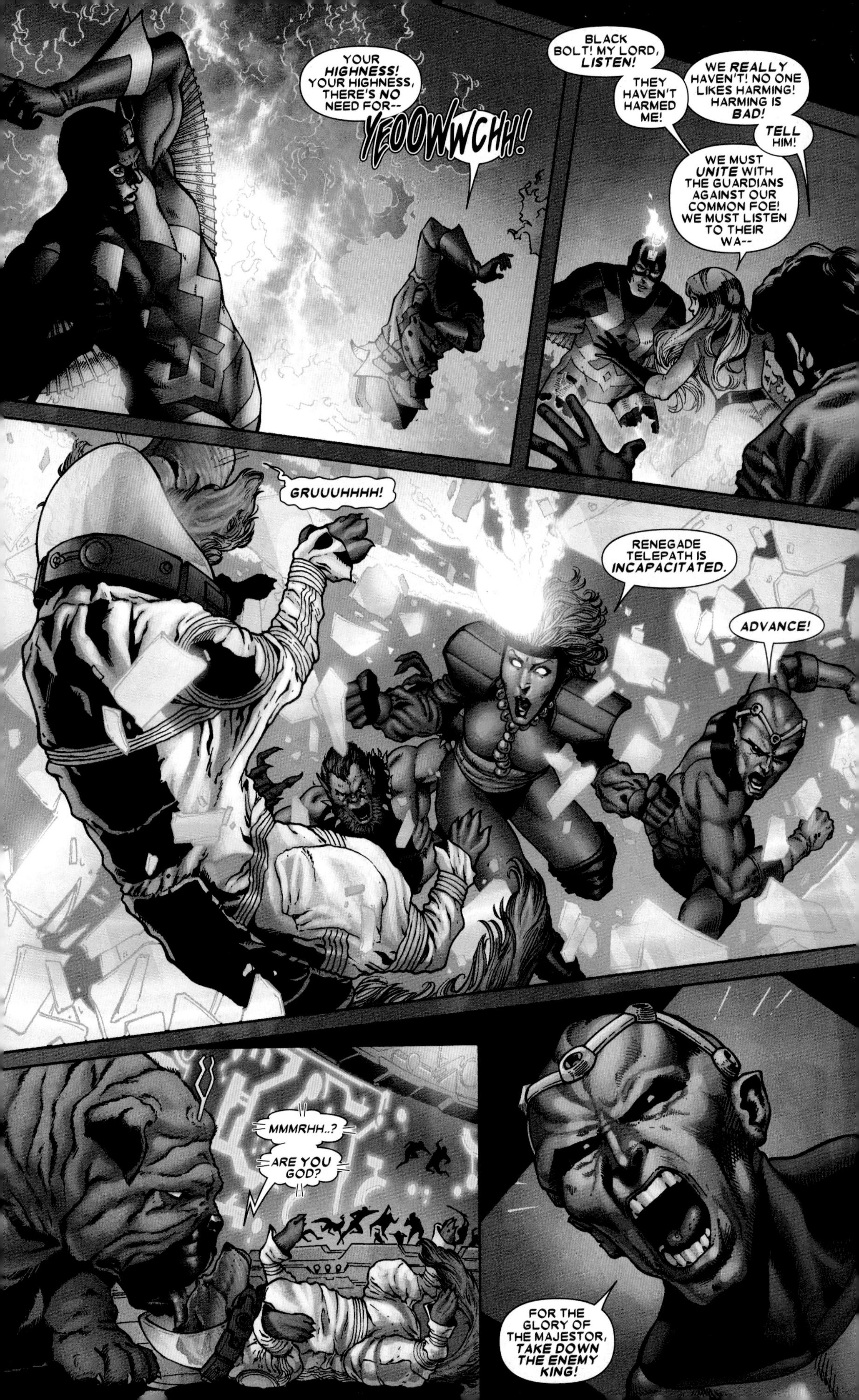
YOUR HIGHNESS! YOUR HIGHNESS, THERE'S NO NEED FOR--
YEOOWWCHH!
BLACK BOLT! MY LORD, LISTEN!
THEY HAVEN'T HARMED ME!
WE REALLY HAVEN'T! NO ONE LIKES HARMING! HARMING IS BAD!
TELL HIM!
WE MUST UNITE WITH THE GUARDIANS AGAINST OUR COMMON FOE! WE MUST LISTEN TO THEIR WA--
GRUUUHHHH!
RENEGADE TELEPATH IS INCAPACITATED.
ADVANCE!
MMMRHH..?
ARE YOU GOD?
FOR THE GLORY OF THE MAJESTOR, TAKE DOWN THE ENEMY KING!

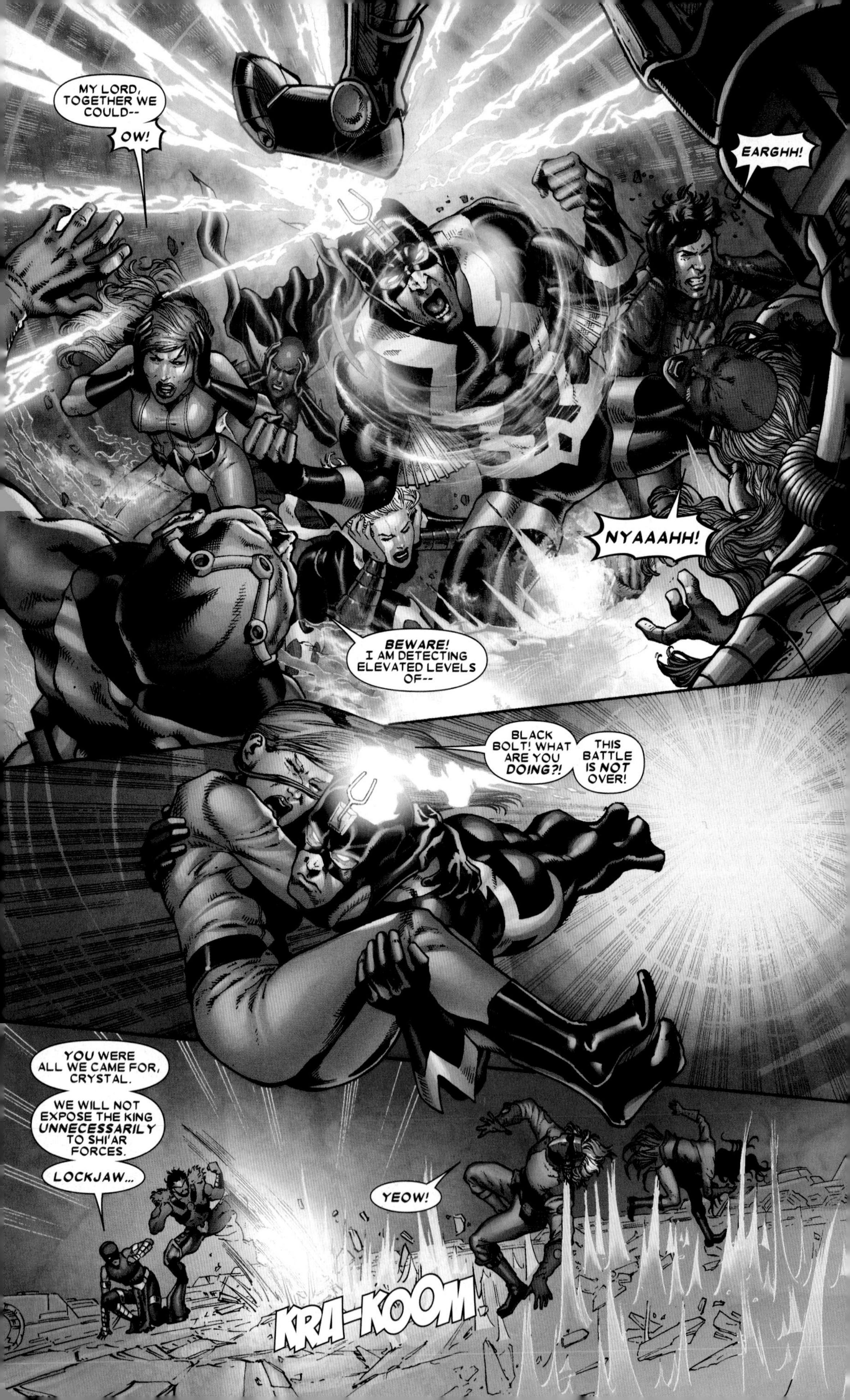
MY LORD, TOGETHER WE COULD--
OW!
EARGHH!
NYAAAHH!
BEWARE! I AM DETECTING ELEVATED LEVELS OF--
BLACK BOLT! WHAT ARE YOU DOING?!
THIS BATTLE IS NOT OVER!
YOU WERE ALL WE CAME FOR, CRYSTAL.
WE WILL NOT EXPOSE THE KING UNNECESSARILY TO SHI'AR FORCES.
LOCKJAW...
YEOW!
KRA-KOOM

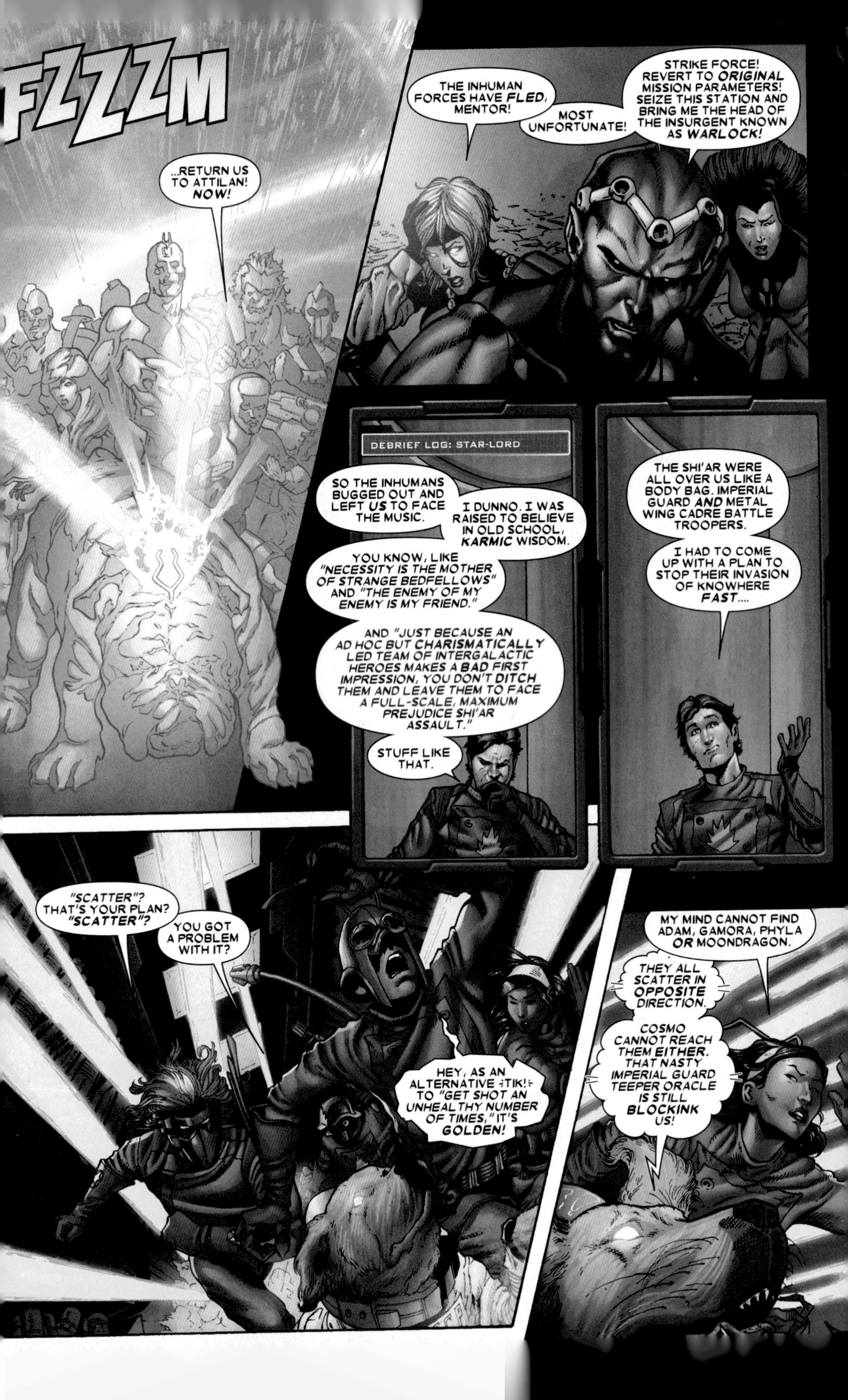
FZZZM
...RETURN US TO ATTILAN! NOW!
THE INHUMAN FORCES HAVE FLED, MENTOR!
MOST UNFORTUNATE!
STRIKE FORCE! REVERT TO ORIGINAL MISSION PARAMETERS! SEIZE THIS STATION AND BRING ME THE HEAD OF THE INSURGENT KNOWN AS WARLOCK!
DEBRIEF LOG: STAR-LORD
SO THE INHUMANS BUGGED OUT AND LEFT US TO FACE THE MUSIC.
I DUNNO. I WAS RAISED TO BELIEVE IN OLD SCHOOL, KARMIC WISDOM.
YOU KNOW, LIKE "NECESSITY IS THE MOTHER OF STRANGE BEDFELLOWS" AND "THE ENEMY OF MY ENEMY IS MY FRIEND."
AND "JUST BECAUSE AN AD HOC BUT CHARISMATICALLY LED TEAM OF INTERGALACTIC HEROES MAKES A BAD FIRST IMPRESSION, YOU DON'T DITCH THEM AND LEAVE THEM TO FACE A FULL-SCALE, MAXIMUM PREJUDICE SHI'AR ASSAULT."
STUFF LIKE THAT.
THE SHI'AR WERE ALL OVER US LIKE A BODY BAG. IMPERIAL GUARD AND METAL WING CADRE BATTLE TROOPERS.
I HAD TO COME UP WITH A PLAN TO STOP THEIR INVASION OF KNOWHERE FAST....
"SCATTER"? THAT'S YOUR PLAN? "SCATTER"?
YOU GOT A PROBLEM WITH IT?
HEY, AS AN ALTERNATIVE -TIK!- TO "GET SHOT AN UNHEALTHY NUMBER OF TIMES," IT'S GOLDEN!
MY MIND CANNOT FIND ADAM, GAMORA, PHYLA OR MOONDRAGON.
THEY ALL SCATTER IN OPPOSITE DIRECTION.
COSMO CANNOT REACH THEM EITHER. THAT NASTY IMPERIAL GUARD TEEPER ORACLE IS STILL BLOCKINK US!

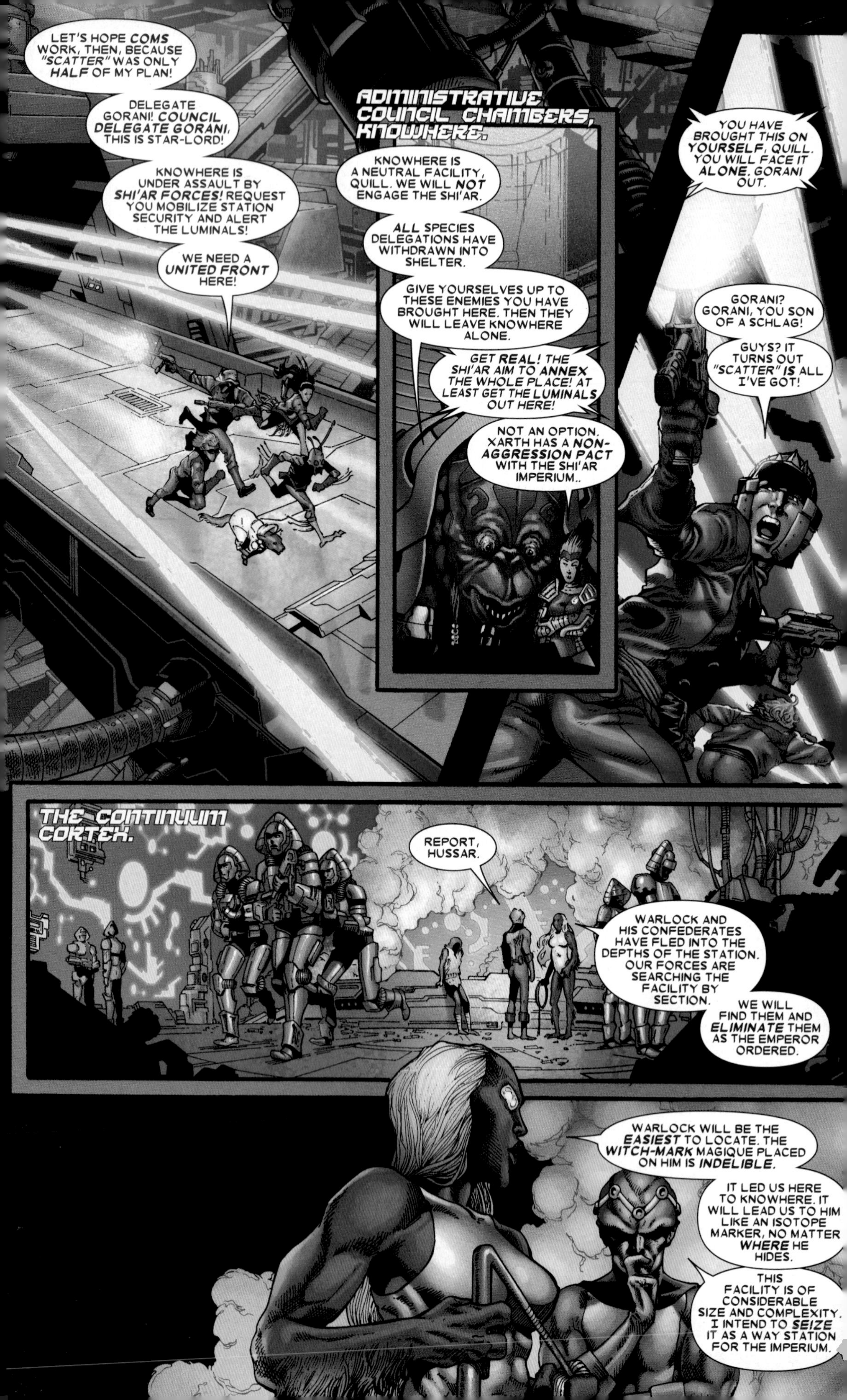
LET'S HOPE COMS WORK, THEN, BECAUSE "SCATTER" WAS ONLY HALF OF MY PLAN!
DELEGATE GORANI! COUNCIL DELEGATE GORANI, THIS IS STAR-LORD!
KNOWHERE IS UNDER ASSAULT BY SHI'AR FORCES! REQUEST YOU MOBILIZE STATION SECURITY AND ALERT THE LUMINALS!
WE NEED A UNITED FRONT HERE!
ADMINISTRATIVE COUNCIL CHAMBERS, KNOWHERE.
KNOWHERE IS A NEUTRAL FACILITY, QUILL. WE WILL NOT ENGAGE THE SHI'AR.
ALL SPECIES DELEGATIONS HAVE WITHDRAWN INTO SHELTER.
GIVE YOURSELVES UP TO THESE ENEMIES YOU HAVE BROUGHT HERE. THEN THEY WILL LEAVE KNOWHERE ALONE.
GET REAL! THE SHI'AR AIM TO ANNEX THE WHOLE PLACE! AT LEAST GET THE LUMINALS OUT HERE!
NOT AN OPTION. XARTH HAS A NON-AGGRESSION PACT WITH THE SHI'AR IMPERIUM..
YOU HAVE BROUGHT THIS ON YOURSELF, QUILL. YOU WILL FACE IT ALONE. GORANI OUT.
GORANI? GORANI, YOU SON OF A SCHLAG!
GUYS? IT TURNS OUT "SCATTER" IS ALL I'VE GOT!
THE CONTINUUM CORTEX.
REPORT, HUSSAR.
WARLOCK AND HIS CONFEDERATES HAVE FLED INTO THE DEPTHS OF THE STATION. OUR FORCES ARE SEARCHING THE FACILITY BY SECTION.
WE WILL FIND THEM AND ELIMINATE THEM AS THE EMPEROR ORDERED.
WARLOCK WILL BE THE EASIEST TO LOCATE. THE WITCH-MARK MAGIQUE PLACED ON HIM IS INDELIBLE.
IT LED US HERE TO KNOWHERE. IT WILL LEAD US TO HIM LIKE AN ISOTOPE MARKER, NO MATTER WHERE HE HIDES.
THIS FACILITY IS OF CONSIDERABLE SIZE AND COMPLEXITY. I INTEND TO SEIZE IT AS A WAY STATION FOR THE IMPERIUM.

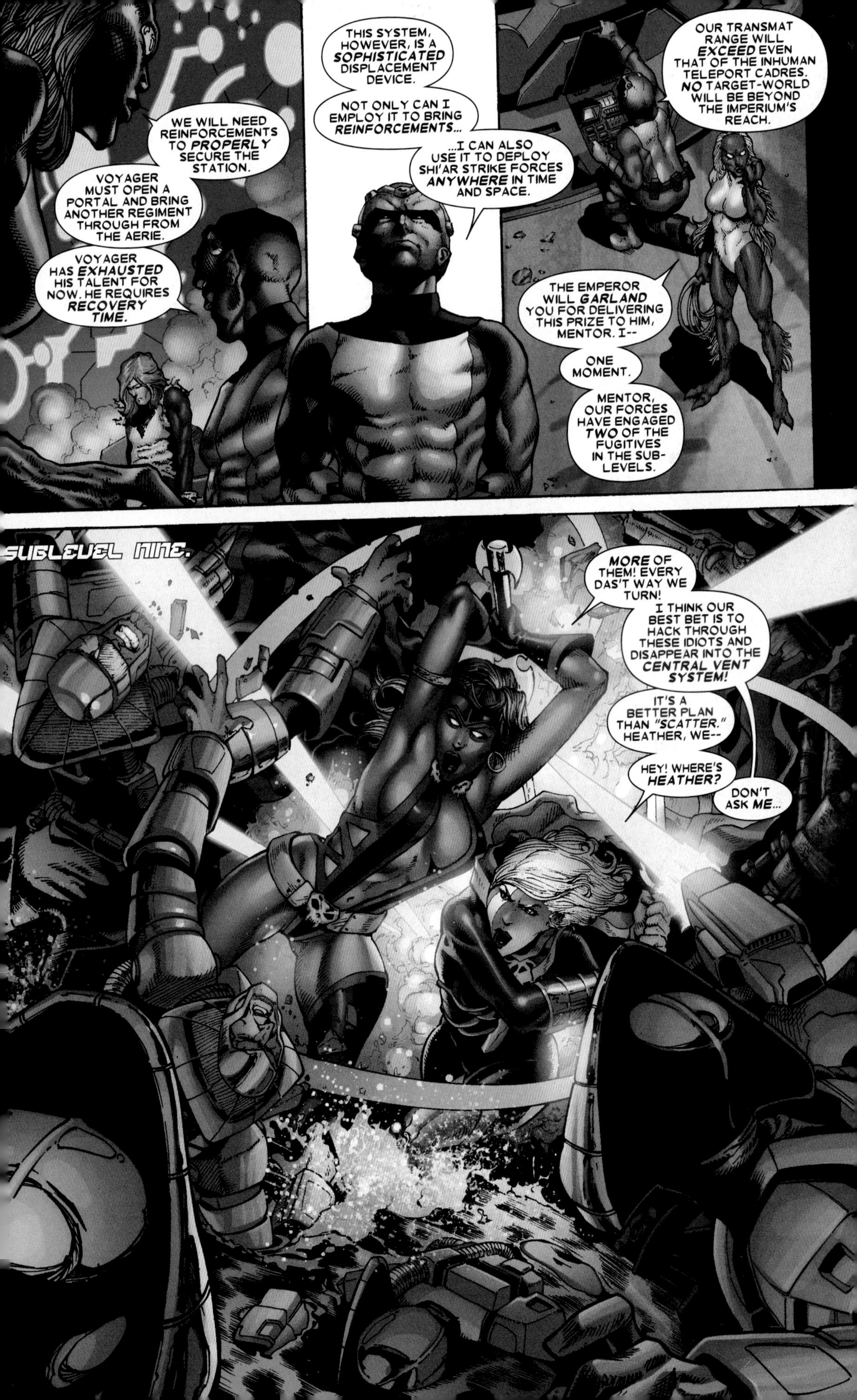
WE WILL NEED REINFORCEMENTS TO PROPERLY SECURE THE STATION.
VOYAGER MUST OPEN A PORTAL AND BRING ANOTHER REGIMENT THROUGH FROM THE AERIE.
VOYAGER HAS EXHAUSTED HIS TALENT FOR NOW. HE REQUIRES RECOVERY TIME.
THIS SYSTEM, HOWEVER, IS A SOPHISTICATED DISPLACEMENT DEVICE.
NOT ONLY CAN I EMPLOY IT TO BRING REINFORCEMENTS...
...I CAN ALSO USE IT TO DEPLOY SHI'AR STRIKE FORCES ANYWHERE IN TIME AND SPACE.
OUR TRANSMAT RANGE WILL EXCEED EVEN THAT OF THE INHUMAN TELEPORT CADRES. NO TARGET-WORLD WILL BE BEYOND THE IMPERIUM'S REACH.
THE EMPEROR WILL GARLAND YOU FOR DELIVERING THIS PRIZE TO HIM, MENTOR. I--
ONE MOMENT.
MENTOR, OUR FORCES HAVE ENGAGED TWO OF THE FUGITIVES IN THE SUB-LEVELS.
SUBLEVEL NINE.
MORE OF THEM! EVERY DAS'T WAY WE TURN!
I THINK OUR BEST BET IS TO HACK THROUGH THESE IDIOTS AND DISAPPEAR INTO THE CENTRAL VENT SYSTEM!
IT'S A BETTER PLAN THAN "SCATTER." HEATHER, WE--
HEY! WHERE'S HEATHER?
DON'T ASK ME...

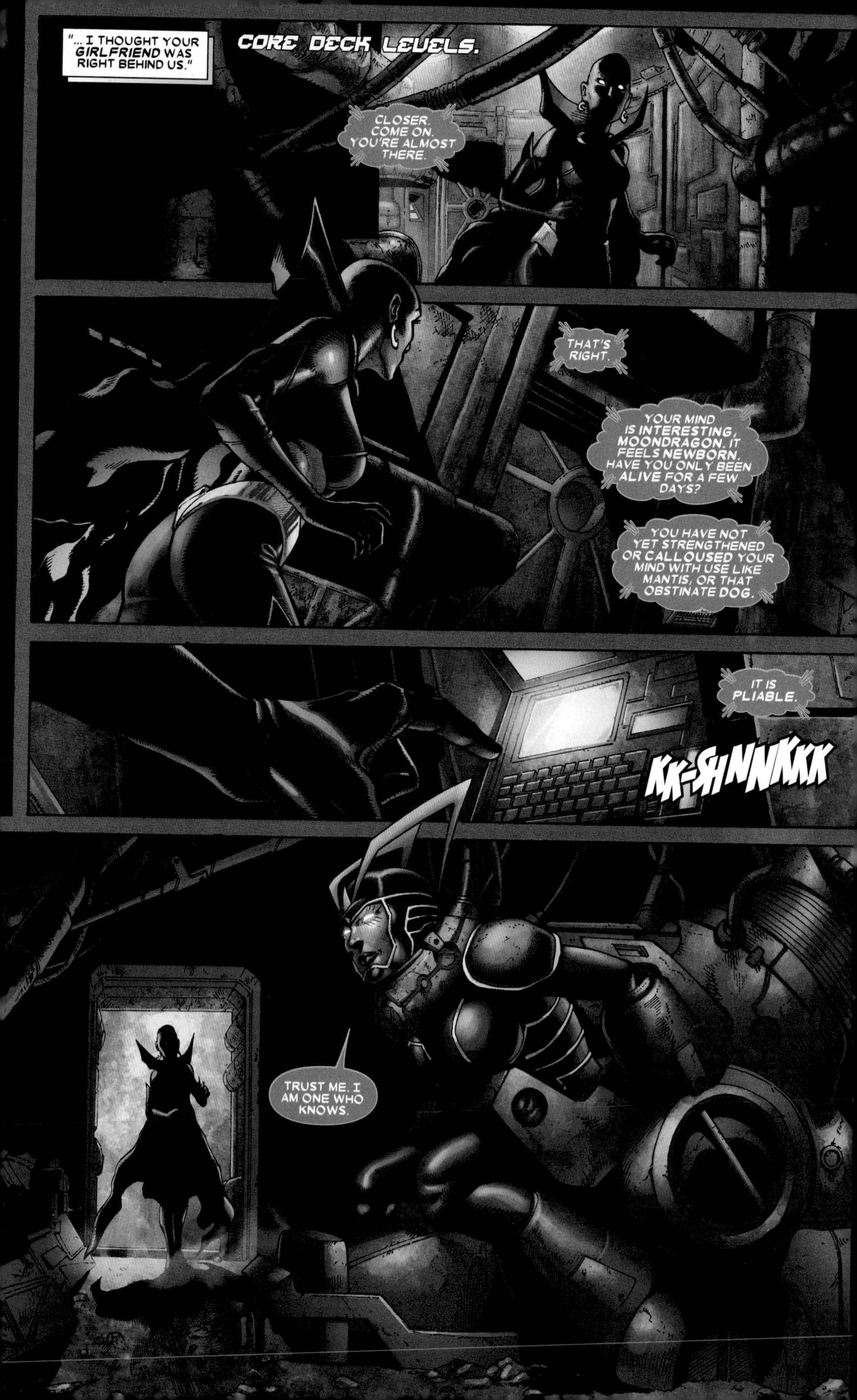
"... I THOUGHT YOUR GIRLFRIEND WAS RIGHT BEHIND US."
CORE DECK LEVELS.
CLOSER. COME ON. YOU'RE ALMOST THERE.
THAT'S RIGHT.
YOUR MIND IS INTERESTING, MOONDRAGON. IT FEELS NEWBORN. HAVE YOU ONLY BEEN ALIVE FOR A FEW DAYS?
YOU HAVE NOT YET STRENGTHENED OR CALLOUSED YOUR MIND WITH USE LIKE MANTIS, OR THAT OBSTINATE DOG.
IT IS PLIABLE.
KK-SHNNKKK
TRUST ME. I AM ONE WHO KNOWS.

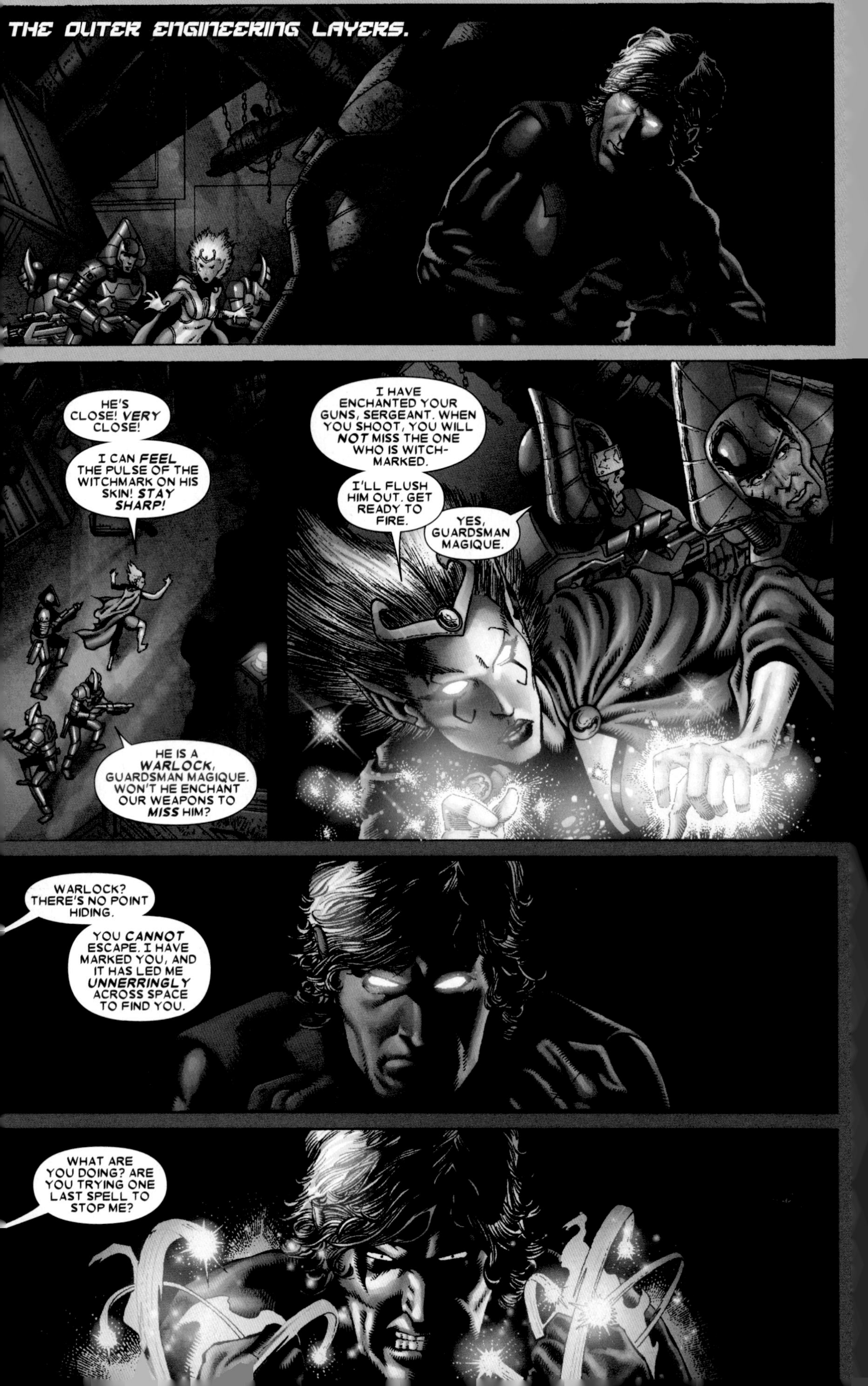
THE OUTER ENGINEERING LAYERS.
HE'S CLOSE! VERY CLOSE!
I CAN FEEL THE PULSE OF THE WITCHMARK ON HIS SKIN! STAY SHARP!
HE IS A WARLOCK, GUARDSMAN MAGIQUE. WON'T HE ENCHANT OUR WEAPONS TO MISS HIM?
I HAVE ENCHANTED YOUR GUNS, SERGEANT. WHEN YOU SHOOT, YOU WILL NOT MISS THE ONE WHO IS WITCH-MARKED.
I'LL FLUSH HIM OUT. GET READY TO FIRE.
YES, GUARDSMAN MAGIQUE.
WARLOCK? THERE'S NO POINT HIDING.
YOU CANNOT ESCAPE. I HAVE MARKED YOU, AND IT HAS LED ME UNNERRINGLY ACROSS SPACE TO FIND YOU.
WHAT ARE YOU DOING? ARE YOU TRYING ONE LAST SPELL TO STOP ME?

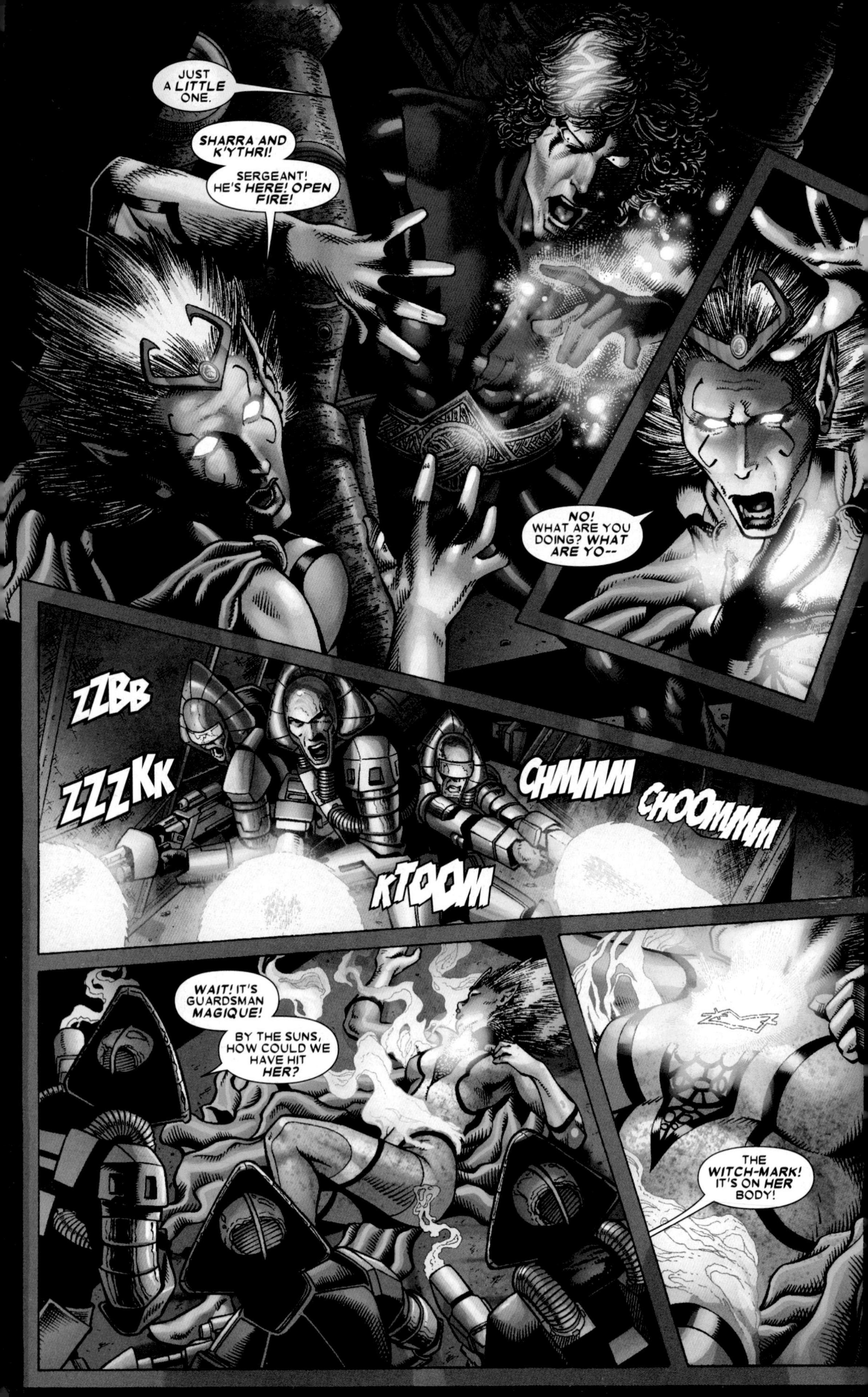
JUST A LITTLE ONE.
SHARRA AND K'YTHRI!
SERGEANT! HE'S HERE! OPEN FIRE!
NO! WHAT ARE YOU DOING? WHAT ARE YO--
ZZBB
ZZZKK
CHMMM
CHOOMMM
KTOOM
WAIT! IT'S GUARDSMAN MAGIQUE!
BY THE SUNS, HOW COULD WE HAVE HIT HER?
THE WITCH-MARK! IT'S ON HER BODY!

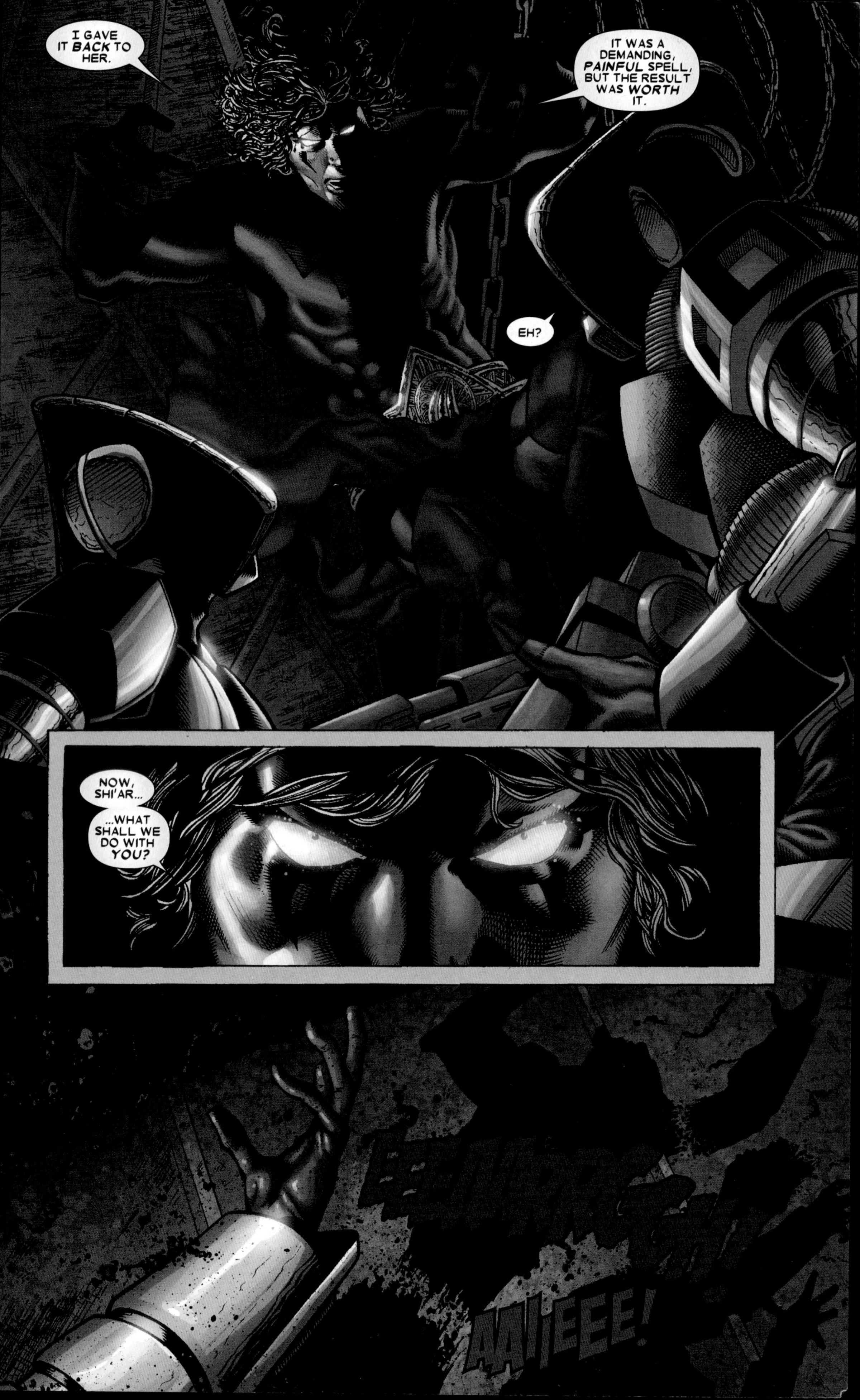
I GAVE IT BACK TO HER.
IT WAS A DEMANDING, PAINFUL SPELL, BUT THE RESULT WAS WORTH IT.
EH?
NOW, SHI'AR...
...WHAT SHALL WE DO WITH YOU?
AAIEEE!

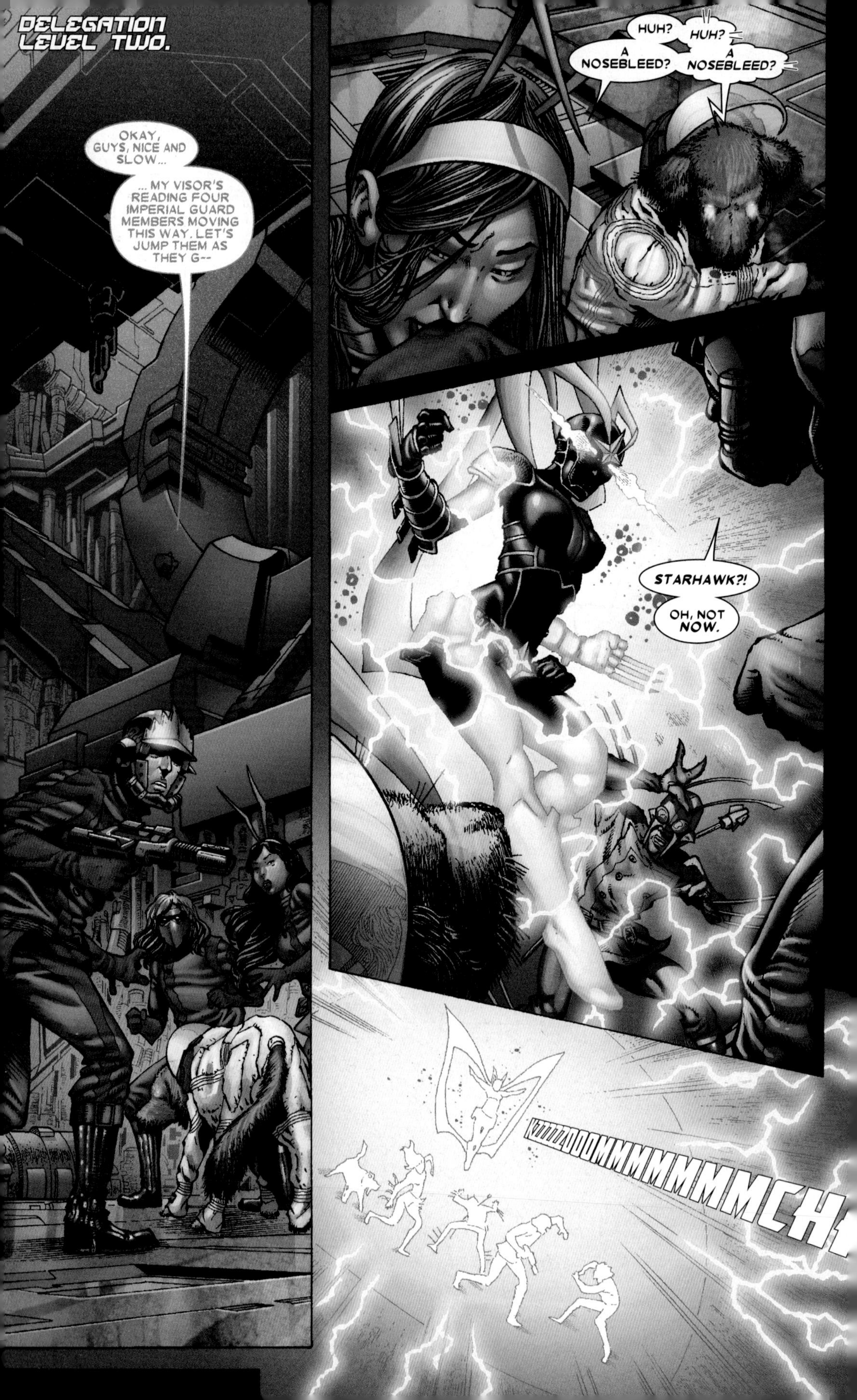
DELEGATION LEVEL TWO.
OKAY, GUYS, NICE AND SLOW...
... MY VISOR'S READING FOUR IMPERIAL GUARD MEMBERS MOVING THIS WAY. LET'S JUMP THEM AS THEY G--
HUH? A NOSEBLEED?
HUH? A NOSEBLEED?
STARHAWK?!
OH, NOT NOW.
KZZZZOOOMMMMMMMMMCH!

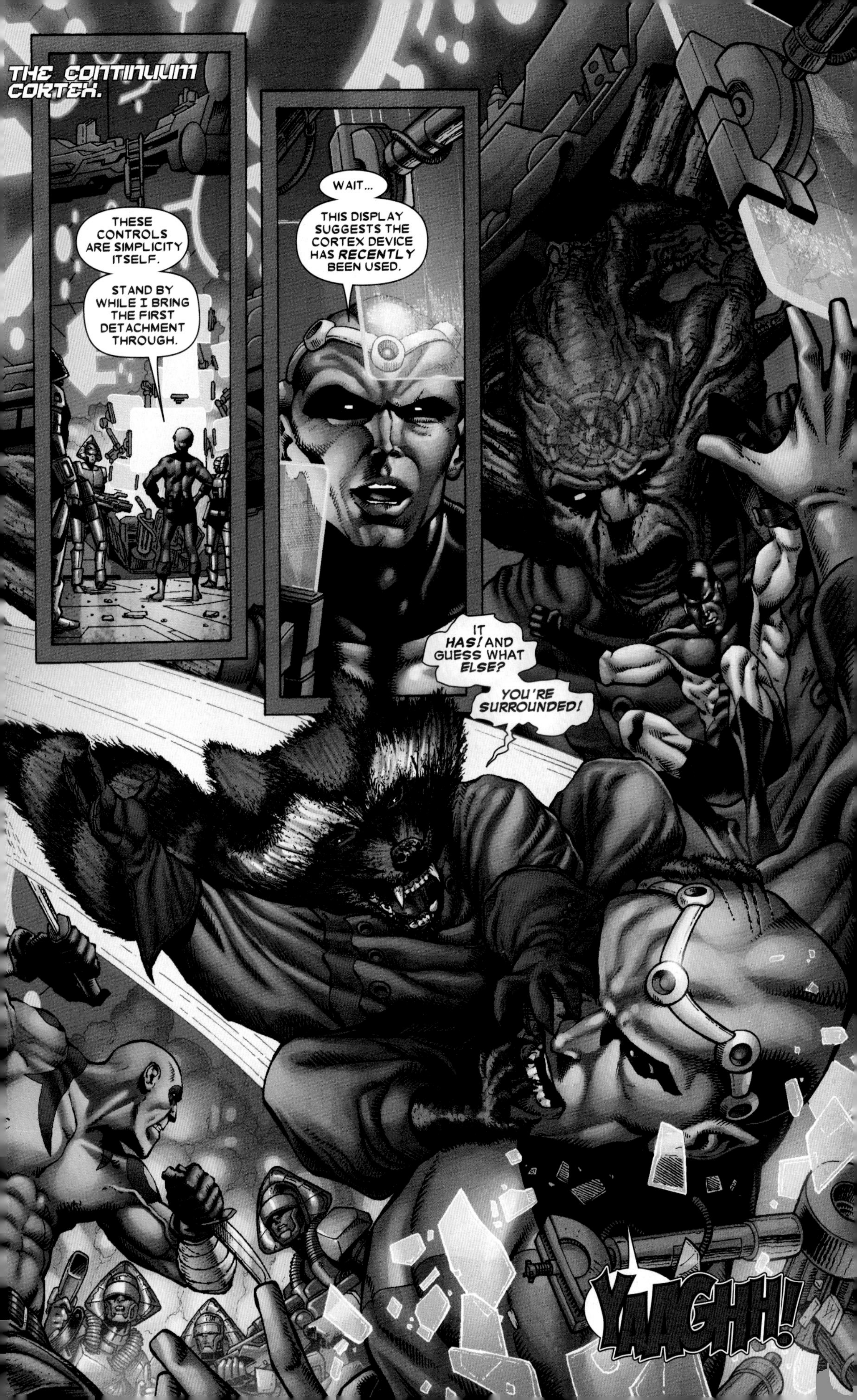
THE CONTINUUM CORTEX.
THESE CONTROLS ARE SIMPLICITY ITSELF.
STAND BY WHILE I BRING THE FIRST DETACHMENT THROUGH.
WAIT...
THIS DISPLAY SUGGESTS THE CORTEX DEVICE HAS RECENTLY BEEN USED.
IT HAS! AND GUESS WHAT ELSE?
YOU'RE SURROUNDED!
YAAGHH!

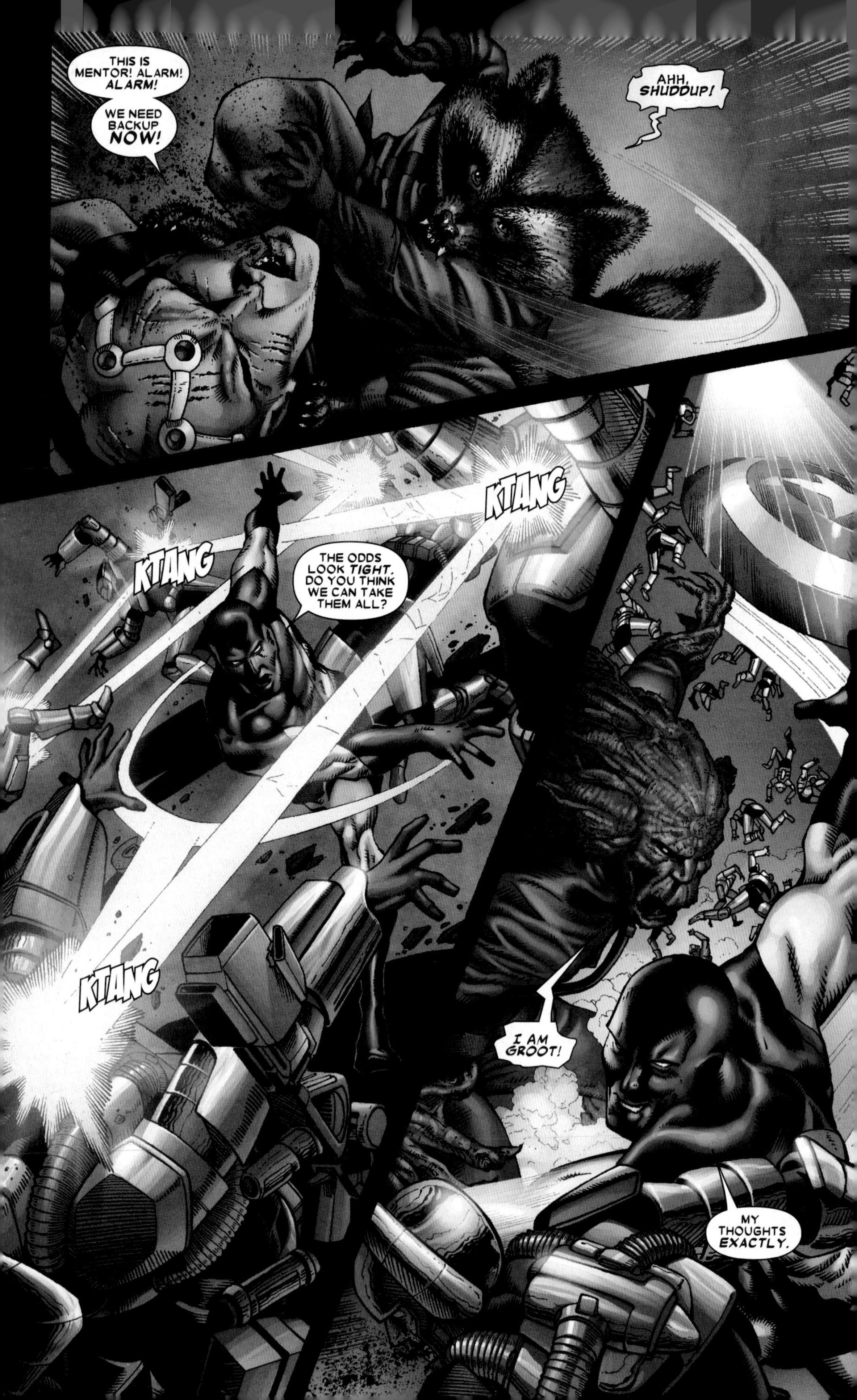
THIS IS MENTOR! ALARM! ALARM!
WE NEED BACKUP NOW!
AHH, SHUDDUP!
KTANG
KTANG
THE ODDS LOOK TIGHT. DO YOU THINK WE CAN TAKE THEM ALL?
KTANG
I AM GROOT!
MY THOUGHTS EXACTLY.

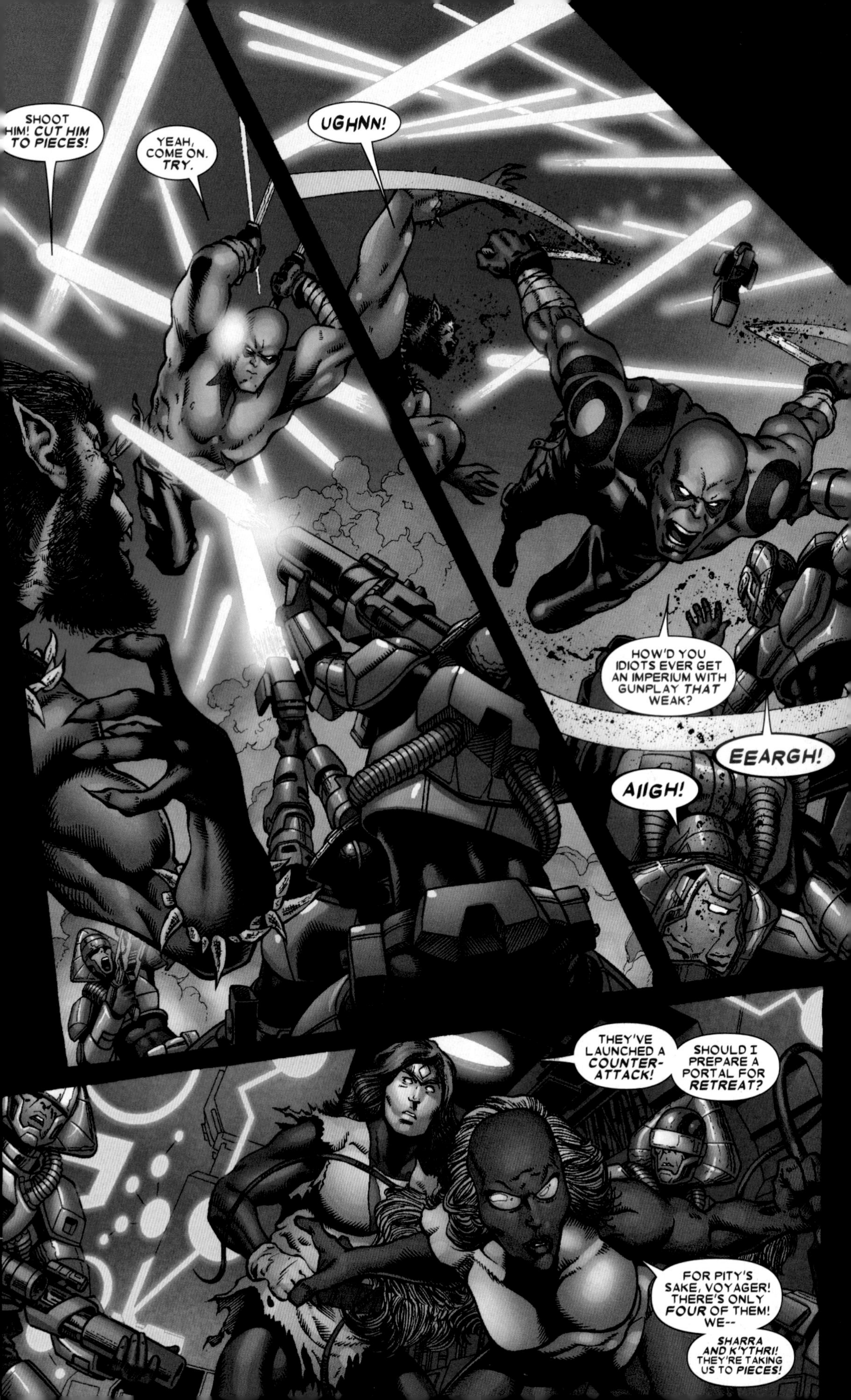
SHOOT HIM! CUT HIM TO PIECES!
YEAH, COME ON. TRY.
UGHNN!
HOW'D YOU IDIOTS EVER GET AN IMPERIUM WITH GUNPLAY THAT WEAK?
EEARGH!
AIIGH!
THEY'VE LAUNCHED A COUNTER-ATTACK!
SHOULD I PREPARE A PORTAL FOR RETREAT?
FOR PITY'S SAKE, VOYAGER! THERE'S ONLY FOUR OF THEM! WE--
SHARRA AND K'YTHRI! THEY'RE TAKING US TO PIECES!

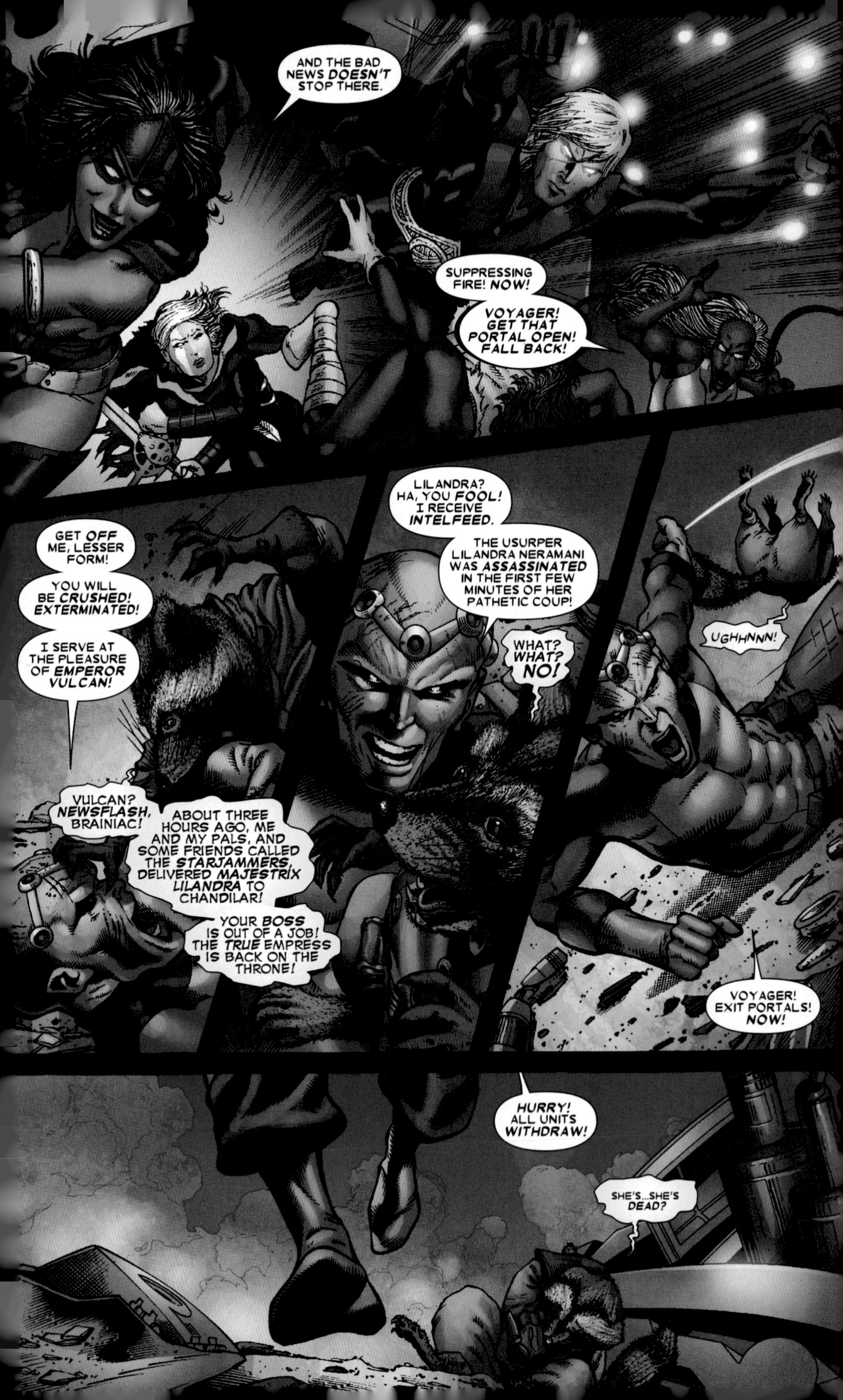
AND THE BAD NEWS DOESN'T STOP THERE.
SUPPRESSING FIRE! NOW!
VOYAGER! GET THAT PORTAL OPEN! FALL BACK!
GET OFF ME, LESSER FORM!
YOU WILL BE CRUSHED! EXTERMINATED!
I SERVE AT THE PLEASURE OF EMPEROR VULCAN!
VULCAN? NEWSFLASH, BRAINIAC!
ABOUT THREE HOURS AGO, ME AND MY PALS, AND SOME FRIENDS CALLED THE STARJAMMERS, DELIVERED MAJESTRIX LILANDRA TO CHANDILAR!
YOUR BOSS IS OUT OF A JOB! THE TRUE EMPRESS IS BACK ON THE THRONE!
LILANDRA? HA, YOU FOOL! I RECEIVE INTELFEED.
THE USURPER LILANDRA NERAMANI WAS ASSASSINATED IN THE FIRST FEW MINUTES OF HER PATHETIC COUP!
WHAT? WHAT? NO!
UGHHNNN!
VOYAGER! EXIT PORTALS! NOW!
HURRY! ALL UNITS WITHDRAW!
SHE'S...SHE'S DEAD?

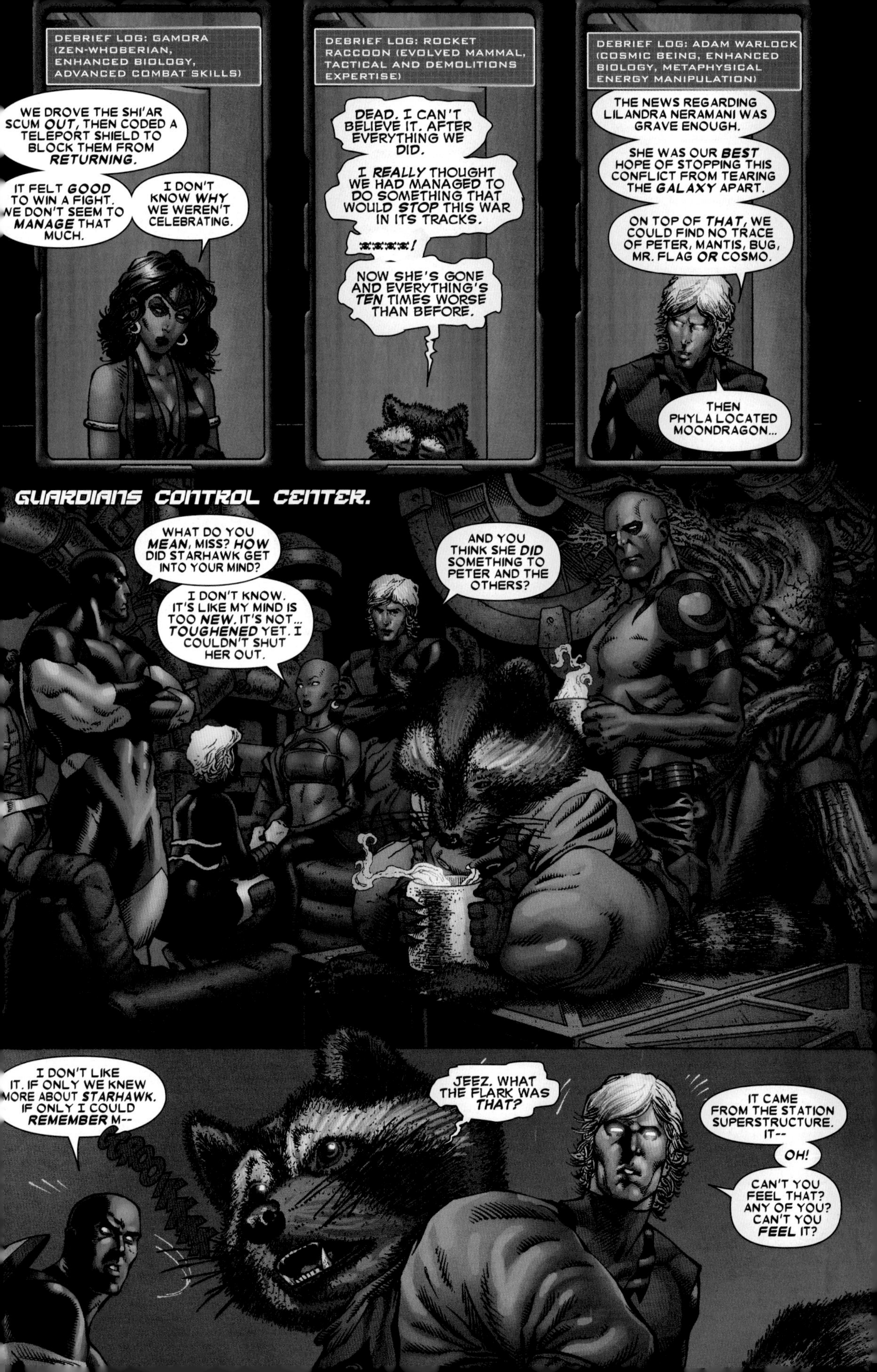
DEBRIEF LOG: GAMORA (ZEN-WHOBERIAN, ENHANCED BIOLOGY, ADVANCED COMBAT SKILLS)
WE DROVE THE SHI'AR SCUM OUT, THEN CODED A TELEPORT SHIELD TO BLOCK THEM FROM RETURNING.
IT FELT GOOD TO WIN A FIGHT. WE DON'T SEEM TO MANAGE THAT MUCH.
I DON'T KNOW WHY WE WEREN'T CELEBRATING.
DEBRIEF LOG: ROCKET RACCOON (EVOLVED MAMMAL, TACTICAL AND DEMOLITIONS EXPERTISE)
DEAD. I CAN'T BELIEVE IT. AFTER EVERYTHING WE DID.
I REALLY THOUGHT WE HAD MANAGED TO DO SOMETHING THAT WOULD STOP THIS WAR IN ITS TRACKS.
NOW SHE'S GONE AND EVERYTHING'S TEN TIMES WORSE THAN BEFORE.
DEBRIEF LOG: ADAM WARLOCK (COSMIC BEING, ENHANCED BIOLOGY, METAPHYSICAL ENERGY MANIPULATION)
THE NEWS REGARDING LILANDRA NERAMANI WAS GRAVE ENOUGH.
SHE WAS OUR BEST HOPE OF STOPPING THIS CONFLICT FROM TEARING THE GALAXY APART.
ON TOP OF THAT, WE COULD FIND NO TRACE OF PETER, MANTIS, BUG, MR. FLAG OR COSMO.
THEN PHYLA LOCATED MOONDRAGON...
GUARDIANS CONTROL CENTER.
WHAT DO YOU MEAN, MISS? HOW DID STARHAWK GET INTO YOUR MIND?
I DON'T KNOW. IT'S LIKE MY MIND IS TOO NEW. IT'S NOT... TOUGHENED YET. I COULDN'T SHUT HER OUT.
AND YOU THINK SHE DID SOMETHING TO PETER AND THE OTHERS?
I DON'T LIKE IT. IF ONLY WE KNEW MORE ABOUT STARHAWK. IF ONLY I COULD REMEMBER M--
JEEZ. WHAT THE FLARK WAS THAT?
IT CAME FROM THE STATION SUPERSTRUCTURE. IT--
OH!
CAN'T YOU FEEL THAT? ANY OF YOU? CAN'T YOU FEEL IT?

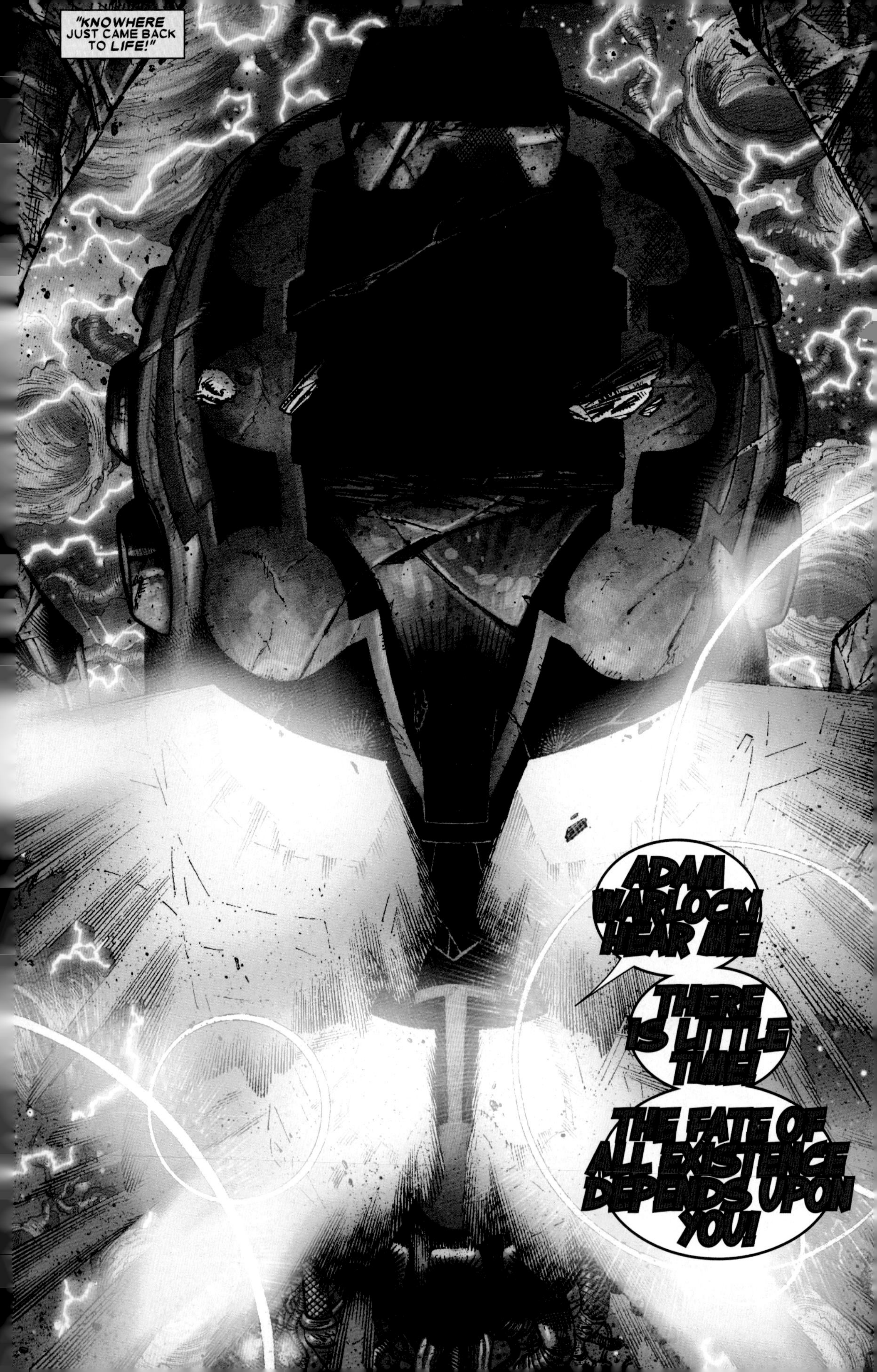
"KNOWHERE JUST CAME BACK TO LIFE!"
ADAM WARLOCK! HEAR ME!
THERE IS LITTLE TIME!
THE FATE OF ALL EXISTENCE DEPENDS UPON YOU!

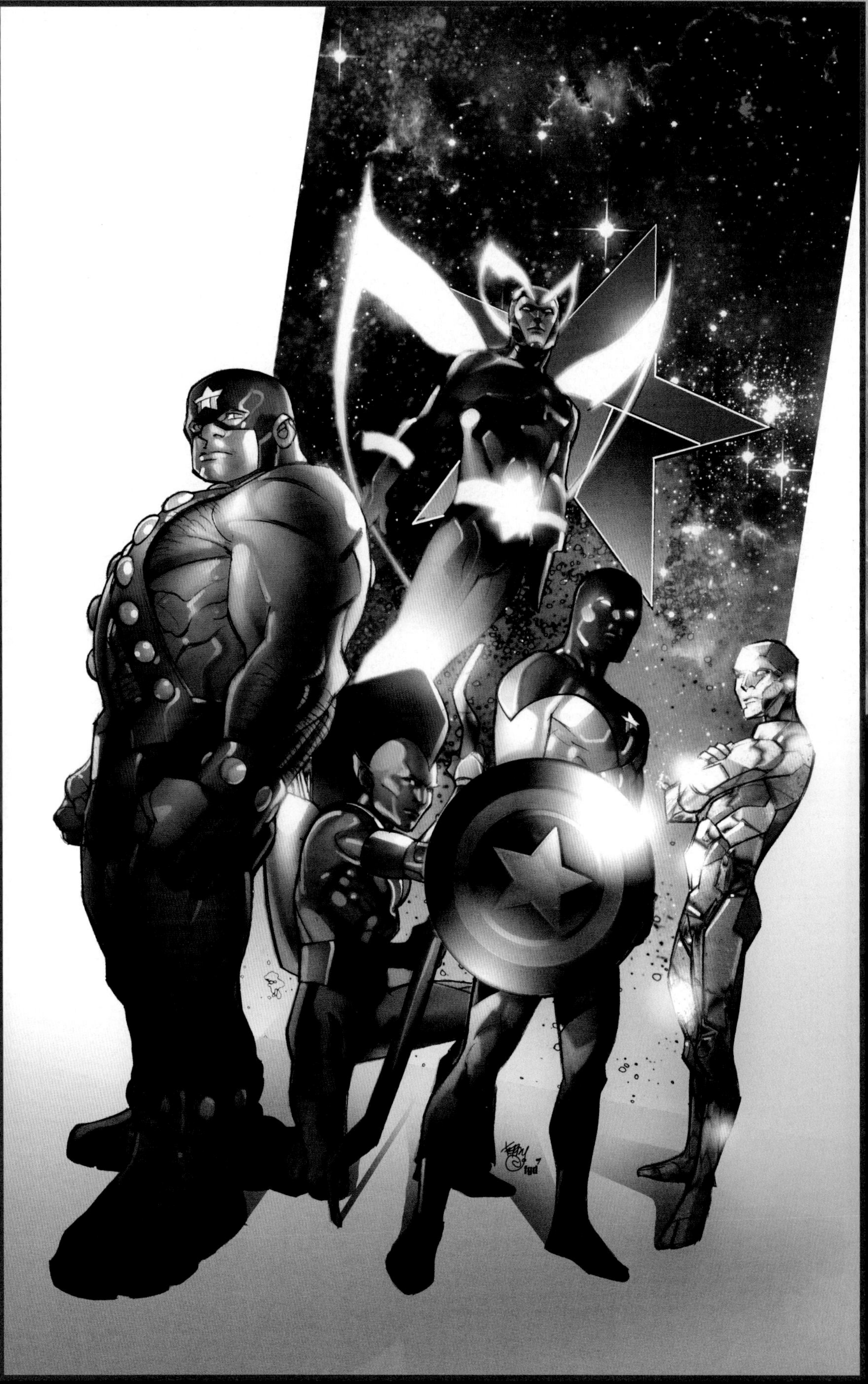

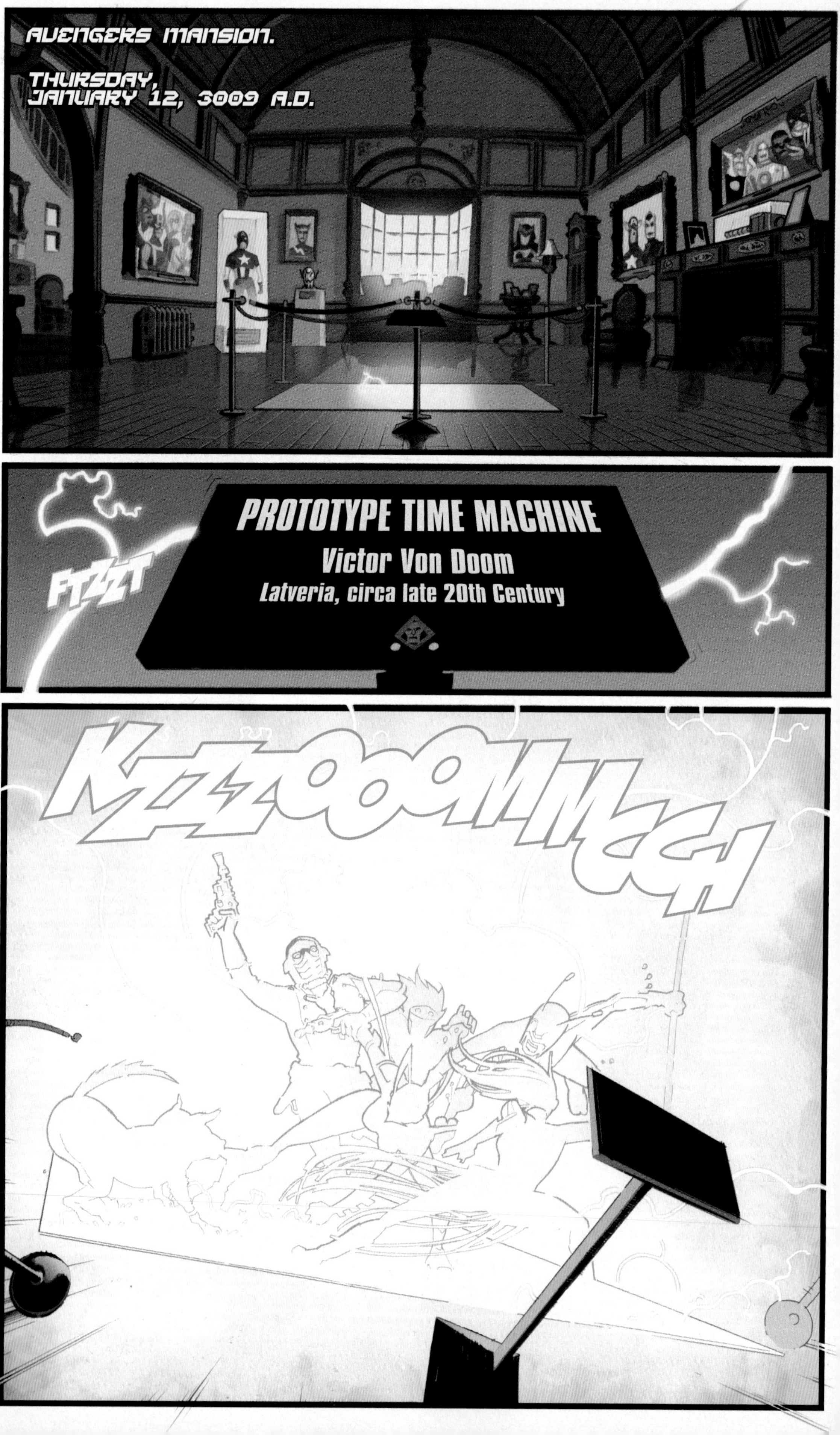
AVENGERS MANSION.
THURSDAY, JANUARY 12, 3009 A.D.
PROTOTYPE TIME MACHINE
Victor Von Doom
Latveria, circa late 20th Century
FTZZT
KZZOOOMMCCH

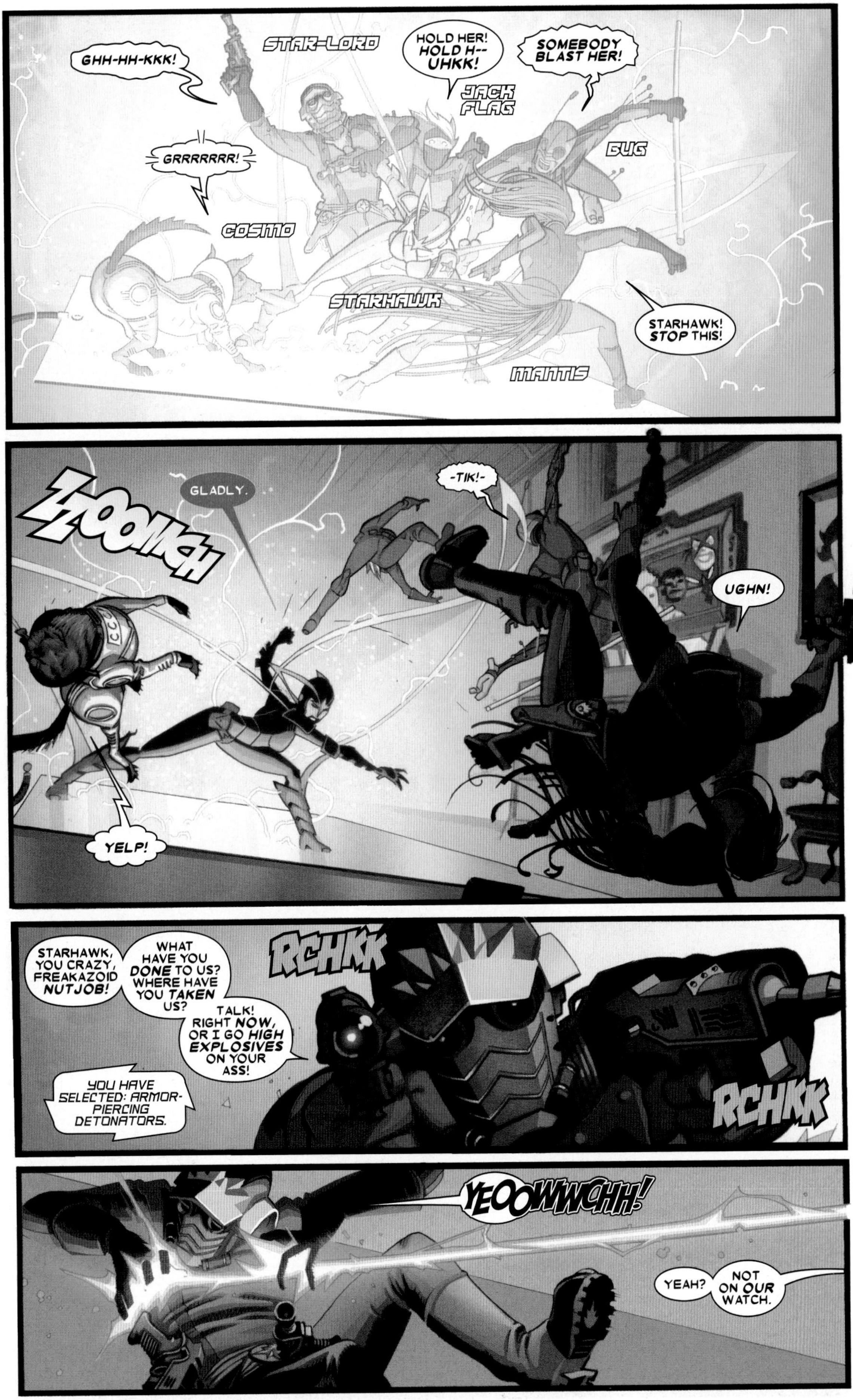
GHH-HH-KKK!
STAR-LORD
HOLD HER! HOLD H-- UHKK!
SOMEBODY BLAST HER!
JACK FLAG
GRRRRRRR!
BUG
COSMO
STARHAWK
STARHAWK! STOP THIS!
MANTIS
ZOOMCH
GLADLY.
-TIK!-
UGHN!
YELP!
STARHAWK, YOU CRAZY, FREAKAZOID NUTJOB!
WHAT HAVE YOU DONE TO US? WHERE HAVE YOU TAKEN US?
RCHKK
TALK! RIGHT NOW, OR I GO HIGH EXPLOSIVES ON YOUR ASS!
YOU HAVE SELECTED: ARMOR-PIERCING DETONATORS.
RCHKK
YEOOWWCHH!
YEAH?
NOT ON OUR WATCH.

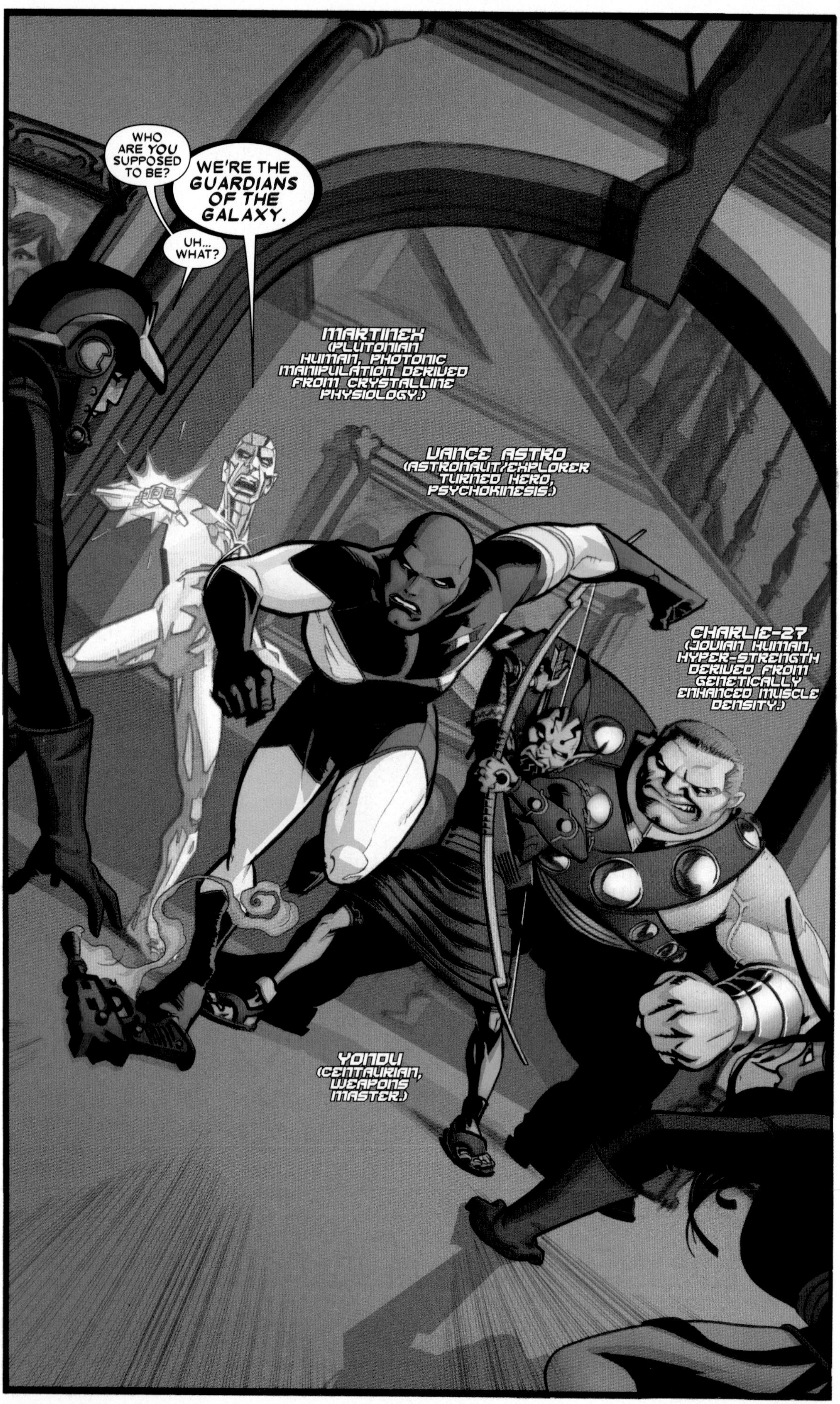
WHO ARE YOU SUPPOSED TO BE?
WE'RE THE GUARDIANS OF THE GALAXY.
UH... WHAT?
MARTINEX (PLUTONIAN HUMAN, PHOTONIC MANIPULATION DERIVED FROM CRYSTALLINE PHYSIOLOGY.)
VANCE ASTRO (ASTRONAUT/EXPLORER TURNED HERO, PSYCHOKINESIS.)
CHARLIE-27 (JOVIAN HUMAN, HYPER-STRENGTH DERIVED FROM GENETICALLY ENHANCED MUSCLE DENSITY.)
YONDU (CENTAURIAN, WEAPONS MASTER.)

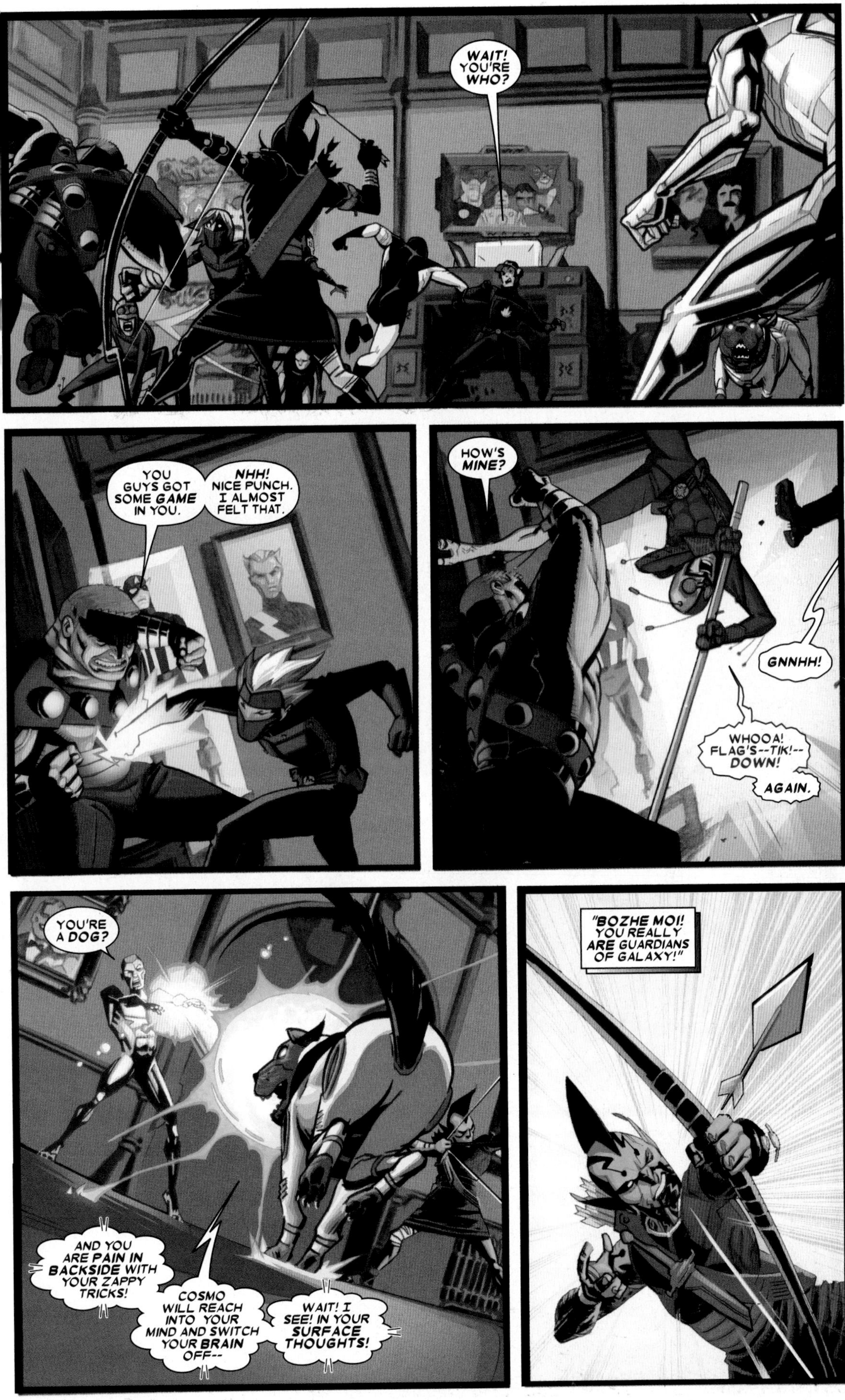

WAIT! YOU'RE WHO?
YOU GUYS GOT SOME GAME IN YOU.
NHH! NICE PUNCH. I ALMOST FELT THAT.
HOW'S MINE?
GNNHH!
WHOOA! FLAG'S--TIK!--DOWN!
AGAIN.
YOU'RE A DOG?
AND YOU ARE PAIN IN BACKSIDE WITH YOUR ZAPPY TRICKS!
COSMO WILL REACH INTO YOUR MIND AND SWITCH YOUR BRAIN OFF--
WAIT! I SEE! IN YOUR SURFACE THOUGHTS!
"BOZHE MOI! YOU REALLY ARE GUARDIANS OF GALAXY!"

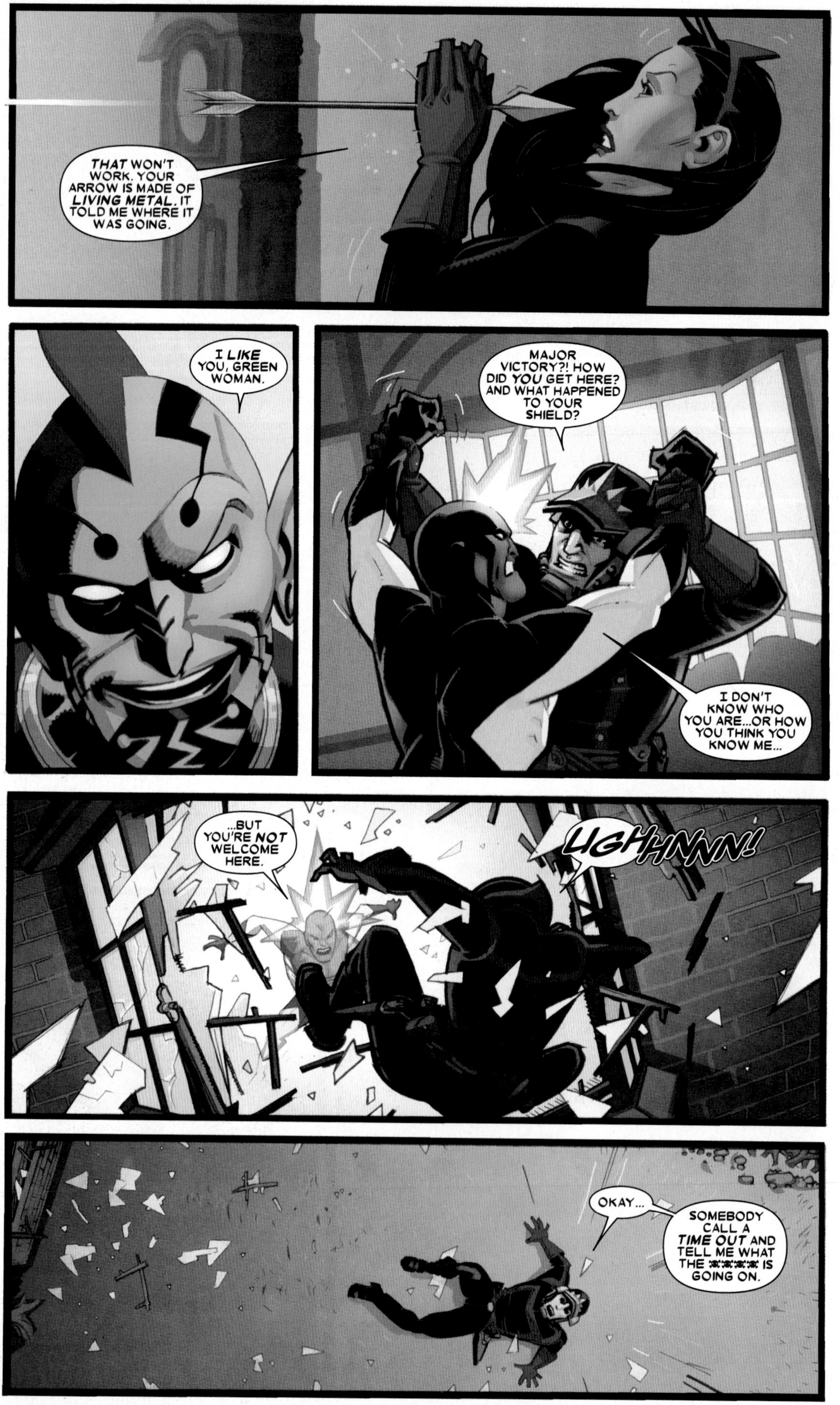
THAT WON'T WORK. YOUR ARROW IS MADE OF LIVING METAL. IT TOLD ME WHERE IT WAS GOING.
I LIKE YOU, GREEN WOMAN.
MAJOR VICTORY?! HOW DID YOU GET HERE? AND WHAT HAPPENED TO YOUR SHIELD?
I DON'T KNOW WHO YOU ARE...OR HOW YOU THINK YOU KNOW ME...
...BUT YOU'RE NOT WELCOME HERE.
UGHHNNN!
OKAY...
SOMEBODY CALL A TIME OUT AND TELL ME WHAT THE ✱✱✱ IS GOING ON.

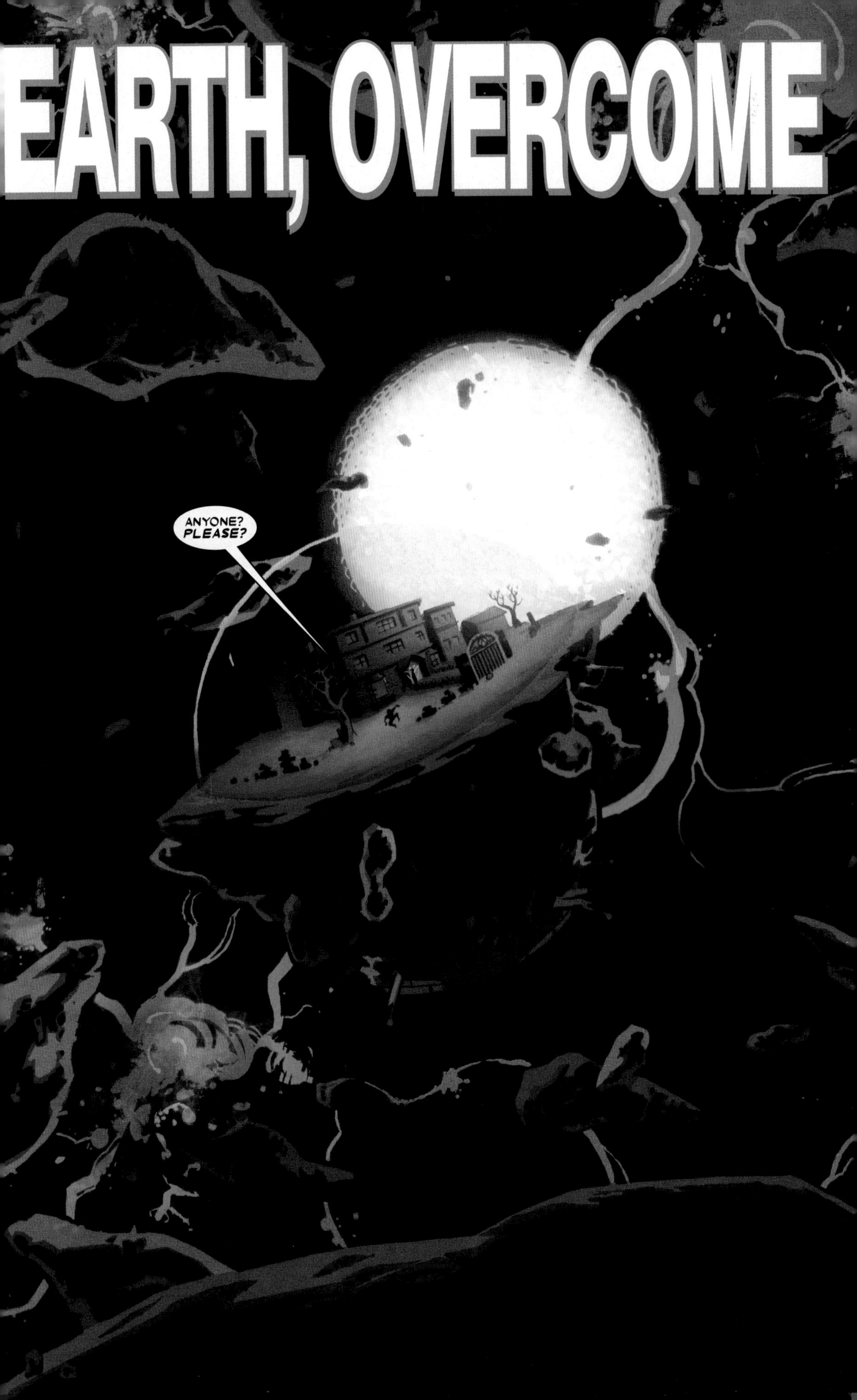
EARTH, OVERCOME
ANYONE? PLEASE?

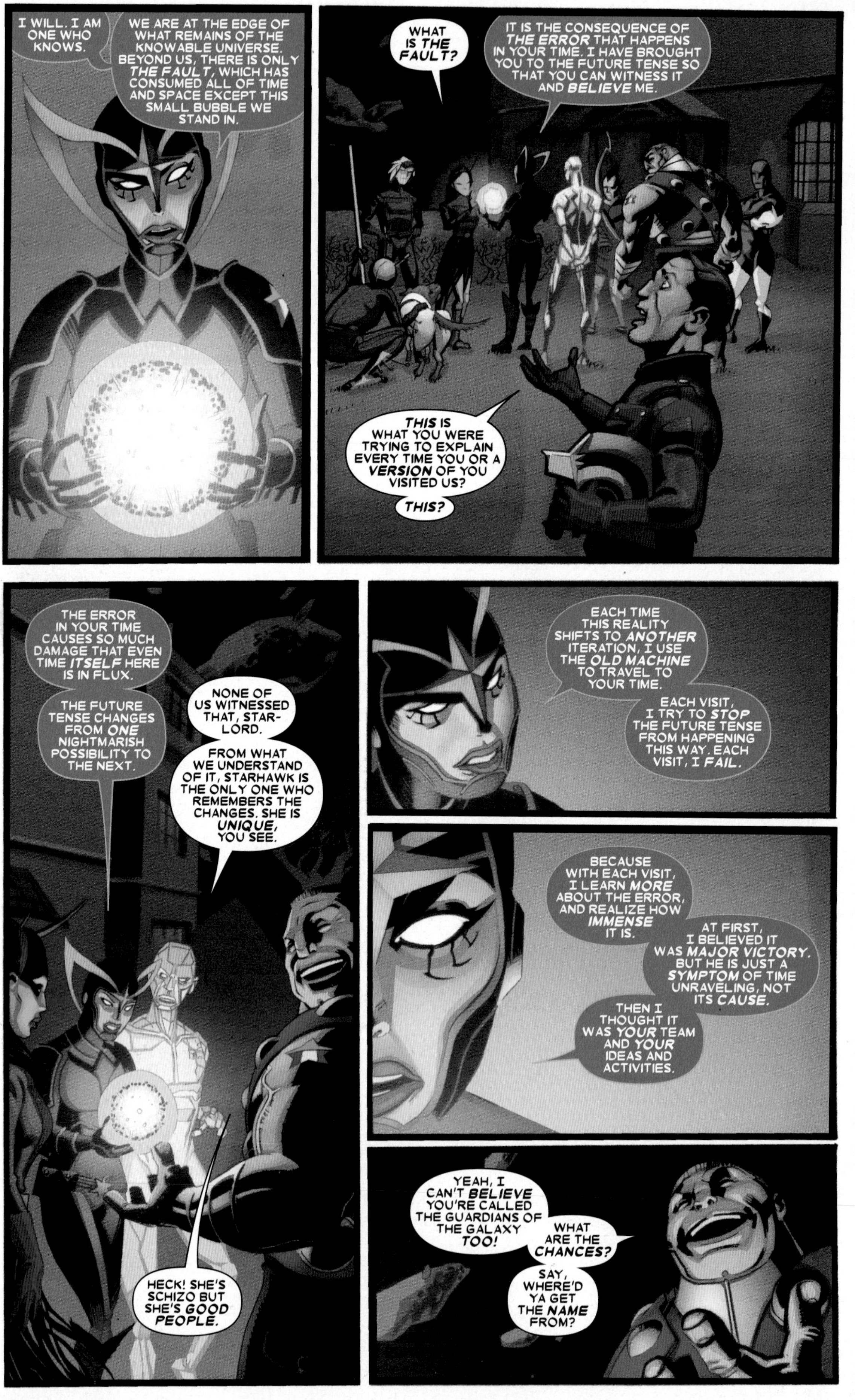
I WILL. I AM ONE WHO KNOWS.
WE ARE AT THE EDGE OF WHAT REMAINS OF THE KNOWABLE UNIVERSE. BEYOND US, THERE IS ONLY THE FAULT, WHICH HAS CONSUMED ALL OF TIME AND SPACE EXCEPT THIS SMALL BUBBLE WE STAND IN.
WHAT IS THE FAULT?
IT IS THE CONSEQUENCE OF THE ERROR THAT HAPPENS IN YOUR TIME. I HAVE BROUGHT YOU TO THE FUTURE TENSE SO THAT YOU CAN WITNESS IT AND BELIEVE ME.
THIS IS WHAT YOU WERE TRYING TO EXPLAIN EVERY TIME YOU OR A VERSION OF YOU VISITED US?
THIS?
THE ERROR IN YOUR TIME CAUSES SO MUCH DAMAGE THAT EVEN TIME ITSELF HERE IS IN FLUX.
THE FUTURE TENSE CHANGES FROM ONE NIGHTMARISH POSSIBILITY TO THE NEXT.
NONE OF US WITNESSED THAT, STAR-LORD.
FROM WHAT WE UNDERSTAND OF IT, STARHAWK IS THE ONLY ONE WHO REMEMBERS THE CHANGES. SHE IS UNIQUE, YOU SEE.
HECK! SHE'S SCHIZO BUT SHE'S GOOD PEOPLE.
EACH TIME THIS REALITY SHIFTS TO ANOTHER ITERATION, I USE THE OLD MACHINE TO TRAVEL TO YOUR TIME.
EACH VISIT, I TRY TO STOP THE FUTURE TENSE FROM HAPPENING THIS WAY. EACH VISIT, I FAIL.
BECAUSE WITH EACH VISIT, I LEARN MORE ABOUT THE ERROR, AND REALIZE HOW IMMENSE IT IS.
AT FIRST, I BELIEVED IT WAS MAJOR VICTORY. BUT HE IS JUST A SYMPTOM OF TIME UNRAVELING, NOT ITS CAUSE.
THEN I THOUGHT IT WAS YOUR TEAM AND YOUR IDEAS AND ACTIVITIES.
YEAH, I CAN'T BELIEVE YOU'RE CALLED THE GUARDIANS OF THE GALAXY TOO!
WHAT ARE THE CHANCES?
SAY, WHERE'D YA GET THE NAME FROM?

OH, *RIGHT*. I GET IT. "*NOT THE TIME FOR CHIT-CHAT, CHARLIE.*" IT'S JUST THAT WE HAVEN'T HAD VISITORS IN THE *LONGEST* TIME.

ON MY LAST VISIT, YOU *DETAINED* ME.

THIS GAVE ME TIME TO STUDY, TO *PROBE*.

THEN THE FORCES OF THE *SHI'AR* AND THE *INHUMANS* ARRIVED ON YOUR STATION, AND MY MIND WAS BROUGHT INTO *CLOSE* PROXIMITY TO THE THOUGHTS OF THE INHUMAN KING.

AND AT LAST I SAW THE *TRUTH*.

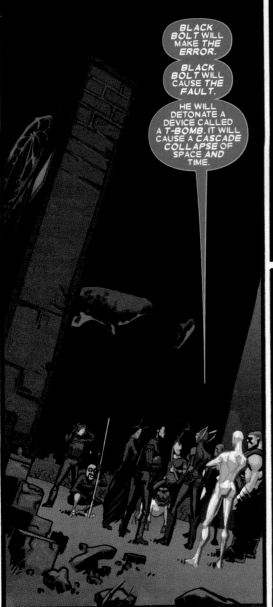

BLACK BOLT WILL MAKE *THE ERROR*.

BLACK BOLT WILL CAUSE *THE FAULT*.

HE WILL DETONATE A DEVICE CALLED A *T-BOMB*. IT WILL CAUSE A *CASCADE COLLAPSE* OF SPACE *AND* TIME.

THOSE STUPID ✱✱✱✱✱✱✱✱✱!

THIS IS *EXACTLY* WHAT ADAM WARLOCK HAS BEEN WARNING US OF ALL ALONG. THE UNIVERSE IS TOO *FRAGILE* TO WITHSTAND THE PUNISHMENT OF A STELLAR WAR.

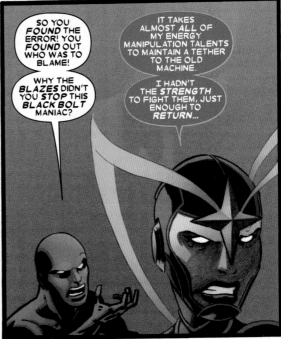

SO YOU *FOUND* THE ERROR! YOU *FOUND* OUT WHO WAS TO BLAME!

WHY THE *BLAZES* DIDN'T YOU *STOP* THIS BLACK BOLT MANIAC?

IT TAKES ALMOST *ALL* OF MY ENERGY MANIPULATION TALENTS TO MAINTAIN A TETHER TO THE OLD MACHINE.

I HADN'T THE *STRENGTH* TO FIGHT THEM, JUST ENOUGH TO *RETURN...*

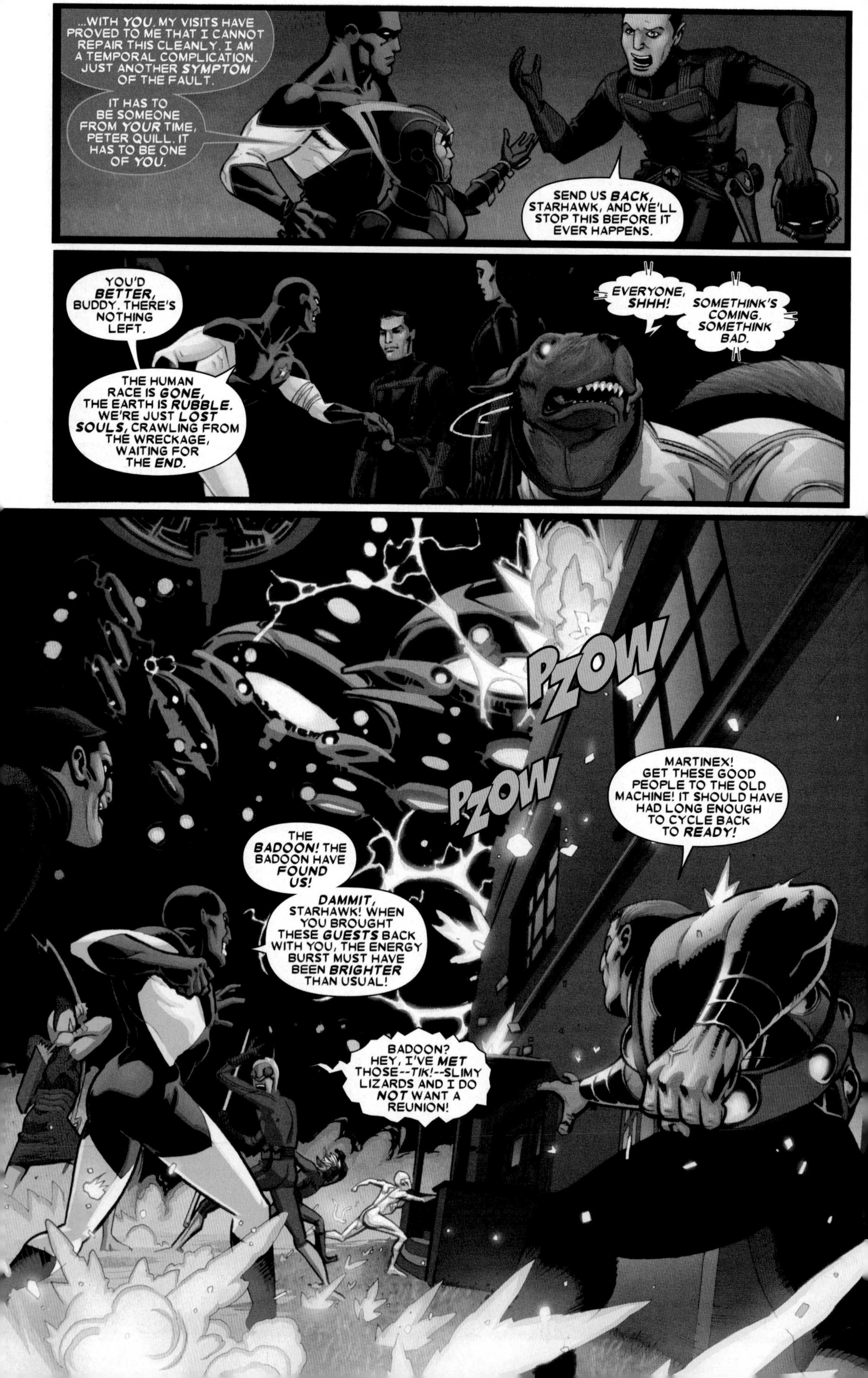
...WITH YOU. MY VISITS HAVE PROVED TO ME THAT I CANNOT REPAIR THIS CLEANLY. I AM A TEMPORAL COMPLICATION. JUST ANOTHER SYMPTOM OF THE FAULT.
IT HAS TO BE SOMEONE FROM YOUR TIME, PETER QUILL. IT HAS TO BE ONE OF YOU.
SEND US BACK, STARHAWK, AND WE'LL STOP THIS BEFORE IT EVER HAPPENS.
YOU'D BETTER, BUDDY. THERE'S NOTHING LEFT.
THE HUMAN RACE IS GONE, THE EARTH IS RUBBLE. WE'RE JUST LOST SOULS, CRAWLING FROM THE WRECKAGE, WAITING FOR THE END.
EVERYONE, SHHH!
SOMETHINK'S COMING. SOMETHINK BAD.
PZOW
PZOW
MARTINEX! GET THESE GOOD PEOPLE TO THE OLD MACHINE! IT SHOULD HAVE HAD LONG ENOUGH TO CYCLE BACK TO READY!
THE BADOON! THE BADOON HAVE FOUND US!
DAMMIT, STARHAWK! WHEN YOU BROUGHT THESE GUESTS BACK WITH YOU, THE ENERGY BURST MUST HAVE BEEN BRIGHTER THAN USUAL!
BADOON? HEY, I'VE MET THOSE--TIK!--SLIMY LIZARDS AND I DO NOT WANT A REUNION!

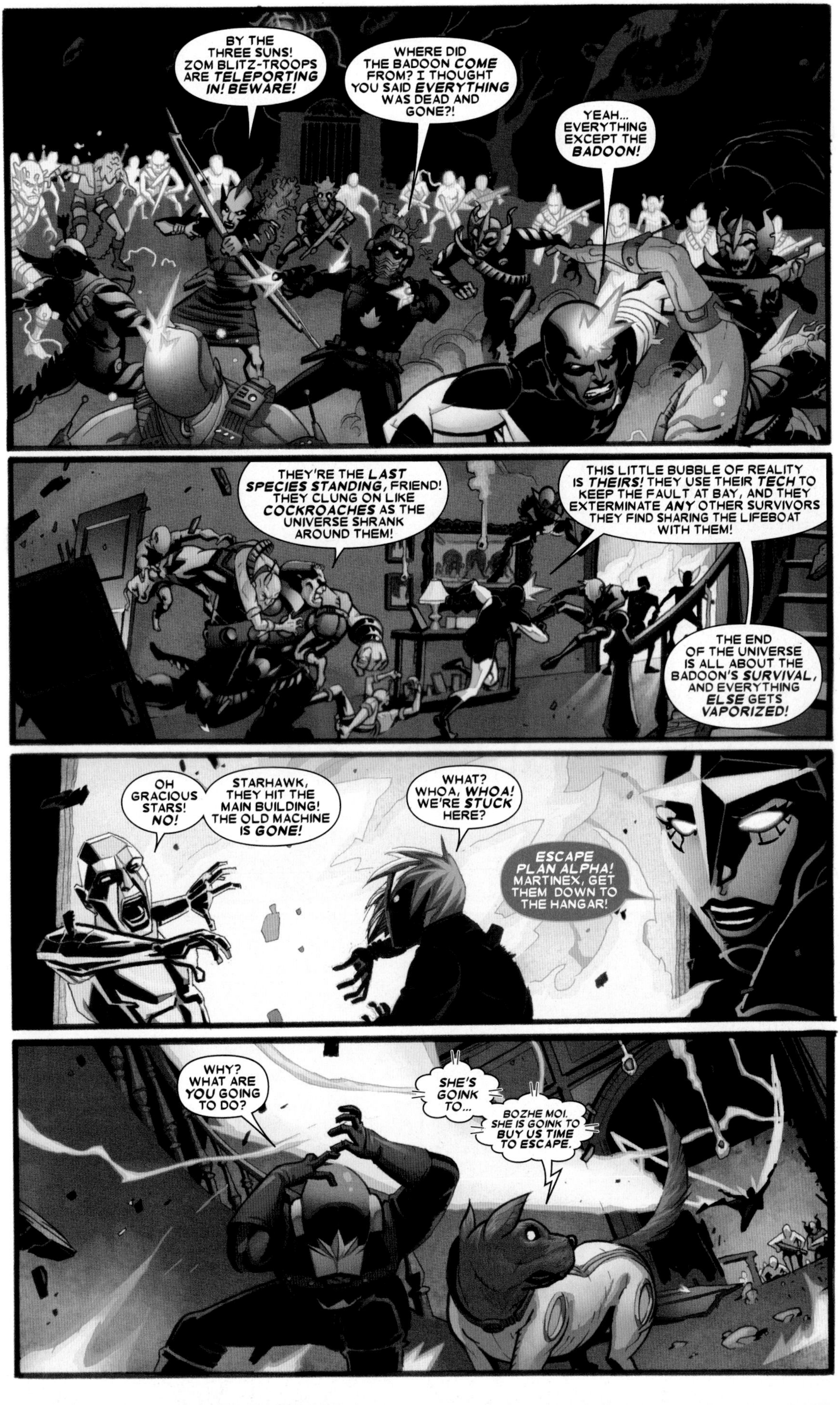
BY THE THREE SUNS! ZOM BLITZ-TROOPS ARE TELEPORTING IN! BEWARE!
WHERE DID THE BADOON COME FROM? I THOUGHT YOU SAID EVERYTHING WAS DEAD AND GONE?!
YEAH... EVERYTHING EXCEPT THE BADOON!
THEY'RE THE LAST SPECIES STANDING, FRIEND! THEY CLUNG ON LIKE COCKROACHES AS THE UNIVERSE SHRANK AROUND THEM!
THIS LITTLE BUBBLE OF REALITY IS THEIRS! THEY USE THEIR TECH TO KEEP THE FAULT AT BAY, AND THEY EXTERMINATE ANY OTHER SURVIVORS THEY FIND SHARING THE LIFEBOAT WITH THEM!
THE END OF THE UNIVERSE IS ALL ABOUT THE BADOON'S SURVIVAL, AND EVERYTHING ELSE GETS VAPORIZED!
OH GRACIOUS STARS! NO!
STARHAWK, THEY HIT THE MAIN BUILDING! THE OLD MACHINE IS GONE!
WHAT? WHOA, WHOA! WE'RE STUCK HERE?
ESCAPE PLAN ALPHA! MARTINEX, GET THEM DOWN TO THE HANGAR!
WHY? WHAT ARE YOU GOING TO DO?
SHE'S GOINK TO...
BOZHE MOI. SHE IS GOINK TO BUY US TIME TO ESCAPE.

BADOON! MOST OF YOU WILL *NOT* SURVIVE THE NEXT THIRTY SECONDS!

TRUST ME ON THIS...

...I AM ONE WHO KNOWS.

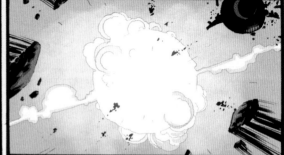

WHOOOOMMMM!!

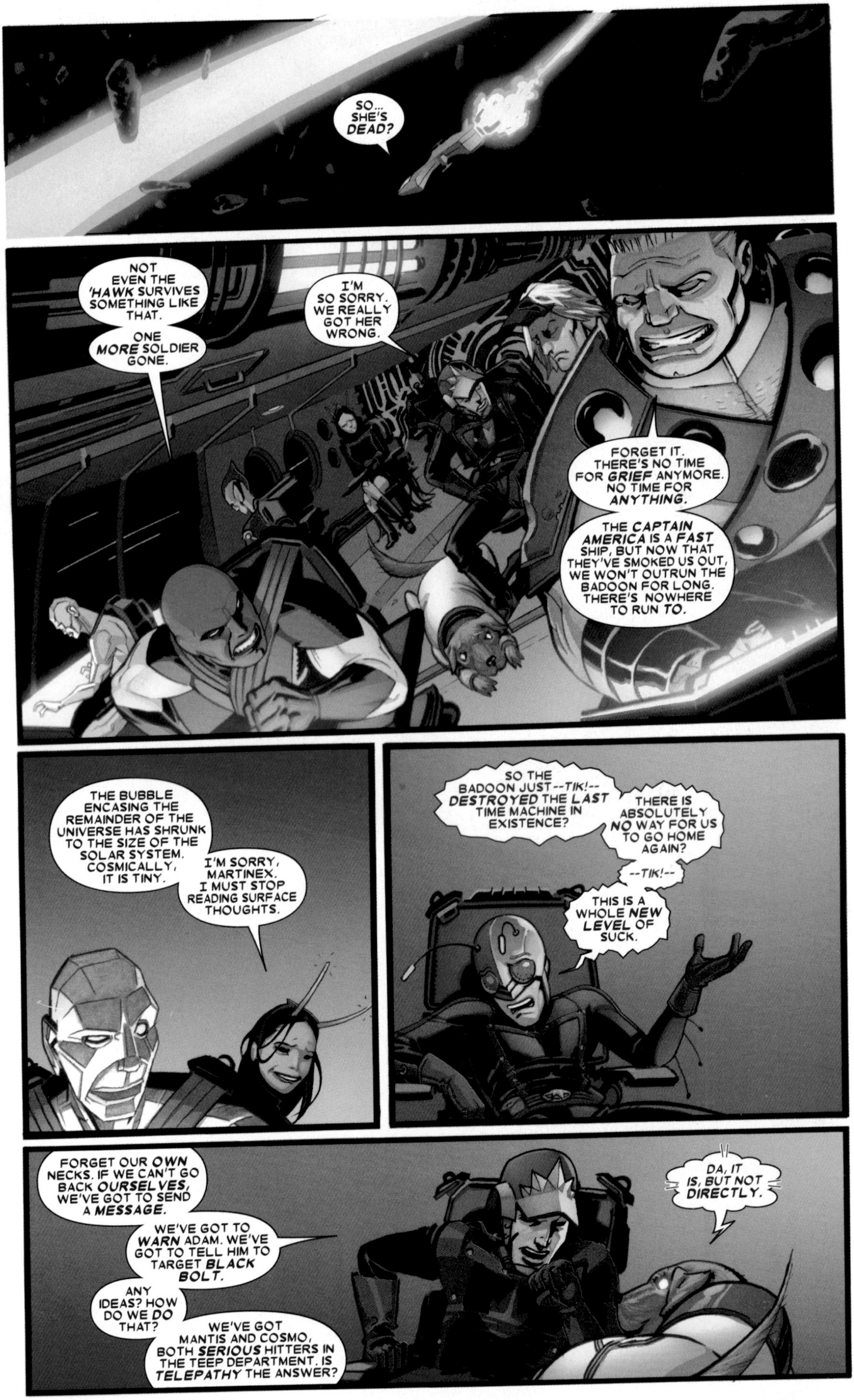
SO... SHE'S DEAD?
NOT EVEN THE 'HAWK SURVIVES SOMETHING LIKE THAT.
ONE MORE SOLDIER GONE.
I'M SO SORRY. WE REALLY GOT HER WRONG.
FORGET IT. THERE'S NO TIME FOR GRIEF ANYMORE. NO TIME FOR ANYTHING.
THE CAPTAIN AMERICA IS A FAST SHIP, BUT NOW THAT THEY'VE SMOKED US OUT, WE WON'T OUTRUN THE BADOON FOR LONG. THERE'S NOWHERE TO RUN TO.
THE BUBBLE ENCASING THE REMAINDER OF THE UNIVERSE HAS SHRUNK TO THE SIZE OF THE SOLAR SYSTEM. COSMICALLY, IT IS TINY.
I'M SORRY, MARTINEX. I MUST STOP READING SURFACE THOUGHTS.
SO THE BADOON JUST --TIK!-- DESTROYED THE LAST TIME MACHINE IN EXISTENCE?
THERE IS ABSOLUTELY NO WAY FOR US TO GO HOME AGAIN?
--TIK!--
THIS IS A WHOLE NEW LEVEL OF SUCK.
FORGET OUR OWN NECKS. IF WE CAN'T GO BACK OURSELVES, WE'VE GOT TO SEND A MESSAGE.
WE'VE GOT TO WARN ADAM. WE'VE GOT TO TELL HIM TO TARGET BLACK BOLT.
ANY IDEAS? HOW DO WE DO THAT?
WE'VE GOT MANTIS AND COSMO, BOTH SERIOUS HITTERS IN THE TEEP DEPARTMENT. IS TELEPATHY THE ANSWER?
DA, IT IS, BUT NOT DIRECTLY.

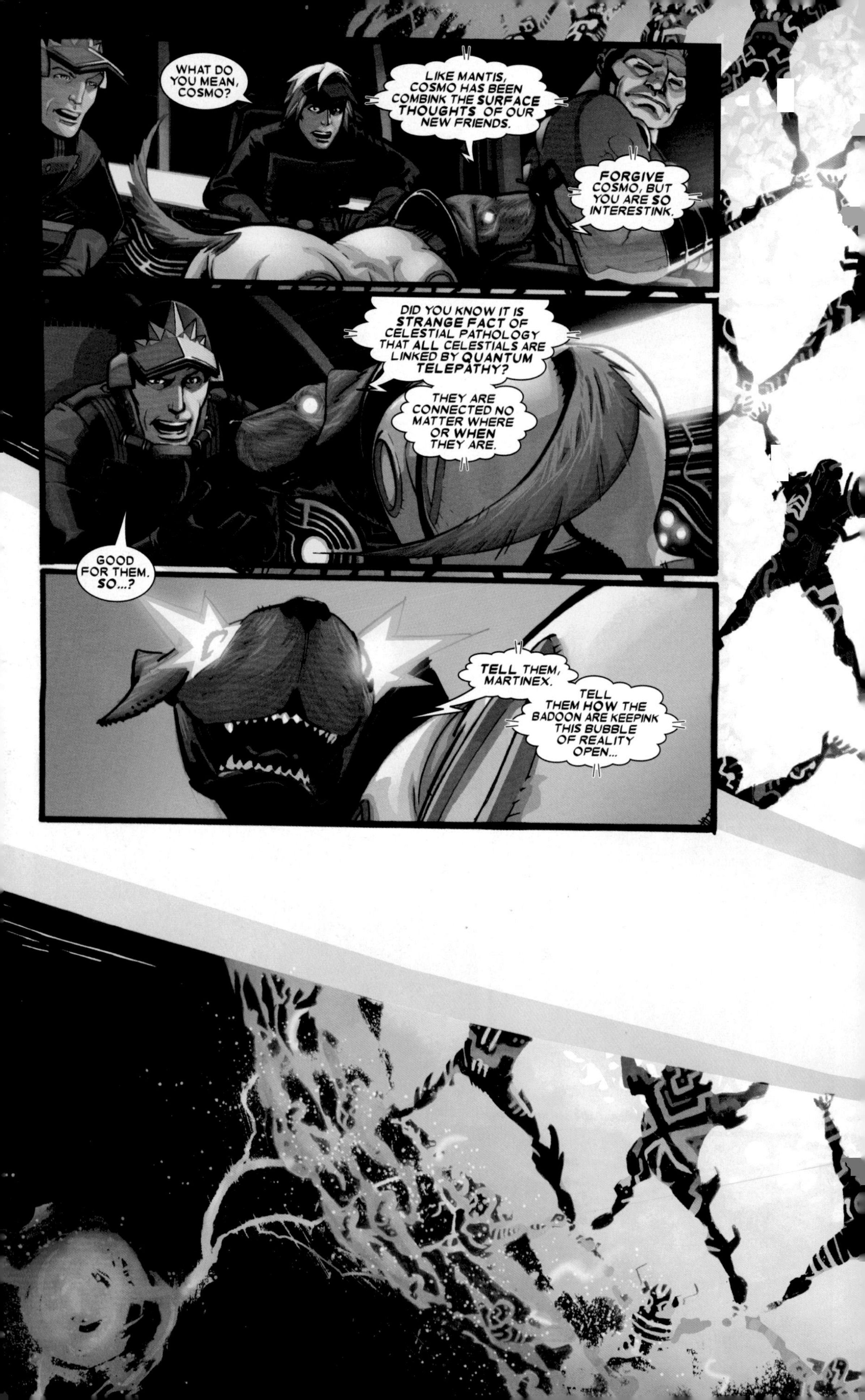
WHAT DO YOU MEAN, COSMO?
LIKE MANTIS, COSMO HAS BEEN COMBINK THE SURFACE THOUGHTS OF OUR NEW FRIENDS.
FORGIVE COSMO, BUT YOU ARE SO INTERESTINK.
DID YOU KNOW IT IS STRANGE FACT OF CELESTIAL PATHOLOGY THAT ALL CELESTIALS ARE LINKED BY QUANTUM TELEPATHY?
THEY ARE CONNECTED NO MATTER WHERE OR WHEN THEY ARE.
GOOD FOR THEM. SO...?
TELL THEM, MARTINEX.
TELL THEM HOW THE BADOON ARE KEEPINK THIS BUBBLE OF REALITY OPEN...

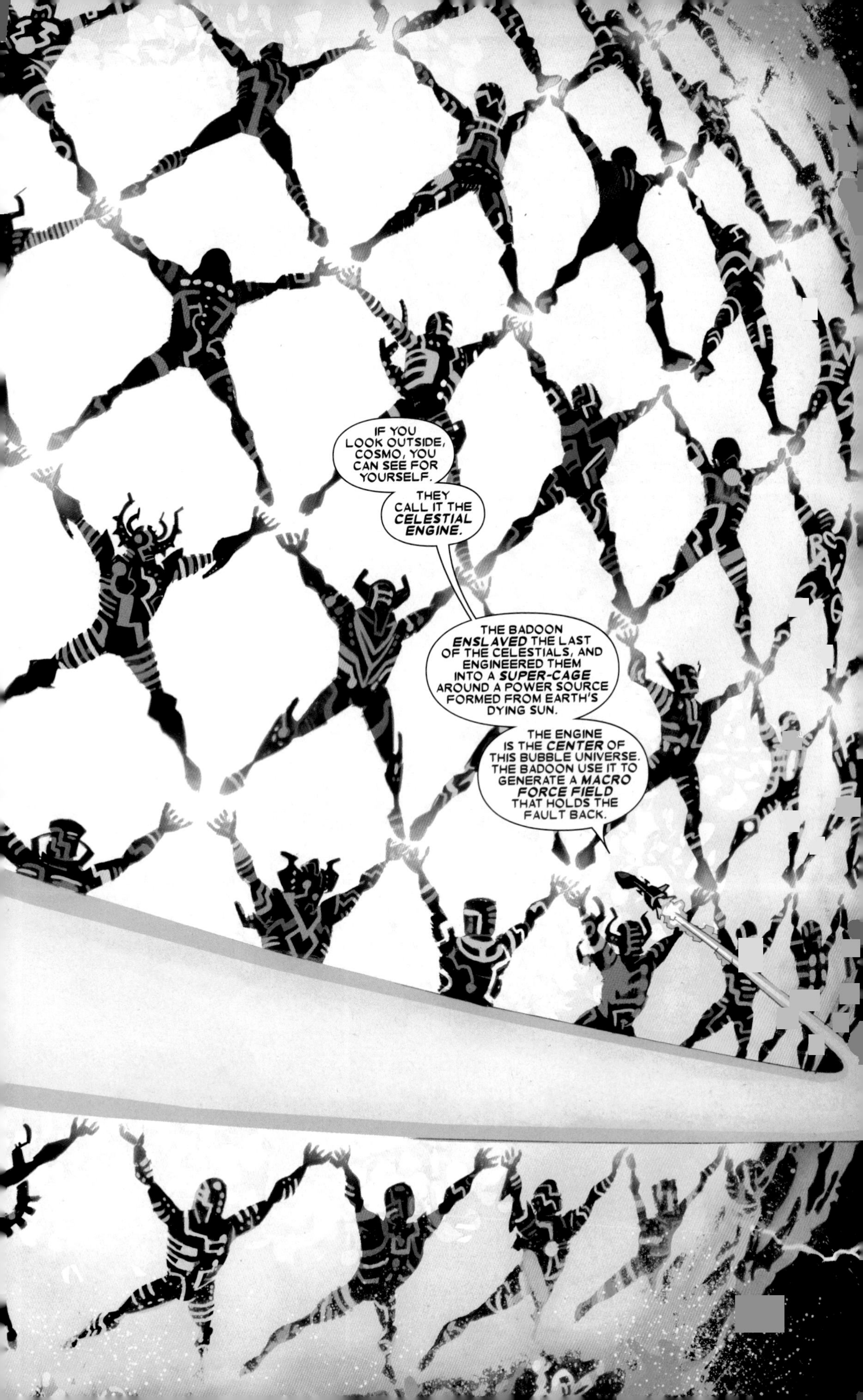
IF YOU LOOK OUTSIDE, COSMO, YOU CAN SEE FOR YOURSELF.
THEY CALL IT THE CELESTIAL ENGINE.
THE BADOON ENSLAVED THE LAST OF THE CELESTIALS, AND ENGINEERED THEM INTO A SUPER-CAGE AROUND A POWER SOURCE FORMED FROM EARTH'S DYING SUN.
THE ENGINE IS THE CENTER OF THIS BUBBLE UNIVERSE. THE BADOON USE IT TO GENERATE A MACRO FORCE FIELD THAT HOLDS THE FAULT BACK.

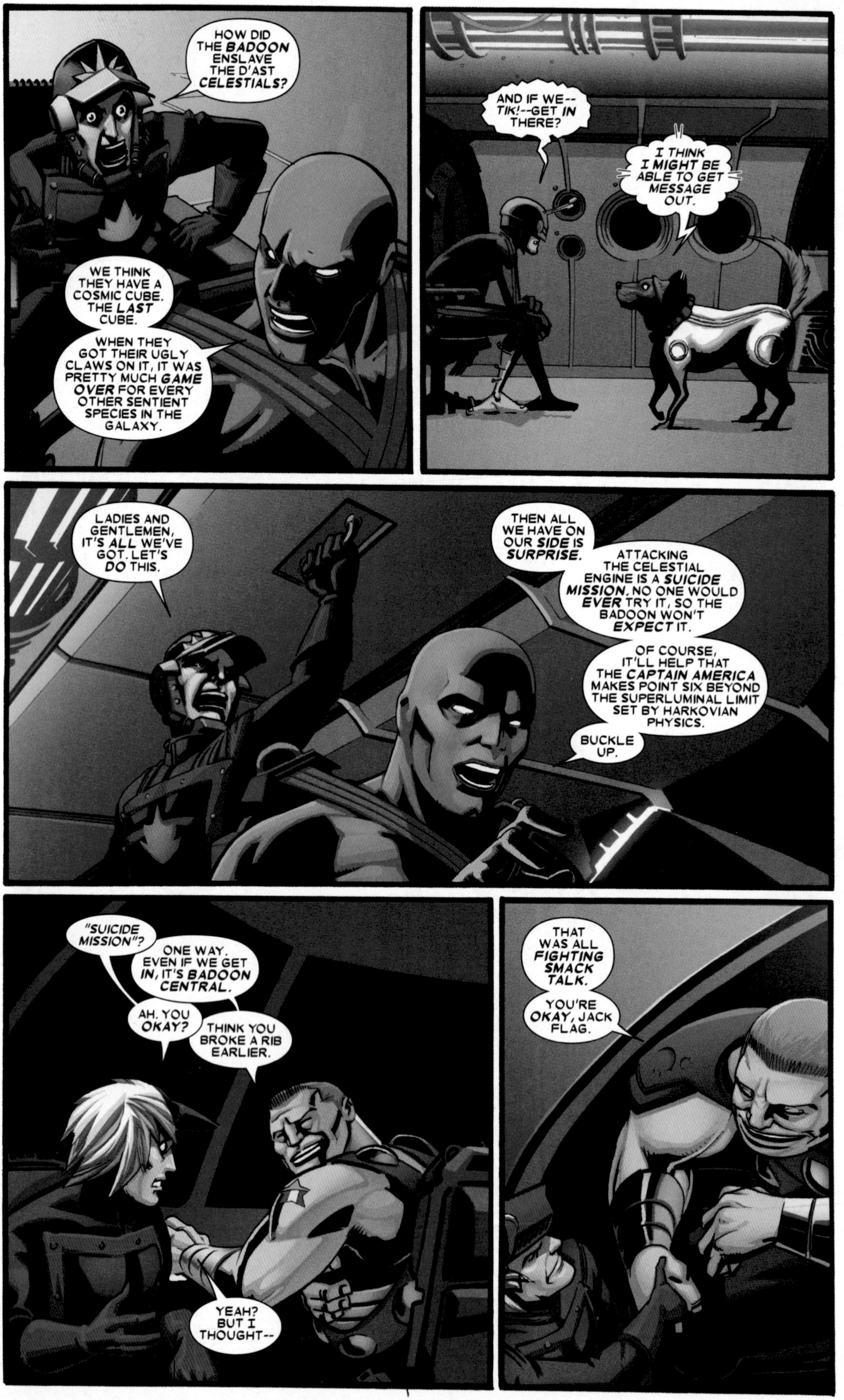
HOW DID THE BADOON ENSLAVE THE D'AST CELESTIALS?
WE THINK THEY HAVE A COSMIC CUBE. THE LAST CUBE.
WHEN THEY GOT THEIR UGLY CLAWS ON IT, IT WAS PRETTY MUCH GAME OVER FOR EVERY OTHER SENTIENT SPECIES IN THE GALAXY.
AND IF WE--TIK!--GET IN THERE?
I THINK I MIGHT BE ABLE TO GET MESSAGE OUT.
LADIES AND GENTLEMEN, IT'S ALL WE'VE GOT. LET'S DO THIS.
THEN ALL WE HAVE ON OUR SIDE IS SURPRISE.
ATTACKING THE CELESTIAL ENGINE IS A SUICIDE MISSION. NO ONE WOULD EVER TRY IT, SO THE BADOON WON'T EXPECT IT.
OF COURSE, IT'LL HELP THAT THE CAPTAIN AMERICA MAKES POINT SIX BEYOND THE SUPERLUMINAL LIMIT SET BY HARKOVIAN PHYSICS.
BUCKLE UP.
"SUICIDE MISSION"?
ONE WAY. EVEN IF WE GET IN, IT'S BADOON CENTRAL.
AH. YOU OKAY?
THINK YOU BROKE A RIB EARLIER.
YEAH? BUT I THOUGHT--
THAT WAS ALL FIGHTING SMACK TALK.
YOU'RE OKAY, JACK FLAG.

YES, I THINK SO, TOO.

TWENTY SECONDS TO TARGET.

THEY'VE *SCOPED* US. WARSHIPS CLOSING!

MAX THE SHIELDS!

MARTINEX! MAIN GUN-BANKS *NOW!*

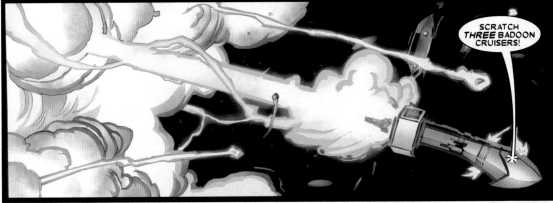

SCRATCH *THREE* BADOON CRUISERS!

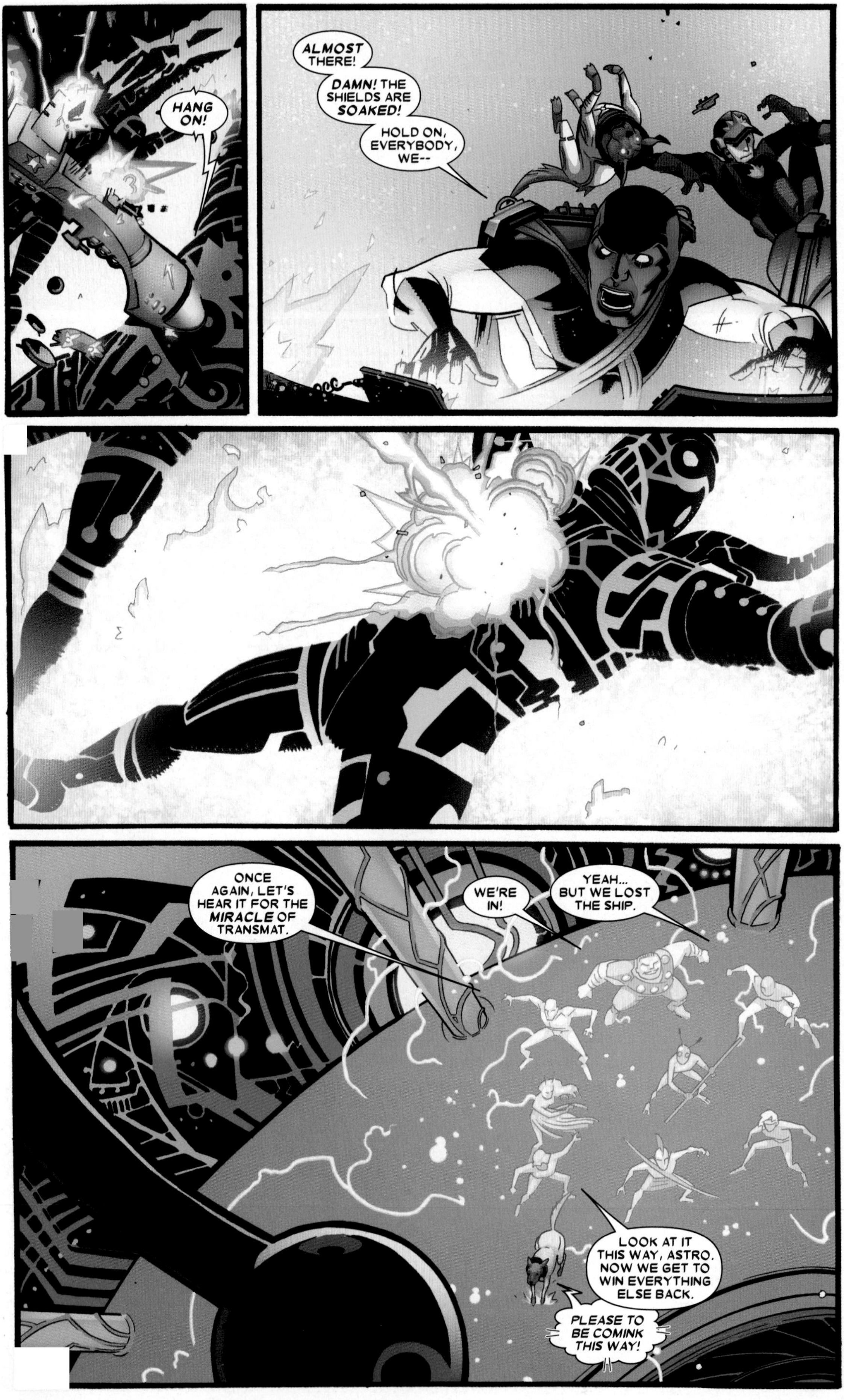
HANG ON!
ALMOST THERE!
DAMN! THE SHIELDS ARE SOAKED!
HOLD ON, EVERYBODY, WE--
ONCE AGAIN, LET'S HEAR IT FOR THE MIRACLE OF TRANSMAT.
WE'RE IN!
YEAH... BUT WE LOST THE SHIP.
LOOK AT IT THIS WAY, ASTRO. NOW WE GET TO WIN EVERYTHING ELSE BACK.
PLEASE TO BE COMINK THIS WAY!

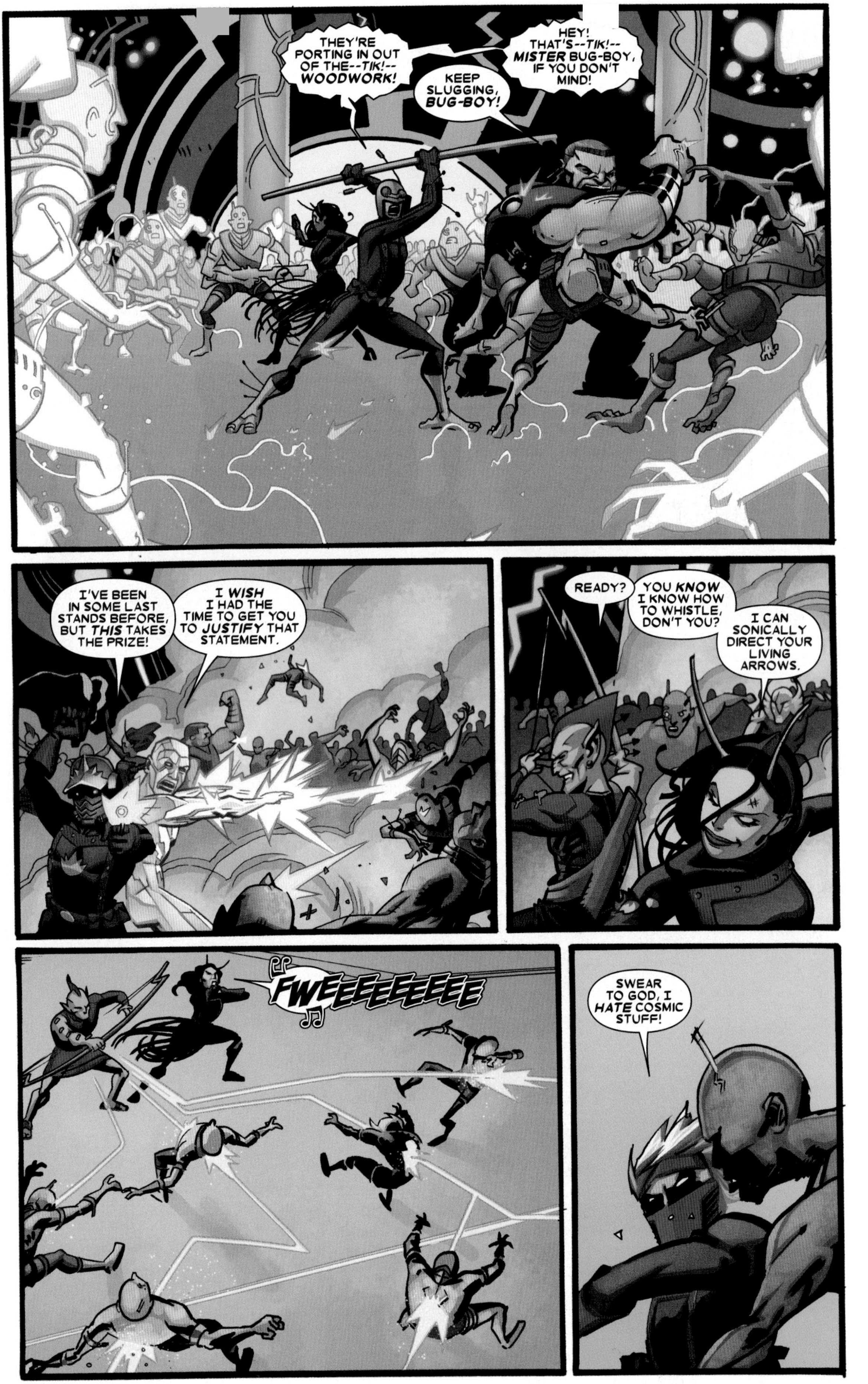
THEY'RE PORTING IN OUT OF THE--*TIK!*--**WOODWORK!**
KEEP SLUGGING, **BUG-BOY!**
HEY! THAT'S--*TIK!*--**MISTER** BUG-BOY, IF YOU DON'T MIND!
I'VE BEEN IN SOME LAST STANDS BEFORE, BUT *THIS* TAKES THE PRIZE!
I *WISH* I HAD THE TIME TO GET YOU TO *JUSTIFY* THAT STATEMENT.
READY?
YOU *KNOW* I KNOW HOW TO WHISTLE, DON'T YOU?
I CAN SONICALLY DIRECT YOUR LIVING ARROWS.
FWEEEEEEEEE
SWEAR TO GOD, I *HATE* COSMIC STUFF!

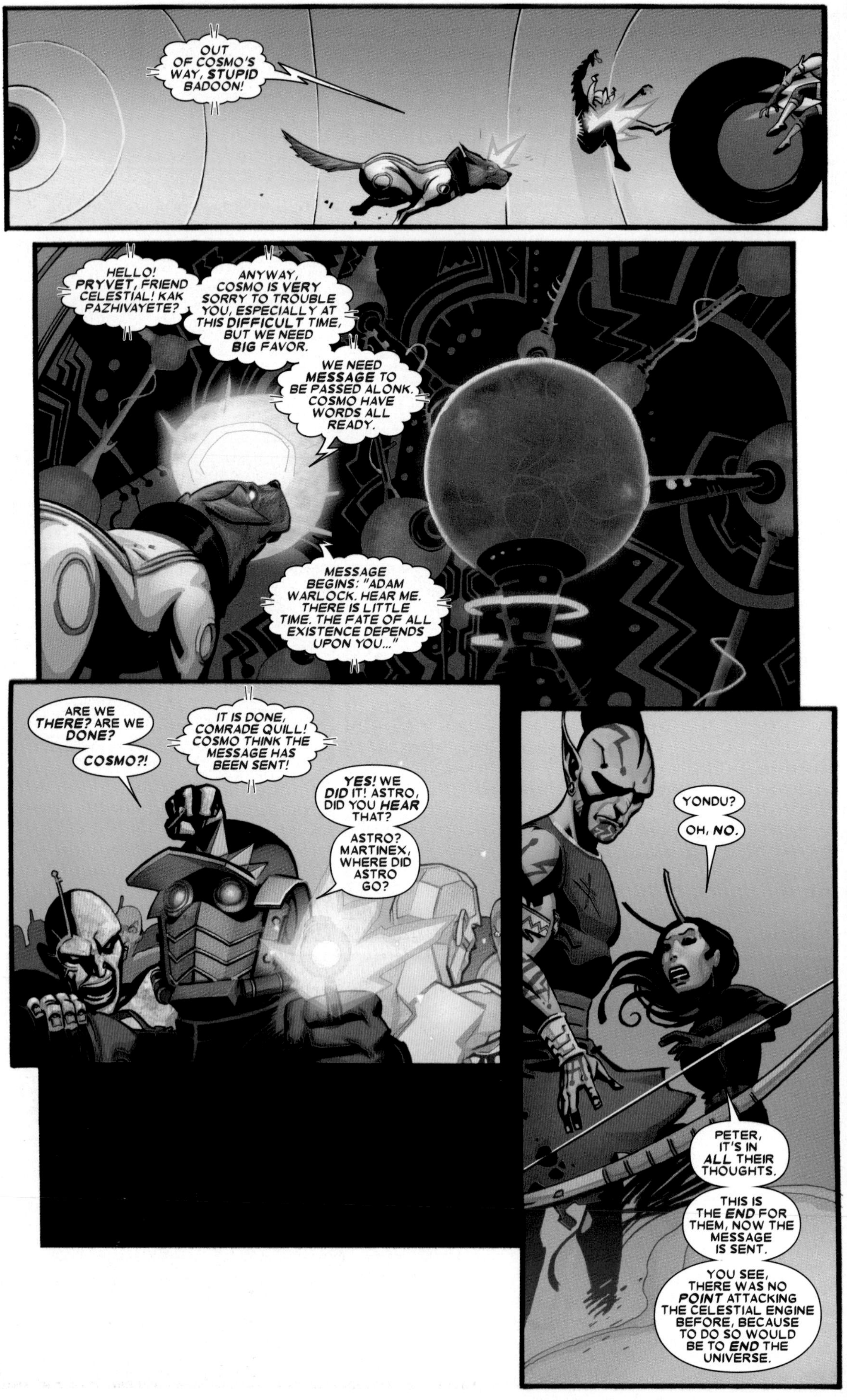
OUT OF COSMO'S WAY, STUPID BADOON!
HELLO! PRYVET, FRIEND CELESTIAL! KAK PAZHIVAYETE?
ANYWAY, COSMO IS VERY SORRY TO TROUBLE YOU, ESPECIALLY AT THIS DIFFICULT TIME, BUT WE NEED BIG FAVOR.
WE NEED MESSAGE TO BE PASSED ALONK. COSMO HAVE WORDS ALL READY.
MESSAGE BEGINS: "ADAM WARLOCK. HEAR ME. THERE IS LITTLE TIME. THE FATE OF ALL EXISTENCE DEPENDS UPON YOU..."
ARE WE THERE? ARE WE DONE?
COSMO?!
IT IS DONE, COMRADE QUILL! COSMO THINK THE MESSAGE HAS BEEN SENT!
YES! WE DID IT! ASTRO, DID YOU HEAR THAT?
ASTRO? MARTINEX, WHERE DID ASTRO GO?
YONDU?
OH, NO.
PETER, IT'S IN ALL THEIR THOUGHTS.
THIS IS THE END FOR THEM, NOW THE MESSAGE IS SENT.
YOU SEE, THERE WAS NO POINT ATTACKING THE CELESTIAL ENGINE BEFORE, BECAUSE TO DO SO WOULD BE TO END THE UNIVERSE.

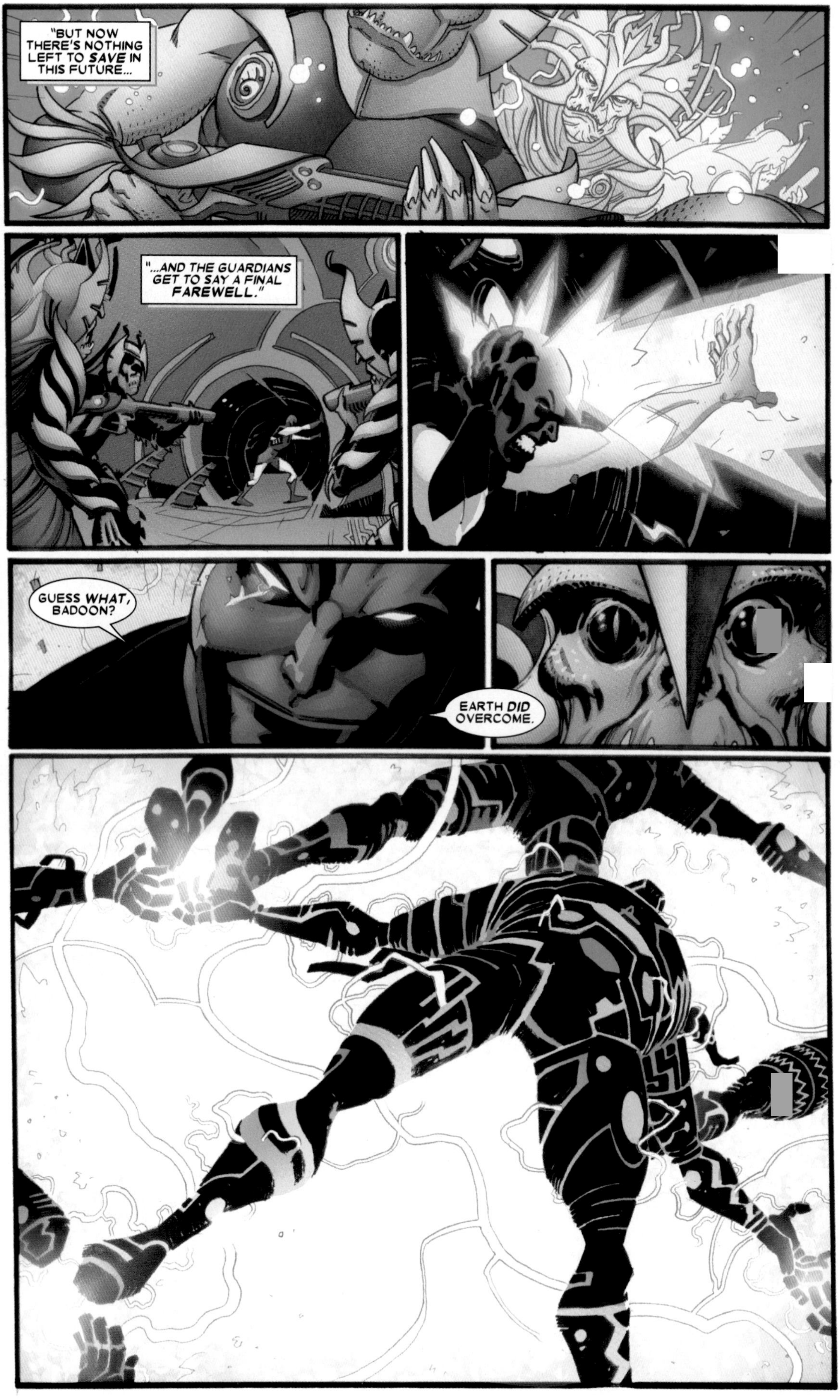
"BUT NOW THERE'S NOTHING LEFT TO *SAVE* IN THIS FUTURE...
"...AND THE GUARDIANS GET TO SAY A FINAL *FAREWELL*."
GUESS *WHAT*, BADOON?
EARTH *DID* OVERCOME.

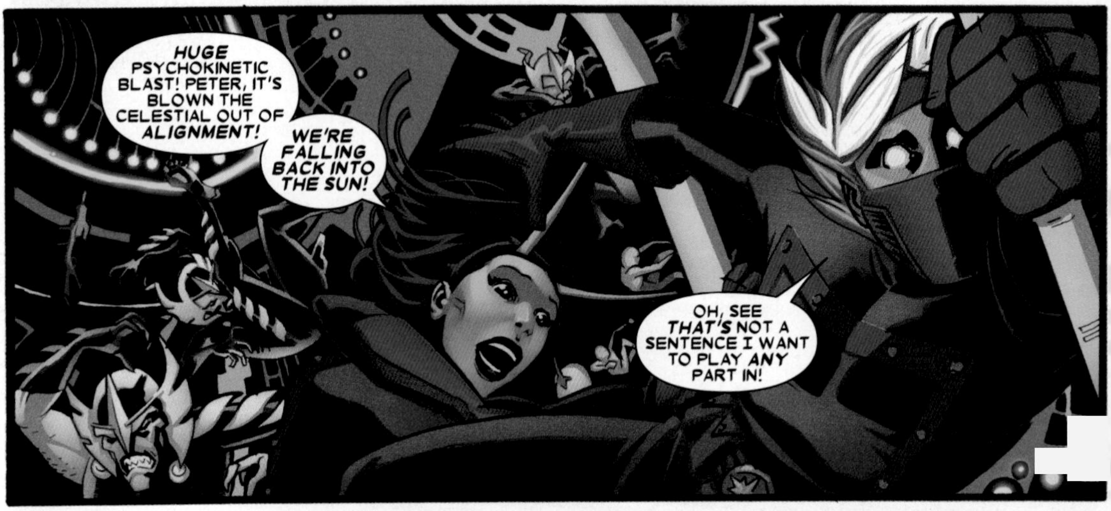
HUGE PSYCHOKINETIC BLAST! PETER, IT'S BLOWN THE CELESTIAL OUT OF ALIGNMENT!
WE'RE FALLING BACK INTO THE SUN!
OH, SEE THAT'S NOT A SENTENCE I WANT TO PLAY ANY PART IN!

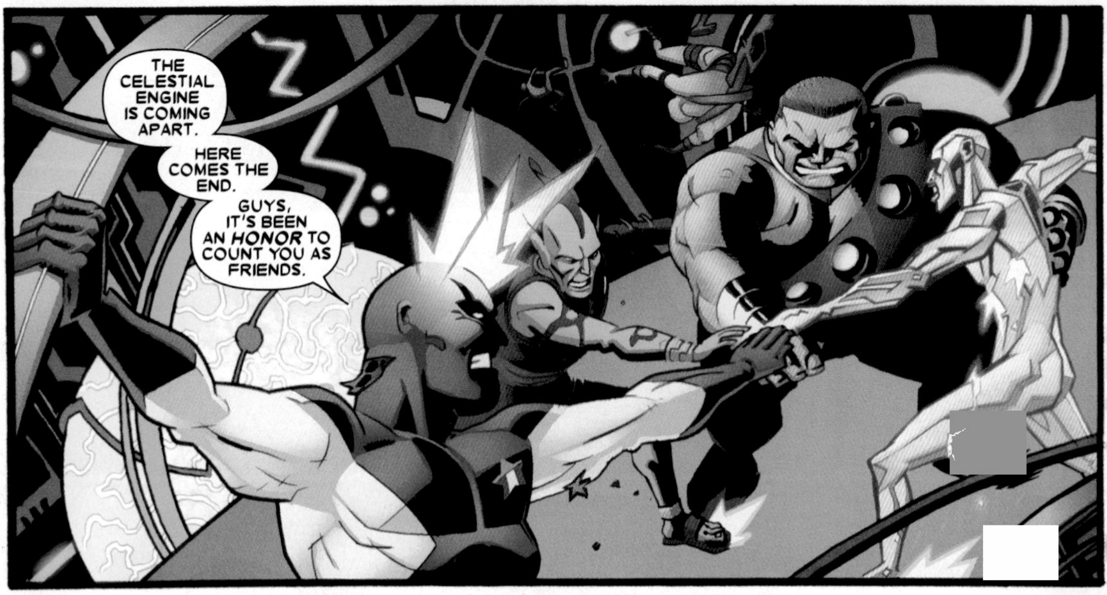
THE CELESTIAL ENGINE IS COMING APART.
HERE COMES THE END.
GUYS, IT'S BEEN AN HONOR TO COUNT YOU AS FRIENDS.

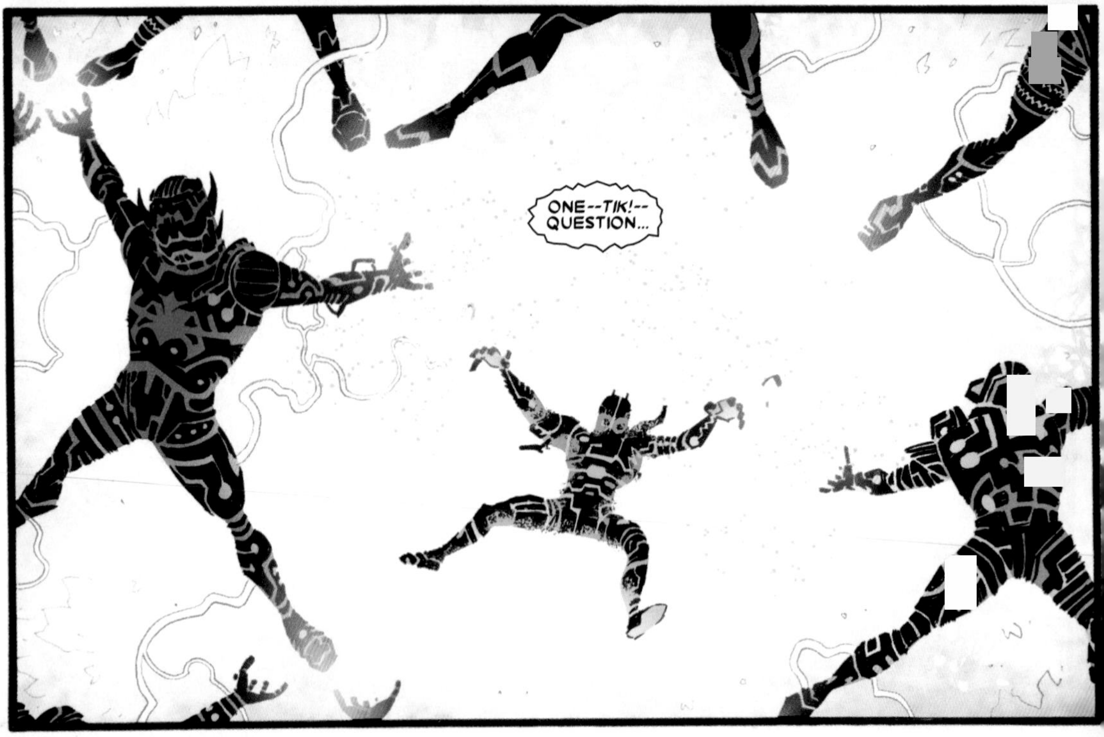
ONE--TIK!--QUESTION...

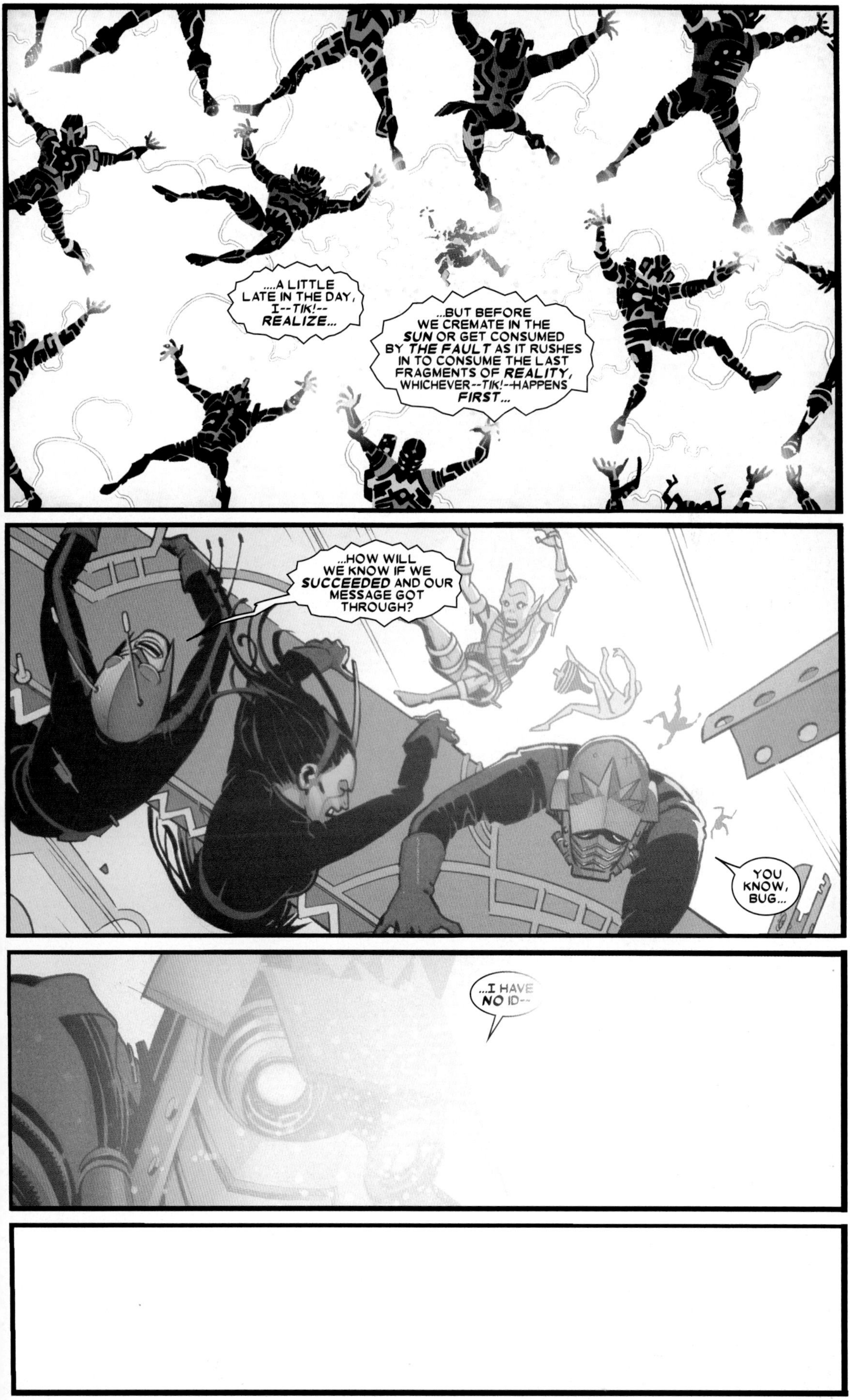
....A LITTLE LATE IN THE DAY, I--TIK!--REALIZE...
...BUT BEFORE WE CREMATE IN THE SUN OR GET CONSUMED BY THE FAULT AS IT RUSHES IN TO CONSUME THE LAST FRAGMENTS OF REALITY, WHICHEVER--TIK!--HAPPENS FIRST...
...HOW WILL WE KNOW IF WE SUCCEEDED AND OUR MESSAGE GOT THROUGH?
YOU KNOW, BUG...
...I HAVE NO ID--

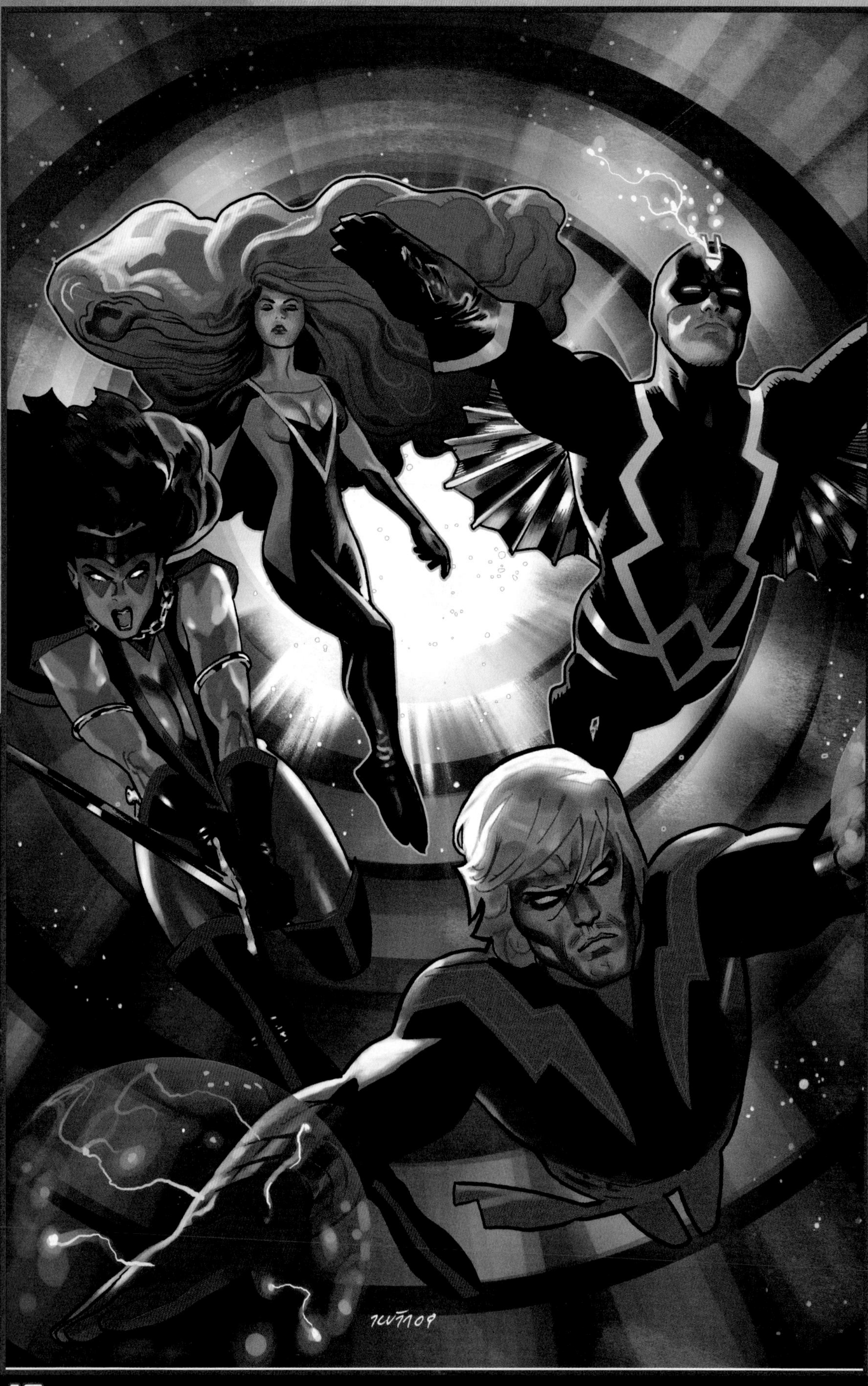

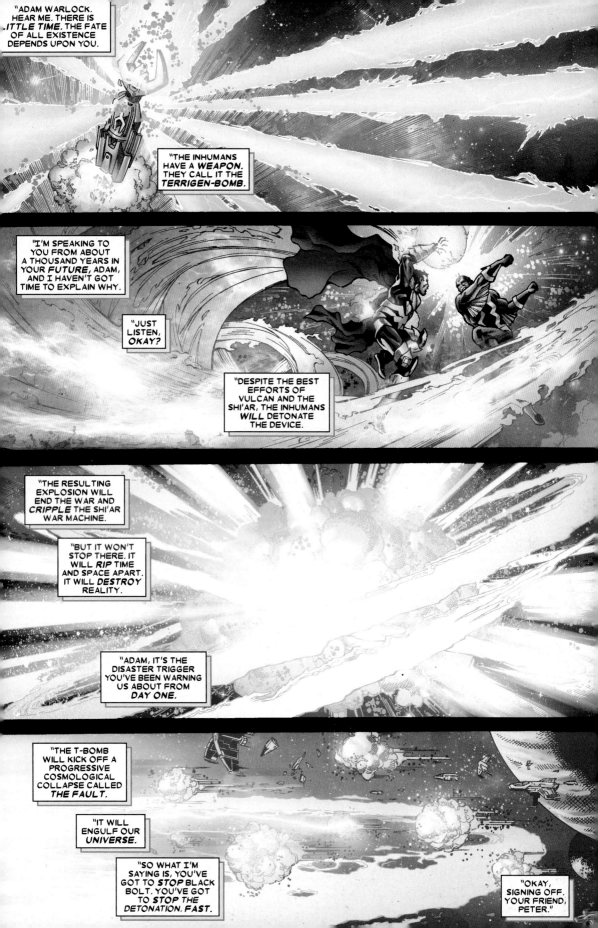

"ADAM WARLOCK. HEAR ME. THERE IS *LITTLE TIME*. THE FATE OF ALL EXISTENCE DEPENDS UPON YOU.

"THE INHUMANS HAVE A *WEAPON*. THEY CALL IT THE *TERRIGEN-BOMB*.

"I'M SPEAKING TO YOU FROM ABOUT A THOUSAND YEARS IN YOUR *FUTURE*, ADAM, AND I HAVEN'T GOT TIME TO EXPLAIN WHY.

"JUST LISTEN, OKAY?

"DESPITE THE BEST EFFORTS OF VULCAN AND THE SHI'AR, THE INHUMANS *WILL* DETONATE THE DEVICE.

"THE RESULTING EXPLOSION WILL END THE WAR AND *CRIPPLE* THE SHI'AR WAR MACHINE.

"BUT IT WON'T STOP THERE. IT WILL *RIP* TIME AND SPACE APART. IT WILL *DESTROY* REALITY.

"ADAM, IT'S THE DISASTER TRIGGER YOU'VE BEEN WARNING US ABOUT FROM *DAY ONE*.

"THE T-BOMB WILL KICK OFF A PROGRESSIVE COSMOLOGICAL COLLAPSE CALLED *THE FAULT*.

"IT WILL ENGULF OUR *UNIVERSE*.

"SO WHAT I'M SAYING IS, YOU'VE GOT TO *STOP* BLACK BOLT. YOU'VE GOT TO *STOP* THE DETONATION. *FAST*.

"OKAY, SIGNING OFF. YOUR FRIEND, PETER."

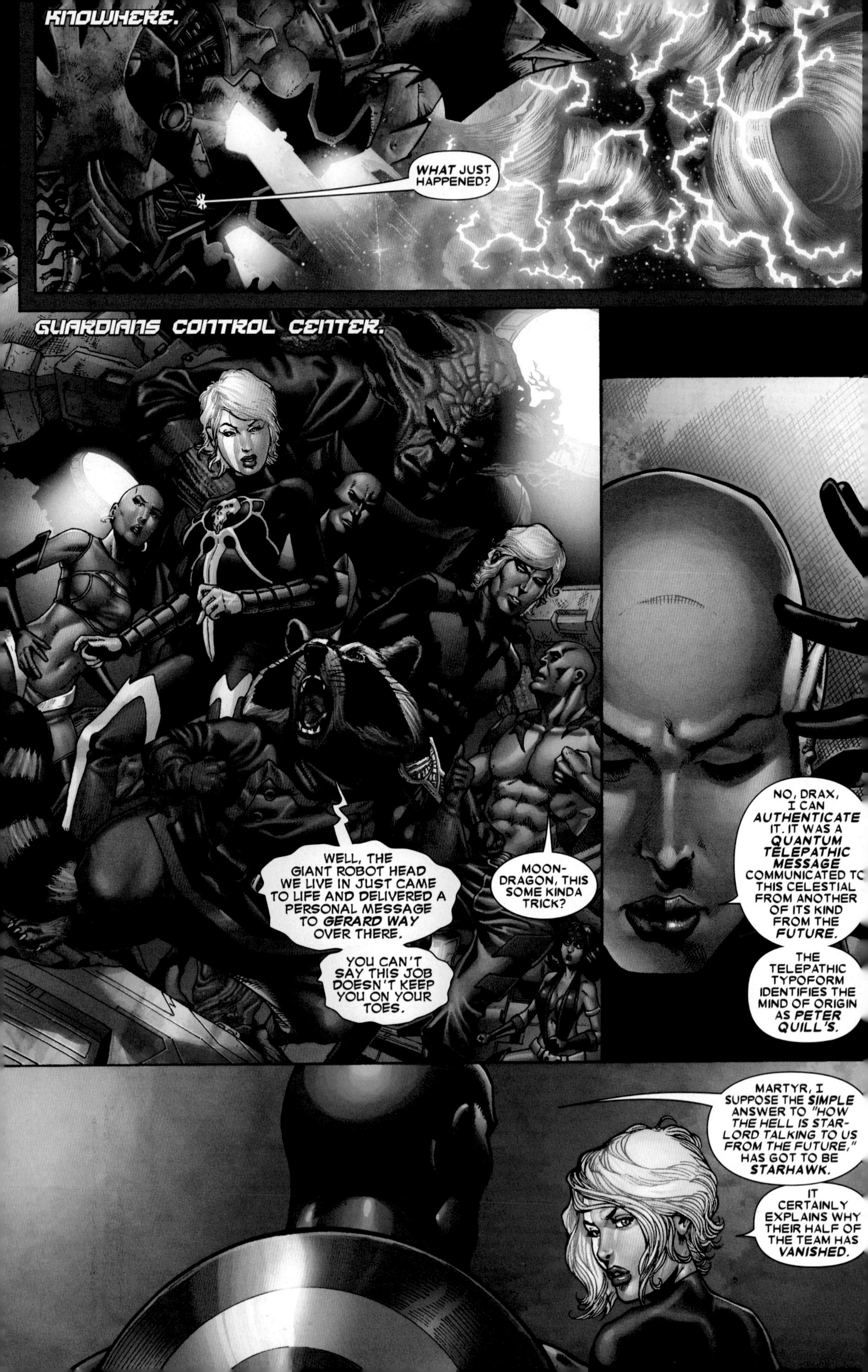
KNOWHERE.
WHAT JUST HAPPENED?
GUARDIANS CONTROL CENTER.
WELL, THE GIANT ROBOT HEAD WE LIVE IN JUST CAME TO LIFE AND DELIVERED A PERSONAL MESSAGE TO GERARD WAY OVER THERE.
YOU CAN'T SAY THIS JOB DOESN'T KEEP YOU ON YOUR TOES.
MOON-DRAGON, THIS SOME KINDA TRICK?
NO, DRAX, I CAN AUTHENTICATE IT. IT WAS A QUANTUM TELEPATHIC MESSAGE COMMUNICATED TO THIS CELESTIAL FROM ANOTHER OF ITS KIND FROM THE FUTURE.
THE TELEPATHIC TYPOFORM IDENTIFIES THE MIND OF ORIGIN AS PETER QUILL'S.
MARTYR, I SUPPOSE THE SIMPLE ANSWER TO "HOW THE HELL IS STAR-LORD TALKING TO US FROM THE FUTURE," HAS GOT TO BE STARHAWK.
IT CERTAINLY EXPLAINS WHY THEIR HALF OF THE TEAM HAS VANISHED.

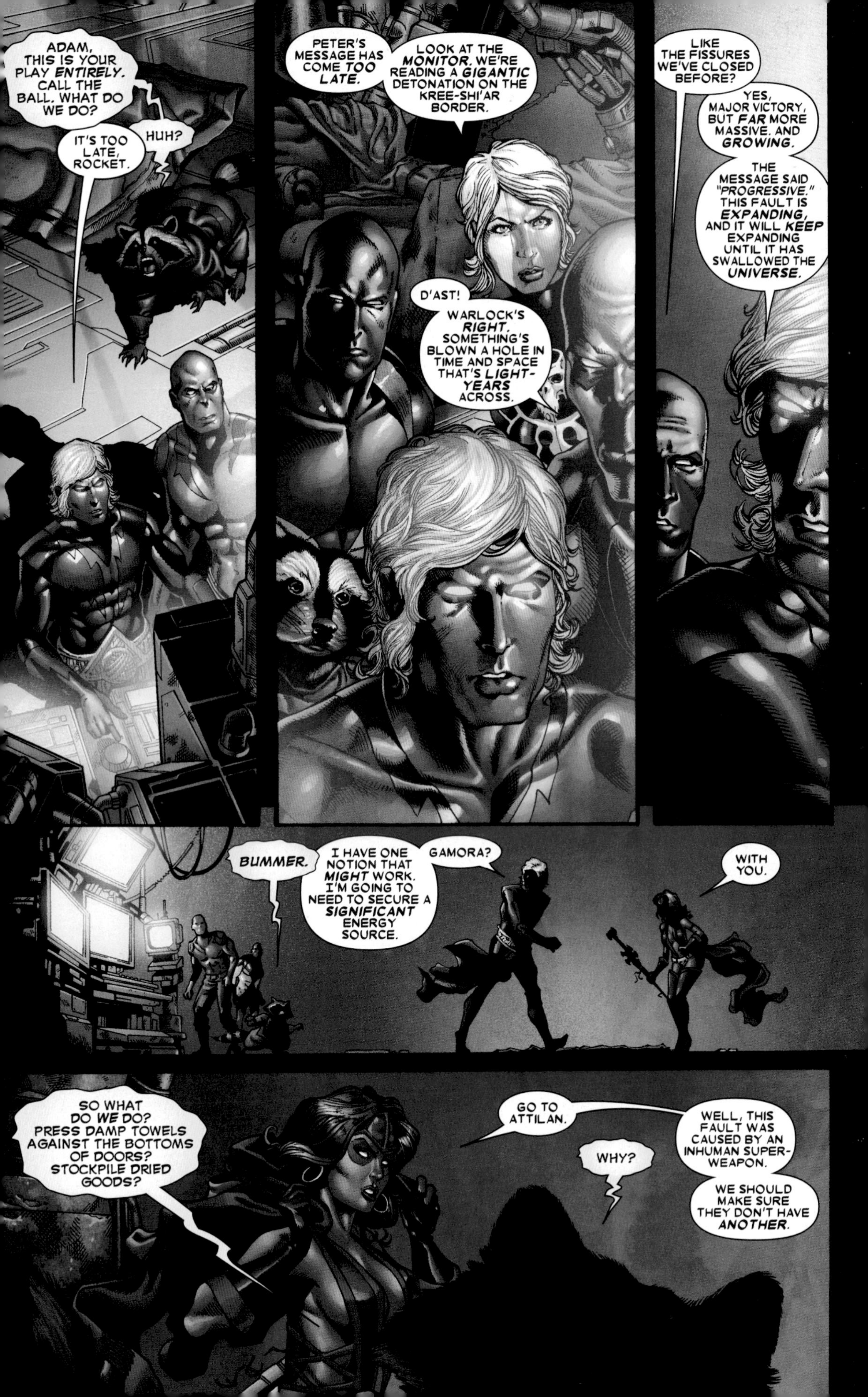

ADAM, THIS IS YOUR PLAY ENTIRELY. CALL THE BALL. WHAT DO WE DO?
IT'S TOO LATE, ROCKET.
HUH?
PETER'S MESSAGE HAS COME TOO LATE.
LOOK AT THE MONITOR. WE'RE READING A GIGANTIC DETONATION ON THE KREE-SHI'AR BORDER.
D'AST!
WARLOCK'S RIGHT. SOMETHING'S BLOWN A HOLE IN TIME AND SPACE THAT'S LIGHT-YEARS ACROSS.
LIKE THE FISSURES WE'VE CLOSED BEFORE?
YES, MAJOR VICTORY, BUT FAR MORE MASSIVE, AND GROWING.
THE MESSAGE SAID "PROGRESSIVE." THIS FAULT IS EXPANDING, AND IT WILL KEEP EXPANDING UNTIL IT HAS SWALLOWED THE UNIVERSE.
BUMMER.
I HAVE ONE NOTION THAT MIGHT WORK. I'M GOING TO NEED TO SECURE A SIGNIFICANT ENERGY SOURCE.
GAMORA?
WITH YOU.
SO WHAT DO WE DO? PRESS DAMP TOWELS AGAINST THE BOTTOMS OF DOORS? STOCKPILE DRIED GOODS?
GO TO ATTILAN.
WHY?
WELL, THIS FAULT WAS CAUSED BY AN INHUMAN SUPER-WEAPON.
WE SHOULD MAKE SURE THEY DON'T HAVE ANOTHER.

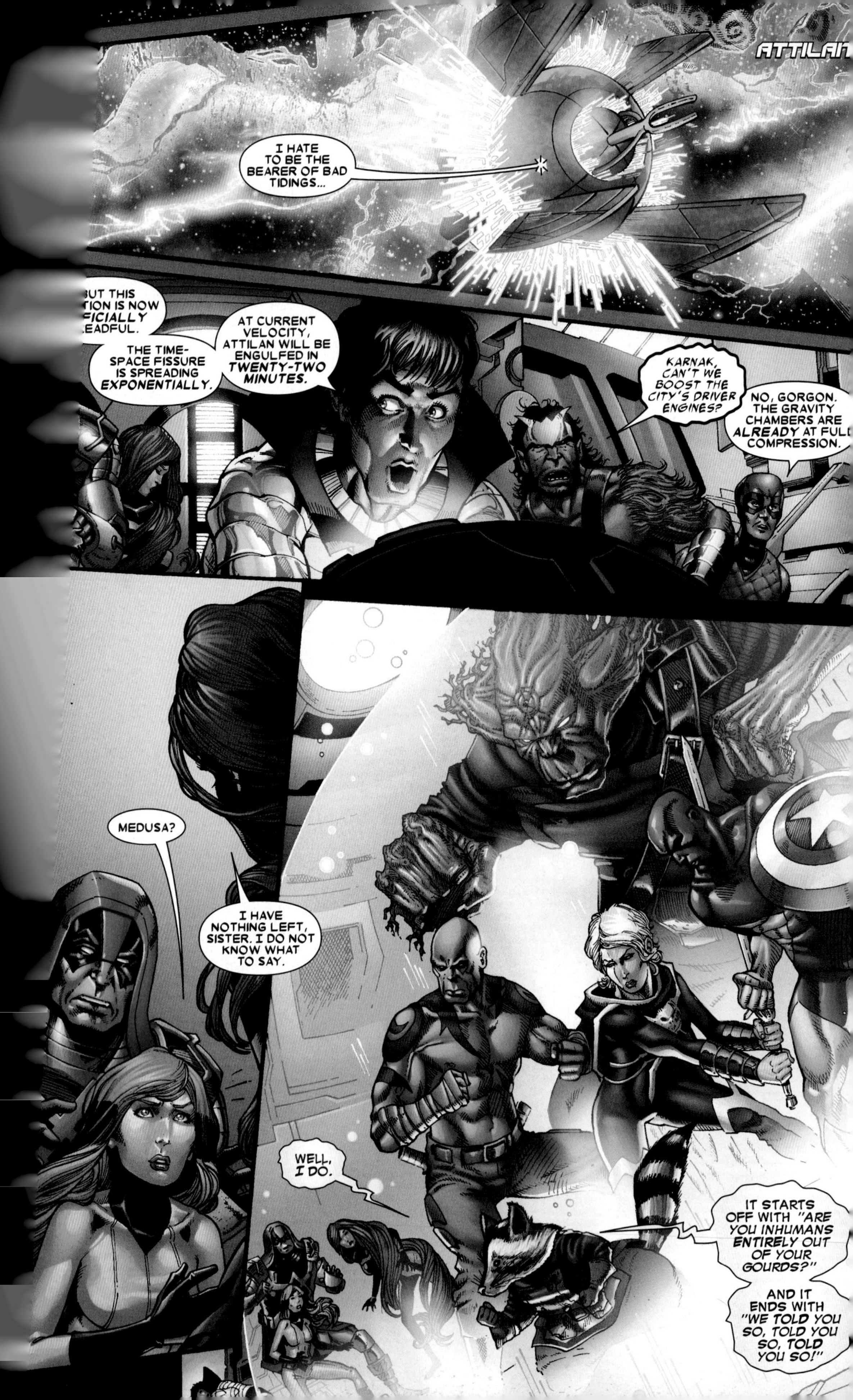
ATTILAN
I HATE TO BE THE BEARER OF BAD TIDINGS...
BUT THIS TION IS NOW FICIALLY EADFUL.
THE TIME-SPACE FISSURE IS SPREADING EXPONENTIALLY.
AT CURRENT VELOCITY, ATTILAN WILL BE ENGULFED IN TWENTY-TWO MINUTES.
KARNAK, CAN'T WE BOOST THE CITY'S DRIVER ENGINES?
NO, GORGON. THE GRAVITY CHAMBERS ARE ALREADY AT FUL COMPRESSION.
MEDUSA?
I HAVE NOTHING LEFT, SISTER. I DO NOT KNOW WHAT TO SAY.
WELL, I DO.
IT STARTS OFF WITH "ARE YOU INHUMANS ENTIRELY OUT OF YOUR GOURDS?"
AND IT ENDS WITH "WE TOLD YOU SO, TOLD YOU SO, TOLD YOU SO!"

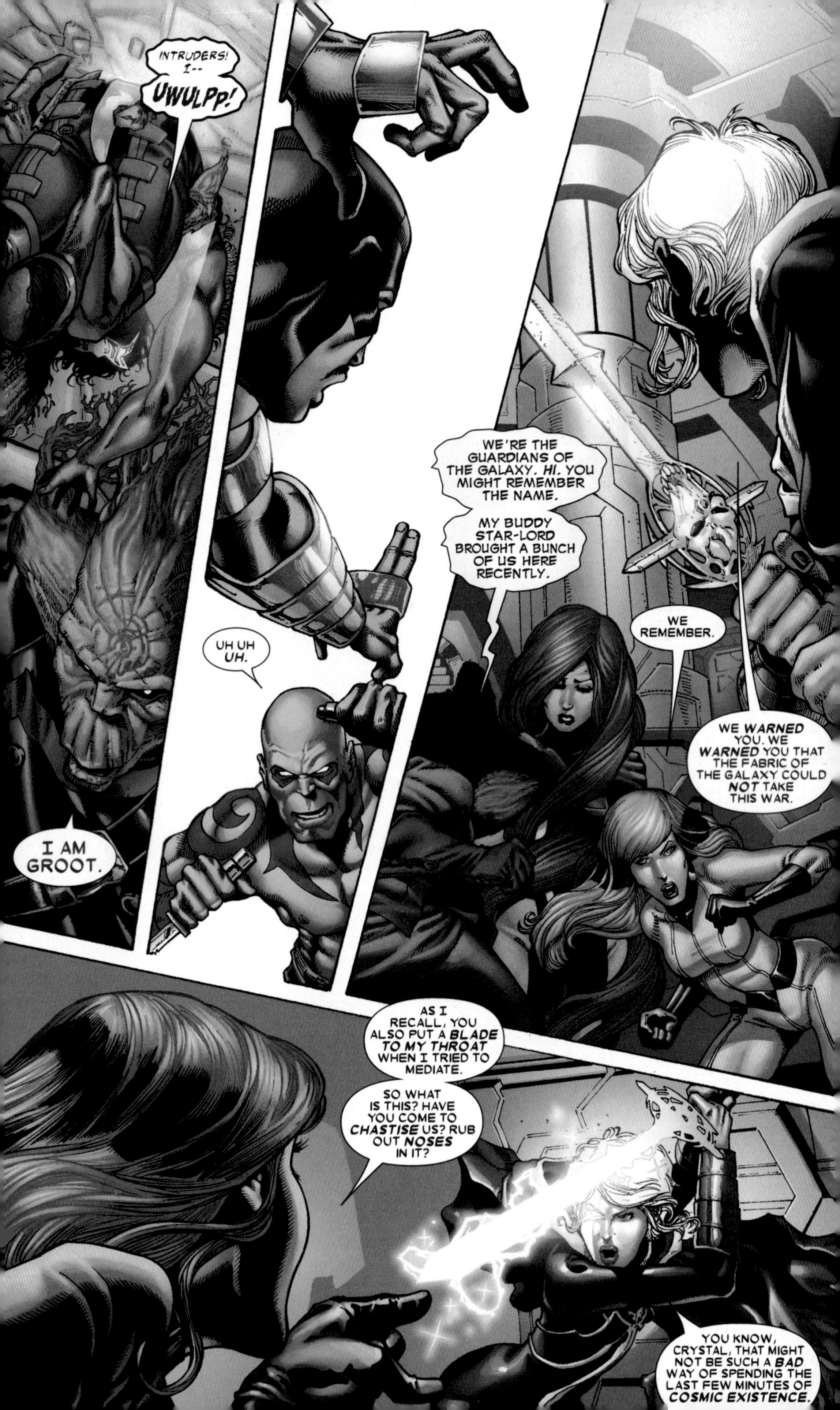
INTRUDERS! I-- UWULPP!
I AM GROOT.
UH UH UH.
WE'RE THE GUARDIANS OF THE GALAXY. HI. YOU MIGHT REMEMBER THE NAME.
MY BUDDY STAR-LORD BROUGHT A BUNCH OF US HERE RECENTLY.
WE REMEMBER.
WE WARNED YOU. WE WARNED YOU THAT THE FABRIC OF THE GALAXY COULD NOT TAKE THIS WAR.
AS I RECALL, YOU ALSO PUT A BLADE TO MY THROAT WHEN I TRIED TO MEDIATE.
SO WHAT IS THIS? HAVE YOU COME TO CHASTISE US? RUB OUT NOSES IN IT?
YOU KNOW, CRYSTAL, THAT MIGHT NOT BE SUCH A BAD WAY OF SPENDING THE LAST FEW MINUTES OF COSMIC EXISTENCE.

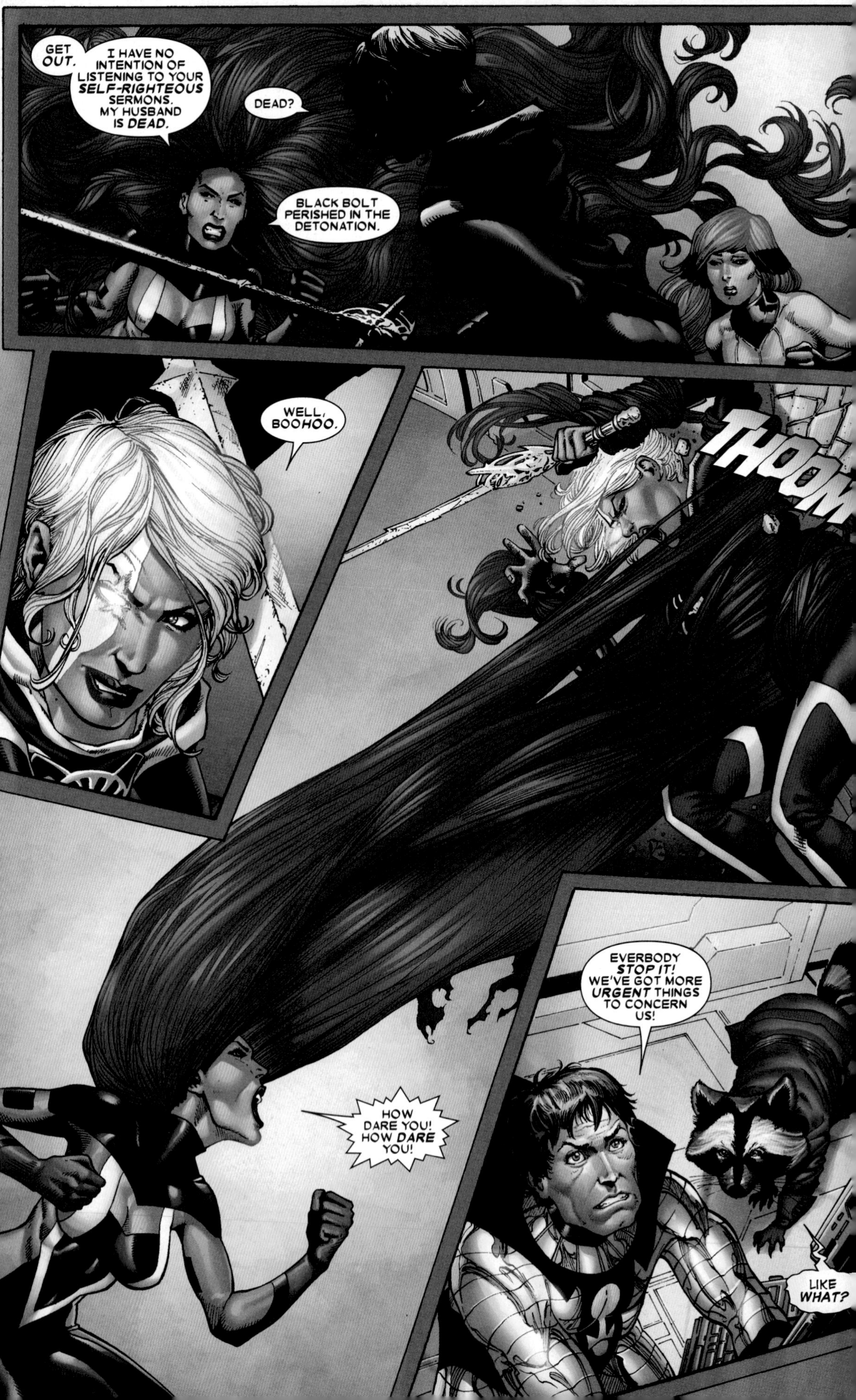
GET OUT.
I HAVE NO INTENTION OF LISTENING TO YOUR SELF-RIGHTEOUS SERMONS. MY HUSBAND IS DEAD.
DEAD?
BLACK BOLT PERISHED IN THE DETONATION.
WELL, BOOHOO.
THOOM
EVERBODY STOP IT! WE'VE GOT MORE URGENT THINGS TO CONCERN US!
HOW DARE YOU! HOW DARE YOU!
LIKE WHAT?

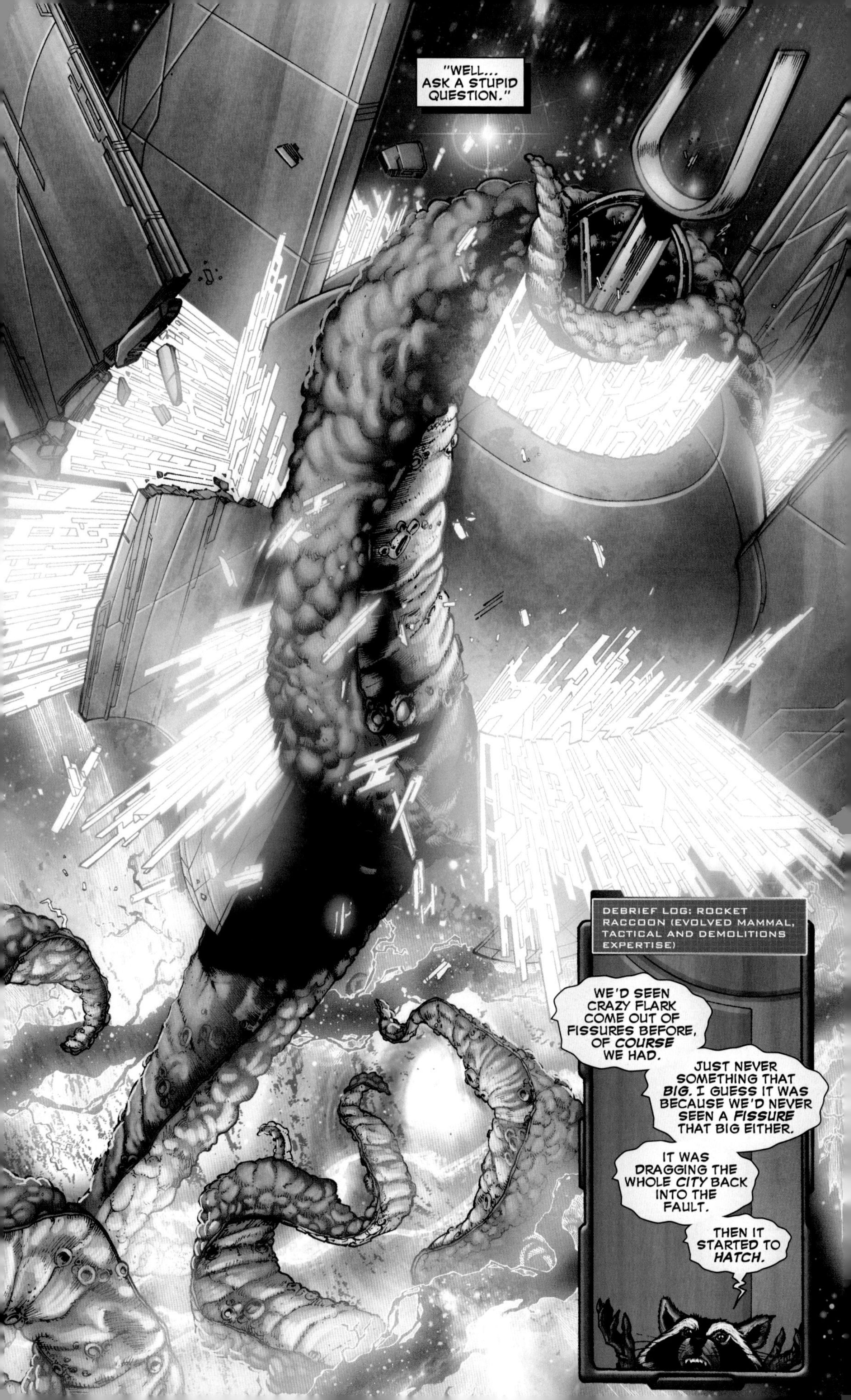
"WELL... ASK A STUPID QUESTION."
DEBRIEF LOG: ROCKET RACCOON (EVOLVED MAMMAL, TACTICAL AND DEMOLITIONS EXPERTISE)
WE'D SEEN CRAZY FLARK COME OUT OF FISSURES BEFORE, OF COURSE WE HAD.
JUST NEVER SOMETHING THAT BIG. I GUESS IT WAS BECAUSE WE'D NEVER SEEN A FISSURE THAT BIG EITHER.
IT WAS DRAGGING THE WHOLE CITY BACK INTO THE FAULT.
THEN IT STARTED TO HATCH.

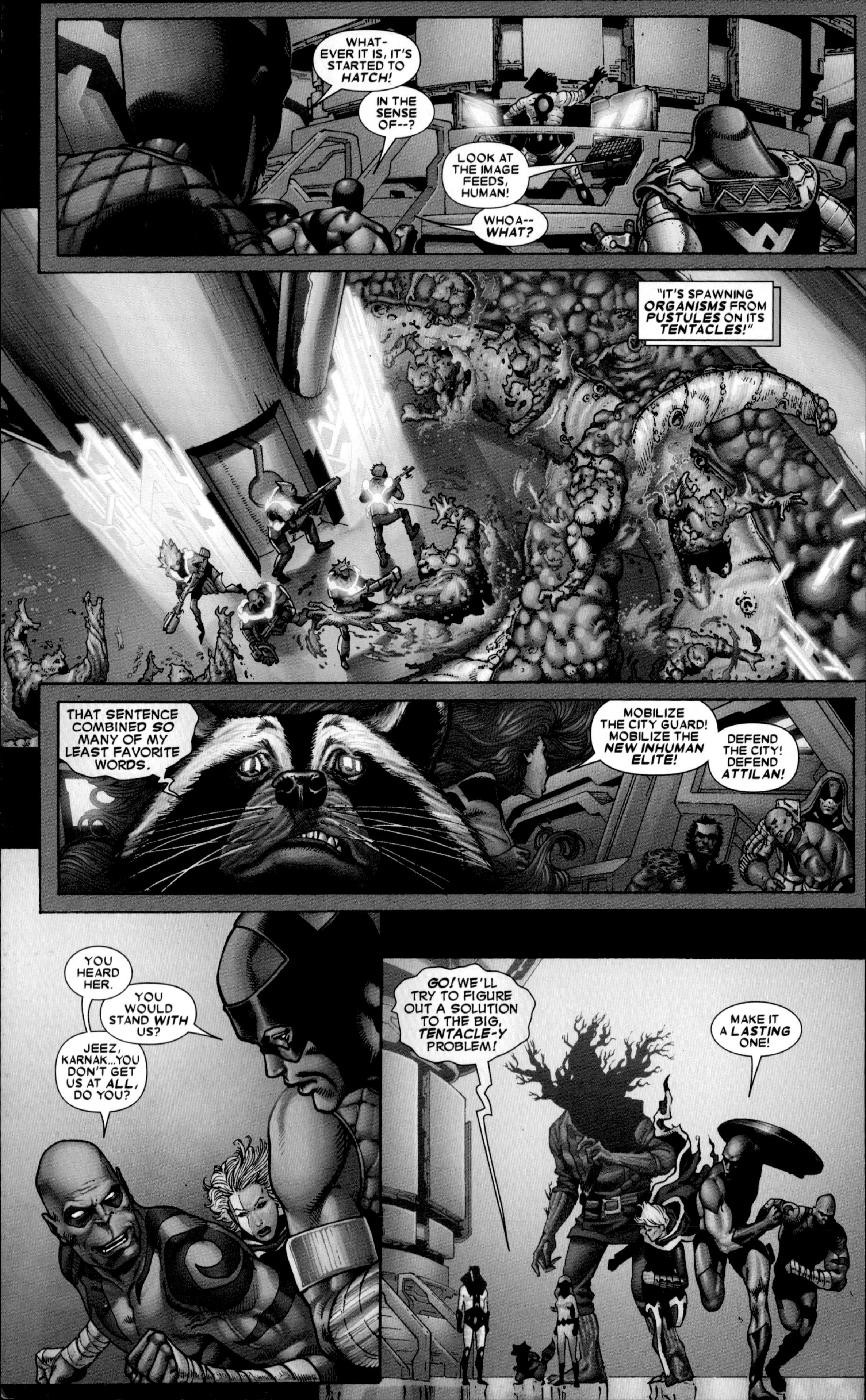
WHAT-EVER IT IS, IT'S STARTED TO HATCH!
IN THE SENSE OF--?
LOOK AT THE IMAGE FEEDS, HUMAN!
WHOA-- WHAT?
"IT'S SPAWNING ORGANISMS FROM PUSTULES ON ITS TENTACLES!"
THAT SENTENCE COMBINED SO MANY OF MY LEAST FAVORITE WORDS.
MOBILIZE THE CITY GUARD! MOBILIZE THE NEW INHUMAN ELITE!
DEFEND THE CITY! DEFEND ATTILAN!
YOU HEARD HER.
YOU WOULD STAND WITH US?
JEEZ, KARNAK...YOU DON'T GET US AT ALL, DO YOU?
GO! WE'LL TRY TO FIGURE OUT A SOLUTION TO THE BIG, TENTACLE-Y PROBLEM!
MAKE IT A LASTING ONE!

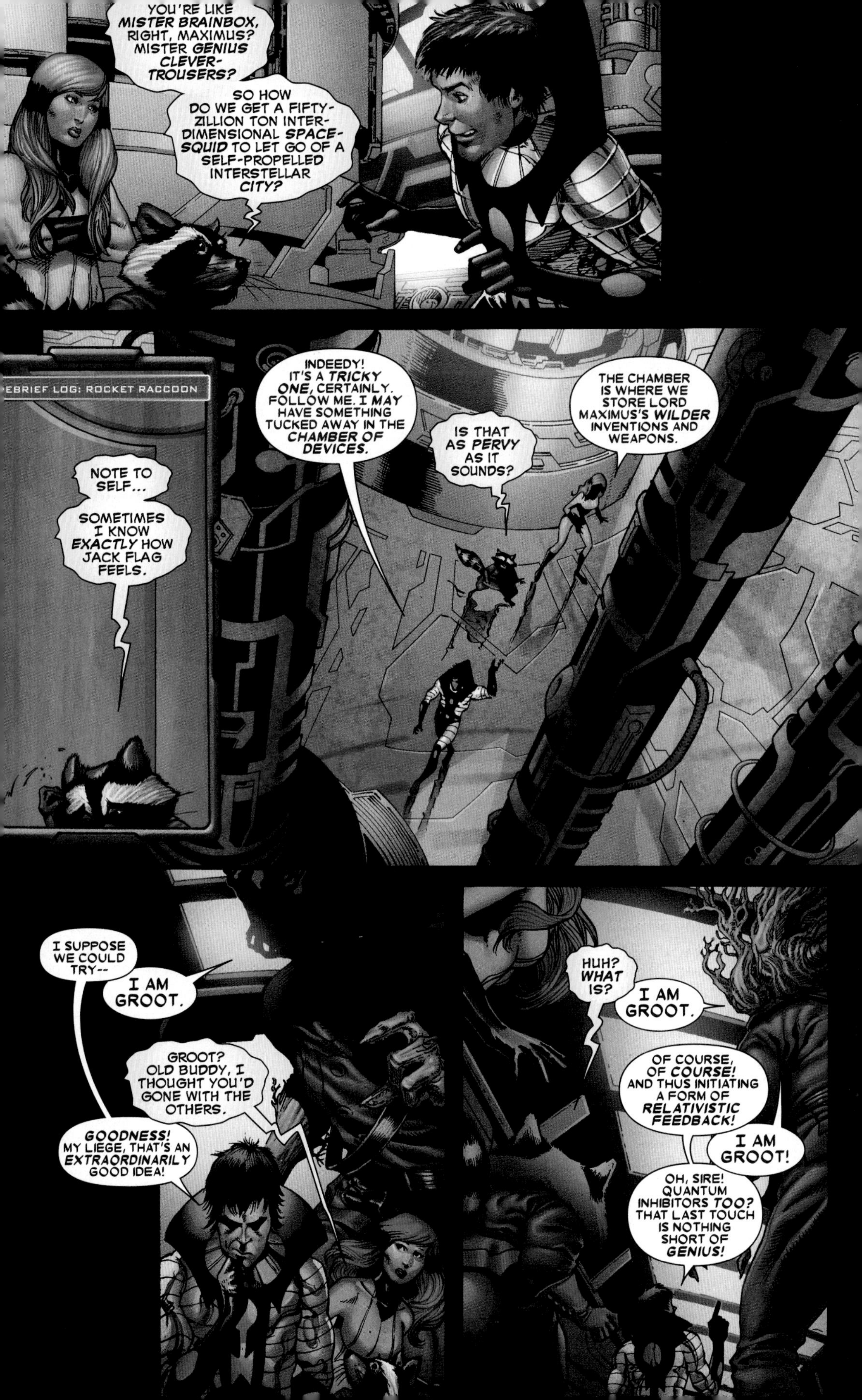
YOU'RE LIKE MISTER BRAINBOX, RIGHT, MAXIMUS? MISTER GENIUS CLEVER-TROUSERS?
SO HOW DO WE GET A FIFTY-ZILLION TON INTER-DIMENSIONAL SPACE-SQUID TO LET GO OF A SELF-PROPELLED INTERSTELLAR CITY?
EBRIEF LOG: ROCKET RACCOON
NOTE TO SELF...
SOMETIMES I KNOW EXACTLY HOW JACK FLAG FEELS.
INDEEDY! IT'S A TRICKY ONE, CERTAINLY. FOLLOW ME. I MAY HAVE SOMETHING TUCKED AWAY IN THE CHAMBER OF DEVICES.
IS THAT AS PERVY AS IT SOUNDS?
THE CHAMBER IS WHERE WE STORE LORD MAXIMUS'S WILDER INVENTIONS AND WEAPONS.
I SUPPOSE WE COULD TRY--
I AM GROOT.
GROOT? OLD BUDDY, I THOUGHT YOU'D GONE WITH THE OTHERS.
GOODNESS! MY LIEGE, THAT'S AN EXTRAORDINARILY GOOD IDEA!
HUH? WHAT IS?
I AM GROOT.
OF COURSE, OF COURSE! AND THUS INITIATING A FORM OF RELATIVISTIC FEEDBACK!
I AM GROOT!
OH, SIRE! QUANTUM INHIBITORS TOO? THAT LAST TOUCH IS NOTHING SHORT OF GENIUS!

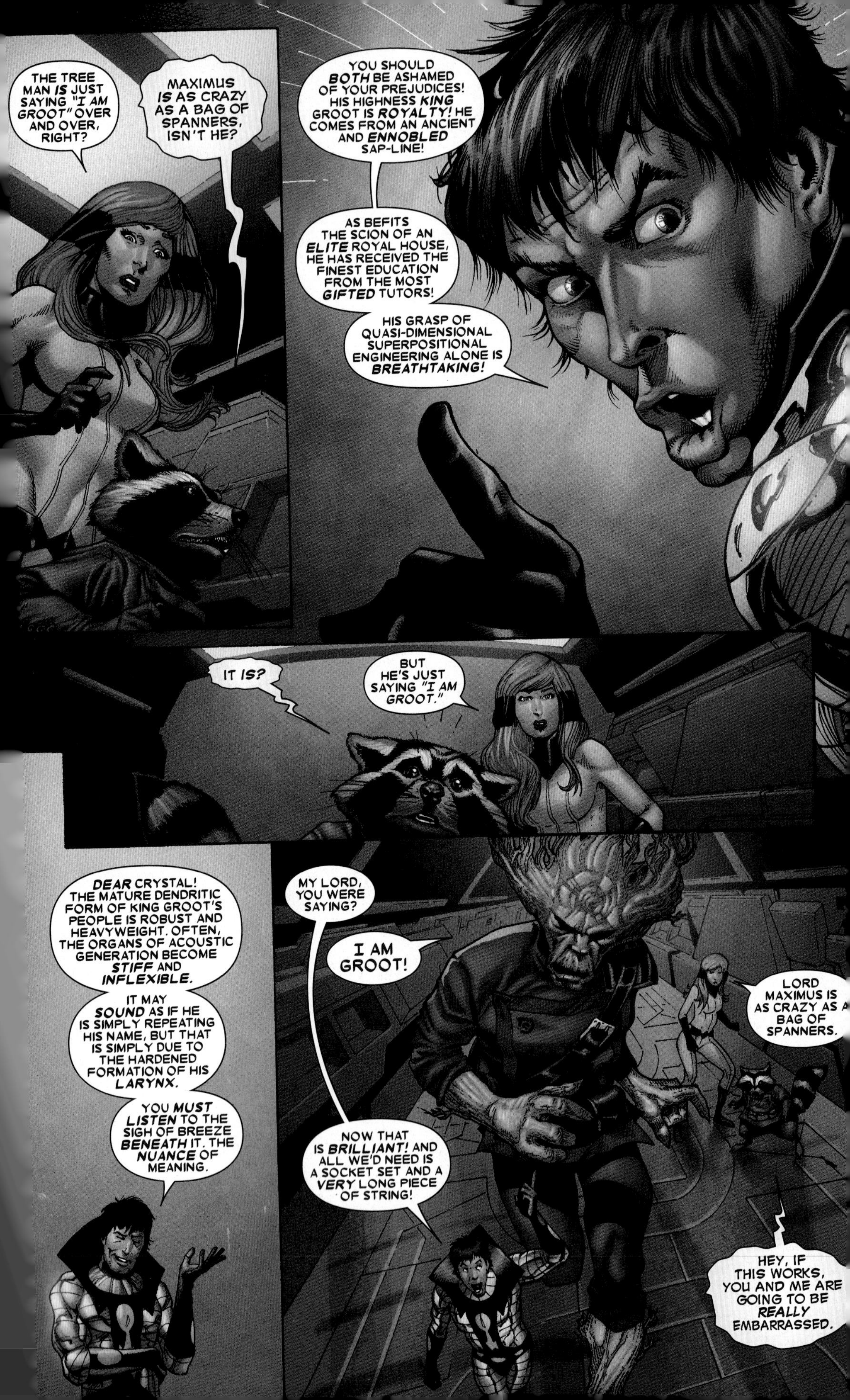
THE TREE MAN IS JUST SAYING "I AM GROOT" OVER AND OVER, RIGHT?
MAXIMUS IS AS CRAZY AS A BAG OF SPANNERS, ISN'T HE?
YOU SHOULD BOTH BE ASHAMED OF YOUR PREJUDICES! HIS HIGHNESS KING GROOT IS ROYALTY! HE COMES FROM AN ANCIENT AND ENNOBLED SAP-LINE!
AS BEFITS THE SCION OF AN ELITE ROYAL HOUSE, HE HAS RECEIVED THE FINEST EDUCATION FROM THE MOST GIFTED TUTORS!
HIS GRASP OF QUASI-DIMENSIONAL SUPERPOSITIONAL ENGINEERING ALONE IS BREATHTAKING!
IT IS?
BUT HE'S JUST SAYING "I AM GROOT."
DEAR CRYSTAL! THE MATURE DENDRITIC FORM OF KING GROOT'S PEOPLE IS ROBUST AND HEAVYWEIGHT. OFTEN, THE ORGANS OF ACOUSTIC GENERATION BECOME STIFF AND INFLEXIBLE.
IT MAY SOUND AS IF HE IS SIMPLY REPEATING HIS NAME, BUT THAT IS SIMPLY DUE TO THE HARDENED FORMATION OF HIS LARYNX.
YOU MUST LISTEN TO THE SIGH OF BREEZE BENEATH IT. THE NUANCE OF MEANING.
MY LORD, YOU WERE SAYING?
I AM GROOT!
NOW THAT IS BRILLIANT! AND ALL WE'D NEED IS A SOCKET SET AND A VERY LONG PIECE OF STRING!
LORD MAXIMUS IS AS CRAZY AS A BAG OF SPANNERS.
HEY, IF THIS WORKS, YOU AND ME ARE GOING TO BE REALLY EMBARRASSED.

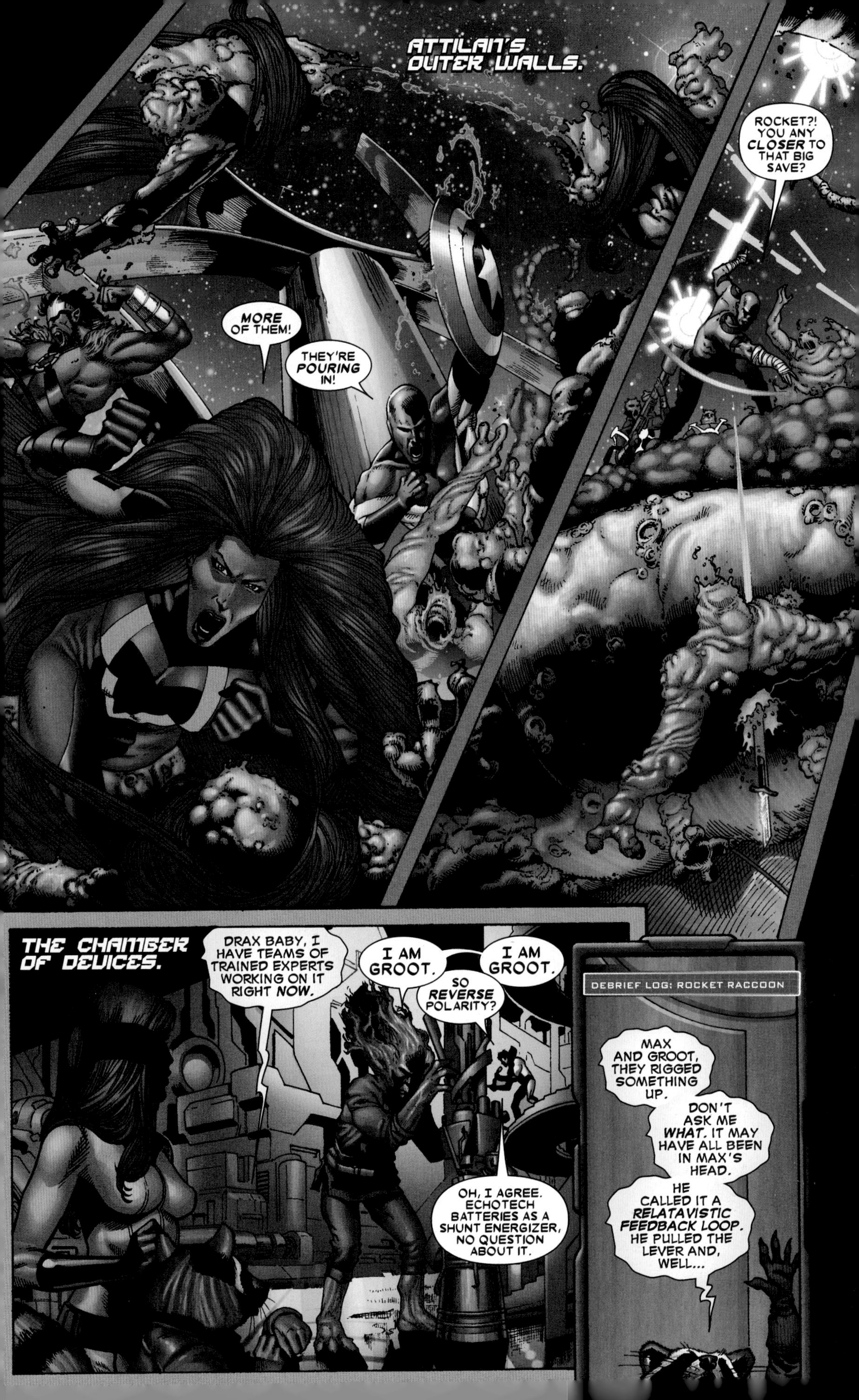
ATTILAN'S OUTER WALLS.
MORE OF THEM!
THEY'RE POURING IN!
ROCKET?! YOU ANY CLOSER TO THAT BIG SAVE?
THE CHAMBER OF DEVICES.
DRAX BABY, I HAVE TEAMS OF TRAINED EXPERTS WORKING ON IT RIGHT NOW.
I AM GROOT.
I AM GROOT.
SO REVERSE POLARITY?
OH, I AGREE. ECHOTECH BATTERIES AS A SHUNT ENERGIZER, NO QUESTION ABOUT IT.
DEBRIEF LOG: ROCKET RACCOON
MAX AND GROOT, THEY RIGGED SOMETHING UP.
DON'T ASK ME WHAT. IT MAY HAVE ALL BEEN IN MAX'S HEAD.
HE CALLED IT A RELATAVISTIC FEEDBACK LOOP. HE PULLED THE LEVER AND, WELL...

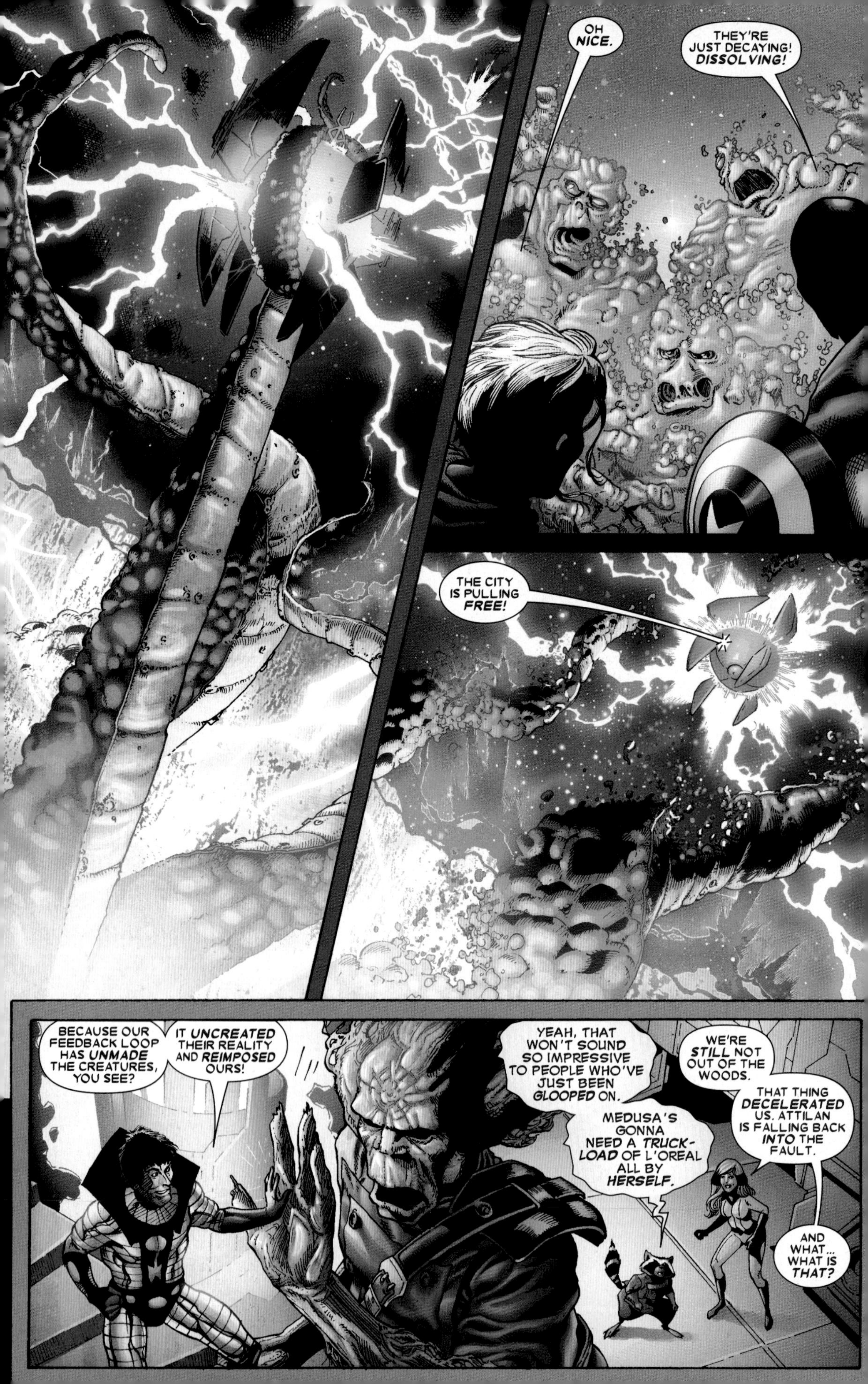
OH NICE.
THEY'RE JUST DECAYING! DISSOLVING!
THE CITY IS PULLING FREE!
BECAUSE OUR FEEDBACK LOOP HAS UNMADE THE CREATURES, YOU SEE?
IT UNCREATED THEIR REALITY AND REIMPOSED OURS!
YEAH, THAT WON'T SOUND SO IMPRESSIVE TO PEOPLE WHO'VE JUST BEEN GLOOPED ON.
MEDUSA'S GONNA NEED A TRUCK-LOAD OF L'OREAL ALL BY HERSELF.
WE'RE STILL NOT OUT OF THE WOODS.
THAT THING DECELERATED US. ATTILAN IS FALLING BACK INTO THE FAULT.
AND WHAT... WHAT IS THAT?

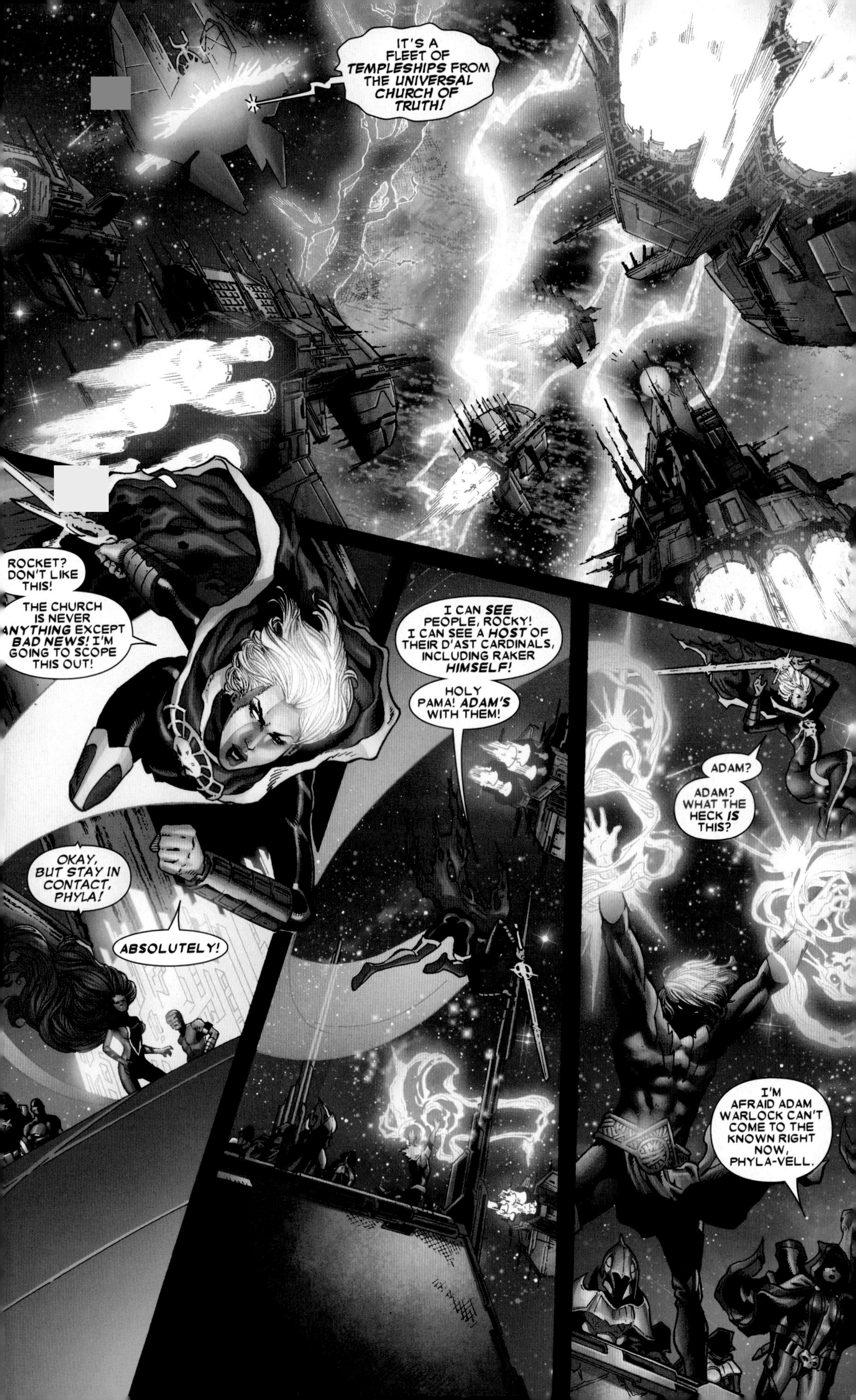
IT'S A FLEET OF *TEMPLESHIPS* FROM THE *UNIVERSAL CHURCH OF TRUTH!*
ROCKET? DON'T LIKE THIS!
THE CHURCH IS NEVER *ANYTHING* EXCEPT *BAD NEWS!* I'M GOING TO SCOPE THIS OUT!
OKAY, BUT STAY IN CONTACT, PHYLA!
ABSOLUTELY!
I CAN *SEE* PEOPLE, ROCKY! I CAN SEE A *HOST* OF THEIR D'AST CARDINALS, INCLUDING RAKER *HIMSELF!*
HOLY PAMA! *ADAM'S* WITH THEM!
ADAM?
ADAM? WHAT THE HECK *IS* THIS?
I'M AFRAID ADAM WARLOCK CAN'T COME TO THE KNOWN RIGHT NOW, PHYLA-VELL.

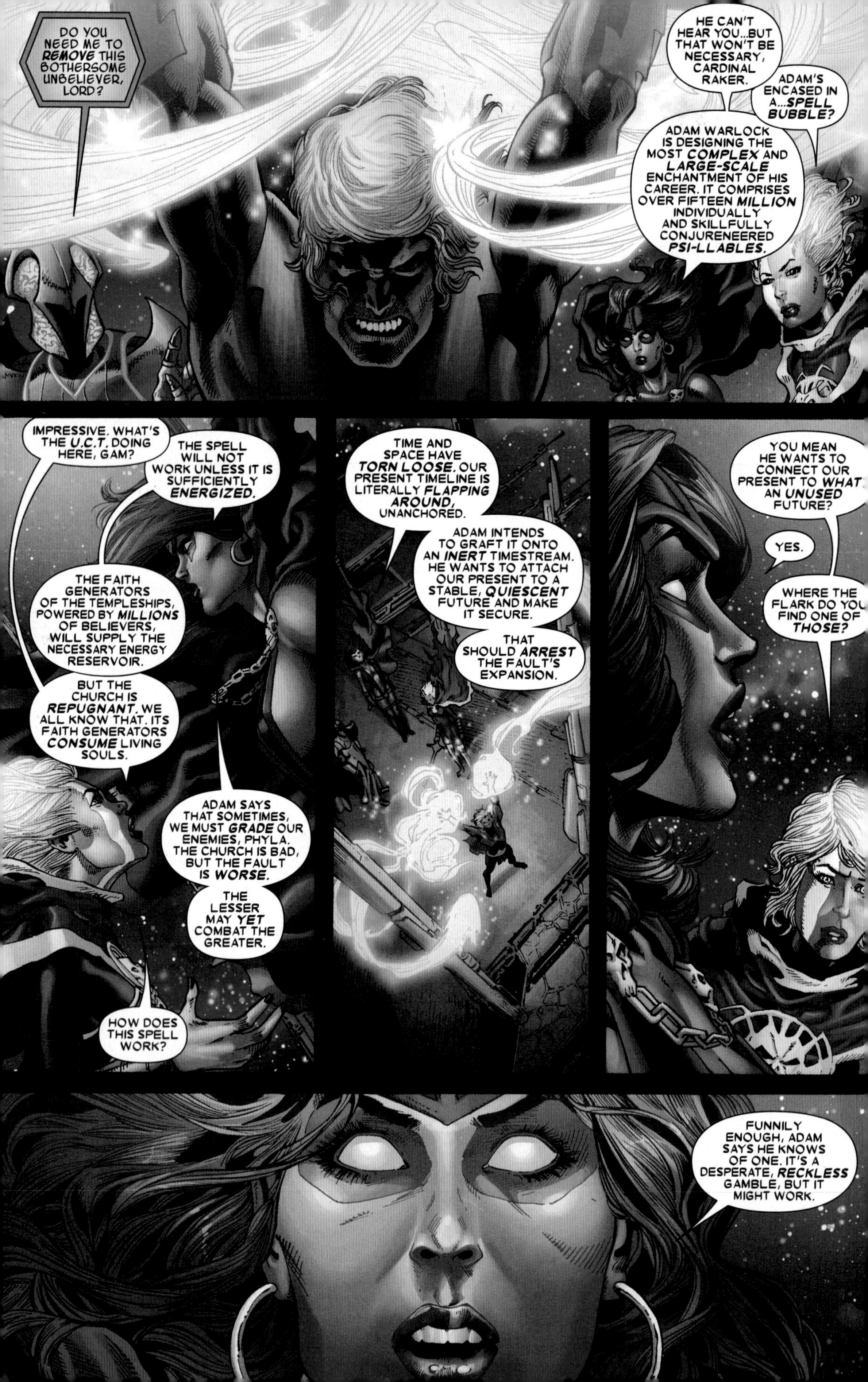
DO YOU NEED ME TO REMOVE THIS BOTHERSOME UNBELIEVER, LORD?
HE CAN'T HEAR YOU...BUT THAT WON'T BE NECESSARY, CARDINAL RAKER.
ADAM'S ENCASED IN A...SPELL BUBBLE?
ADAM WARLOCK IS DESIGNING THE MOST COMPLEX AND LARGE-SCALE ENCHANTMENT OF HIS CAREER. IT COMPRISES OVER FIFTEEN MILLION INDIVIDUALLY AND SKILLFULLY CONJURENEERED PSI-LLABLES.
IMPRESSIVE. WHAT'S THE U.C.T. DOING HERE, GAM?
THE SPELL WILL NOT WORK UNLESS IT IS SUFFICIENTLY ENERGIZED.
THE FAITH GENERATORS OF THE TEMPLESHIPS, POWERED BY MILLIONS OF BELIEVERS, WILL SUPPLY THE NECESSARY ENERGY RESERVOIR.
BUT THE CHURCH IS REPUGNANT. WE ALL KNOW THAT. ITS FAITH GENERATORS CONSUME LIVING SOULS.
ADAM SAYS THAT SOMETIMES, WE MUST GRADE OUR ENEMIES, PHYLA. THE CHURCH IS BAD, BUT THE FAULT IS WORSE.
THE LESSER MAY YET COMBAT THE GREATER.
HOW DOES THIS SPELL WORK?
TIME AND SPACE HAVE TORN LOOSE. OUR PRESENT TIMELINE IS LITERALLY FLAPPING AROUND, UNANCHORED.
ADAM INTENDS TO GRAFT IT ONTO AN INERT TIMESTREAM. HE WANTS TO ATTACH OUR PRESENT TO A STABLE, QUIESCENT FUTURE AND MAKE IT SECURE.
THAT SHOULD ARREST THE FAULT'S EXPANSION.
YOU MEAN HE WANTS TO CONNECT OUR PRESENT TO WHAT? AN UNUSED FUTURE?
YES.
WHERE THE FLARK DO YOU FIND ONE OF THOSE?
FUNNILY ENOUGH, ADAM SAYS HE KNOWS OF ONE. IT'S A DESPERATE, RECKLESS GAMBLE, BUT IT MIGHT WORK.

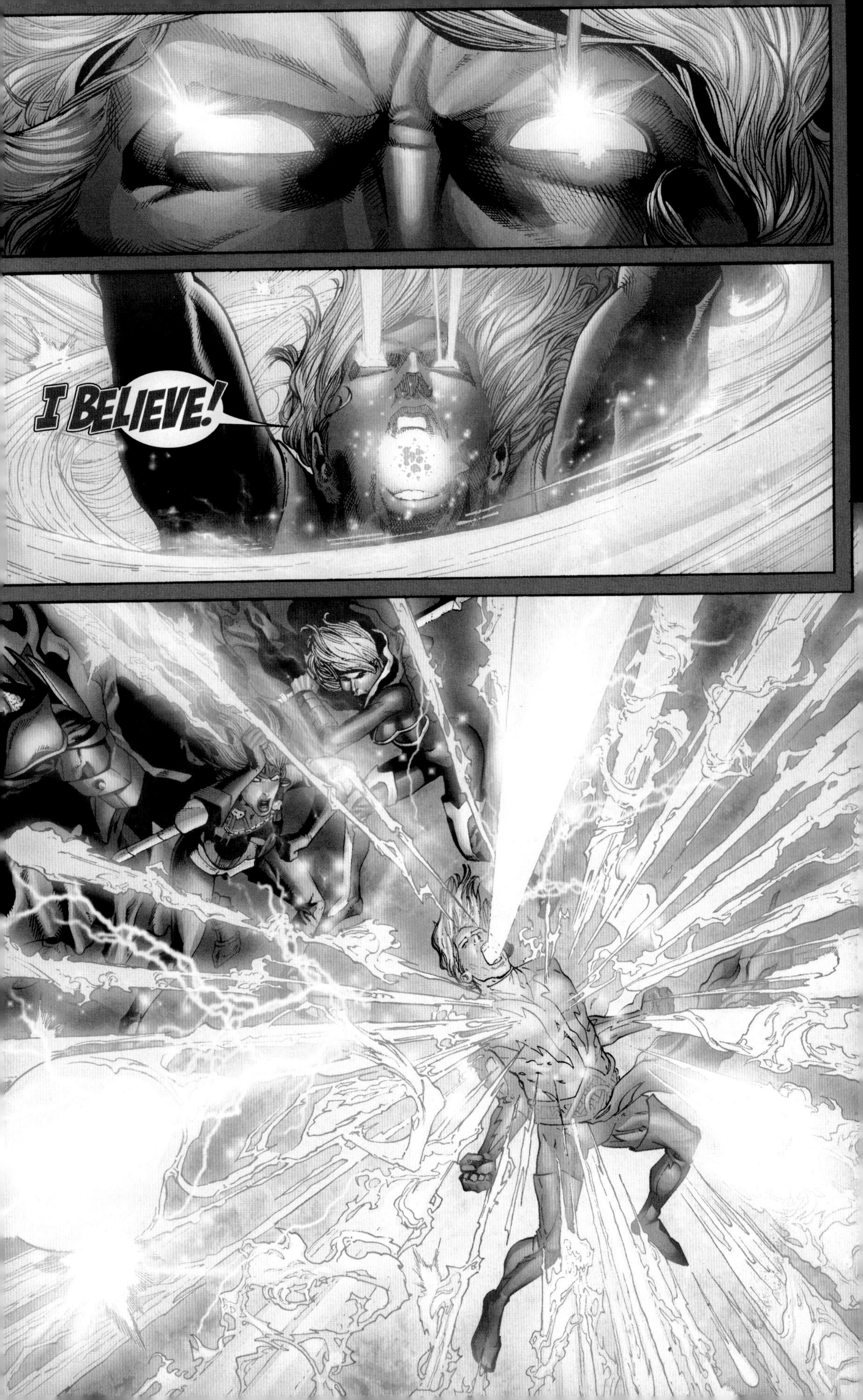
I BELIEVE!

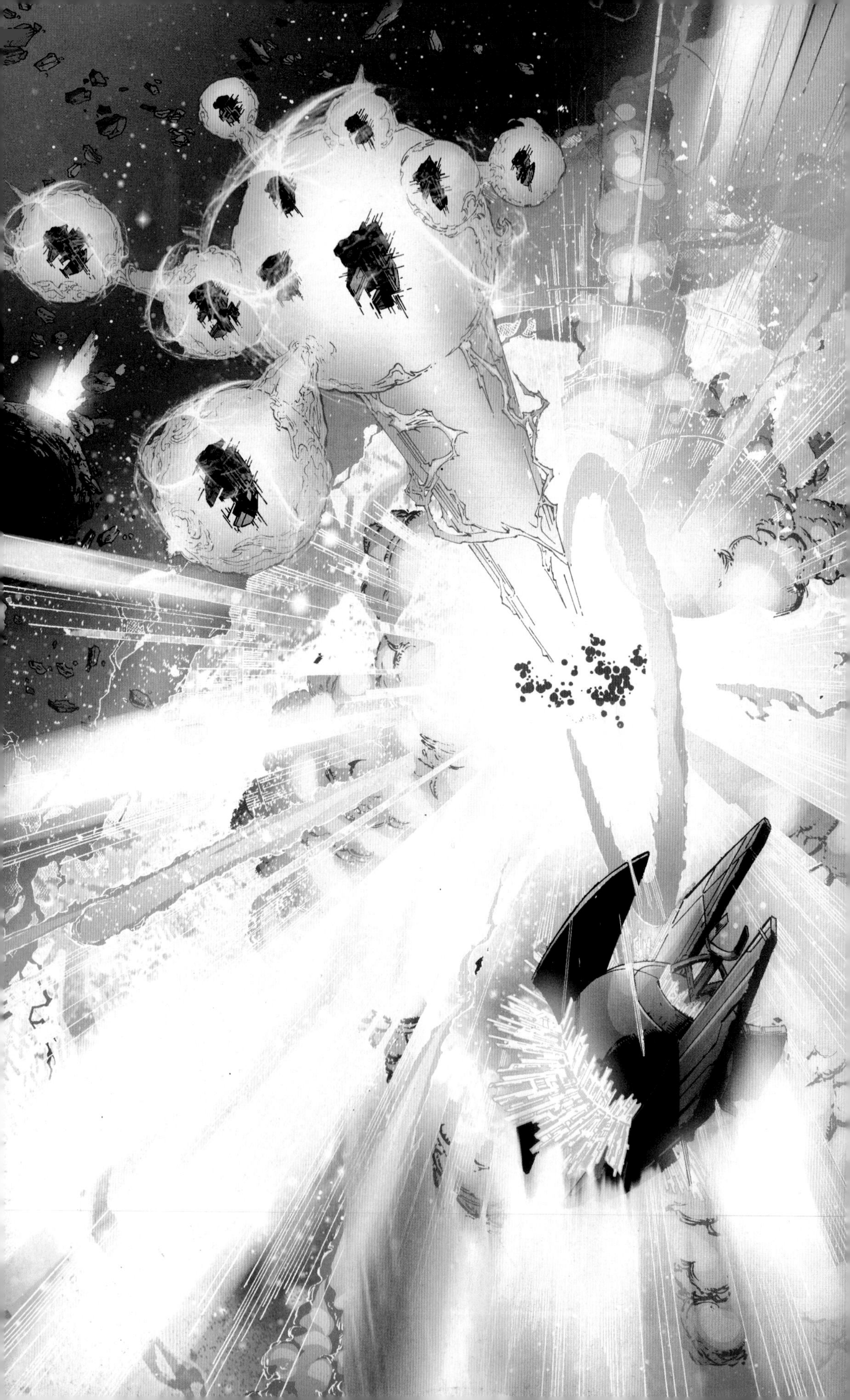

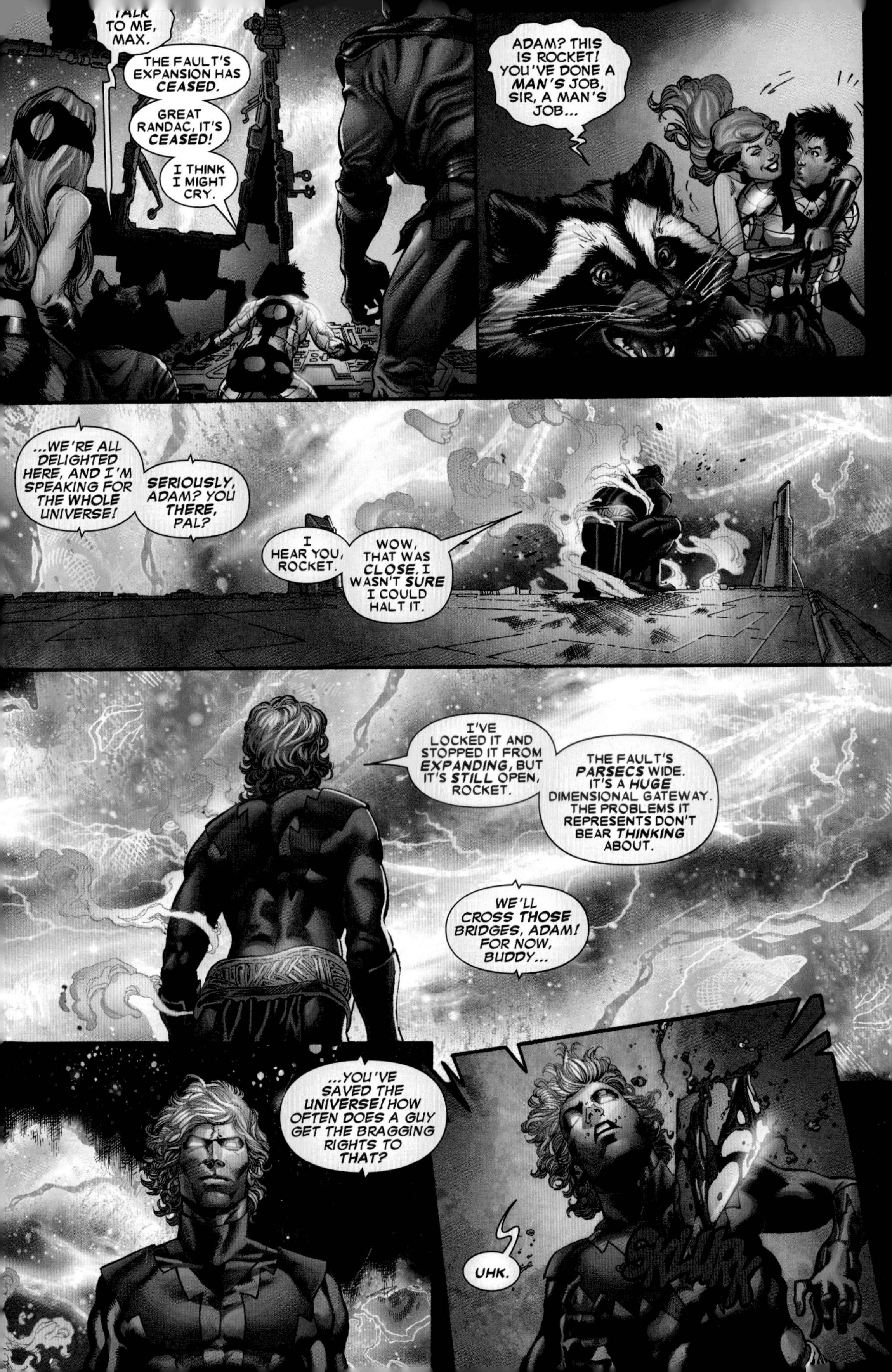
TALK TO ME, MAX.
THE FAULT'S EXPANSION HAS CEASED.
GREAT RANDAC, IT'S CEASED!
I THINK I MIGHT CRY.
ADAM? THIS IS ROCKET! YOU'VE DONE A MAN'S JOB, SIR, A MAN'S JOB...
...WE'RE ALL DELIGHTED HERE, AND I'M SPEAKING FOR THE WHOLE UNIVERSE!
SERIOUSLY, ADAM? YOU THERE, PAL?
I HEAR YOU, ROCKET.
WOW, THAT WAS CLOSE. I WASN'T SURE I COULD HALT IT.
I'VE LOCKED IT AND STOPPED IT FROM EXPANDING, BUT IT'S STILL OPEN, ROCKET.
THE FAULT'S PARSECS WIDE. IT'S A HUGE DIMENSIONAL GATEWAY. THE PROBLEMS IT REPRESENTS DON'T BEAR THINKING ABOUT.
WE'LL CROSS THOSE BRIDGES, ADAM! FOR NOW, BUDDY...
...YOU'VE SAVED THE UNIVERSE! HOW OFTEN DOES A GUY GET THE BRAGGING RIGHTS TO THAT?
UHK.

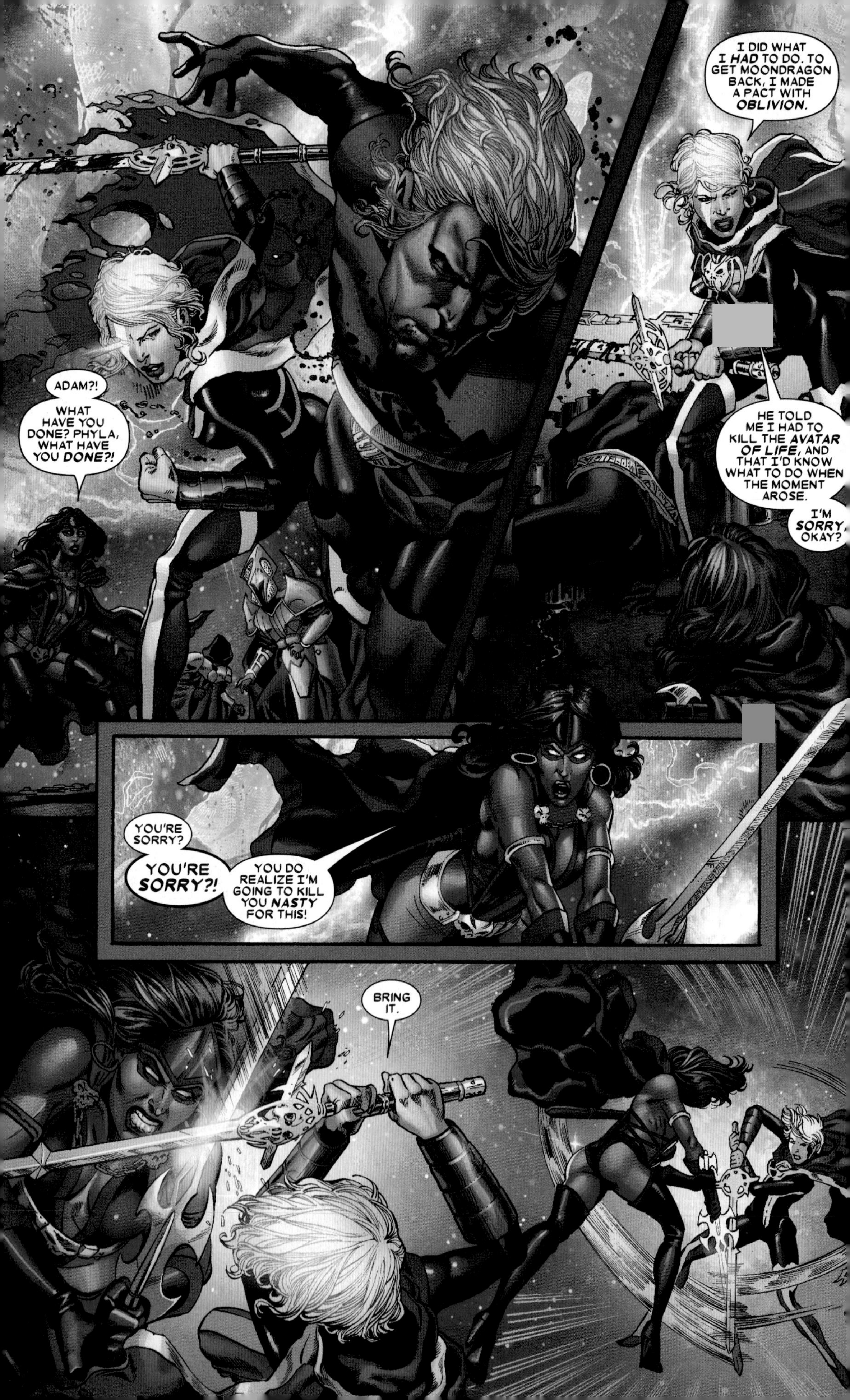

I DID WHAT I HAD TO DO. TO GET MOONDRAGON BACK, I MADE A PACT WITH OBLIVION.
ADAM?!
WHAT HAVE YOU DONE? PHYLA, WHAT HAVE YOU DONE?!
HE TOLD ME I HAD TO KILL THE AVATAR OF LIFE, AND THAT I'D KNOW WHAT TO DO WHEN THE MOMENT AROSE.
I'M SORRY, OKAY?
YOU'RE SORRY?
YOU'RE SORRY?!
YOU DO REALIZE I'M GOING TO KILL YOU NASTY FOR THIS!
BRING IT.

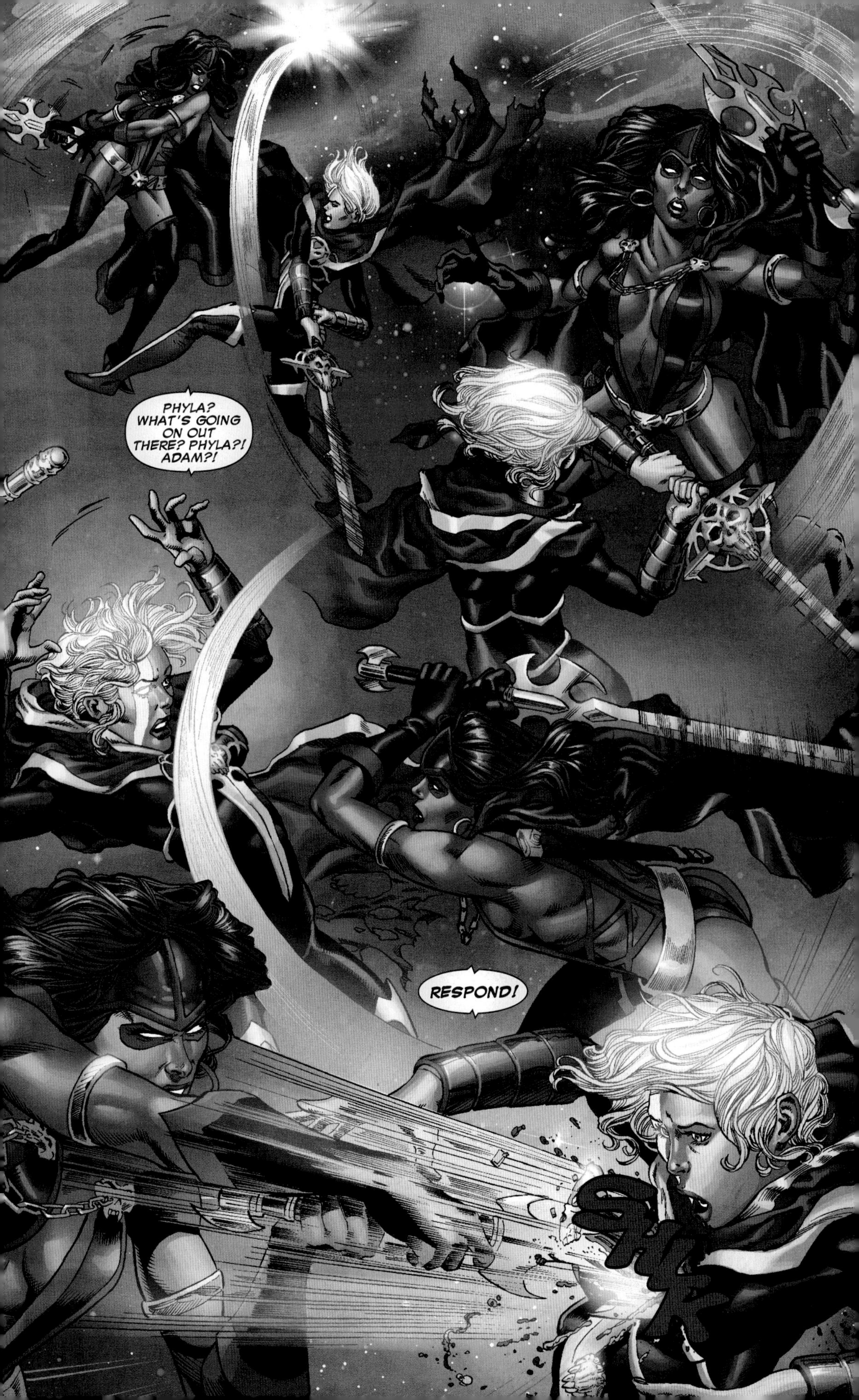
PHYLA? WHAT'S GOING ON OUT THERE? PHYLA?! ADAM?!
RESPOND!

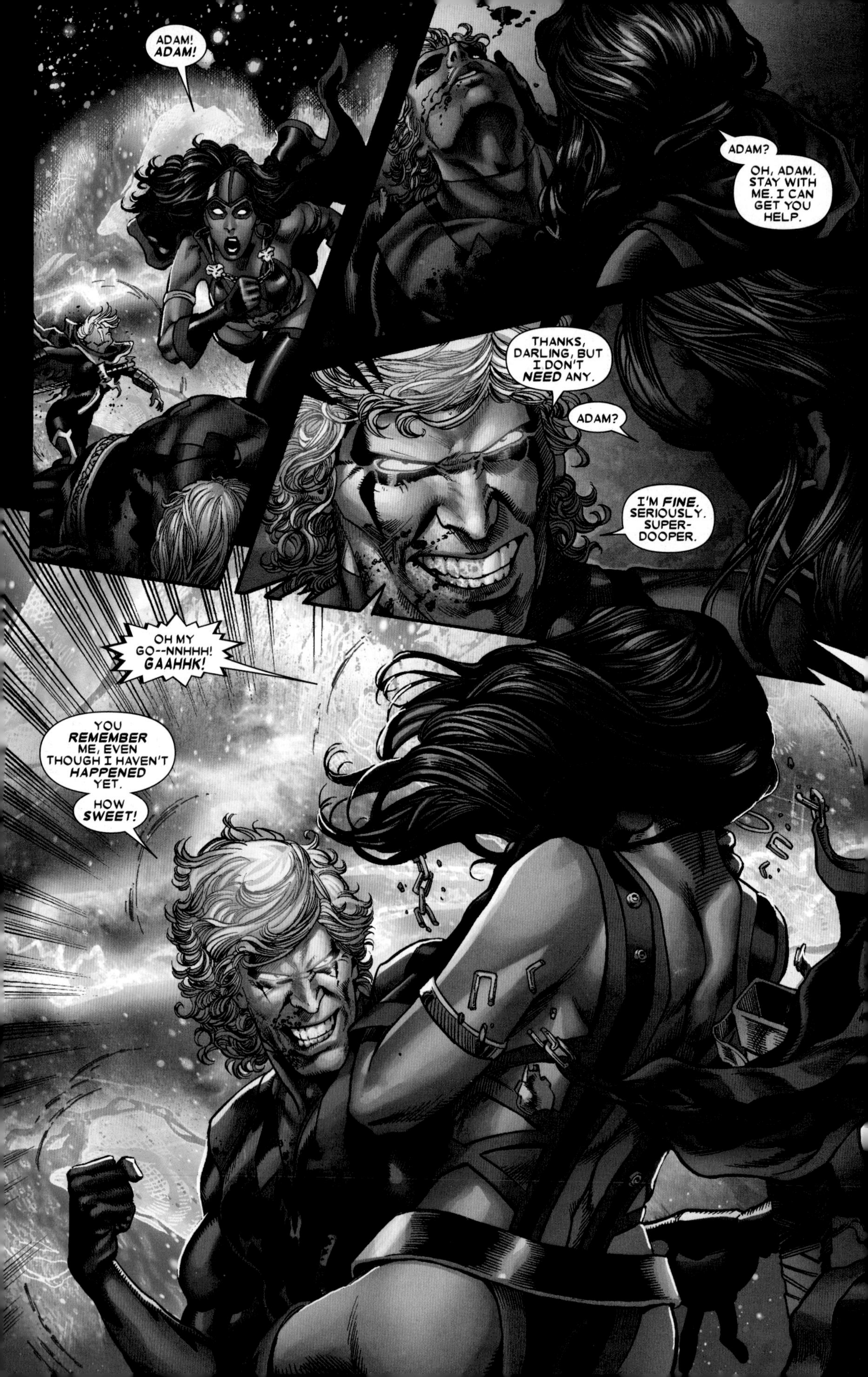
ADAM! ADAM!
ADAM?
OH, ADAM. STAY WITH ME. I CAN GET YOU HELP.
THANKS, DARLING, BUT I DON'T NEED ANY.
ADAM?
I'M FINE. SERIOUSLY. SUPER-DOOPER.
OH MY GO--NNHHH! GAAHHK!
YOU REMEMBER ME, EVEN THOUGH I HAVEN'T HAPPENED YET.
HOW SWEET!

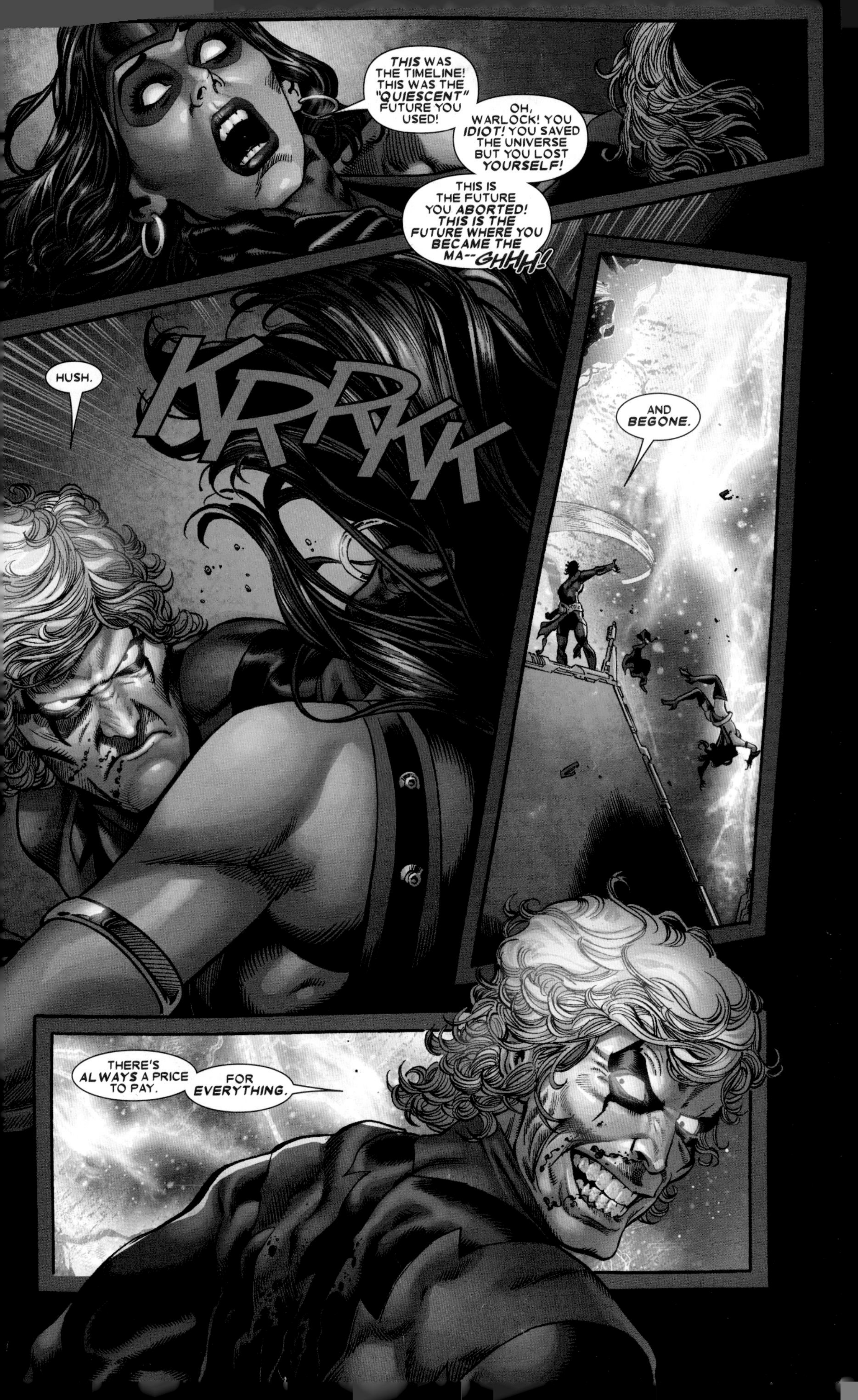
THIS WAS THE TIMELINE! THIS WAS THE "QUIESCENT" FUTURE YOU USED!
OH, WARLOCK! YOU IDIOT! YOU SAVED THE UNIVERSE BUT YOU LOST YOURSELF!
THIS IS THE FUTURE YOU ABORTED! THIS IS THE FUTURE WHERE YOU BECAME THE MA--GHHH!
HUSH.
KRRKK
AND BEGONE.
THERE'S ALWAYS A PRICE TO PAY.
FOR EVERYTHING.

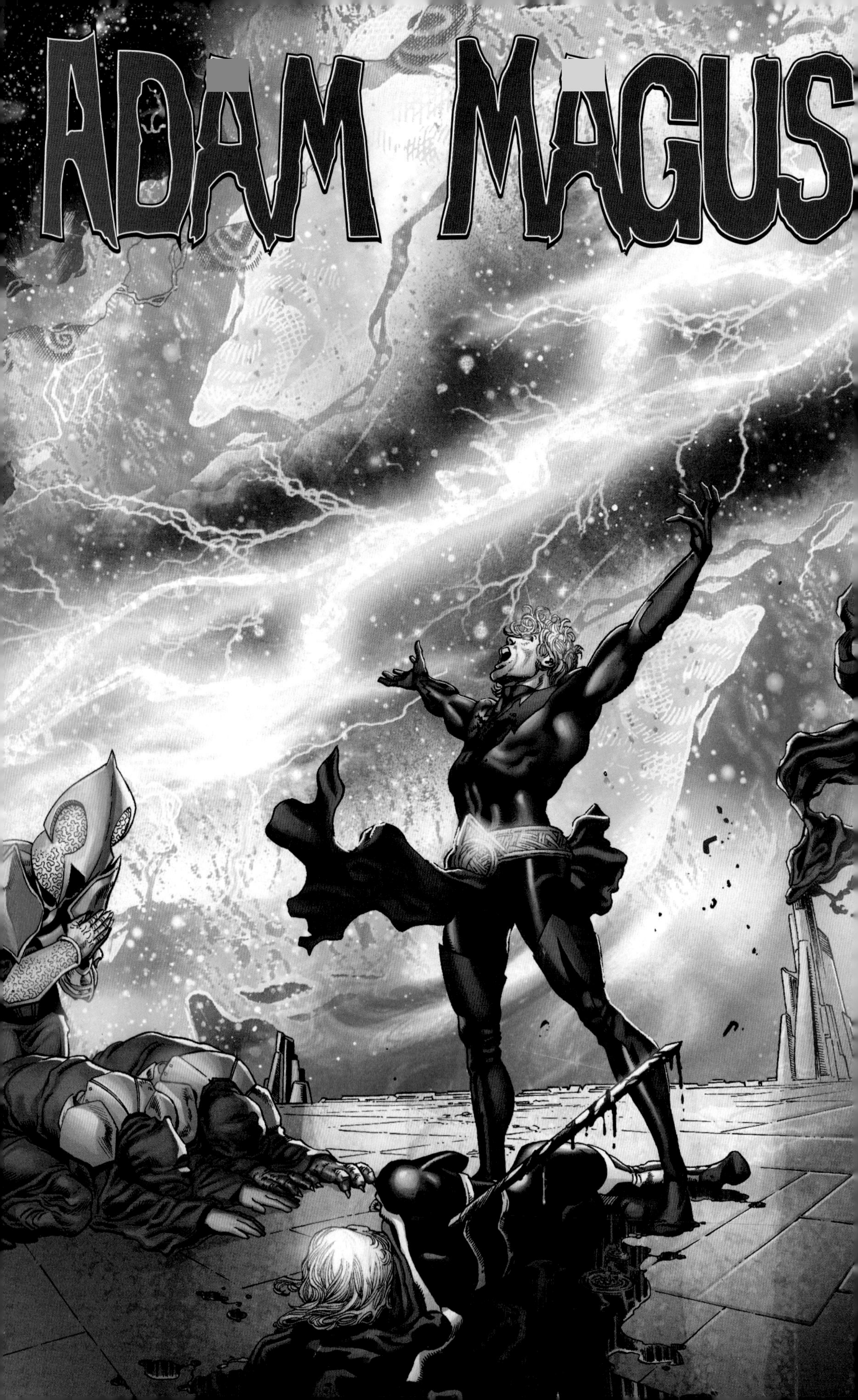
ADAM MAGUS

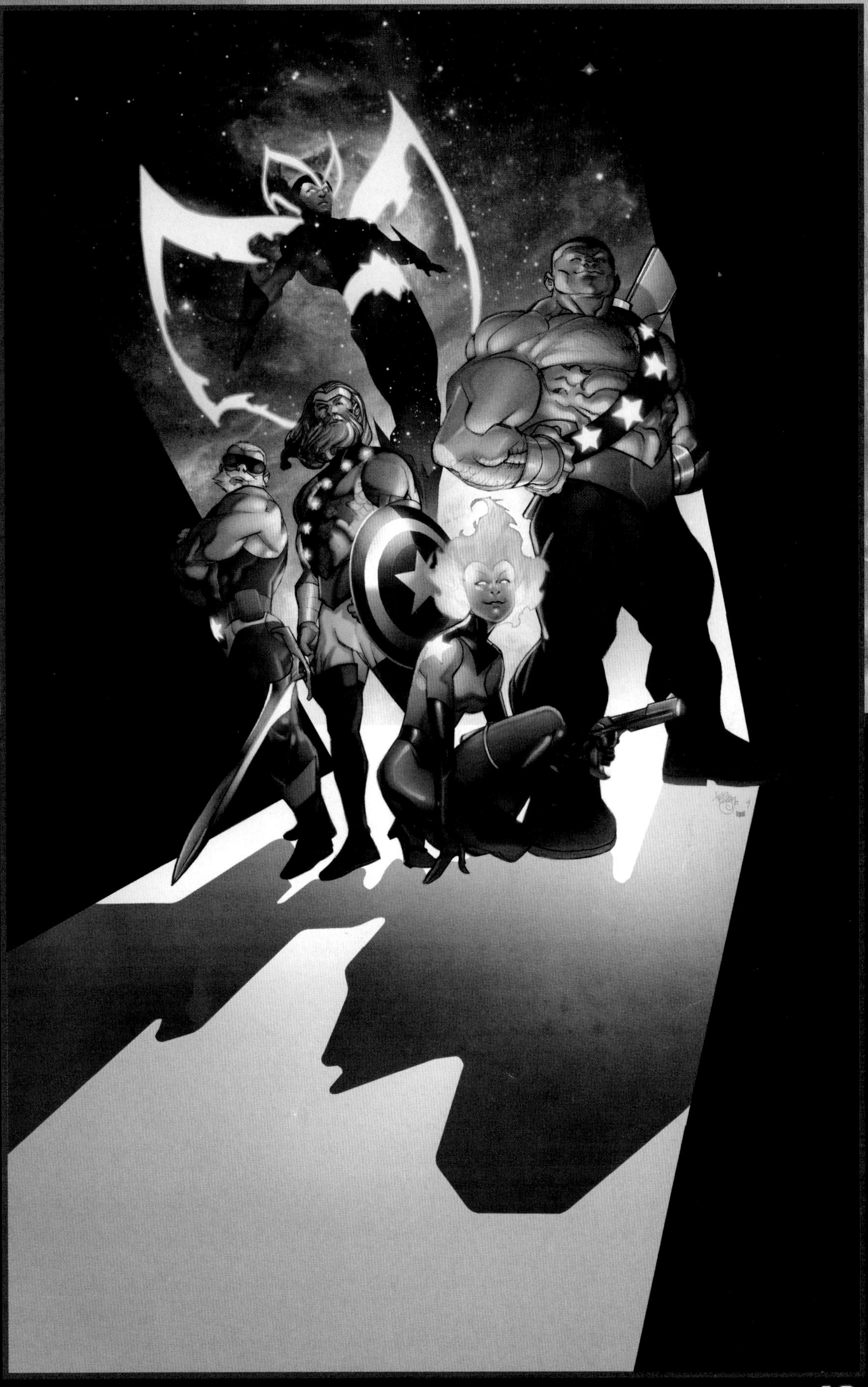

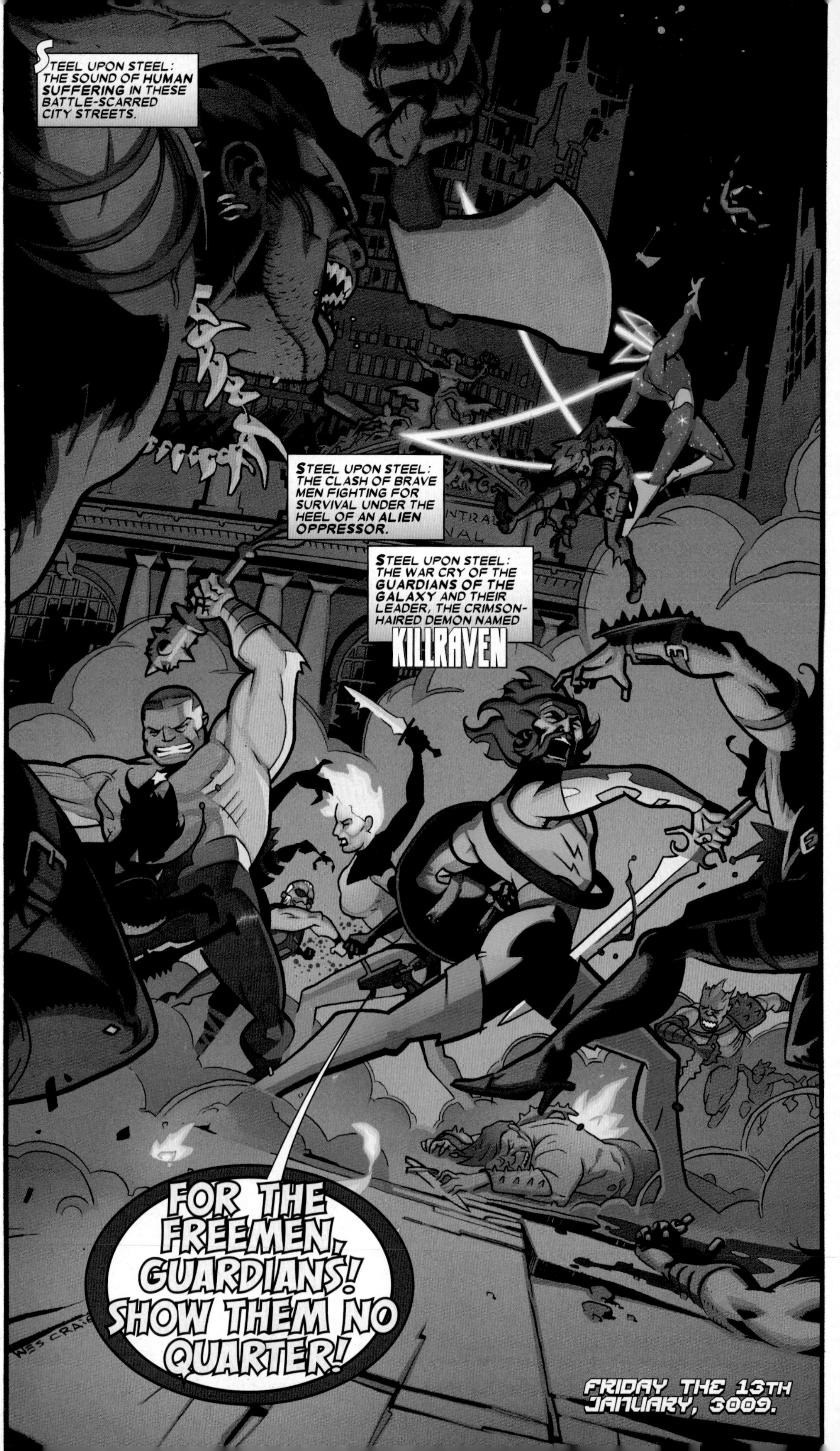
STEEL UPON STEEL: THE SOUND OF HUMAN SUFFERING IN THESE BATTLE-SCARRED CITY STREETS.
STEEL UPON STEEL: THE CLASH OF BRAVE MEN FIGHTING FOR SURVIVAL UNDER THE HEEL OF AN ALIEN OPPRESSOR.
STEEL UPON STEEL: THE WAR CRY OF THE GUARDIANS OF THE GALAXY AND THEIR LEADER, THE CRIMSON-HAIRED DEMON NAMED KILLRAVEN
FOR THE FREEMEN, GUARDIANS! SHOW THEM NO QUARTER!
FRIDAY THE 13TH JANUARY, 3009.
WES CRAIG

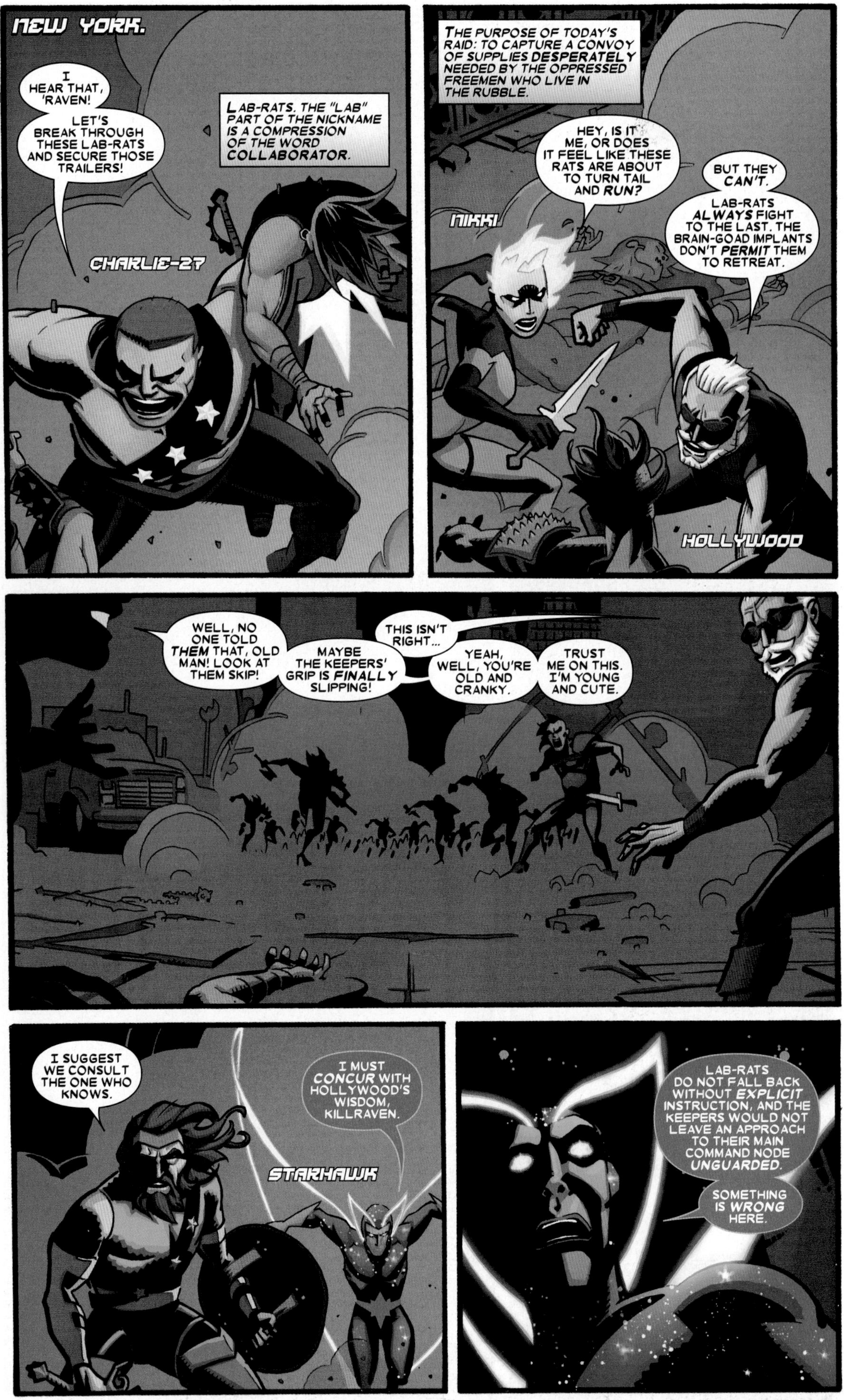
NEW YORK.
I HEAR THAT, 'RAVEN!
LET'S BREAK THROUGH THESE LAB-RATS AND SECURE THOSE TRAILERS!
LAB-RATS. THE "LAB" PART OF THE NICKNAME IS A COMPRESSION OF THE WORD COLLABORATOR.
CHARLIE-27
THE PURPOSE OF TODAY'S RAID: TO CAPTURE A CONVOY OF SUPPLIES DESPERATELY NEEDED BY THE OPPRESSED FREEMEN WHO LIVE IN THE RUBBLE.
HEY, IS IT ME, OR DOES IT FEEL LIKE THESE RATS ARE ABOUT TO TURN TAIL AND RUN?
NIKKI
BUT THEY CAN'T.
LAB-RATS ALWAYS FIGHT TO THE LAST. THE BRAIN-GOAD IMPLANTS DON'T PERMIT THEM TO RETREAT.
HOLLYWOOD
WELL, NO ONE TOLD THEM THAT, OLD MAN! LOOK AT THEM SKIP!
MAYBE THE KEEPERS' GRIP IS FINALLY SLIPPING!
THIS ISN'T RIGHT...
YEAH, WELL, YOU'RE OLD AND CRANKY.
TRUST ME ON THIS. I'M YOUNG AND CUTE.
I SUGGEST WE CONSULT THE ONE WHO KNOWS.
I MUST CONCUR WITH HOLLYWOOD'S WISDOM, KILLRAVEN.
STARHAWK
LAB-RATS DO NOT FALL BACK WITHOUT EXPLICIT INSTRUCTION, AND THE KEEPERS WOULD NOT LEAVE AN APPROACH TO THEIR MAIN COMMAND NODE UNGUARDED.
SOMETHING IS WRONG HERE.

I CAN FEEL IT. THE BURNING SUN. THE AIRLESS HUSH. NOTHING STIRRING.

IT IS AS IF TIME *ITSELF* HAS PAUSED.

IT IS AS IF THE WORLD IS HOLDING ITS BREATH AND--

THOOM

THOOM THOOM

THOOM

IT CAN'T BE...

GOOD GOD! NO!

TRIPODS! MOVE!

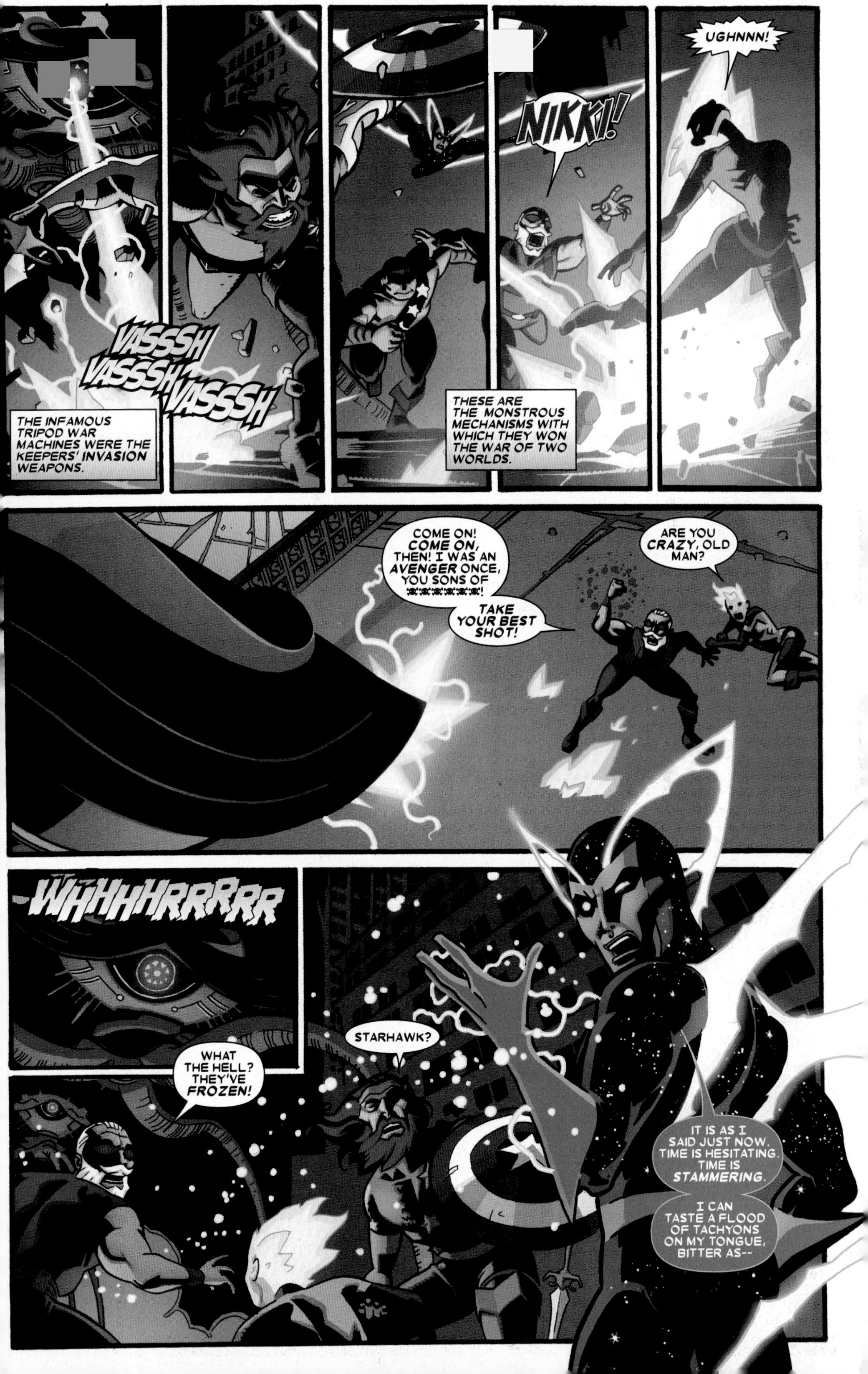
THE INFAMOUS TRIPOD WAR MACHINES WERE THE KEEPERS' INVASION WEAPONS.
VASSSH VASSSH VASSSH
THESE ARE THE MONSTROUS MECHANISMS WITH WHICH THEY WON THE WAR OF TWO WORLDS.
NIKKI!
UGHNNN!
COME ON! COME ON, THEN! I WAS AN AVENGER ONCE, YOU SONS OF ☠☠☠☠☠☠!
TAKE YOUR BEST SHOT!
ARE YOU CRAZY, OLD MAN?
WHHHHRRRRR
WHAT THE HELL? THEY'VE FROZEN!
STARHAWK?
IT IS AS I SAID JUST NOW. TIME IS HESITATING. TIME IS STAMMERING.
I CAN TASTE A FLOOD OF TACHYONS ON MY TONGUE, BITTER AS--

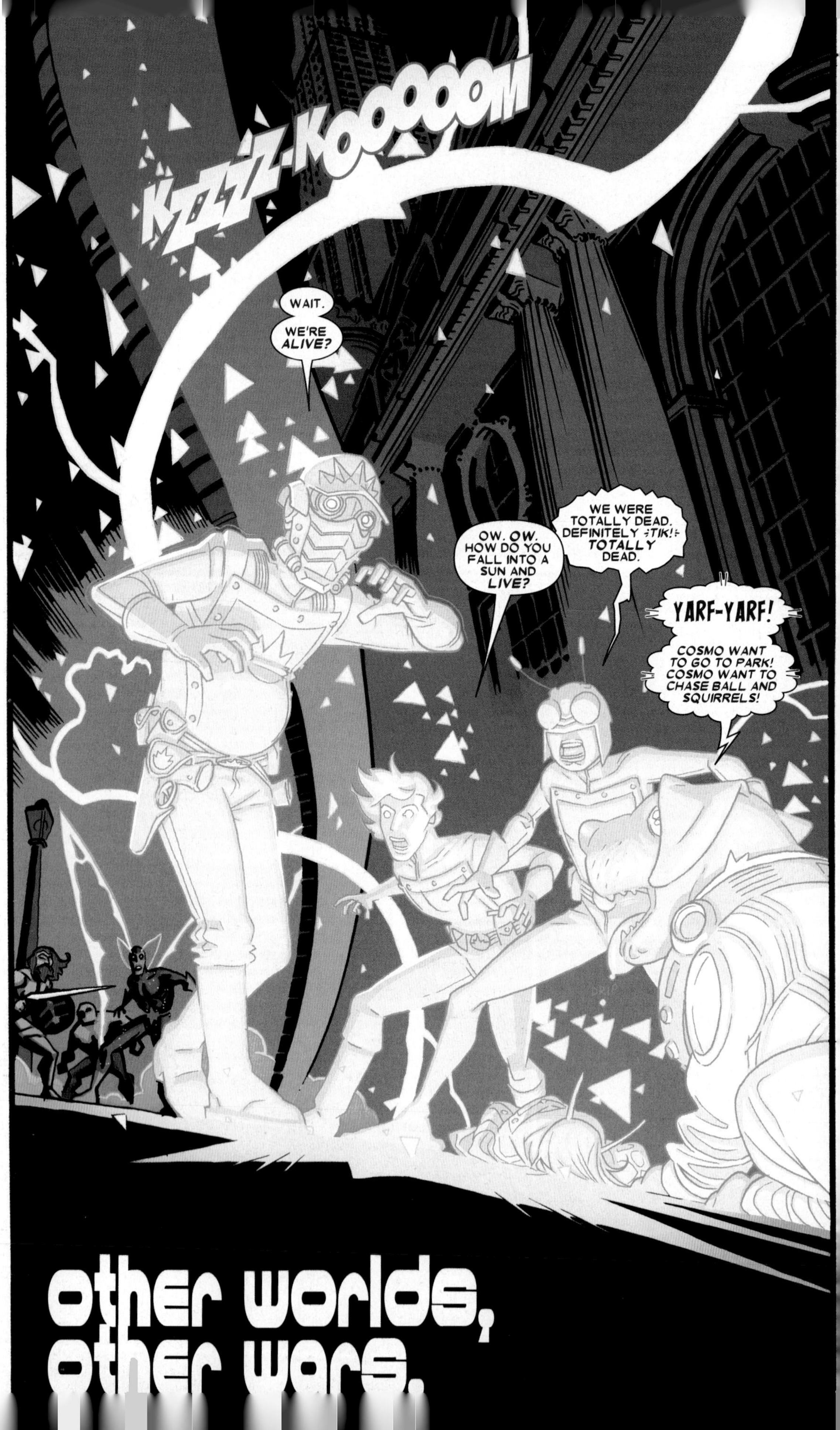
KZZZZ-KOOOOOOM
WAIT.
WE'RE ALIVE?
OW. OW. HOW DO YOU FALL INTO A SUN AND LIVE?
WE WERE TOTALLY DEAD. DEFINITELY ≠TIK!≠ TOTALLY DEAD.
YARF-YARF!
COSMO WANT TO GO TO PARK! COSMO WANT TO CHASE BALL AND SQUIRRELS!
other worlds, other wars.

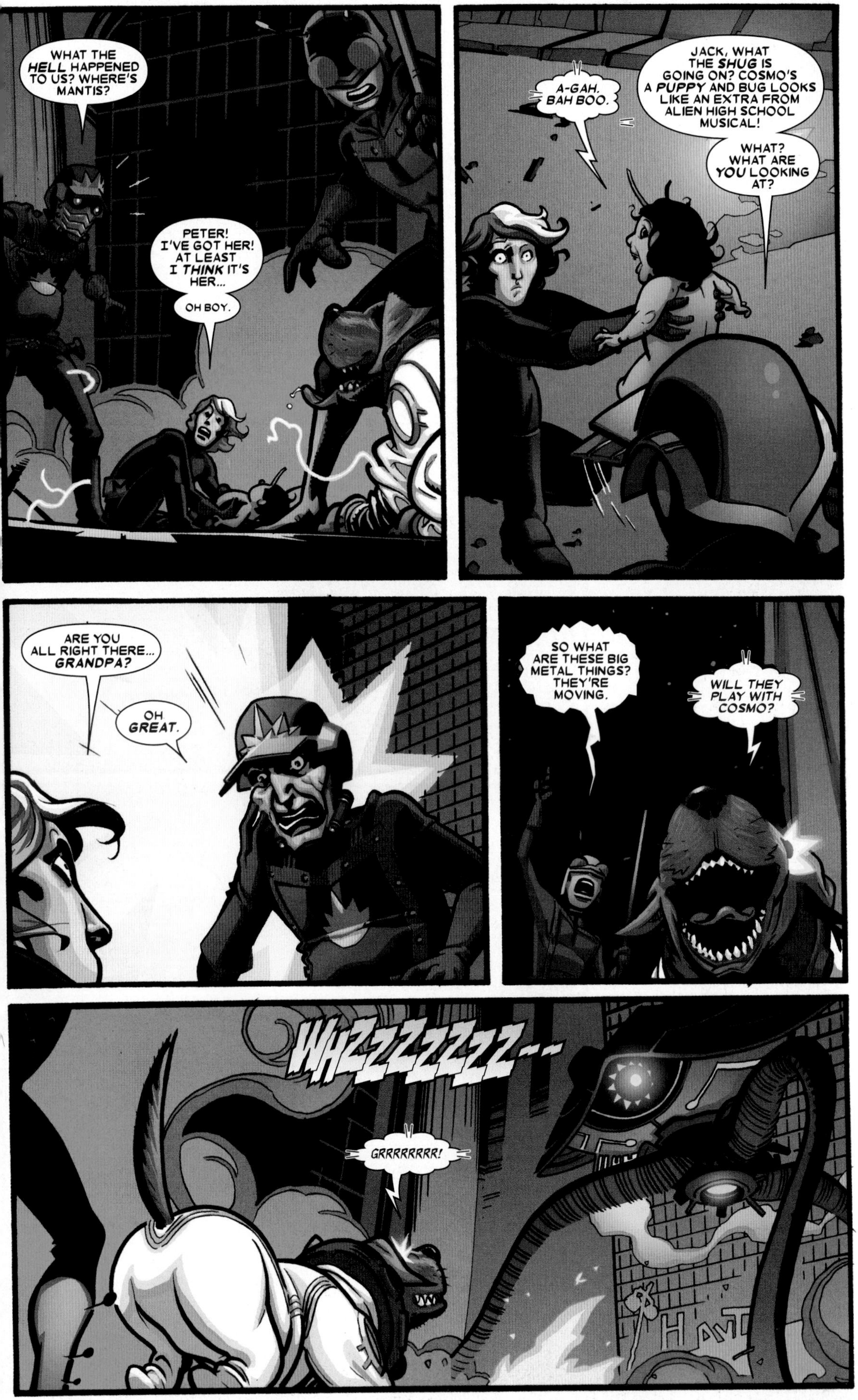
WHAT THE HELL HAPPENED TO US? WHERE'S MANTIS?
PETER! I'VE GOT HER! AT LEAST I THINK IT'S HER...
OH BOY.
A-GAH. BAH BOO.
JACK, WHAT THE SHUG IS GOING ON? COSMO'S A PUPPY AND BUG LOOKS LIKE AN EXTRA FROM ALIEN HIGH SCHOOL MUSICAL!
WHAT? WHAT ARE YOU LOOKING AT?
ARE YOU ALL RIGHT THERE... GRANDPA?
OH. GREAT.
SO WHAT ARE THESE BIG METAL THINGS? THEY'RE MOVING.
WILL THEY PLAY WITH COSMO?
WHZZZZZZZ--
GRRRRRRRR!

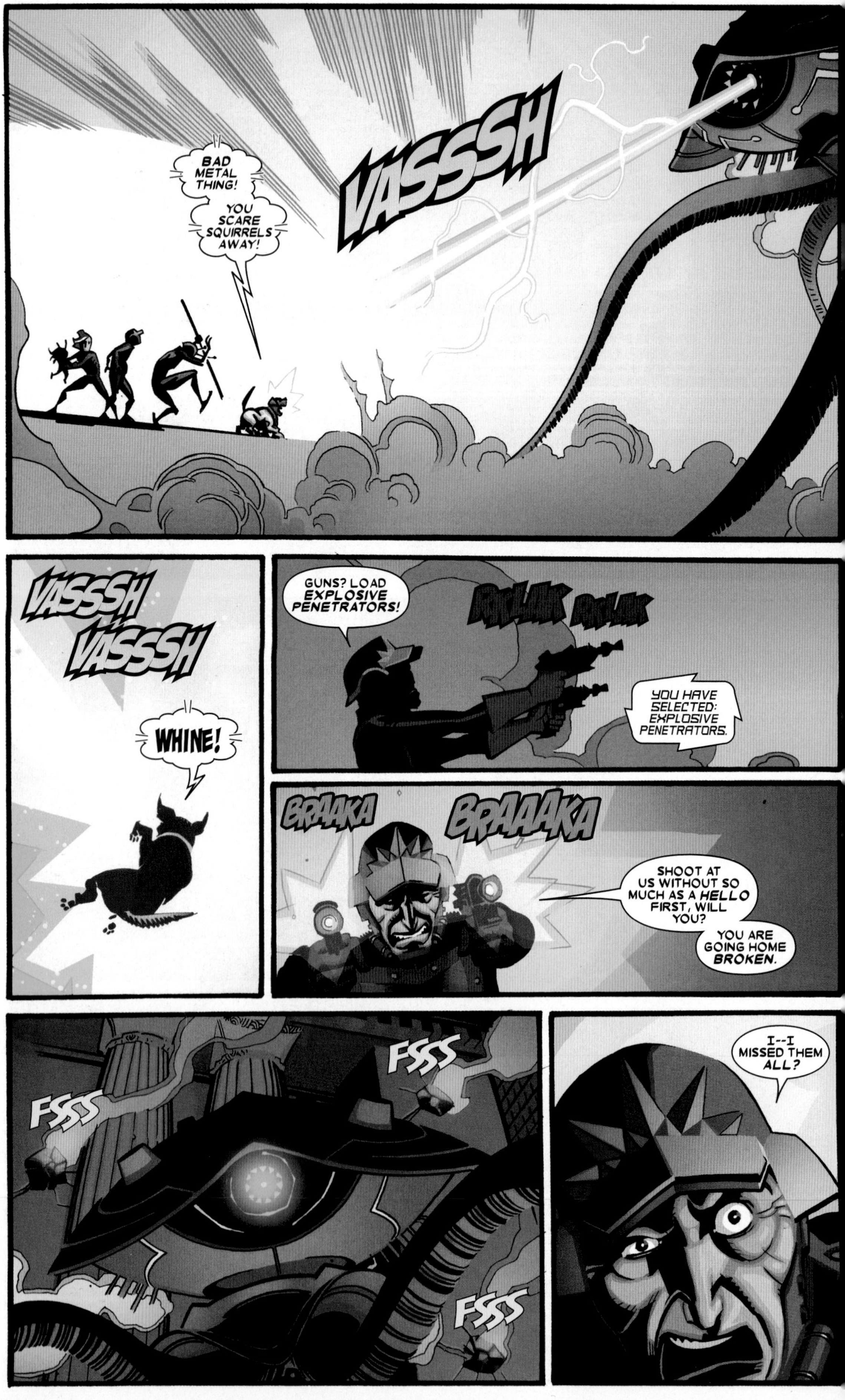
BAD METAL THING!
YOU SCARE SQUIRRELS AWAY!
VASSSH
VASSSH
VASSSH
WHINE!
GUNS? LOAD EXPLOSIVE PENETRATORS!
YOU HAVE SELECTED: EXPLOSIVE PENETRATORS.
BRAAKA
BRAAAKA
SHOOT AT US WITHOUT SO MUCH AS A HELLO FIRST, WILL YOU?
YOU ARE GOING HOME BROKEN.
FSSS
FSSS
FSSS
I--I MISSED THEM ALL?

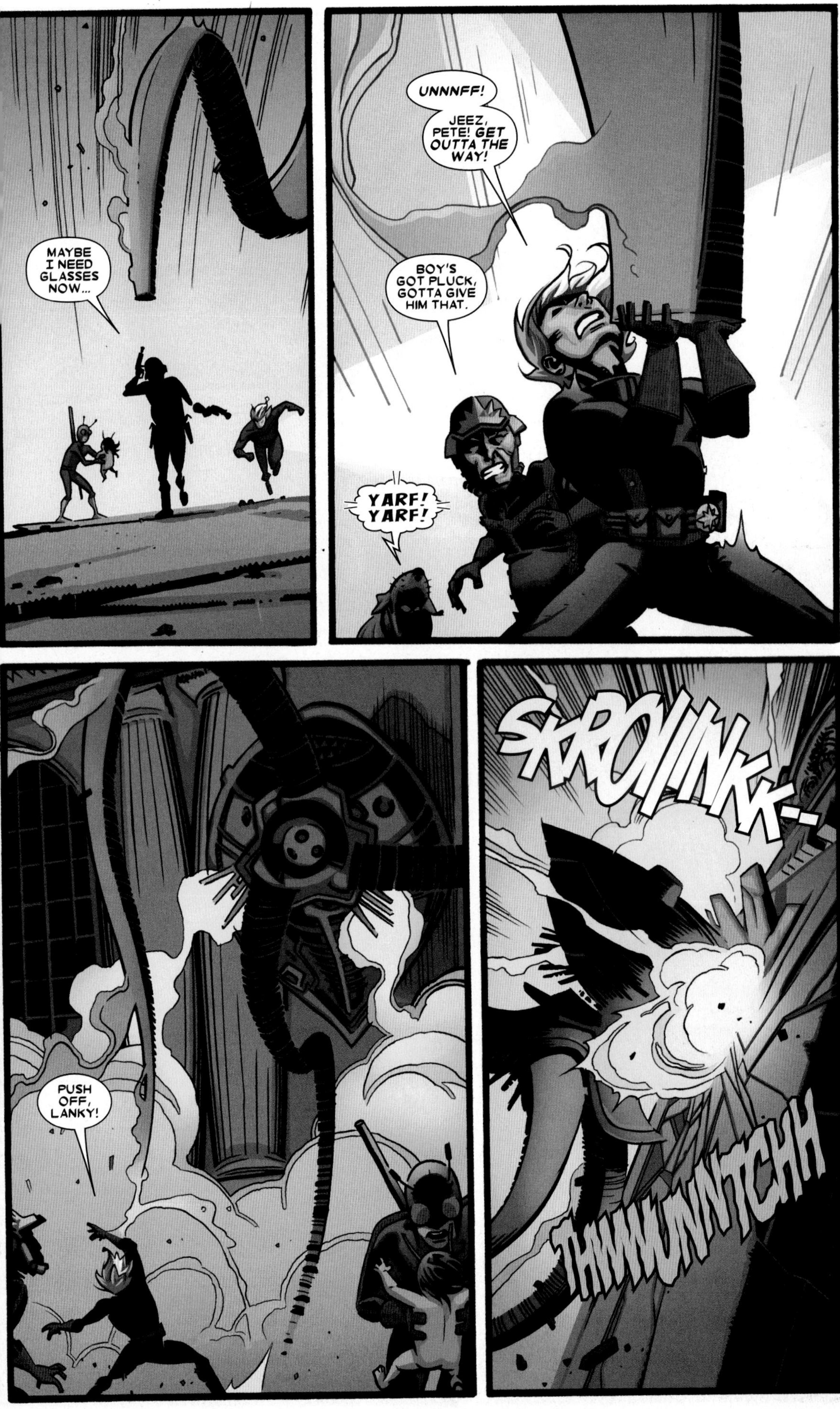
MAYBE I NEED GLASSES NOW...
UNNNFF!
JEEZ, PETE! GET OUTTA THE WAY!
BOY'S GOT PLUCK, GOTTA GIVE HIM THAT.
YARF! YARF!
PUSH OFF, LANKY!
SKROIINKK--
THWUNNTCHH

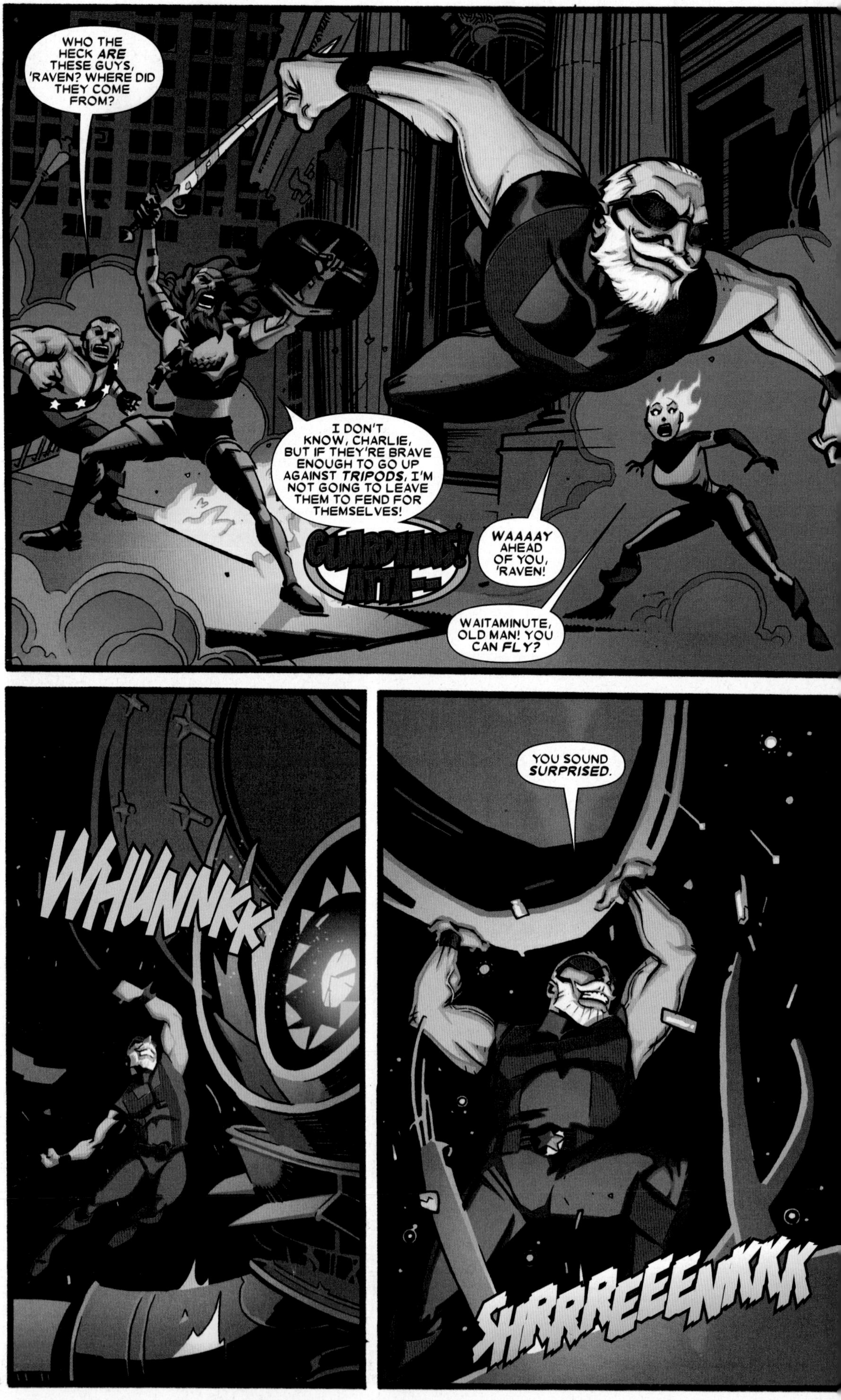
WHO THE HECK *ARE* THESE GUYS, 'RAVEN? WHERE DID THEY COME FROM?
I DON'T KNOW, CHARLIE, BUT IF THEY'RE BRAVE ENOUGH TO GO UP AGAINST *TRIPODS*, I'M NOT GOING TO LEAVE THEM TO FEND FOR THEMSELVES!
GUARDIANS! ATTA
WAAAAY AHEAD OF YOU, 'RAVEN!
WAITAMINUTE, OLD MAN! YOU CAN *FLY*?
WHUNNKK
YOU SOUND *SURPRISED*.
SHRRREEENKKK

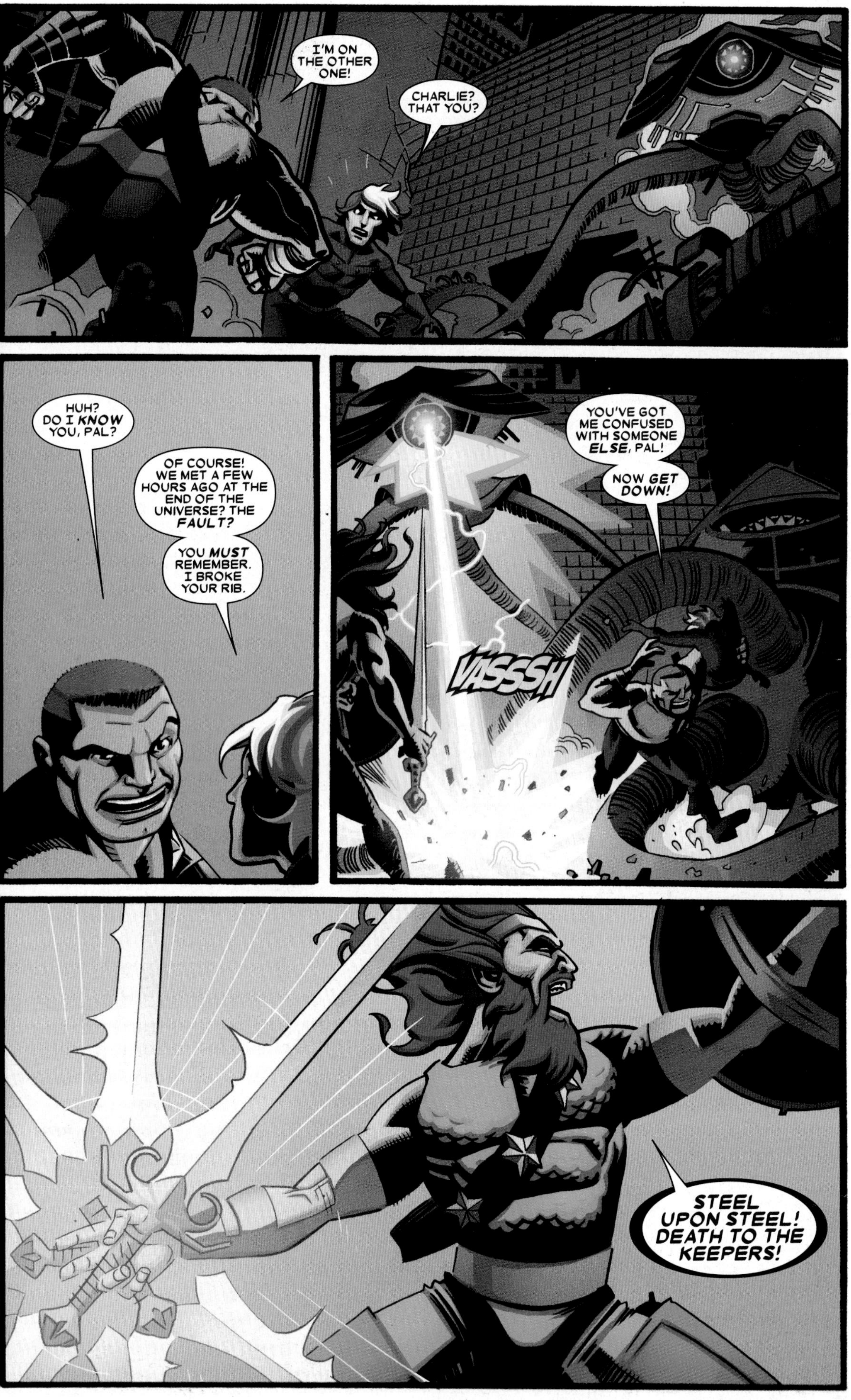
I'M ON THE OTHER ONE!
CHARLIE? THAT YOU?
HUH? DO I KNOW YOU, PAL?
OF COURSE! WE MET A FEW HOURS AGO AT THE END OF THE UNIVERSE? THE FAULT?
YOU MUST REMEMBER. I BROKE YOUR RIB.
YOU'VE GOT ME CONFUSED WITH SOMEONE ELSE, PAL!
NOW GET DOWN!
VASSSH
STEEL UPON STEEL! DEATH TO THE KEEPERS!

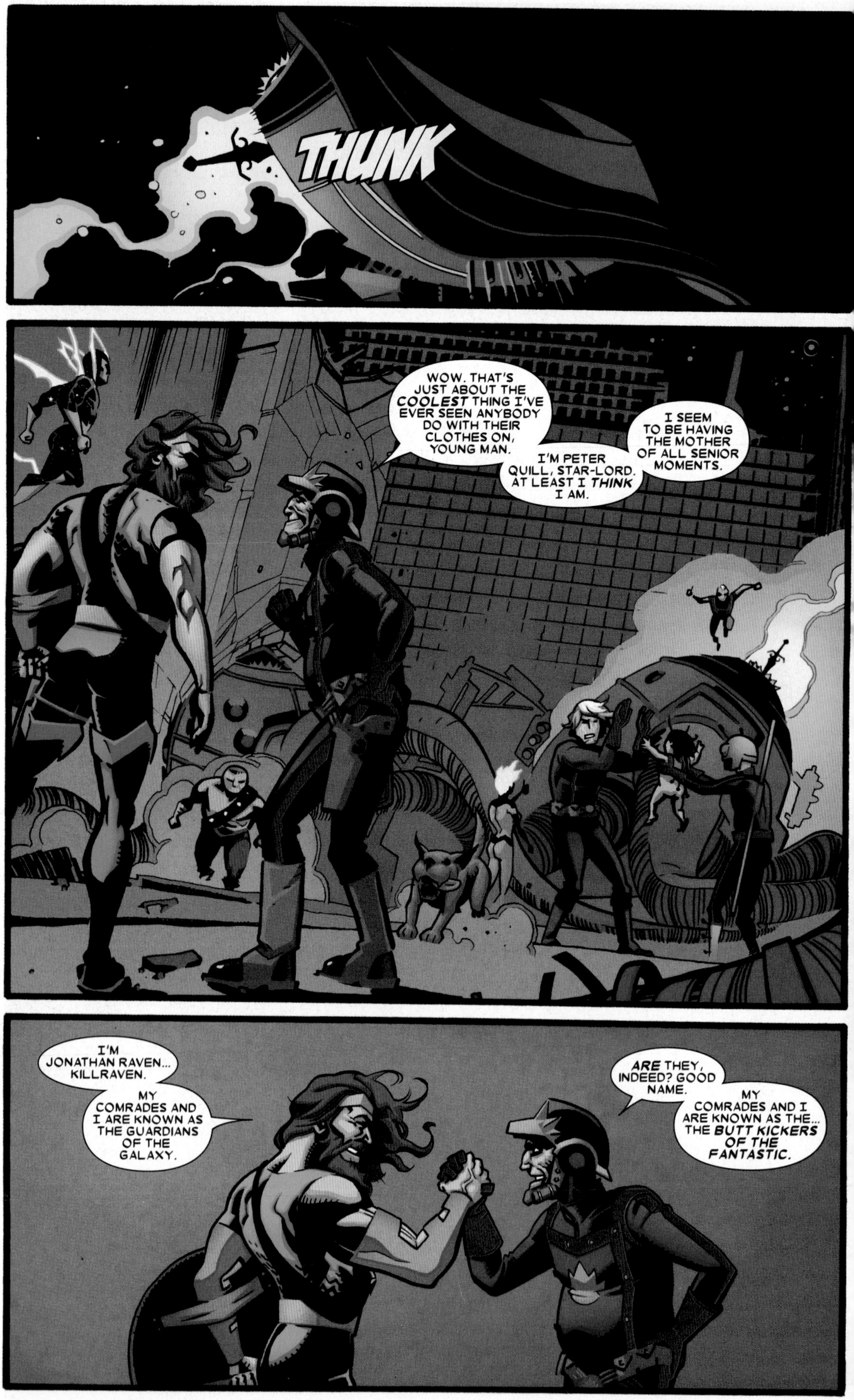
THUNK
WOW. THAT'S JUST ABOUT THE COOLEST THING I'VE EVER SEEN ANYBODY DO WITH THEIR CLOTHES ON, YOUNG MAN.
I'M PETER QUILL, STAR-LORD. AT LEAST I THINK I AM.
I SEEM TO BE HAVING THE MOTHER OF ALL SENIOR MOMENTS.
I'M JONATHAN RAVEN... KILLRAVEN.
MY COMRADES AND I ARE KNOWN AS THE GUARDIANS OF THE GALAXY.
ARE THEY, INDEED? GOOD NAME.
MY COMRADES AND I ARE KNOWN AS THE... THE BUTT KICKERS OF THE FANTASTIC.

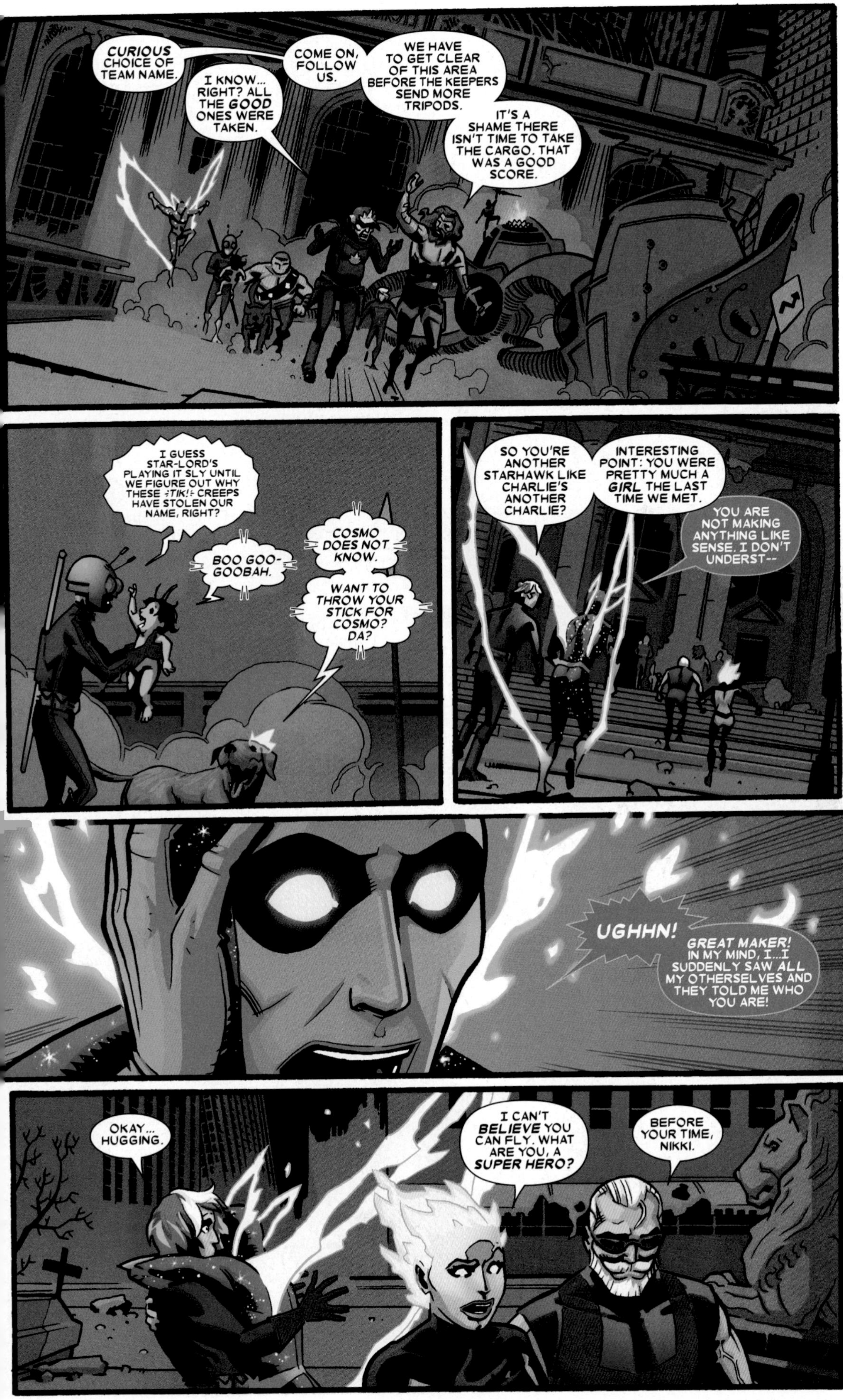
CURIOUS CHOICE OF TEAM NAME.
I KNOW... RIGHT? ALL THE GOOD ONES WERE TAKEN.
COME ON, FOLLOW US.
WE HAVE TO GET CLEAR OF THIS AREA BEFORE THE KEEPERS SEND MORE TRIPODS.
IT'S A SHAME THERE ISN'T TIME TO TAKE THE CARGO. THAT WAS A GOOD SCORE.
I GUESS STAR-LORD'S PLAYING IT SLY UNTIL WE FIGURE OUT WHY THESE -TIK!- CREEPS HAVE STOLEN OUR NAME, RIGHT?
BOO GOO-GOOBAH.
COSMO DOES NOT KNOW.
WANT TO THROW YOUR STICK FOR COSMO? DA?
SO YOU'RE ANOTHER STARHAWK LIKE CHARLIE'S ANOTHER CHARLIE?
INTERESTING POINT: YOU WERE PRETTY MUCH A GIRL THE LAST TIME WE MET.
YOU ARE NOT MAKING ANYTHING LIKE SENSE. I DON'T UNDERST--
UGHHN!
GREAT MAKER! IN MY MIND, I...I SUDDENLY SAW ALL MY OTHERSELVES AND THEY TOLD ME WHO YOU ARE!
OKAY... HUGGING.
I CAN'T BELIEVE YOU CAN FLY. WHAT ARE YOU, A SUPER HERO?
BEFORE YOUR TIME, NIKKI.

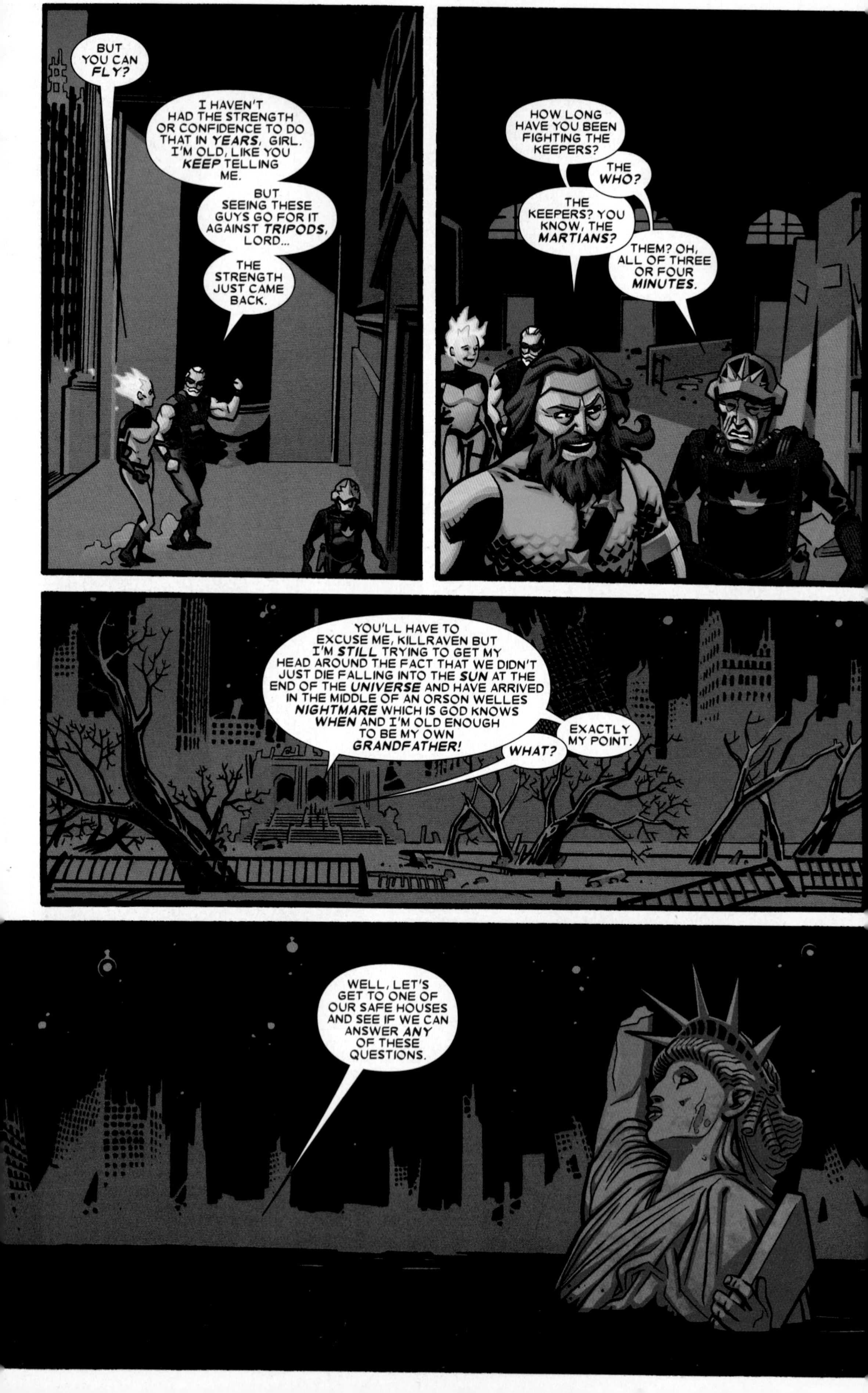
BUT YOU CAN FLY?
I HAVEN'T HAD THE STRENGTH OR CONFIDENCE TO DO THAT IN YEARS, GIRL. I'M OLD, LIKE YOU KEEP TELLING ME.
BUT SEEING THESE GUYS GO FOR IT AGAINST TRIPODS, LORD...
THE STRENGTH JUST CAME BACK.
HOW LONG HAVE YOU BEEN FIGHTING THE KEEPERS?
THE WHO?
THE KEEPERS? YOU KNOW, THE MARTIANS?
THEM? OH, ALL OF THREE OR FOUR MINUTES.
YOU'LL HAVE TO EXCUSE ME, KILLRAVEN BUT I'M STILL TRYING TO GET MY HEAD AROUND THE FACT THAT WE DIDN'T JUST DIE FALLING INTO THE SUN AT THE END OF THE UNIVERSE AND HAVE ARRIVED IN THE MIDDLE OF AN ORSON WELLES NIGHTMARE WHICH IS GOD KNOWS WHEN AND I'M OLD ENOUGH TO BE MY OWN GRANDFATHER!
WHAT?
EXACTLY MY POINT.
WELL, LET'S GET TO ONE OF OUR SAFE HOUSES AND SEE IF WE CAN ANSWER ANY OF THESE QUESTIONS.

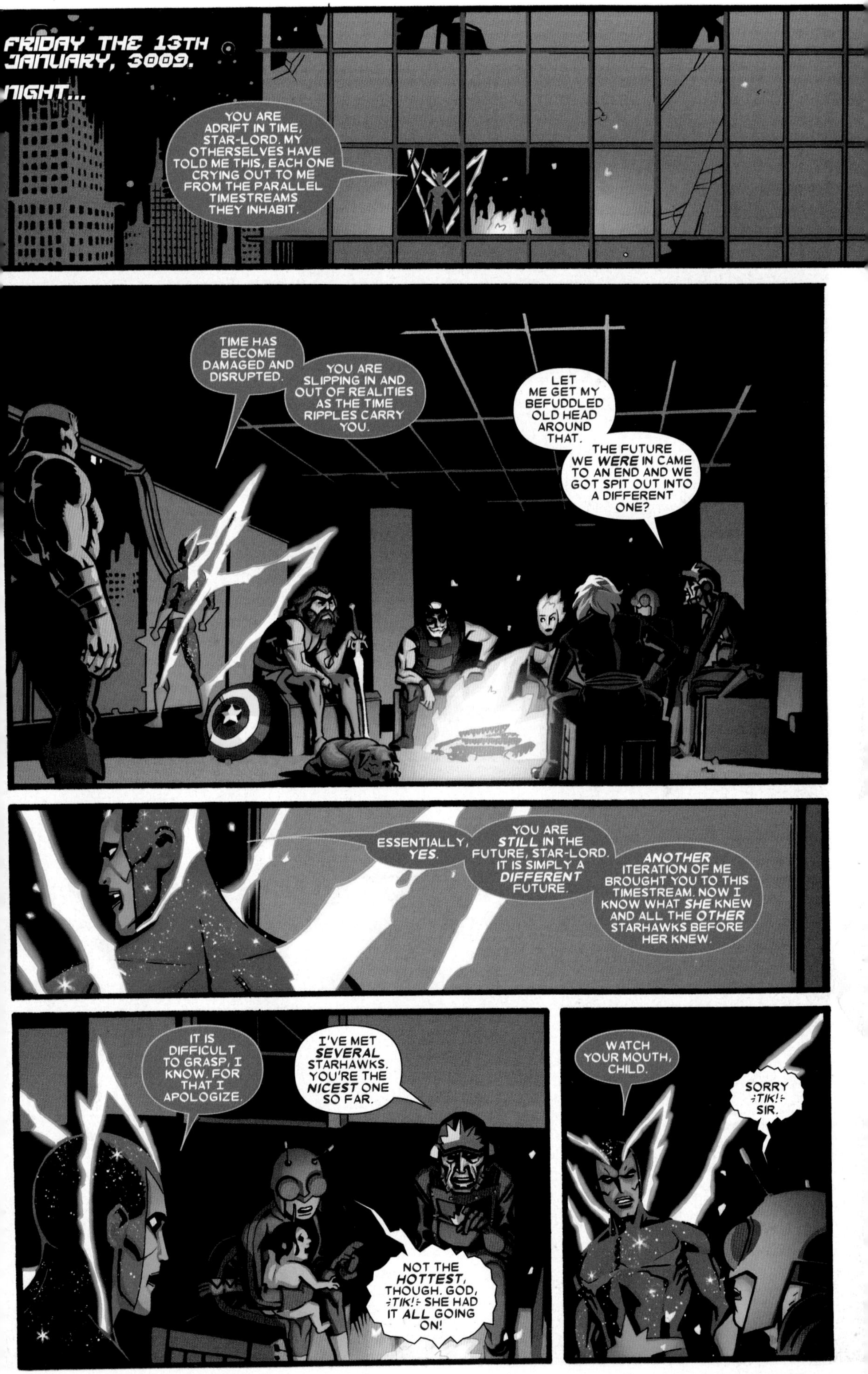
FRIDAY THE 13TH JANUARY, 3009.
NIGHT...
YOU ARE ADRIFT IN TIME, STAR-LORD. MY OTHERSELVES HAVE TOLD ME THIS, EACH ONE CRYING OUT TO ME FROM THE PARALLEL TIMESTREAMS THEY INHABIT.
TIME HAS BECOME DAMAGED AND DISRUPTED.
YOU ARE SLIPPING IN AND OUT OF REALITIES AS THE TIME RIPPLES CARRY YOU.
LET ME GET MY BEFUDDLED OLD HEAD AROUND THAT.
THE FUTURE WE *WERE* IN CAME TO AN END AND WE GOT SPIT OUT INTO A DIFFERENT ONE?
ESSENTIALLY, *YES*.
YOU ARE *STILL* IN THE FUTURE, STAR-LORD. IT IS SIMPLY A *DIFFERENT* FUTURE.
ANOTHER ITERATION OF ME BROUGHT YOU TO THIS TIMESTREAM. NOW I KNOW WHAT *SHE* KNEW AND ALL THE *OTHER* STARHAWKS BEFORE HER KNEW.
IT IS DIFFICULT TO GRASP, I KNOW. FOR THAT I APOLOGIZE.
I'VE MET *SEVERAL* STARHAWKS. YOU'RE THE *NICEST* ONE SO FAR.
NOT THE *HOTTEST*, THOUGH. GOD, *TIK!* SHE HAD IT *ALL* GOING ON!
WATCH YOUR MOUTH, CHILD.
SORRY *TIK!* SIR.

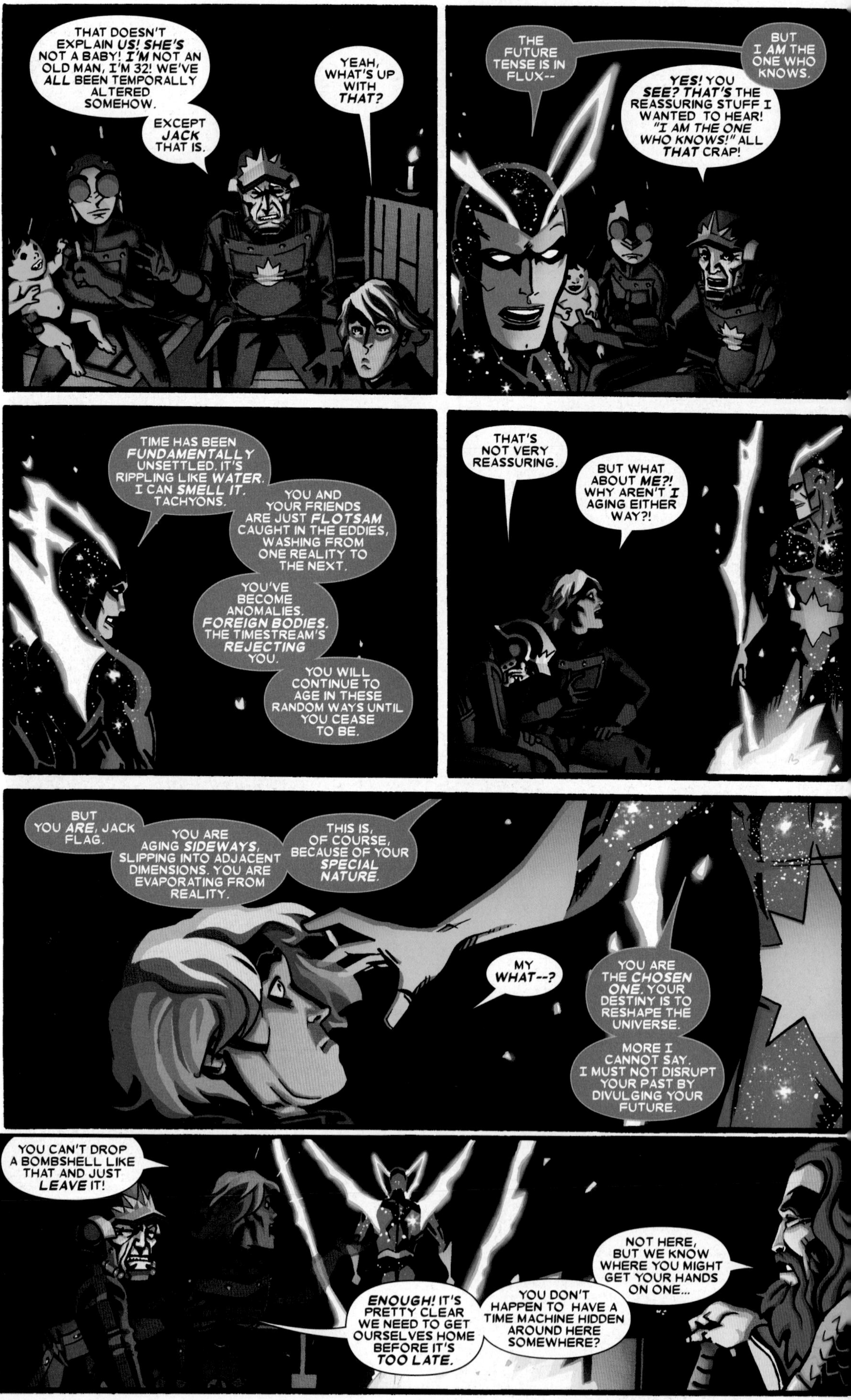
THAT DOESN'T EXPLAIN US! SHE'S NOT A BABY! I'M NOT AN OLD MAN, I'M 32! WE'VE ALL BEEN TEMPORALLY ALTERED SOMEHOW.
EXCEPT JACK THAT IS.
YEAH, WHAT'S UP WITH THAT?
THE FUTURE TENSE IS IN FLUX--
BUT I AM THE ONE WHO KNOWS.
YES! YOU SEE? THAT'S THE REASSURING STUFF I WANTED TO HEAR! "I AM THE ONE WHO KNOWS!" ALL THAT CRAP!
TIME HAS BEEN FUNDAMENTALLY UNSETTLED. IT'S RIPPLING LIKE WATER. I CAN SMELL IT. TACHYONS.
YOU AND YOUR FRIENDS ARE JUST FLOTSAM CAUGHT IN THE EDDIES, WASHING FROM ONE REALITY TO THE NEXT.
YOU'VE BECOME ANOMALIES. FOREIGN BODIES. THE TIMESTREAM'S REJECTING YOU.
YOU WILL CONTINUE TO AGE IN THESE RANDOM WAYS UNTIL YOU CEASE TO BE.
THAT'S NOT VERY REASSURING.
BUT WHAT ABOUT ME?! WHY AREN'T I AGING EITHER WAY?!
BUT YOU ARE, JACK FLAG.
YOU ARE AGING SIDEWAYS, SLIPPING INTO ADJACENT DIMENSIONS. YOU ARE EVAPORATING FROM REALITY.
THIS IS, OF COURSE, BECAUSE OF YOUR SPECIAL NATURE.
MY WHAT--?
YOU ARE THE CHOSEN ONE. YOUR DESTINY IS TO RESHAPE THE UNIVERSE.
MORE I CANNOT SAY. I MUST NOT DISRUPT YOUR PAST BY DIVULGING YOUR FUTURE.
YOU CAN'T DROP A BOMBSHELL LIKE THAT AND JUST LEAVE IT!
ENOUGH! IT'S PRETTY CLEAR WE NEED TO GET OURSELVES HOME BEFORE IT'S TOO LATE.
YOU DON'T HAPPEN TO HAVE A TIME MACHINE HIDDEN AROUND HERE SOMEWHERE?
NOT HERE, BUT WE KNOW WHERE YOU MIGHT GET YOUR HANDS ON ONE...

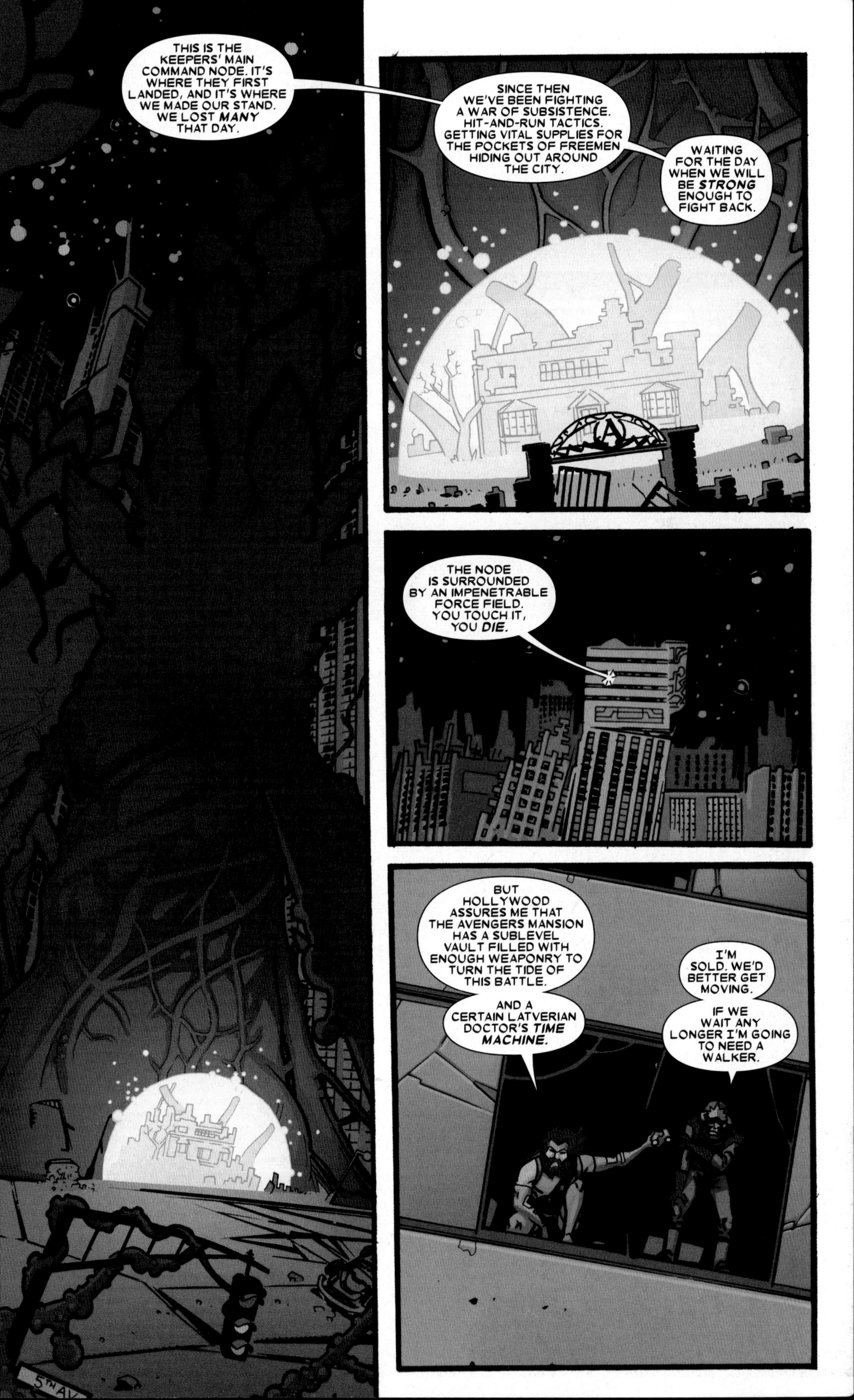
THIS IS THE KEEPERS' MAIN COMMAND NODE. IT'S WHERE THEY FIRST LANDED, AND IT'S WHERE WE MADE OUR STAND. WE LOST *MANY* THAT DAY.
SINCE THEN WE'VE BEEN FIGHTING A WAR OF SUBSISTENCE. HIT-AND-RUN TACTICS. GETTING VITAL SUPPLIES FOR THE POCKETS OF FREEMEN HIDING OUT AROUND THE CITY.
WAITING FOR THE DAY WHEN WE WILL BE *STRONG* ENOUGH TO FIGHT BACK.
THE NODE IS SURROUNDED BY AN IMPENETRABLE FORCE FIELD. YOU TOUCH IT, YOU *DIE.*
BUT HOLLYWOOD ASSURES ME THAT THE AVENGERS MANSION HAS A SUBLEVEL VAULT FILLED WITH ENOUGH WEAPONRY TO TURN THE TIDE OF THIS BATTLE.
AND A CERTAIN LATVERIAN DOCTOR'S *TIME MACHINE.*
I'M SOLD. WE'D BETTER GET MOVING.
IF WE WAIT ANY LONGER I'M GOING TO NEED A WALKER.
5TH AV

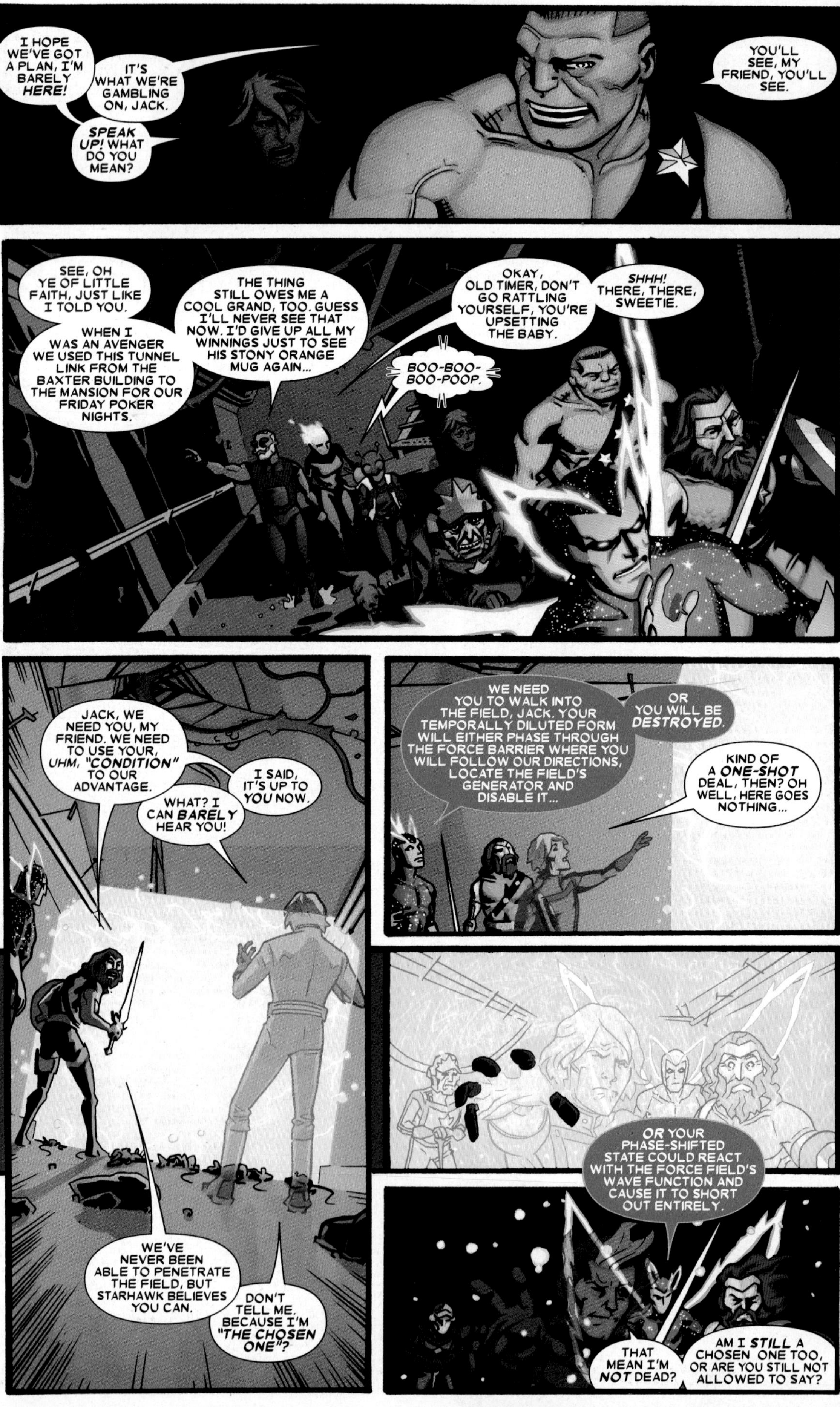

I HOPE WE'VE GOT A PLAN, I'M BARELY *HERE!*
IT'S WHAT WE'RE GAMBLING ON, JACK.
SPEAK UP! WHAT DO YOU MEAN?
YOU'LL SEE, MY FRIEND, YOU'LL SEE.
SEE, OH YE OF LITTLE FAITH, JUST LIKE I TOLD YOU.
WHEN I WAS AN AVENGER WE USED THIS TUNNEL LINK FROM THE BAXTER BUILDING TO THE MANSION FOR OUR FRIDAY POKER NIGHTS.
THE THING STILL OWES ME A COOL GRAND, TOO. GUESS I'LL NEVER SEE THAT NOW. I'D GIVE UP ALL MY WINNINGS JUST TO SEE HIS STONY ORANGE MUG AGAIN...
BOO-BOO-BOO-POOP.
OKAY, OLD TIMER, DON'T GO RATTLING YOURSELF, YOU'RE UPSETTING THE BABY.
SHHH! THERE, THERE, SWEETIE.
JACK, WE NEED YOU, MY FRIEND. WE NEED TO USE YOUR, *UHM, "CONDITION"* TO OUR ADVANTAGE.
I SAID, IT'S UP TO *YOU* NOW.
WHAT? I CAN *BARELY* HEAR YOU!
WE'VE NEVER BEEN ABLE TO PENETRATE THE FIELD, BUT STARHAWK BELIEVES YOU CAN.
DON'T TELL ME. BECAUSE I'M *"THE CHOSEN ONE"*?
WE NEED YOU TO WALK INTO THE FIELD, JACK. YOUR TEMPORALLY DILUTED FORM WILL EITHER PHASE THROUGH THE FORCE BARRIER WHERE YOU WILL FOLLOW OUR DIRECTIONS, LOCATE THE FIELD'S GENERATOR AND DISABLE IT...
OR YOU WILL BE *DESTROYED.*
KIND OF A *ONE-SHOT* DEAL, THEN? OH WELL, HERE GOES NOTHING...
OR YOUR PHASE-SHIFTED STATE COULD REACT WITH THE FORCE FIELD'S WAVE FUNCTION AND CAUSE IT TO SHORT OUT ENTIRELY.
THAT MEAN I'M *NOT* DEAD?
AM I *STILL* A CHOSEN ONE TOO, OR ARE YOU STILL NOT ALLOWED TO SAY?

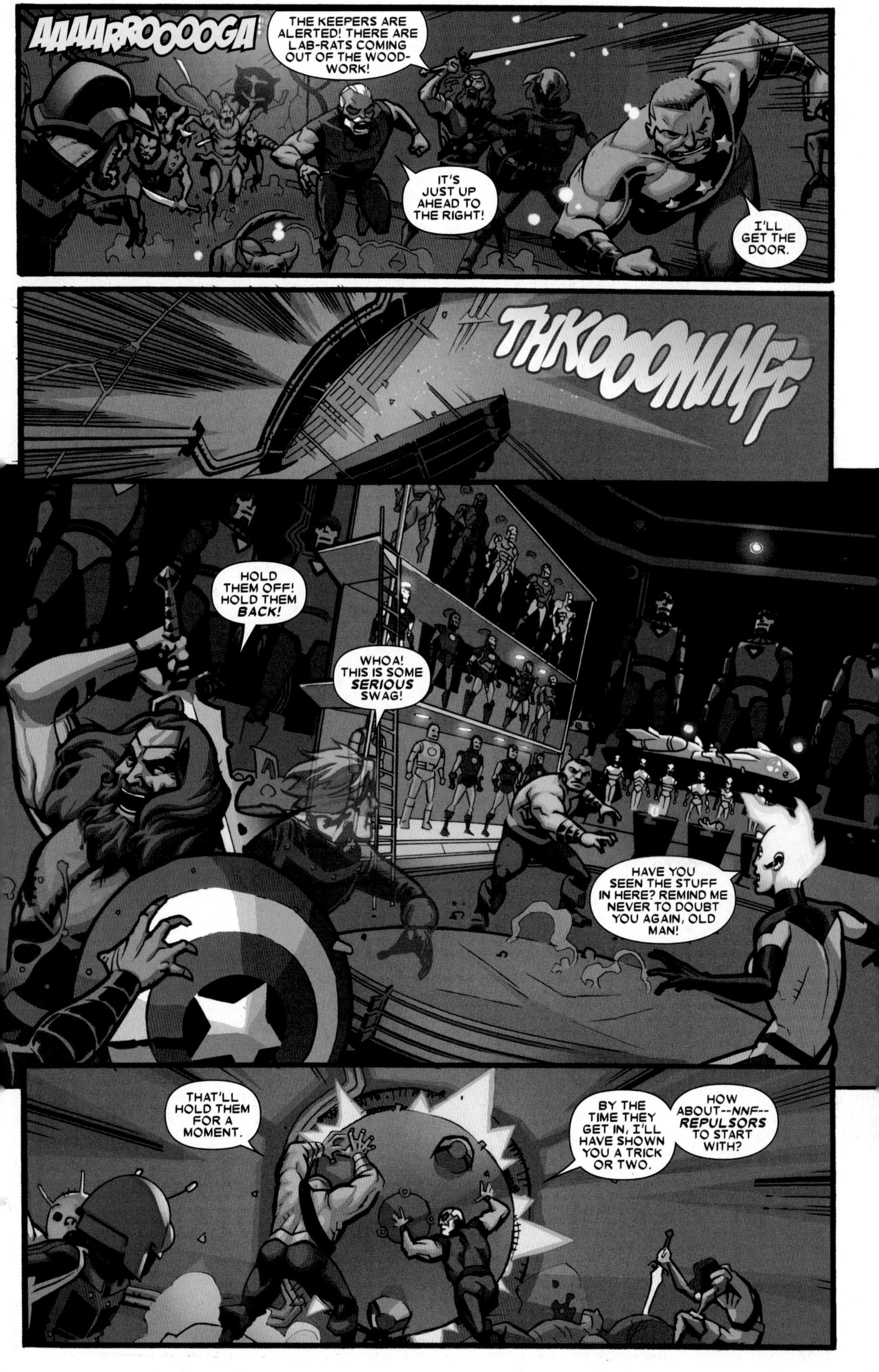
AAAARROOOOGA
THE KEEPERS ARE ALERTED! THERE ARE LAB-RATS COMING OUT OF THE WOOD-WORK!
IT'S JUST UP AHEAD TO THE RIGHT!
I'LL GET THE DOOR.
THKOOOMMFF
HOLD THEM OFF! HOLD THEM BACK!
WHOA! THIS IS SOME SERIOUS SWAG!
HAVE YOU SEEN THE STUFF IN HERE? REMIND ME NEVER TO DOUBT YOU AGAIN, OLD MAN!
THAT'LL HOLD THEM FOR A MOMENT.
BY THE TIME THEY GET IN, I'LL HAVE SHOWN YOU A TRICK OR TWO.
HOW ABOUT--NNF-- REPULSORS TO START WITH?

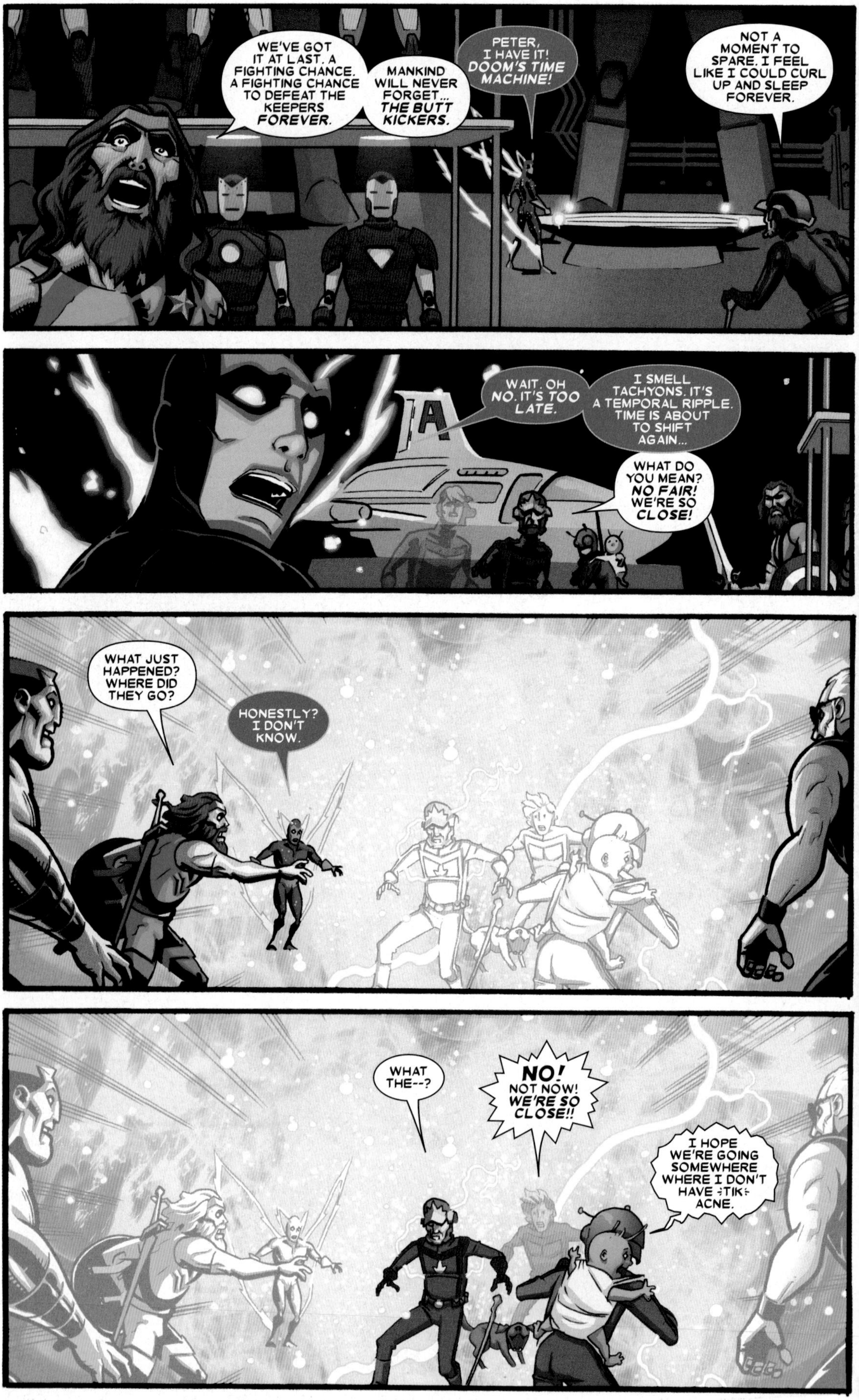
WE'VE GOT IT AT LAST. A FIGHTING CHANCE. A FIGHTING CHANCE TO DEFEAT THE KEEPERS FOREVER.
MANKIND WILL NEVER FORGET... THE BUTT KICKERS.
PETER, I HAVE IT! DOOM'S TIME MACHINE!
NOT A MOMENT TO SPARE. I FEEL LIKE I COULD CURL UP AND SLEEP FOREVER.
WAIT. OH NO. IT'S TOO LATE.
I SMELL TACHYONS. IT'S A TEMPORAL RIPPLE. TIME IS ABOUT TO SHIFT AGAIN...
WHAT DO YOU MEAN? NO FAIR! WE'RE SO CLOSE!
WHAT JUST HAPPENED? WHERE DID THEY GO?
HONESTLY? I DON'T KNOW.
WHAT THE--?
NO! NOT NOW! WE'RE SO CLOSE!!
I HOPE WE'RE GOING SOMEWHERE WHERE I DON'T HAVE ⫶TIK⫶ ACNE.

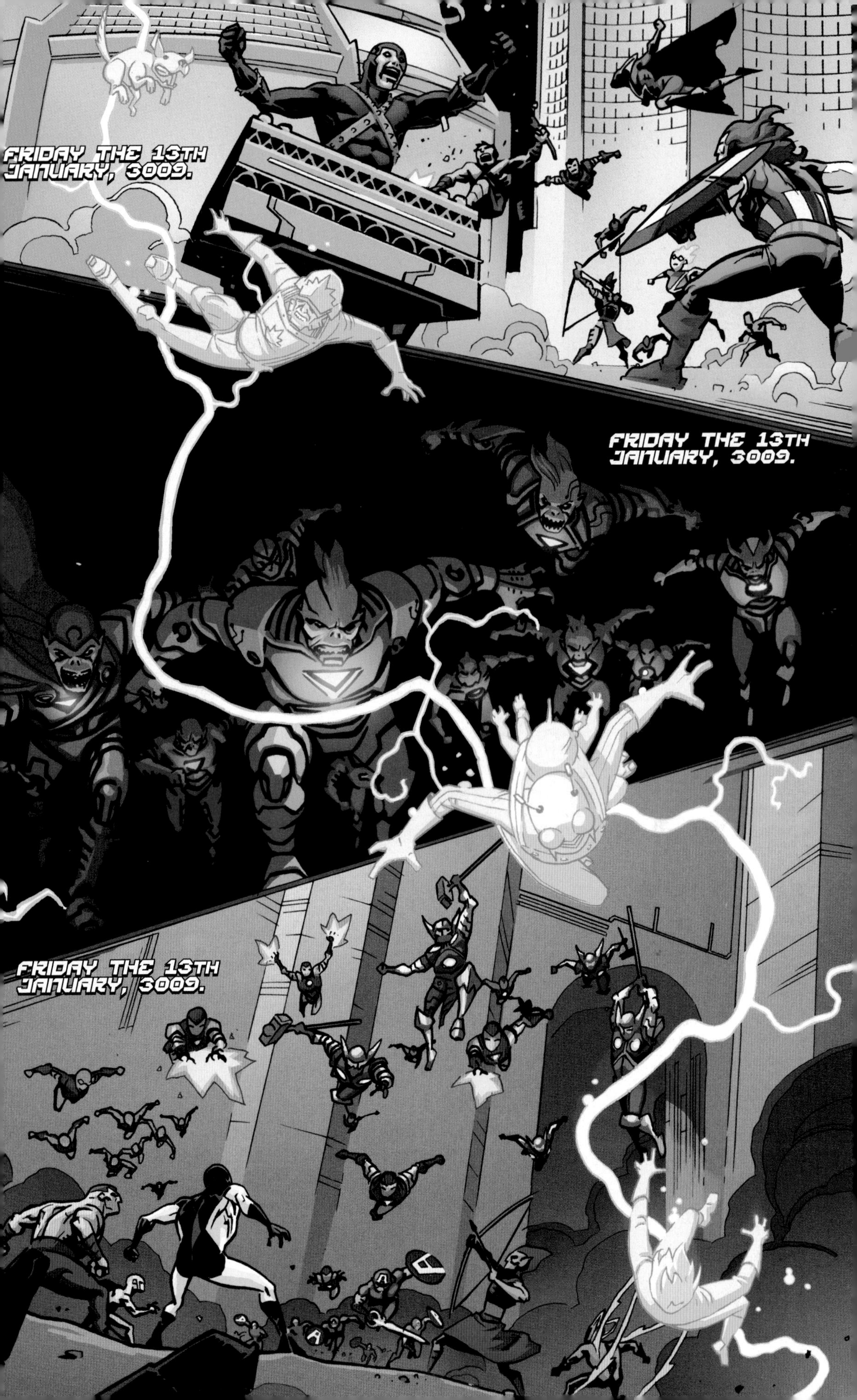

FRIDAY THE 13TH JANUARY, 3009.
FRIDAY THE 13TH JANUARY, 3009.
FRIDAY THE 13TH JANUARY, 3009.

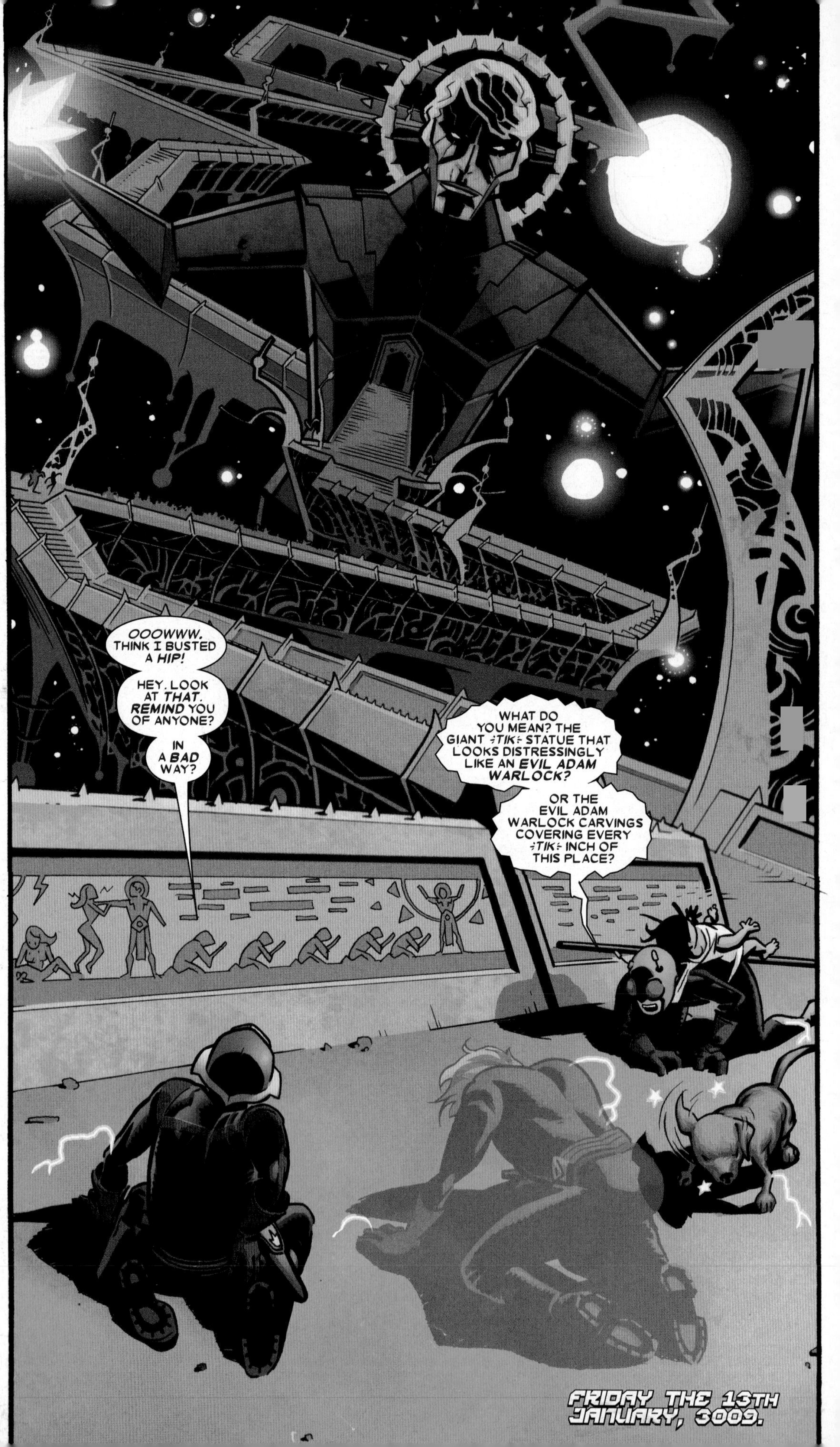
OOOWWW. THINK I BUSTED A HIP!
HEY. LOOK AT THAT. REMIND YOU OF ANYONE?
IN A BAD WAY?
WHAT DO YOU MEAN? THE GIANT ╪TIK╪ STATUE THAT LOOKS DISTRESSINGLY LIKE AN EVIL ADAM WARLOCK?
OR THE EVIL ADAM WARLOCK CARVINGS COVERING EVERY ╪TIK╪ INCH OF THIS PLACE?
FRIDAY THE 13TH JANUARY, 3009.

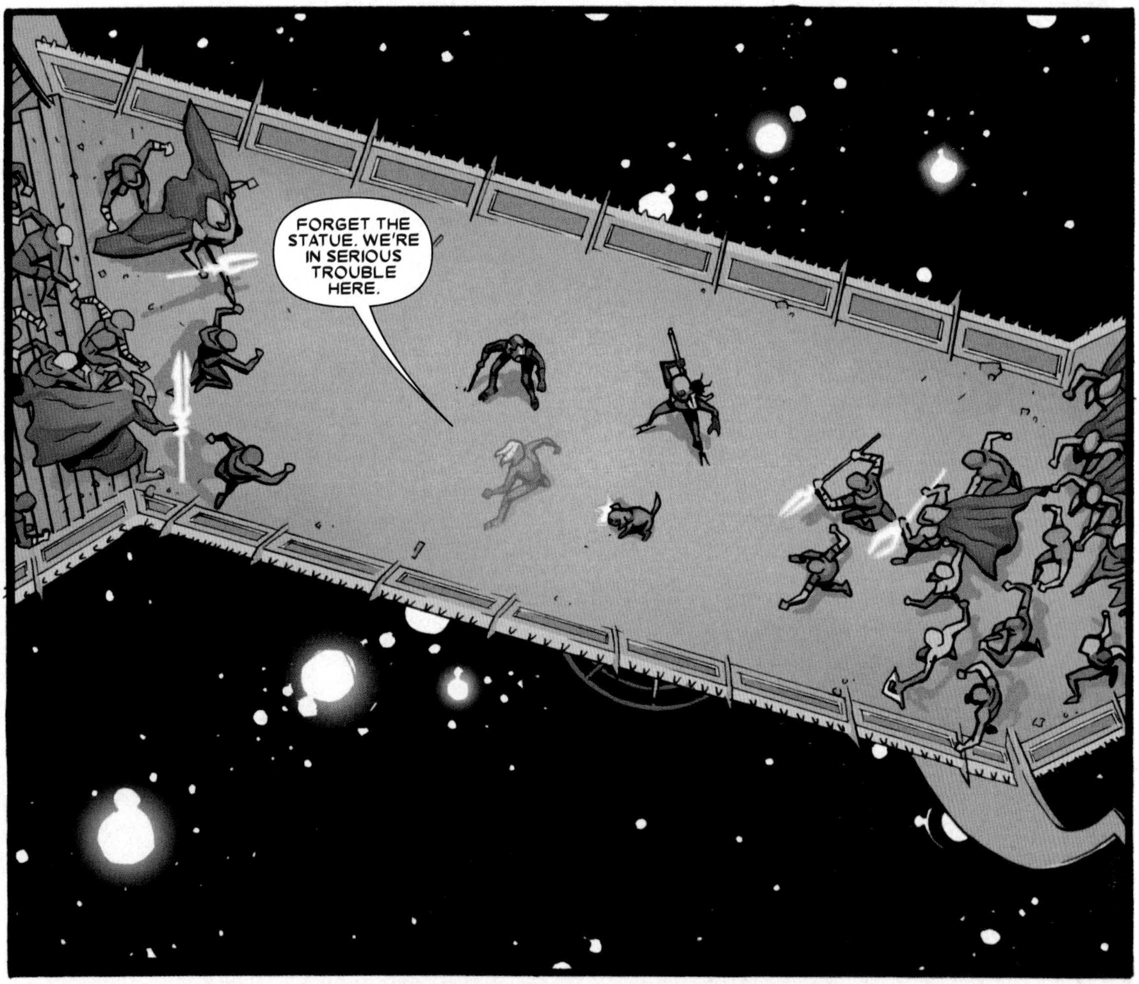
FORGET THE STATUE. WE'RE IN SERIOUS TROUBLE HERE.

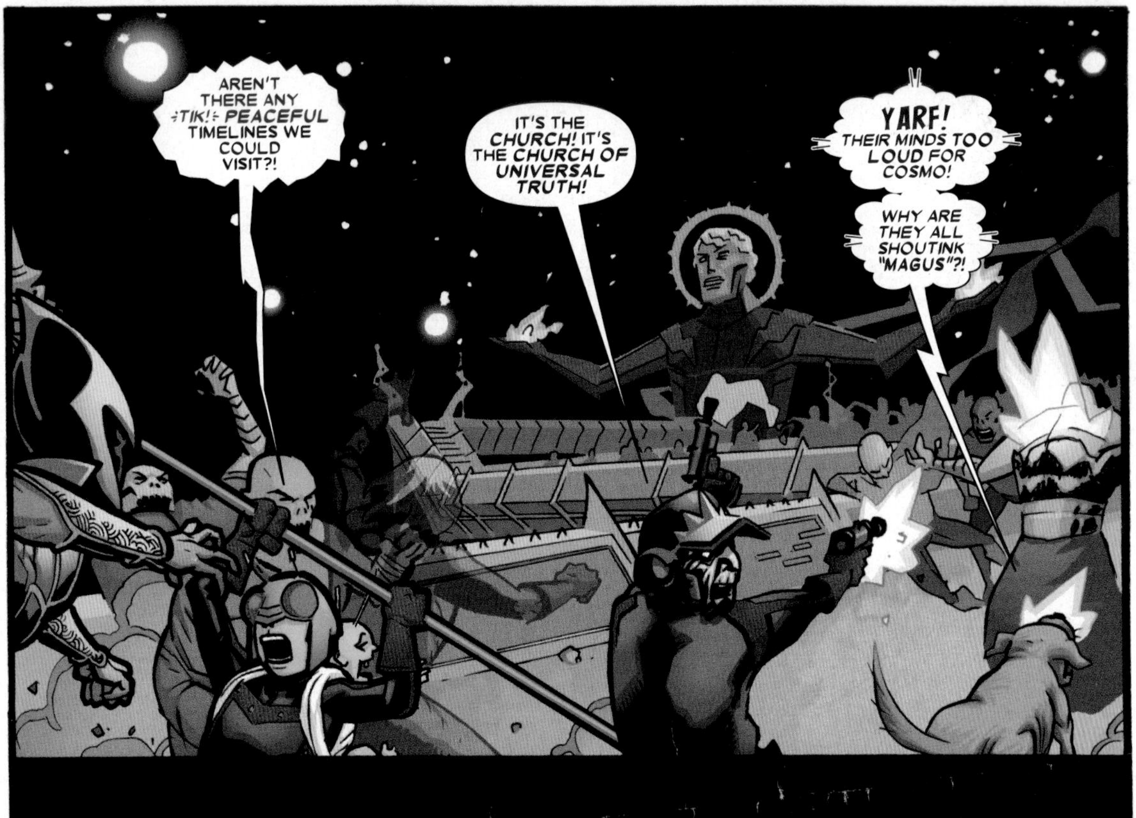
AREN'T THERE ANY ‡TIK!‡ PEACEFUL TIMELINES WE COULD VISIT?!
IT'S THE CHURCH! IT'S THE CHURCH OF UNIVERSAL TRUTH!
YARF! THEIR MINDS TOO LOUD FOR COSMO!
WHY ARE THEY ALL SHOUTINK "MAGUS"?!

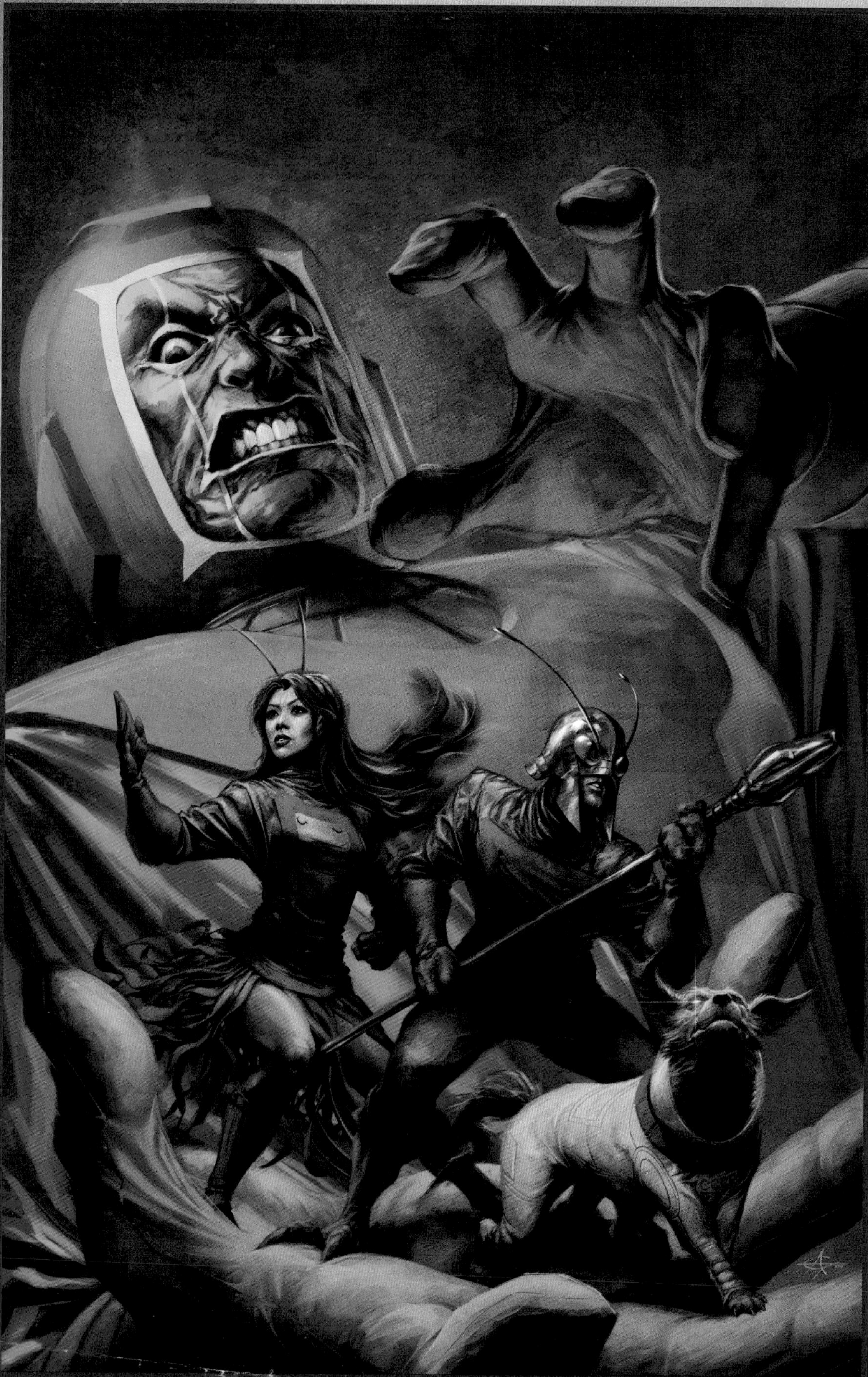

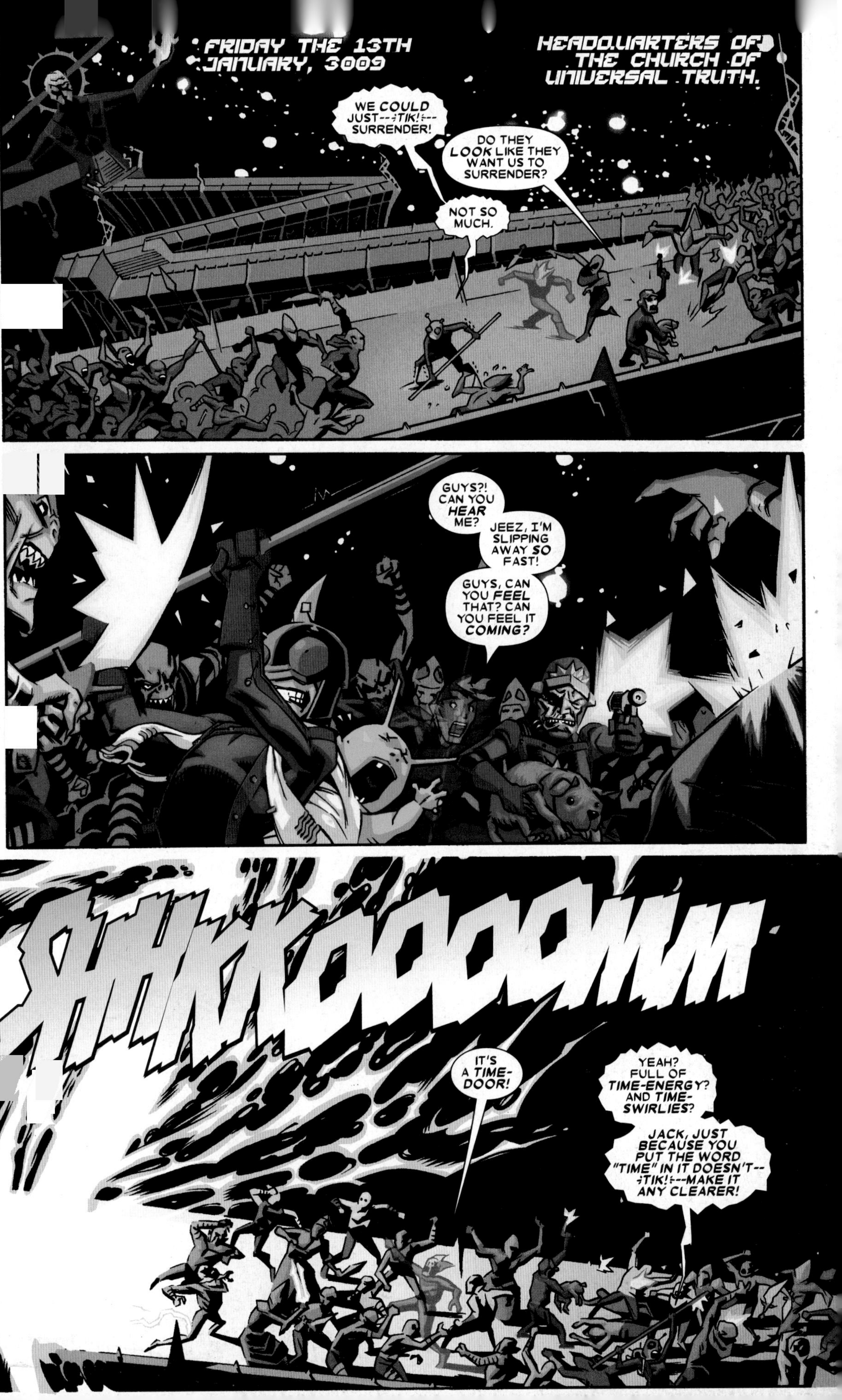
FRIDAY THE 13TH JANUARY, 3009
HEADQUARTERS OF THE CHURCH OF UNIVERSAL TRUTH.
WE COULD JUST--+TIK!+--SURRENDER!
DO THEY LOOK LIKE THEY WANT US TO SURRENDER?
NOT SO MUCH.
GUYS?! CAN YOU HEAR ME?
JEEZ, I'M SLIPPING AWAY SO FAST!
GUYS, CAN YOU FEEL THAT? CAN YOU FEEL IT COMING?
SHHOOOOMM
IT'S A TIME-DOOR!
YEAH? FULL OF TIME-ENERGY? AND TIME-SWIRLIES?
JACK, JUST BECAUSE YOU PUT THE WORD "TIME" IN IT DOESN'T--+TIK!+--MAKE IT ANY CLEARER!

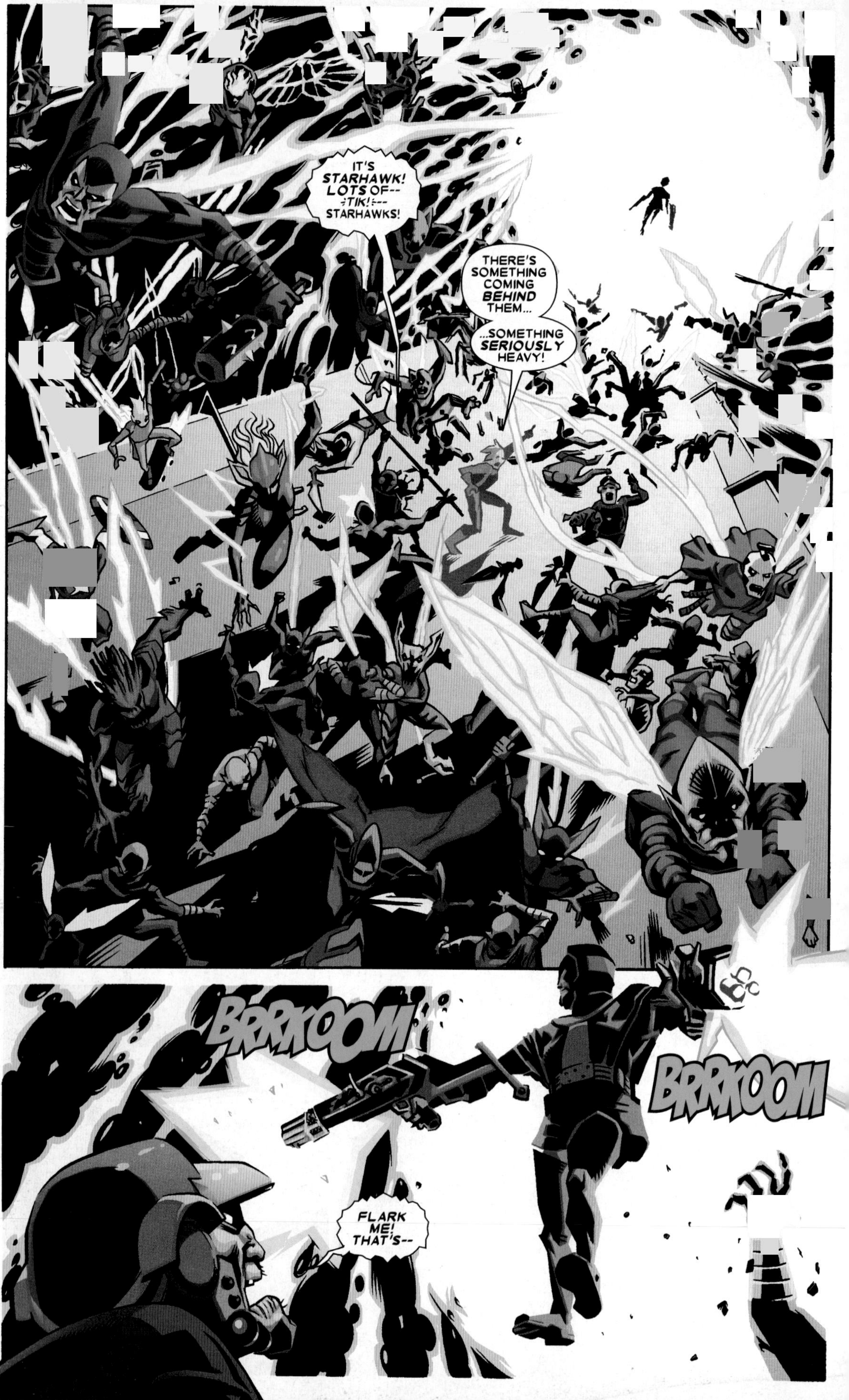
IT'S STARHAWK! LOTS OF-- ÷TIK!÷-- STARHAWKS!
THERE'S SOMETHING COMING BEHIND THEM...
...SOMETHING SERIOUSLY HEAVY!
BRRKOOM
BRRKOOM
FLARK ME! THAT'S--

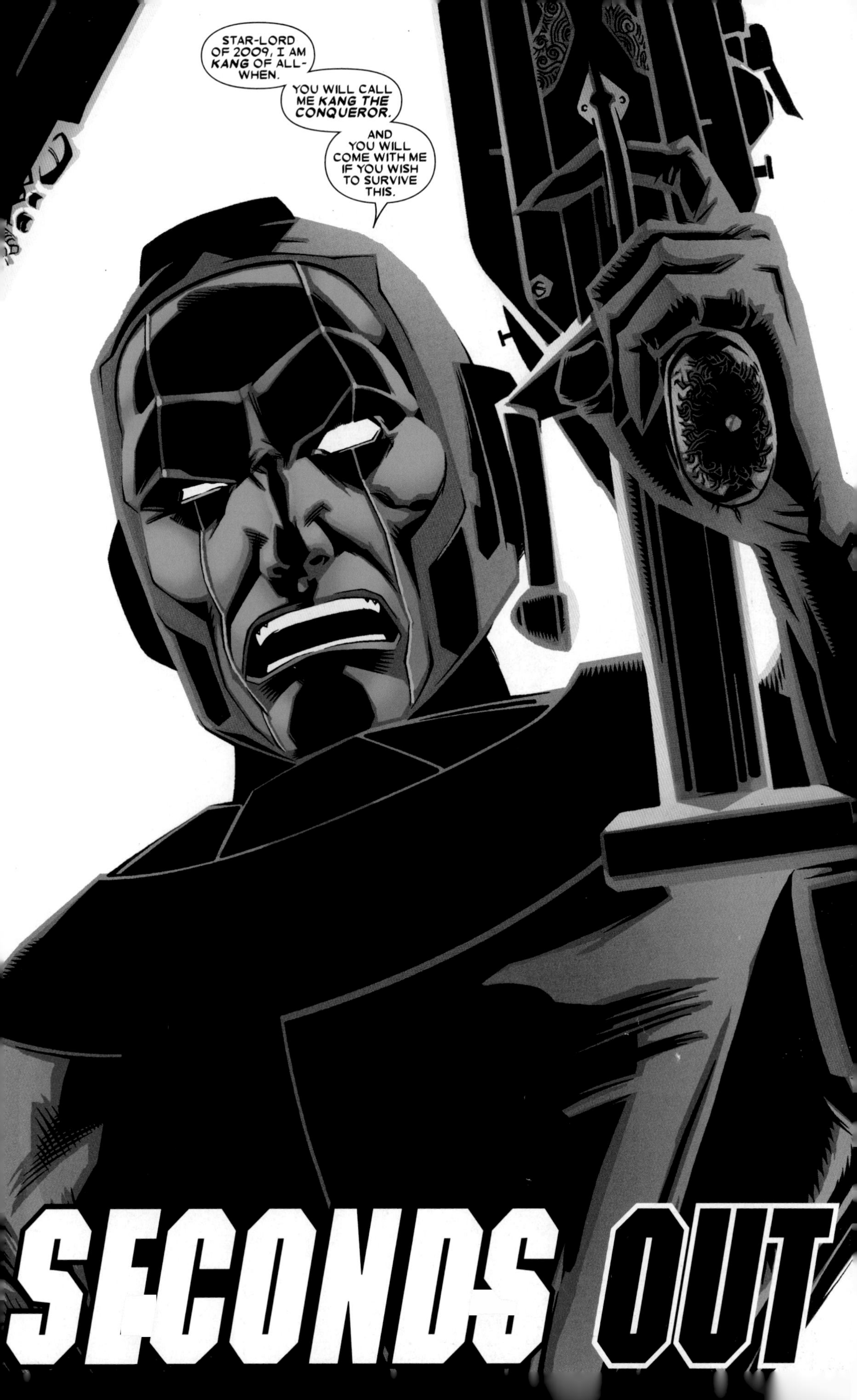
STAR-LORD OF 2009, I AM KANG OF ALL-WHEN.
YOU WILL CALL ME KANG THE CONQUEROR.
AND YOU WILL COME WITH ME IF YOU WISH TO SURVIVE THIS.
SECONDS OUT

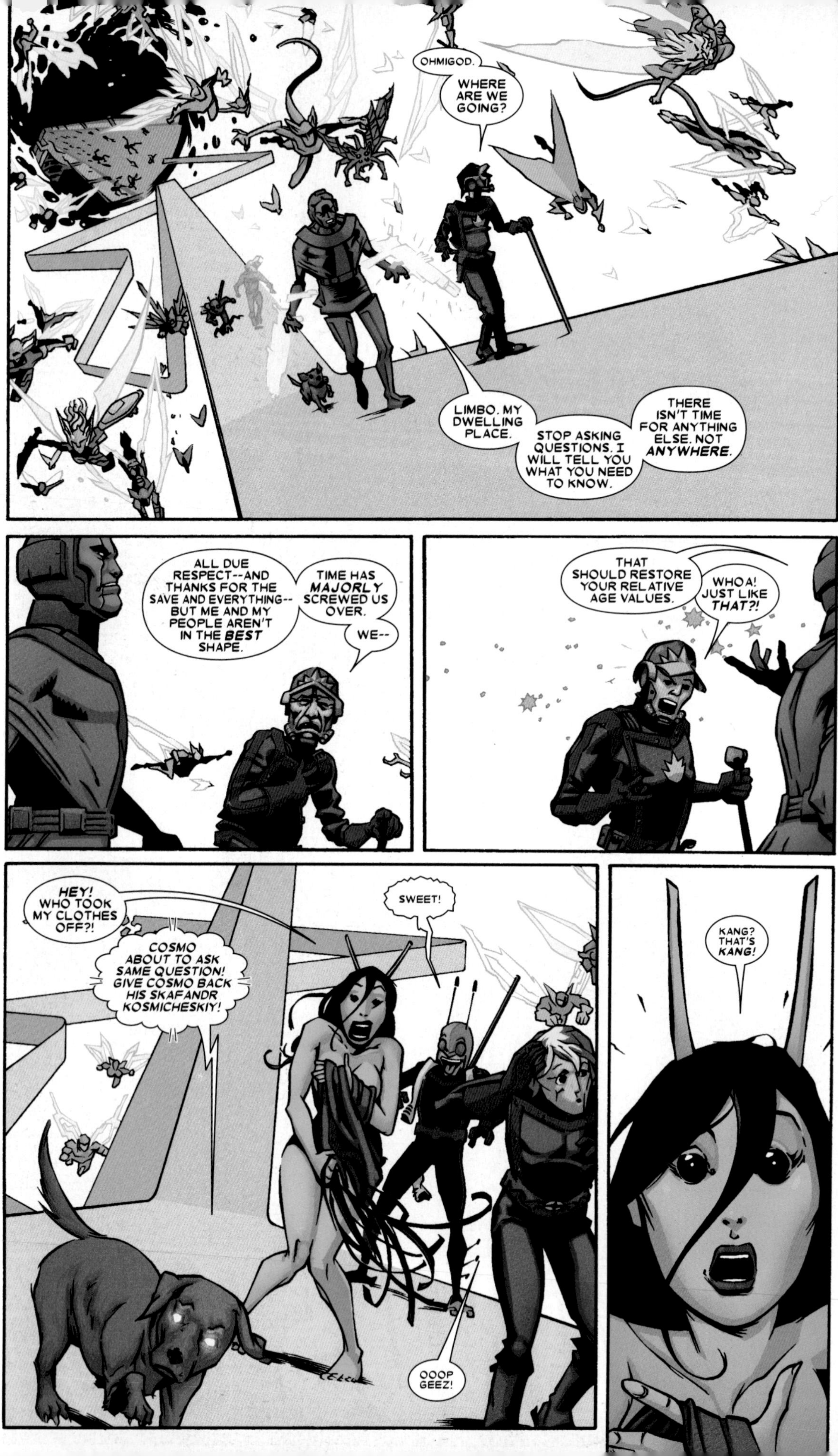

OHMIGOD.
WHERE ARE WE GOING?
LIMBO. MY DWELLING PLACE.
STOP ASKING QUESTIONS. I WILL TELL YOU WHAT YOU NEED TO KNOW.
THERE ISN'T TIME FOR ANYTHING ELSE. NOT *ANYWHERE.*
ALL DUE RESPECT--AND THANKS FOR THE SAVE AND EVERYTHING--BUT ME AND MY PEOPLE AREN'T IN THE *BEST* SHAPE.
TIME HAS *MAJORLY* SCREWED US OVER.
WE--
THAT SHOULD RESTORE YOUR RELATIVE AGE VALUES.
WHOA! JUST LIKE *THAT?!*
HEY! WHO TOOK MY CLOTHES OFF?!
COSMO ABOUT TO ASK SAME QUESTION! GIVE COSMO BACK HIS SKAFANDR KOSMICHESKIY!
SWEET!
OOOP GEEZ!
KANG? THAT'S *KANG!*

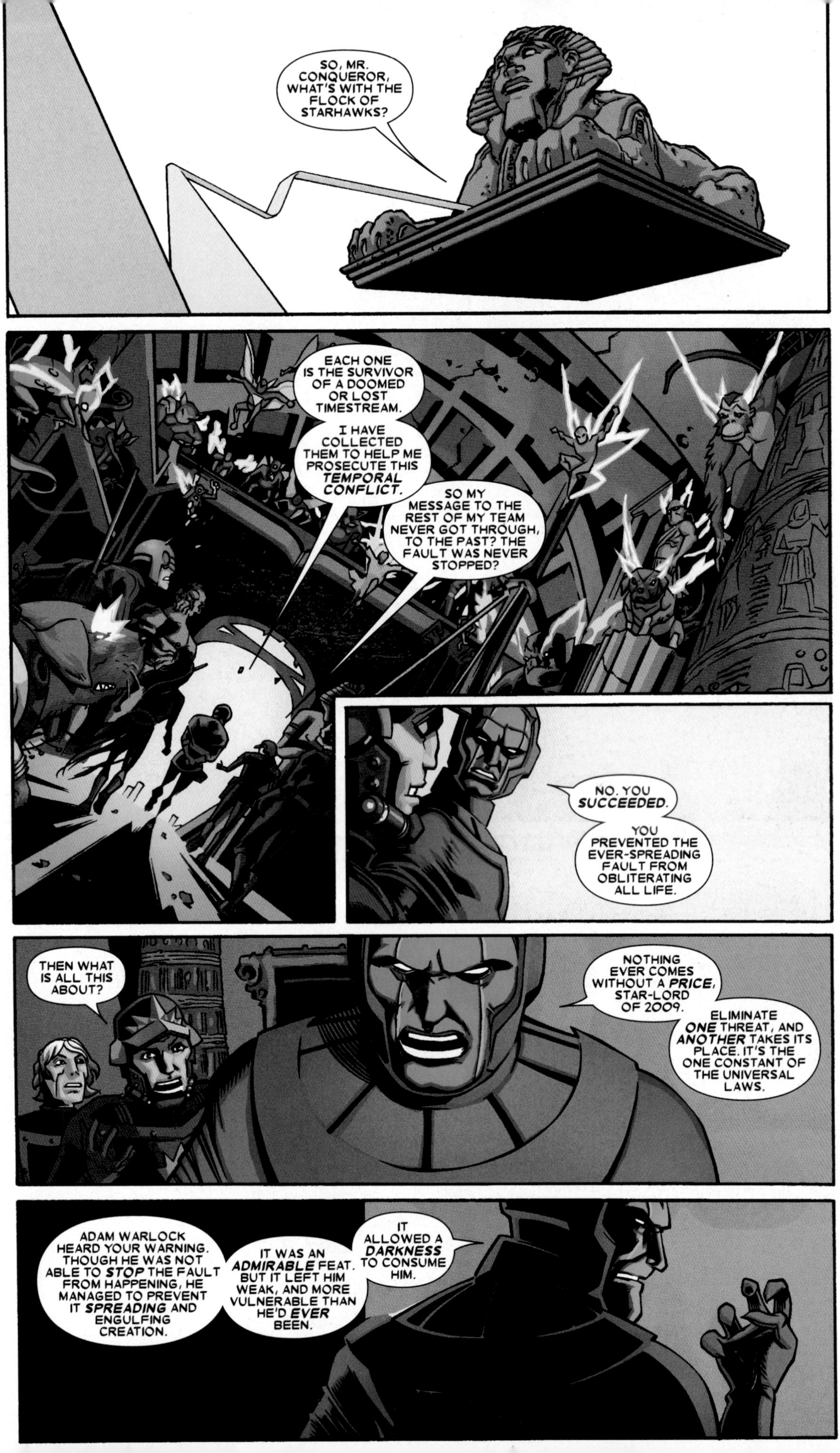
SO, MR. CONQUEROR, WHAT'S WITH THE FLOCK OF STARHAWKS?
EACH ONE IS THE SURVIVOR OF A DOOMED OR LOST TIMESTREAM.
I HAVE COLLECTED THEM TO HELP ME PROSECUTE THIS *TEMPORAL CONFLICT*.
SO MY MESSAGE TO THE REST OF MY TEAM NEVER GOT THROUGH, TO THE PAST? THE FAULT WAS NEVER STOPPED?
NO. YOU *SUCCEEDED*.
YOU PREVENTED THE EVER-SPREADING FAULT FROM OBLITERATING ALL LIFE.
THEN WHAT IS ALL THIS ABOUT?
NOTHING EVER COMES WITHOUT A *PRICE*, STAR-LORD OF 2009.
ELIMINATE *ONE* THREAT, AND *ANOTHER* TAKES ITS PLACE. IT'S THE ONE CONSTANT OF THE UNIVERSAL LAWS.
ADAM WARLOCK HEARD YOUR WARNING. THOUGH HE WAS NOT ABLE TO *STOP* THE FAULT FROM HAPPENING, HE MANAGED TO PREVENT IT *SPREADING* AND ENGULFING CREATION.
IT WAS AN *ADMIRABLE* FEAT. BUT IT LEFT HIM WEAK, AND MORE VULNERABLE THAN HE'D *EVER* BEEN.
IT ALLOWED A *DARKNESS* TO CONSUME HIM.

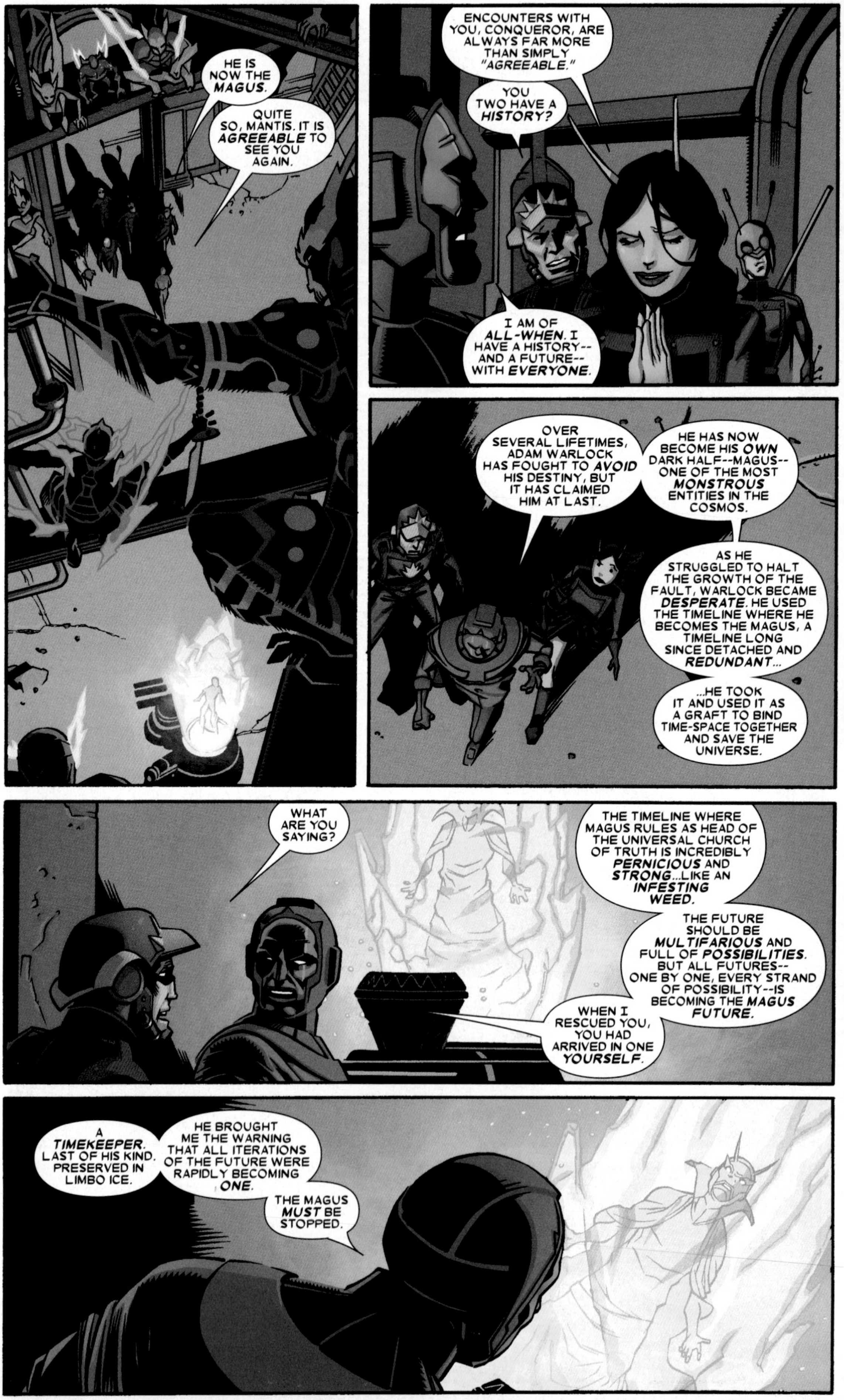
HE IS NOW THE MAGUS.
QUITE SO, MANTIS. IT IS AGREEABLE TO SEE YOU AGAIN.
ENCOUNTERS WITH YOU, CONQUEROR, ARE ALWAYS FAR MORE THAN SIMPLY "AGREEABLE."
YOU TWO HAVE A HISTORY?
I AM OF ALL-WHEN. I HAVE A HISTORY-- AND A FUTURE-- WITH EVERYONE.
OVER SEVERAL LIFETIMES, ADAM WARLOCK HAS FOUGHT TO AVOID HIS DESTINY, BUT IT HAS CLAIMED HIM AT LAST.
HE HAS NOW BECOME HIS OWN DARK HALF--MAGUS-- ONE OF THE MOST MONSTROUS ENTITIES IN THE COSMOS.
AS HE STRUGGLED TO HALT THE GROWTH OF THE FAULT, WARLOCK BECAME DESPERATE. HE USED THE TIMELINE WHERE HE BECOMES THE MAGUS, A TIMELINE LONG SINCE DETACHED AND REDUNDANT...
...HE TOOK IT AND USED IT AS A GRAFT TO BIND TIME-SPACE TOGETHER AND SAVE THE UNIVERSE.
WHAT ARE YOU SAYING?
THE TIMELINE WHERE MAGUS RULES AS HEAD OF THE UNIVERSAL CHURCH OF TRUTH IS INCREDIBLY PERNICIOUS AND STRONG...LIKE AN INFESTING WEED.
THE FUTURE SHOULD BE MULTIFARIOUS AND FULL OF POSSIBILITIES. BUT ALL FUTURES-- ONE BY ONE, EVERY STRAND OF POSSIBILITY--IS BECOMING THE MAGUS FUTURE.
WHEN I RESCUED YOU, YOU HAD ARRIVED IN ONE YOURSELF.
A TIMEKEEPER. LAST OF HIS KIND. PRESERVED IN LIMBO ICE.
HE BROUGHT ME THE WARNING THAT ALL ITERATIONS OF THE FUTURE WERE RAPIDLY BECOMING ONE.
THE MAGUS MUST BE STOPPED.

MAGUS CONTROLS SO *MUCH* OF THE TIME-STREAM THAT IF I MOVE *DIRECTLY* AGAINST HIM, HE WILL SEE ME COMING.

BUT YOU ARE *ANOMALIES*, UNTETHERED IN TIME. I INTEND TO SEND YOU BACK, *THROUGH* HIS DEFENSES, TO THE POINT OF HIS CREATION.

TO DO *WHAT?*

STOP HIM WITH *THIS.*

A *COSMIC CUBE!*

THE *LAST* ONE. I'VE CALIBRATED IT TO ASSIST YOU.

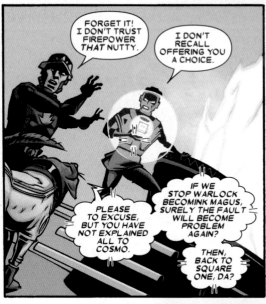

FORGET IT! I DON'T TRUST FIREPOWER *THAT* NUTTY.

I DON'T RECALL OFFERING YOU A CHOICE.

PLEASE TO EXCUSE, BUT YOU HAVE NOT EXPLAINED ALL TO COSMO.

IF WE STOP WARLOCK BECOMINK MAGUS, SURELY THE FAULT WILL BECOME PROBLEM AGAIN?

THEN, BACK TO SQUARE ONE, DA?

I HAVE CALCULATED THAT THERE IS A VERY SMALL WINDOW OF OPPORTUNITY...JUST A MATTER OF *SECONDS.*

WARLOCK SEALS THE FAULT. LESS THAN A MINUTE LATER, HE *BECOMES* THE MAGUS.

THAT IS WHEN YOU STRIKE.

AND DO WHAT? LIKE PETER ASK, WHAT ARE YOU *SUGGESTINK* WE DO?

WHATEVER IT TAKES TO SAVE THE UNIVERSE.

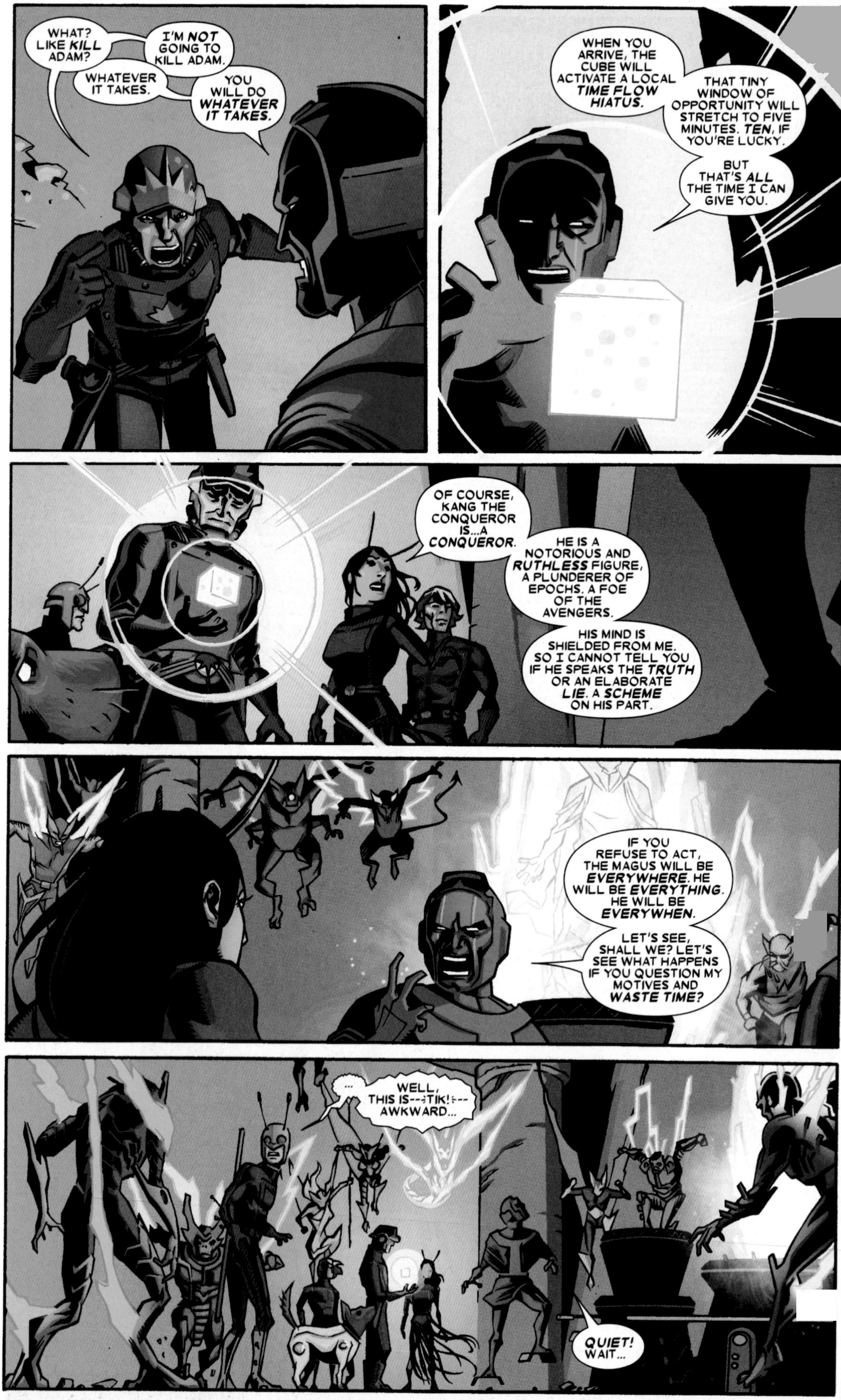

WHAT? LIKE KILL ADAM?
I'M NOT GOING TO KILL ADAM.
WHATEVER IT TAKES.
YOU WILL DO WHATEVER IT TAKES.
WHEN YOU ARRIVE, THE CUBE WILL ACTIVATE A LOCAL TIME FLOW HIATUS.
THAT TINY WINDOW OF OPPORTUNITY WILL STRETCH TO FIVE MINUTES. TEN, IF YOU'RE LUCKY.
BUT THAT'S ALL THE TIME I CAN GIVE YOU.
OF COURSE, KANG THE CONQUEROR IS...A CONQUEROR.
HE IS A NOTORIOUS AND RUTHLESS FIGURE, A PLUNDERER OF EPOCHS. A FOE OF THE AVENGERS.
HIS MIND IS SHIELDED FROM ME. SO I CANNOT TELL YOU IF HE SPEAKS THE TRUTH OR AN ELABORATE LIE. A SCHEME ON HIS PART.
IF YOU REFUSE TO ACT, THE MAGUS WILL BE EVERYWHERE. HE WILL BE EVERYTHING. HE WILL BE EVERYWHEN.
LET'S SEE, SHALL WE? LET'S SEE WHAT HAPPENS IF YOU QUESTION MY MOTIVES AND WASTE TIME?
...
WELL, THIS IS--TIK!--AWKWARD...
QUIET! WAIT...

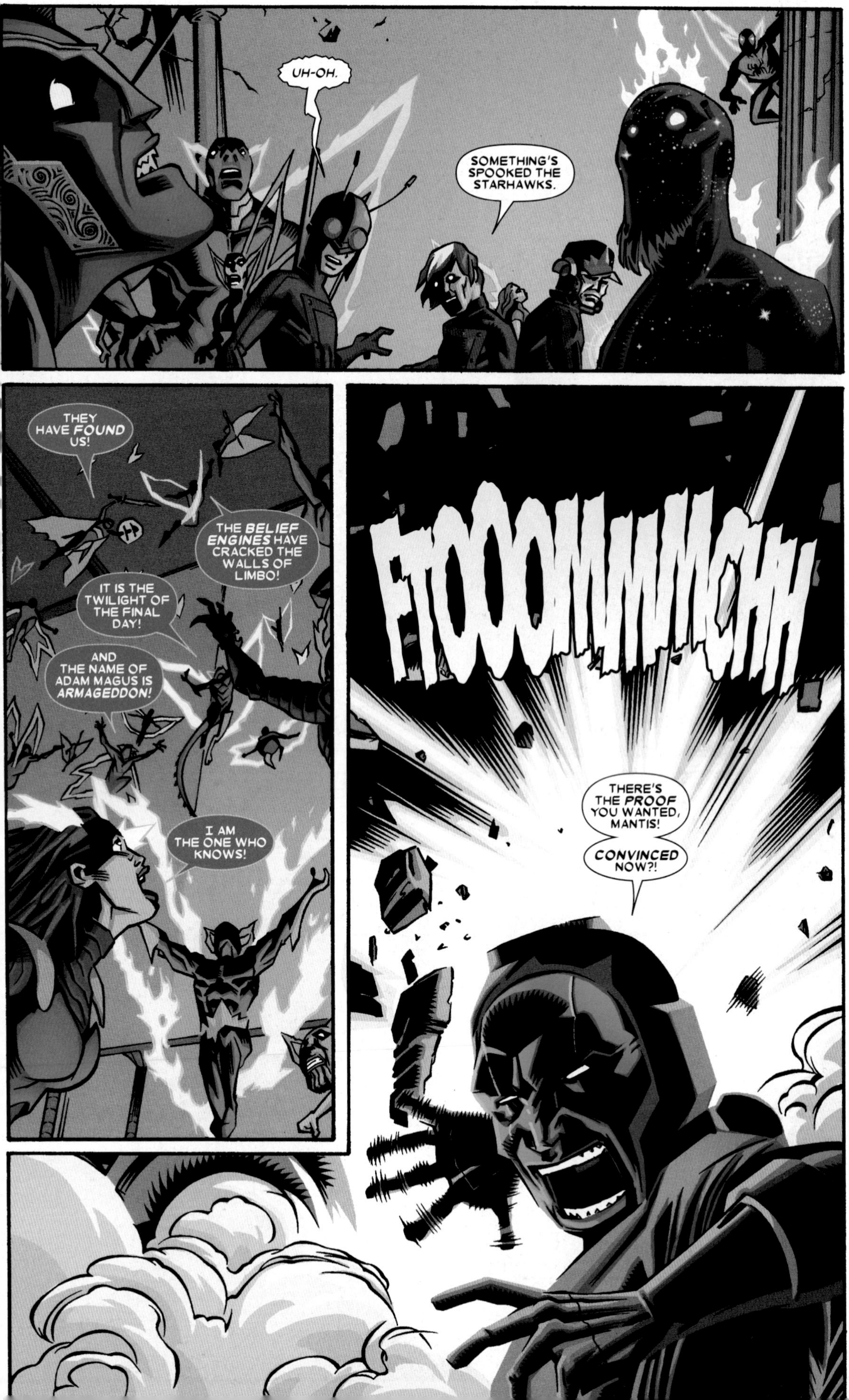
UH-OH.
SOMETHING'S SPOOKED THE STARHAWKS.
THEY HAVE FOUND US!
THE BELIEF ENGINES HAVE CRACKED THE WALLS OF LIMBO!
IT IS THE TWILIGHT OF THE FINAL DAY!
AND THE NAME OF ADAM MAGUS IS ARMAGEDDON!
I AM THE ONE WHO KNOWS!
FTOOOMMMCHH
THERE'S THE PROOF YOU WANTED, MANTIS!
CONVINCED NOW?!

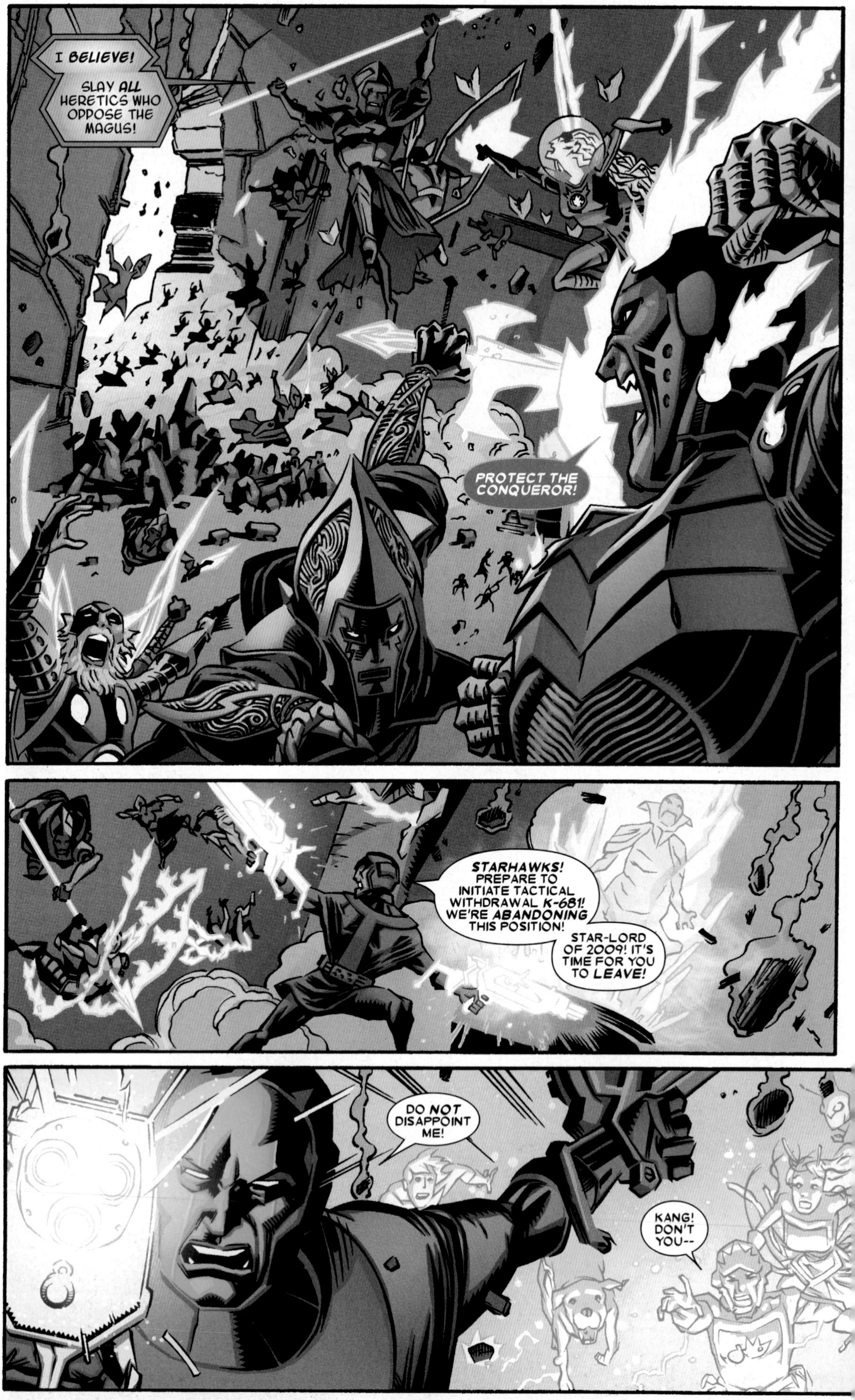

I BELIEVE!
SLAY ALL HERETICS WHO OPPOSE THE MAGUS!
PROTECT THE CONQUEROR!
STARHAWKS! PREPARE TO INITIATE TACTICAL WITHDRAWAL K-681! WE'RE ABANDONING THIS POSITION!
STAR-LORD OF 2009! IT'S TIME FOR YOU TO LEAVE!
DO NOT DISAPPOINT ME!
KANG! DON'T YOU--

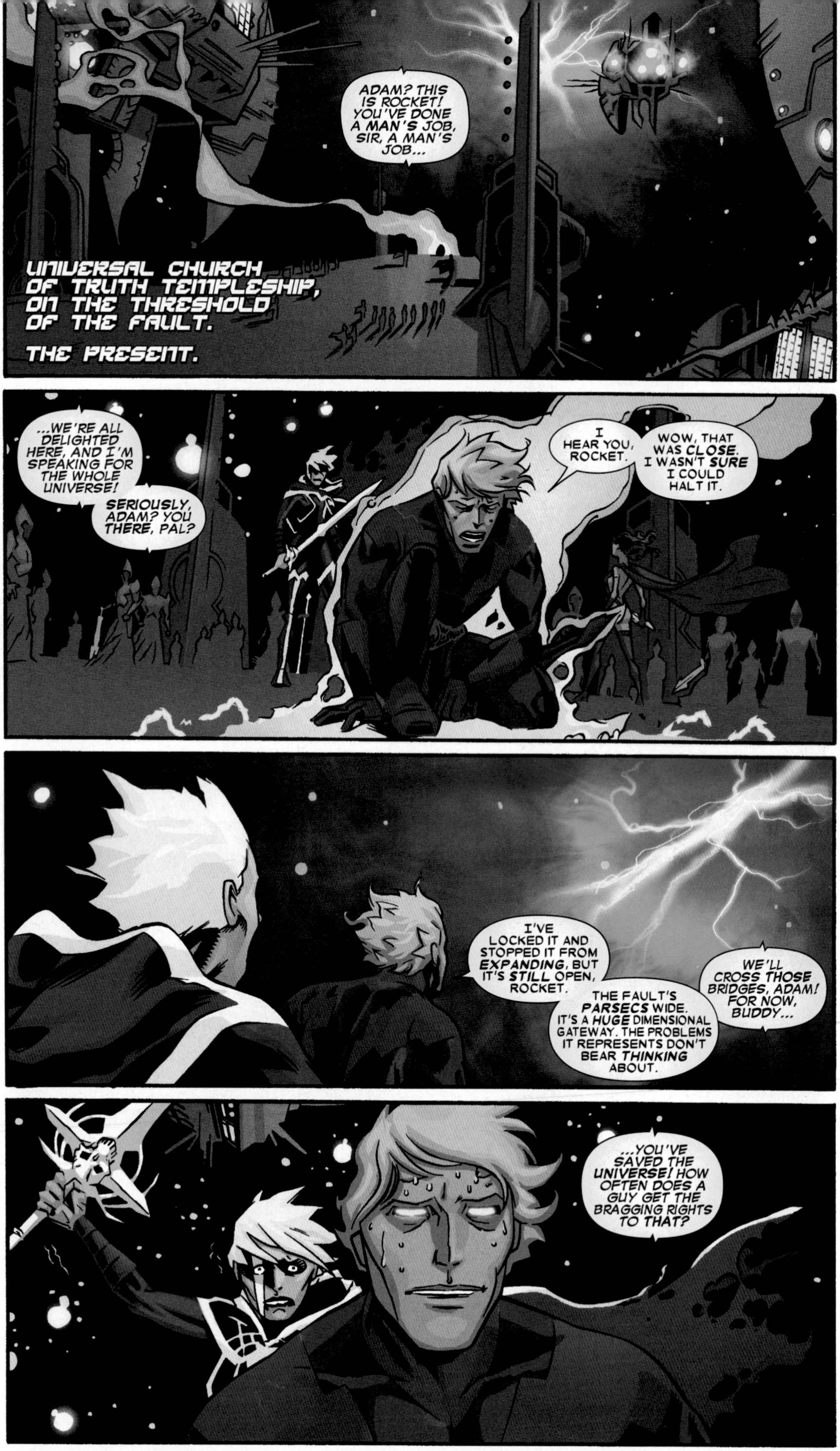

UNIVERSAL CHURCH OF TRUTH TEMPLESHIP, ON THE THRESHOLD OF THE FAULT.
THE PRESENT.
ADAM? THIS IS ROCKET! YOU'VE DONE A MAN'S JOB, SIR, A MAN'S JOB...
...WE'RE ALL DELIGHTED HERE, AND I'M SPEAKING FOR THE WHOLE UNIVERSE!
SERIOUSLY, ADAM? YOU THERE, PAL?
I HEAR YOU, ROCKET.
WOW, THAT WAS CLOSE. I WASN'T SURE I COULD HALT IT.
I'VE LOCKED IT AND STOPPED IT FROM EXPANDING, BUT IT'S STILL OPEN, ROCKET.
THE FAULT'S PARSECS WIDE. IT'S A HUGE DIMENSIONAL GATEWAY. THE PROBLEMS IT REPRESENTS DON'T BEAR THINKING ABOUT.
WE'LL CROSS THOSE BRIDGES, ADAM! FOR NOW, BUDDY...
...YOU'VE SAVED THE UNIVERSE! HOW OFTEN DOES A GUY GET THE BRAGGING RIGHTS TO THAT?

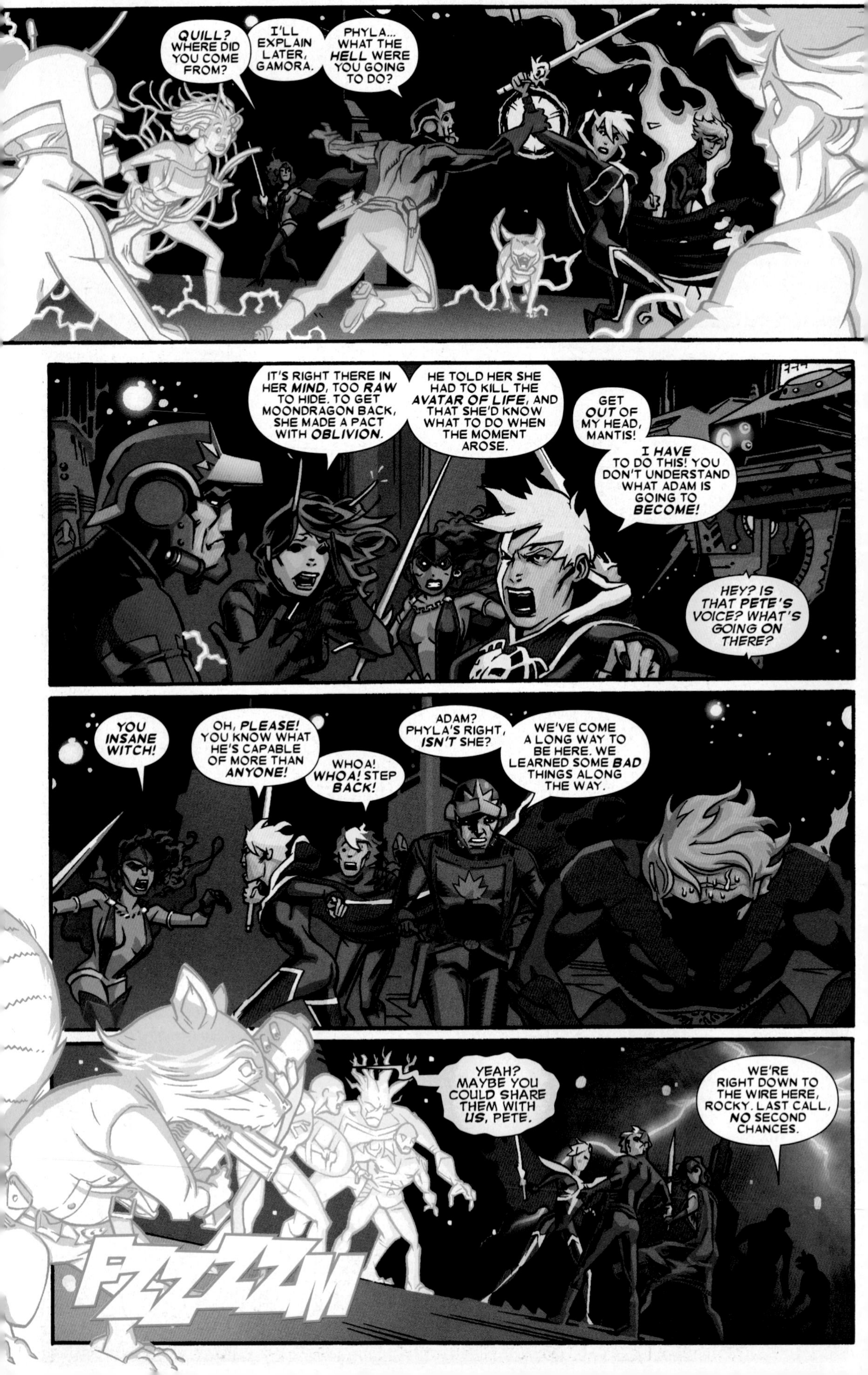
QUILL? WHERE DID YOU COME FROM?
I'LL EXPLAIN LATER, GAMORA.
PHYLA... WHAT THE HELL WERE YOU GOING TO DO?
IT'S RIGHT THERE IN HER MIND, TOO RAW TO HIDE. TO GET MOONDRAGON BACK, SHE MADE A PACT WITH OBLIVION.
HE TOLD HER SHE HAD TO KILL THE AVATAR OF LIFE, AND THAT SHE'D KNOW WHAT TO DO WHEN THE MOMENT AROSE.
GET OUT OF MY HEAD, MANTIS!
I HAVE TO DO THIS! YOU DON'T UNDERSTAND WHAT ADAM IS GOING TO BECOME!
HEY? IS THAT PETE'S VOICE? WHAT'S GOING ON THERE?
YOU INSANE WITCH!
OH, PLEASE! YOU KNOW WHAT HE'S CAPABLE OF MORE THAN ANYONE!
WHOA! WHOA! STEP BACK!
ADAM? PHYLA'S RIGHT, ISN'T SHE?
WE'VE COME A LONG WAY TO BE HERE. WE LEARNED SOME BAD THINGS ALONG THE WAY.
YEAH? MAYBE YOU COULD SHARE THEM WITH US, PETE.
WE'RE RIGHT DOWN TO THE WIRE HERE, ROCKY. LAST CALL, NO SECOND CHANCES.
FZZZZM

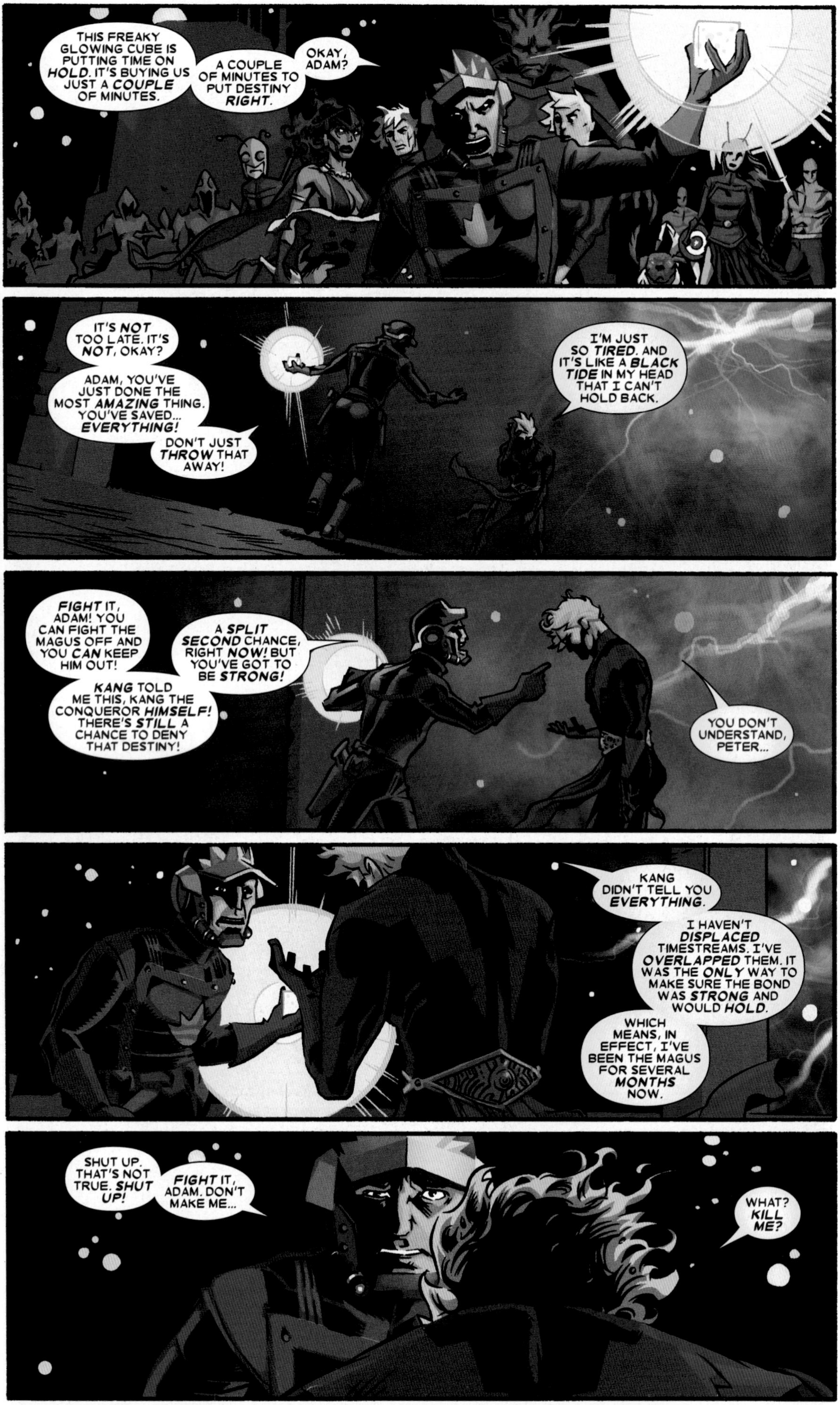
THIS FREAKY GLOWING CUBE IS PUTTING TIME ON HOLD. IT'S BUYING US JUST A COUPLE OF MINUTES.
A COUPLE OF MINUTES TO PUT DESTINY RIGHT.
OKAY, ADAM?
IT'S NOT TOO LATE. IT'S NOT, OKAY?
ADAM, YOU'VE JUST DONE THE MOST AMAZING THING. YOU'VE SAVED... EVERYTHING!
DON'T JUST THROW THAT AWAY!
I'M JUST SO TIRED. AND IT'S LIKE A BLACK TIDE IN MY HEAD THAT I CAN'T HOLD BACK.
FIGHT IT, ADAM! YOU CAN FIGHT THE MAGUS OFF AND YOU CAN KEEP HIM OUT!
A SPLIT SECOND CHANCE, RIGHT NOW! BUT YOU'VE GOT TO BE STRONG!
KANG TOLD ME THIS, KANG THE CONQUEROR HIMSELF! THERE'S STILL A CHANCE TO DENY THAT DESTINY!
YOU DON'T UNDERSTAND, PETER...
KANG DIDN'T TELL YOU EVERYTHING.
I HAVEN'T DISPLACED TIMESTREAMS. I'VE OVERLAPPED THEM. IT WAS THE ONLY WAY TO MAKE SURE THE BOND WAS STRONG AND WOULD HOLD.
WHICH MEANS, IN EFFECT, I'VE BEEN THE MAGUS FOR SEVERAL MONTHS NOW.
SHUT UP. THAT'S NOT TRUE. SHUT UP!
FIGHT IT, ADAM. DON'T MAKE ME...
WHAT? KILL ME?

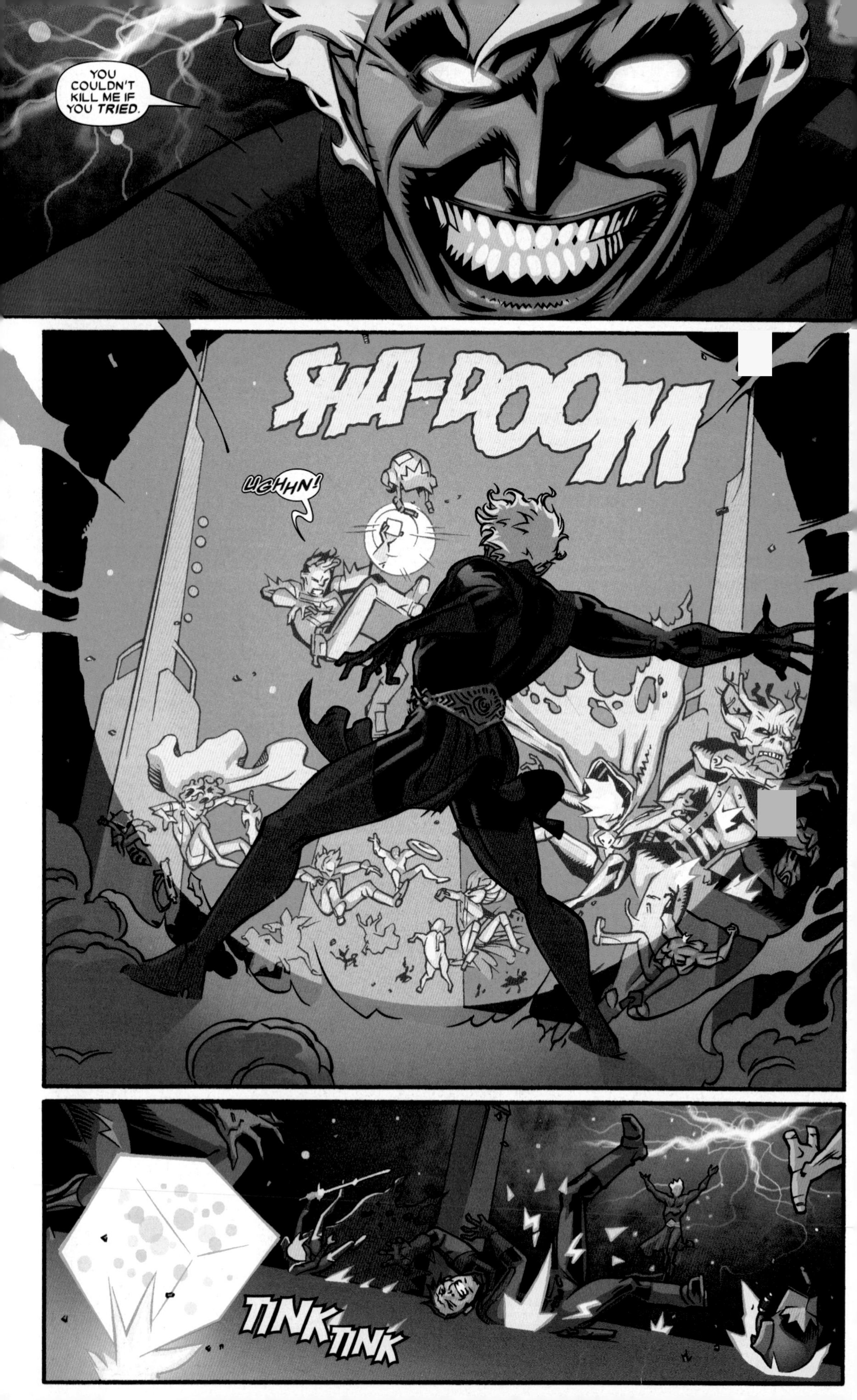
YOU COULDN'T KILL ME IF YOU TRIED.
SHA-DOOM
UGHHN!
TINK TINK

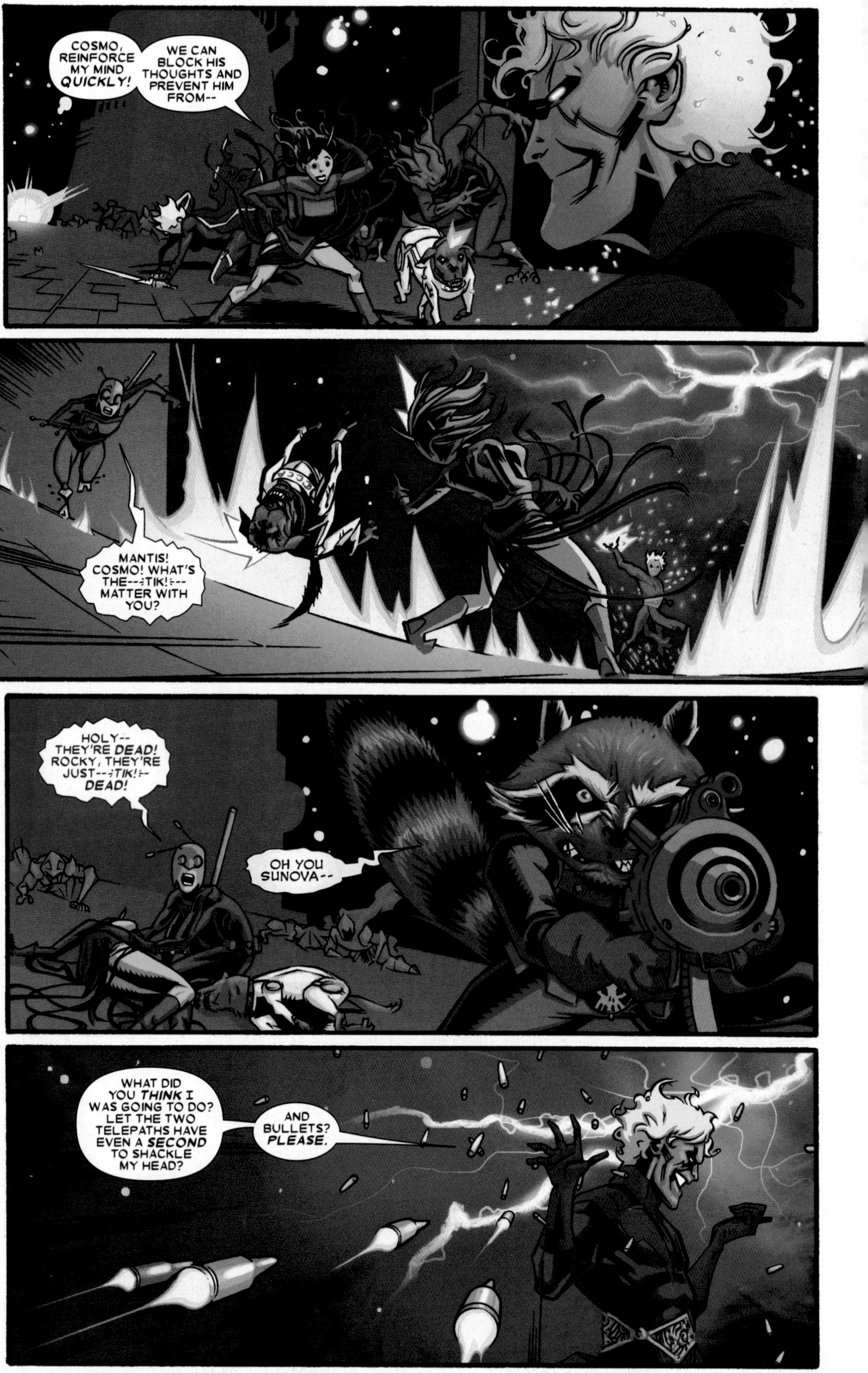

COSMO, REINFORCE MY MIND *QUICKLY!*
WE CAN BLOCK HIS THOUGHTS AND PREVENT HIM FROM--
MANTIS! COSMO! WHAT'S THE--*TIK!*--MATTER WITH YOU?
HOLY--THEY'RE *DEAD!* ROCKY, THEY'RE JUST--*TIK!*--*DEAD!*
OH YOU SUNOVA--
WHAT DID YOU *THINK* I WAS GOING TO DO? LET THE TWO TELEPATHS HAVE EVEN A *SECOND* TO SHACKLE MY HEAD?
AND BULLETS? *PLEASE.*

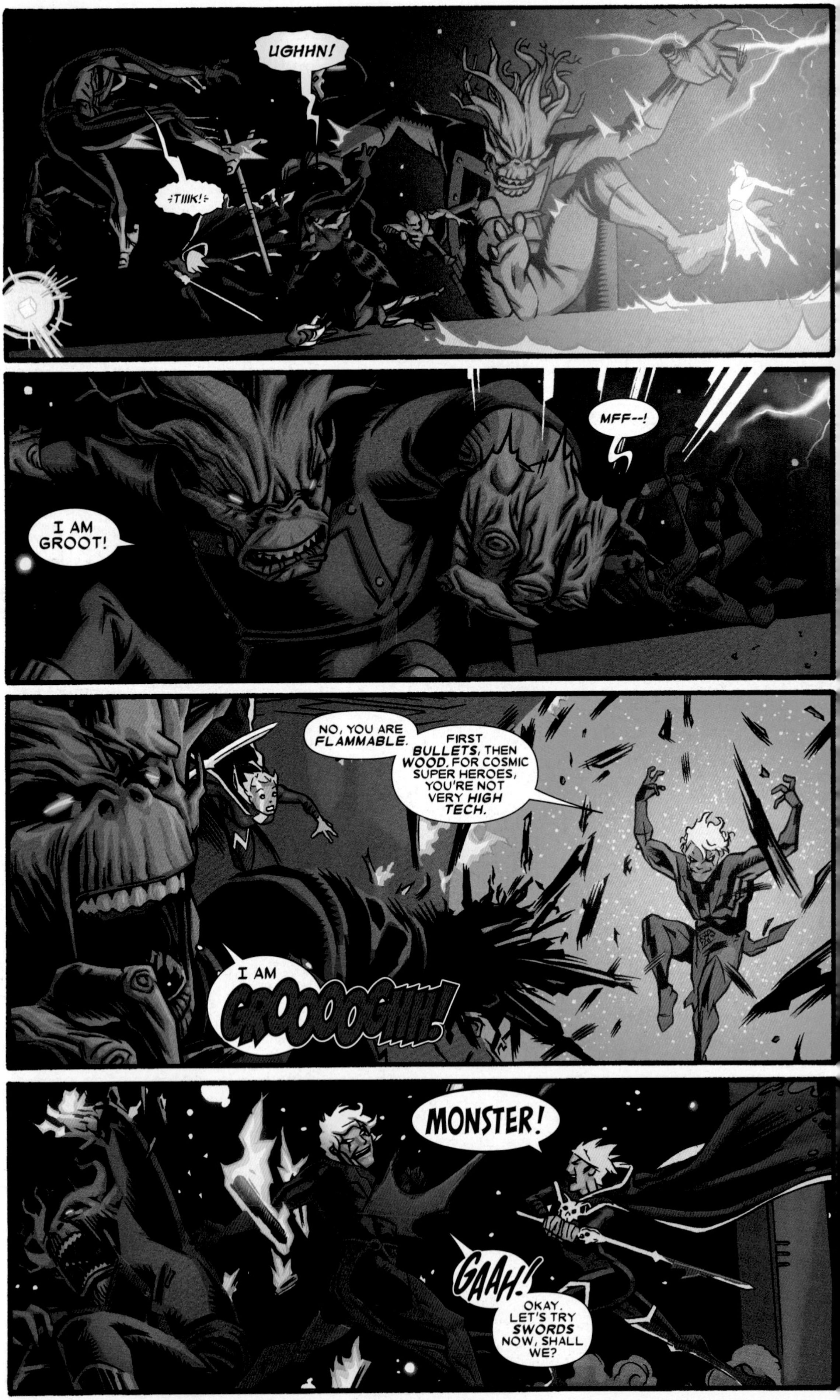
UGHHN!
=TIIIK!=
MFF--!
I AM GROOT!
NO, YOU ARE FLAMMABLE.
FIRST BULLETS, THEN WOOD. FOR COSMIC SUPER HEROES, YOU'RE NOT VERY HIGH TECH.
I AM GROOOOOGHH!
MONSTER!
GAAH!
OKAY. LET'S TRY SWORDS NOW, SHALL WE?

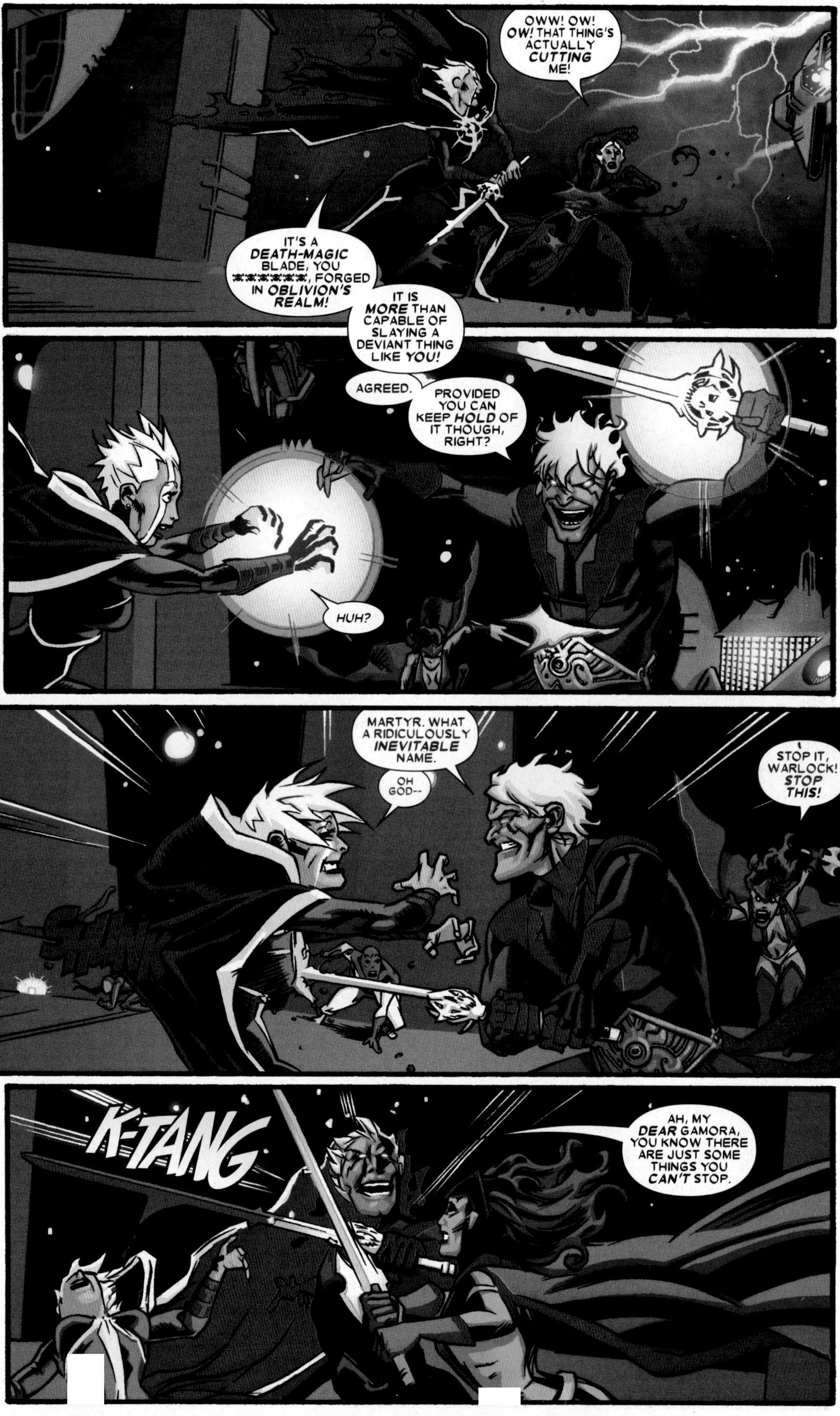
OWW! OW! OW! THAT THING'S ACTUALLY CUTTING ME!
IT'S A DEATH-MAGIC BLADE, YOU ※※※※※※, FORGED IN OBLIVION'S REALM!
IT IS MORE THAN CAPABLE OF SLAYING A DEVIANT THING LIKE YOU!
AGREED.
PROVIDED YOU CAN KEEP HOLD OF IT THOUGH, RIGHT?
HUH?
MARTYR. WHAT A RIDICULOUSLY INEVITABLE NAME.
OH GOD--
STOP IT, WARLOCK! STOP THIS!
K-TANG
AH, MY DEAR GAMORA, YOU KNOW THERE ARE JUST SOME THINGS YOU CAN'T STOP.

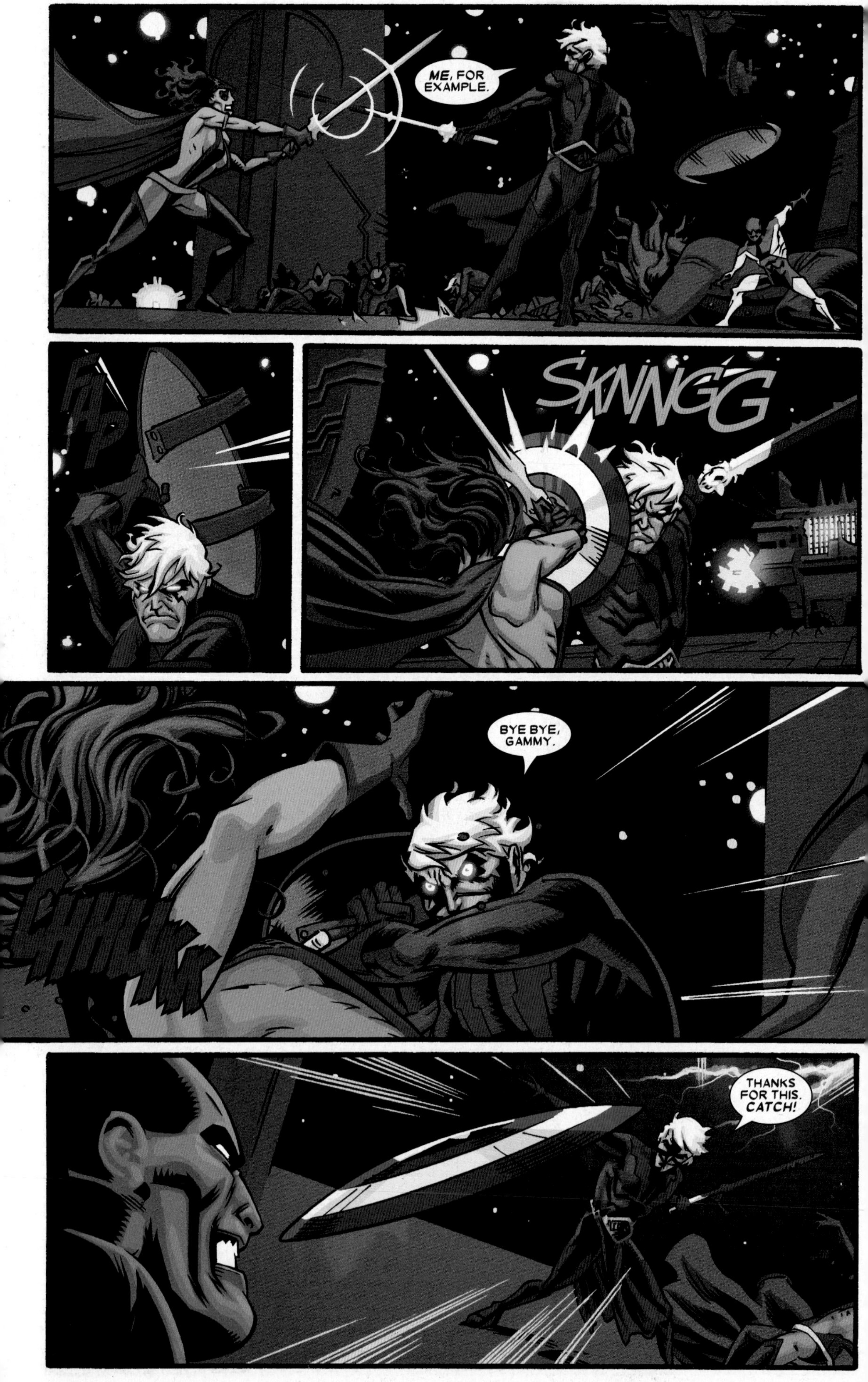
ME, FOR EXAMPLE.
SKNNGG
BYE BYE, GAMMY.
THANKS FOR THIS. CATCH!

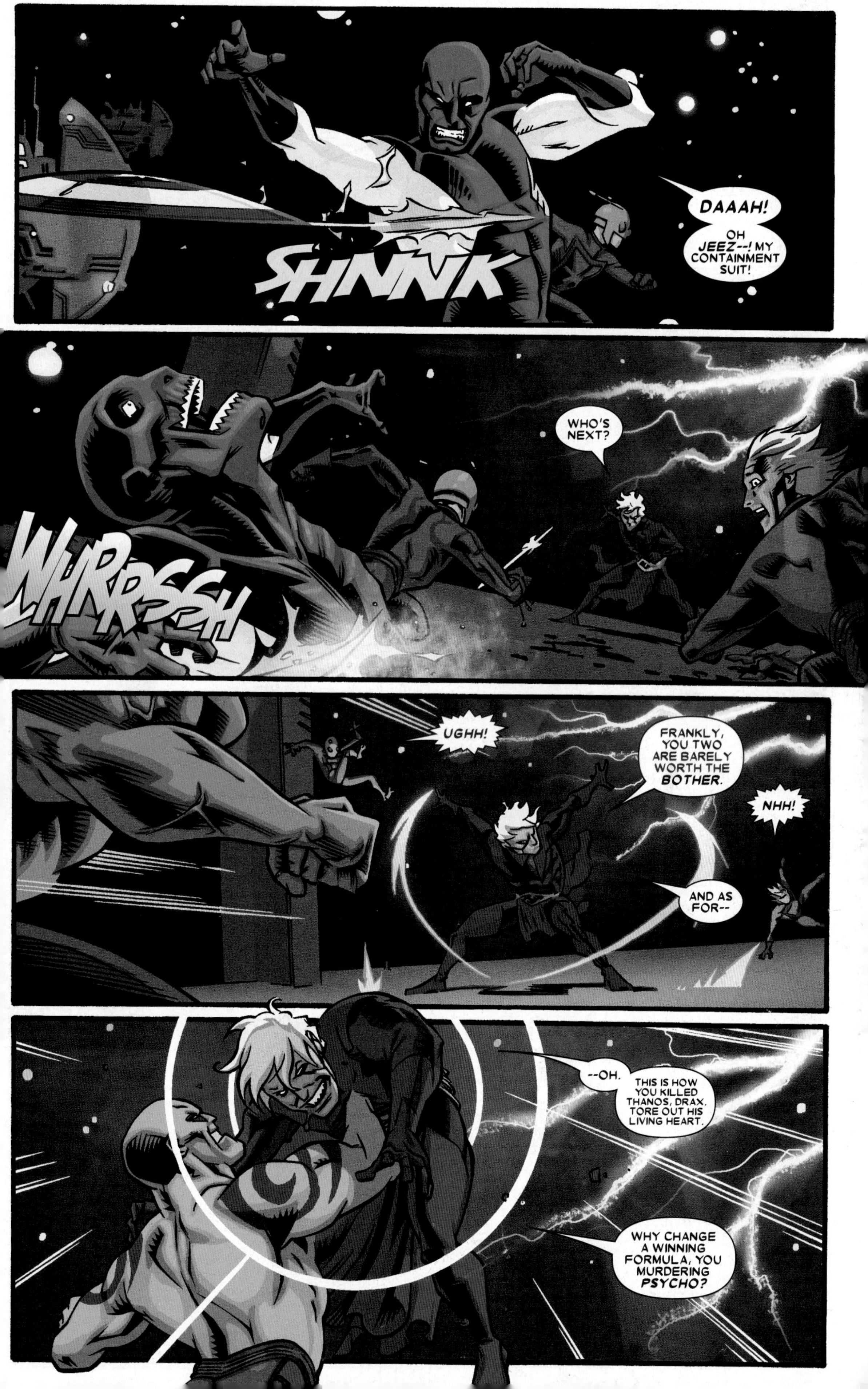
SHNNK
DAAAH!
OH JEEZ--! MY CONTAINMENT SUIT!
WHARRSSH
WHO'S NEXT?
UGHH!
FRANKLY, YOU TWO ARE BARELY WORTH THE BOTHER.
NHH!
AND AS FOR--
--OH.
THIS IS HOW YOU KILLED THANOS, DRAX. TORE OUT HIS LIVING HEART.
WHY CHANGE A WINNING FORMULA, YOU MURDERING PSYCHO?

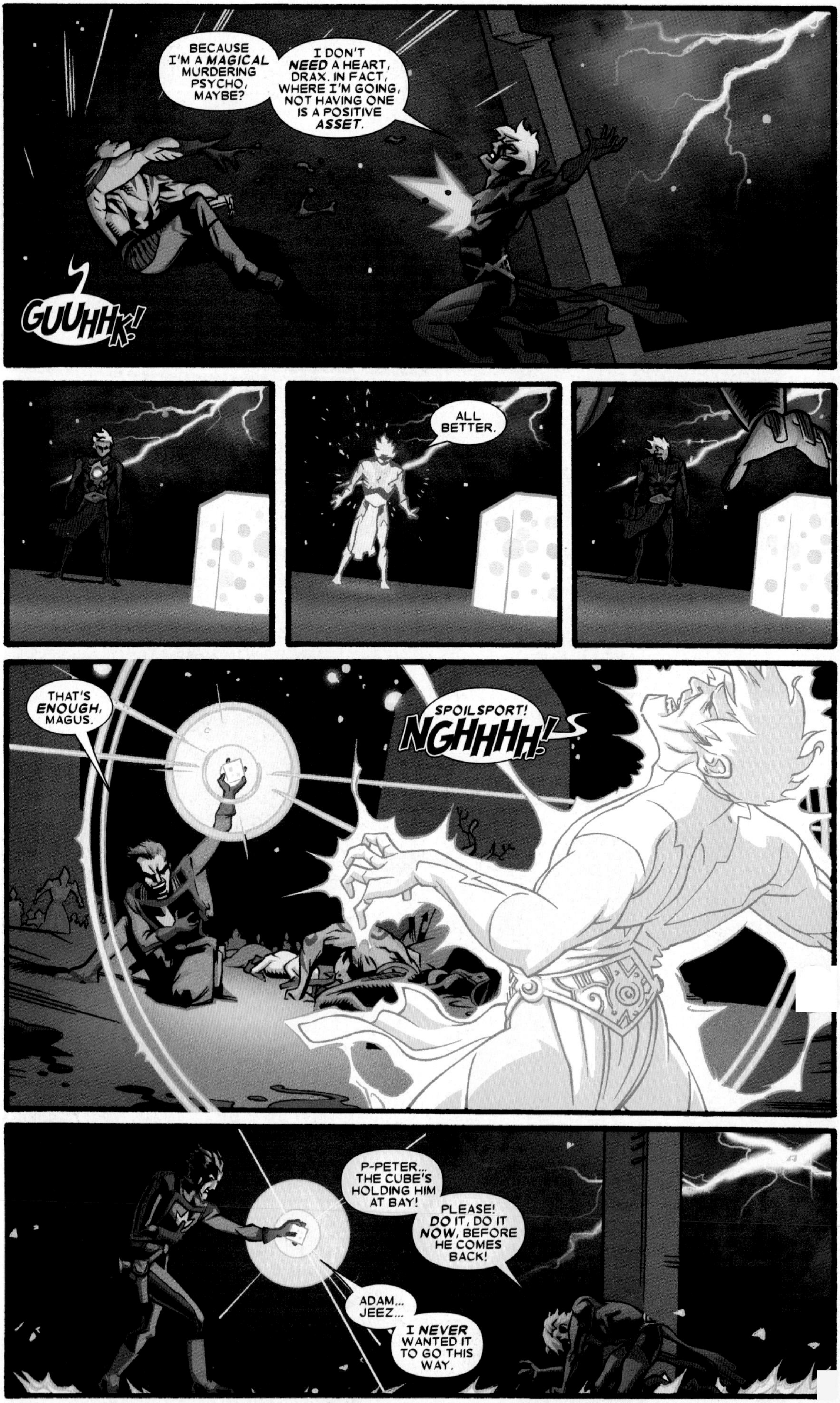
BECAUSE I'M A MAGICAL MURDERING PSYCHO, MAYBE?
I DON'T NEED A HEART, DRAX. IN FACT, WHERE I'M GOING, NOT HAVING ONE IS A POSITIVE ASSET.
GUUHHK!
ALL BETTER.
THAT'S ENOUGH, MAGUS.
SPOILSPORT!
NGHHHH!
P-PETER... THE CUBE'S HOLDING HIM AT BAY!
PLEASE! DO IT, DO IT NOW, BEFORE HE COMES BACK!
ADAM... JEEZ...
I NEVER WANTED IT TO GO THIS WAY.

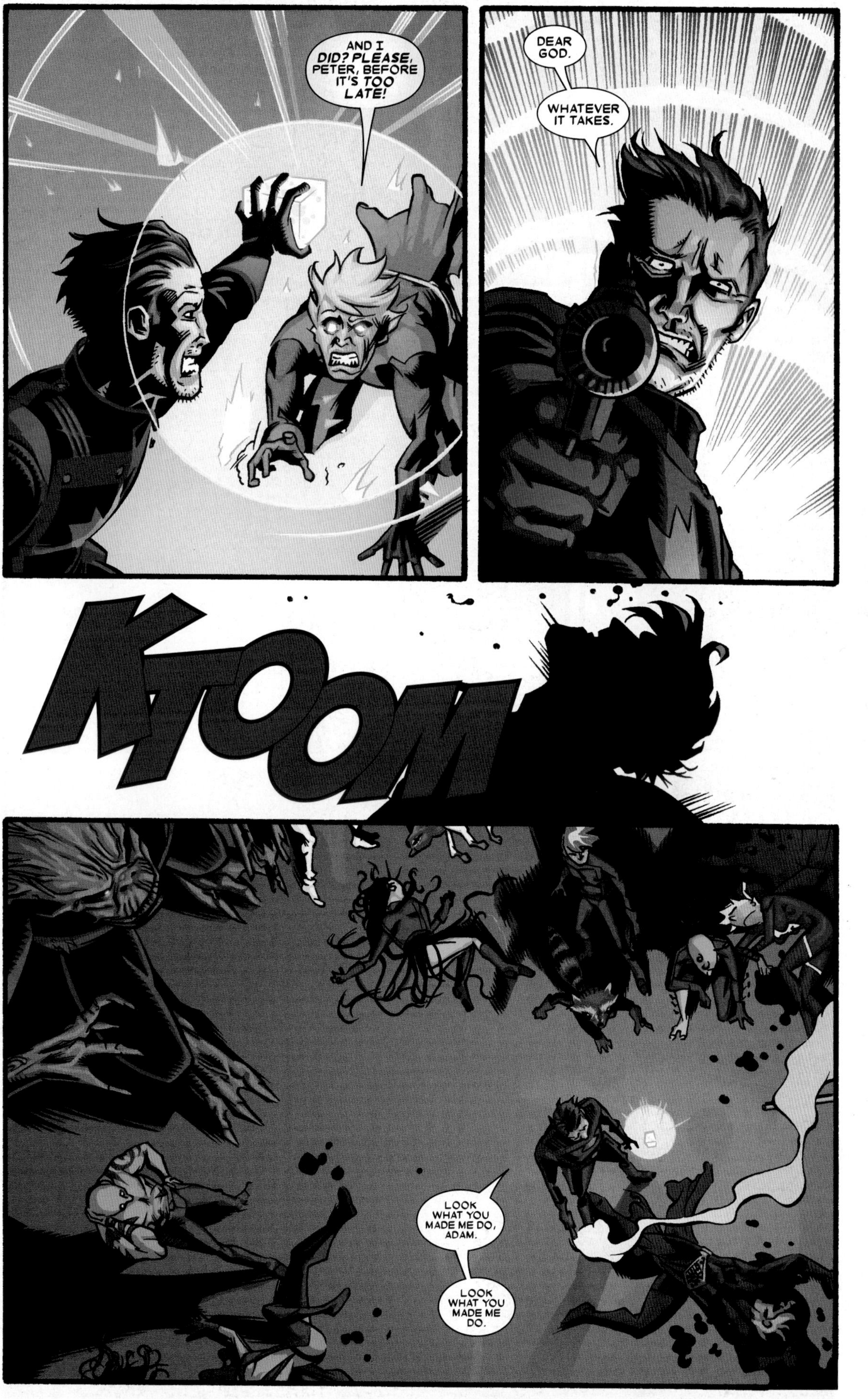
AND I *DID? PLEASE,* PETER, BEFORE IT'S *TOO LATE!*
DEAR GOD.
WHATEVER IT TAKES.
KTOOM
LOOK WHAT YOU MADE ME DO, ADAM.
LOOK WHAT YOU MADE ME DO.

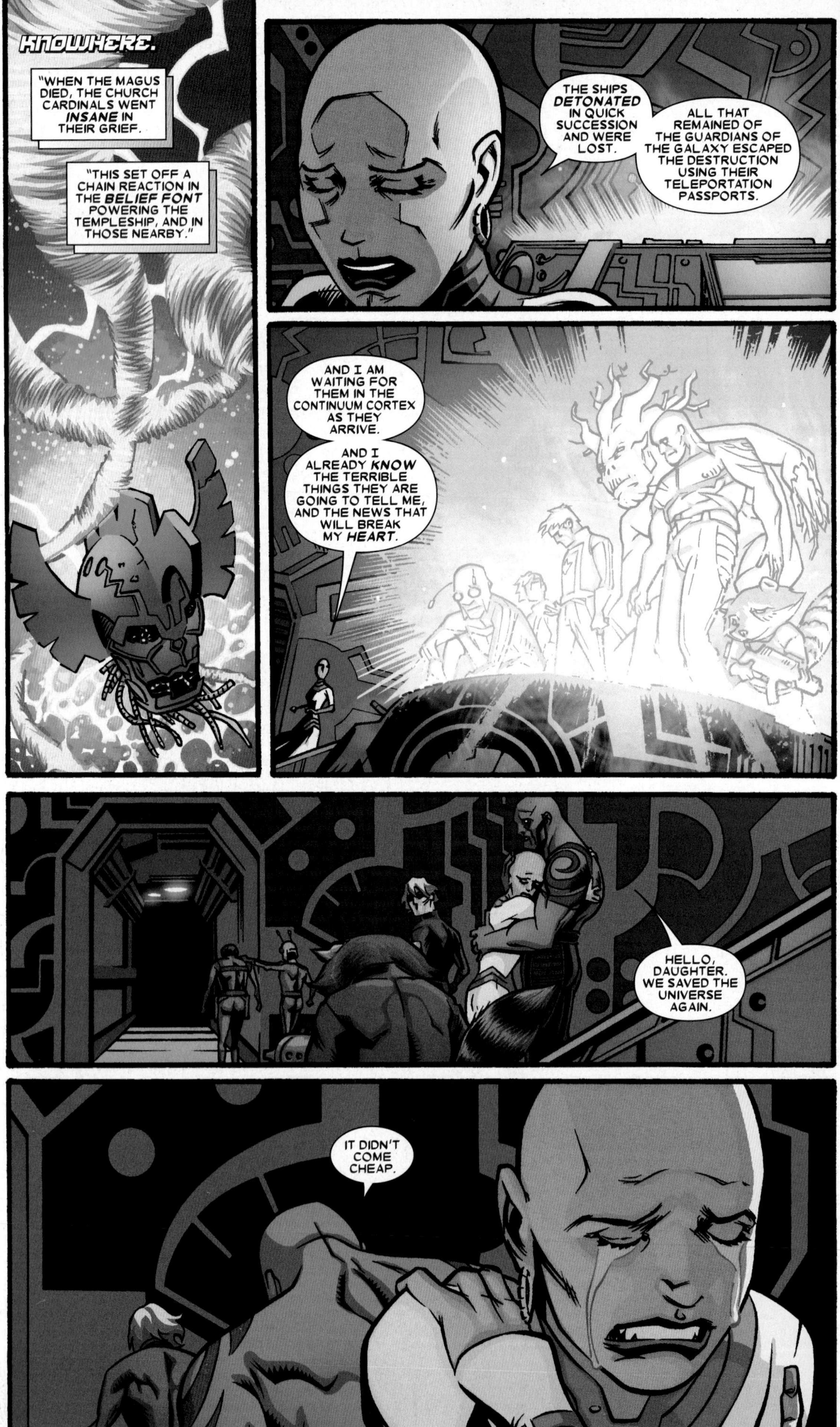
KNOWHERE.
"WHEN THE MAGUS DIED, THE CHURCH CARDINALS WENT INSANE IN THEIR GRIEF.
"THIS SET OFF A CHAIN REACTION IN THE BELIEF FONT POWERING THE TEMPLESHIP, AND IN THOSE NEARBY."
THE SHIPS DETONATED IN QUICK SUCCESSION AND WERE LOST.
ALL THAT REMAINED OF THE GUARDIANS OF THE GALAXY ESCAPED THE DESTRUCTION USING THEIR TELEPORTATION PASSPORTS.
AND I AM WAITING FOR THEM IN THE CONTINUUM CORTEX AS THEY ARRIVE.
AND I ALREADY KNOW THE TERRIBLE THINGS THEY ARE GOING TO TELL ME, AND THE NEWS THAT WILL BREAK MY HEART.
HELLO, DAUGHTER. WE SAVED THE UNIVERSE AGAIN.
IT DIDN'T COME CHEAP.

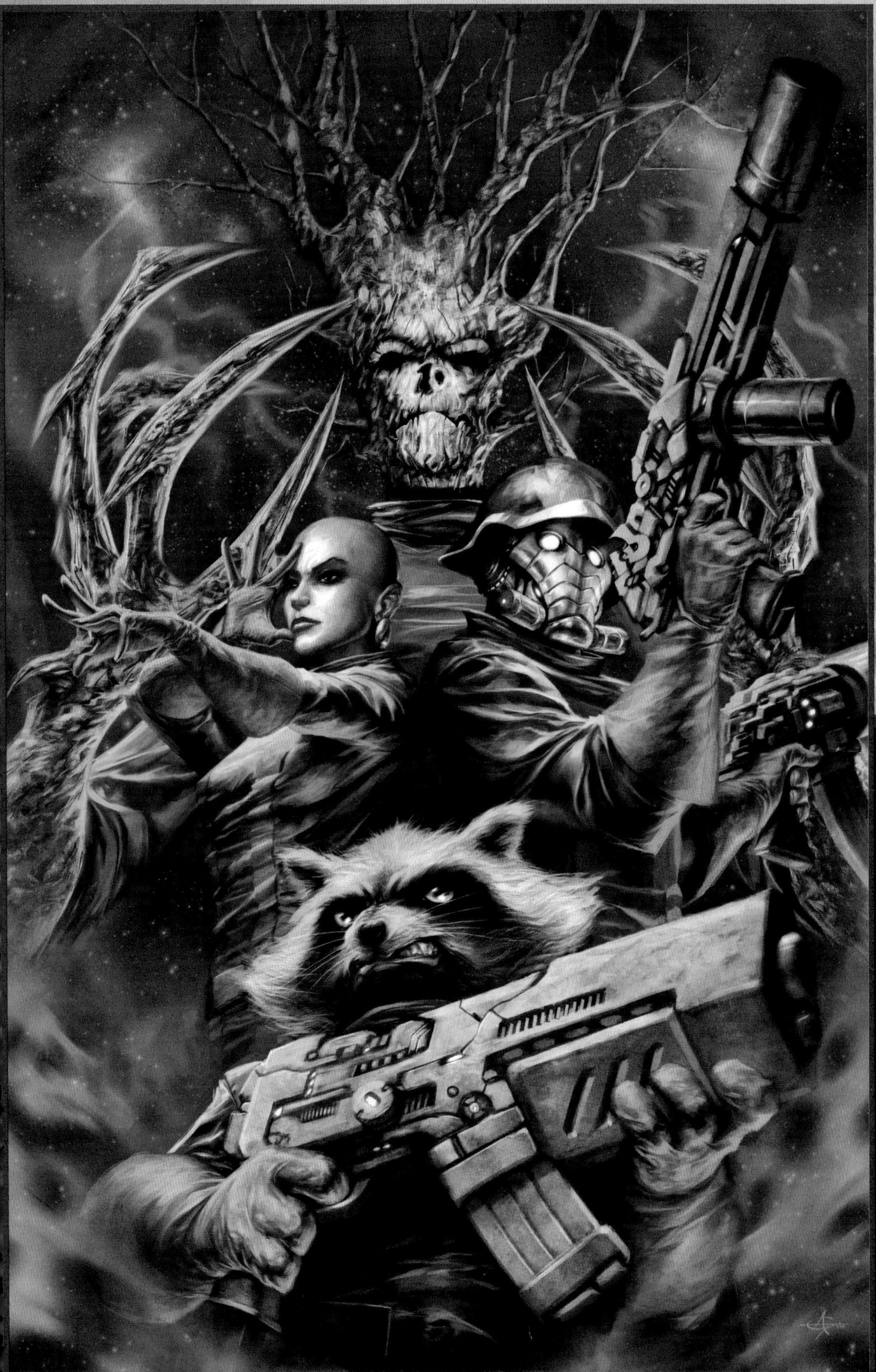

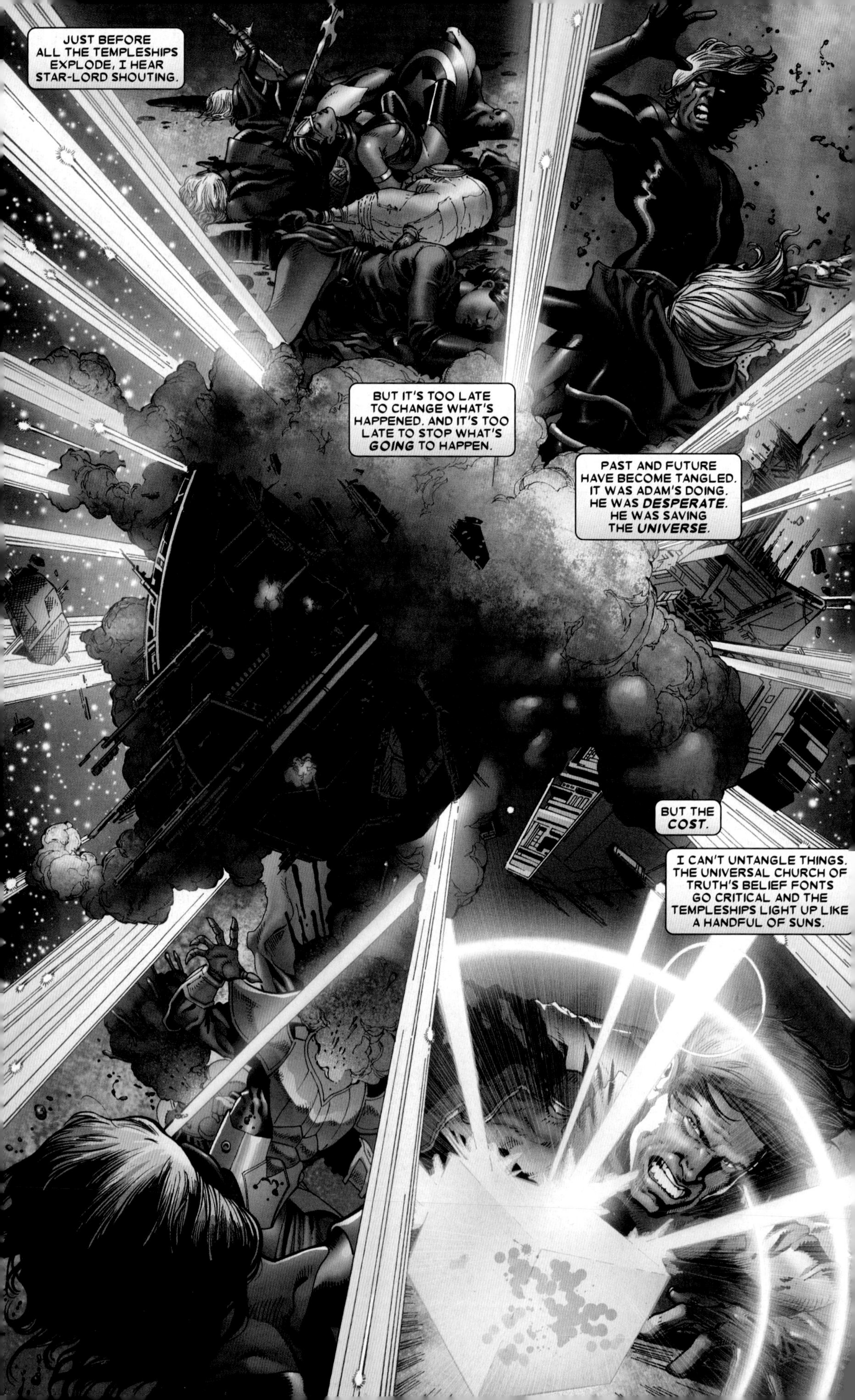
JUST BEFORE ALL THE TEMPLESHIPS EXPLODE, I HEAR STAR-LORD SHOUTING.
BUT IT'S TOO LATE TO CHANGE WHAT'S HAPPENED. AND IT'S TOO LATE TO STOP WHAT'S *GOING* TO HAPPEN.
PAST AND FUTURE HAVE BECOME TANGLED. IT WAS ADAM'S DOING. HE WAS *DESPERATE*. HE WAS SAVING THE *UNIVERSE*.
BUT THE *COST*.
I CAN'T UNTANGLE THINGS. THE UNIVERSAL CHURCH OF TRUTH'S BELIEF FONTS GO CRITICAL AND THE TEMPLESHIPS LIGHT UP LIKE A HANDFUL OF SUNS.

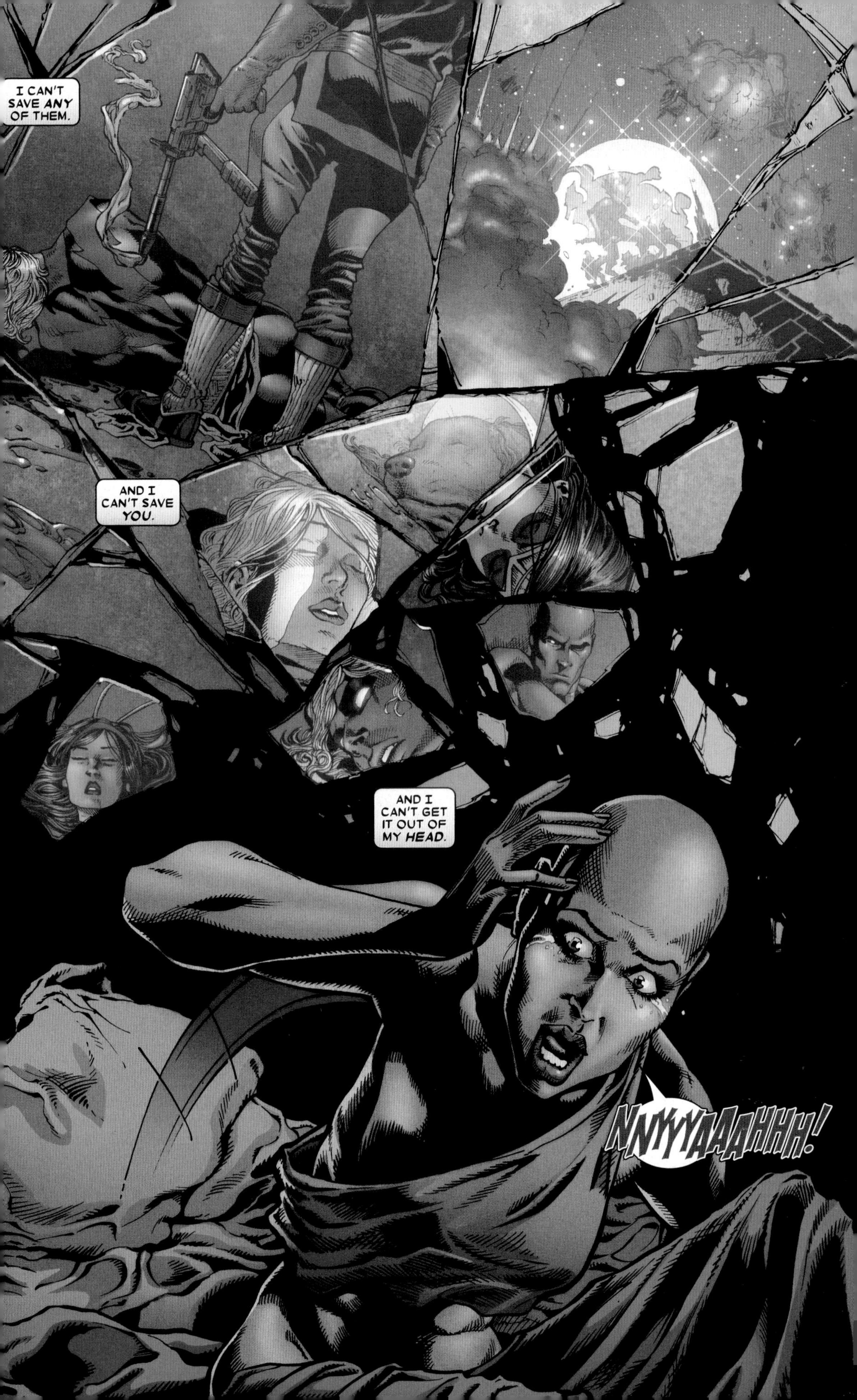
I CAN'T SAVE ANY OF THEM.
AND I CAN'T SAVE YOU.
AND I CAN'T GET IT OUT OF MY HEAD.
NNYYAAAHHH!

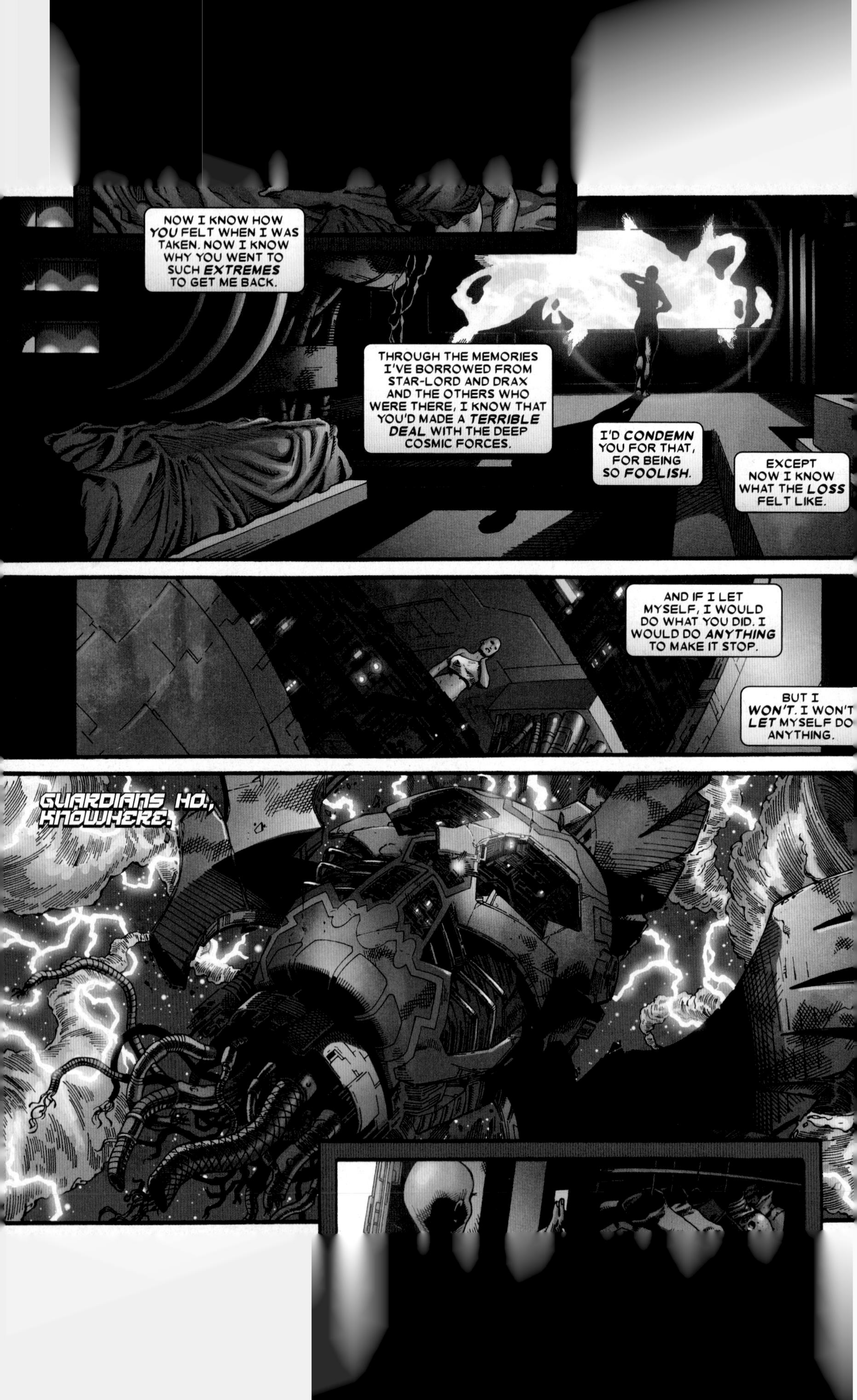
NOW I KNOW HOW YOU FELT WHEN I WAS TAKEN. NOW I KNOW WHY YOU WENT TO SUCH EXTREMES TO GET ME BACK.
THROUGH THE MEMORIES I'VE BORROWED FROM STAR-LORD AND DRAX AND THE OTHERS WHO WERE THERE, I KNOW THAT YOU'D MADE A TERRIBLE DEAL WITH THE DEEP COSMIC FORCES.
I'D CONDEMN YOU FOR THAT, FOR BEING SO FOOLISH.
EXCEPT NOW I KNOW WHAT THE LOSS FELT LIKE.
AND IF I LET MYSELF, I WOULD DO WHAT YOU DID. I WOULD DO ANYTHING TO MAKE IT STOP.
BUT I WON'T. I WON'T LET MYSELF DO ANYTHING.
GUARDIANS HQ., KNOWHERE.

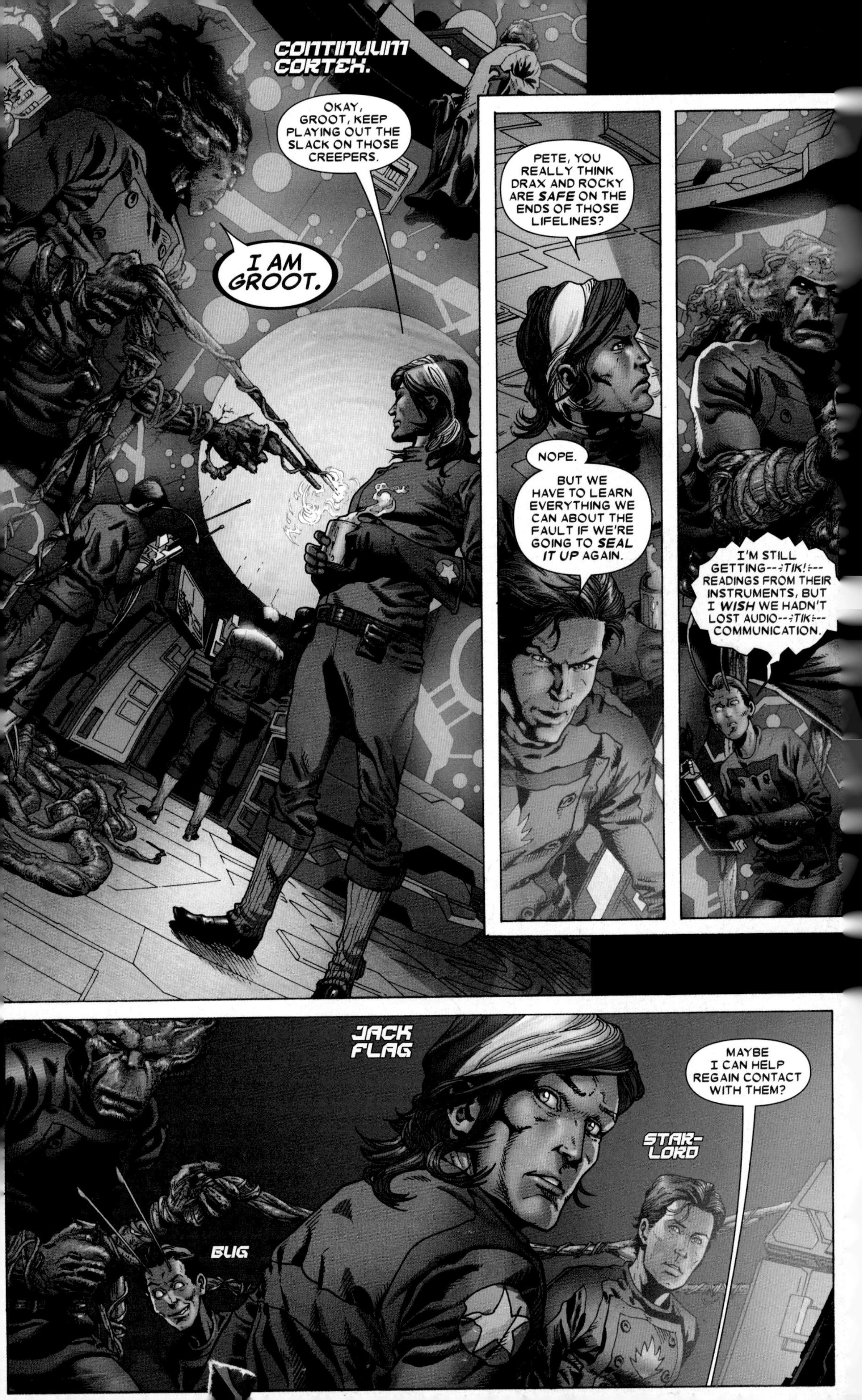
CONTINUUM CORTEX.
OKAY, GROOT, KEEP PLAYING OUT THE SLACK ON THOSE CREEPERS.
I AM GROOT.
PETE, YOU REALLY THINK DRAX AND ROCKY ARE SAFE ON THE ENDS OF THOSE LIFELINES?
NOPE.
BUT WE HAVE TO LEARN EVERYTHING WE CAN ABOUT THE FAULT IF WE'RE GOING TO SEAL IT UP AGAIN.
I'M STILL GETTING--TIK!--READINGS FROM THEIR INSTRUMENTS, BUT I WISH WE HADN'T LOST AUDIO--TIK!--COMMUNICATION.
JACK FLAG
STAR-LORD
BUG
MAYBE I CAN HELP REGAIN CONTACT WITH THEM?

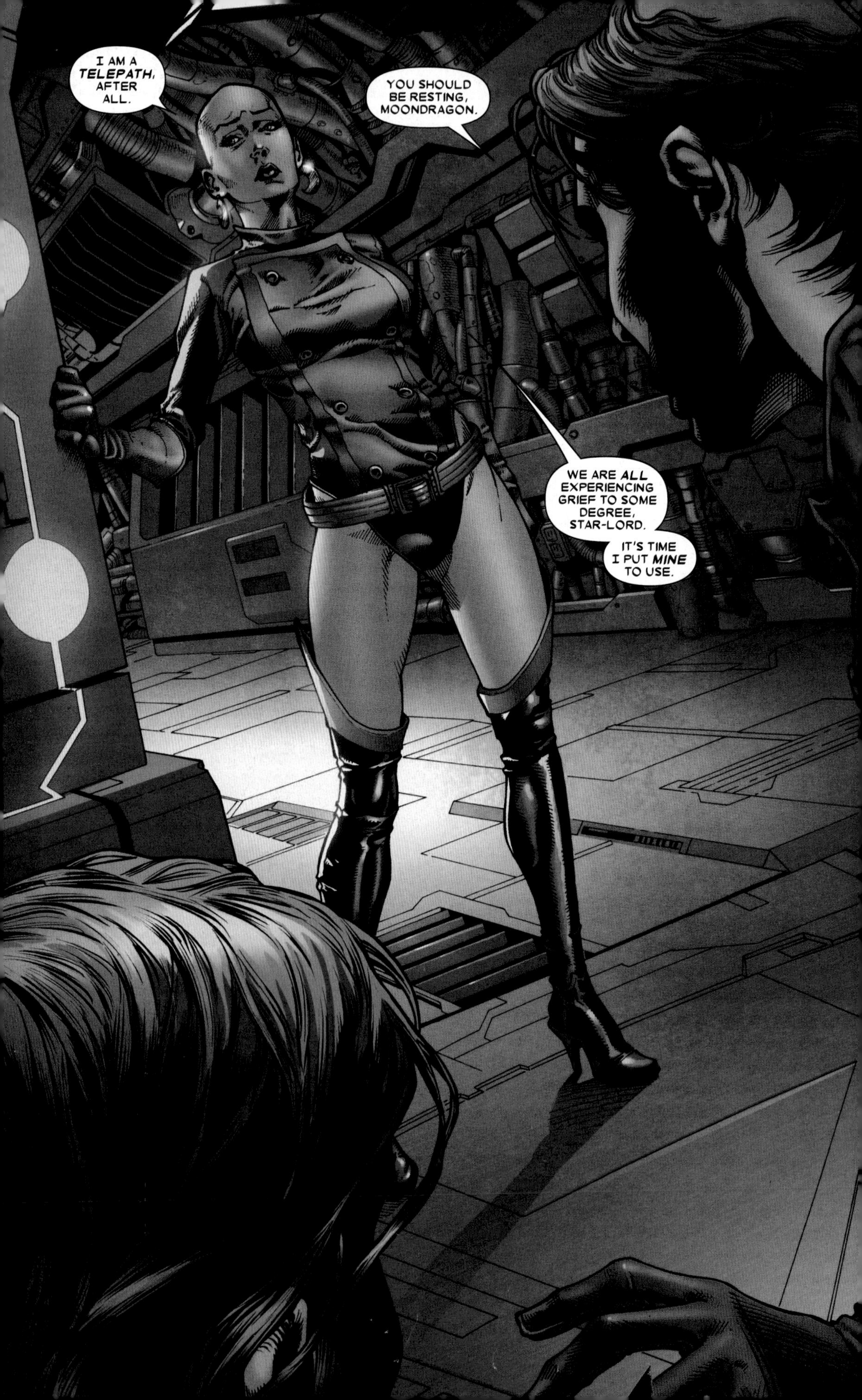
I AM A TELEPATH, AFTER ALL.
YOU SHOULD BE RESTING, MOONDRAGON.
WE ARE ALL EXPERIENCING GRIEF TO SOME DEGREE, STAR-LORD.
IT'S TIME I PUT MINE TO USE.

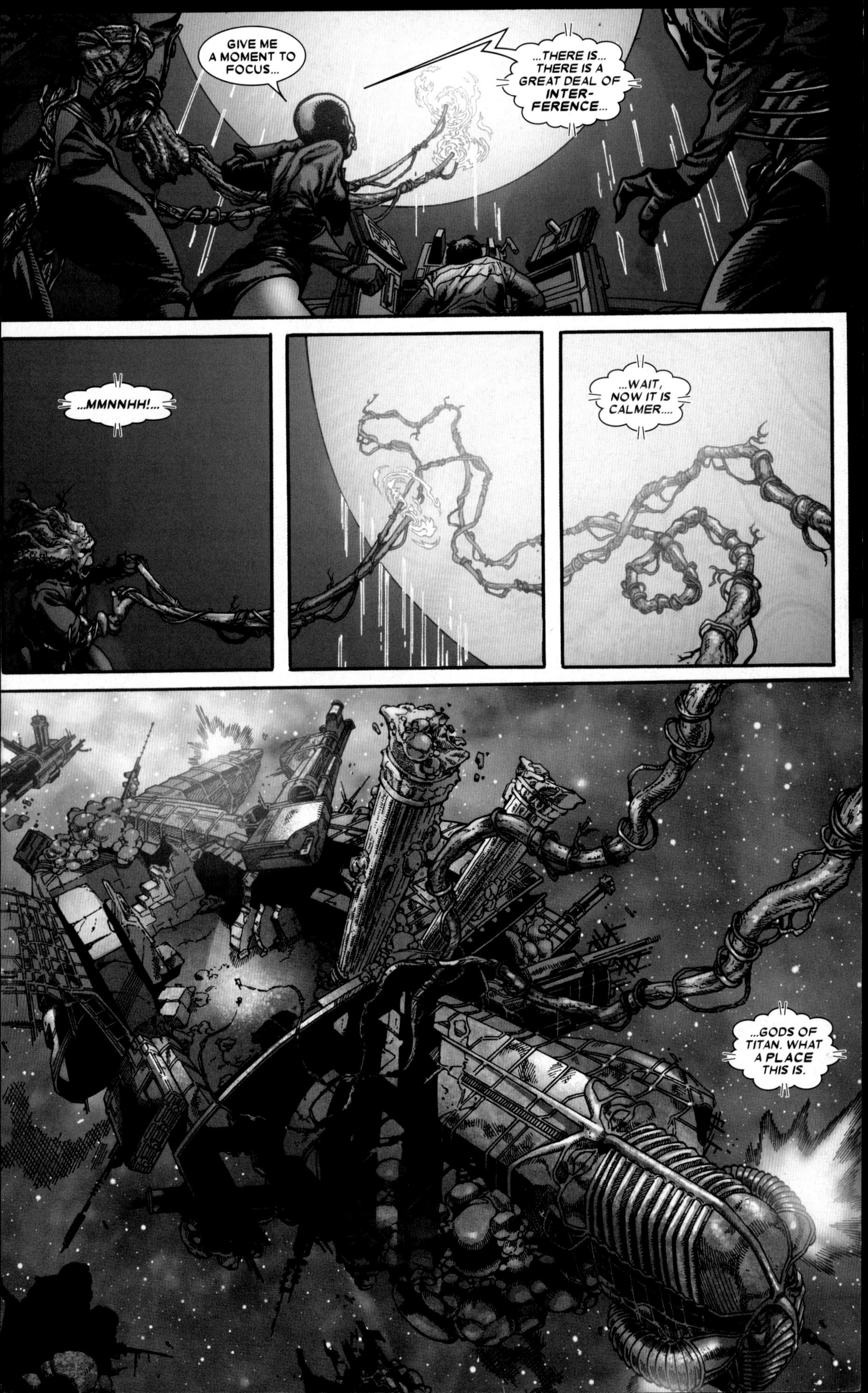
GIVE ME A MOMENT TO FOCUS...
...THERE IS... THERE IS A GREAT DEAL OF INTER-FERENCE...
...MMNNHH!...
...WAIT, NOW IT IS CALMER....
...GODS OF TITAN. WHAT A PLACE THIS IS.

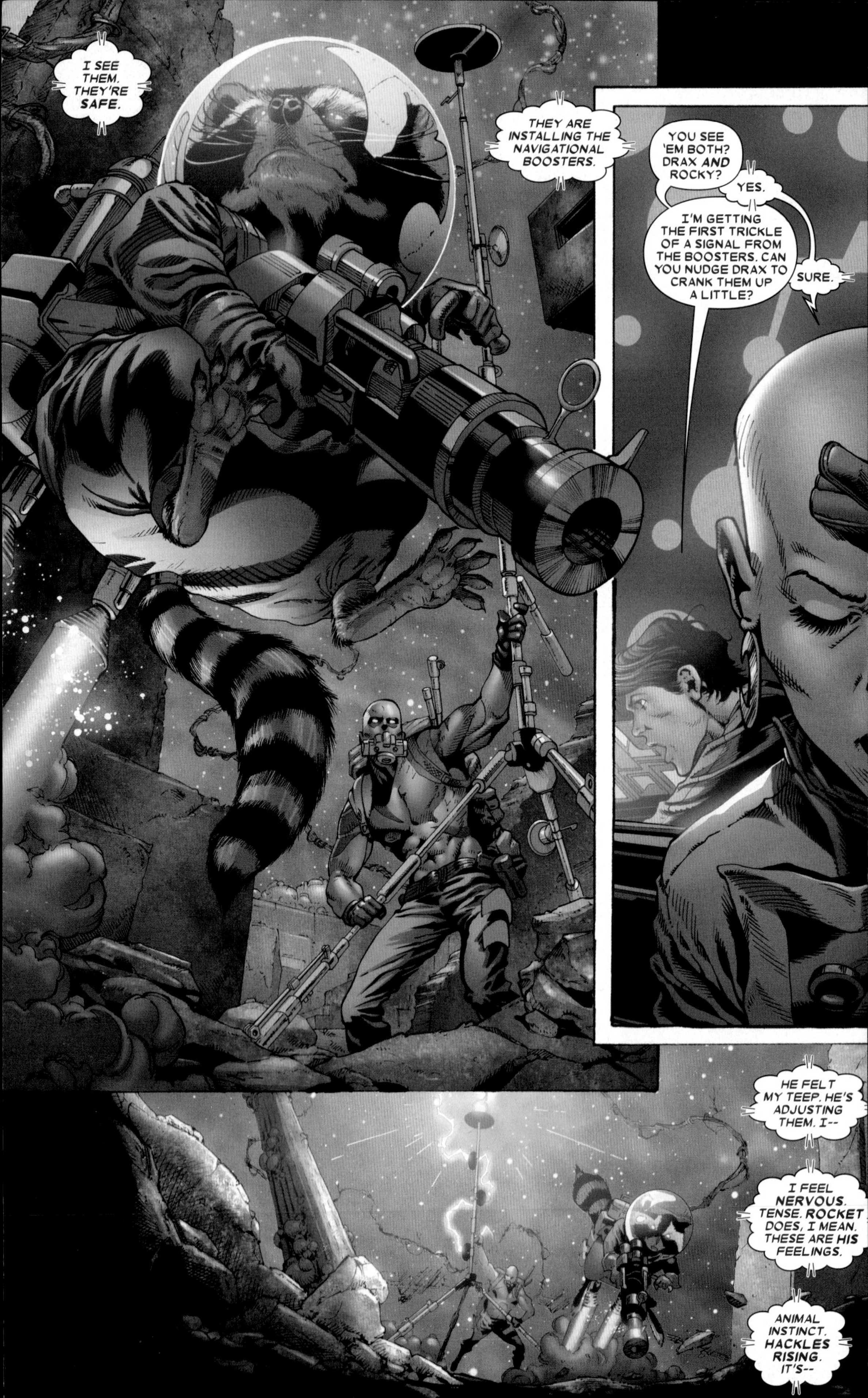
I SEE THEM. THEY'RE SAFE.
THEY ARE INSTALLING THE NAVIGATIONAL BOOSTERS.
YOU SEE 'EM BOTH? DRAX AND ROCKY?
YES.
I'M GETTING THE FIRST TRICKLE OF A SIGNAL FROM THE BOOSTERS. CAN YOU NUDGE DRAX TO CRANK THEM UP A LITTLE?
SURE.
HE FELT MY TEEP. HE'S ADJUSTING THEM. I--
I FEEL NERVOUS. TENSE. ROCKET DOES, I MEAN. THESE ARE HIS FEELINGS.
ANIMAL INSTINCT. HACKLES RISING. IT'S--

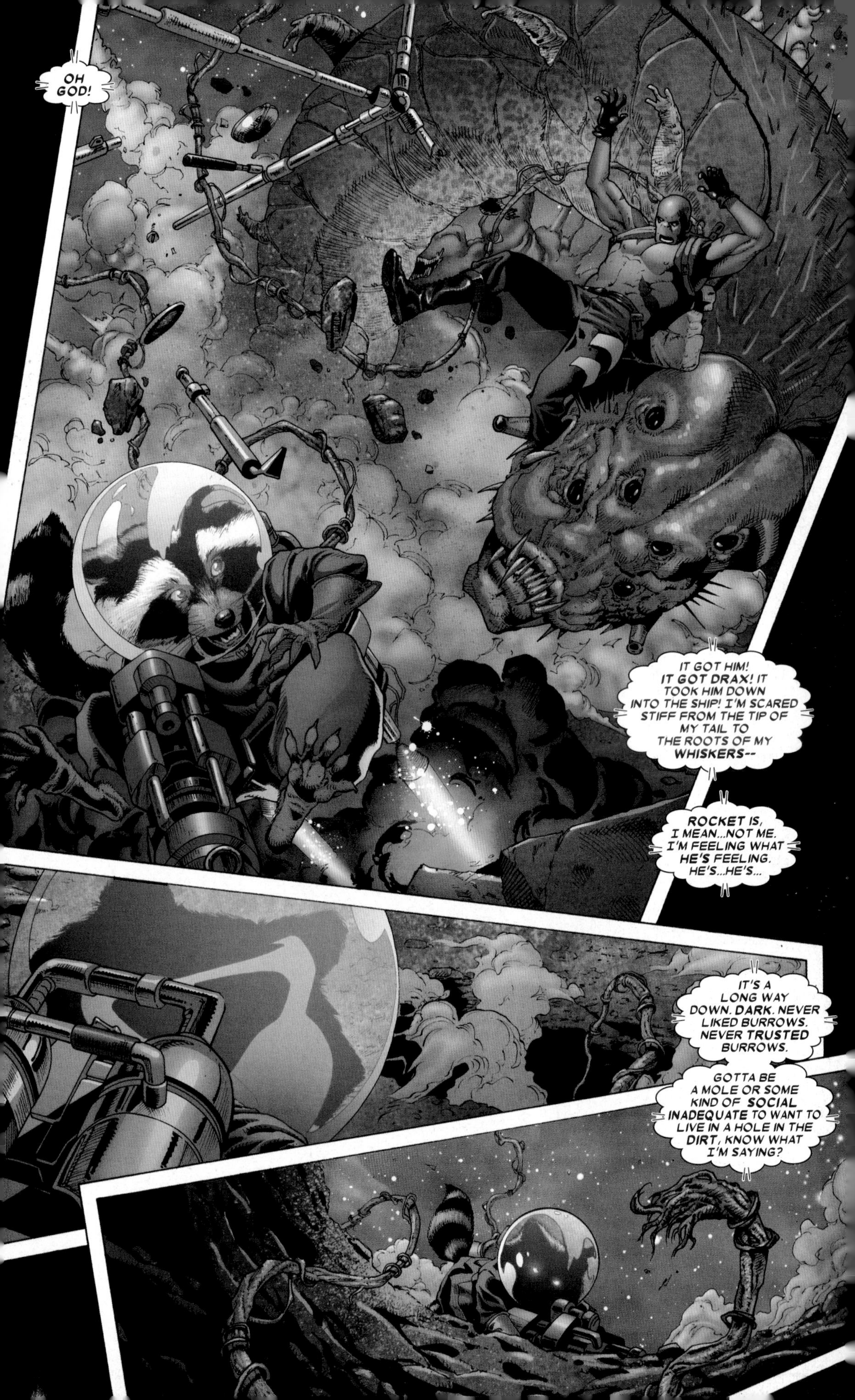
OH GOD!
IT GOT HIM! IT GOT DRAX! IT TOOK HIM DOWN INTO THE SHIP! I'M SCARED STIFF FROM THE TIP OF MY TAIL TO THE ROOTS OF MY WHISKERS--
ROCKET IS, I MEAN...NOT ME. I'M FEELING WHAT HE'S FEELING. HE'S...HE'S...
IT'S A LONG WAY DOWN. DARK. NEVER LIKED BURROWS. NEVER TRUSTED BURROWS.
GOTTA BE A MOLE OR SOME KIND OF SOCIAL INADEQUATE TO WANT TO LIVE IN A HOLE IN THE DIRT, KNOW WHAT I'M SAYING?

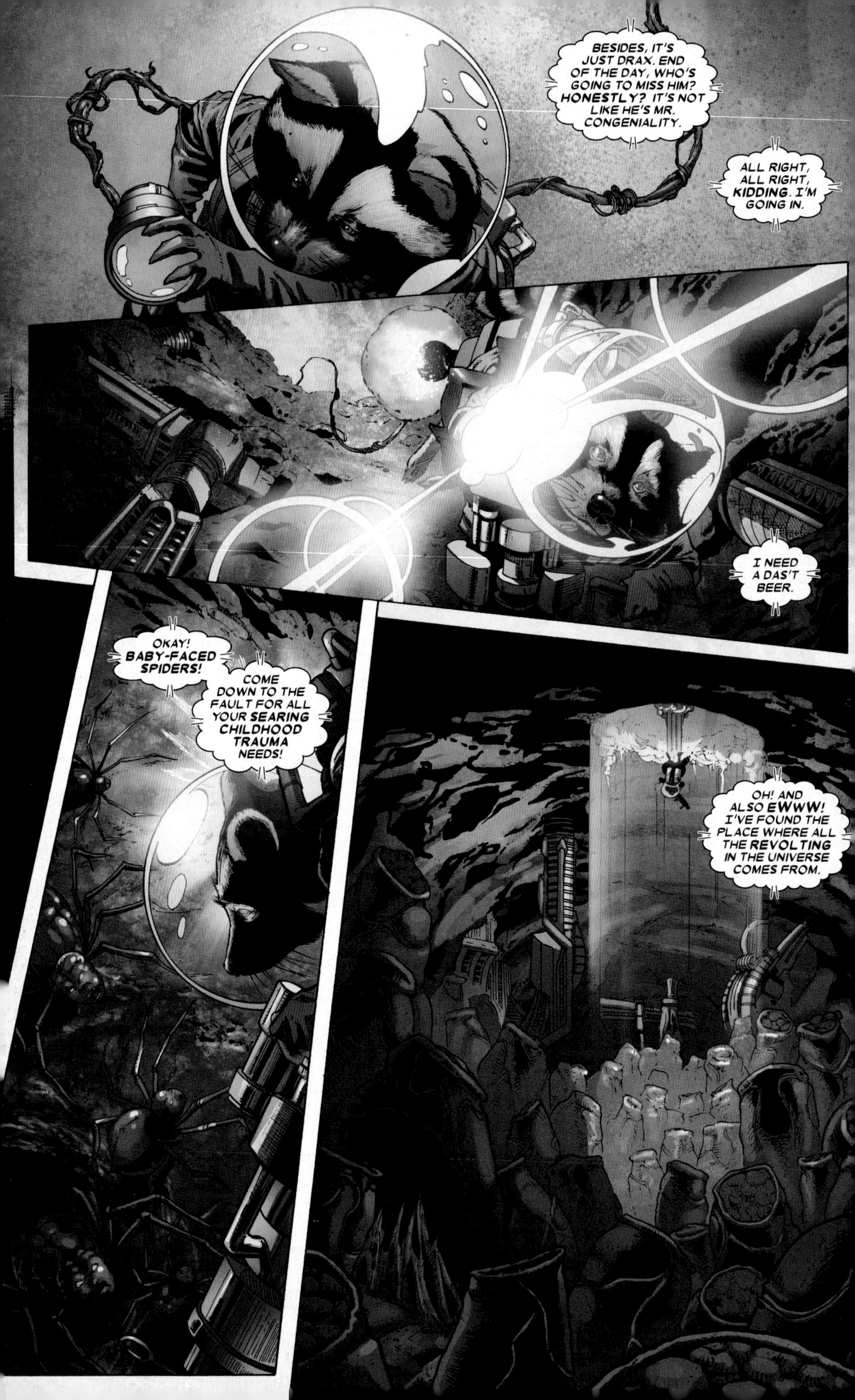
BESIDES, IT'S JUST DRAX. END OF THE DAY, WHO'S GOING TO MISS HIM? HONESTLY? IT'S NOT LIKE HE'S MR. CONGENIALITY.
ALL RIGHT, ALL RIGHT, KIDDING. I'M GOING IN.
I NEED A DAS'T BEER.
OKAY! BABY-FACED SPIDERS!
COME DOWN TO THE FAULT FOR ALL YOUR SEARING CHILDHOOD TRAUMA NEEDS!
OH! AND ALSO EWWW! I'VE FOUND THE PLACE WHERE ALL THE REVOLTING IN THE UNIVERSE COMES FROM.

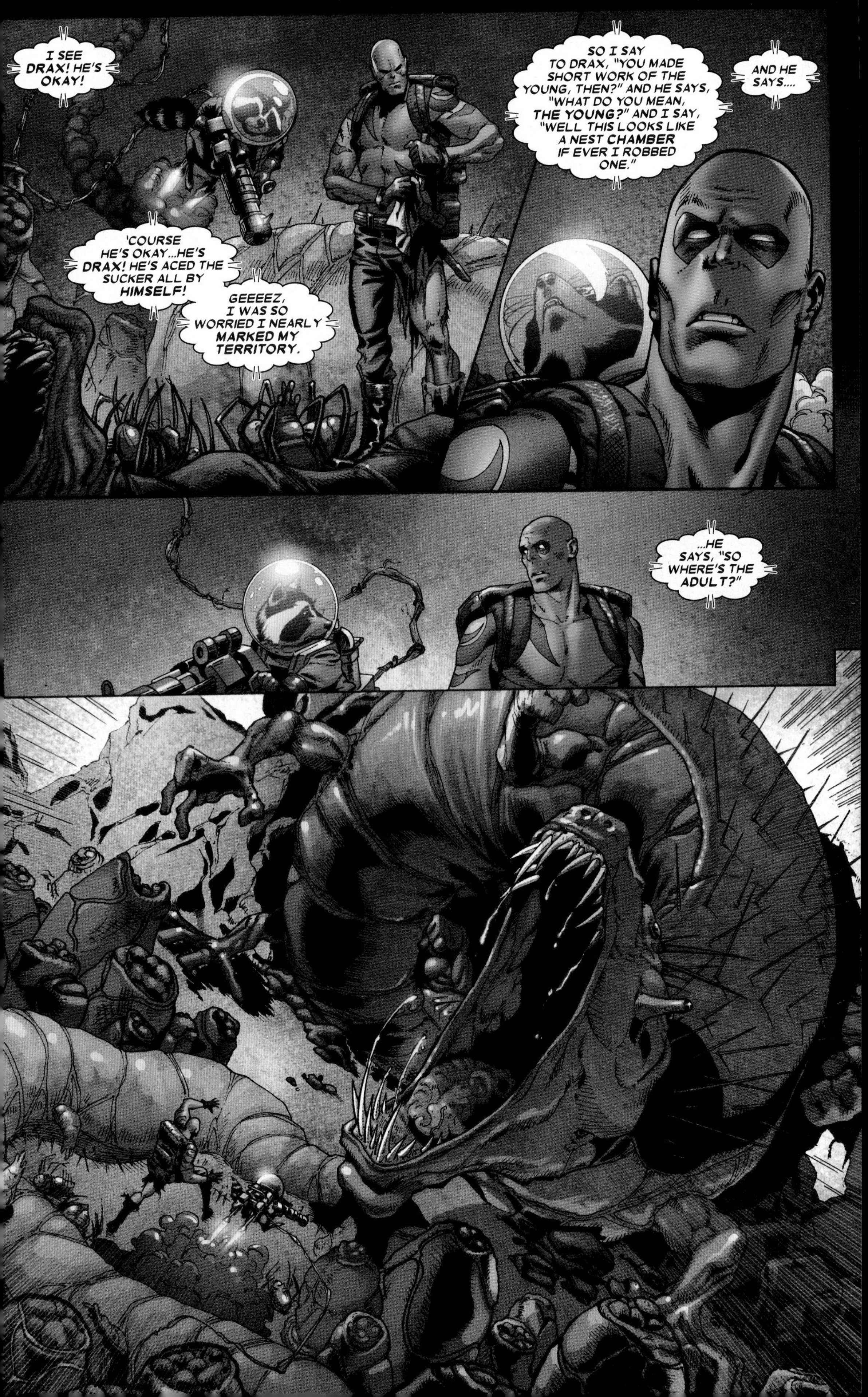
I SEE DRAX! HE'S OKAY!
'COURSE HE'S OKAY...HE'S DRAX! HE'S ACED THE SUCKER ALL BY HIMSELF!
GEEEEZ, I WAS SO WORRIED I NEARLY MARKED MY TERRITORY.
SO I SAY TO DRAX, "YOU MADE SHORT WORK OF THE YOUNG, THEN?" AND HE SAYS, "WHAT DO YOU MEAN, THE YOUNG?" AND I SAY, "WELL THIS LOOKS LIKE A NEST CHAMBER IF EVER I ROBBED ONE."
AND HE SAYS....
...HE SAYS, "SO WHERE'S THE ADULT?"

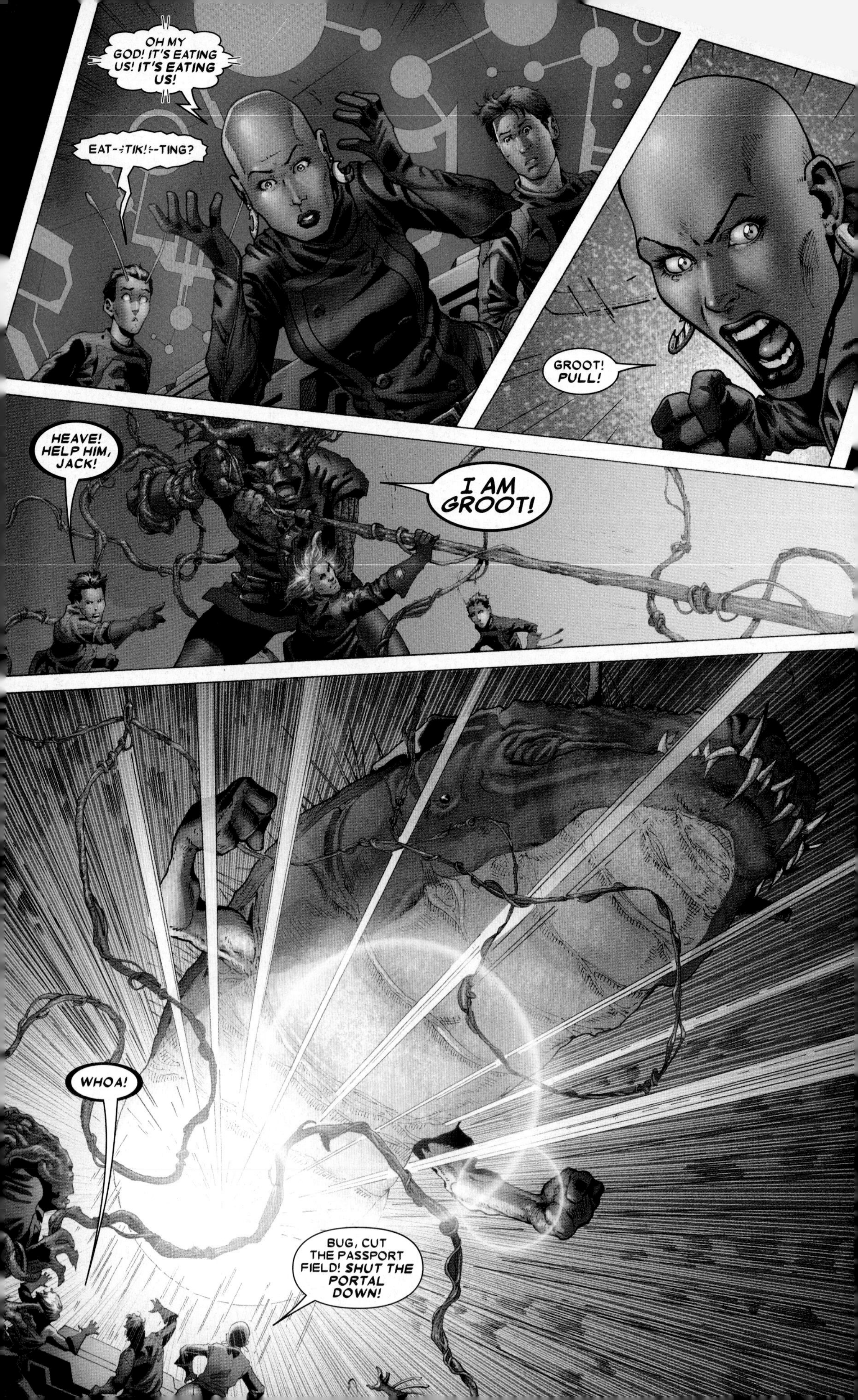
OH MY GOD! IT'S EATING US! IT'S EATING US!
EAT-⫶TIK!⫶-TING?
GROOT! PULL!
HEAVE! HELP HIM, JACK!
I AM GROOT!
WHOA!
BUG, CUT THE PASSPORT FIELD! SHUT THE PORTAL DOWN!

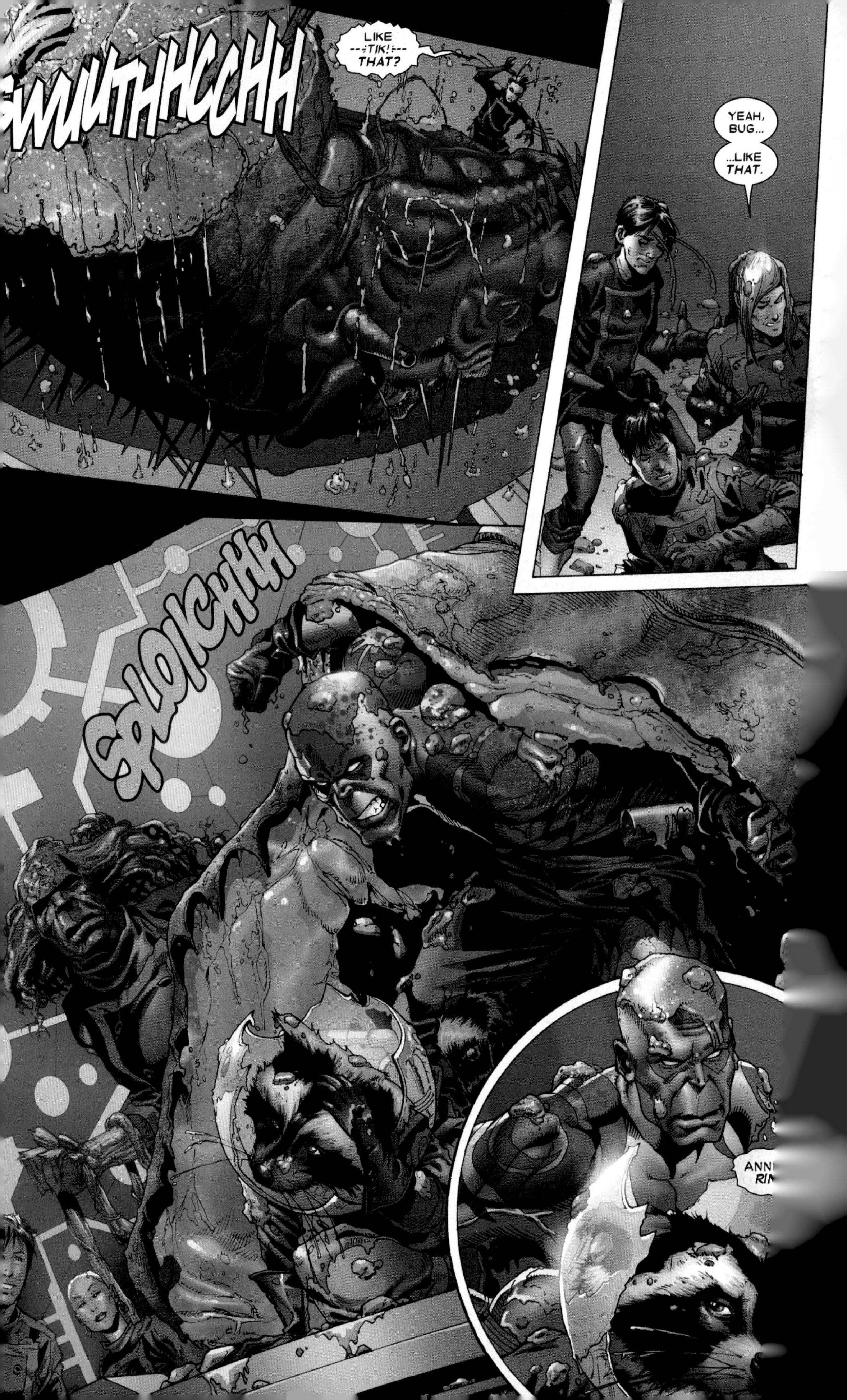
SWUUTHHCCHH
LIKE --TIK!-- THAT?
YEAH, BUG...
...LIKE THAT.
SPLOICHHH

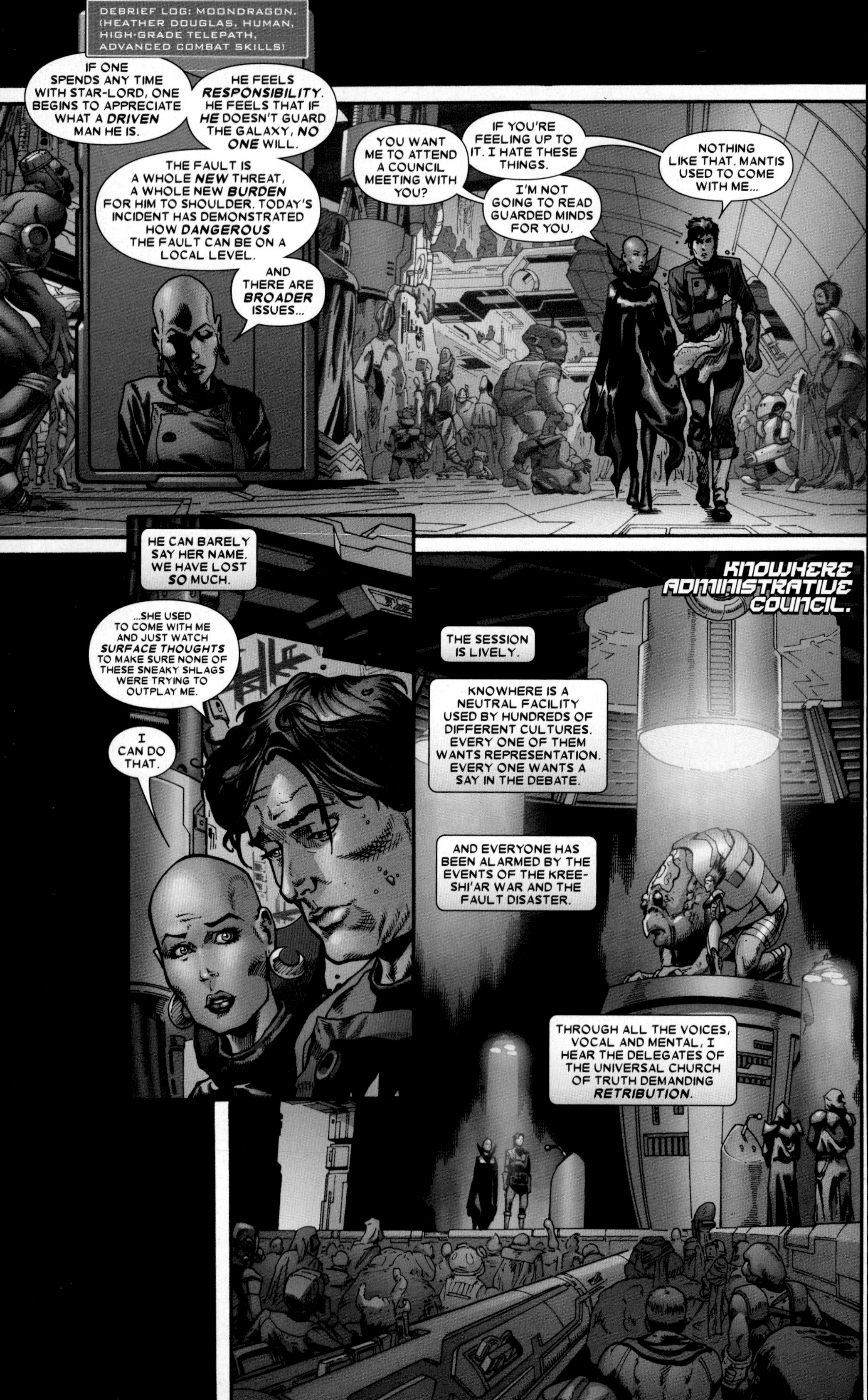
DEBRIEF LOG: MOONDRAGON. (HEATHER DOUGLAS, HUMAN, HIGH-GRADE TELEPATH, ADVANCED COMBAT SKILLS)
IF ONE SPENDS ANY TIME WITH STAR-LORD, ONE BEGINS TO APPRECIATE WHAT A DRIVEN MAN HE IS.
HE FEELS RESPONSIBILITY. HE FEELS THAT IF HE DOESN'T GUARD THE GALAXY, NO ONE WILL.
THE FAULT IS A WHOLE NEW THREAT, A WHOLE NEW BURDEN FOR HIM TO SHOULDER. TODAY'S INCIDENT HAS DEMONSTRATED HOW DANGEROUS THE FAULT CAN BE ON A LOCAL LEVEL.
AND THERE ARE BROADER ISSUES...
YOU WANT ME TO ATTEND A COUNCIL MEETING WITH YOU?
IF YOU'RE FEELING UP TO IT. I HATE THESE THINGS.
I'M NOT GOING TO READ GUARDED MINDS FOR YOU.
NOTHING LIKE THAT. MANTIS USED TO COME WITH ME...
HE CAN BARELY SAY HER NAME. WE HAVE LOST SO MUCH.
...SHE USED TO COME WITH ME AND JUST WATCH SURFACE THOUGHTS TO MAKE SURE NONE OF THESE SNEAKY SHLAGS WERE TRYING TO OUTPLAY ME.
I CAN DO THAT.
KNOWHERE ADMINISTRATIVE COUNCIL.
THE SESSION IS LIVELY.
KNOWHERE IS A NEUTRAL FACILITY USED BY HUNDREDS OF DIFFERENT CULTURES. EVERY ONE OF THEM WANTS REPRESENTATION. EVERY ONE WANTS A SAY IN THE DEBATE.
AND EVERYONE HAS BEEN ALARMED BY THE EVENTS OF THE KREE-SHI'AR WAR AND THE FAULT DISASTER.
THROUGH ALL THE VOICES, VOCAL AND MENTAL, I HEAR THE DELEGATES OF THE UNIVERSAL CHURCH OF TRUTH DEMANDING RETRIBUTION.

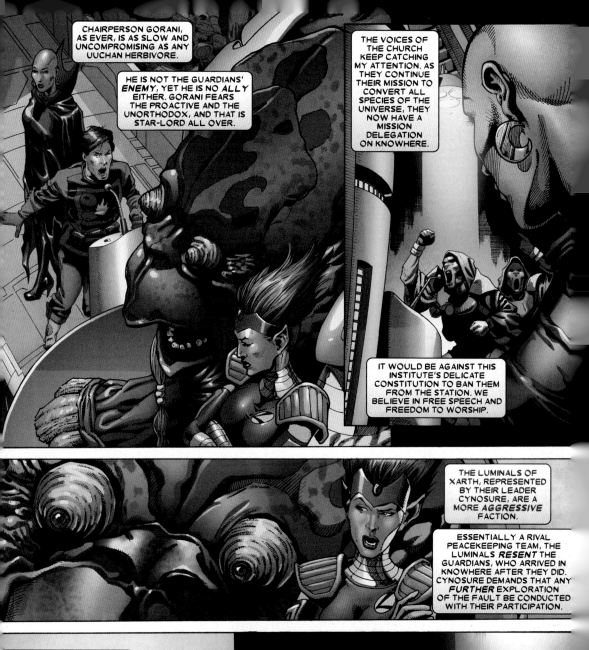

CHAIRPERSON GORANI, AS EVER, IS AS SLOW AND UNCOMPROMISING AS ANY UUCHAN HERBIVORE.

HE IS NOT THE GUARDIANS' *ENEMY*, YET HE IS NO *ALLY* EITHER. GORANI FEARS THE PROACTIVE AND THE UNORTHODOX, AND THAT IS STAR-LORD ALL OVER.

THE VOICES OF THE CHURCH KEEP CATCHING MY ATTENTION. AS THEY CONTINUE THEIR MISSION TO CONVERT ALL SPECIES OF THE UNIVERSE, THEY NOW HAVE A MISSION DELEGATION ON KNOWHERE.

IT WOULD BE AGAINST THIS INSTITUTE'S DELICATE CONSTITUTION TO BAN THEM FROM THE STATION. WE BELIEVE IN FREE SPEECH AND FREEDOM TO WORSHIP.

THE LUMINALS OF XARTH, REPRESENTED BY THEIR LEADER CYNOSURE, ARE A MORE *AGGRESSIVE* FACTION.

ESSENTIALLY A RIVAL PEACEKEEPING TEAM, THE LUMINALS *RESENT* THE GUARDIANS, WHO ARRIVED IN KNOWHERE AFTER THEY DID. CYNOSURE DEMANDS THAT ANY *FURTHER* EXPLORATION OF THE FAULT BE CONDUCTED WITH THEIR PARTICIPATION.

STAR-LORD HAS NO CHOICE BUT TO AGREE. HE NEEDS CYNOSURE AND THE LUMINALS ON OUR SIDE IF HE IS GOING TO KEEP ON TOP OF THE FAULT SITUATION.

I CAN TASTE HIS RELUCTANCE. I--

AGAIN, THE ACOLYTES OF THE CHURCH. WHY ARE THEIR THOUGHTS SO *PIERCING...* SO *INSISTENT?*

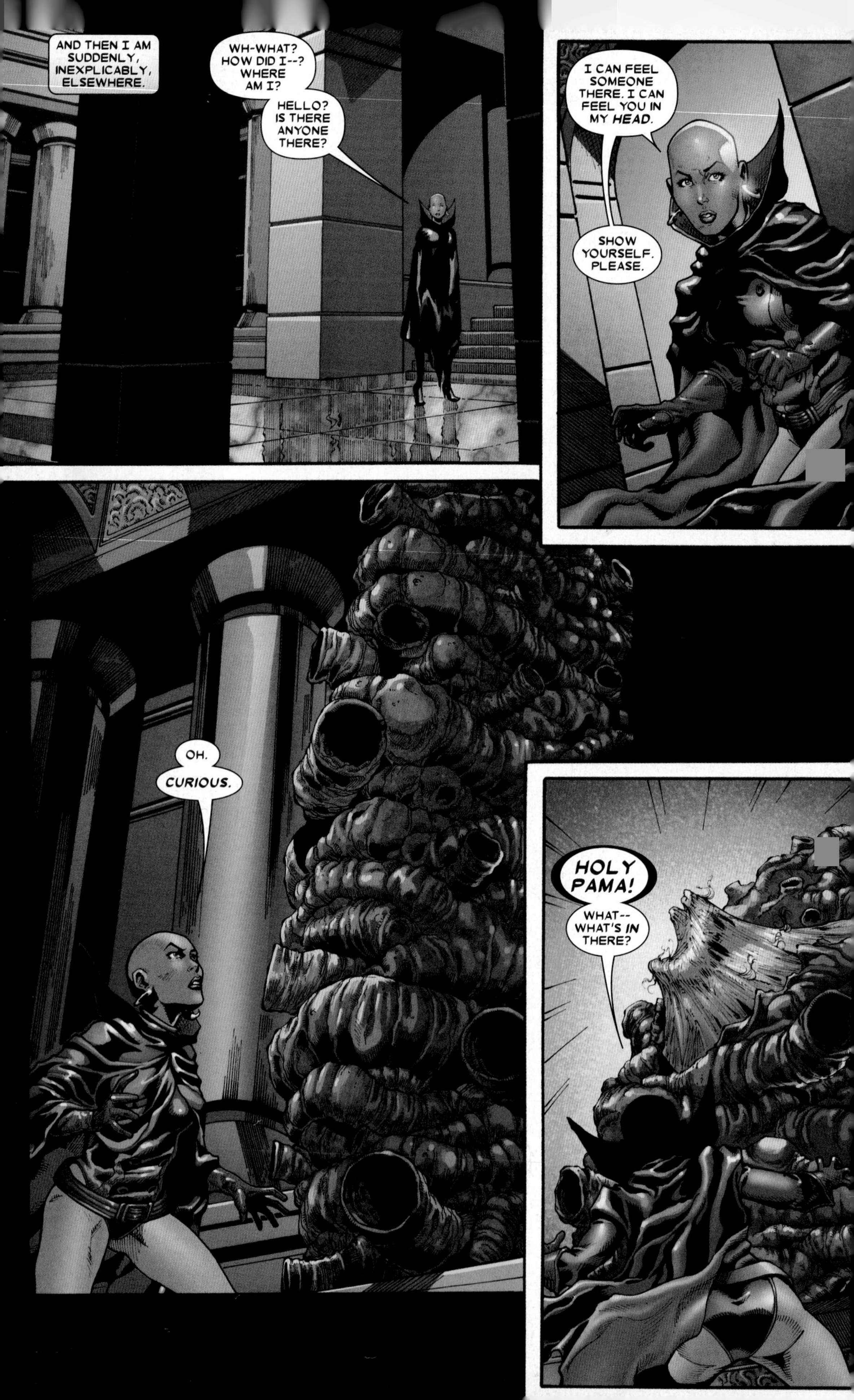
AND THEN I AM SUDDENLY, INEXPLICABLY, ELSEWHERE.
WH-WHAT? HOW DID I--? WHERE AM I?
HELLO? IS THERE ANYONE THERE?
I CAN FEEL SOMEONE THERE. I CAN FEEL YOU IN MY HEAD.
SHOW YOURSELF. PLEASE.
OH. CURIOUS.
HOLY PAMA!
WHAT-- WHAT'S IN THERE?

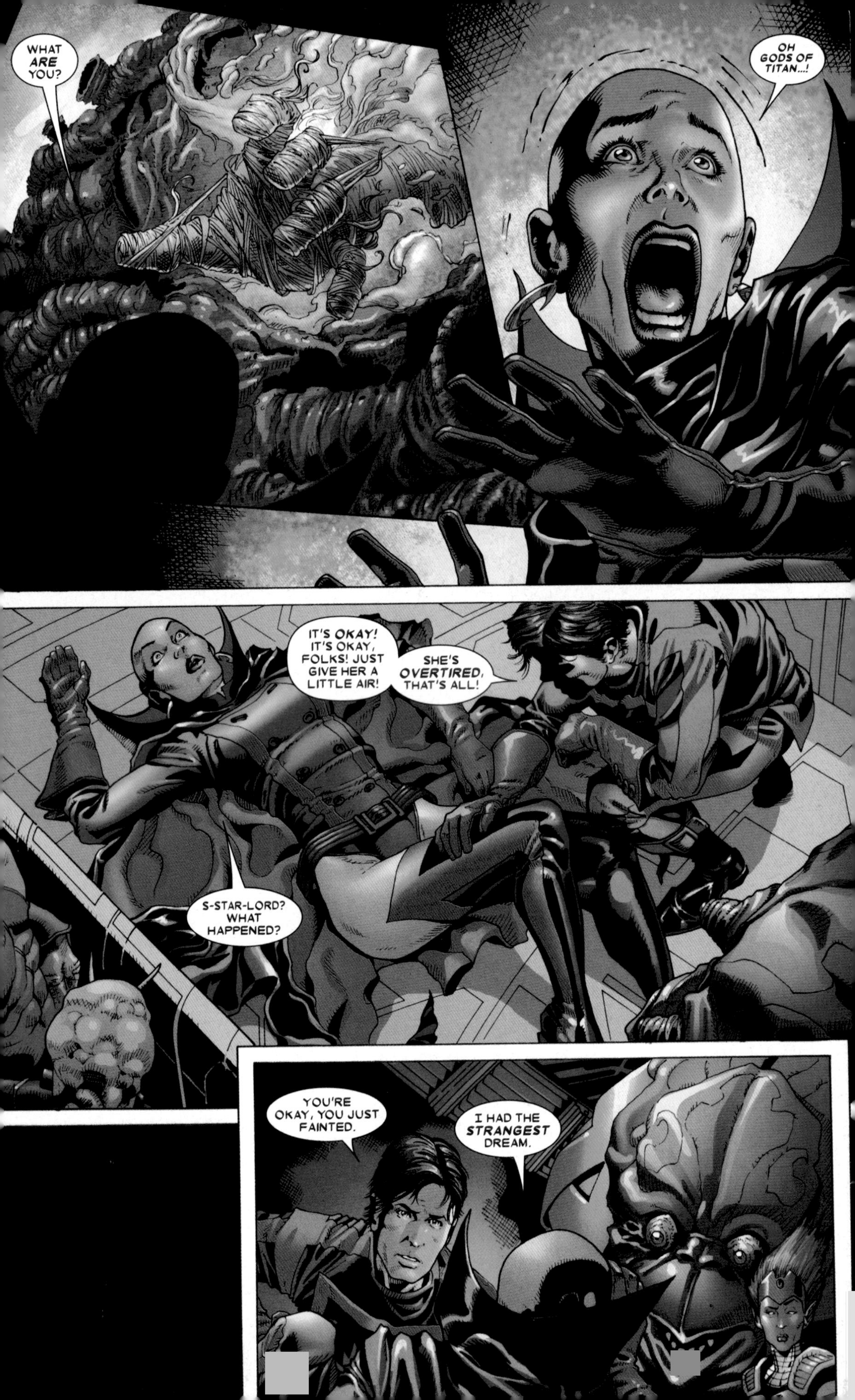
WHAT ARE YOU?
OH GODS OF TITAN...!
IT'S OKAY! IT'S OKAY, FOLKS! JUST GIVE HER A LITTLE AIR!
SHE'S OVERTIRED, THAT'S ALL!
S-STAR-LORD? WHAT HAPPENED?
YOU'RE OKAY, YOU JUST FAINTED.
I HAD THE STRANGEST DREAM.

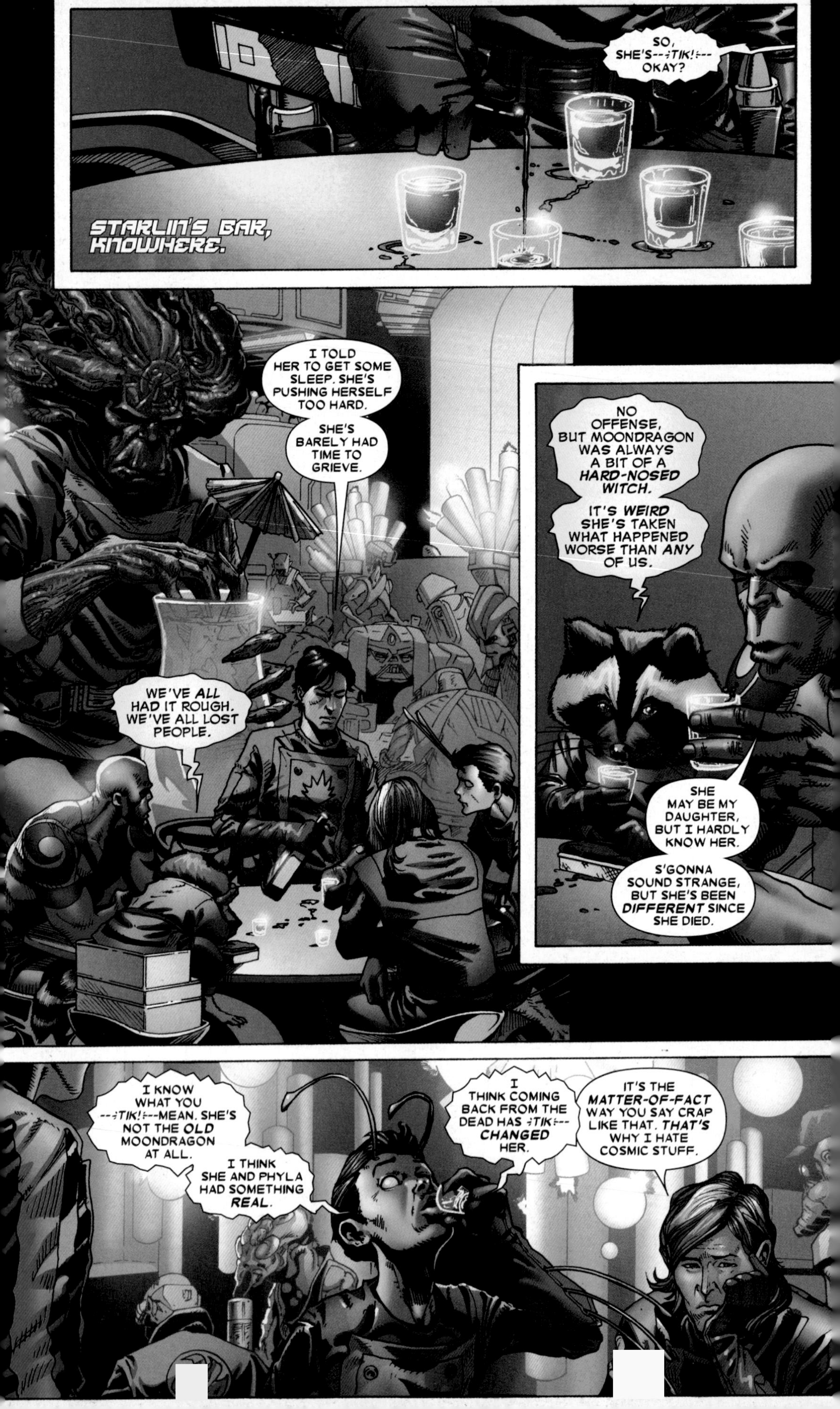
SO, SHE'S--TIK!--OKAY?
STARLIN'S BAR, KNOWHERE.
I TOLD HER TO GET SOME SLEEP. SHE'S PUSHING HERSELF TOO HARD.
SHE'S BARELY HAD TIME TO GRIEVE.
WE'VE ALL HAD IT ROUGH. WE'VE ALL LOST PEOPLE.
NO OFFENSE, BUT MOONDRAGON WAS ALWAYS A BIT OF A HARD-NOSED WITCH.
IT'S WEIRD SHE'S TAKEN WHAT HAPPENED WORSE THAN ANY OF US.
SHE MAY BE MY DAUGHTER, BUT I HARDLY KNOW HER.
S'GONNA SOUND STRANGE, BUT SHE'S BEEN DIFFERENT SINCE SHE DIED.
I KNOW WHAT YOU --TIK!--MEAN. SHE'S NOT THE OLD MOONDRAGON AT ALL.
I THINK SHE AND PHYLA HAD SOMETHING REAL.
I THINK COMING BACK FROM THE DEAD HAS TIK!-- CHANGED HER.
IT'S THE MATTER-OF-FACT WAY YOU SAY CRAP LIKE THAT. THAT'S WHY I HATE COSMIC STUFF.

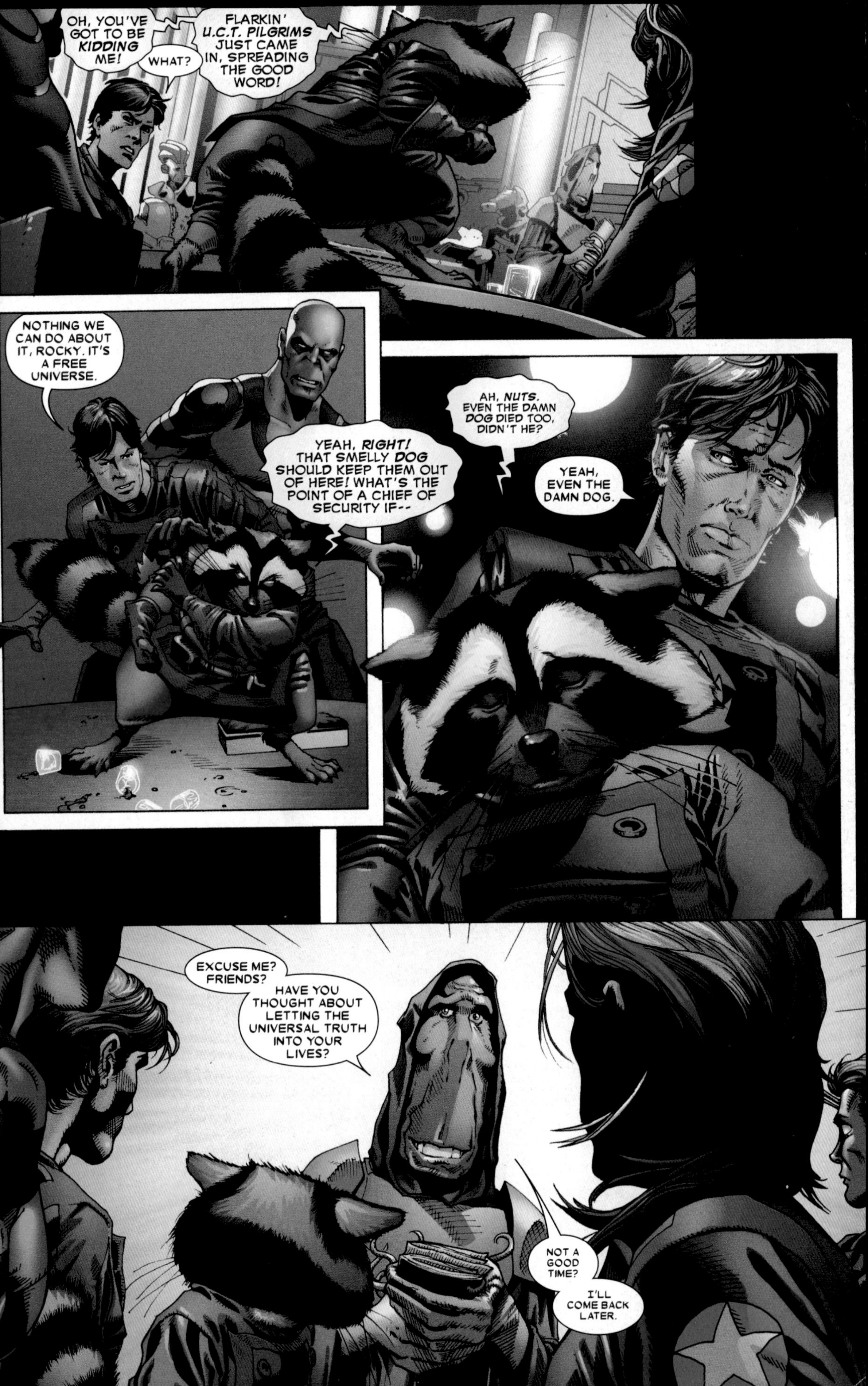
OH, YOU'VE GOT TO BE KIDDING ME!
WHAT?
FLARKIN' U.C.T. PILGRIMS JUST CAME IN, SPREADING THE GOOD WORD!
NOTHING WE CAN DO ABOUT IT, ROCKY. IT'S A FREE UNIVERSE.
YEAH, RIGHT! THAT SMELLY DOG SHOULD KEEP THEM OUT OF HERE! WHAT'S THE POINT OF A CHIEF OF SECURITY IF--
AH, NUTS. EVEN THE DAMN DOG DIED TOO, DIDN'T HE?
YEAH, EVEN THE DAMN DOG.
EXCUSE ME? FRIENDS?
HAVE YOU THOUGHT ABOUT LETTING THE UNIVERSAL TRUTH INTO YOUR LIVES?
NOT A GOOD TIME?
I'LL COME BACK LATER.

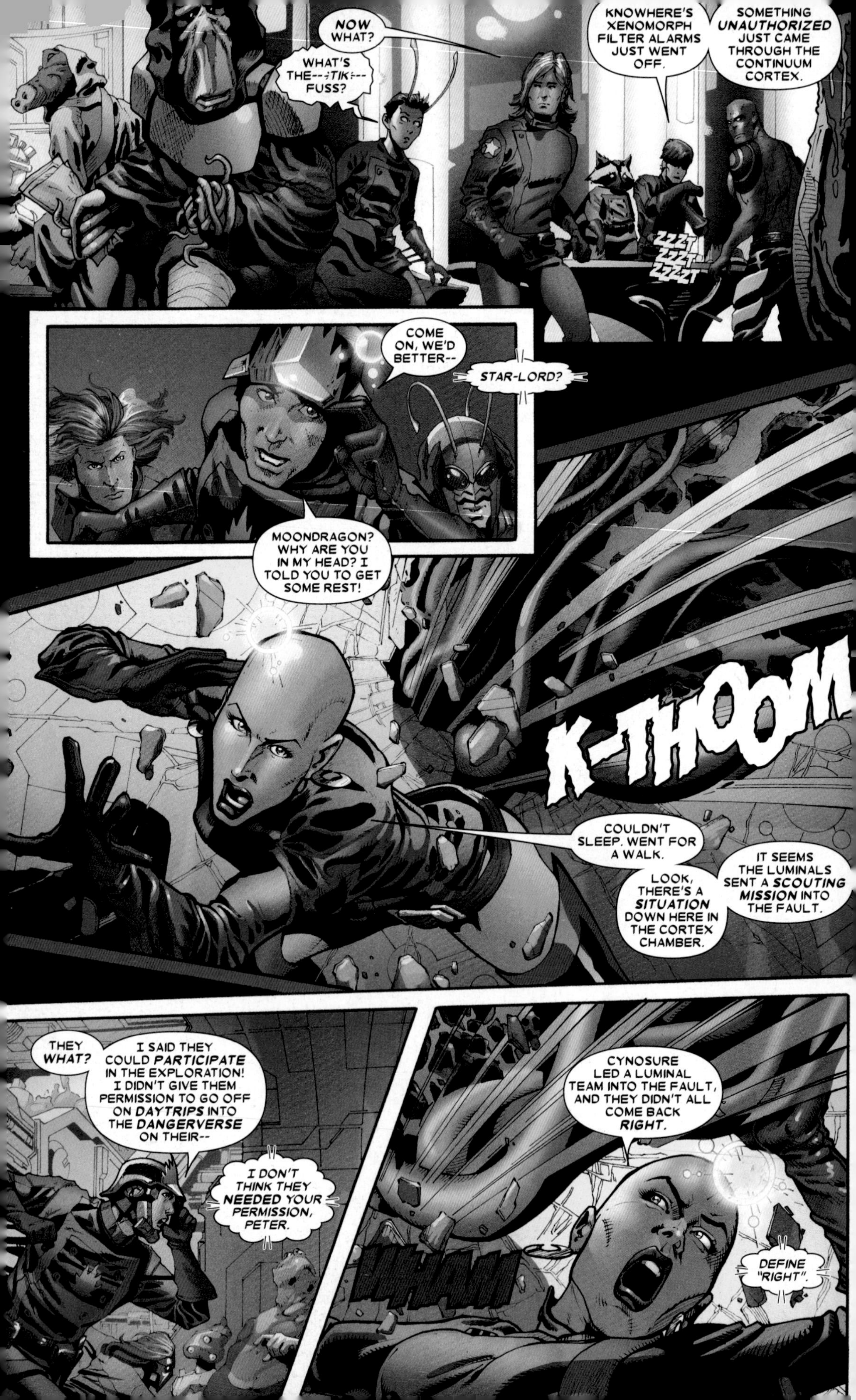
NOW WHAT?
WHAT'S THE--tik--FUSS?
KNOWHERE'S XENOMORPH FILTER ALARMS JUST WENT OFF.
SOMETHING UNAUTHORIZED JUST CAME THROUGH THE CONTINUUM CORTEX.
ZZZT ZZZT ZZZZT
COME ON, WE'D BETTER--
STAR-LORD?
MOONDRAGON? WHY ARE YOU IN MY HEAD? I TOLD YOU TO GET SOME REST!
K-THOOM
COULDN'T SLEEP. WENT FOR A WALK.
LOOK, THERE'S A SITUATION DOWN HERE IN THE CORTEX CHAMBER.
IT SEEMS THE LUMINALS SENT A SCOUTING MISSION INTO THE FAULT.
THEY WHAT?
I SAID THEY COULD PARTICIPATE IN THE EXPLORATION! I DIDN'T GIVE THEM PERMISSION TO GO OFF ON DAYTRIPS INTO THE DANGERVERSE ON THEIR--
I DON'T THINK THEY NEEDED YOUR PERMISSION, PETER.
CYNOSURE LED A LUMINAL TEAM INTO THE FAULT, AND THEY DIDN'T ALL COME BACK RIGHT.
DEFINE "RIGHT".

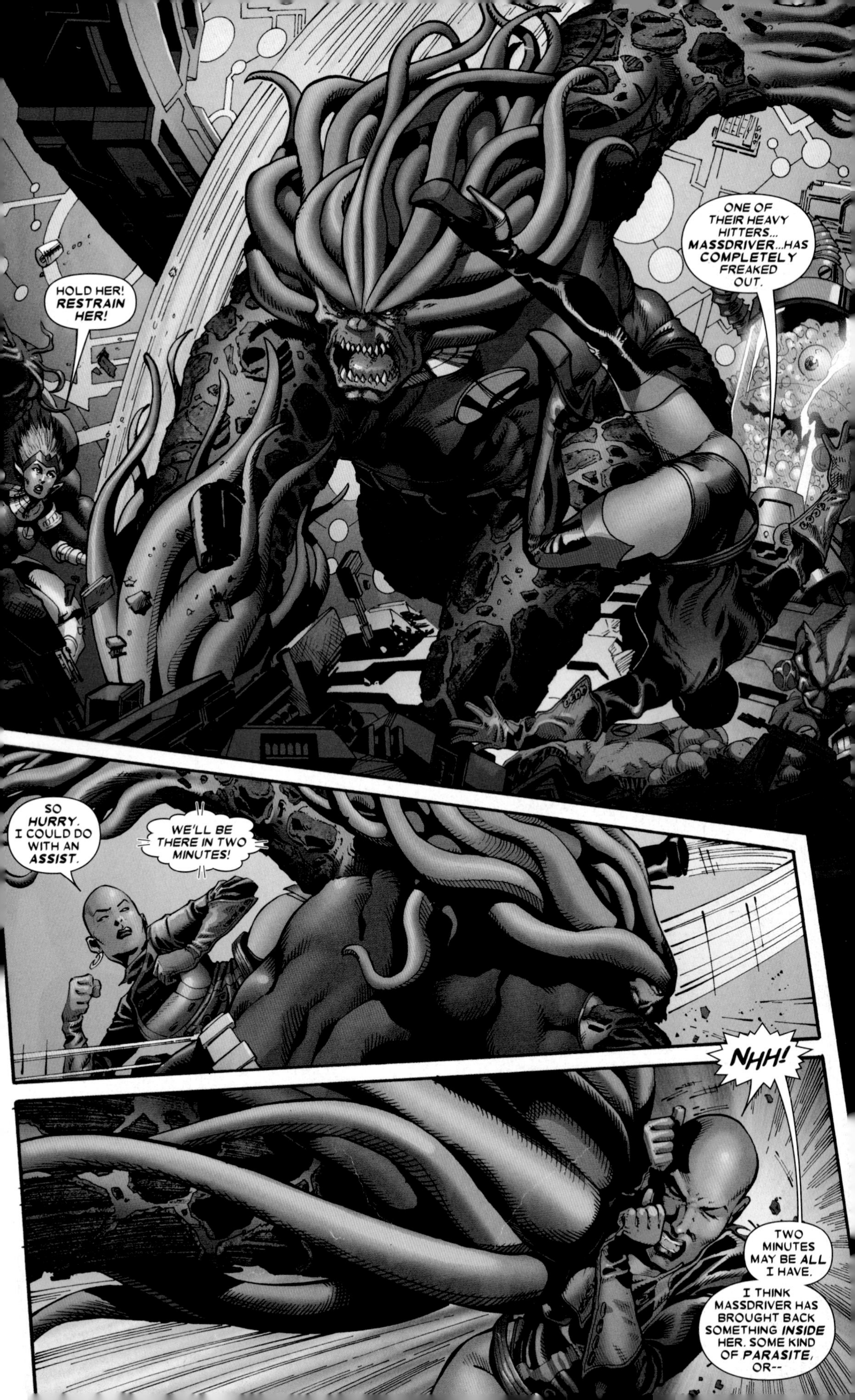
HOLD HER! RESTRAIN HER!
ONE OF THEIR HEAVY HITTERS... MASSDRIVER...HAS COMPLETELY FREAKED OUT.
SO HURRY. I COULD DO WITH AN ASSIST.
WE'LL BE THERE IN TWO MINUTES!
NHH!
TWO MINUTES MAY BE ALL I HAVE.
I THINK MASSDRIVER HAS BROUGHT BACK SOMETHING INSIDE HER. SOME KIND OF PARASITE, OR--

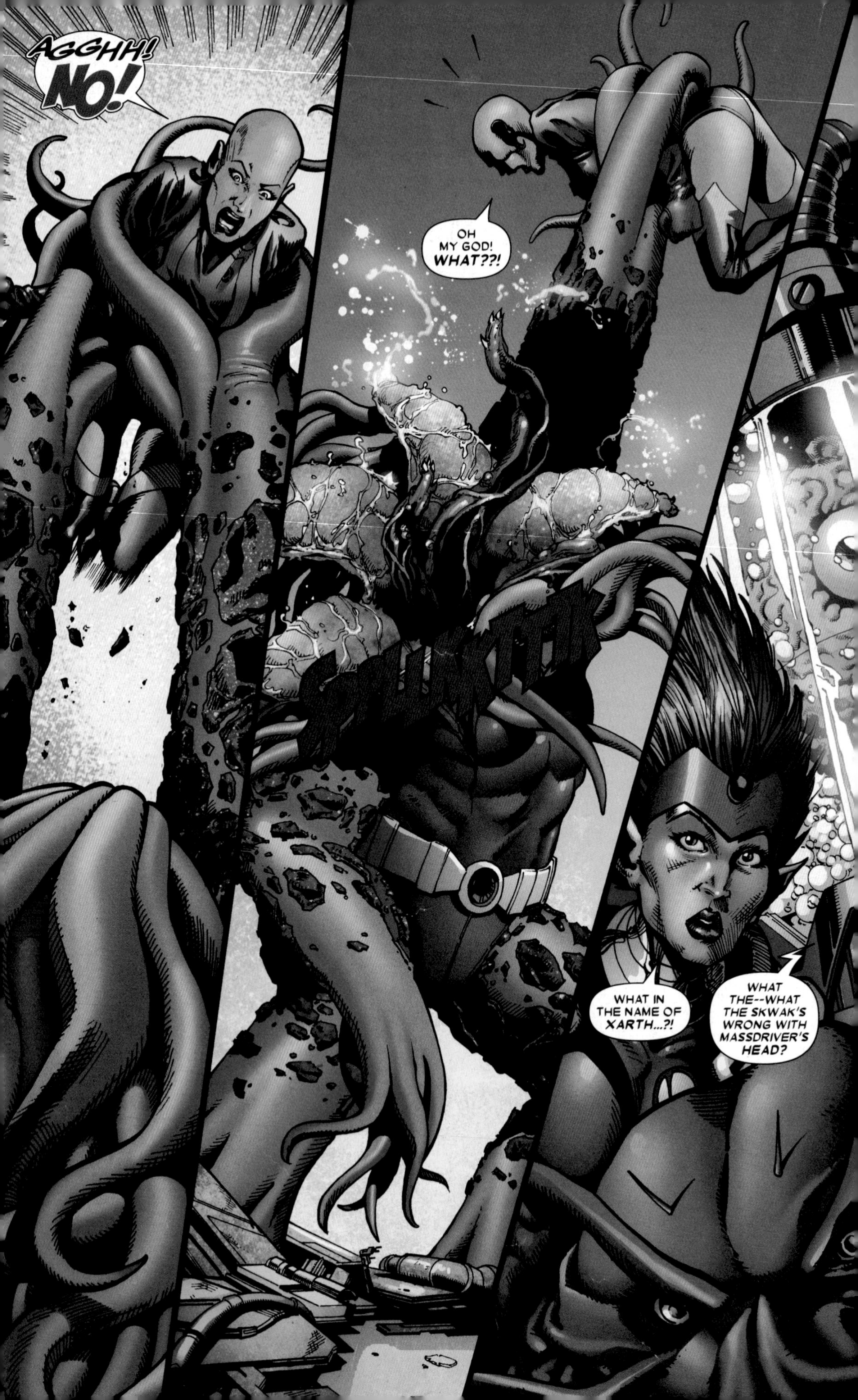
AGGHH! NO!
OH MY GOD! WHAT??!
WHAT IN THE NAME OF XARTH...?!
WHAT THE--WHAT THE SKWAK'S WRONG WITH MASSDRIVER'S HEAD?

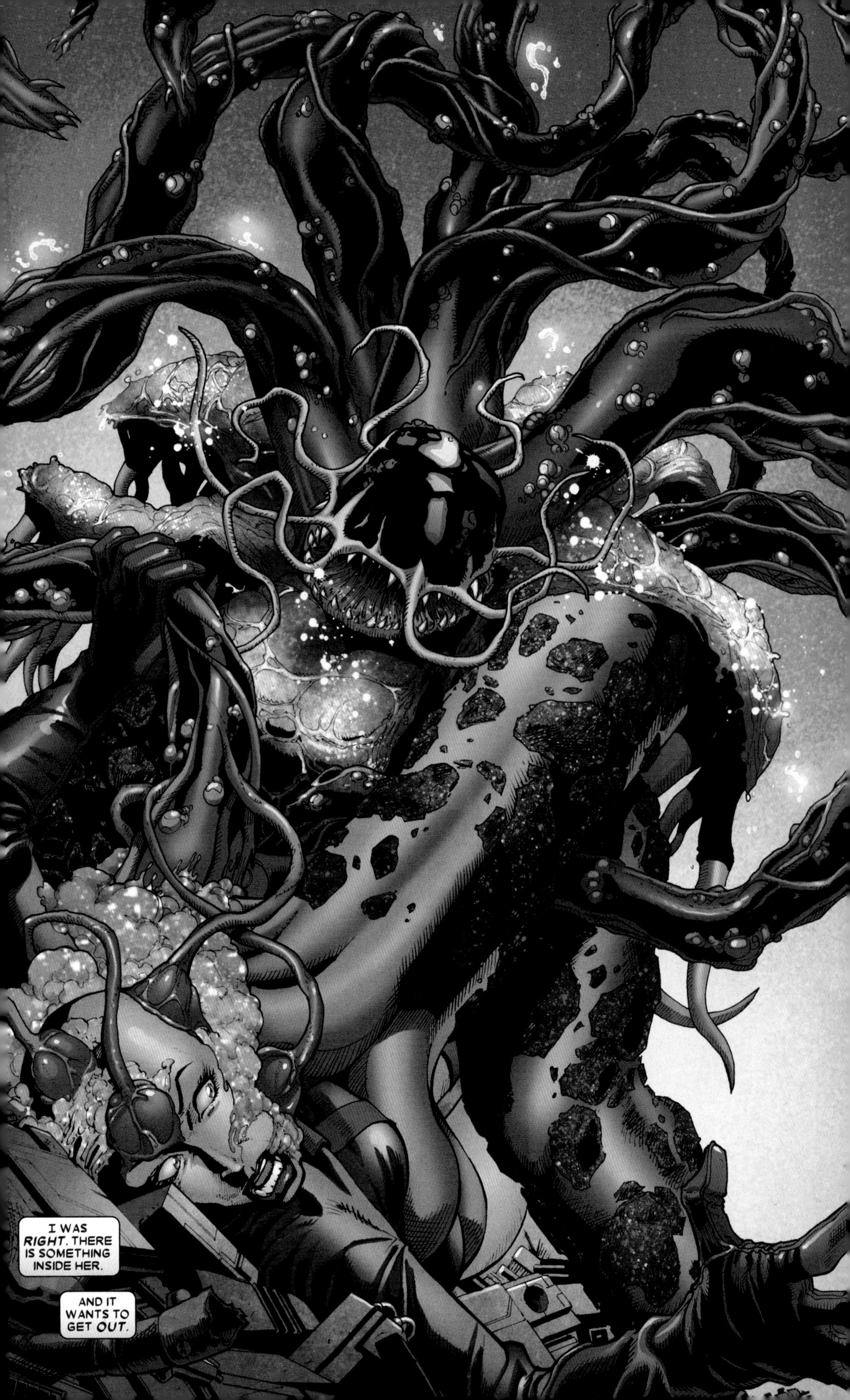
I WAS RIGHT. THERE IS SOMETHING INSIDE HER.
AND IT WANTS TO GET OUT.

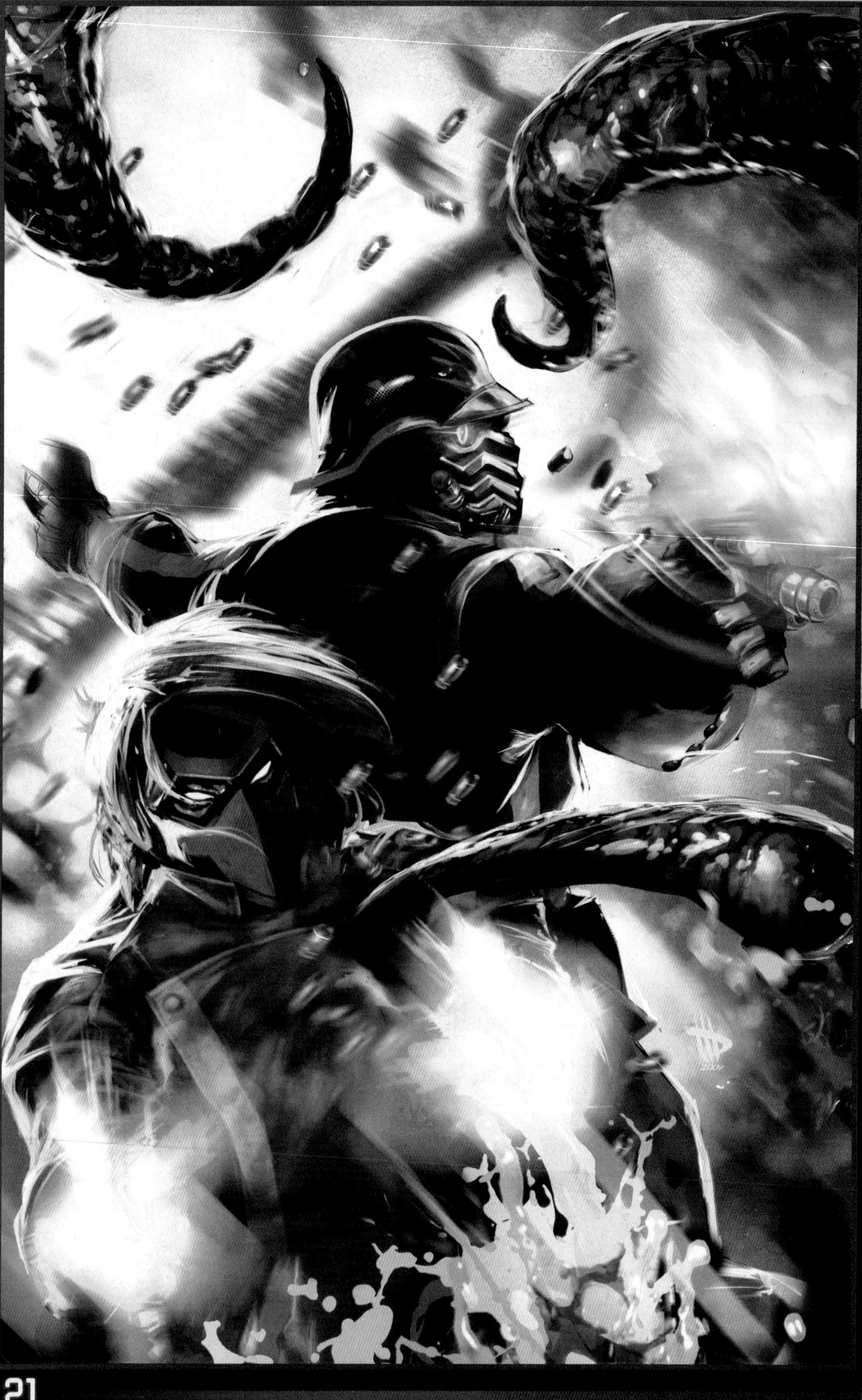

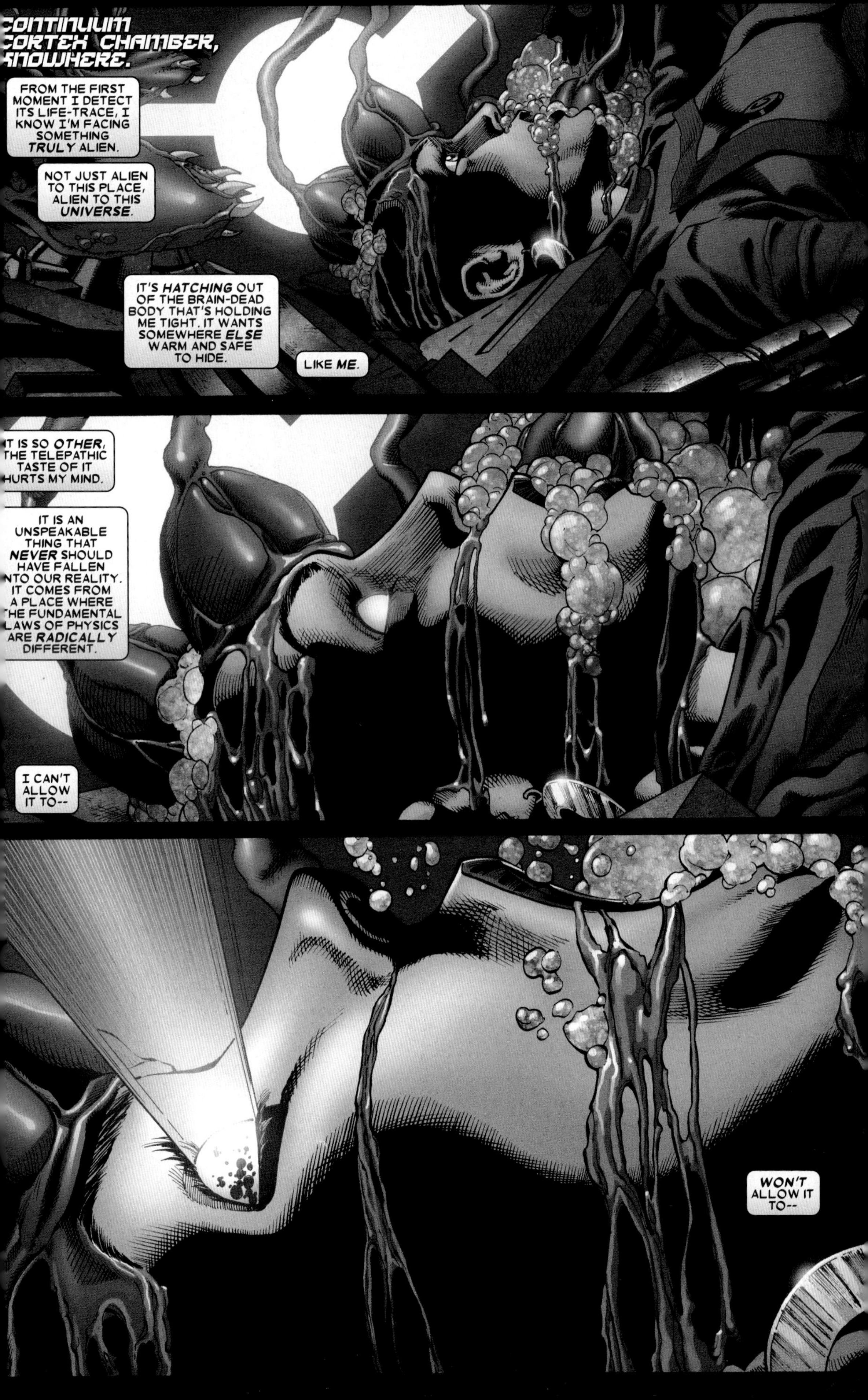
CONTINUUM CORTEX CHAMBER, KNOWHERE.
FROM THE FIRST MOMENT I DETECT ITS LIFE-TRACE, I KNOW I'M FACING SOMETHING TRULY ALIEN.
NOT JUST ALIEN TO THIS PLACE, ALIEN TO THIS UNIVERSE.
IT'S HATCHING OUT OF THE BRAIN-DEAD BODY THAT'S HOLDING ME TIGHT. IT WANTS SOMEWHERE ELSE WARM AND SAFE TO HIDE.
LIKE ME.
IT IS SO OTHER, THE TELEPATHIC TASTE OF IT HURTS MY MIND.
IT IS AN UNSPEAKABLE THING THAT NEVER SHOULD HAVE FALLEN INTO OUR REALITY. IT COMES FROM A PLACE WHERE THE FUNDAMENTAL LAWS OF PHYSICS ARE RADICALLY DIFFERENT.
I CAN'T ALLOW IT TO--
WON'T ALLOW IT TO--

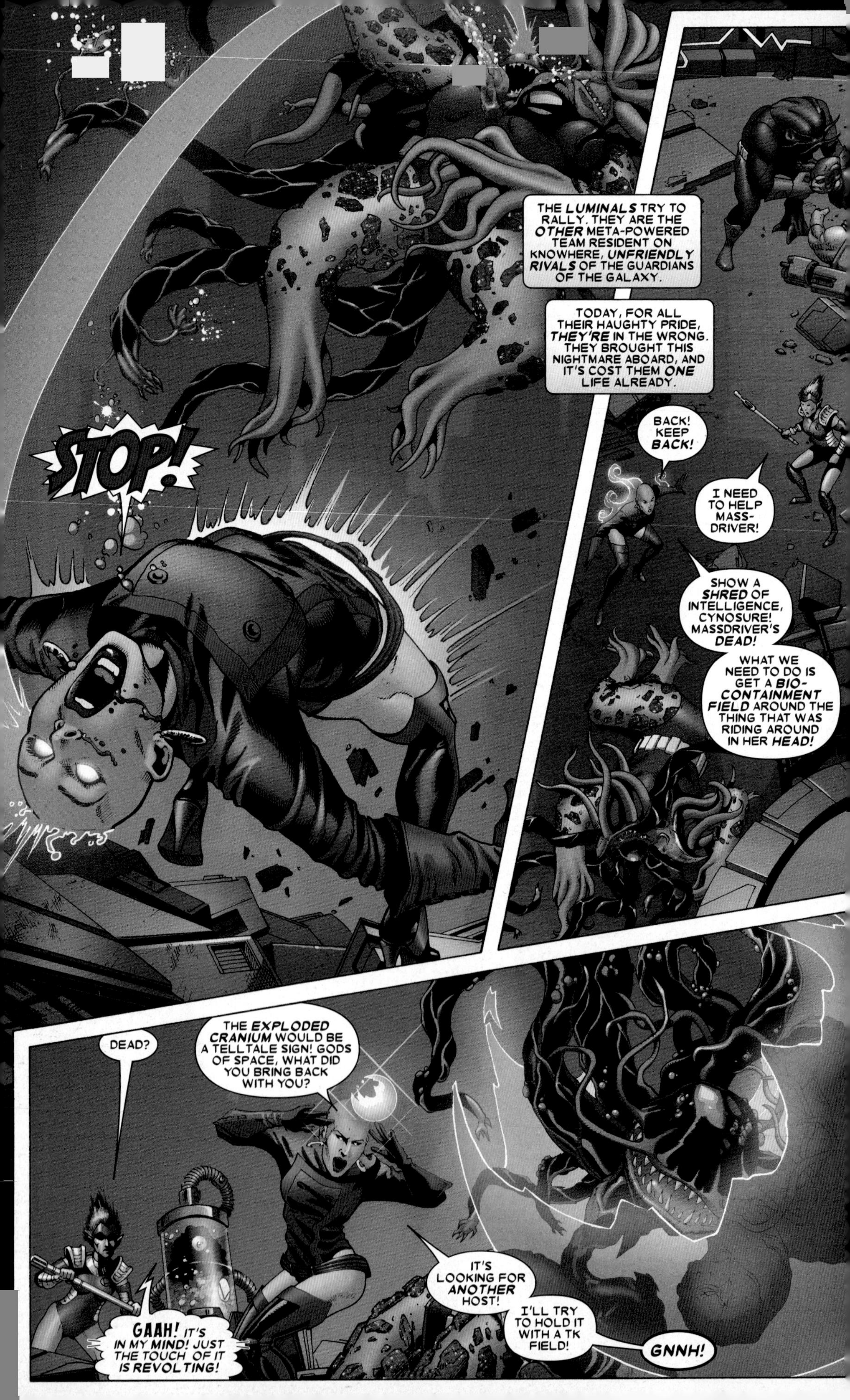
THE LUMINALS TRY TO RALLY. THEY ARE THE OTHER META-POWERED TEAM RESIDENT ON KNOWHERE, UNFRIENDLY RIVALS OF THE GUARDIANS OF THE GALAXY.
TODAY, FOR ALL THEIR HAUGHTY PRIDE, THEY'RE IN THE WRONG. THEY BROUGHT THIS NIGHTMARE ABOARD, AND IT'S COST THEM ONE LIFE ALREADY.
STOP!
BACK! KEEP BACK!
I NEED TO HELP MASS-DRIVER!
SHOW A SHRED OF INTELLIGENCE, CYNOSURE! MASSDRIVER'S DEAD!
WHAT WE NEED TO DO IS GET A BIO-CONTAINMENT FIELD AROUND THE THING THAT WAS RIDING AROUND IN HER HEAD!
DEAD?
THE EXPLODED CRANIUM WOULD BE A TELLTALE SIGN! GODS OF SPACE, WHAT DID YOU BRING BACK WITH YOU?
GAAH! IT'S IN MY MIND! JUST THE TOUCH OF IT IS REVOLTING!
IT'S LOOKING FOR ANOTHER HOST!
I'LL TRY TO HOLD IT WITH A TK FIELD!
GNNH!

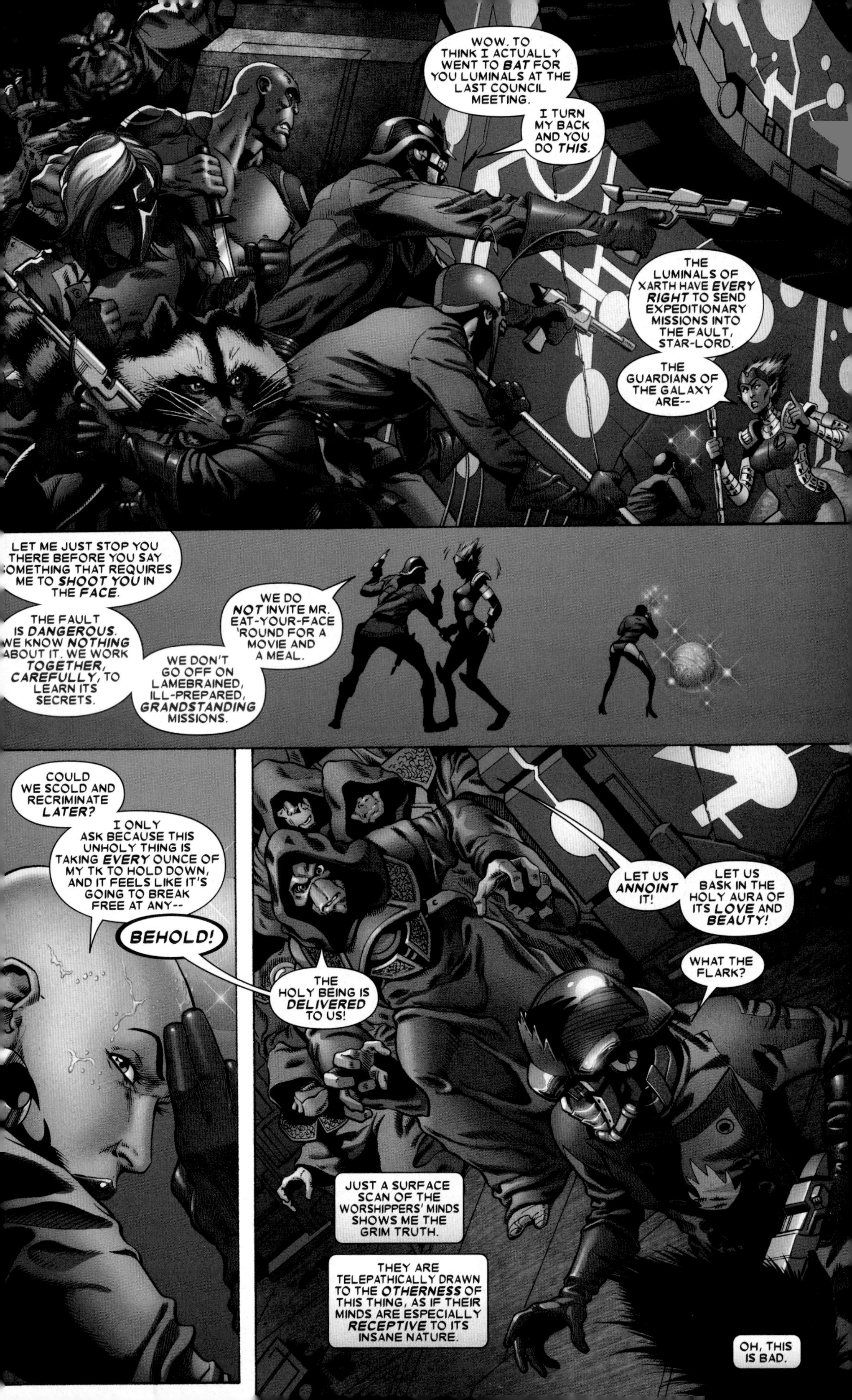
WOW. TO THINK I ACTUALLY WENT TO BAT FOR YOU LUMINALS AT THE LAST COUNCIL MEETING.
I TURN MY BACK AND YOU DO THIS.
THE LUMINALS OF XARTH HAVE EVERY RIGHT TO SEND EXPEDITIONARY MISSIONS INTO THE FAULT, STAR-LORD.
THE GUARDIANS OF THE GALAXY ARE--
LET ME JUST STOP YOU THERE BEFORE YOU SAY SOMETHING THAT REQUIRES ME TO SHOOT YOU IN THE FACE.
THE FAULT IS DANGEROUS. WE KNOW NOTHING ABOUT IT. WE WORK TOGETHER, CAREFULLY, TO LEARN ITS SECRETS.
WE DON'T GO OFF ON LAMEBRAINED, ILL-PREPARED, GRANDSTANDING MISSIONS.
WE DO NOT INVITE MR. EAT-YOUR-FACE 'ROUND FOR A MOVIE AND A MEAL.
COULD WE SCOLD AND RECRIMINATE LATER?
I ONLY ASK BECAUSE THIS UNHOLY THING IS TAKING EVERY OUNCE OF MY TK TO HOLD DOWN, AND IT FEELS LIKE IT'S GOING TO BREAK FREE AT ANY--
BEHOLD!
THE HOLY BEING IS DELIVERED TO US!
LET US ANNOINT IT!
LET US BASK IN THE HOLY AURA OF ITS LOVE AND BEAUTY!
WHAT THE FLARK?
JUST A SURFACE SCAN OF THE WORSHIPPERS' MINDS SHOWS ME THE GRIM TRUTH.
THEY ARE TELEPATHICALLY DRAWN TO THE OTHERNESS OF THIS THING, AS IF THEIR MINDS ARE ESPECIALLY RECEPTIVE TO ITS INSANE NATURE.
OH, THIS IS BAD.

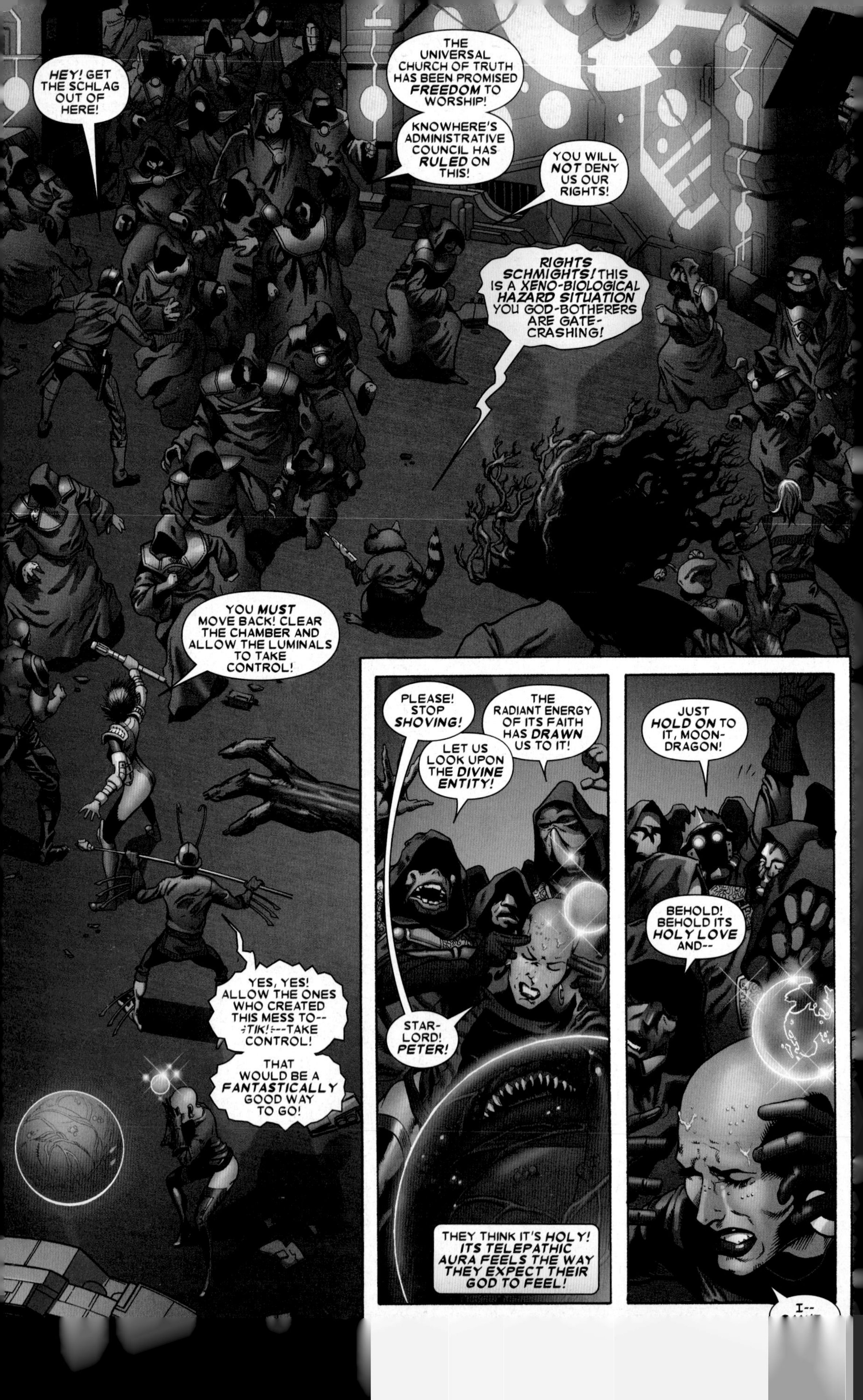
HEY! GET THE SCHLAG OUT OF HERE!
THE UNIVERSAL CHURCH OF TRUTH HAS BEEN PROMISED FREEDOM TO WORSHIP!
KNOWHERE'S ADMINISTRATIVE COUNCIL HAS RULED ON THIS!
YOU WILL NOT DENY US OUR RIGHTS!
RIGHTS SCHMIGHTS! THIS IS A XENO-BIOLOGICAL HAZARD SITUATION YOU GOD-BOTHERERS ARE GATE-CRASHING!
YOU MUST MOVE BACK! CLEAR THE CHAMBER AND ALLOW THE LUMINALS TO TAKE CONTROL!
YES, YES! ALLOW THE ONES WHO CREATED THIS MESS TO-- ÷TIK!÷--TAKE CONTROL!
THAT WOULD BE A FANTASTICALLY GOOD WAY TO GO!
PLEASE! STOP SHOVING!
THE RADIANT ENERGY OF ITS FAITH HAS DRAWN US TO IT!
LET US LOOK UPON THE DIVINE ENTITY!
STAR-LORD! PETER!
THEY THINK IT'S HOLY! ITS TELEPATHIC AURA FEELS THE WAY THEY EXPECT THEIR GOD TO FEEL!
JUST HOLD ON TO IT, MOON-DRAGON!
BEHOLD! BEHOLD ITS HOLY LOVE AND--
I--

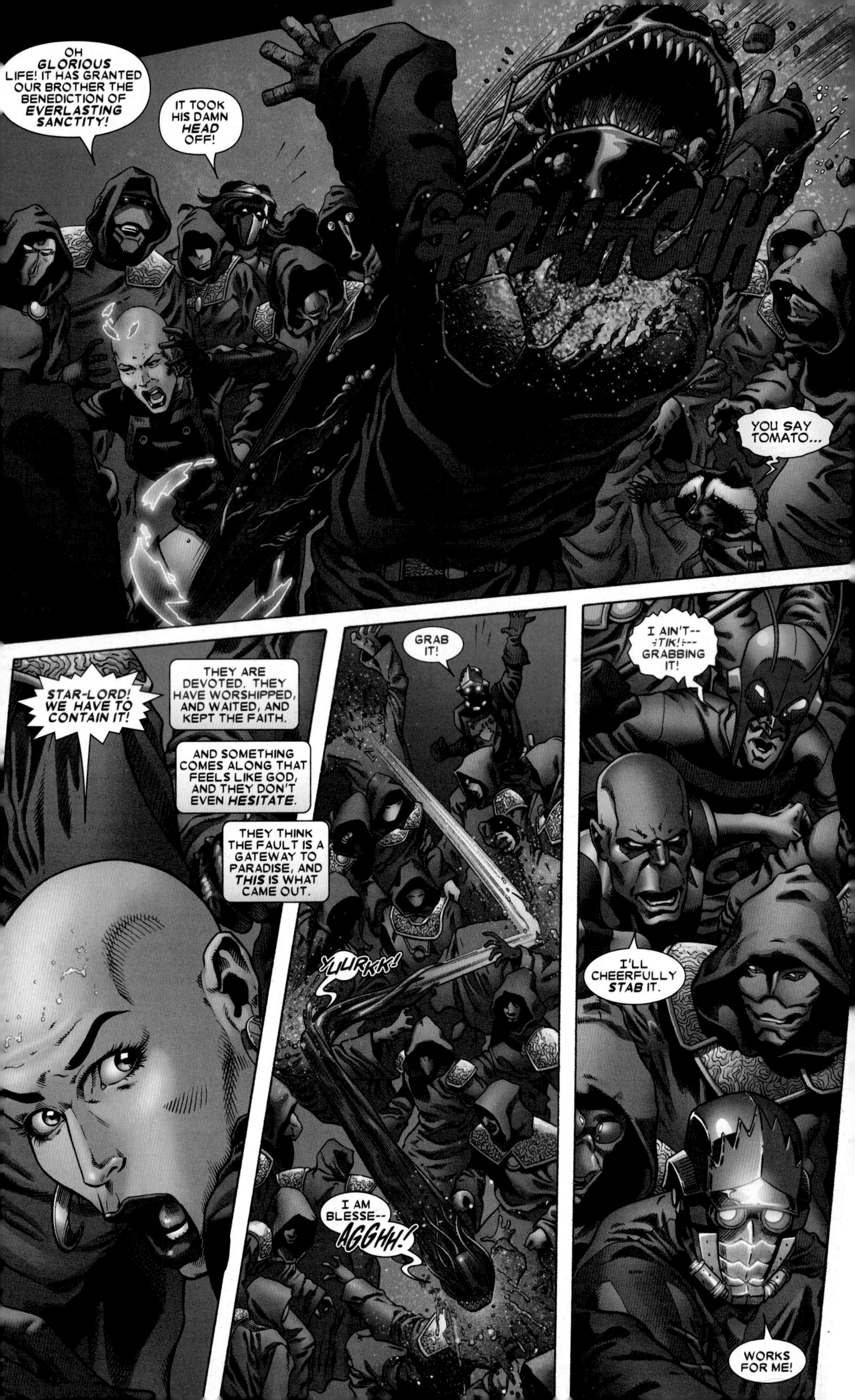
OH GLORIOUS LIFE! IT HAS GRANTED OUR BROTHER THE BENEDICTION OF EVERLASTING SANCTITY!
IT TOOK HIS DAMN HEAD OFF!
SPPLLTCHH
YOU SAY TOMATO...
STAR-LORD! WE HAVE TO CONTAIN IT!
THEY ARE DEVOTED. THEY HAVE WORSHIPPED, AND WAITED, AND KEPT THE FAITH.
AND SOMETHING COMES ALONG THAT FEELS LIKE GOD, AND THEY DON'T EVEN HESITATE.
THEY THINK THE FAULT IS A GATEWAY TO PARADISE, AND THIS IS WHAT CAME OUT.
GRAB IT!
YUURKK!
I AM BLESSE-- AGGHH!
I AIN'T-- -TIK!- -- GRABBING IT!
I'LL CHEERFULLY STAB IT.
WORKS FOR ME!

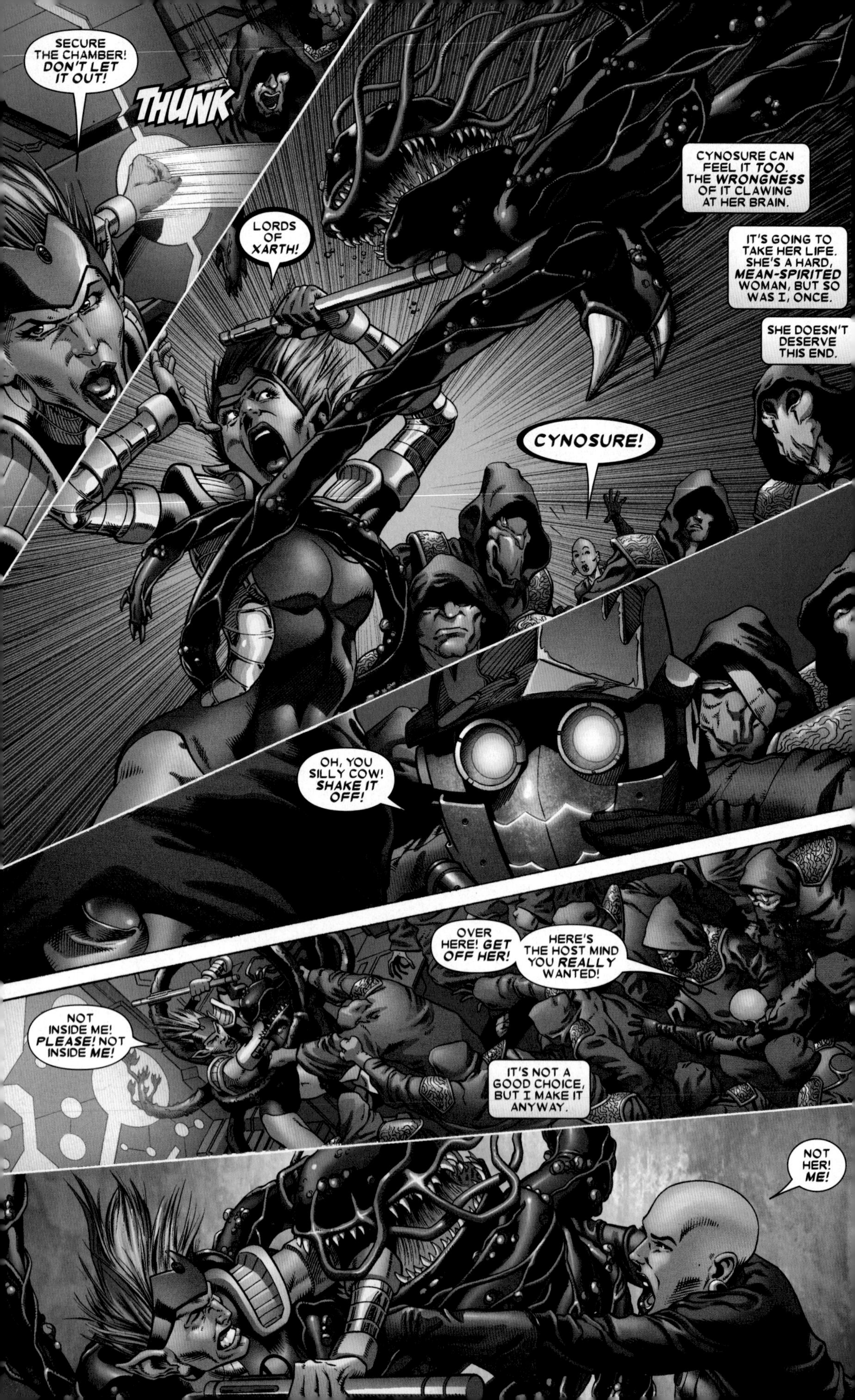
SECURE THE CHAMBER! DON'T LET IT OUT!
THUNK
LORDS OF XARTH!
CYNOSURE CAN FEEL IT TOO. THE WRONGNESS OF IT CLAWING AT HER BRAIN.
IT'S GOING TO TAKE HER LIFE. SHE'S A HARD, MEAN-SPIRITED WOMAN, BUT SO WAS I, ONCE.
SHE DOESN'T DESERVE THIS END.
CYNOSURE!
OH, YOU SILLY COW! SHAKE IT OFF!
OVER HERE! GET OFF HER!
HERE'S THE HOST MIND YOU REALLY WANTED!
NOT INSIDE ME! PLEASE! NOT INSIDE ME!
IT'S NOT A GOOD CHOICE, BUT I MAKE IT ANYWAY.
NOT HER! ME!

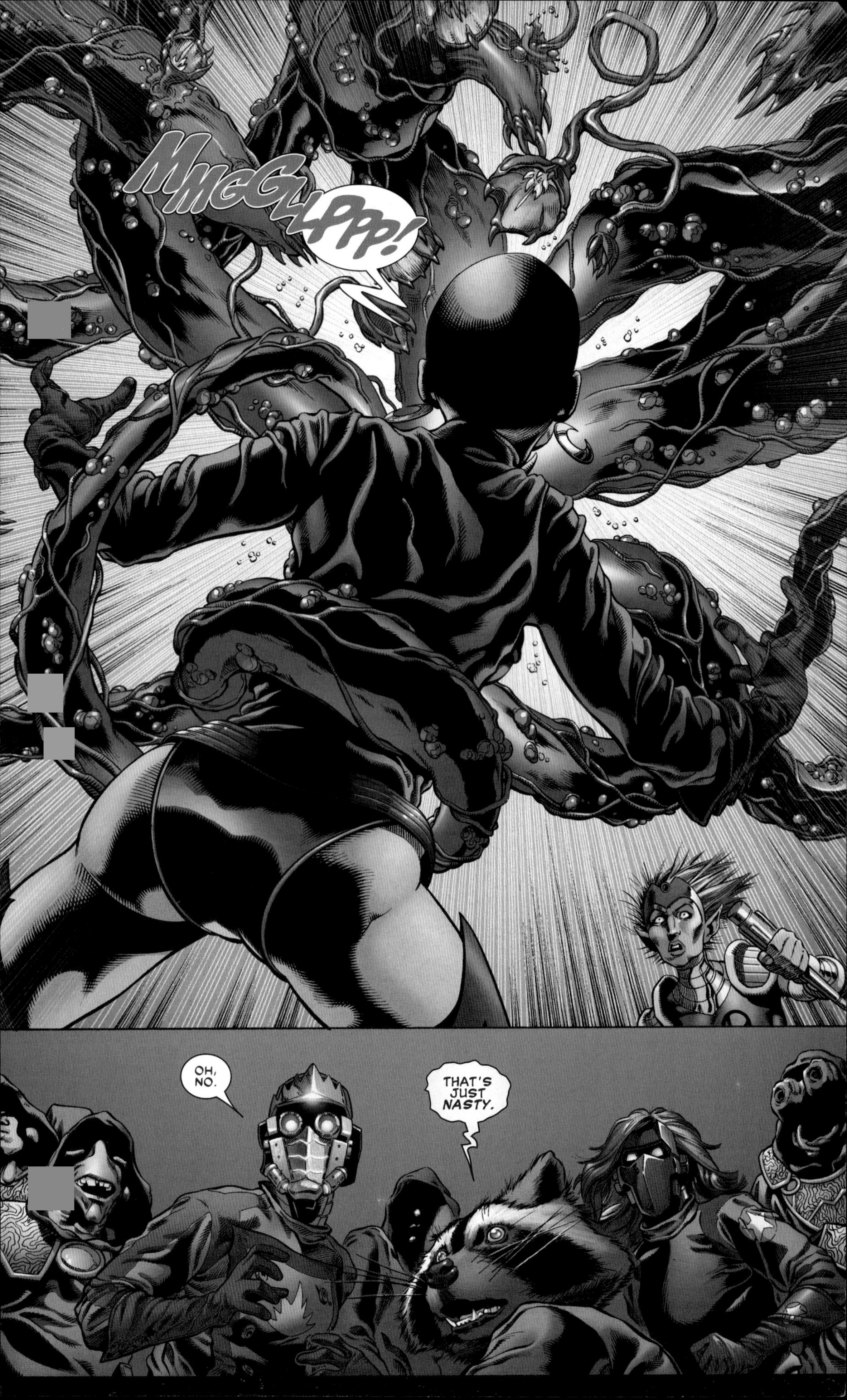
MMGGLLPPP!
OH, NO.
THAT'S JUST NASTY.

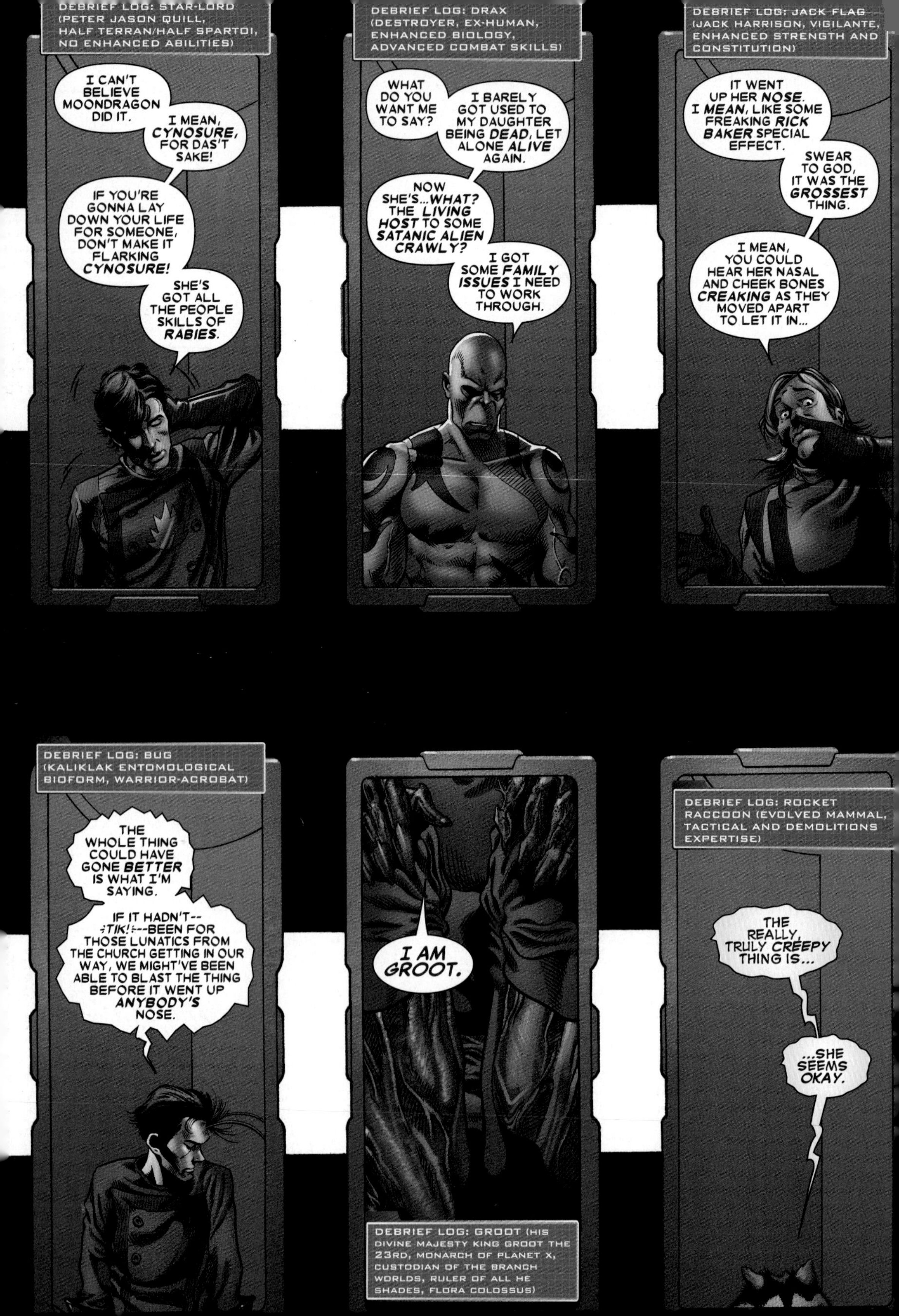

DEBRIEF LOG: STAR-LORD (PETER JASON QUILL, HALF TERRAN/HALF SPARTOI, NO ENHANCED ABILITIES)
I CAN'T BELIEVE MOONDRAGON DID IT.
I MEAN, CYNOSURE, FOR DAS'T SAKE!
IF YOU'RE GONNA LAY DOWN YOUR LIFE FOR SOMEONE, DON'T MAKE IT FLARKING CYNOSURE!
SHE'S GOT ALL THE PEOPLE SKILLS OF RABIES.
DEBRIEF LOG: DRAX (DESTROYER, EX-HUMAN, ENHANCED BIOLOGY, ADVANCED COMBAT SKILLS)
WHAT DO YOU WANT ME TO SAY?
I BARELY GOT USED TO MY DAUGHTER BEING DEAD, LET ALONE ALIVE AGAIN.
NOW SHE'S...WHAT? THE LIVING HOST TO SOME SATANIC ALIEN CRAWLY?
I GOT SOME FAMILY ISSUES I NEED TO WORK THROUGH.
DEBRIEF LOG: JACK FLAG (JACK HARRISON, VIGILANTE, ENHANCED STRENGTH AND CONSTITUTION)
IT WENT UP HER NOSE. I MEAN, LIKE SOME FREAKING RICK BAKER SPECIAL EFFECT.
SWEAR TO GOD, IT WAS THE GROSSEST THING.
I MEAN, YOU COULD HEAR HER NASAL AND CHEEK BONES CREAKING AS THEY MOVED APART TO LET IT IN...
DEBRIEF LOG: BUG (KALIKLAK ENTOMOLOGICAL BIOFORM, WARRIOR-ACROBAT)
THE WHOLE THING COULD HAVE GONE BETTER IS WHAT I'M SAYING.
IF IT HADN'T-- ‡TIK!‡--BEEN FOR THOSE LUNATICS FROM THE CHURCH GETTING IN OUR WAY, WE MIGHT'VE BEEN ABLE TO BLAST THE THING BEFORE IT WENT UP ANYBODY'S NOSE.
I AM GROOT.
DEBRIEF LOG: GROOT (HIS DIVINE MAJESTY KING GROOT THE 23RD, MONARCH OF PLANET X, CUSTODIAN OF THE BRANCH WORLDS, RULER OF ALL HE SHADES, FLORA COLOSSUS)
DEBRIEF LOG: ROCKET RACCOON (EVOLVED MAMMAL, TACTICAL AND DEMOLITIONS EXPERTISE)
THE REALLY, TRULY CREEPY THING IS...
...SHE SEEMS OKAY.

I'M OKAY.

YOU LOOK LIKE...

NAH.

GO ON?

I'M A TELEPATH. YOU WERE *GOING* TO SAY "I LOOK LIKE I'M CARRYING A *LITTLE EXTRA WEIGHT.*"

WHICH IS *UNDER-STANDABLE*, GIVEN THE ALIEN BIOMASS INSIDE ME.

IF YOU CAN READ MY MIND, WHY'D YOU ASK?

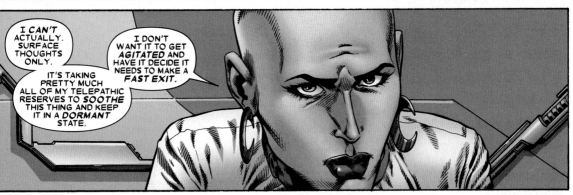

I *CAN'T* ACTUALLY. SURFACE THOUGHTS ONLY.

I DON'T WANT IT TO GET *AGITATED* AND HAVE IT DECIDE IT NEEDS TO MAKE A *FAST EXIT.*

IT'S TAKING PRETTY MUCH ALL OF MY TELEPATHIC RESERVES TO *SOOTHE* THIS THING AND KEEP IT IN A *DORMANT* STATE.

GUH. THAT'S NOTHING ANY OF US NEEDS TO SEE.

HEATHER, WHY DID YOU DO IT?

IT WAS ABOUT TO INSERT ITSELF INTO CYNOSURE.

AND WE'D HAVE BEEN *RID* OF HER FOREVER.

I KNOW YOU DON'T *MEAN* THAT. YOU DON'T SEE EYE-TO-EYE WITH THE LUMINALS, BUT THEY *ARE* GOOD GUYS TOO IN THE GRAND SCHEME OF THINGS.

MAYBE. BUT STILL... *WHY?*

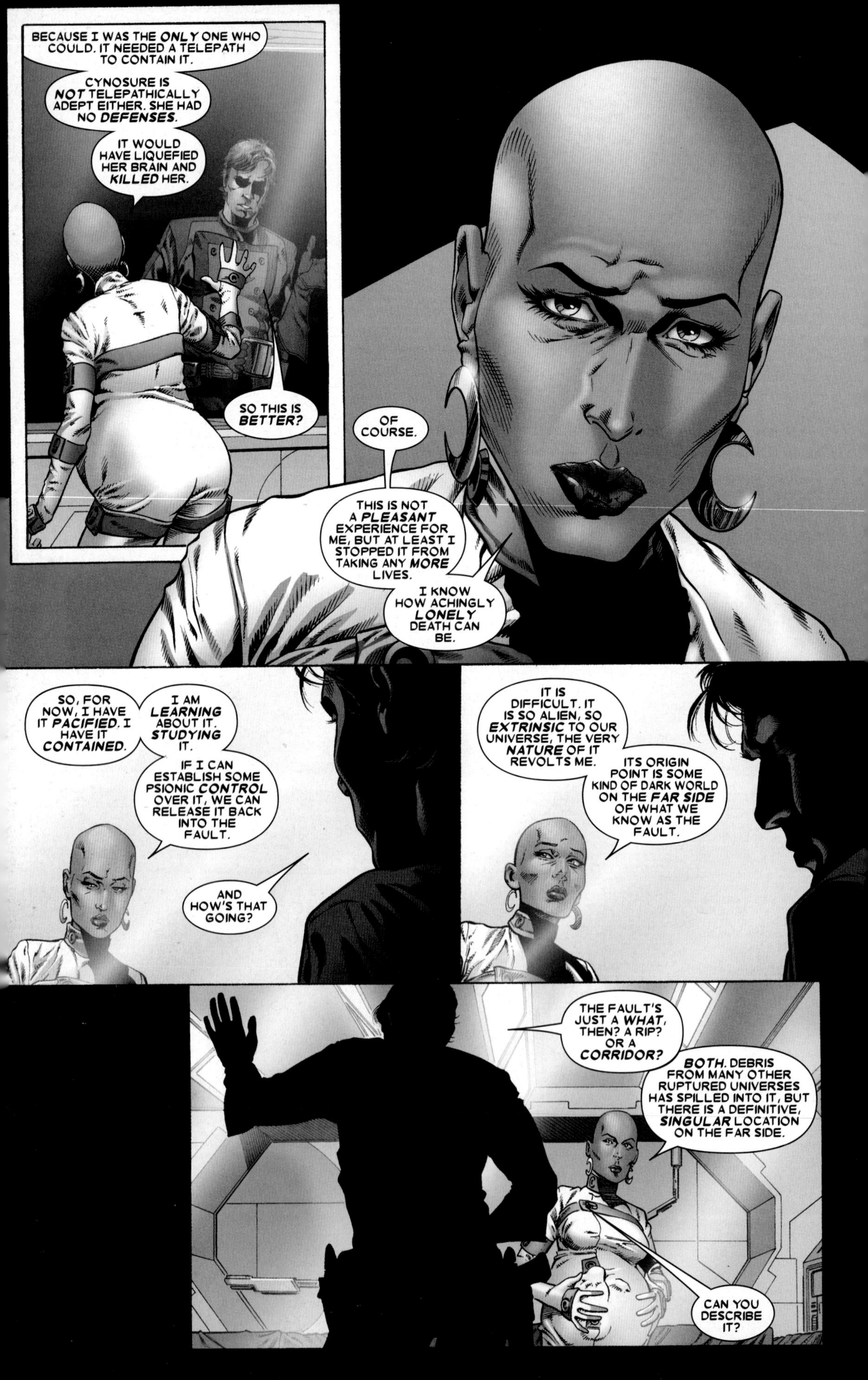

BECAUSE I WAS THE ONLY ONE WHO COULD. IT NEEDED A TELEPATH TO CONTAIN IT.
CYNOSURE IS NOT TELEPATHICALLY ADEPT EITHER. SHE HAD NO DEFENSES.
IT WOULD HAVE LIQUEFIED HER BRAIN AND KILLED HER.
SO THIS IS BETTER?
OF COURSE.
THIS IS NOT A PLEASANT EXPERIENCE FOR ME, BUT AT LEAST I STOPPED IT FROM TAKING ANY MORE LIVES.
I KNOW HOW ACHINGLY LONELY DEATH CAN BE.
SO, FOR NOW, I HAVE IT PACIFIED. I HAVE IT CONTAINED.
I AM LEARNING ABOUT IT. STUDYING IT.
IF I CAN ESTABLISH SOME PSIONIC CONTROL OVER IT, WE CAN RELEASE IT BACK INTO THE FAULT.
AND HOW'S THAT GOING?
IT IS DIFFICULT. IT IS SO ALIEN, SO EXTRINSIC TO OUR UNIVERSE, THE VERY NATURE OF IT REVOLTS ME.
ITS ORIGIN POINT IS SOME KIND OF DARK WORLD ON THE FAR SIDE OF WHAT WE KNOW AS THE FAULT.
THE FAULT'S JUST A WHAT, THEN? A RIP? OR A CORRIDOR?
BOTH. DEBRIS FROM MANY OTHER RUPTURED UNIVERSES HAS SPILLED INTO IT, BUT THERE IS A DEFINITIVE, SINGULAR LOCATION ON THE FAR SIDE.
CAN YOU DESCRIBE IT?

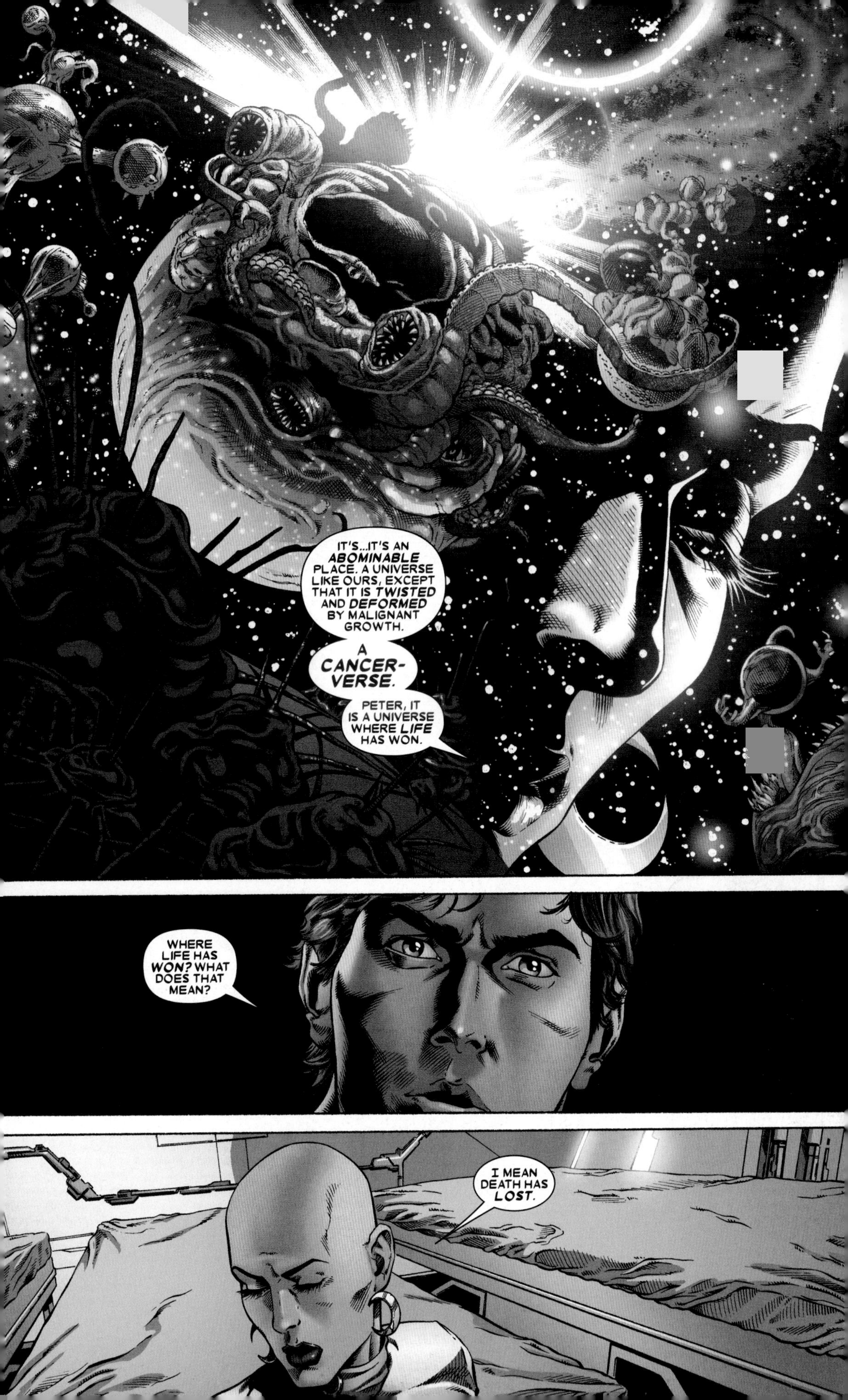
IT'S...IT'S AN ABOMINABLE PLACE. A UNIVERSE LIKE OURS, EXCEPT THAT IT IS TWISTED AND DEFORMED BY MALIGNANT GROWTH.
A CANCER-VERSE.
PETER, IT IS A UNIVERSE WHERE LIFE HAS WON.
WHERE LIFE HAS WON? WHAT DOES THAT MEAN?
I MEAN DEATH HAS LOST.

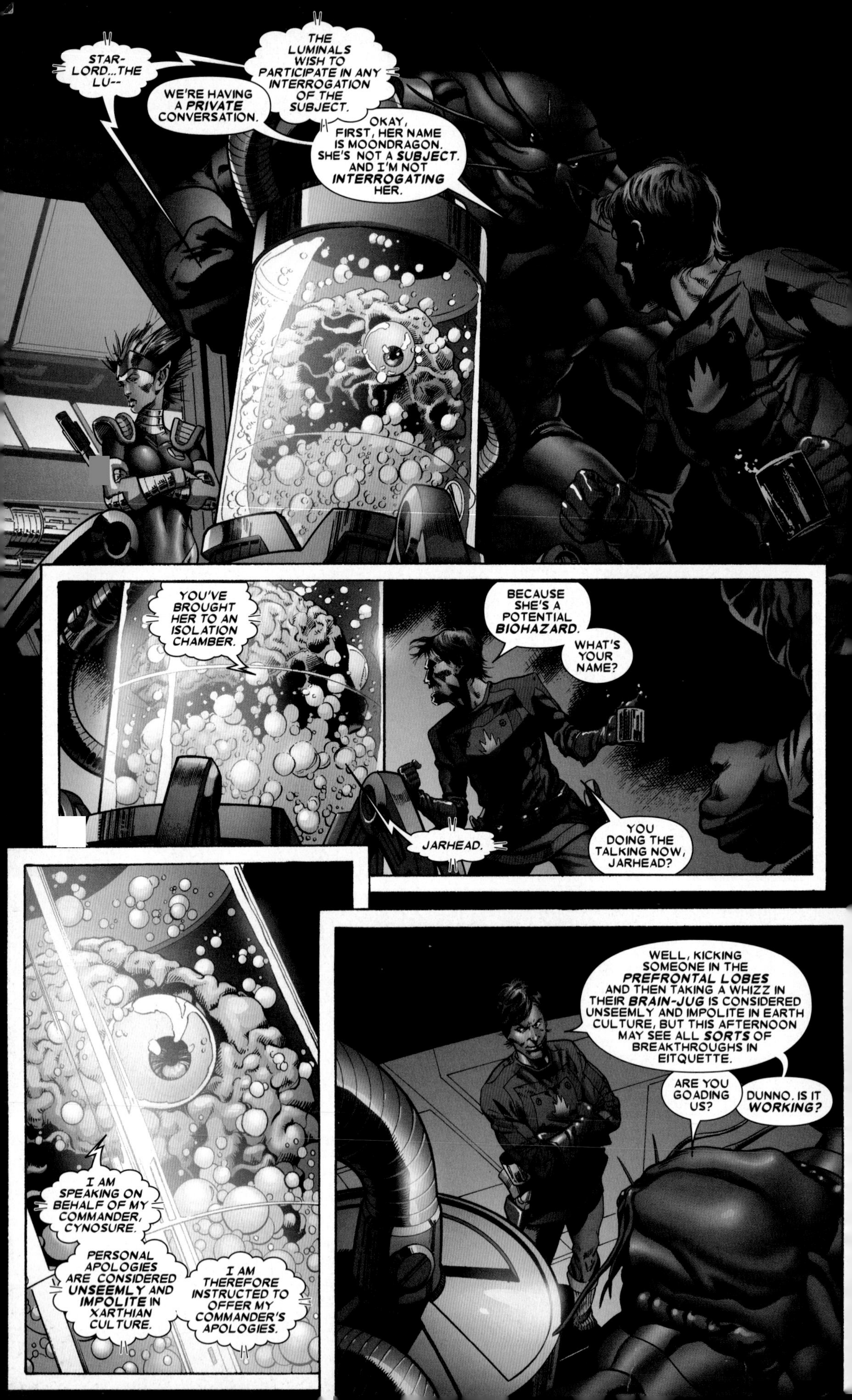
STAR-LORD...THE LU--
THE LUMINALS WISH TO PARTICIPATE IN ANY INTERROGATION OF THE SUBJECT.
WE'RE HAVING A PRIVATE CONVERSATION.
OKAY, FIRST, HER NAME IS MOONDRAGON. SHE'S NOT A SUBJECT. AND I'M NOT INTERROGATING HER.
YOU'VE BROUGHT HER TO AN ISOLATION CHAMBER.
BECAUSE SHE'S A POTENTIAL BIOHAZARD.
WHAT'S YOUR NAME?
JARHEAD.
YOU DOING THE TALKING NOW, JARHEAD?
I AM SPEAKING ON BEHALF OF MY COMMANDER, CYNOSURE.
PERSONAL APOLOGIES ARE CONSIDERED UNSEEMLY AND IMPOLITE IN XARTHIAN CULTURE.
I AM THEREFORE INSTRUCTED TO OFFER MY COMMANDER'S APOLOGIES.
WELL, KICKING SOMEONE IN THE PREFRONTAL LOBES AND THEN TAKING A WHIZZ IN THEIR BRAIN-JUG IS CONSIDERED UNSEEMLY AND IMPOLITE IN EARTH CULTURE, BUT THIS AFTERNOON MAY SEE ALL SORTS OF BREAKTHROUGHS IN EITQUETTE.
ARE YOU GOADING US?
DUNNO. IS IT WORKING?

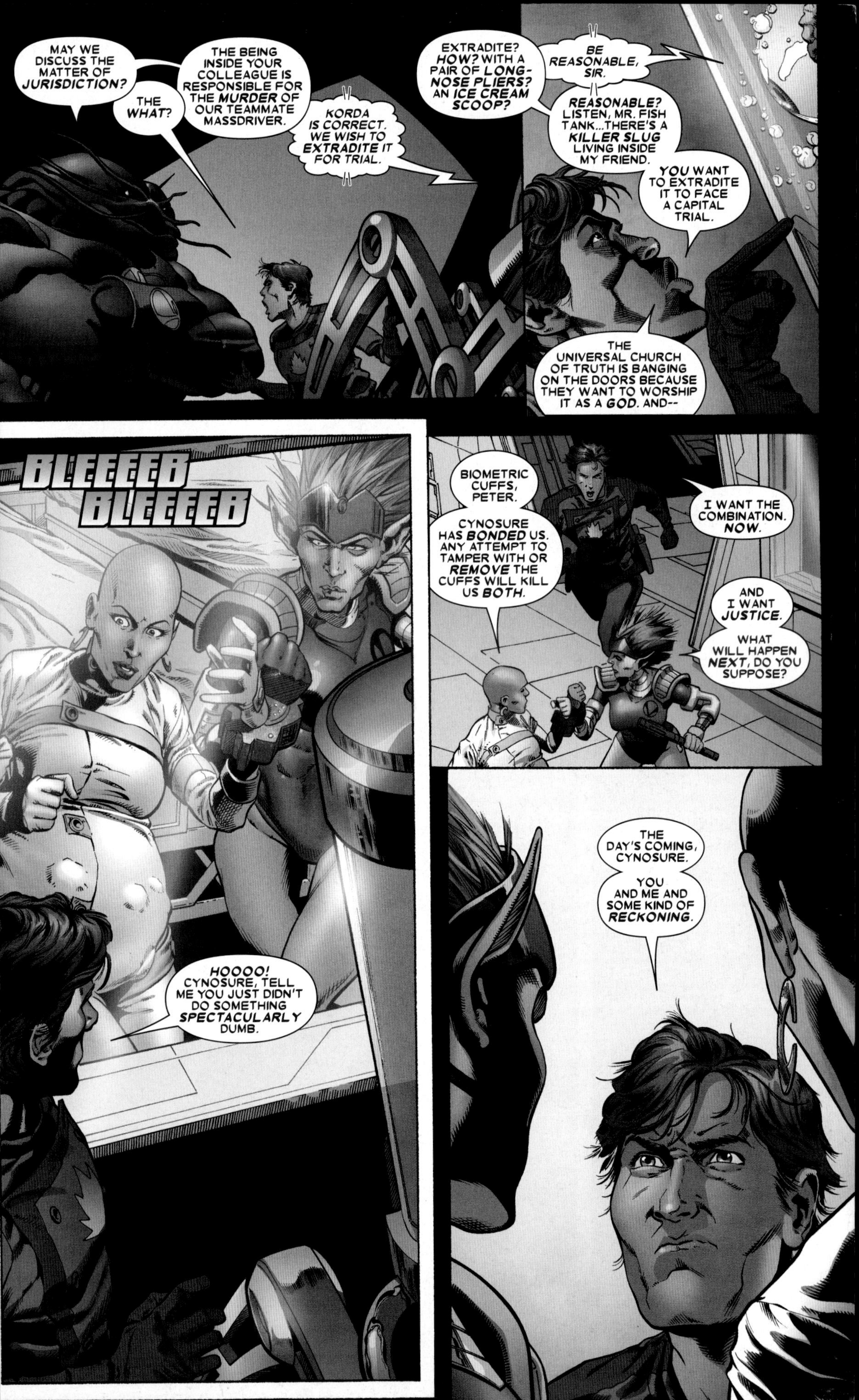
MAY WE DISCUSS THE MATTER OF JURISDICTION?
THE WHAT?
THE BEING INSIDE YOUR COLLEAGUE IS RESPONSIBLE FOR THE MURDER OF OUR TEAMMATE MASSDRIVER.
KORDA IS CORRECT. WE WISH TO EXTRADITE IT FOR TRIAL.
EXTRADITE? HOW? WITH A PAIR OF LONG-NOSE PLIERS? AN ICE CREAM SCOOP?
BE REASONABLE, SIR.
REASONABLE? LISTEN, MR. FISH TANK...THERE'S A KILLER SLUG LIVING INSIDE MY FRIEND.
YOU WANT TO EXTRADITE IT TO FACE A CAPITAL TRIAL.
THE UNIVERSAL CHURCH OF TRUTH IS BANGING ON THE DOORS BECAUSE THEY WANT TO WORSHIP IT AS A GOD. AND--
BLEEEEB BLEEEEB
HOOOO! CYNOSURE, TELL ME YOU JUST DIDN'T DO SOMETHING SPECTACULARLY DUMB.
BIOMETRIC CUFFS, PETER.
CYNOSURE HAS BONDED US. ANY ATTEMPT TO TAMPER WITH OR REMOVE THE CUFFS WILL KILL US BOTH.
I WANT THE COMBINATION. NOW.
AND I WANT JUSTICE.
WHAT WILL HAPPEN NEXT, DO YOU SUPPOSE?
THE DAY'S COMING, CYNOSURE.
YOU AND ME AND SOME KIND OF RECKONING.

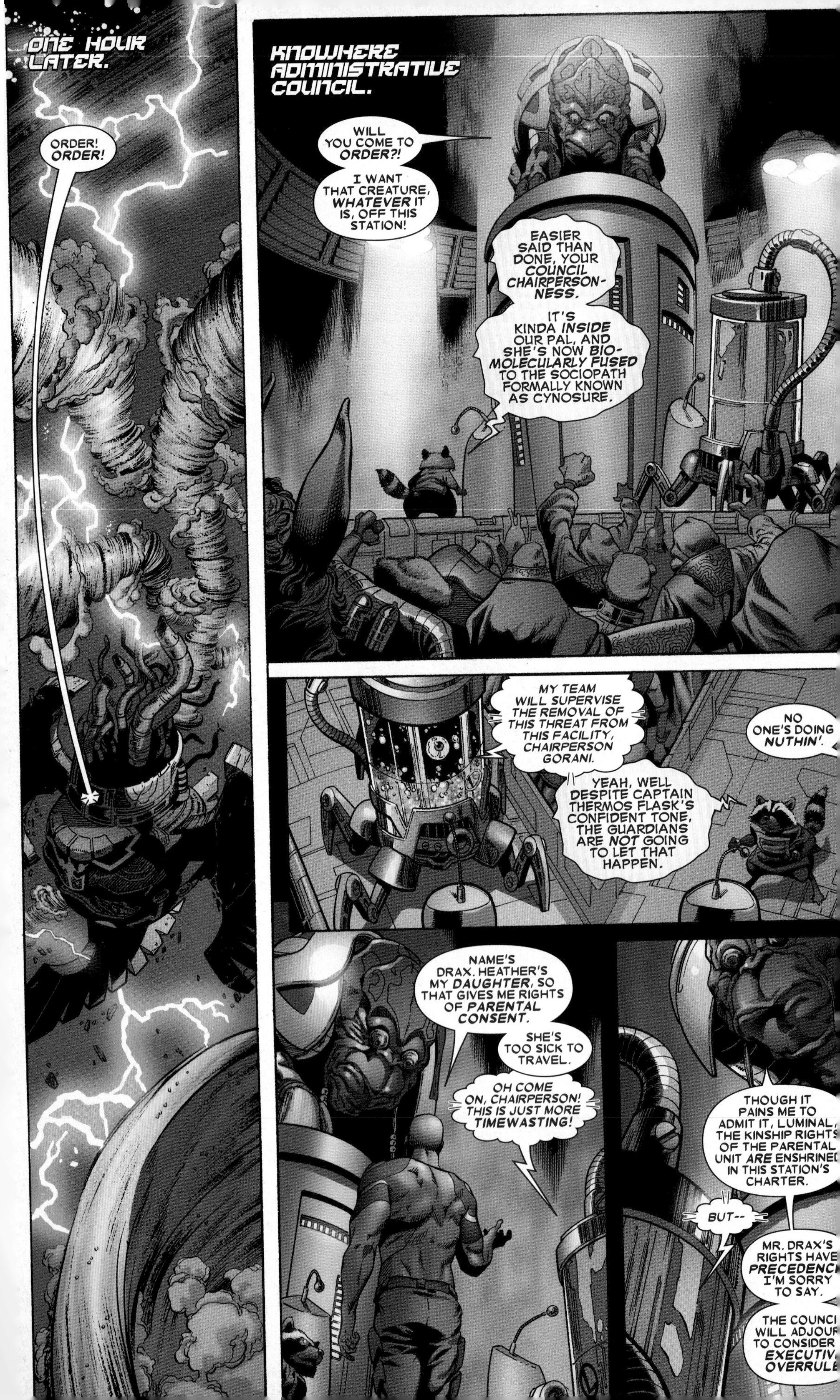
ONE HOUR LATER.
ORDER! ORDER!
KNOWHERE ADMINISTRATIVE COUNCIL.
WILL YOU COME TO ORDER?!
I WANT THAT CREATURE, WHATEVER IT IS, OFF THIS STATION!
EASIER SAID THAN DONE, YOUR COUNCIL CHAIRPERSON-NESS.
IT'S KINDA INSIDE OUR PAL, AND SHE'S NOW BIO-MOLECULARLY FUSED TO THE SOCIOPATH FORMALLY KNOWN AS CYNOSURE.
MY TEAM WILL SUPERVISE THE REMOVAL OF THIS THREAT FROM THIS FACILITY, CHAIRPERSON GORANI.
NO ONE'S DOING NUTHIN'.
YEAH, WELL DESPITE CAPTAIN THERMOS FLASK'S CONFIDENT TONE, THE GUARDIANS ARE NOT GOING TO LET THAT HAPPEN.
NAME'S DRAX. HEATHER'S MY DAUGHTER, SO THAT GIVES ME RIGHTS OF PARENTAL CONSENT.
SHE'S TOO SICK TO TRAVEL.
OH COME ON, CHAIRPERSON! THIS IS JUST MORE TIMEWASTING!
THOUGH IT PAINS ME TO ADMIT IT, LUMINAL, THE KINSHIP RIGHTS OF THE PARENTAL UNIT ARE ENSHRINED IN THIS STATION'S CHARTER.
BUT--
MR. DRAX'S RIGHTS HAVE PRECEDENC I'M SORRY TO SAY.
THE COUNCI WILL ADJOUR TO CONSIDER EXECUTIV OVERRUL

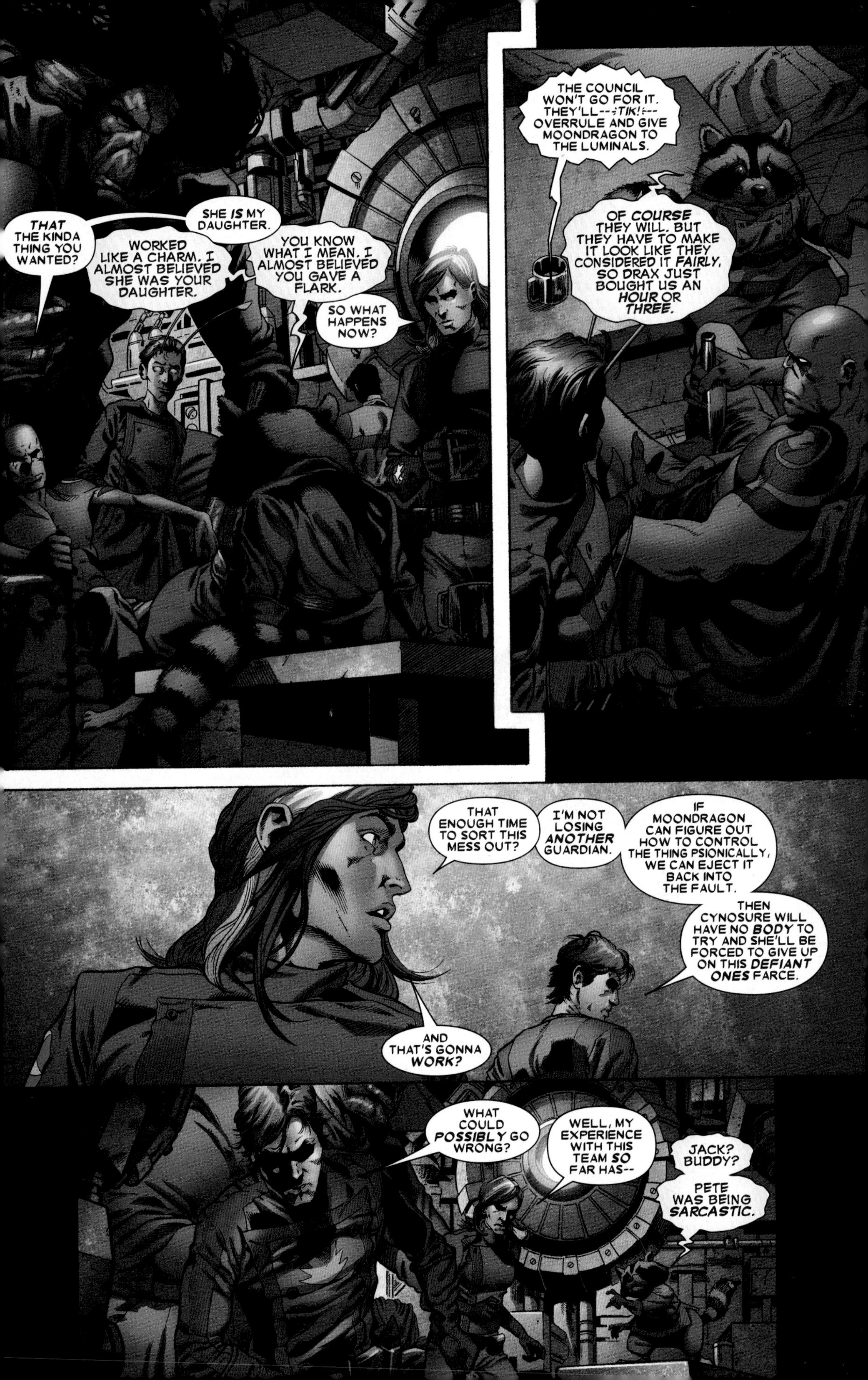
THAT THE KINDA THING YOU WANTED?
SHE IS MY DAUGHTER.
WORKED LIKE A CHARM. I ALMOST BELIEVED SHE WAS YOUR DAUGHTER.
YOU KNOW WHAT I MEAN. I ALMOST BELIEVED YOU GAVE A FLARK.
SO WHAT HAPPENS NOW?
THE COUNCIL WON'T GO FOR IT. THEY'LL--¡TIK!--OVERRULE AND GIVE MOONDRAGON TO THE LUMINALS.
OF COURSE THEY WILL, BUT THEY HAVE TO MAKE IT LOOK LIKE THEY CONSIDERED IT FAIRLY, SO DRAX JUST BOUGHT US AN HOUR OR THREE.
THAT ENOUGH TIME TO SORT THIS MESS OUT?
I'M NOT LOSING ANOTHER GUARDIAN.
IF MOONDRAGON CAN FIGURE OUT HOW TO CONTROL THE THING PSIONICALLY, WE CAN EJECT IT BACK INTO THE FAULT.
THEN CYNOSURE WILL HAVE NO BODY TO TRY AND SHE'LL BE FORCED TO GIVE UP ON THIS DEFIANT ONES FARCE.
AND THAT'S GONNA WORK?
WHAT COULD POSSIBLY GO WRONG?
WELL, MY EXPERIENCE WITH THIS TEAM SO FAR HAS--
JACK? BUDDY?
PETE WAS BEING SARCASTIC.

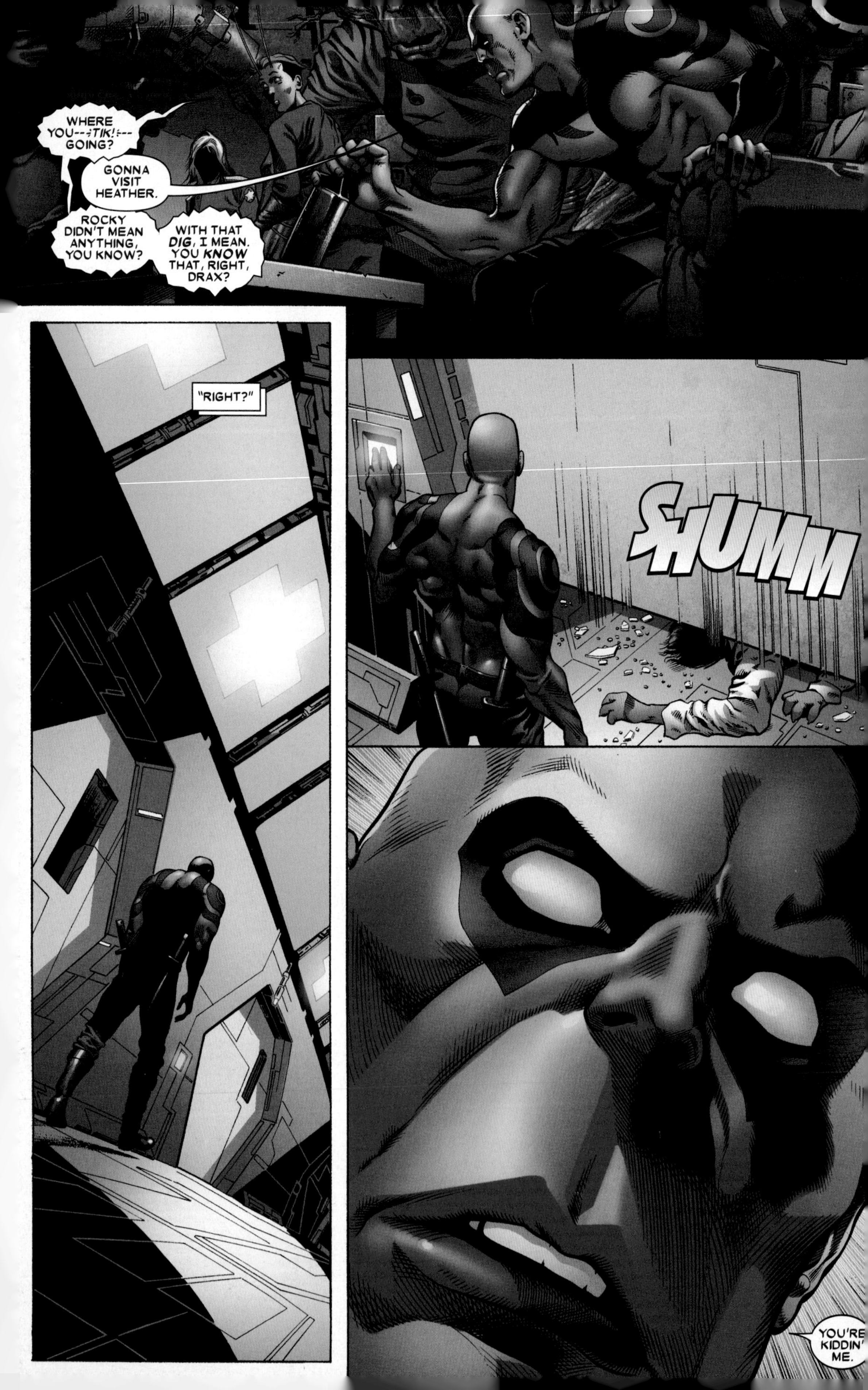
WHERE YOU--¡TIK!¡--GOING?
GONNA VISIT HEATHER.
ROCKY DIDN'T MEAN ANYTHING, YOU KNOW?
WITH THAT DIG, I MEAN. YOU KNOW THAT, RIGHT, DRAX?
"RIGHT?"
SHUMM
YOU'RE KIDDIN' ME.

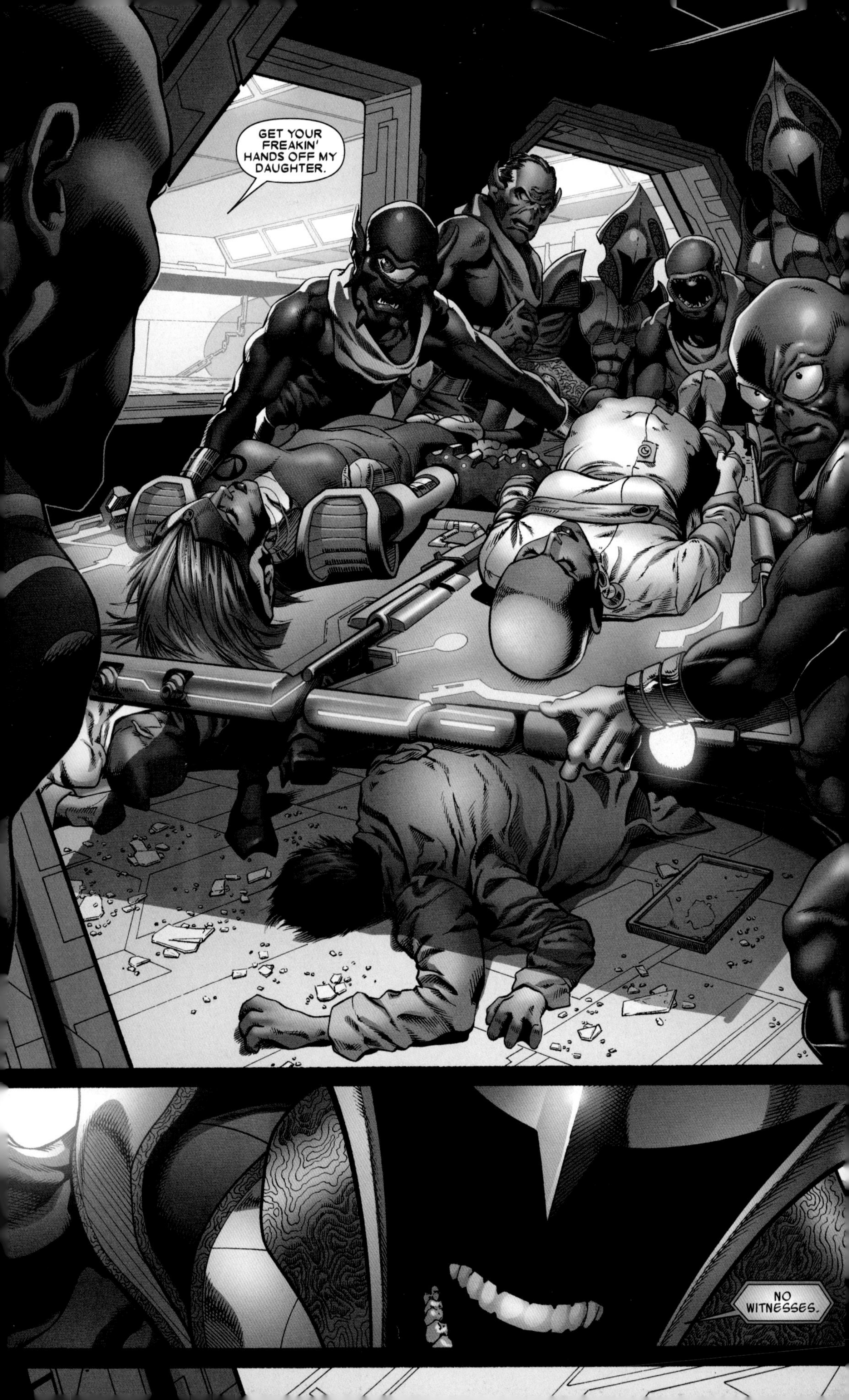
GET YOUR FREAKIN' HANDS OFF MY DAUGHTER.
NO WITNESSES.

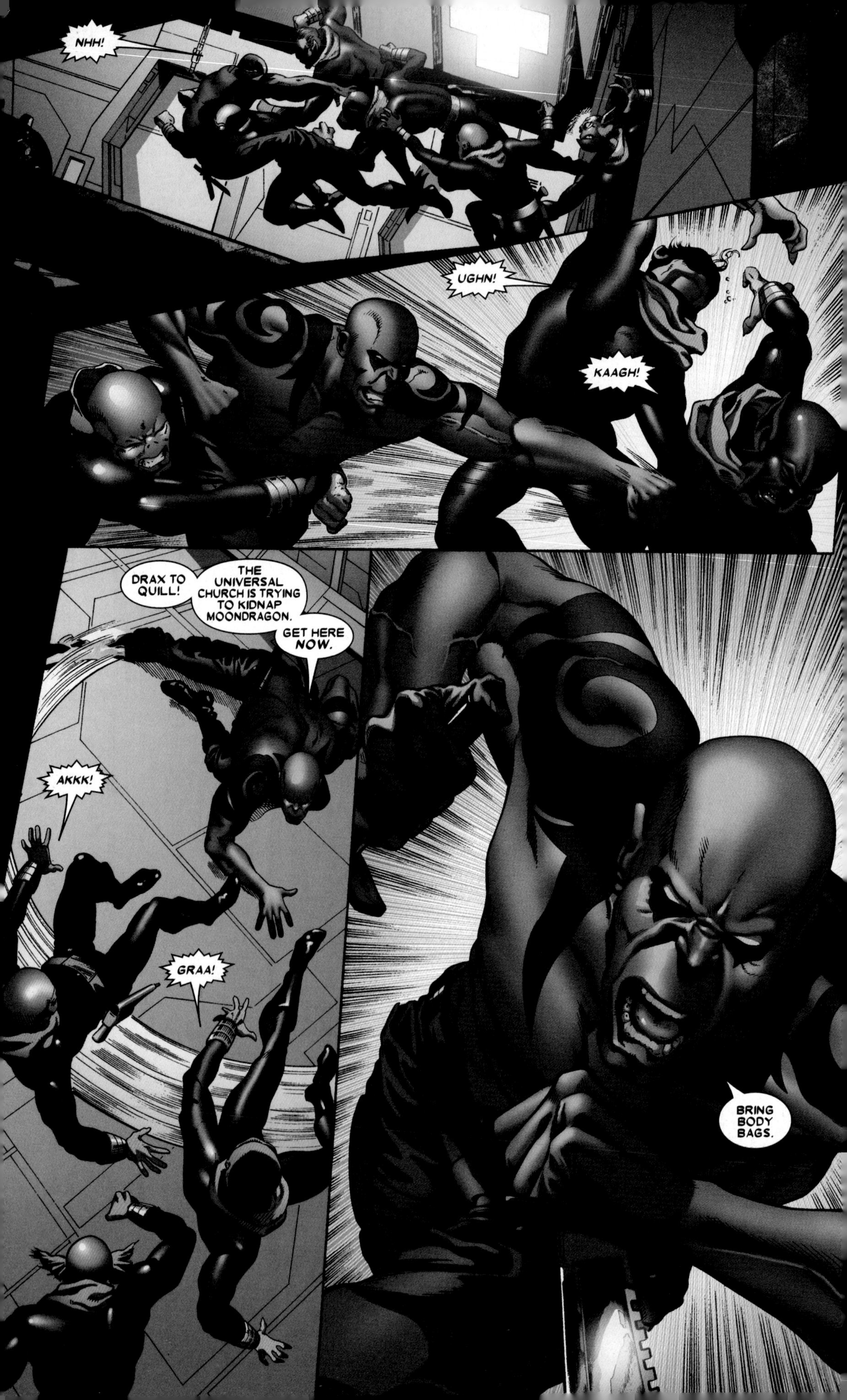
NHH!
UGHN!
KAAGH!
DRAX TO QUILL!
THE UNIVERSAL CHURCH IS TRYING TO KIDNAP MOONDRAGON.
GET HERE NOW.
AKKK!
GRAA!
BRING BODY BAGS.

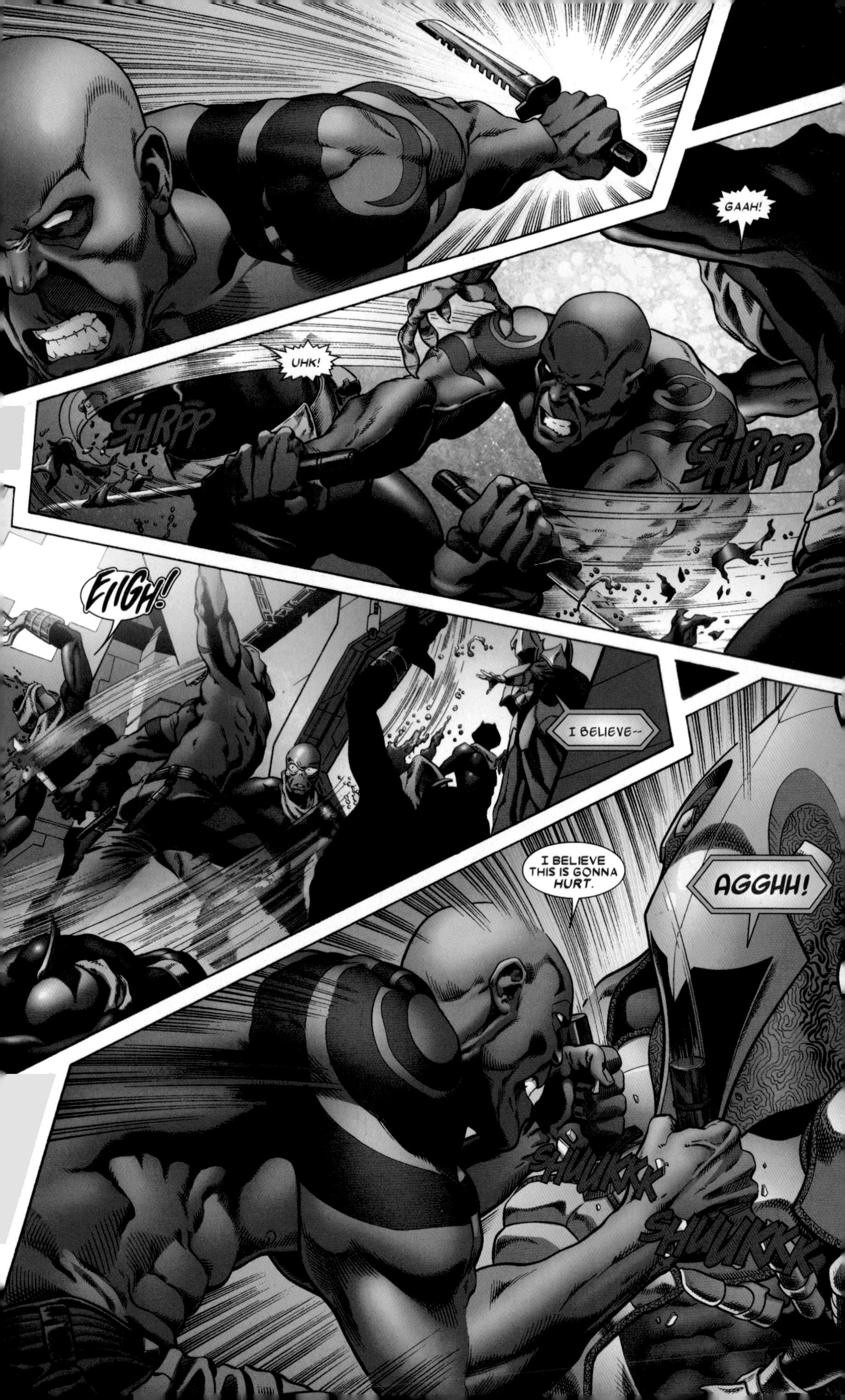
GAAH!
UHK!
SHRPP
SHRPP
EIIGH!
I BELIEVE--
I BELIEVE THIS IS GONNA HURT.
AGGHH!
SHUKK
SHUKK

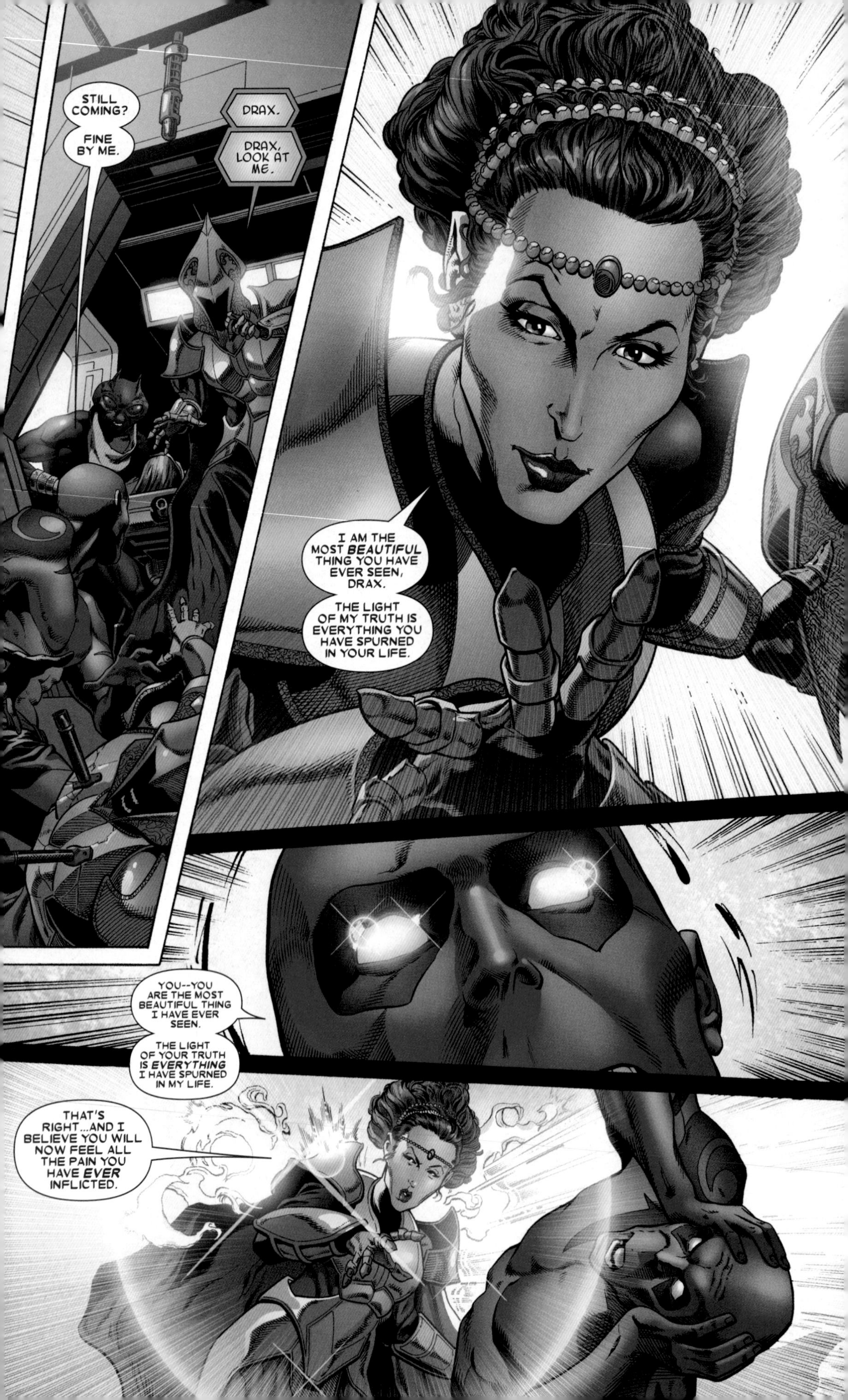
STILL COMING?
FINE BY ME.
DRAX.
DRAX, LOOK AT ME.
I AM THE MOST BEAUTIFUL THING YOU HAVE EVER SEEN, DRAX.
THE LIGHT OF MY TRUTH IS EVERYTHING YOU HAVE SPURNED IN YOUR LIFE.
YOU--YOU ARE THE MOST BEAUTIFUL THING I HAVE EVER SEEN.
THE LIGHT OF YOUR TRUTH IS EVERYTHING I HAVE SPURNED IN MY LIFE.
THAT'S RIGHT...AND I BELIEVE YOU WILL NOW FEEL ALL THE PAIN YOU HAVE EVER INFLICTED.

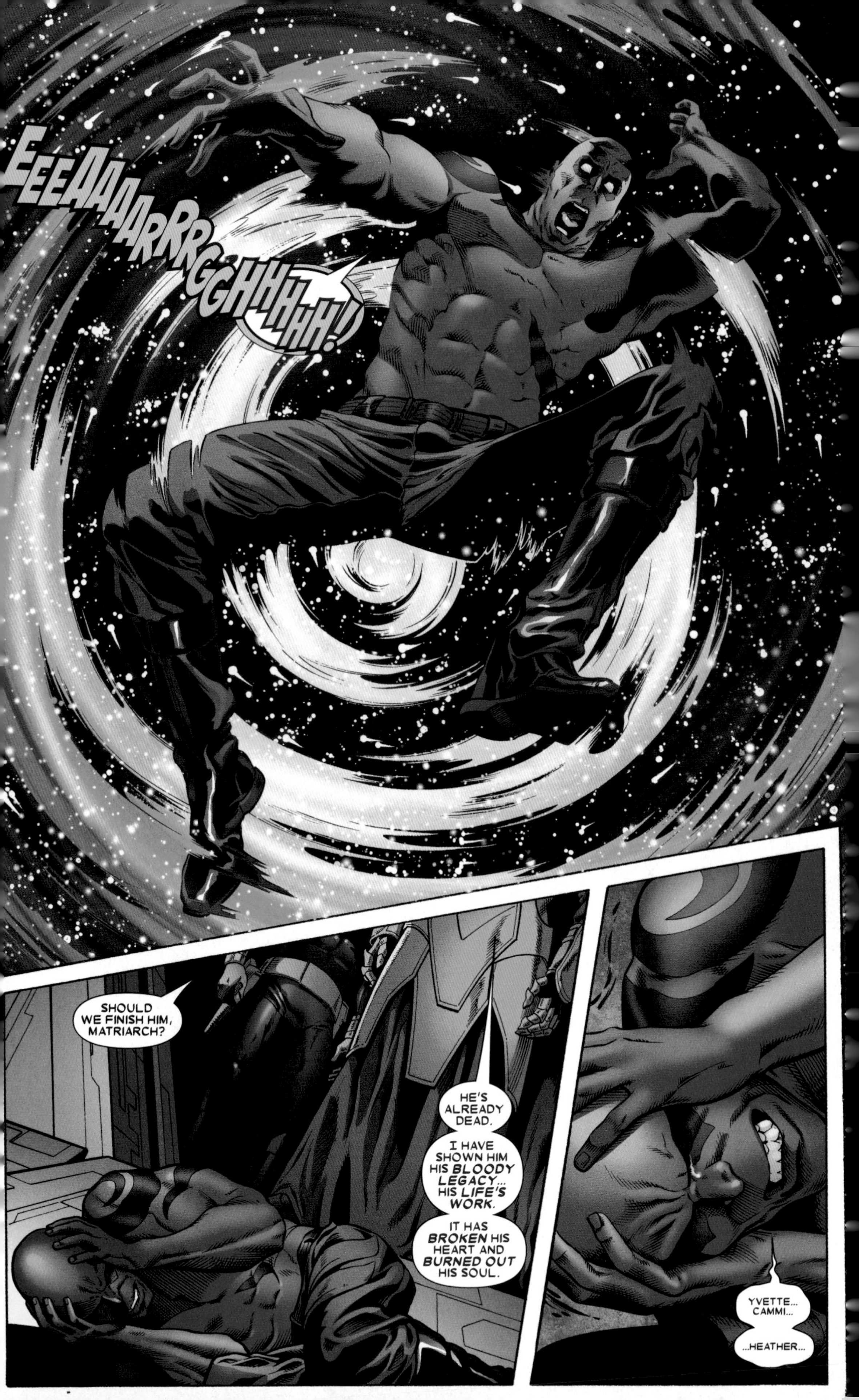
EEEAAAARRRGGHHHHH!!
SHOULD WE FINISH HIM, MATRIARCH?
HE'S ALREADY DEAD.
I HAVE SHOWN HIM HIS BLOODY LEGACY... HIS LIFE'S WORK.
IT HAS BROKEN HIS HEART AND BURNED OUT HIS SOUL.
YVETTE... CAMMI...
...HEATHER...

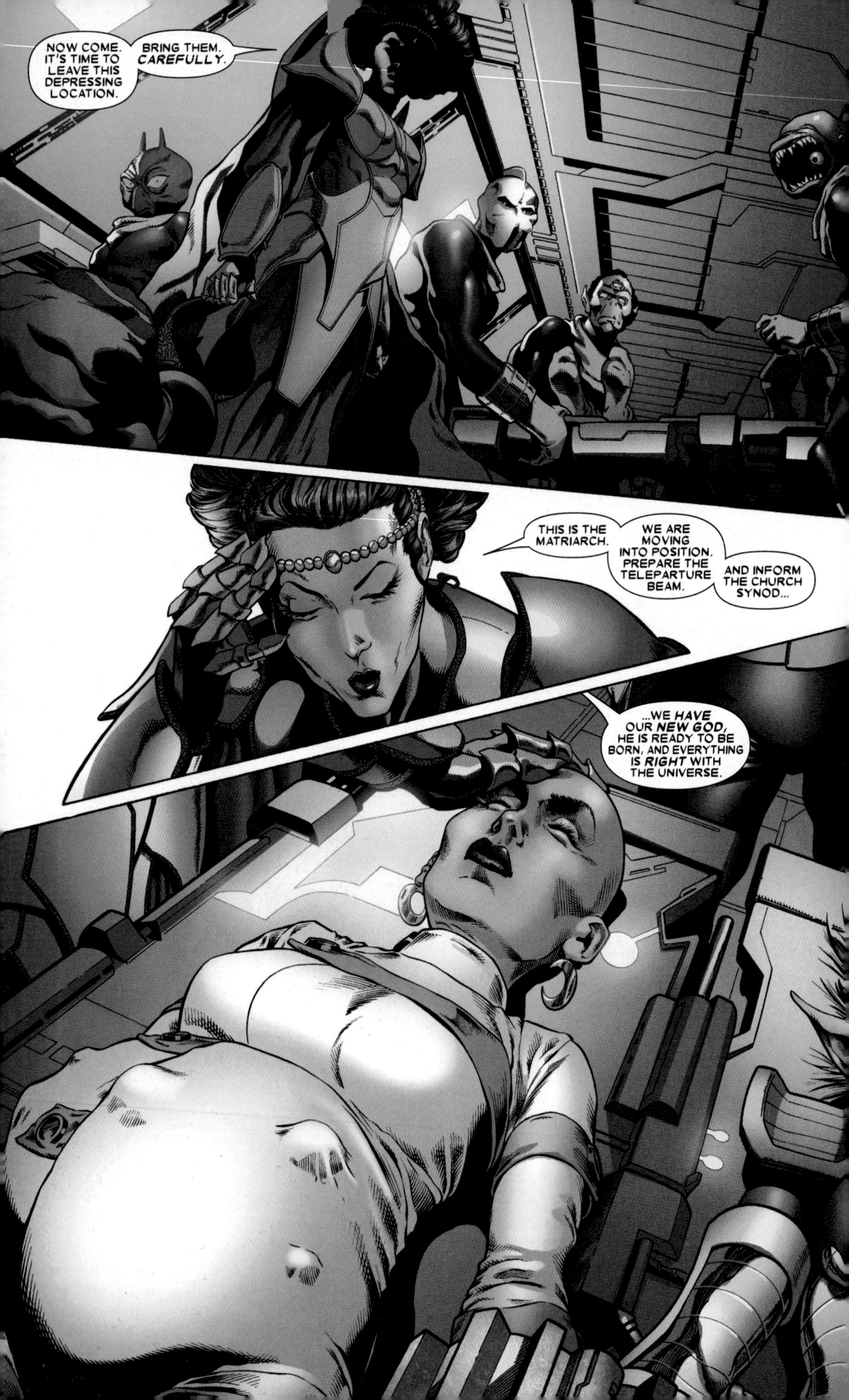
NOW COME. IT'S TIME TO LEAVE THIS DEPRESSING LOCATION.
BRING THEM. CAREFULLY.
THIS IS THE MATRIARCH.
WE ARE MOVING INTO POSITION. PREPARE THE TELEPARTURE BEAM.
AND INFORM THE CHURCH SYNOD...
...WE HAVE OUR NEW GOD, HE IS READY TO BE BORN, AND EVERYTHING IS RIGHT WITH THE UNIVERSE.

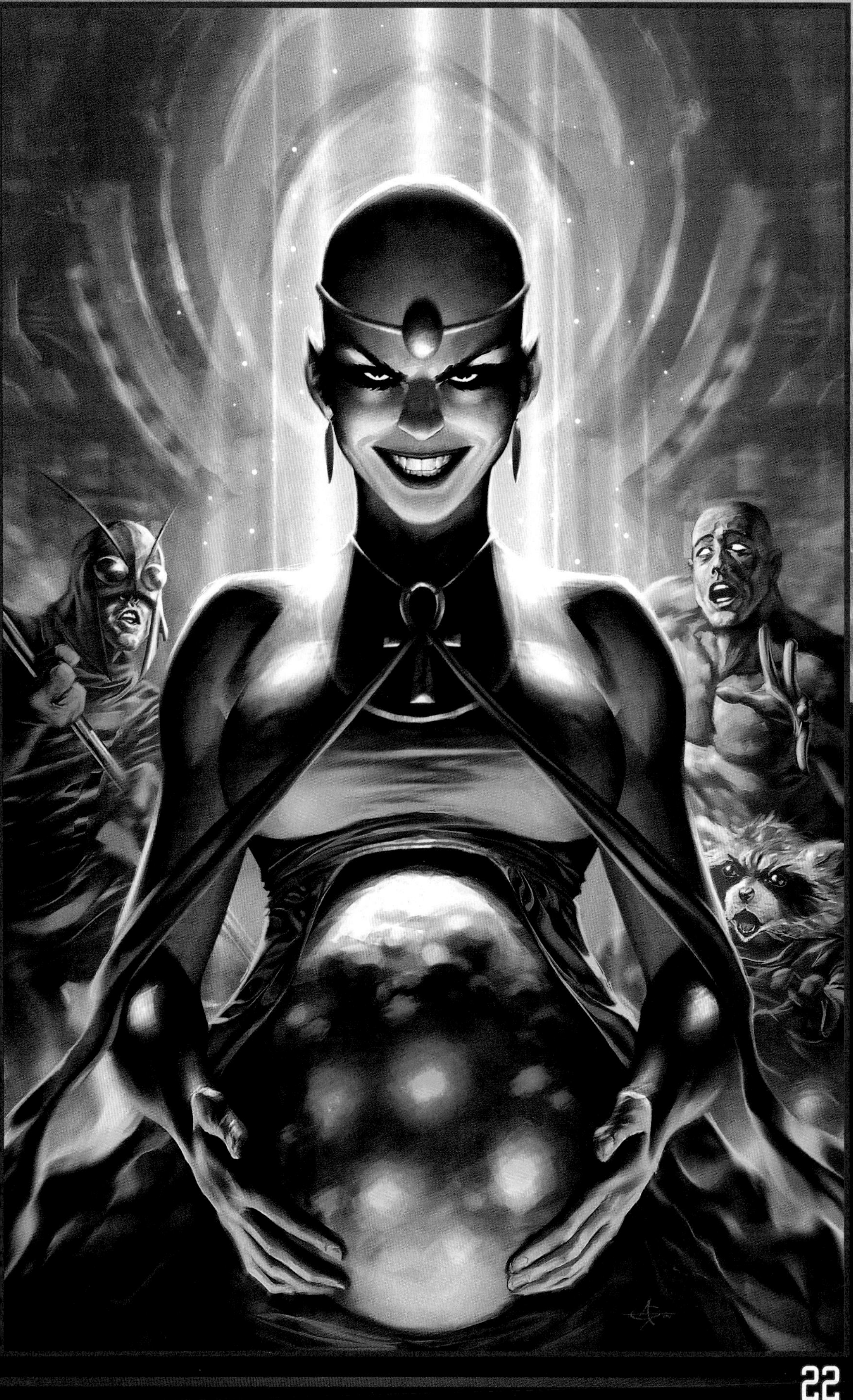

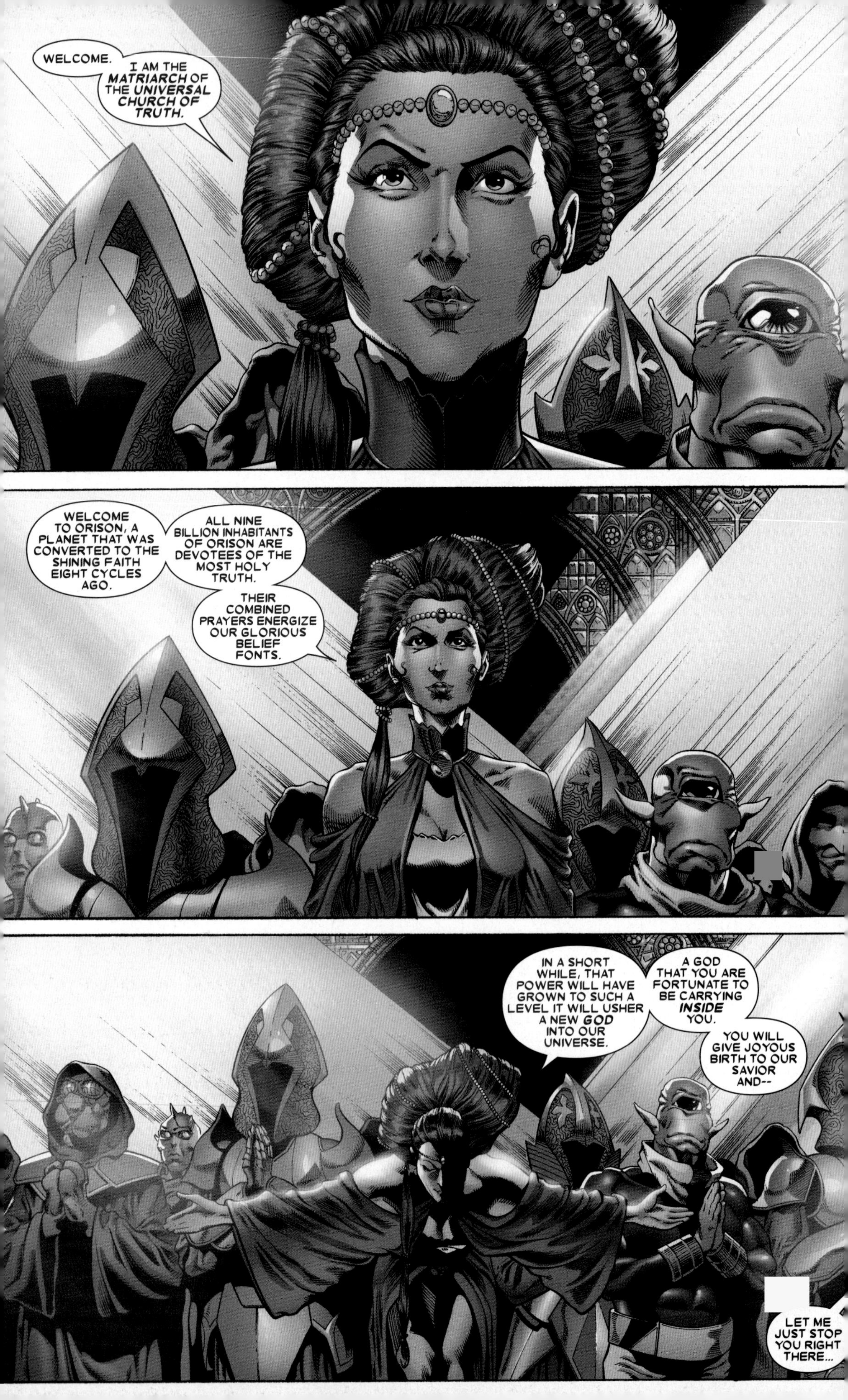
WELCOME.
I AM THE MATRIARCH OF THE UNIVERSAL CHURCH OF TRUTH.
WELCOME TO ORISON, A PLANET THAT WAS CONVERTED TO THE SHINING FAITH EIGHT CYCLES AGO.
ALL NINE BILLION INHABITANTS OF ORISON ARE DEVOTEES OF THE MOST HOLY TRUTH.
THEIR COMBINED PRAYERS ENERGIZE OUR GLORIOUS BELIEF FONTS.
IN A SHORT WHILE, THAT POWER WILL HAVE GROWN TO SUCH A LEVEL IT WILL USHER A NEW GOD INTO OUR UNIVERSE.
A GOD THAT YOU ARE FORTUNATE TO BE CARRYING INSIDE YOU.
YOU WILL GIVE JOYOUS BIRTH TO OUR SAVIOR AND--
LET ME JUST STOP YOU RIGHT THERE...

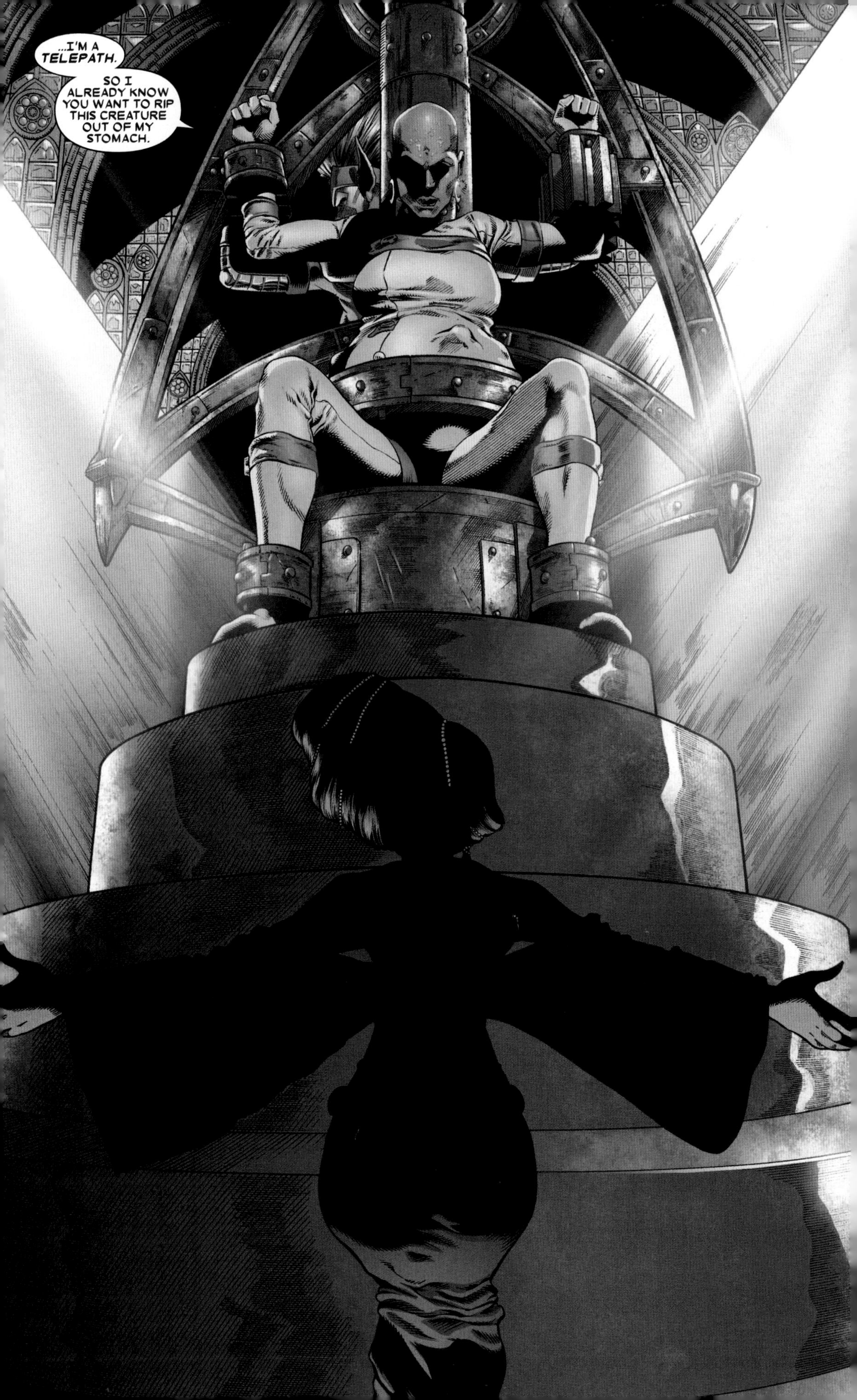
...I'M A TELEPATH.
SO I ALREADY KNOW YOU WANT TO RIP THIS CREATURE OUT OF MY STOMACH.

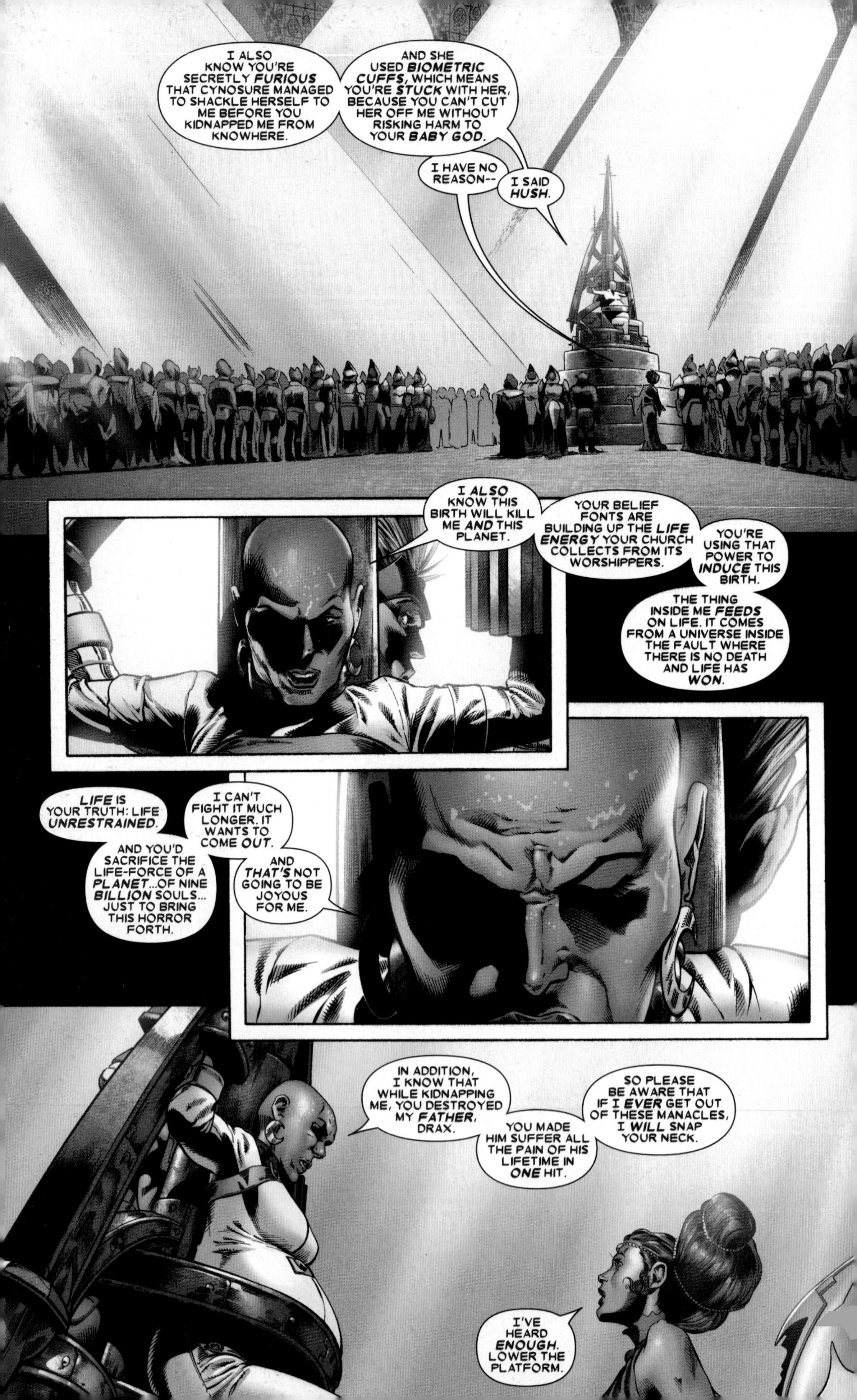
I ALSO KNOW YOU'RE SECRETLY FURIOUS THAT CYNOSURE MANAGED TO SHACKLE HERSELF TO ME BEFORE YOU KIDNAPPED ME FROM KNOWHERE.
AND SHE USED BIOMETRIC CUFFS, WHICH MEANS YOU'RE STUCK WITH HER, BECAUSE YOU CAN'T CUT HER OFF ME WITHOUT RISKING HARM TO YOUR BABY GOD.
I HAVE NO REASON--
I SAID HUSH.
I ALSO KNOW THIS BIRTH WILL KILL ME AND THIS PLANET.
YOUR BELIEF FONTS ARE BUILDING UP THE LIFE ENERGY YOUR CHURCH COLLECTS FROM ITS WORSHIPPERS.
YOU'RE USING THAT POWER TO INDUCE THIS BIRTH.
THE THING INSIDE ME FEEDS ON LIFE. IT COMES FROM A UNIVERSE INSIDE THE FAULT WHERE THERE IS NO DEATH AND LIFE HAS WON.
LIFE IS YOUR TRUTH: LIFE UNRESTRAINED.
AND YOU'D SACRIFICE THE LIFE-FORCE OF A PLANET...OF NINE BILLION SOULS... JUST TO BRING THIS HORROR FORTH.
I CAN'T FIGHT IT MUCH LONGER. IT WANTS TO COME OUT.
AND THAT'S NOT GOING TO BE JOYOUS FOR ME.
IN ADDITION, I KNOW THAT WHILE KIDNAPPING ME, YOU DESTROYED MY FATHER, DRAX.
YOU MADE HIM SUFFER ALL THE PAIN OF HIS LIFETIME IN ONE HIT.
SO PLEASE BE AWARE THAT IF I EVER GET OUT OF THESE MANACLES, I WILL SNAP YOUR NECK.
I'VE HEARD ENOUGH. LOWER THE PLATFORM.

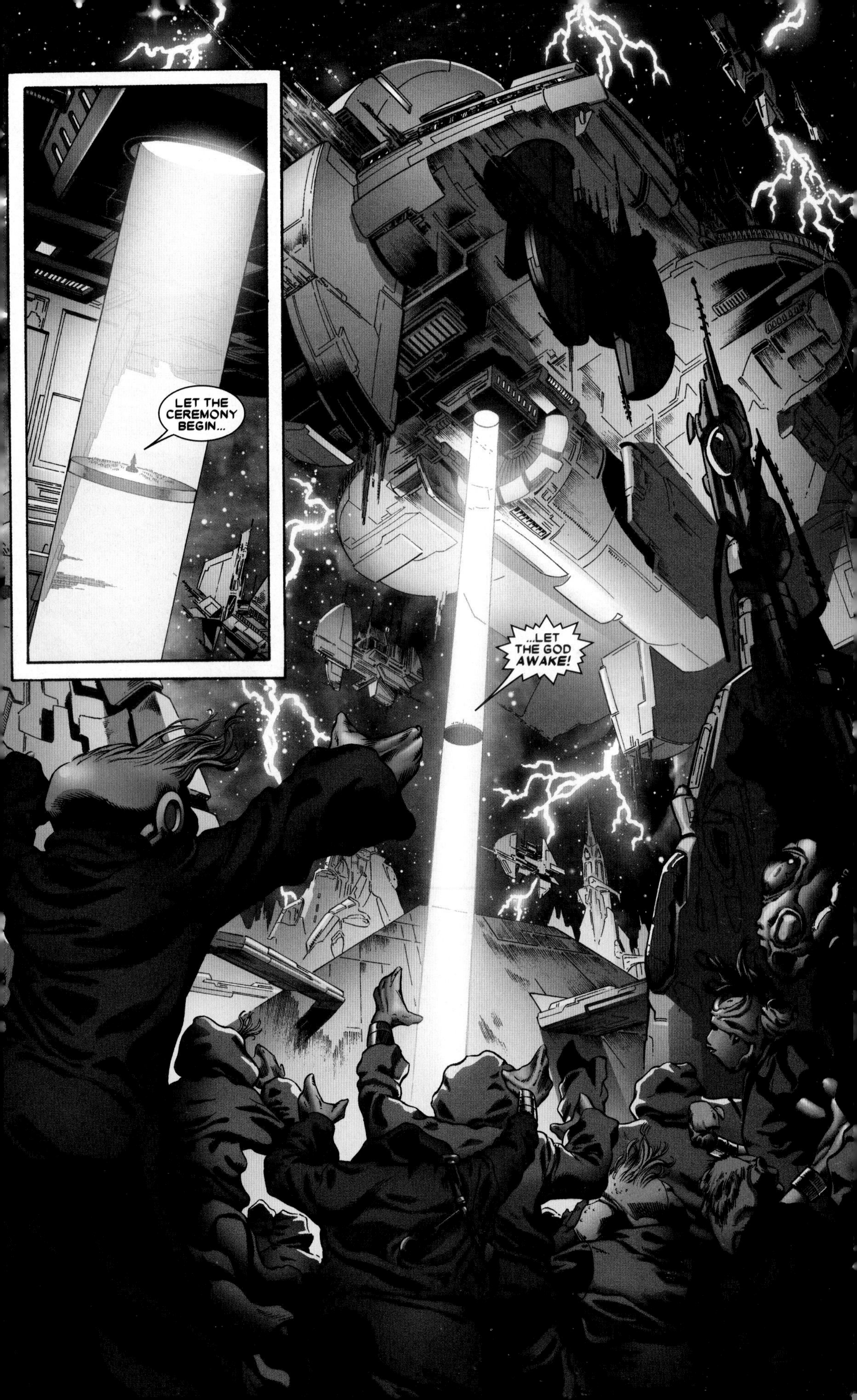
LET THE CEREMONY BEGIN...
...LET THE GOD AWAKE!

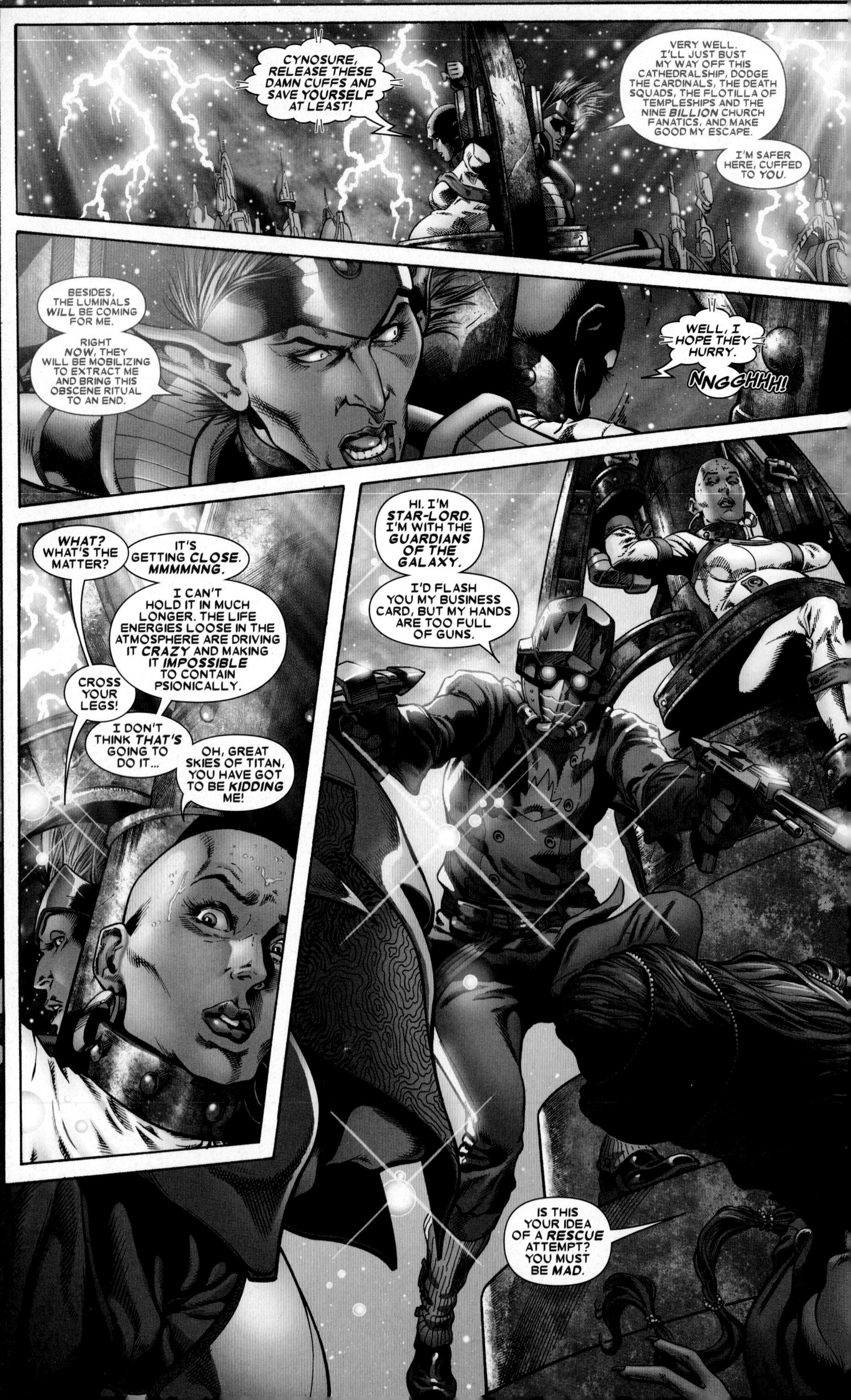
CYNOSURE, RELEASE THESE DAMN CUFFS AND SAVE YOURSELF AT LEAST!
VERY WELL. I'LL JUST BUST MY WAY OFF THIS CATHEDRALSHIP, DODGE THE CARDINALS, THE DEATH SQUADS, THE FLOTILLA OF TEMPLESHIPS AND THE NINE BILLION CHURCH FANATICS, AND MAKE GOOD MY ESCAPE.
I'M SAFER HERE, CUFFED TO YOU.
BESIDES, THE LUMINALS WILL BE COMING FOR ME.
RIGHT NOW, THEY WILL BE MOBILIZING TO EXTRACT ME AND BRING THIS OBSCENE RITUAL TO AN END.
WELL, I HOPE THEY HURRY.
NNGGHHH!
WHAT? WHAT'S THE MATTER?
IT'S GETTING CLOSE. MMMMNNG.
I CAN'T HOLD IT IN MUCH LONGER. THE LIFE ENERGIES LOOSE IN THE ATMOSPHERE ARE DRIVING IT CRAZY AND MAKING IT IMPOSSIBLE TO CONTAIN PSIONICALLY.
CROSS YOUR LEGS!
I DON'T THINK THAT'S GOING TO DO IT...
OH, GREAT SKIES OF TITAN, YOU HAVE GOT TO BE KIDDING ME!
HI. I'M STAR-LORD. I'M WITH THE GUARDIANS OF THE GALAXY.
I'D FLASH YOU MY BUSINESS CARD, BUT MY HANDS ARE TOO FULL OF GUNS.
IS THIS YOUR IDEA OF A RESCUE ATTEMPT? YOU MUST BE MAD.

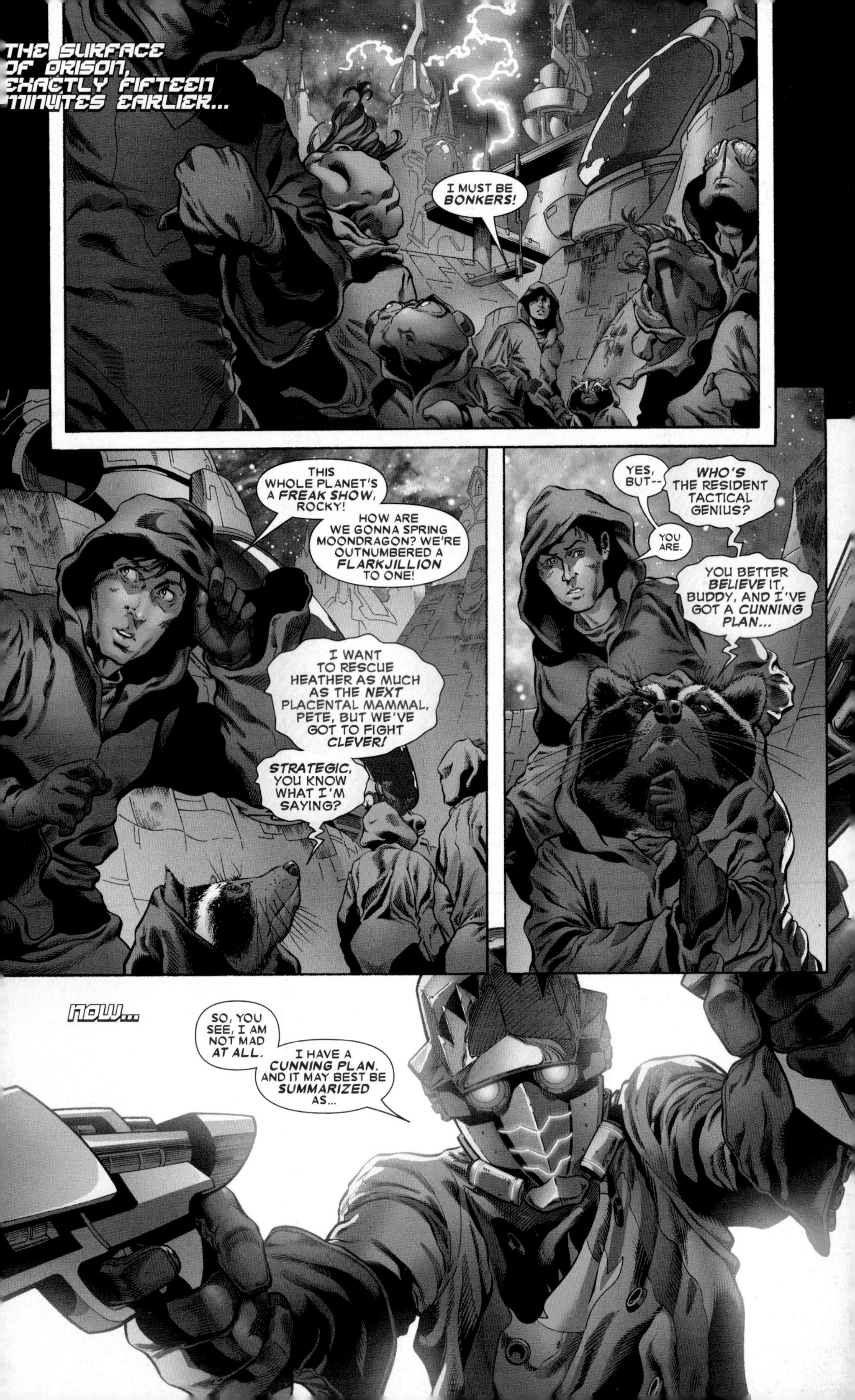
THE SURFACE OF ORISON, EXACTLY FIFTEEN MINUTES EARLIER...
I MUST BE BONKERS!
THIS WHOLE PLANET'S A FREAK SHOW, ROCKY!
HOW ARE WE GONNA SPRING MOONDRAGON? WE'RE OUTNUMBERED A FLARKJILLION TO ONE!
I WANT TO RESCUE HEATHER AS MUCH AS THE NEXT PLACENTAL MAMMAL, PETE, BUT WE'VE GOT TO FIGHT CLEVER!
STRATEGIC, YOU KNOW WHAT I'M SAYING?
YES, BUT--
WHO'S THE RESIDENT TACTICAL GENIUS?
YOU ARE.
YOU BETTER BELIEVE IT, BUDDY, AND I'VE GOT A CUNNING PLAN...
NOW...
SO, YOU SEE, I AM NOT MAD AT ALL.
I HAVE A CUNNING PLAN. AND IT MAY BEST BE SUMMARIZED AS...

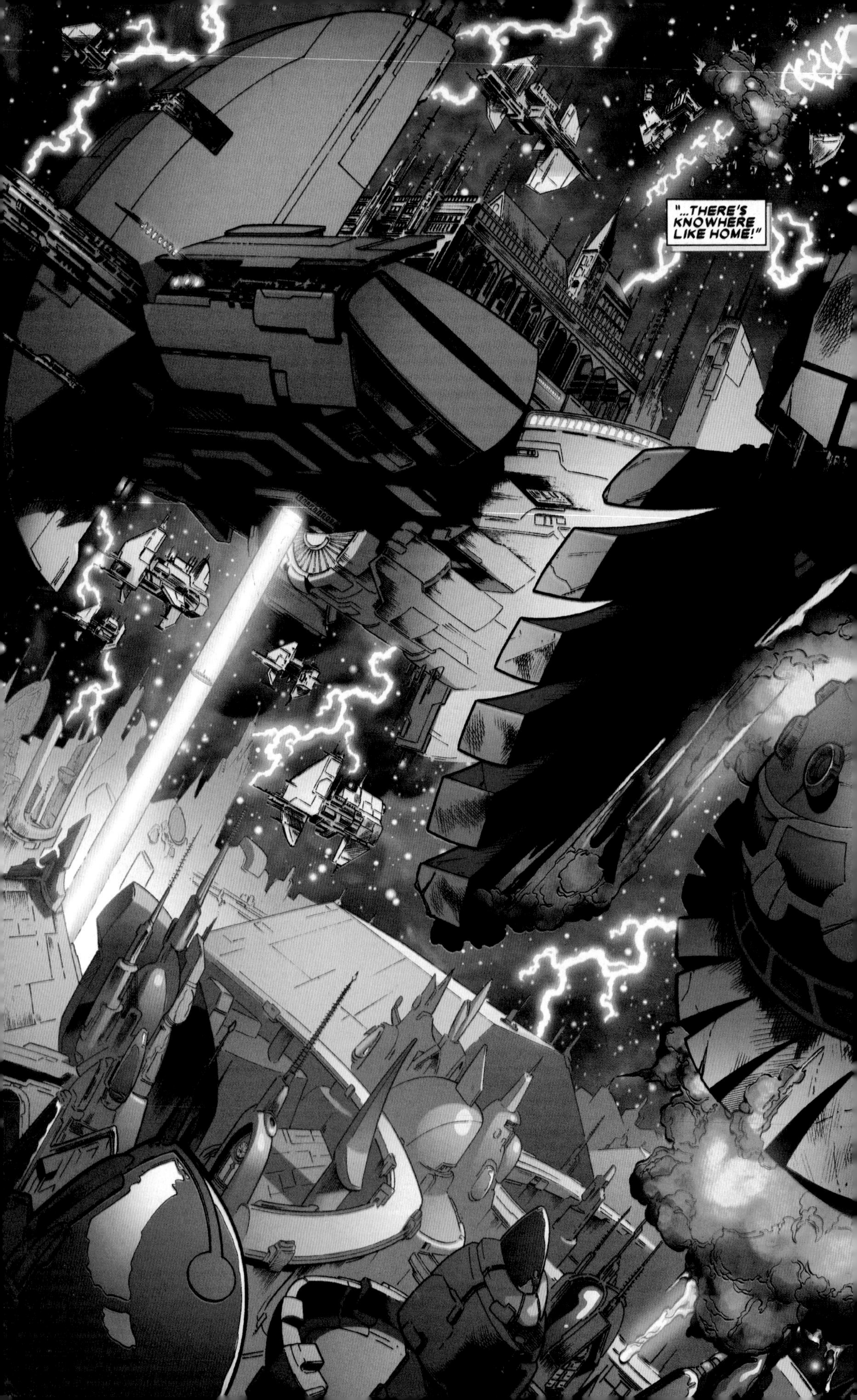
"...THERE'S KNOWHERE LIKE HOME!"

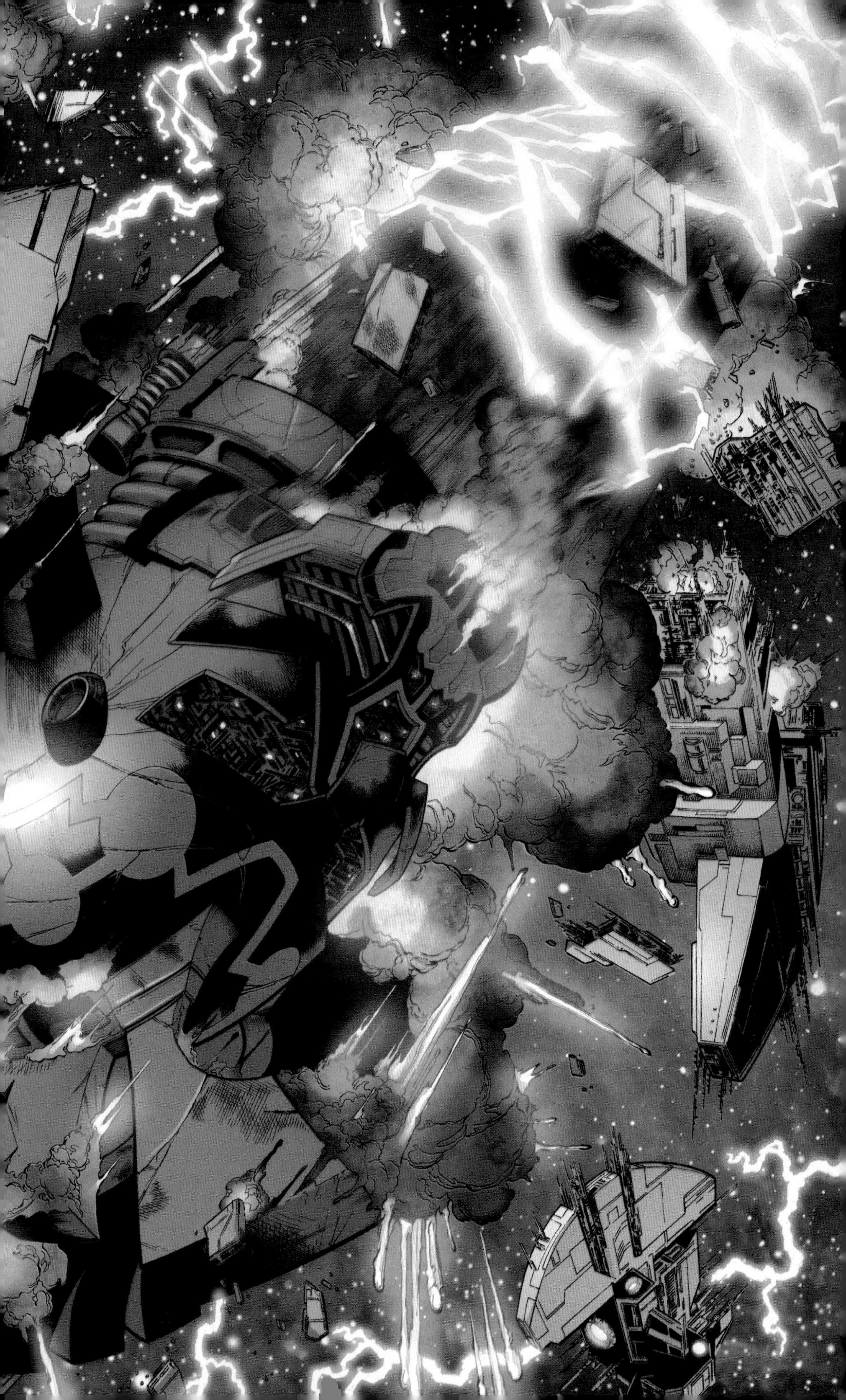

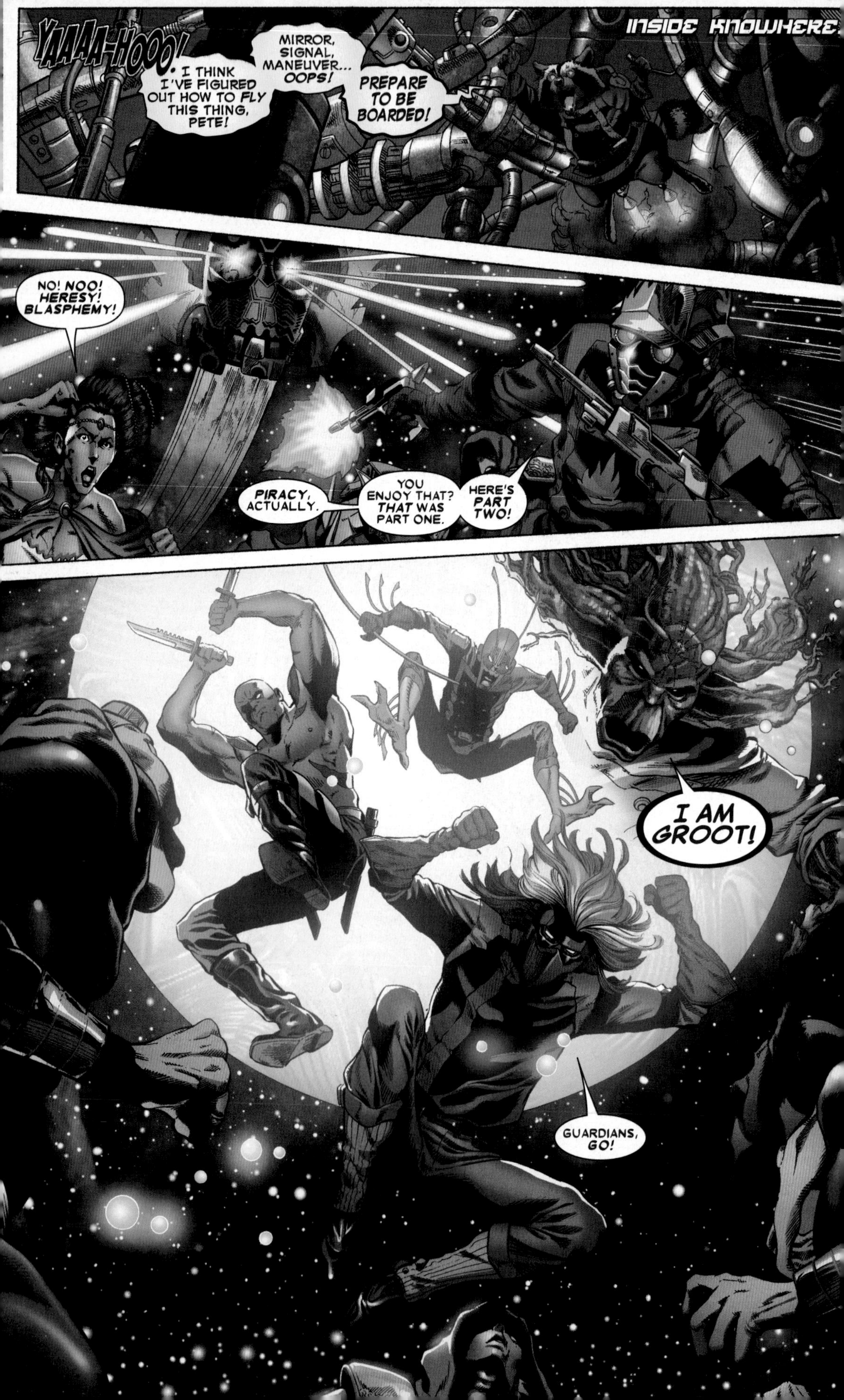
INSIDE KNOWHERE.
YAAAA-HOOO!
I THINK I'VE FIGURED OUT HOW TO FLY THIS THING, PETE!
MIRROR, SIGNAL, MANEUVER... OOPS!
PREPARE TO BE BOARDED!
NO! NOO! HERESY! BLASPHEMY!
PIRACY, ACTUALLY.
YOU ENJOY THAT? THAT WAS PART ONE.
HERE'S PART TWO!
I AM GROOT!
GUARDIANS, GO!

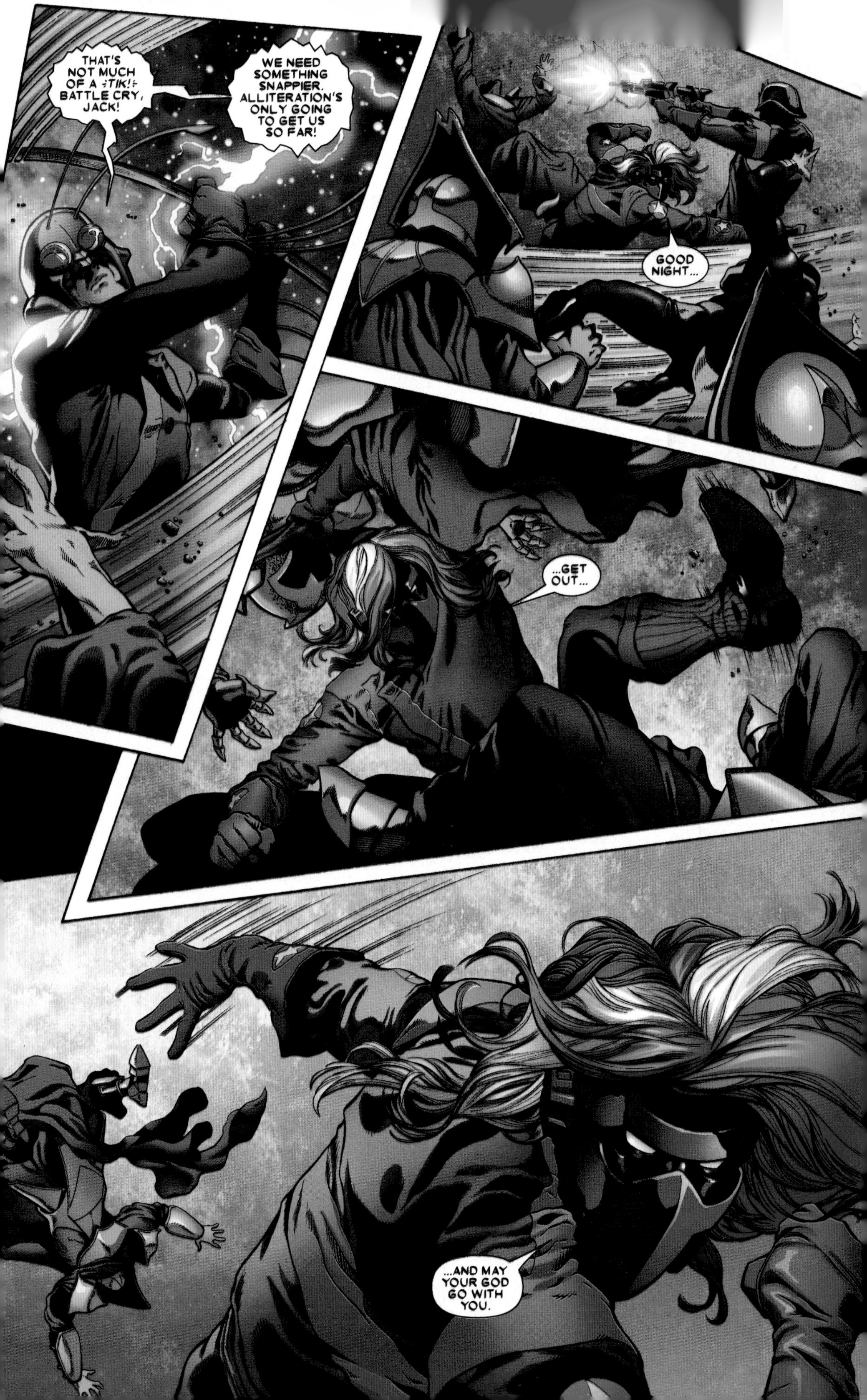
THAT'S NOT MUCH OF A ‡TIK!‡ BATTLE CRY, JACK!
WE NEED SOMETHING SNAPPIER. ALLITERATION'S ONLY GOING TO GET US SO FAR!
GOOD NIGHT...
...GET OUT...
...AND MAY YOUR GOD GO WITH YOU.

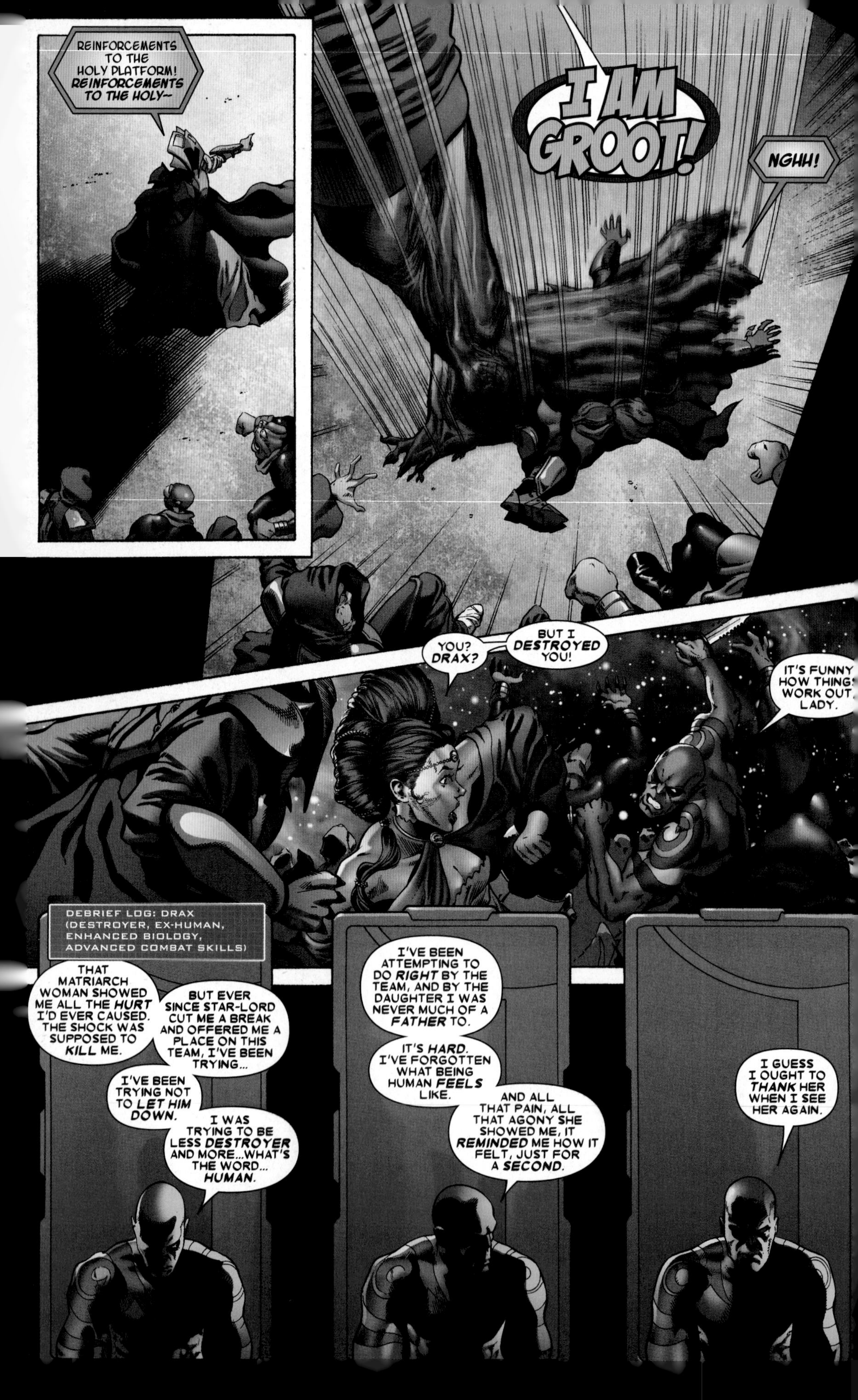
REINFORCEMENTS TO THE HOLY PLATFORM! REINFORCEMENTS TO THE HOLY--
I AM GROOT!
NGHH!
YOU? DRAX?
BUT I DESTROYED YOU!
IT'S FUNNY HOW THINGS WORK OUT, LADY.
DEBRIEF LOG: DRAX (DESTROYER, EX-HUMAN, ENHANCED BIOLOGY, ADVANCED COMBAT SKILLS)
THAT MATRIARCH WOMAN SHOWED ME ALL THE HURT I'D EVER CAUSED. THE SHOCK WAS SUPPOSED TO KILL ME.
BUT EVER SINCE STAR-LORD CUT ME A BREAK AND OFFERED ME A PLACE ON THIS TEAM, I'VE BEEN TRYING...
I'VE BEEN TRYING NOT TO LET HIM DOWN.
I WAS TRYING TO BE LESS DESTROYER AND MORE...WHAT'S THE WORD... HUMAN.
I'VE BEEN ATTEMPTING TO DO RIGHT BY THE TEAM, AND BY THE DAUGHTER I WAS NEVER MUCH OF A FATHER TO.
IT'S HARD. I'VE FORGOTTEN WHAT BEING HUMAN FEELS LIKE.
AND ALL THAT PAIN, ALL THAT AGONY SHE SHOWED ME, IT REMINDED ME HOW IT FELT, JUST FOR A SECOND.
I GUESS I OUGHT TO THANK HER WHEN I SEE HER AGAIN.

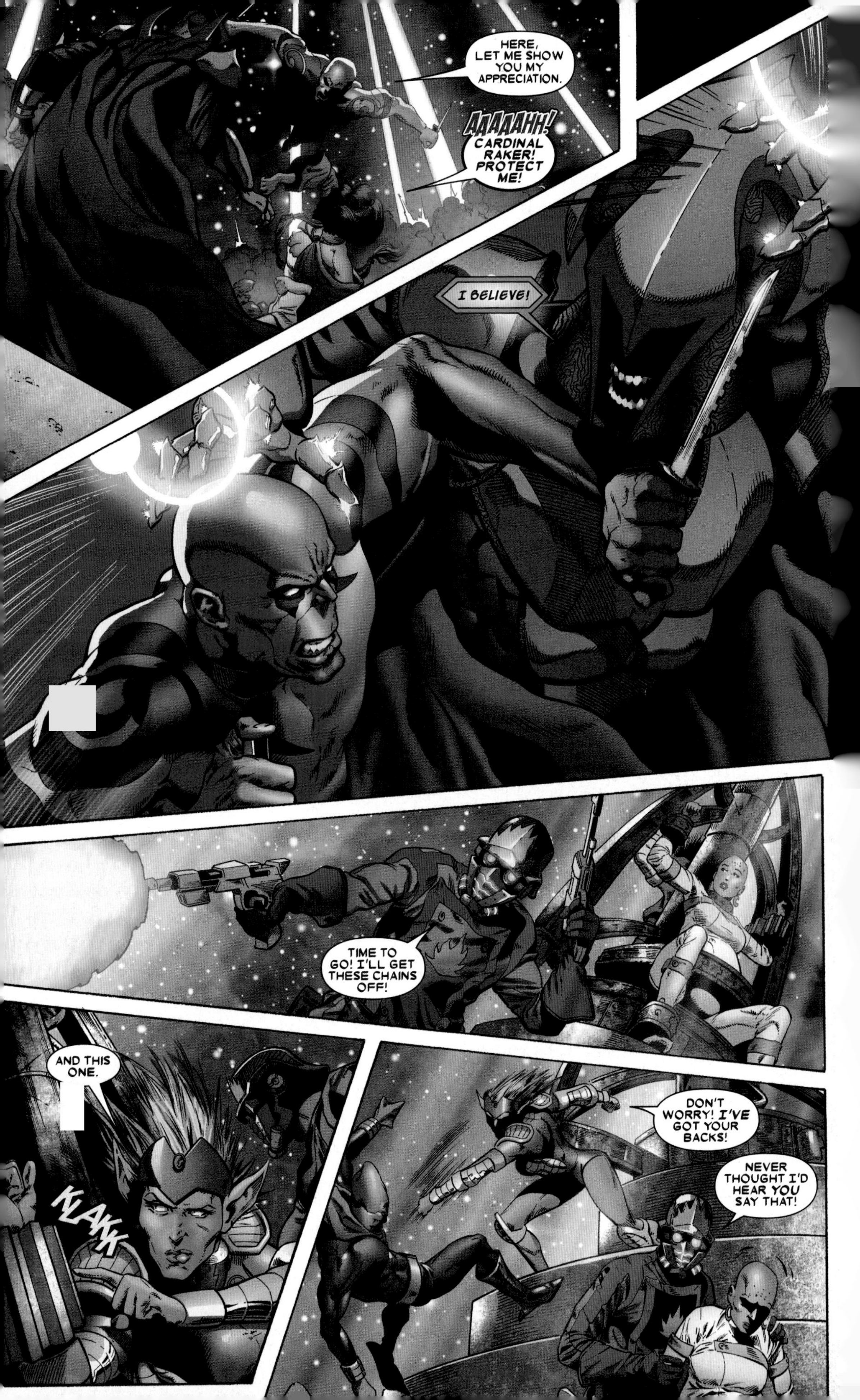
HERE, LET ME SHOW YOU MY APPRECIATION.
AAAAAHH! CARDINAL RAKER! PROTECT ME!
I BELIEVE!
TIME TO GO! I'LL GET THESE CHAINS OFF!
AND THIS ONE.
KLAKK
DON'T WORRY! I'VE GOT YOUR BACKS!
NEVER THOUGHT I'D HEAR YOU SAY THAT!

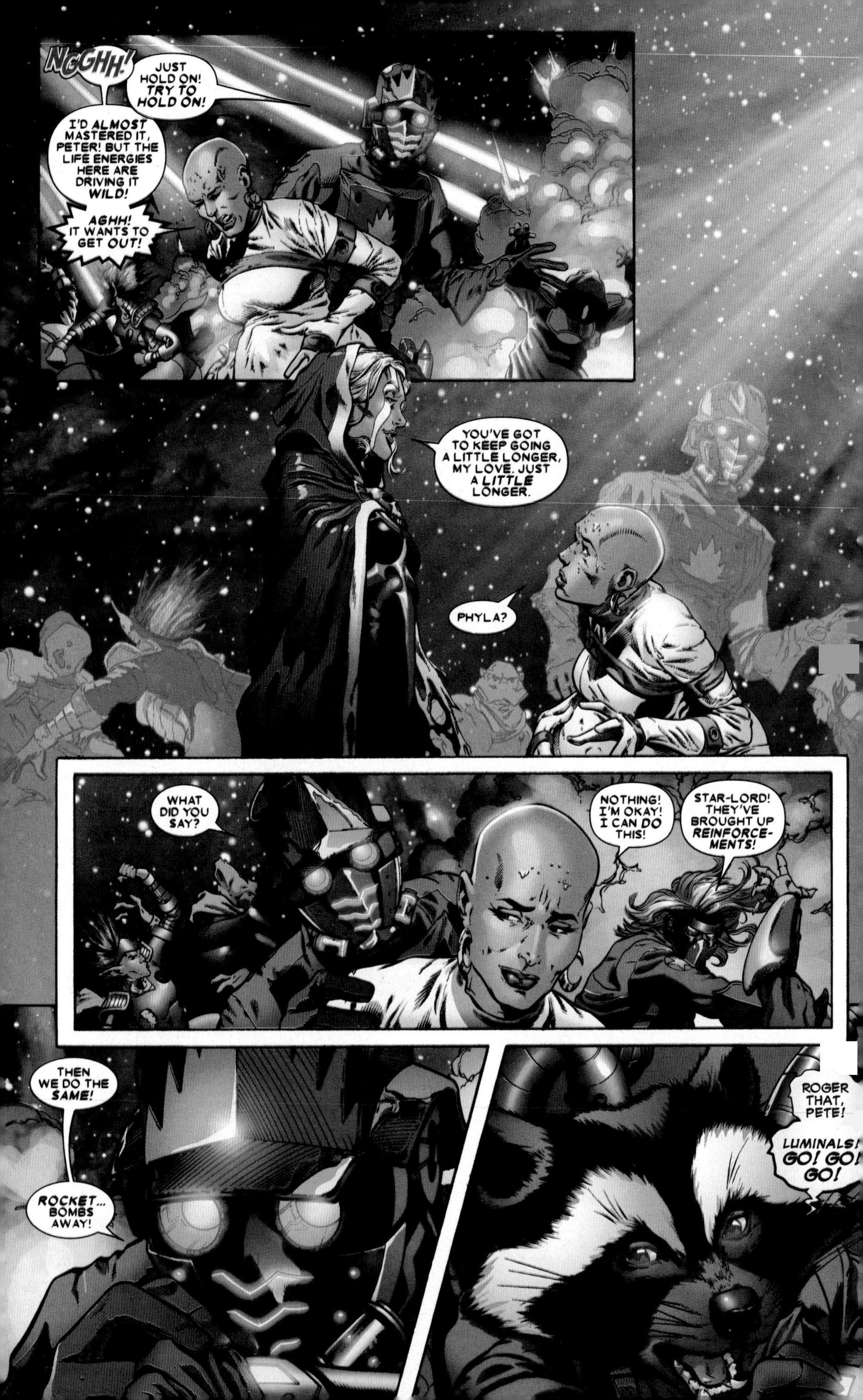
NGGHH!
JUST HOLD ON! TRY TO HOLD ON!
I'D ALMOST MASTERED IT, PETER! BUT THE LIFE ENERGIES HERE ARE DRIVING IT WILD!
AGHH! IT WANTS TO GET OUT!
YOU'VE GOT TO KEEP GOING A LITTLE LONGER, MY LOVE. JUST A LITTLE LONGER.
PHYLA?
WHAT DID YOU SAY?
NOTHING! I'M OKAY! I CAN DO THIS!
STAR-LORD! THEY'VE BROUGHT UP REINFORCE-MENTS!
THEN WE DO THE SAME!
ROCKET... BOMBS AWAY!
ROGER THAT, PETE!
LUMINALS! GO! GO! GO!

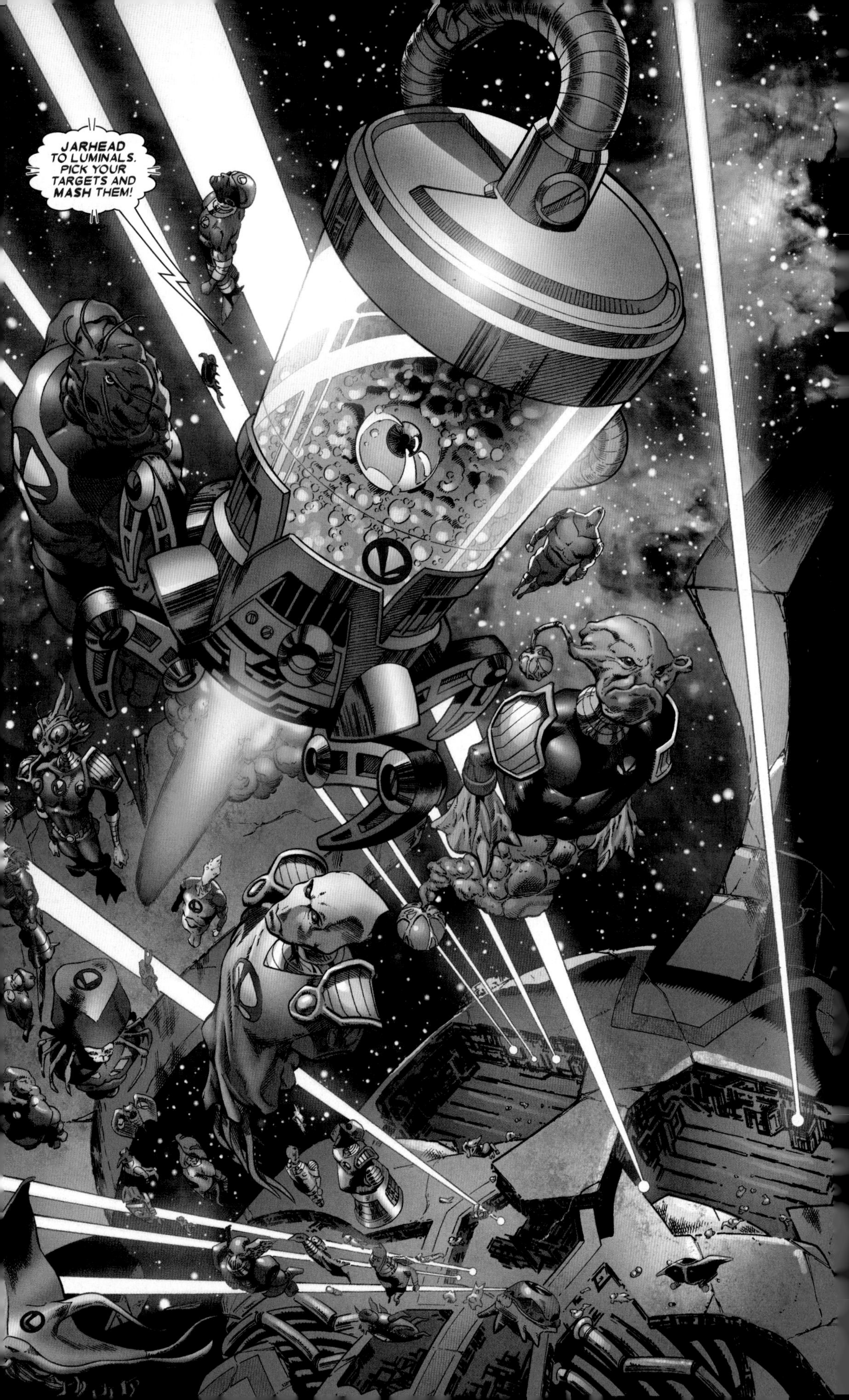
JARHEAD TO LUMINALS. PICK YOUR TARGETS AND MASH THEM!

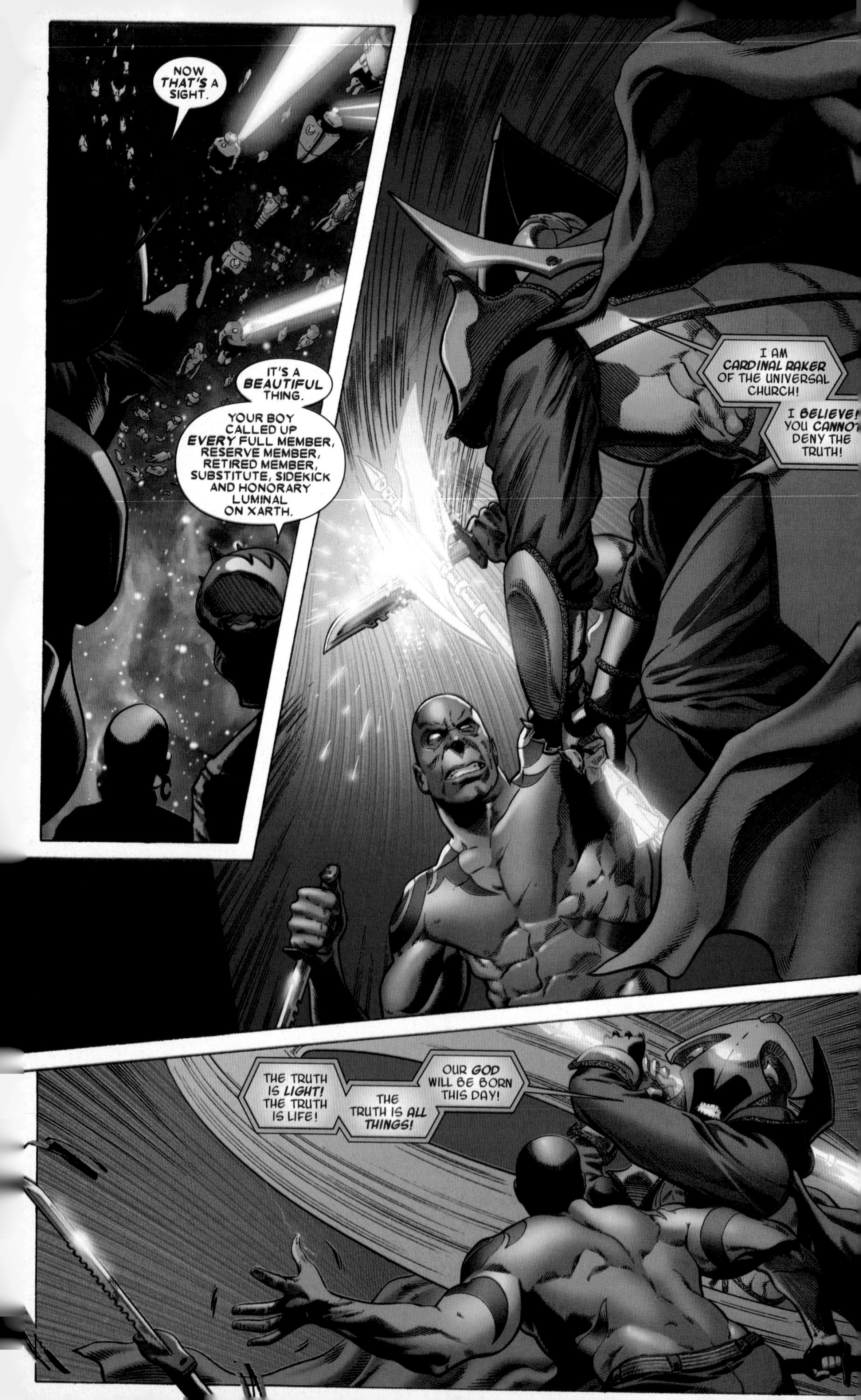
NOW THAT'S A SIGHT.
IT'S A BEAUTIFUL THING.
YOUR BOY CALLED UP EVERY FULL MEMBER, RESERVE MEMBER, RETIRED MEMBER, SUBSTITUTE, SIDEKICK AND HONORARY LUMINAL ON XARTH.
I AM CARDINAL RAKER OF THE UNIVERSAL CHURCH!
I BELIEVE! YOU CANNOT DENY THE TRUTH!
THE TRUTH IS LIGHT! THE TRUTH IS LIFE!
THE TRUTH IS ALL THINGS!
OUR GOD WILL BE BORN THIS DAY!

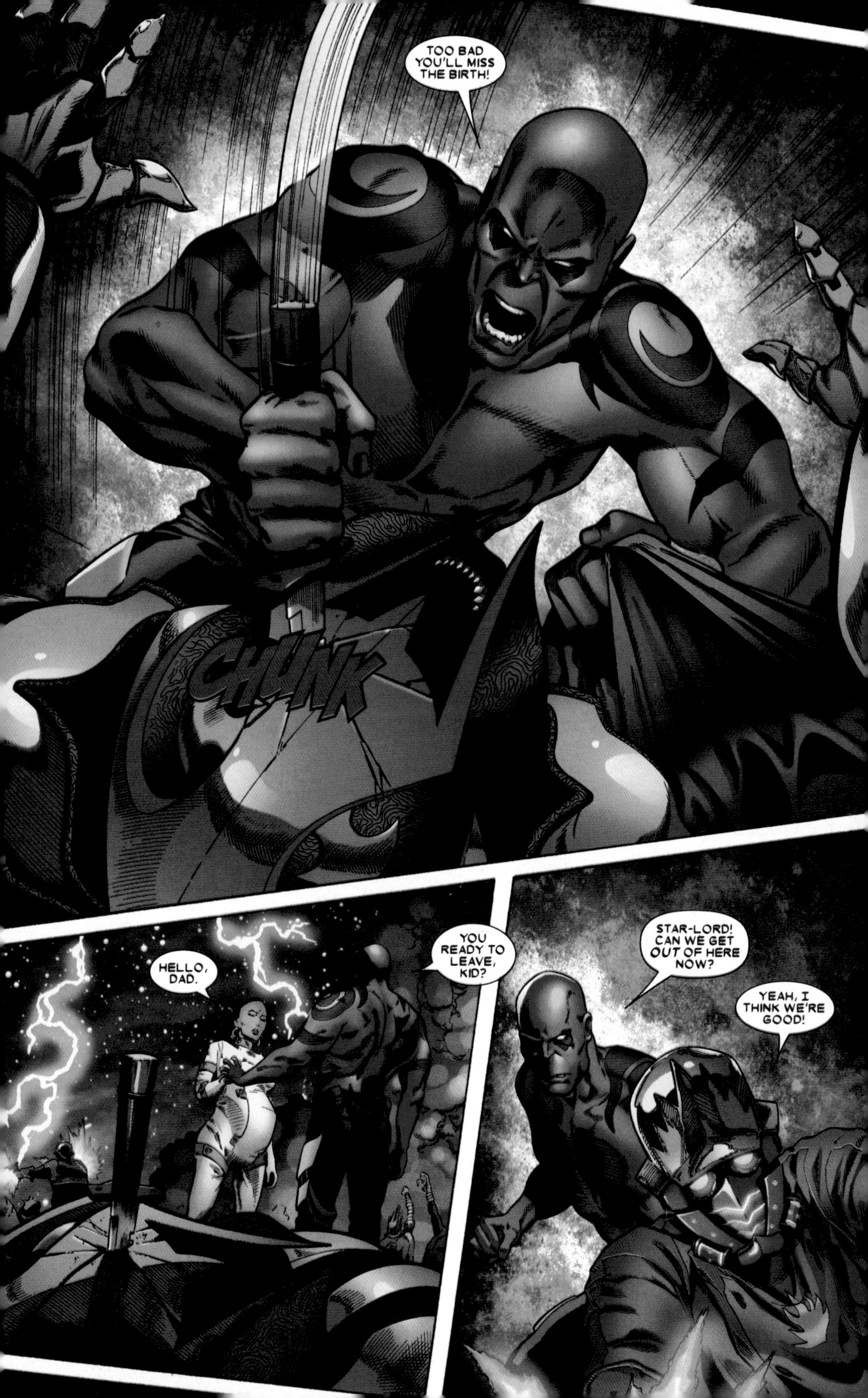
TOO BAD YOU'LL MISS THE BIRTH!
CHUNK
HELLO, DAD.
YOU READY TO LEAVE, KID?
STAR-LORD! CAN WE GET OUT OF HERE NOW?
YEAH, I THINK WE'RE GOOD!

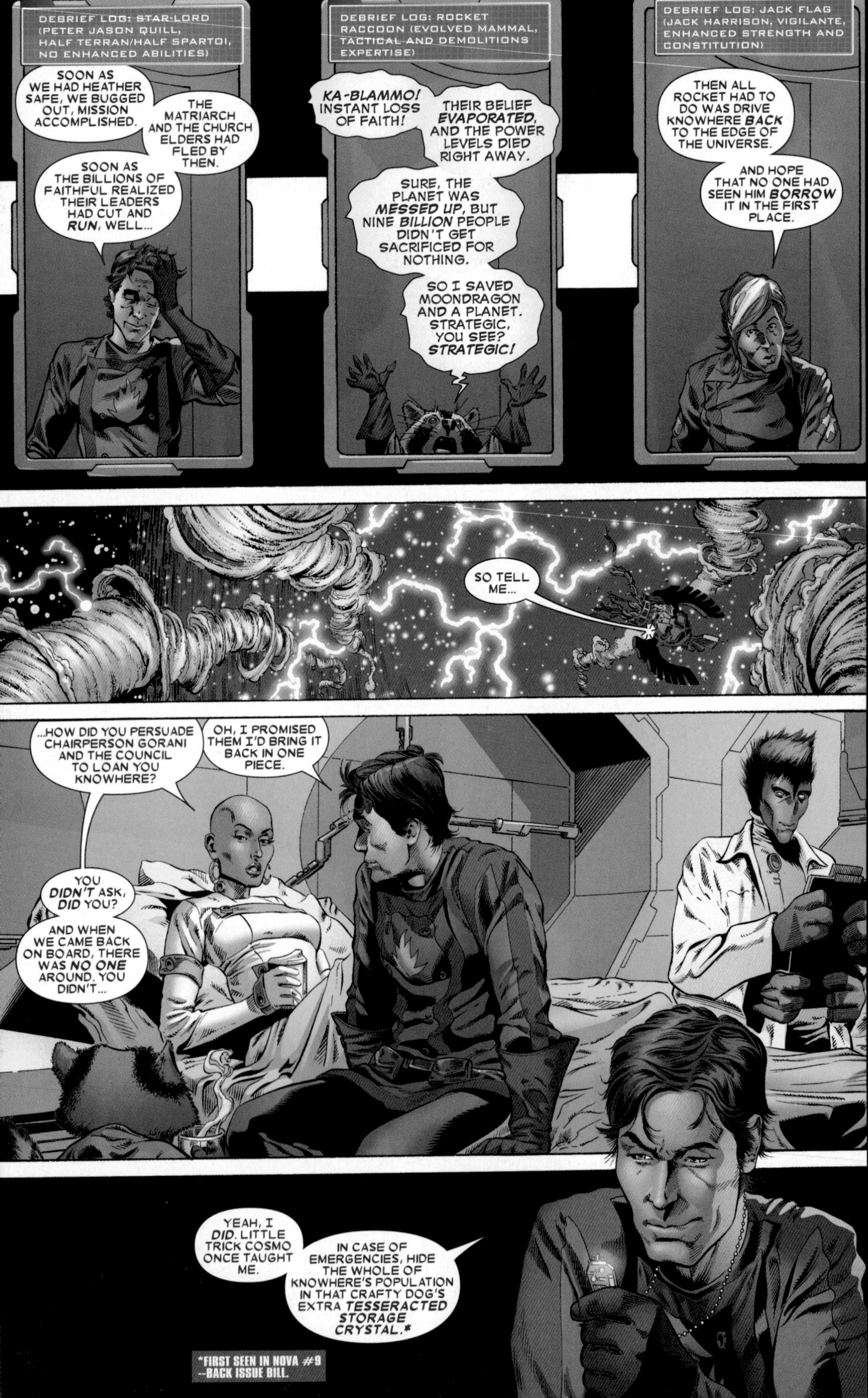
DEBRIEF LOG: STAR-LORD (PETER JASON QUILL, HALF TERRAN/HALF SPARTOI, NO ENHANCED ABILITIES)
SOON AS WE HAD HEATHER SAFE, WE BUGGED OUT, MISSION ACCOMPLISHED.
THE MATRIARCH AND THE CHURCH ELDERS HAD FLED BY THEN.
SOON AS THE BILLIONS OF FAITHFUL REALIZED THEIR LEADERS HAD CUT AND RUN, WELL...
DEBRIEF LOG: ROCKET RACCOON (EVOLVED MAMMAL, TACTICAL AND DEMOLITIONS EXPERTISE)
KA-BLAMMO! INSTANT LOSS OF FAITH!
THEIR BELIEF EVAPORATED, AND THE POWER LEVELS DIED RIGHT AWAY.
SURE, THE PLANET WAS MESSED UP, BUT NINE BILLION PEOPLE DIDN'T GET SACRIFICED FOR NOTHING.
SO I SAVED MOONDRAGON AND A PLANET. STRATEGIC, YOU SEE? STRATEGIC!
DEBRIEF LOG: JACK FLAG (JACK HARRISON, VIGILANTE, ENHANCED STRENGTH AND CONSTITUTION)
THEN ALL ROCKET HAD TO DO WAS DRIVE KNOWHERE BACK TO THE EDGE OF THE UNIVERSE.
AND HOPE THAT NO ONE HAD SEEN HIM BORROW IT IN THE FIRST PLACE.
SO TELL ME...
...HOW DID YOU PERSUADE CHAIRPERSON GORANI AND THE COUNCIL TO LOAN YOU KNOWHERE?
OH, I PROMISED THEM I'D BRING IT BACK IN ONE PIECE.
YOU DIDN'T ASK, DID YOU?
AND WHEN WE CAME BACK ON BOARD, THERE WAS NO ONE AROUND. YOU DIDN'T...
YEAH, I DID. LITTLE TRICK COSMO ONCE TAUGHT ME.
IN CASE OF EMERGENCIES, HIDE THE WHOLE OF KNOWHERE'S POPULATION IN THAT CRAFTY DOG'S EXTRA TESSERACTED STORAGE CRYSTAL.*
*FIRST SEEN IN NOVA #9 --BACK ISSUE BILL.

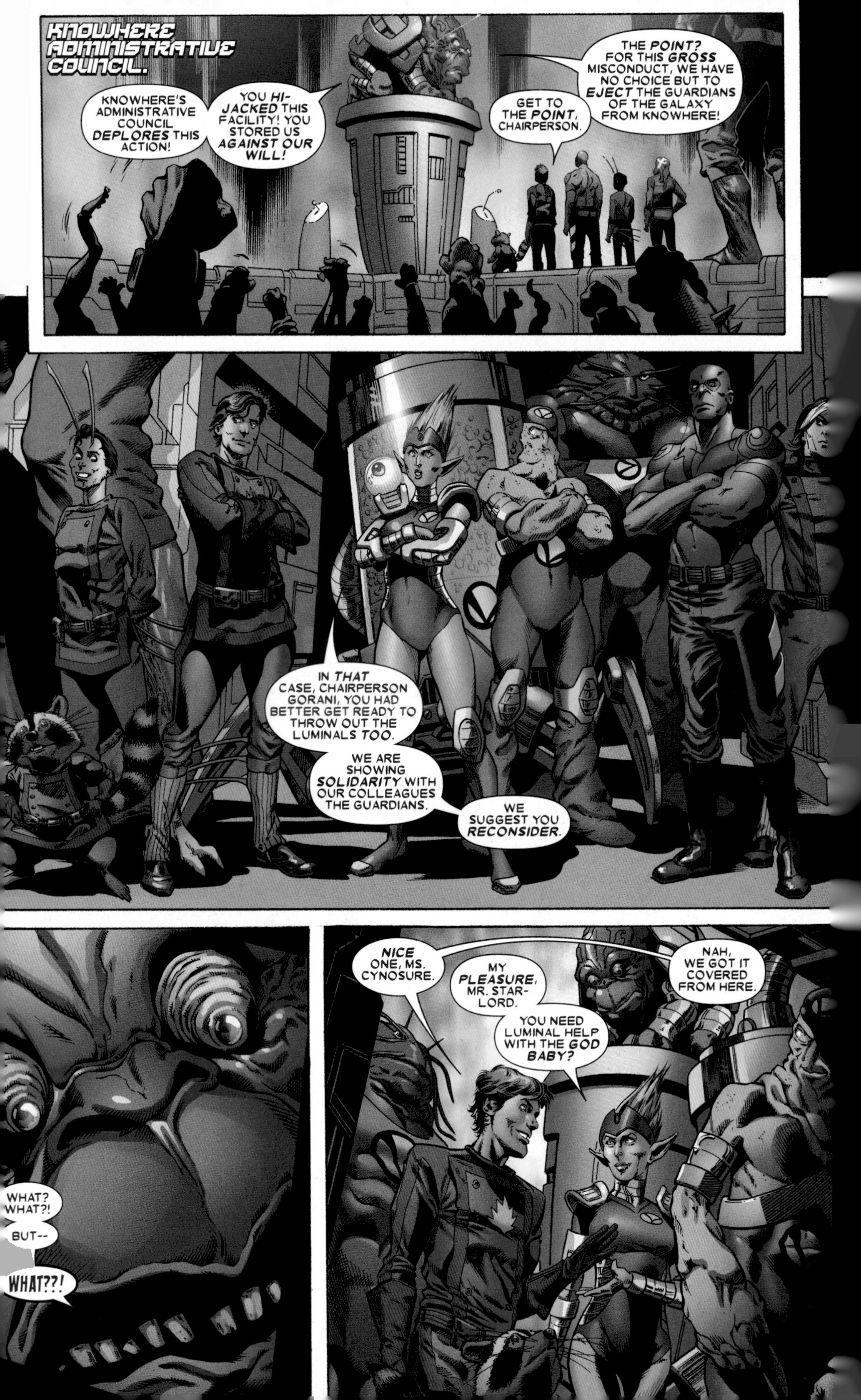
KNOWHERE ADMINISTRATIVE COUNCIL.
KNOWHERE'S ADMINISTRATIVE COUNCIL DEPLORES THIS ACTION!
YOU HI-JACKED THIS FACILITY! YOU STORED US AGAINST OUR WILL!
GET TO THE POINT, CHAIRPERSON.
THE POINT? FOR THIS GROSS MISCONDUCT, WE HAVE NO CHOICE BUT TO EJECT THE GUARDIANS OF THE GALAXY FROM KNOWHERE!
IN THAT CASE, CHAIRPERSON GORANI, YOU HAD BETTER GET READY TO THROW OUT THE LUMINALS TOO.
WE ARE SHOWING SOLIDARITY WITH OUR COLLEAGUES THE GUARDIANS.
WE SUGGEST YOU RECONSIDER.
WHAT? WHAT?!
BUT--
WHAT??!
NICE ONE, MS. CYNOSURE.
MY PLEASURE, MR. STAR-LORD.
YOU NEED LUMINAL HELP WITH THE GOD BABY?
NAH, WE GOT IT COVERED FROM HERE.

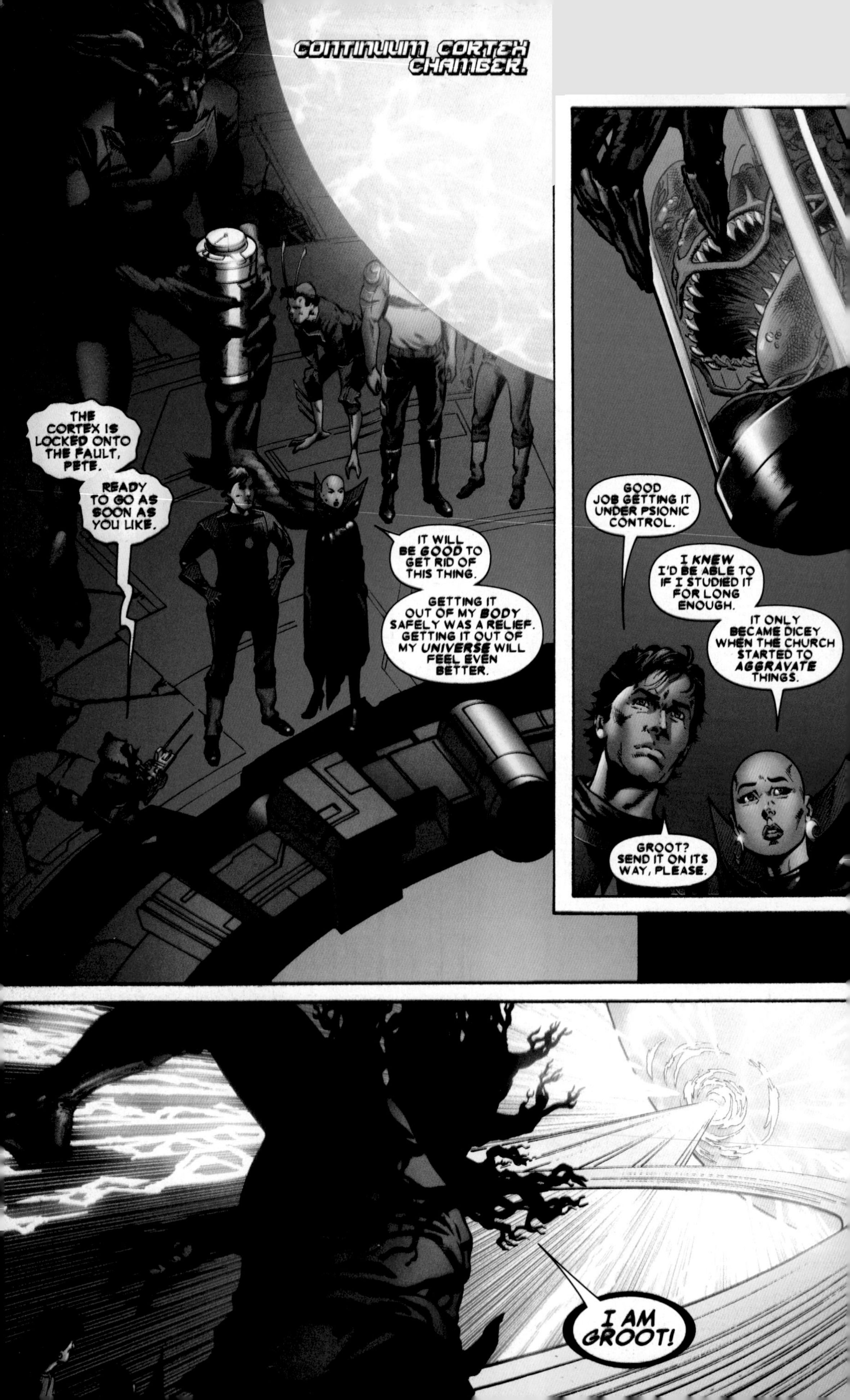
CONTINUUM CORTEX CHAMBER.
THE CORTEX IS LOCKED ONTO THE FAULT, PETE.
READY TO GO AS SOON AS YOU LIKE.
IT WILL BE GOOD TO GET RID OF THIS THING.
GETTING IT OUT OF MY BODY SAFELY WAS A RELIEF. GETTING IT OUT OF MY UNIVERSE WILL FEEL EVEN BETTER.
GOOD JOB GETTING IT UNDER PSIONIC CONTROL.
I KNEW I'D BE ABLE TO IF I STUDIED IT FOR LONG ENOUGH.
IT ONLY BECAME DICEY WHEN THE CHURCH STARTED TO AGGRAVATE THINGS.
GROOT? SEND IT ON ITS WAY, PLEASE.
I AM GROOT!

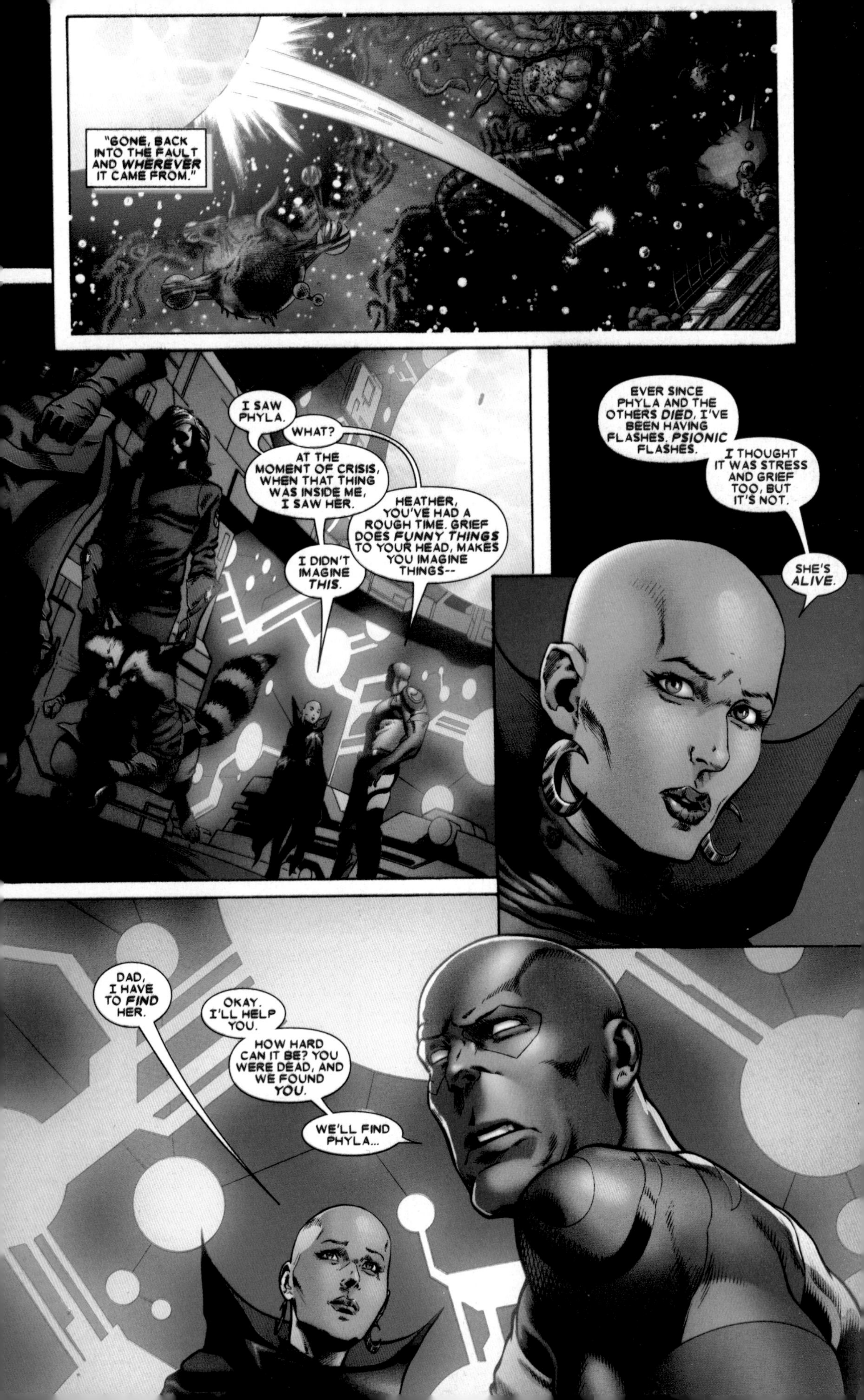

"GONE, BACK INTO THE FAULT AND WHEREVER IT CAME FROM."
I SAW PHYLA.
WHAT?
AT THE MOMENT OF CRISIS, WHEN THAT THING WAS INSIDE ME, I SAW HER.
HEATHER, YOU'VE HAD A ROUGH TIME. GRIEF DOES FUNNY THINGS TO YOUR HEAD, MAKES YOU IMAGINE THINGS--
I DIDN'T IMAGINE THIS.
EVER SINCE PHYLA AND THE OTHERS DIED, I'VE BEEN HAVING FLASHES. PSIONIC FLASHES.
I THOUGHT IT WAS STRESS AND GRIEF TOO, BUT IT'S NOT.
SHE'S ALIVE.
DAD, I HAVE TO FIND HER.
OKAY. I'LL HELP YOU.
HOW HARD CAN IT BE? YOU WERE DEAD, AND WE FOUND YOU.
WE'LL FIND PHYLA...

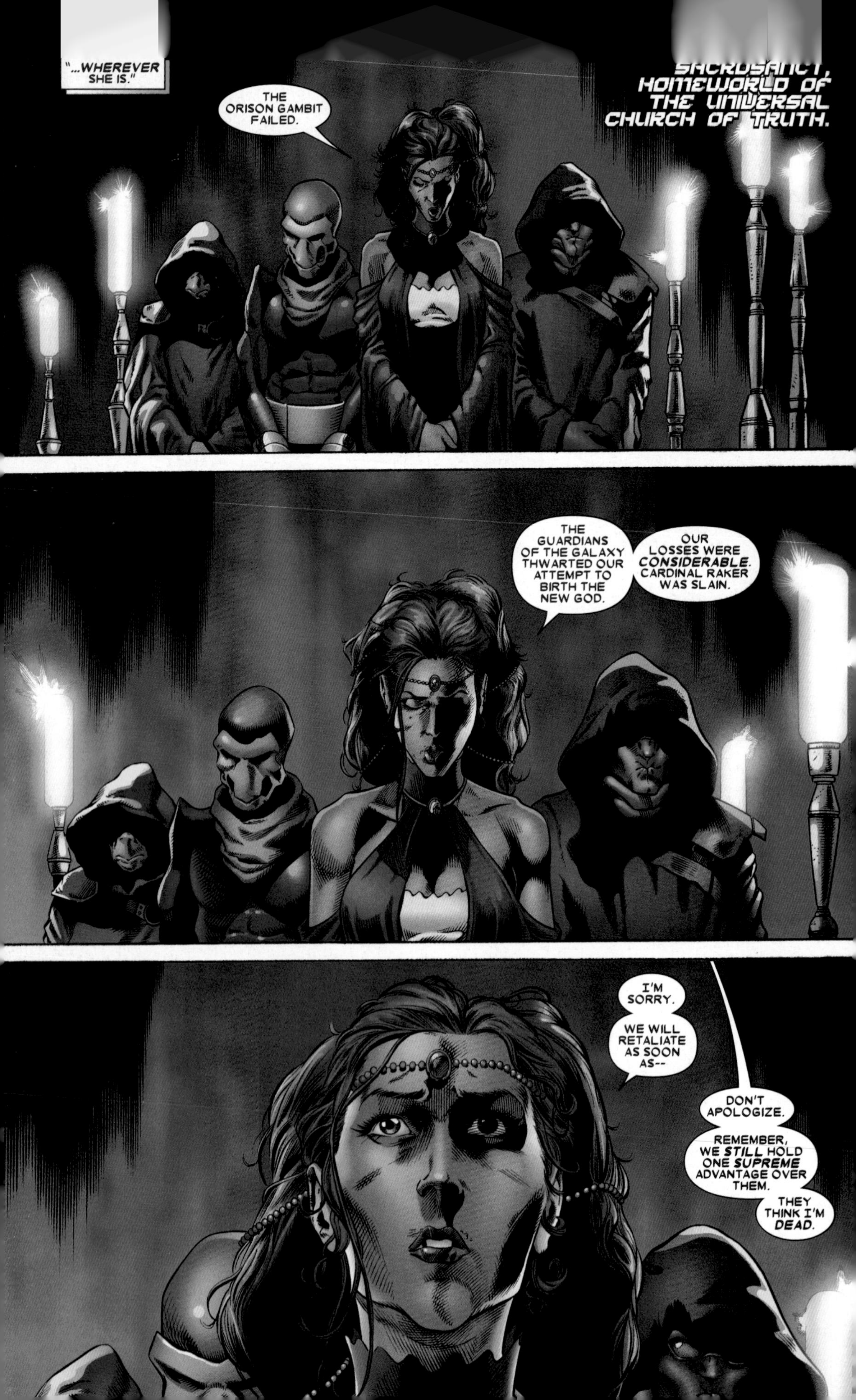
"...WHEREVER SHE IS."
SACROSANCT, HOMEWORLD OF THE UNIVERSAL CHURCH OF TRUTH.
THE ORISON GAMBIT FAILED.
THE GUARDIANS OF THE GALAXY THWARTED OUR ATTEMPT TO BIRTH THE NEW GOD.
OUR LOSSES WERE CONSIDERABLE. CARDINAL RAKER WAS SLAIN.
I'M SORRY.
WE WILL RETALIATE AS SOON AS--
DON'T APOLOGIZE.
REMEMBER, WE STILL HOLD ONE SUPREME ADVANTAGE OVER THEM.
THEY THINK I'M DEAD.

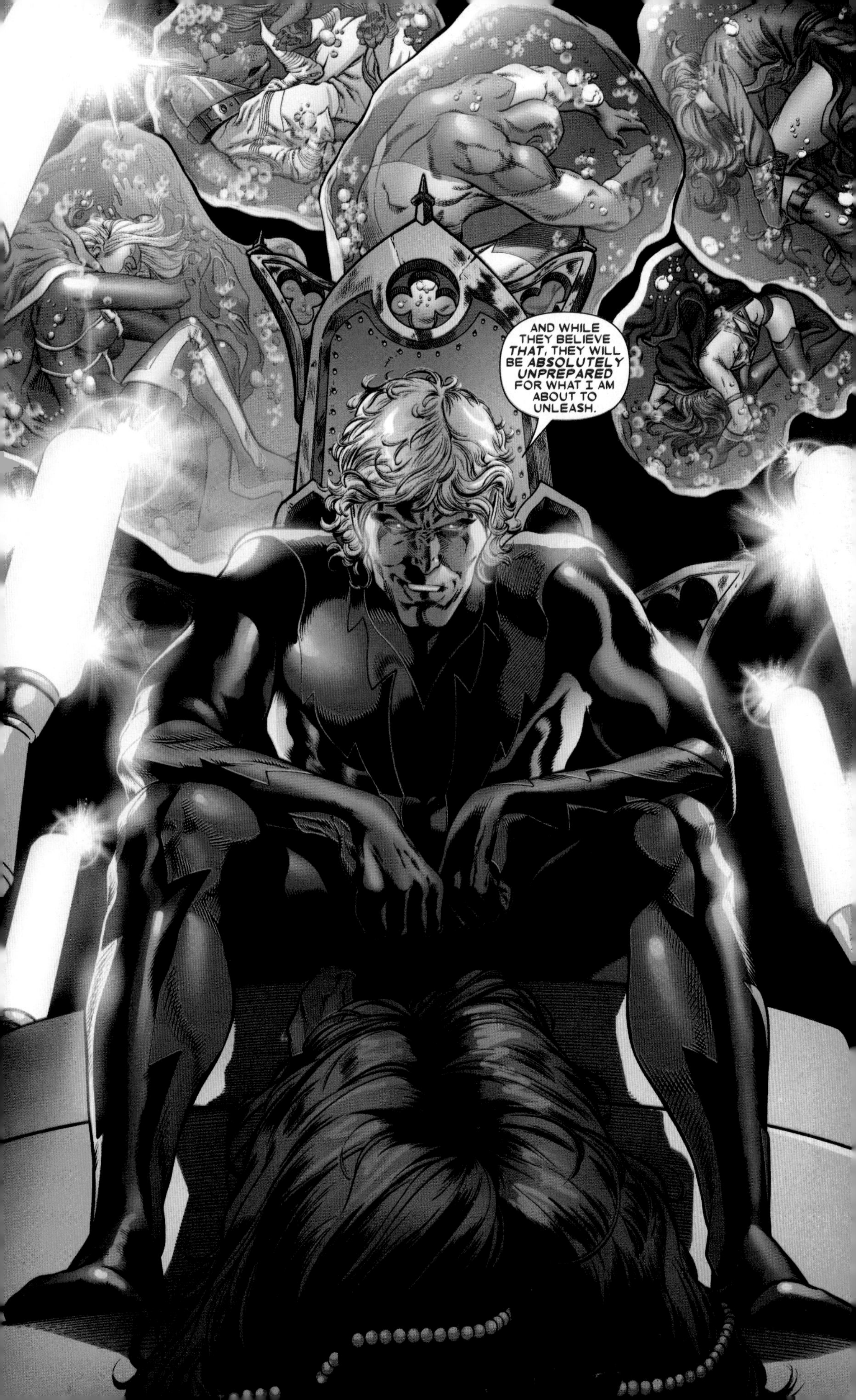
AND WHILE THEY BELIEVE *THAT*, THEY WILL BE ***ABSOLUTELY UNPREPARED*** FOR WHAT I AM ABOUT TO UNLEASH.

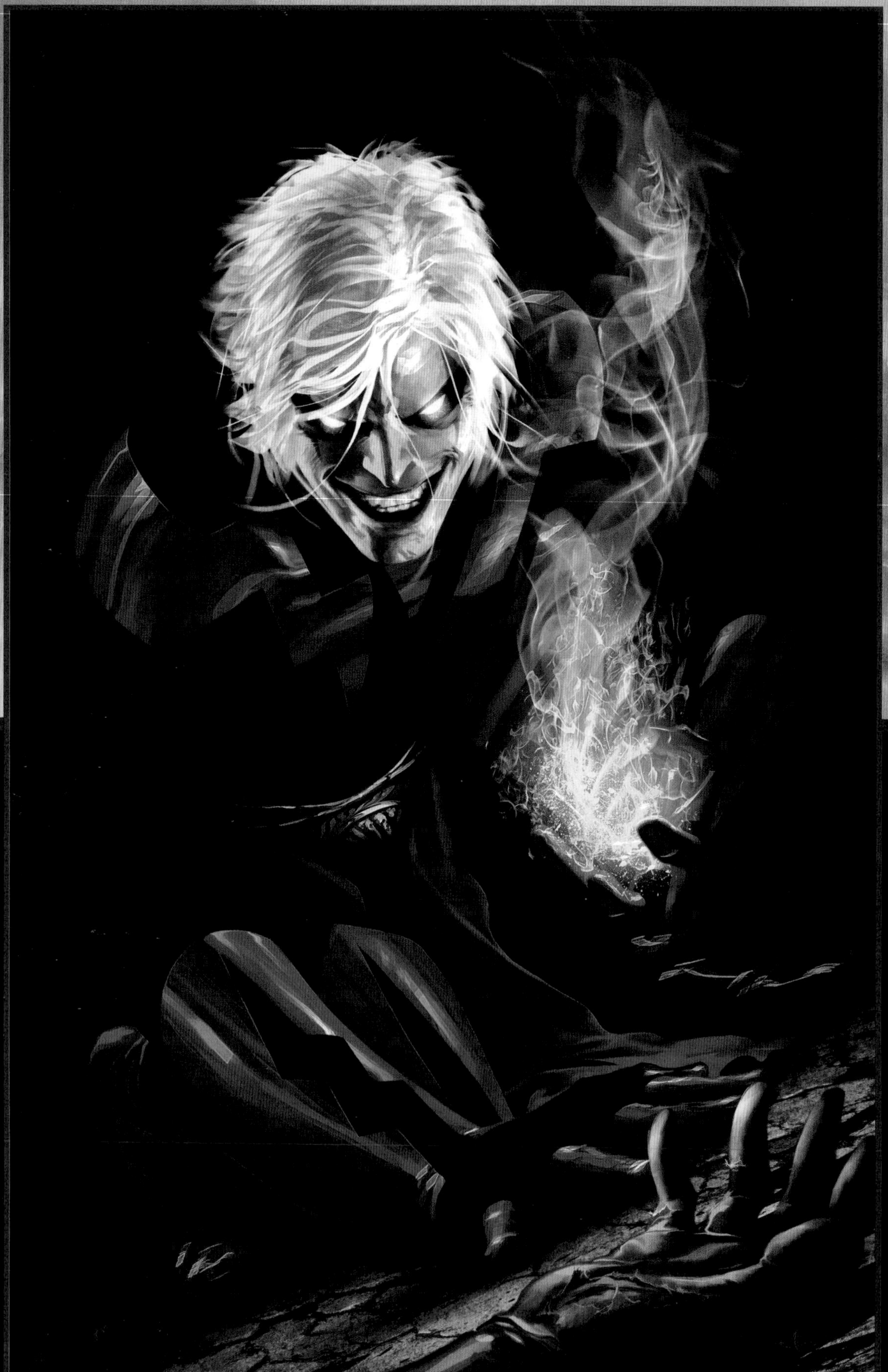

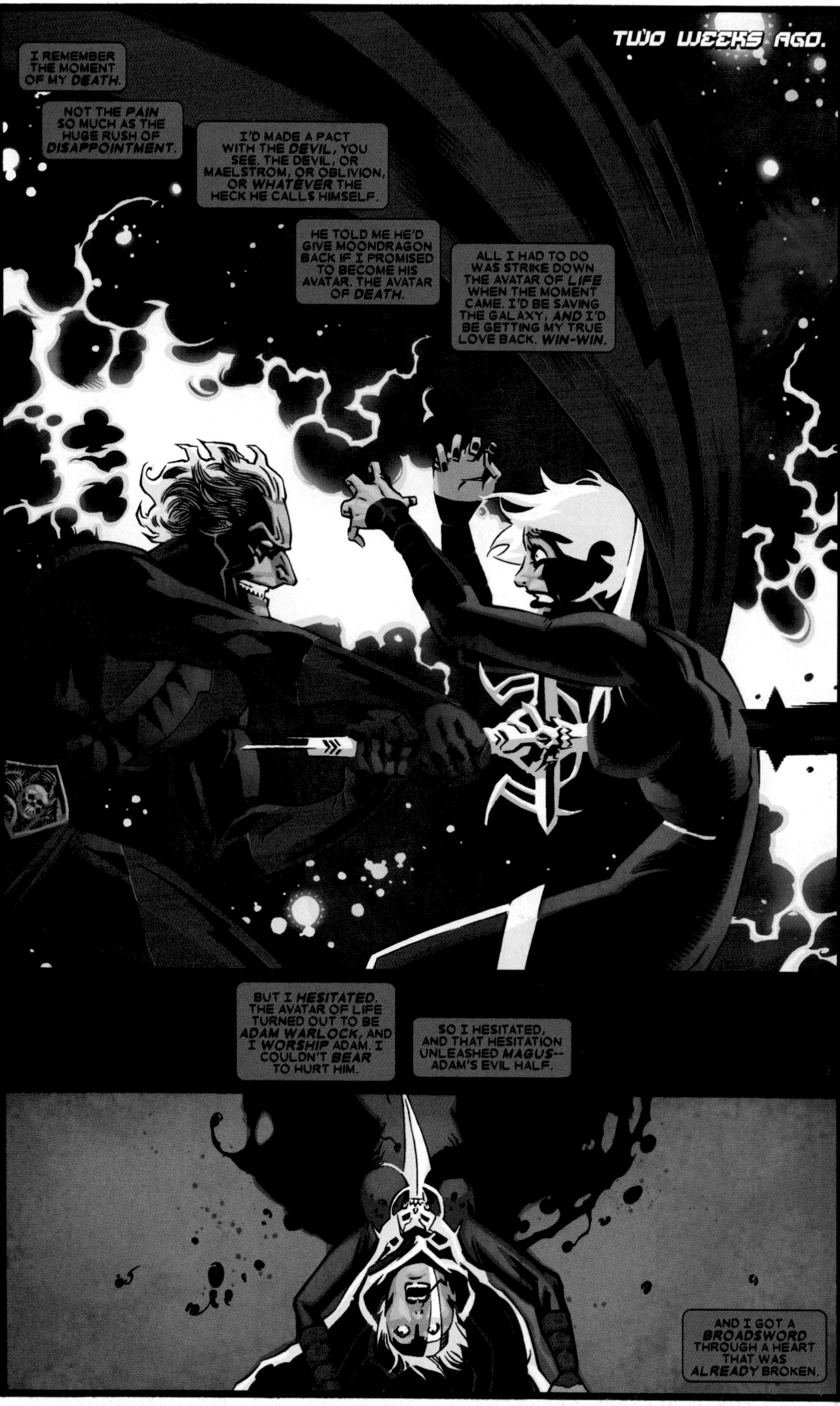
TWO WEEKS AGO.
I REMEMBER THE MOMENT OF MY DEATH.
NOT THE PAIN SO MUCH AS THE HUGE RUSH OF DISAPPOINTMENT.
I'D MADE A PACT WITH THE DEVIL, YOU SEE. THE DEVIL, OR MAELSTROM, OR OBLIVION, OR WHATEVER THE HECK HE CALLS HIMSELF.
HE TOLD ME HE'D GIVE MOONDRAGON BACK IF I PROMISED TO BECOME HIS AVATAR. THE AVATAR OF DEATH.
ALL I HAD TO DO WAS STRIKE DOWN THE AVATAR OF LIFE WHEN THE MOMENT CAME. I'D BE SAVING THE GALAXY, AND I'D BE GETTING MY TRUE LOVE BACK. WIN-WIN.
BUT I HESITATED. THE AVATAR OF LIFE TURNED OUT TO BE ADAM WARLOCK, AND I WORSHIP ADAM. I COULDN'T BEAR TO HURT HIM.
SO I HESITATED, AND THAT HESITATION UNLEASHED MAGUS-- ADAM'S EVIL HALF.
AND I GOT A BROADSWORD THROUGH A HEART THAT WAS ALREADY BROKEN.

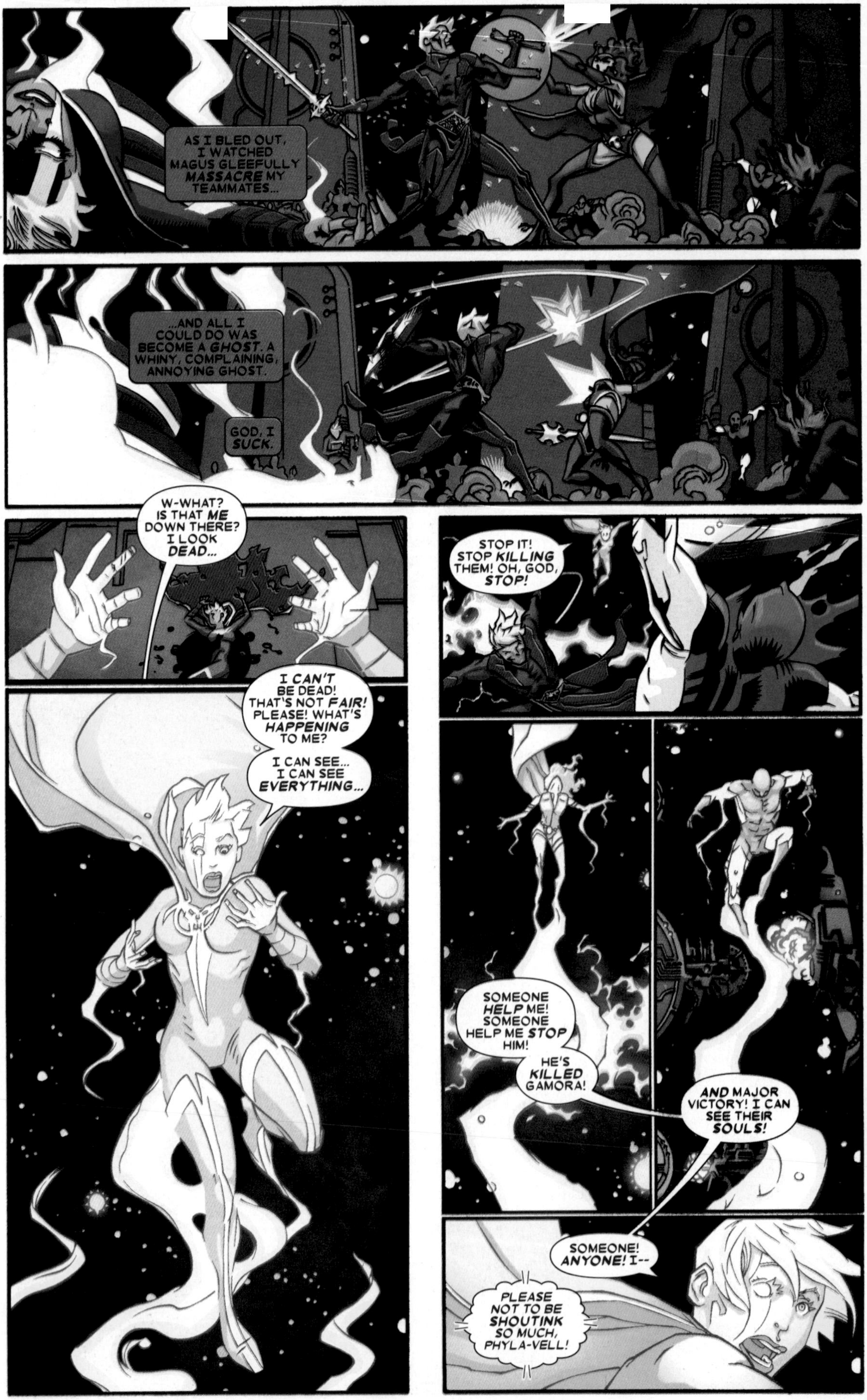
AS I BLED OUT, I WATCHED MAGUS GLEEFULLY MASSACRE MY TEAMMATES...
...AND ALL I COULD DO WAS BECOME A GHOST. A WHINY, COMPLAINING, ANNOYING GHOST.
GOD, I SUCK.
W-WHAT? IS THAT ME DOWN THERE? I LOOK DEAD...
STOP IT! STOP KILLING THEM! OH, GOD, STOP!
I CAN'T BE DEAD! THAT'S NOT FAIR! PLEASE! WHAT'S HAPPENING TO ME?
I CAN SEE... I CAN SEE EVERYTHING...
SOMEONE HELP ME! SOMEONE HELP ME STOP HIM!
HE'S KILLED GAMORA!
AND MAJOR VICTORY! I CAN SEE THEIR SOULS!
SOMEONE! ANYONE! I--
PLEASE NOT TO BE SHOUTINK SO MUCH, PHYLA-VELL!

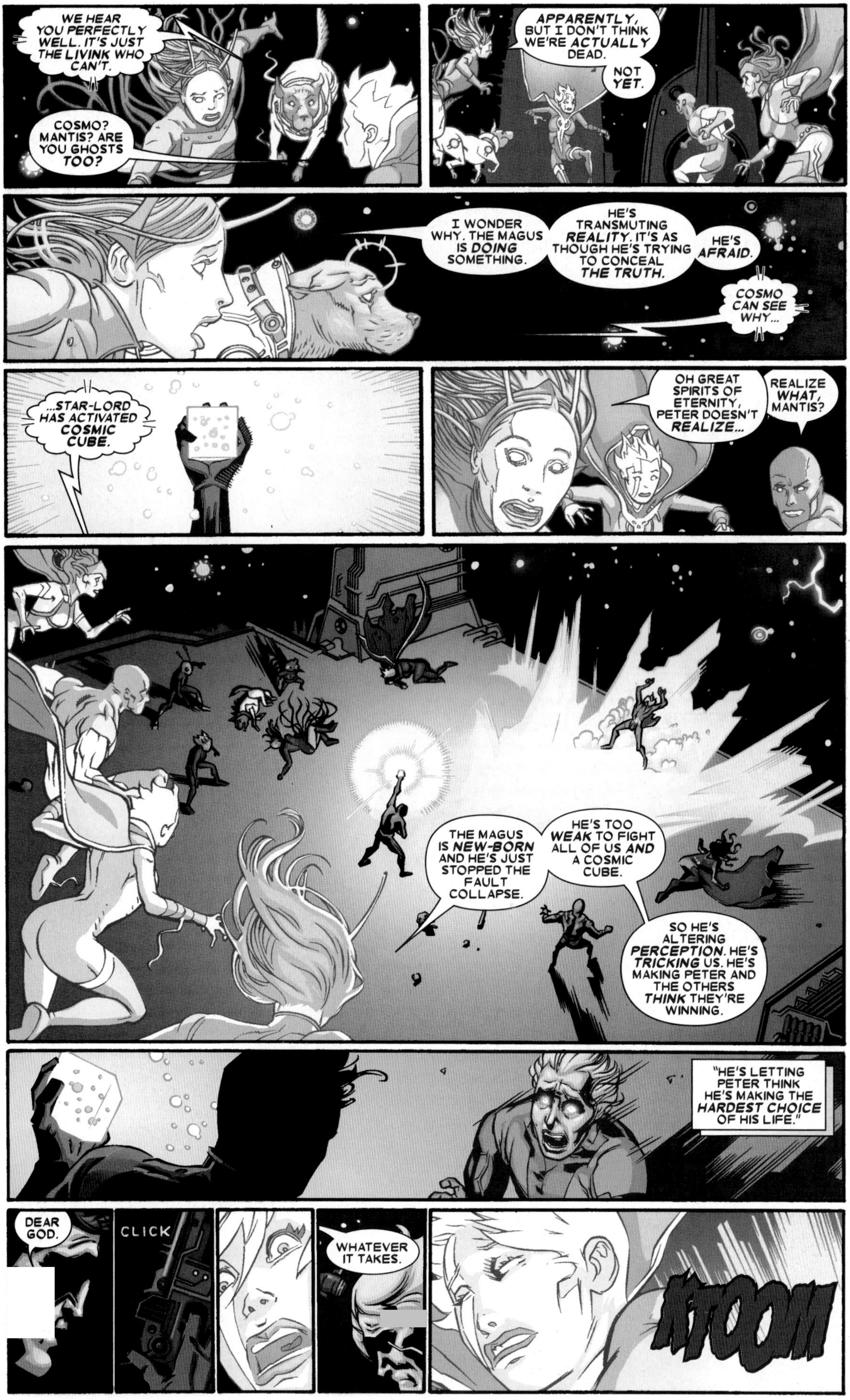
WE HEAR YOU PERFECTLY WELL. IT'S JUST THE LIVINK WHO CAN'T.
COSMO? MANTIS? ARE YOU GHOSTS TOO?
APPARENTLY, BUT I DON'T THINK WE'RE ACTUALLY DEAD.
NOT YET.
I WONDER WHY. THE MAGUS IS DOING SOMETHING.
HE'S TRANSMUTING REALITY. IT'S AS THOUGH HE'S TRYING TO CONCEAL THE TRUTH.
HE'S AFRAID.
COSMO CAN SEE WHY...
...STAR-LORD HAS ACTIVATED COSMIC CUBE.
OH GREAT SPIRITS OF ETERNITY, PETER DOESN'T REALIZE...
REALIZE WHAT, MANTIS?
THE MAGUS IS NEW-BORN AND HE'S JUST STOPPED THE FAULT COLLAPSE.
HE'S TOO WEAK TO FIGHT ALL OF US AND A COSMIC CUBE.
SO HE'S ALTERING PERCEPTION. HE'S TRICKING US. HE'S MAKING PETER AND THE OTHERS THINK THEY'RE WINNING.
"HE'S LETTING PETER THINK HE'S MAKING THE HARDEST CHOICE OF HIS LIFE."
DEAR GOD.
CLICK
WHATEVER IT TAKES.
KTOOM

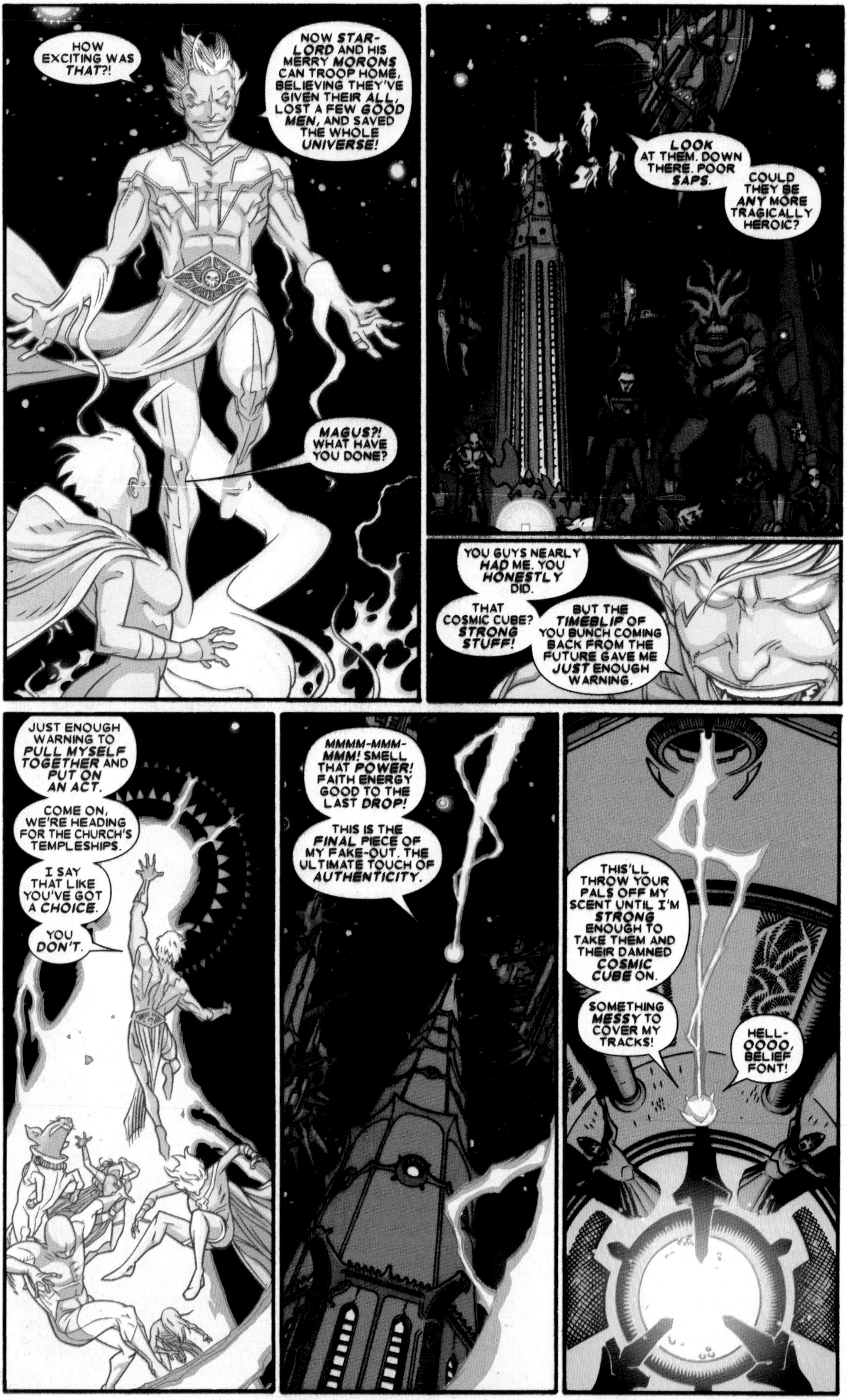
HOW EXCITING WAS THAT?!
NOW STAR-LORD AND HIS MERRY MORONS CAN TROOP HOME, BELIEVING THEY'VE GIVEN THEIR ALL, LOST A FEW GOOD MEN, AND SAVED THE WHOLE UNIVERSE!
MAGUS?! WHAT HAVE YOU DONE?
LOOK AT THEM. DOWN THERE. POOR SAPS.
COULD THEY BE ANY MORE TRAGICALLY HEROIC?
YOU GUYS NEARLY HAD ME. YOU HONESTLY DID.
THAT COSMIC CUBE? STRONG STUFF!
BUT THE TIMEBLIP OF YOU BUNCH COMING BACK FROM THE FUTURE GAVE ME JUST ENOUGH WARNING.
JUST ENOUGH WARNING TO PULL MYSELF TOGETHER AND PUT ON AN ACT.
COME ON, WE'RE HEADING FOR THE CHURCH'S TEMPLESHIPS.
I SAY THAT LIKE YOU'VE GOT A CHOICE.
YOU DON'T.
MMMM-MMM-MMM! SMELL THAT POWER! FAITH ENERGY GOOD TO THE LAST DROP!
THIS IS THE FINAL PIECE OF MY FAKE-OUT. THE ULTIMATE TOUCH OF AUTHENTICITY.
THIS'LL THROW YOUR PALS OFF MY SCENT UNTIL I'M STRONG ENOUGH TO TAKE THEM AND THEIR DAMNED COSMIC CUBE ON.
SOMETHING MESSY TO COVER MY TRACKS!
HELL-OOOO, BELIEF FONT!

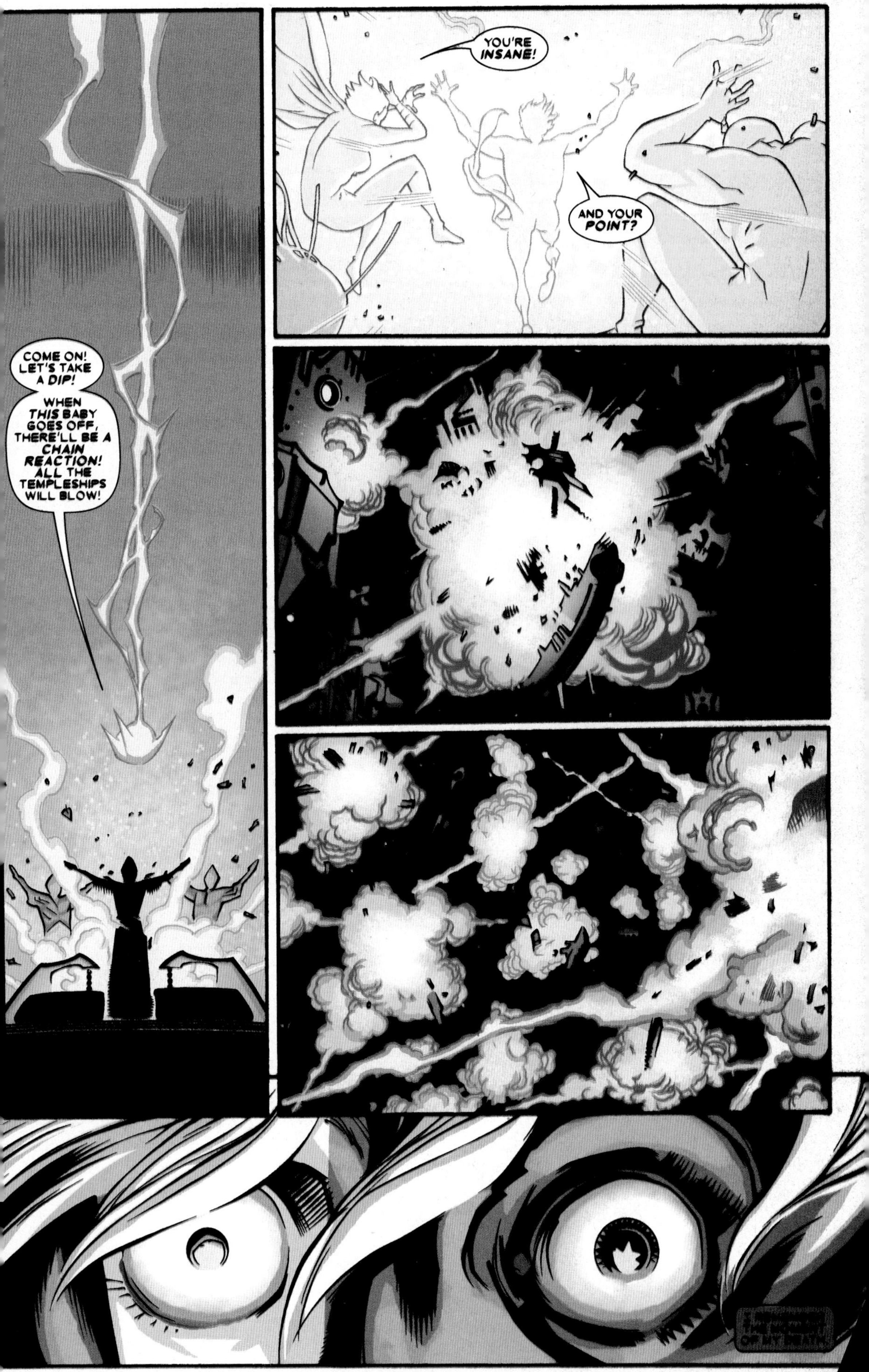
YOU'RE INSANE!
AND YOUR POINT?
COME ON! LET'S TAKE A DIP!
WHEN THIS BABY GOES OFF, THERE'LL BE A CHAIN REACTION! ALL THE TEMPLESHIPS WILL BLOW!
OF MY DEATH.

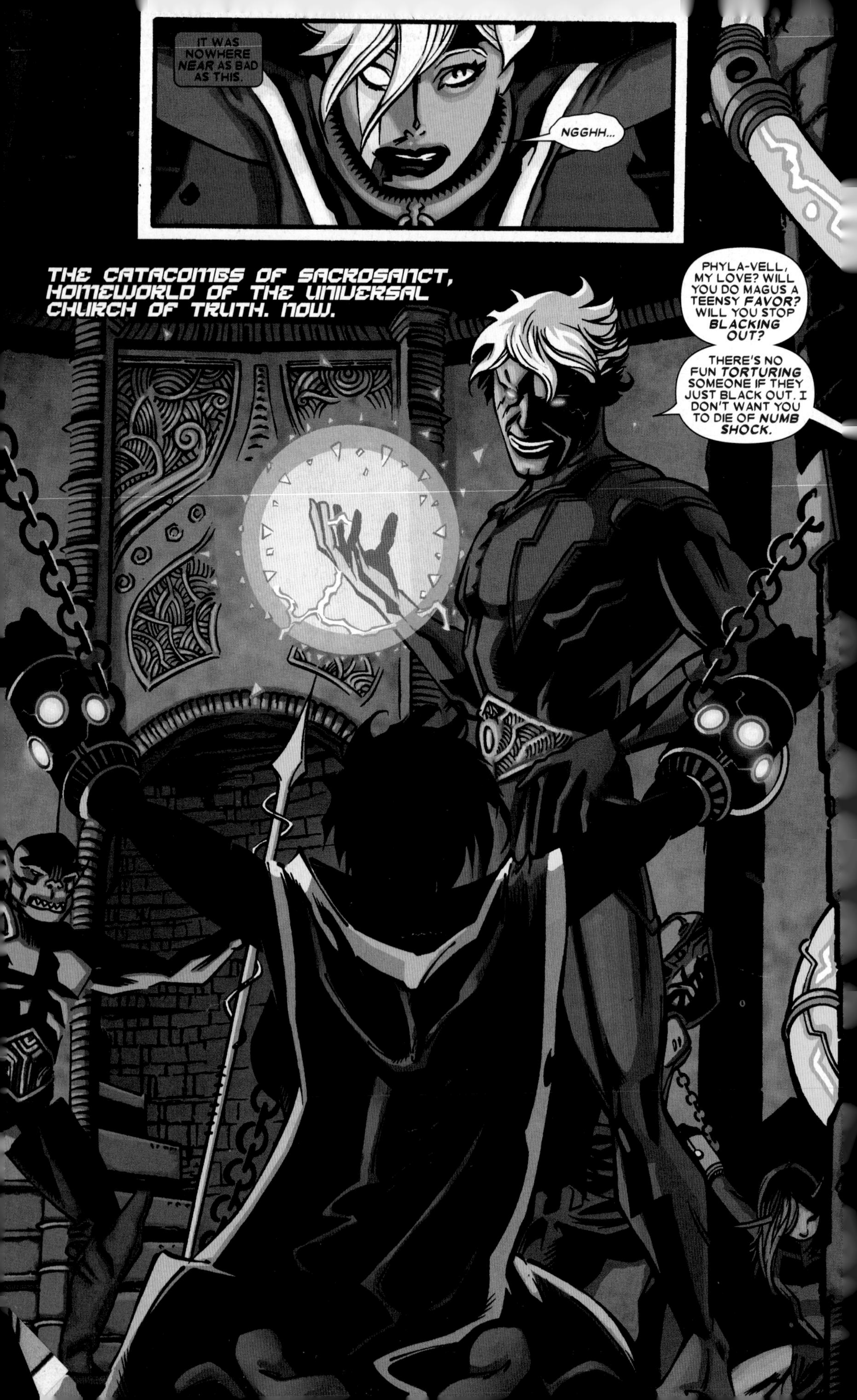
IT WAS NOWHERE NEAR AS BAD AS THIS.
NGGHH...
THE CATACOMBS OF SACROSANCT, HOMEWORLD OF THE UNIVERSAL CHURCH OF TRUTH. NOW.
PHYLA-VELL, MY LOVE? WILL YOU DO MAGUS A TEENSY FAVOR? WILL YOU STOP BLACKING OUT?
THERE'S NO FUN TORTURING SOMEONE IF THEY JUST BLACK OUT. I DON'T WANT YOU TO DIE OF NUMB SHOCK.

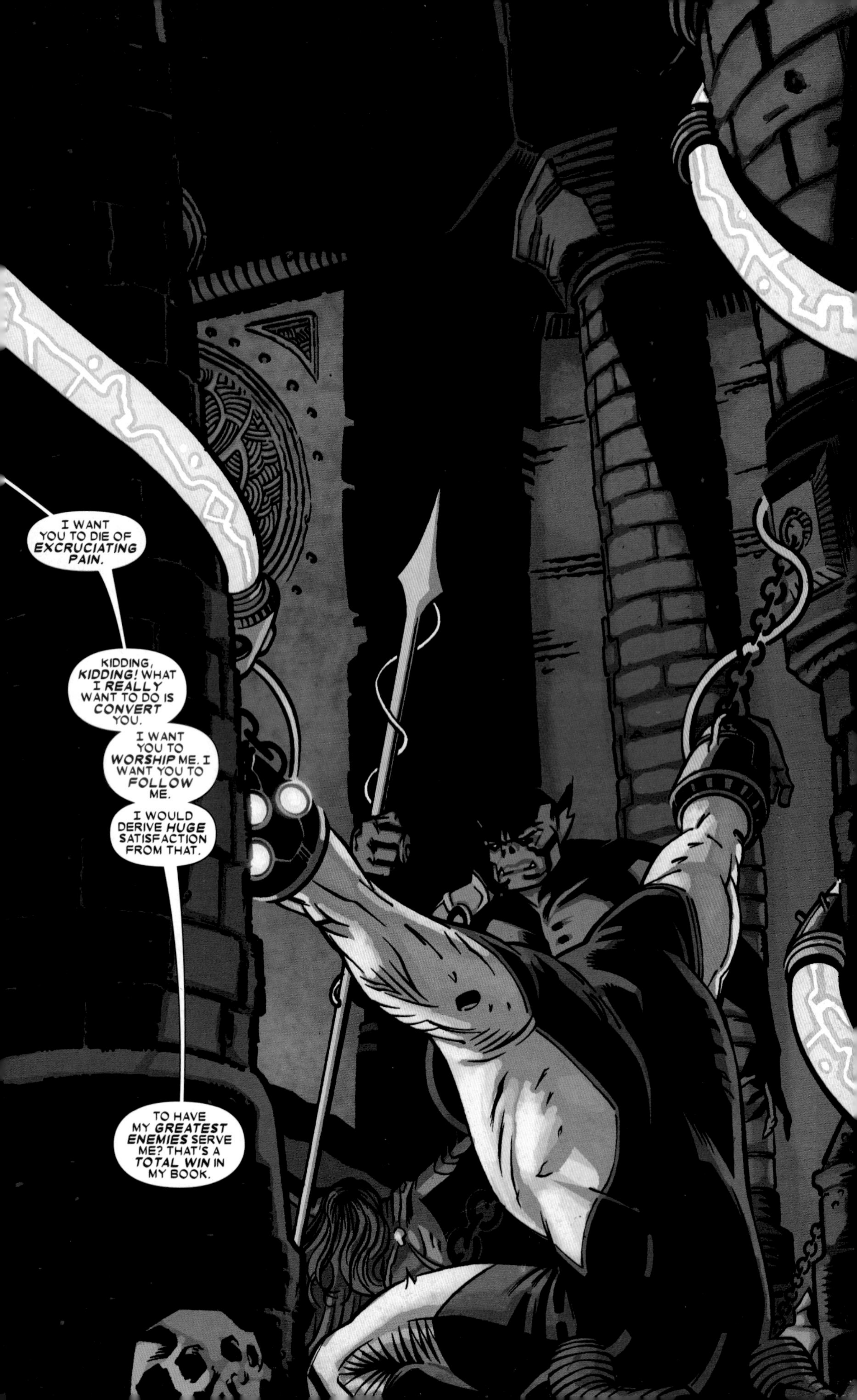
I WANT YOU TO DIE OF EXCRUCIATING PAIN.
KIDDING, KIDDING! WHAT I REALLY WANT TO DO IS CONVERT YOU.
I WANT YOU TO WORSHIP ME. I WANT YOU TO FOLLOW ME.
I WOULD DERIVE HUGE SATISFACTION FROM THAT.
TO HAVE MY GREATEST ENEMIES SERVE ME? THAT'S A TOTAL WIN IN MY BOOK.

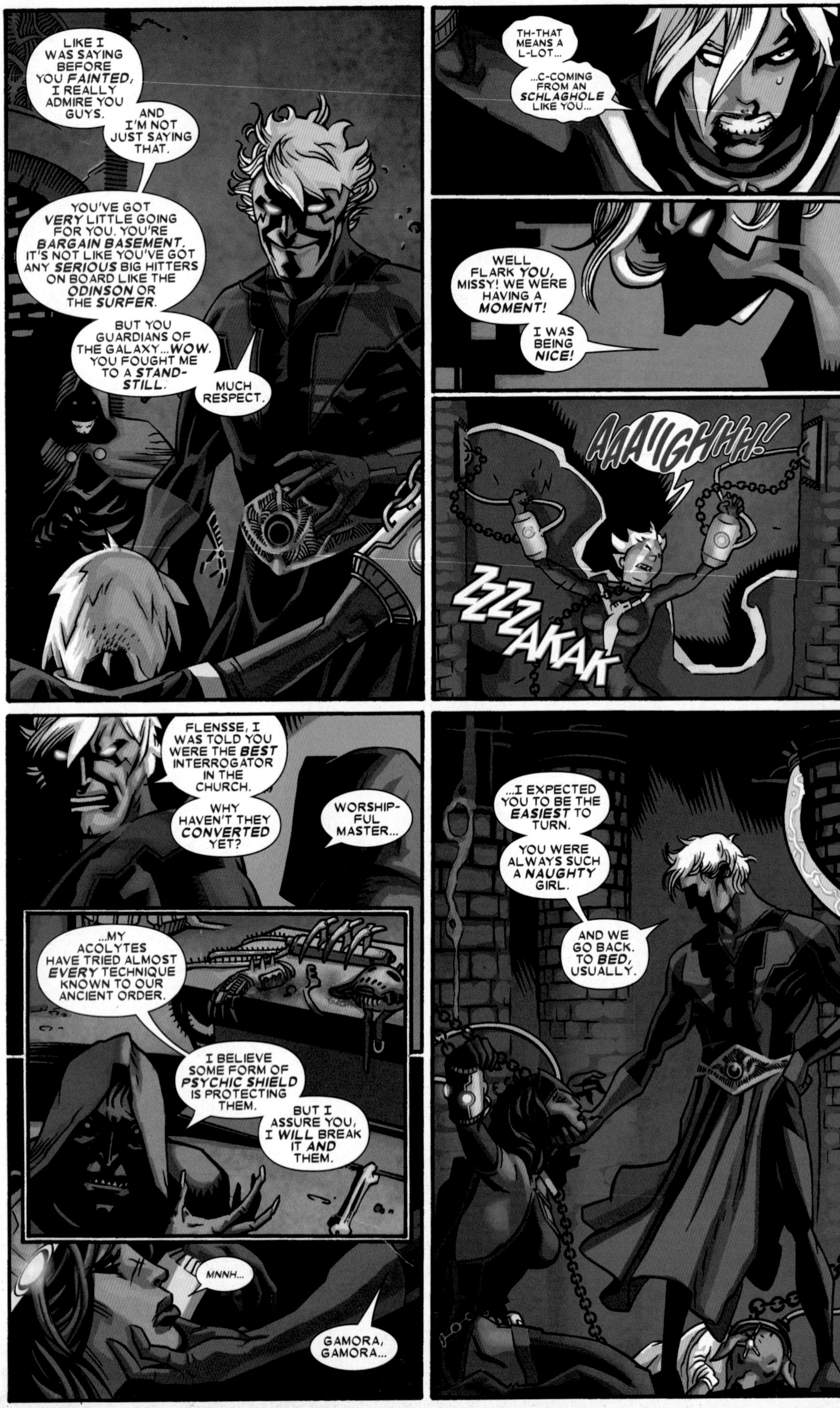
LIKE I WAS SAYING BEFORE YOU FAINTED, I REALLY ADMIRE YOU GUYS.
AND I'M NOT JUST SAYING THAT.
YOU'VE GOT VERY LITTLE GOING FOR YOU. YOU'RE BARGAIN BASEMENT. IT'S NOT LIKE YOU'VE GOT ANY SERIOUS BIG HITTERS ON BOARD LIKE THE ODINSON OR THE SURFER.
BUT YOU GUARDIANS OF THE GALAXY...WOW. YOU FOUGHT ME TO A STAND-STILL.
MUCH RESPECT.
TH-THAT MEANS A L-LOT...
...C-COMING FROM AN SCHLAGHOLE LIKE YOU...
WELL FLARK YOU, MISSY! WE WERE HAVING A MOMENT!
I WAS BEING NICE!
AAAIIGHHH!
ZZZZAKAK
FLENSSE, I WAS TOLD YOU WERE THE BEST INTERROGATOR IN THE CHURCH.
WHY HAVEN'T THEY CONVERTED YET?
WORSHIP-FUL MASTER...
...MY ACOLYTES HAVE TRIED ALMOST EVERY TECHNIQUE KNOWN TO OUR ANCIENT ORDER.
I BELIEVE SOME FORM OF PSYCHIC SHIELD IS PROTECTING THEM.
BUT I ASSURE YOU, I WILL BREAK IT AND THEM.
MNNH...
GAMORA, GAMORA...
...I EXPECTED YOU TO BE THE EASIEST TO TURN.
YOU WERE ALWAYS SUCH A NAUGHTY GIRL.
AND WE GO BACK. TO BED, USUALLY.

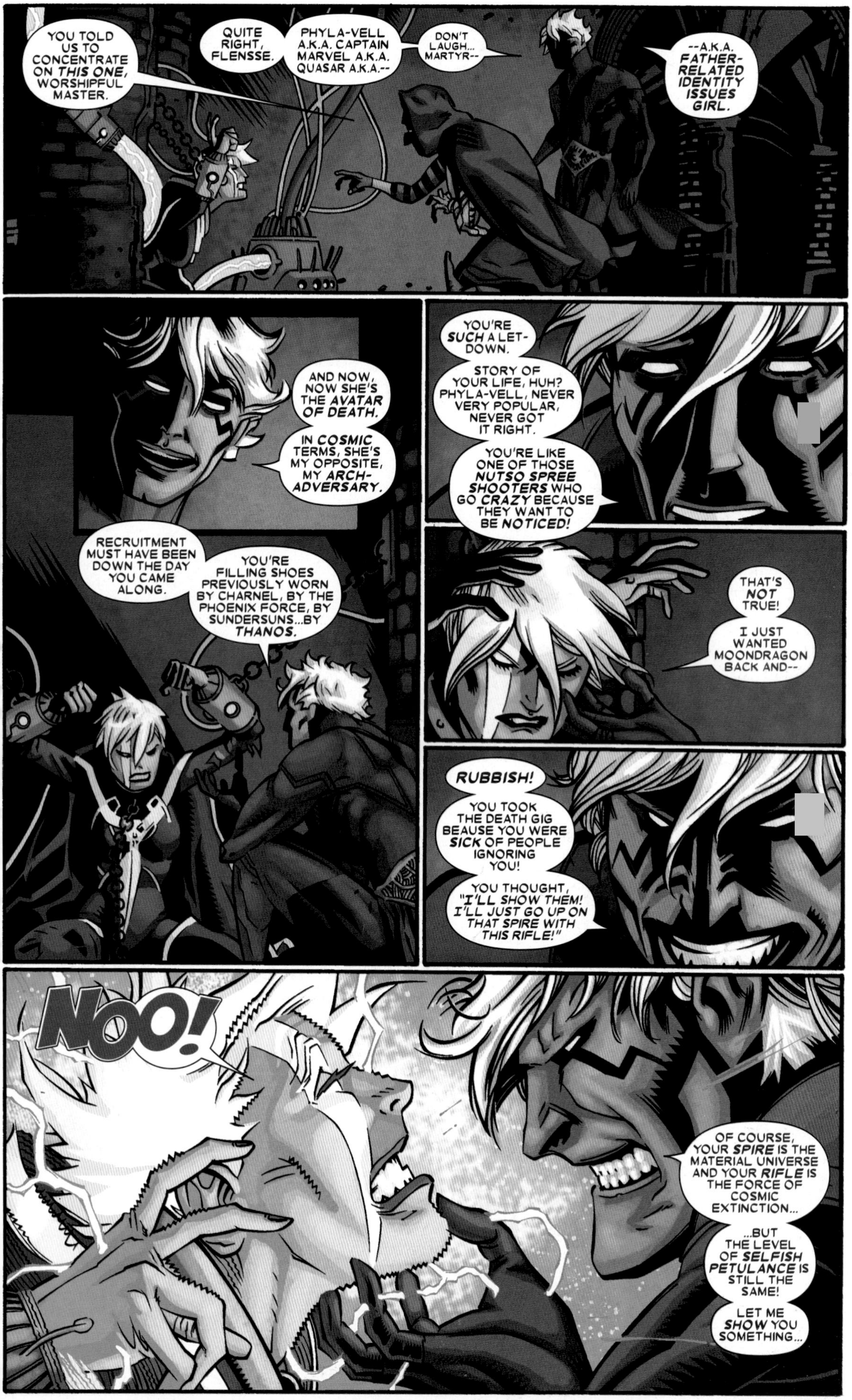
YOU TOLD US TO CONCENTRATE ON THIS ONE, WORSHIPFUL MASTER.
QUITE RIGHT, FLENSSE.
PHYLA-VELL A.K.A. CAPTAIN MARVEL A.K.A. QUASAR A.K.A.--
DON'T LAUGH... MARTYR--
--A.K.A. FATHER-RELATED IDENTITY ISSUES GIRL.
AND NOW, NOW SHE'S THE AVATAR OF DEATH.
IN COSMIC TERMS, SHE'S MY OPPOSITE, MY ARCH-ADVERSARY.
RECRUITMENT MUST HAVE BEEN DOWN THE DAY YOU CAME ALONG.
YOU'RE FILLING SHOES PREVIOUSLY WORN BY CHARNEL, BY THE PHOENIX FORCE, BY SUNDERSUNS...BY THANOS.
YOU'RE SUCH A LET-DOWN.
STORY OF YOUR LIFE, HUH? PHYLA-VELL, NEVER VERY POPULAR, NEVER GOT IT RIGHT.
YOU'RE LIKE ONE OF THOSE NUTSO SPREE SHOOTERS WHO GO CRAZY BECAUSE THEY WANT TO BE NOTICED!
THAT'S NOT TRUE!
I JUST WANTED MOONDRAGON BACK AND--
RUBBISH!
YOU TOOK THE DEATH GIG BEAUSE YOU WERE SICK OF PEOPLE IGNORING YOU!
YOU THOUGHT, "I'LL SHOW THEM! I'LL JUST GO UP ON THAT SPIRE WITH THIS RIFLE!"
NOO!
OF COURSE, YOUR SPIRE IS THE MATERIAL UNIVERSE AND YOUR RIFLE IS THE FORCE OF COSMIC EXTINCTION...
...BUT THE LEVEL OF SELFISH PETULANCE IS STILL THE SAME!
LET ME SHOW YOU SOMETHING...

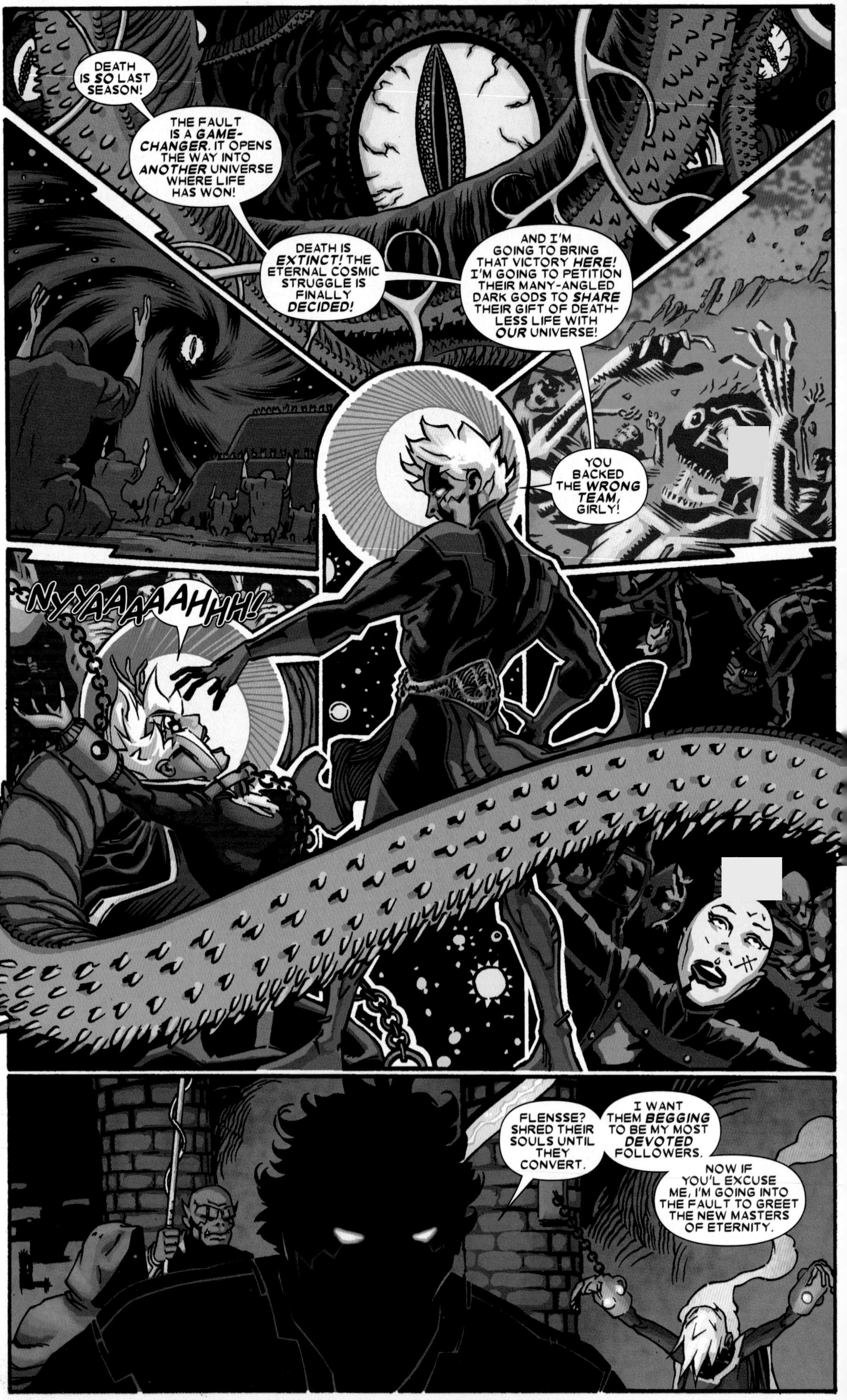
DEATH IS SO LAST SEASON!
THE FAULT IS A GAME-CHANGER. IT OPENS THE WAY INTO ANOTHER UNIVERSE WHERE LIFE HAS WON!
DEATH IS EXTINCT! THE ETERNAL COSMIC STRUGGLE IS FINALLY DECIDED!
AND I'M GOING TO BRING THAT VICTORY HERE! I'M GOING TO PETITION THEIR MANY-ANGLED DARK GODS TO SHARE THEIR GIFT OF DEATH-LESS LIFE WITH OUR UNIVERSE!
YOU BACKED THE WRONG TEAM, GIRLY!
NyYAAAAAHHH!
FLENSSE? SHRED THEIR SOULS UNTIL THEY CONVERT.
I WANT THEM BEGGING TO BE MY MOST DEVOTED FOLLOWERS.
NOW IF YOU'L EXCUSE ME, I'M GOING INTO THE FAULT TO GREET THE NEW MASTERS OF ETERNITY.

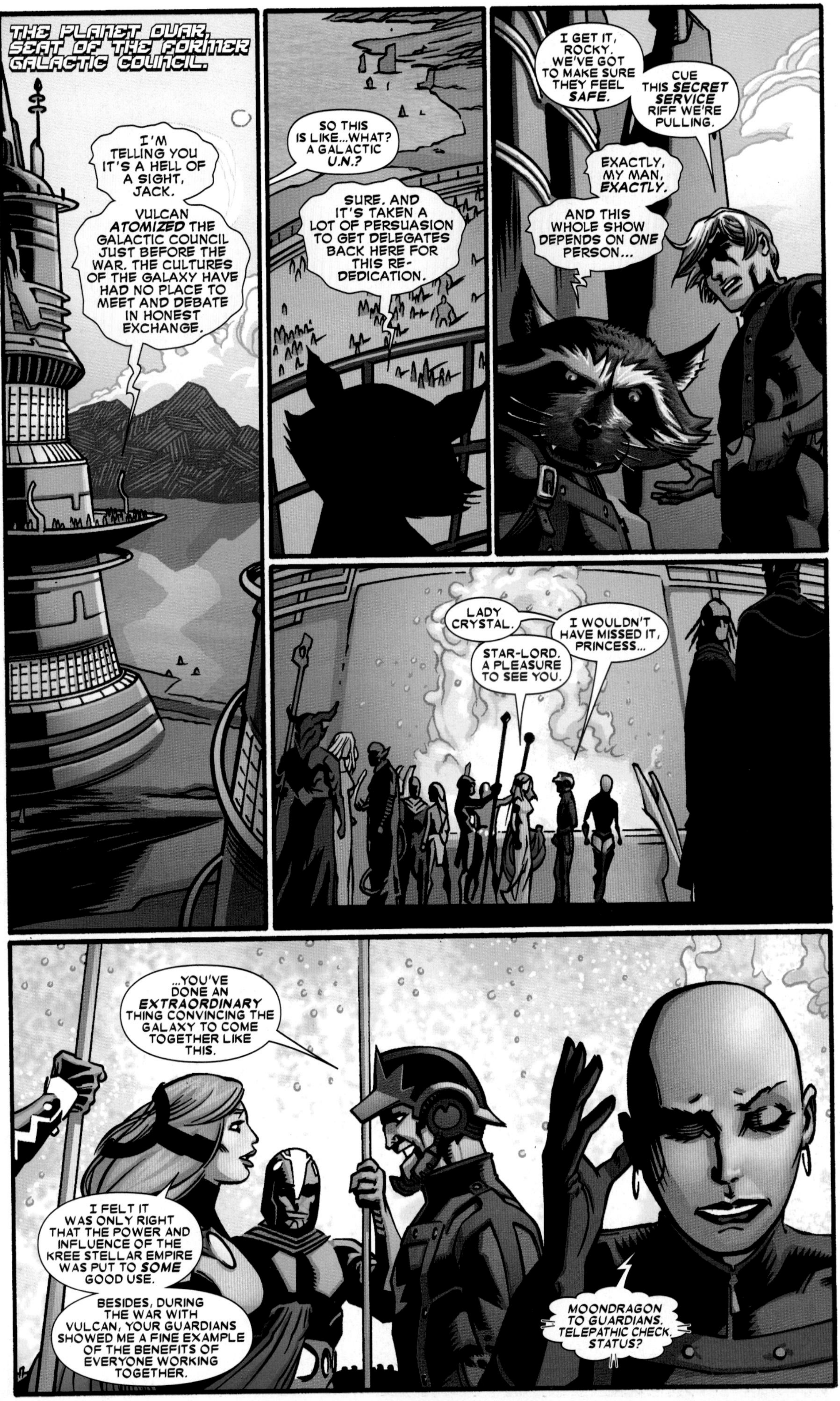
THE PLANET QUAR, SEAT OF THE FORMER GALACTIC COUNCIL.
I'M TELLING YOU IT'S A HELL OF A SIGHT, JACK.
VULCAN ATOMIZED THE GALACTIC COUNCIL JUST BEFORE THE WAR. THE CULTURES OF THE GALAXY HAVE HAD NO PLACE TO MEET AND DEBATE IN HONEST EXCHANGE.
SO THIS IS LIKE...WHAT? A GALACTIC U.N.?
SURE. AND IT'S TAKEN A LOT OF PERSUASION TO GET DELEGATES BACK HERE FOR THIS RE-DEDICATION.
I GET IT, ROCKY. WE'VE GOT TO MAKE SURE THEY FEEL SAFE.
CUE THIS SECRET SERVICE RIFF WE'RE PULLING.
EXACTLY, MY MAN, EXACTLY.
AND THIS WHOLE SHOW DEPENDS ON ONE PERSON...
LADY CRYSTAL.
I WOULDN'T HAVE MISSED IT, PRINCESS...
STAR-LORD. A PLEASURE TO SEE YOU.
...YOU'VE DONE AN EXTRAORDINARY THING CONVINCING THE GALAXY TO COME TOGETHER LIKE THIS.
I FELT IT WAS ONLY RIGHT THAT THE POWER AND INFLUENCE OF THE KREE STELLAR EMPIRE WAS PUT TO SOME GOOD USE.
BESIDES, DURING THE WAR WITH VULCAN, YOUR GUARDIANS SHOWED ME A FINE EXAMPLE OF THE BENEFITS OF EVERYONE WORKING TOGETHER.
MOONDRAGON TO GUARDIANS. TELEPATHIC CHECK. STATUS?

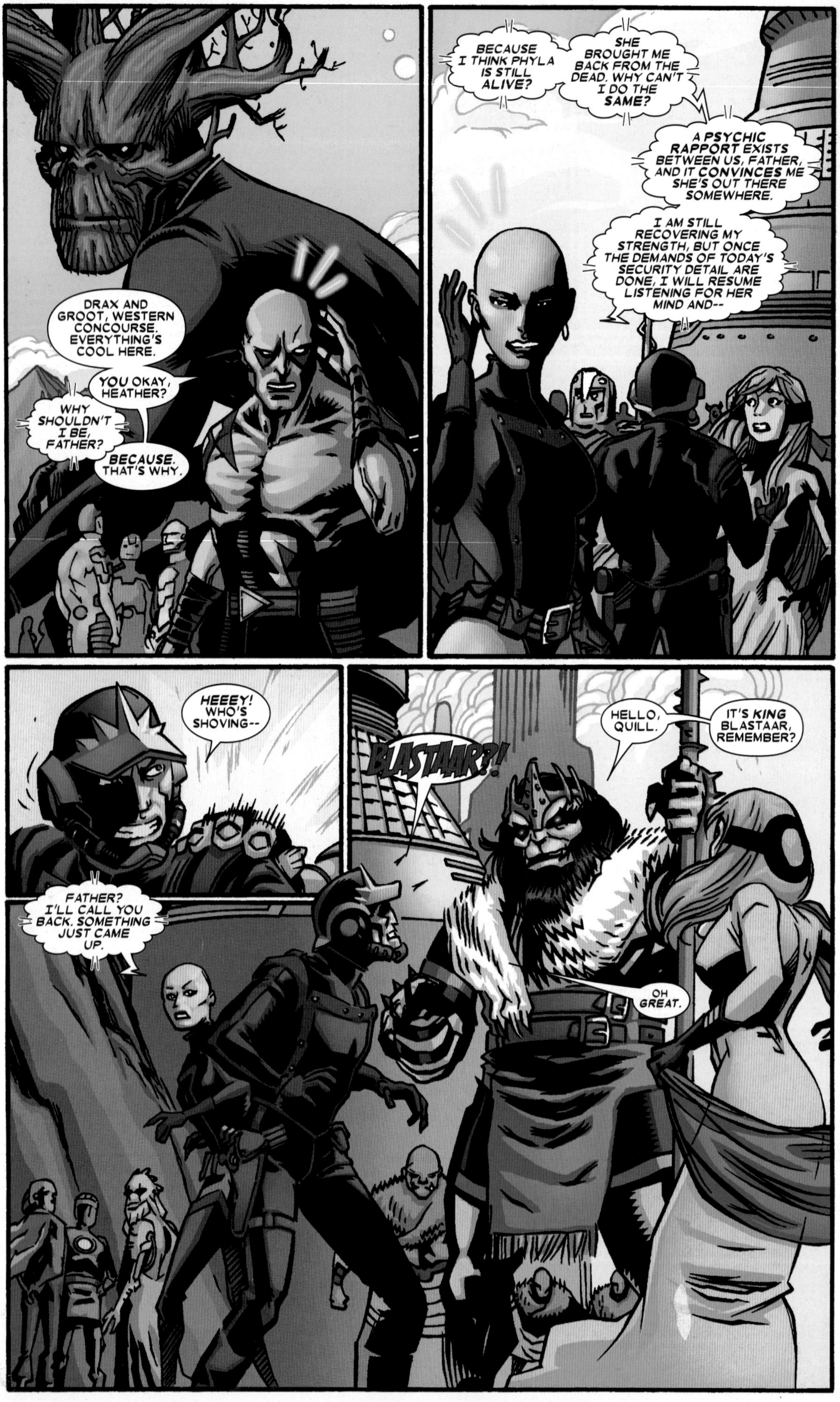
DRAX AND GROOT, WESTERN CONCOURSE. EVERYTHING'S COOL HERE.
YOU OKAY, HEATHER?
WHY SHOULDN'T I BE, FATHER?
BECAUSE. THAT'S WHY.
BECAUSE I THINK PHYLA IS STILL ALIVE?
SHE BROUGHT ME BACK FROM THE DEAD. WHY CAN'T I DO THE SAME?
A PSYCHIC RAPPORT EXISTS BETWEEN US, FATHER, AND IT CONVINCES ME SHE'S OUT THERE SOMEWHERE.
I AM STILL RECOVERING MY STRENGTH, BUT ONCE THE DEMANDS OF TODAY'S SECURITY DETAIL ARE DONE, I WILL RESUME LISTENING FOR HER MIND AND--
HEEEY! WHO'S SHOVING--
BLASTAAR?!
HELLO, QUILL.
IT'S KING BLASTAAR, REMEMBER?
FATHER? I'LL CALL YOU BACK. SOMETHING JUST CAME UP.
OH GREAT.

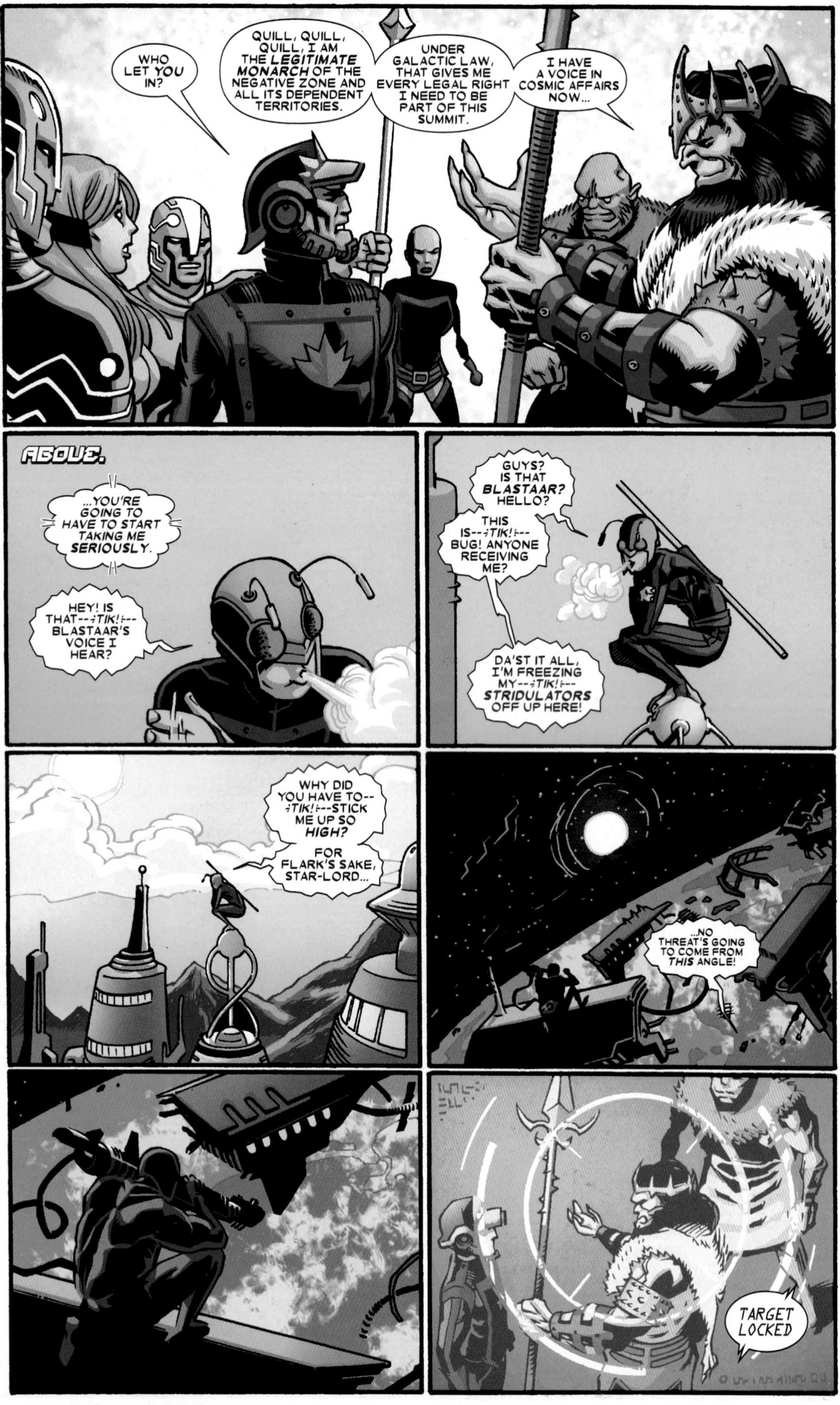

WHO LET YOU IN?
QUILL, QUILL, QUILL, I AM THE LEGITIMATE MONARCH OF THE NEGATIVE ZONE AND ALL ITS DEPENDENT TERRITORIES.
UNDER GALACTIC LAW, THAT GIVES ME EVERY LEGAL RIGHT I NEED TO BE PART OF THIS SUMMIT.
I HAVE A VOICE IN COSMIC AFFAIRS NOW...
ABOVE.
...YOU'RE GOING TO HAVE TO START TAKING ME SERIOUSLY.
HEY! IS THAT--TIK!--BLASTAAR'S VOICE I HEAR?
GUYS? IS THAT BLASTAAR? HELLO?
THIS IS--TIK!--BUG! ANYONE RECEIVING ME?
DA'ST IT ALL, I'M FREEZING MY--TIK!--STRIDULATORS OFF UP HERE!
WHY DID YOU HAVE TO--TIK!--STICK ME UP SO HIGH?
FOR FLARK'S SAKE, STAR-LORD...
...NO THREAT'S GOING TO COME FROM THIS ANGLE!
TARGET LOCKED

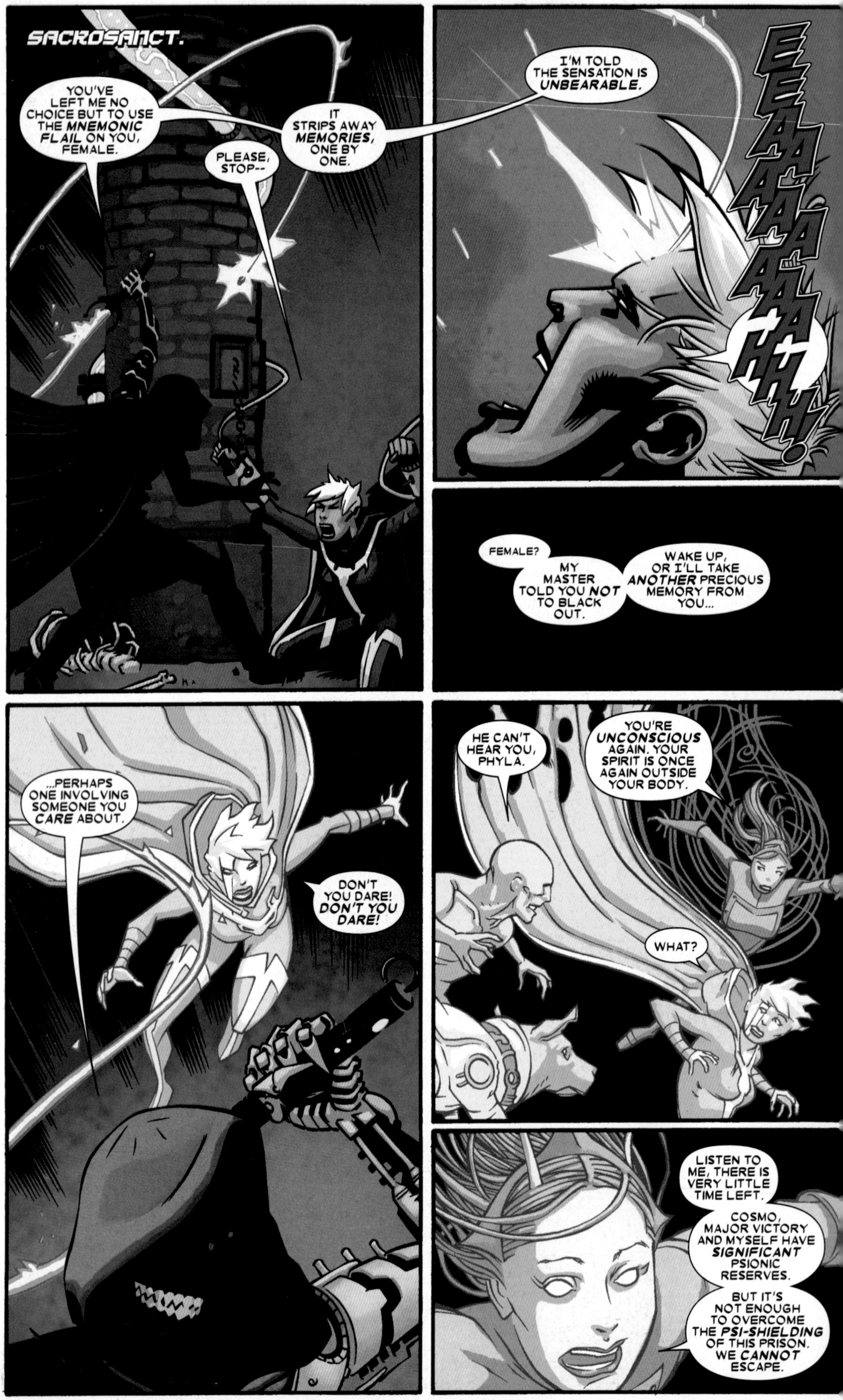
SACROSANCT.
YOU'VE LEFT ME NO CHOICE BUT TO USE THE MNEMONIC FLAIL ON YOU, FEMALE.
PLEASE, STOP--
IT STRIPS AWAY MEMORIES, ONE BY ONE.
I'M TOLD THE SENSATION IS UNBEARABLE.
EEEAAAAAAAAAHHHH!
FEMALE?
MY MASTER TOLD YOU NOT TO BLACK OUT.
WAKE UP, OR I'LL TAKE ANOTHER PRECIOUS MEMORY FROM YOU...
...PERHAPS ONE INVOLVING SOMEONE YOU CARE ABOUT.
DON'T YOU DARE! DON'T YOU DARE!
HE CAN'T HEAR YOU, PHYLA.
YOU'RE UNCONSCIOUS AGAIN. YOUR SPIRIT IS ONCE AGAIN OUTSIDE YOUR BODY.
WHAT?
LISTEN TO ME, THERE IS VERY LITTLE TIME LEFT.
COSMO, MAJOR VICTORY AND MYSELF HAVE SIGNIFICANT PSIONIC RESERVES.
BUT IT'S NOT ENOUGH TO OVERCOME THE PSI-SHIELDING OF THIS PRISON. WE CANNOT ESCAPE.

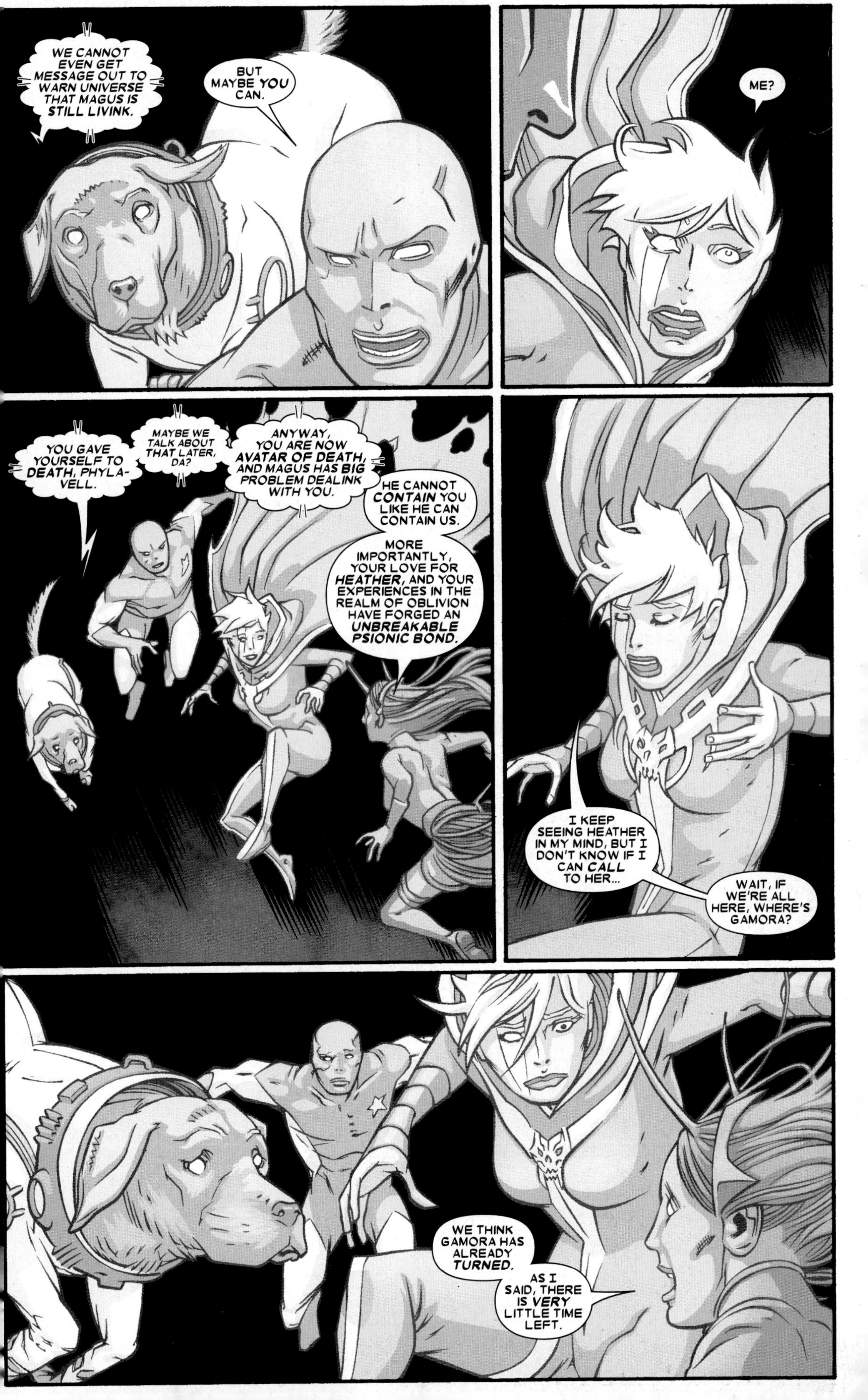
WE CANNOT EVEN GET MESSAGE OUT TO WARN UNIVERSE THAT MAGUS IS STILL LIVINK.
BUT MAYBE YOU CAN.
ME?
YOU GAVE YOURSELF TO DEATH, PHYLA-VELL.
MAYBE WE TALK ABOUT THAT LATER, DA?
ANYWAY, YOU ARE NOW AVATAR OF DEATH, AND MAGUS HAS BIG PROBLEM DEALINK WITH YOU.
HE CANNOT CONTAIN YOU LIKE HE CAN CONTAIN US.
MORE IMPORTANTLY, YOUR LOVE FOR HEATHER, AND YOUR EXPERIENCES IN THE REALM OF OBLIVION HAVE FORGED AN UNBREAKABLE PSIONIC BOND.
I KEEP SEEING HEATHER IN MY MIND, BUT I DON'T KNOW IF I CAN CALL TO HER...
WAIT, IF WE'RE ALL HERE, WHERE'S GAMORA?
WE THINK GAMORA HAS ALREADY TURNED.
AS I SAID, THERE IS VERY LITTLE TIME LEFT.

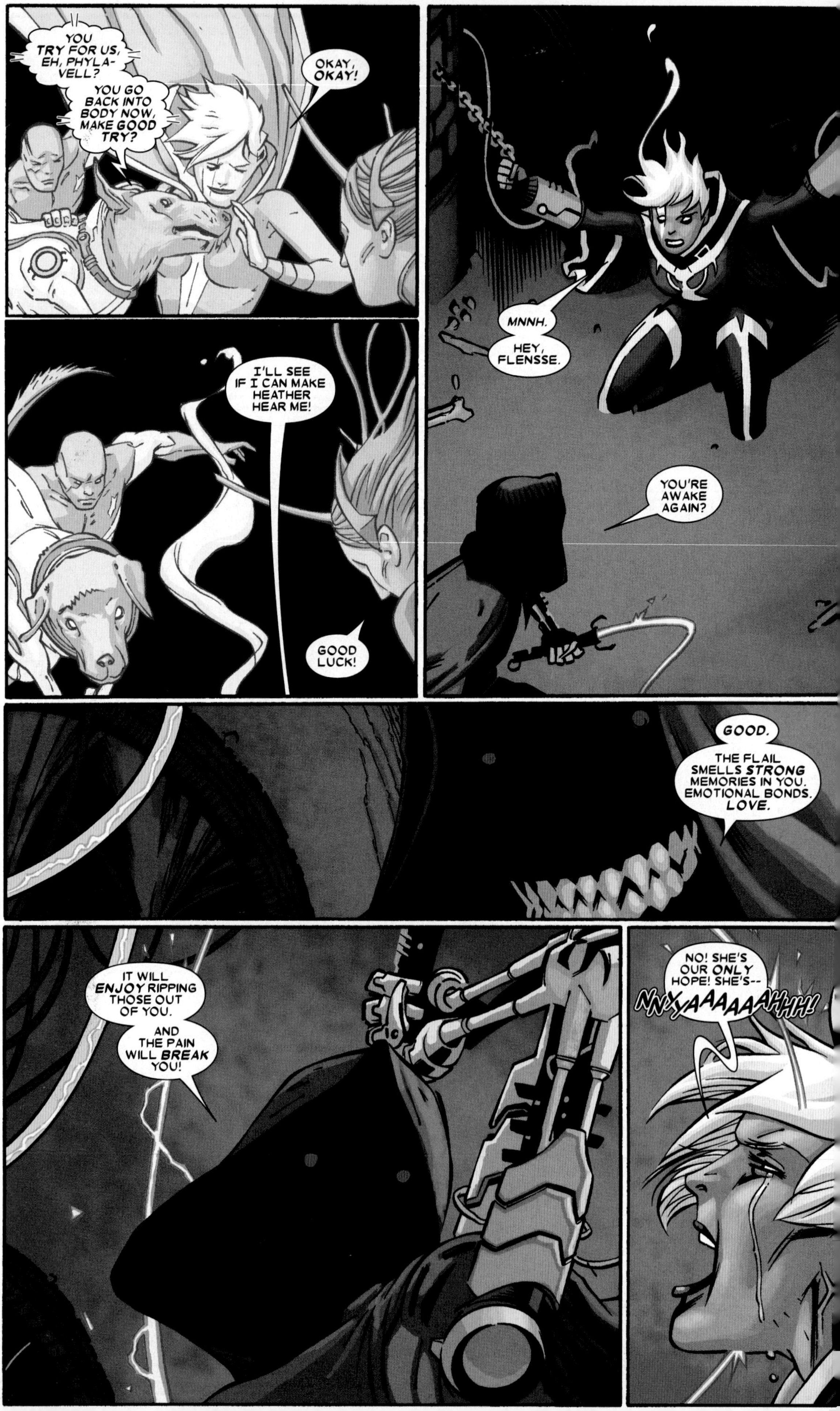
YOU TRY FOR US, EH, PHYLA-VELL?
YOU GO BACK INTO BODY NOW, MAKE GOOD TRY?
OKAY, OKAY!
I'LL SEE IF I CAN MAKE HEATHER HEAR ME!
GOOD LUCK!
MNNH.
HEY, FLENSSE.
YOU'RE AWAKE AGAIN?
GOOD.
THE FLAIL SMELLS STRONG MEMORIES IN YOU. EMOTIONAL BONDS. LOVE.
IT WILL ENJOY RIPPING THOSE OUT OF YOU.
AND THE PAIN WILL BREAK YOU!
NO! SHE'S OUR ONLY HOPE! SHE'S--
NNYYAAAAAAHHH!

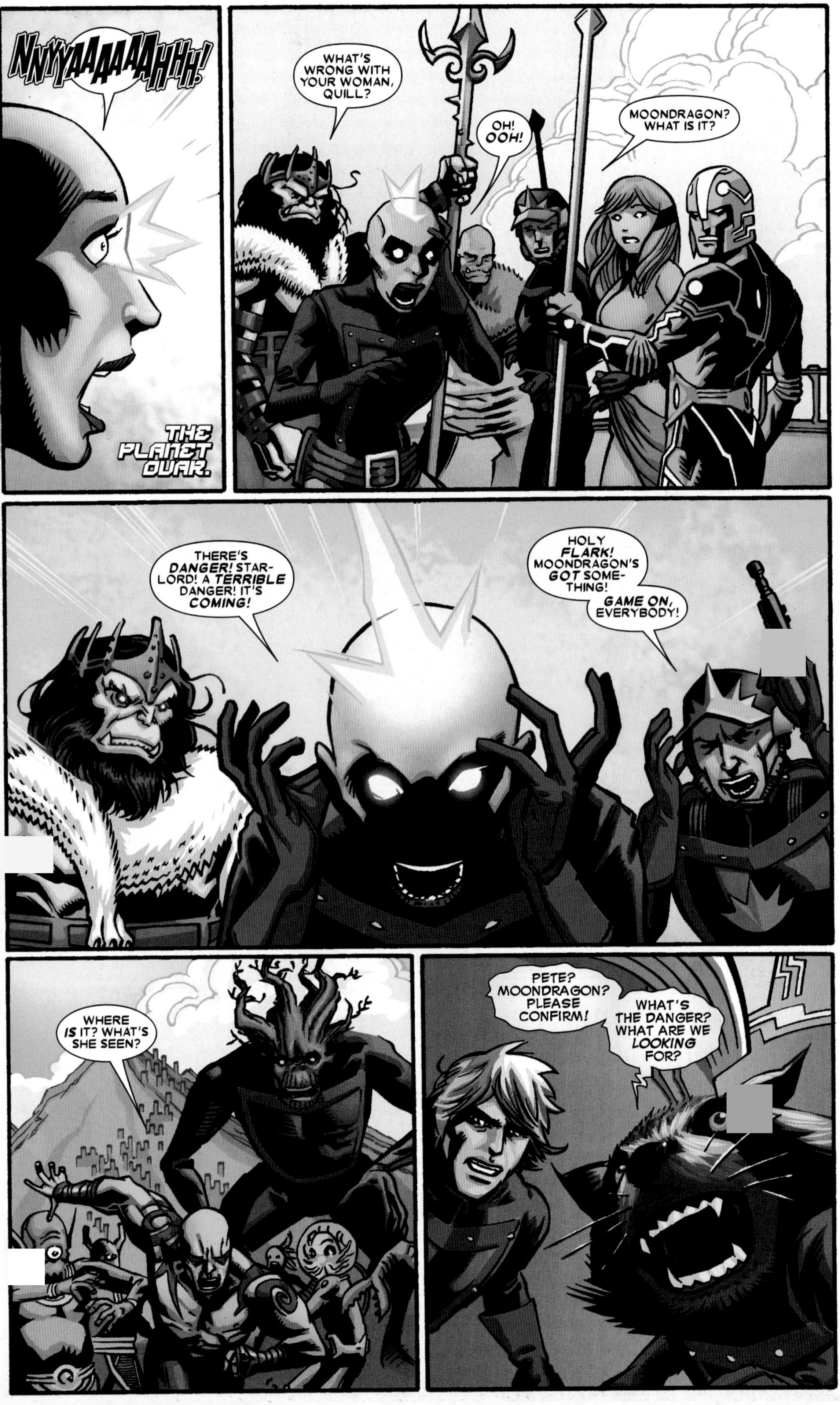

NNYYAAAAAAHHH!
THE PLANET OUAR.
WHAT'S WRONG WITH YOUR WOMAN, QUILL?
OH! OOH!
MOONDRAGON? WHAT IS IT?
THERE'S DANGER! STAR-LORD! A TERRIBLE DANGER! IT'S COMING!
HOLY FLARK! MOONDRAGON'S GOT SOME-THING!
GAME ON, EVERYBODY!
WHERE IS IT? WHAT'S SHE SEEN?
PETE? MOONDRAGON? PLEASE CONFIRM!
WHAT'S THE DANGER? WHAT ARE WE LOOKING FOR?

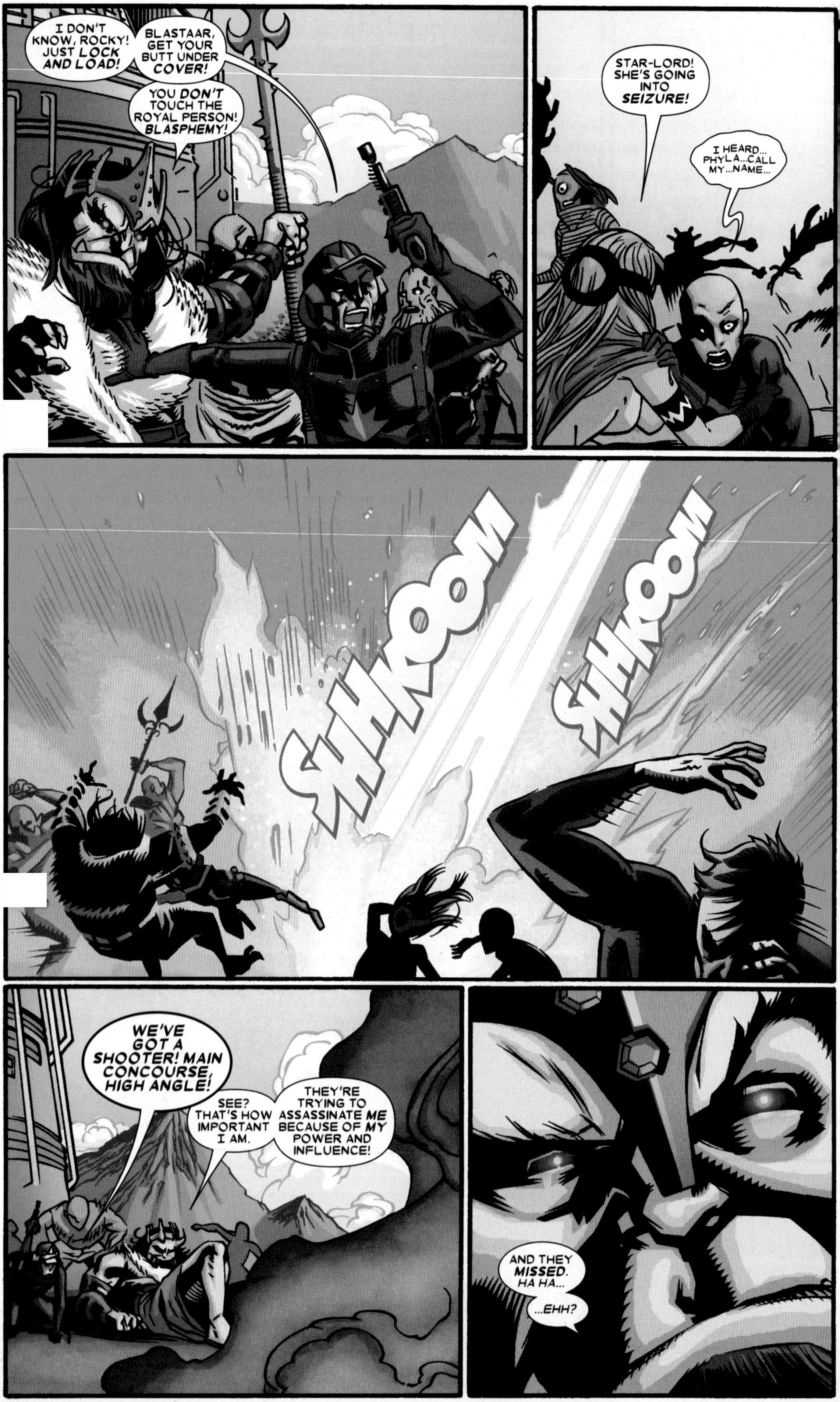
I DON'T KNOW, ROCKY! JUST LOCK AND LOAD!
BLASTAAR, GET YOUR BUTT UNDER COVER!
YOU DON'T TOUCH THE ROYAL PERSON! BLASPHEMY!
STAR-LORD! SHE'S GOING INTO SEIZURE!
I HEARD... PHYLA...CALL MY...NAME...
SHHKOOM
SHHKOOM
WE'VE GOT A SHOOTER! MAIN CONCOURSE, HIGH ANGLE!
SEE? THAT'S HOW IMPORTANT I AM.
THEY'RE TRYING TO ASSASSINATE ME BECAUSE OF MY POWER AND INFLUENCE!
AND THEY MISSED. HA HA...
...EHH?

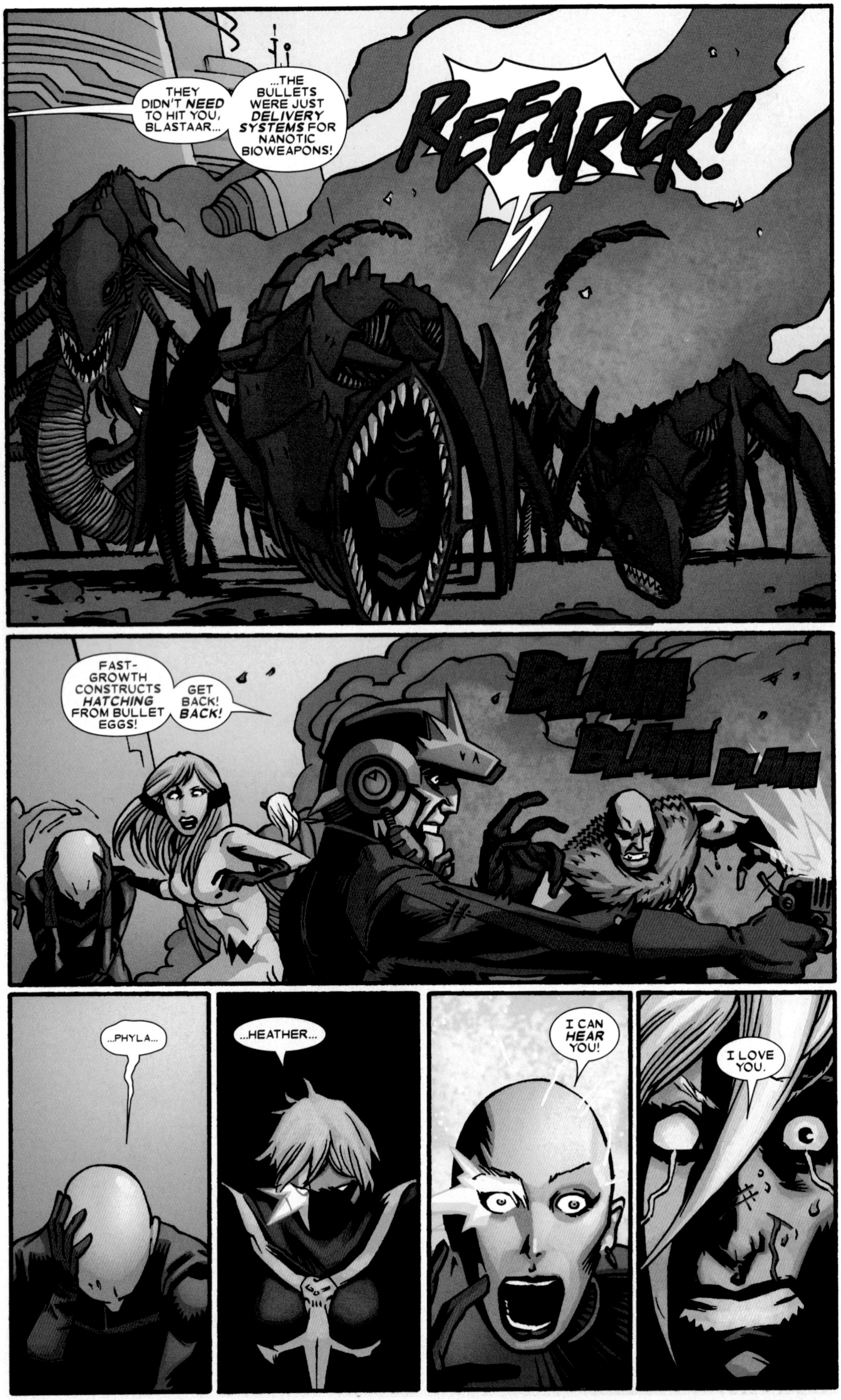
THEY DIDN'T NEED TO HIT YOU, BLASTAAR...
...THE BULLETS WERE JUST DELIVERY SYSTEMS FOR NANOTIC BIOWEAPONS!
REEARCK!
FAST-GROWTH CONSTRUCTS HATCHING FROM BULLET EGGS!
GET BACK! BACK!
...PHYLA...
...HEATHER...
I CAN HEAR YOU!
I LOVE YOU.

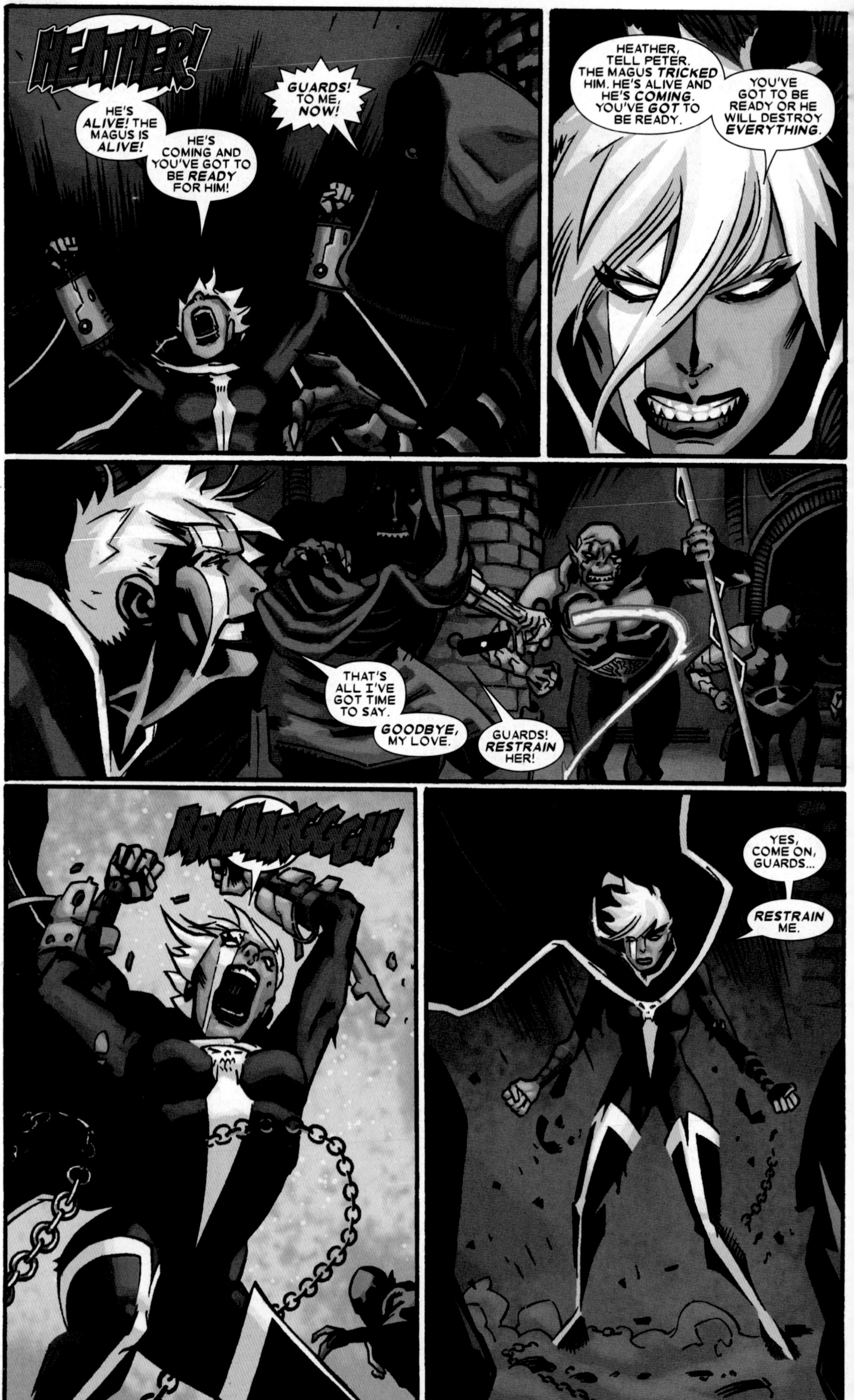
HEATHER!
HE'S ALIVE! THE MAGUS IS ALIVE!
HE'S COMING AND YOU'VE GOT TO BE READY FOR HIM!
GUARDS! TO ME, NOW!
HEATHER, TELL PETER. THE MAGUS TRICKED HIM. HE'S ALIVE AND HE'S COMING. YOU'VE GOT TO BE READY.
YOU'VE GOT TO BE READY OR HE WILL DESTROY EVERYTHING.
THAT'S ALL I'VE GOT TIME TO SAY.
GOODBYE, MY LOVE.
GUARDS! RESTRAIN HER!
RRAAARGGH!
YES, COME ON, GUARDS...
RESTRAIN ME.

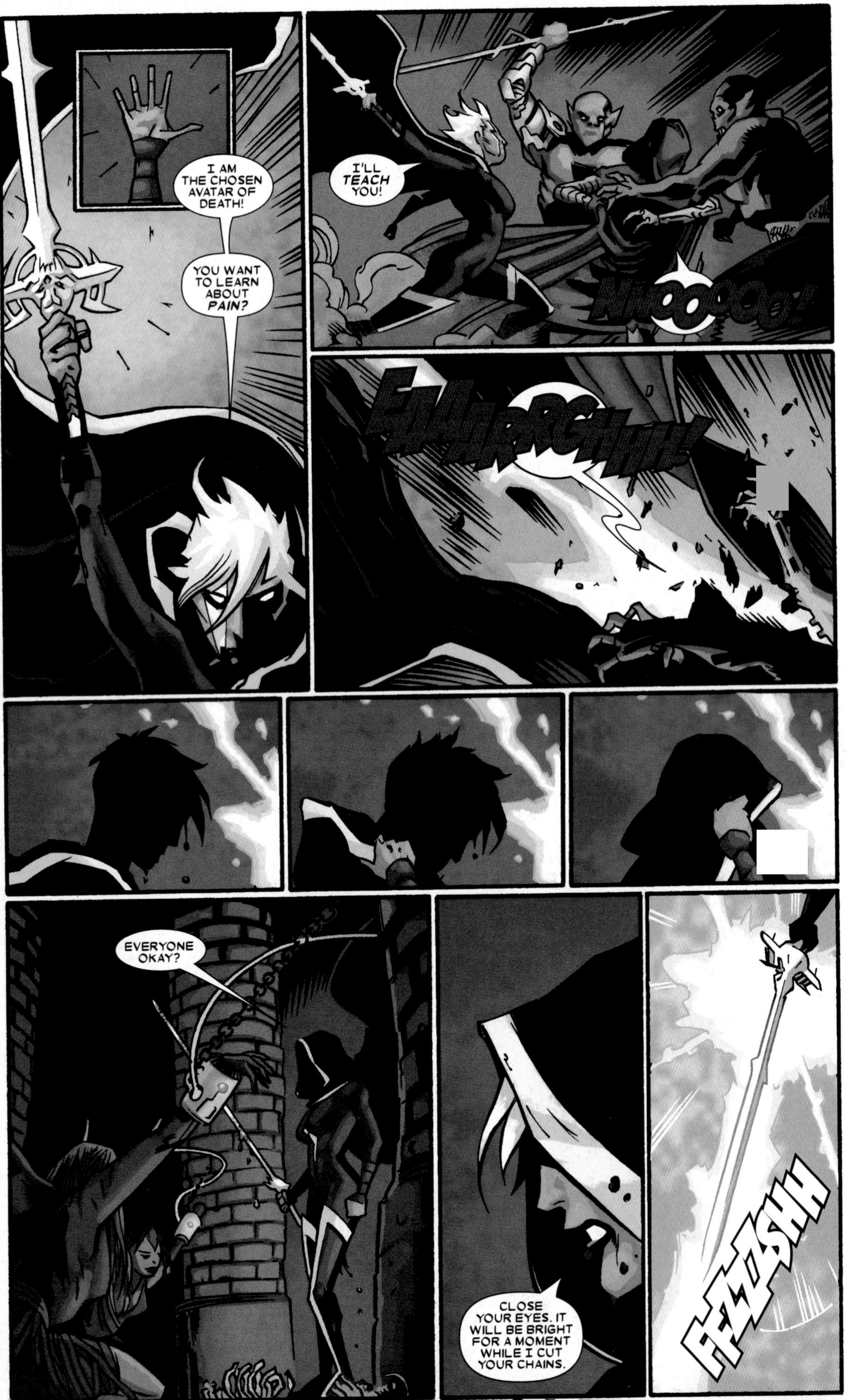
I AM THE CHOSEN AVATAR OF DEATH!
YOU WANT TO LEARN ABOUT *PAIN?*
I'LL *TEACH* YOU!
NHOOOOOO!
EHHHRRRGHHHH!
EVERYONE OKAY?
CLOSE YOUR EYES. IT WILL BE BRIGHT FOR A MOMENT WHILE I CUT YOUR CHAINS.
FFZZSHH

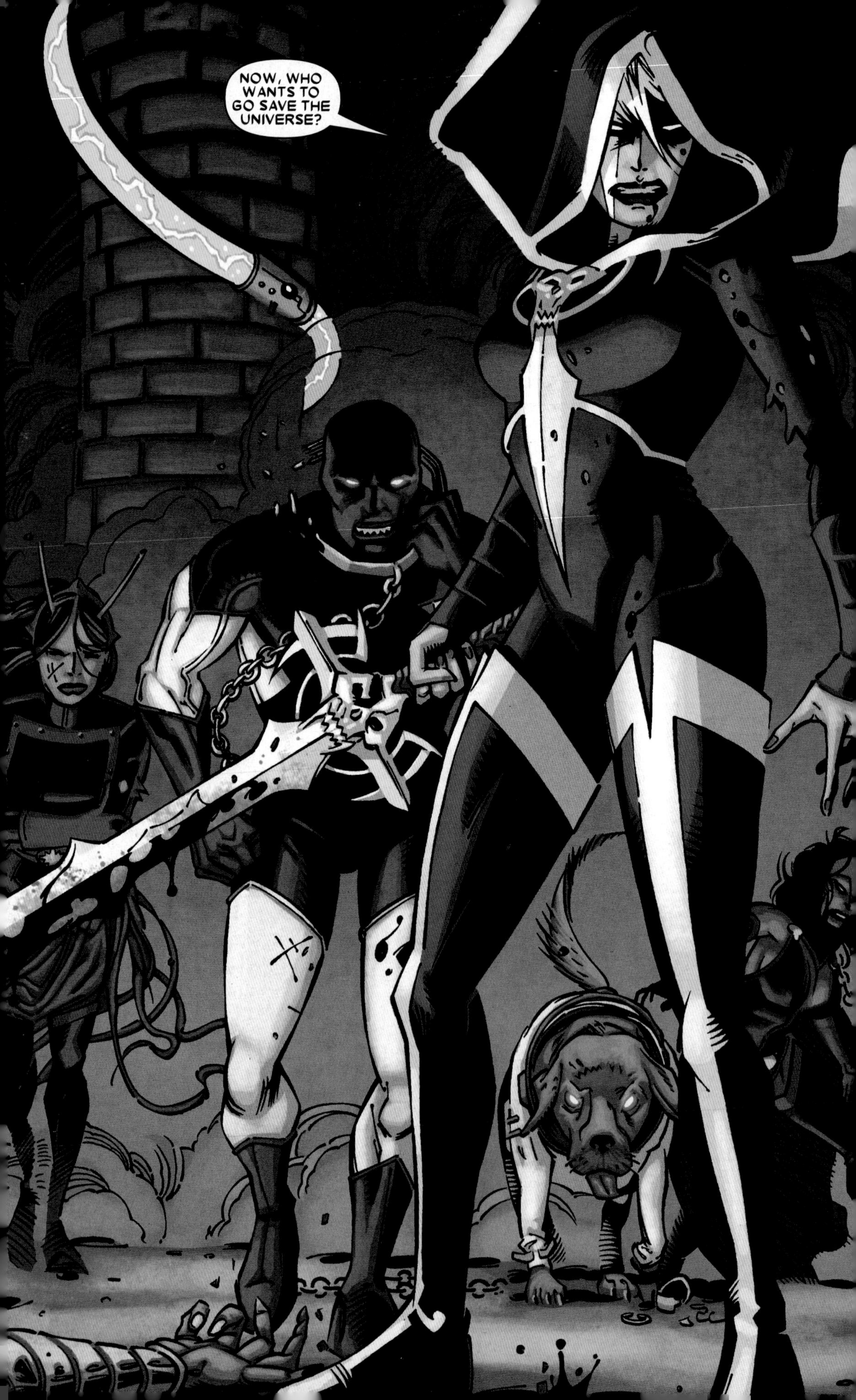
NOW, WHO WANTS TO GO SAVE THE UNIVERSE?

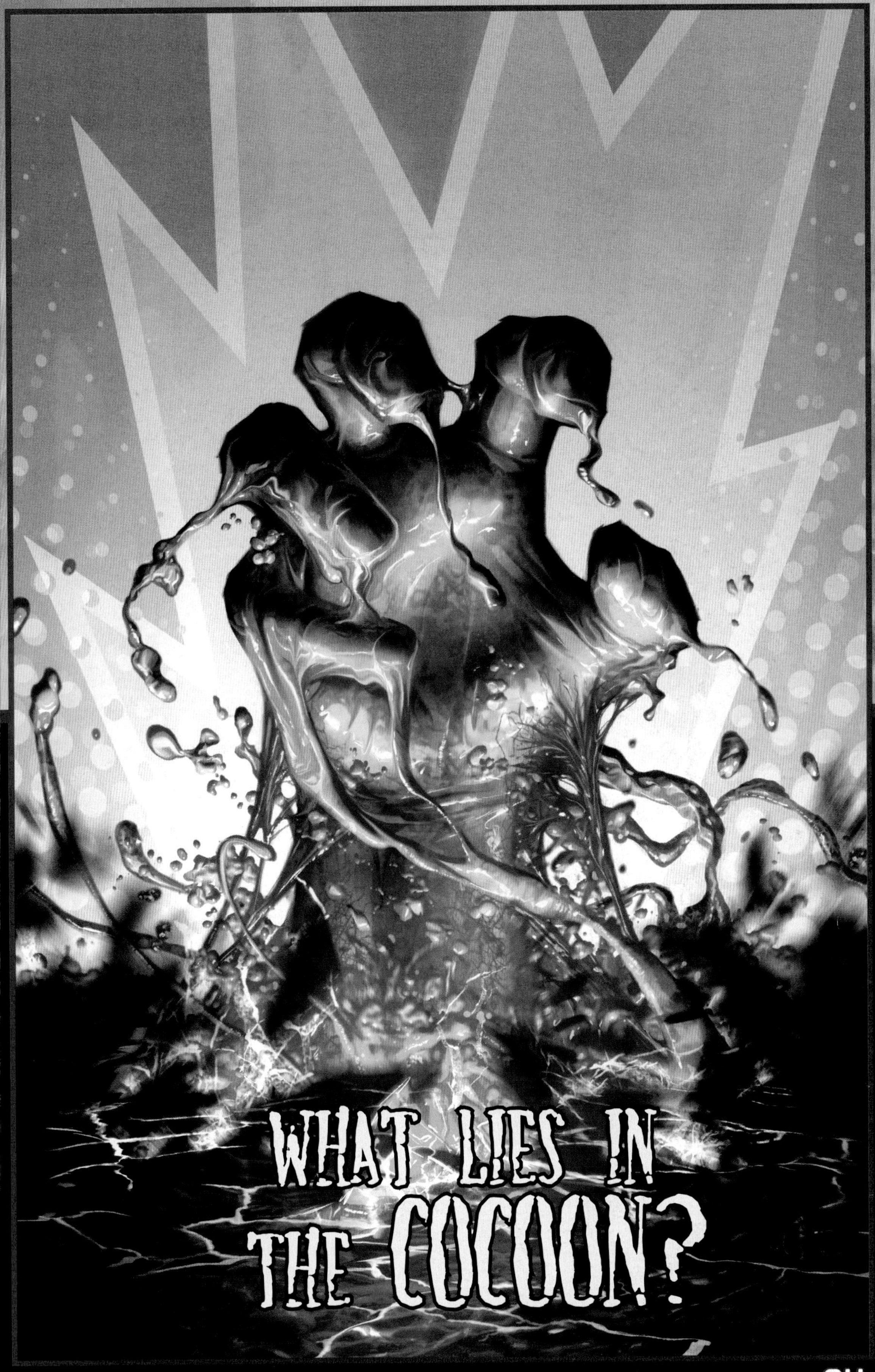
WHAT LIES IN THE COCOON?

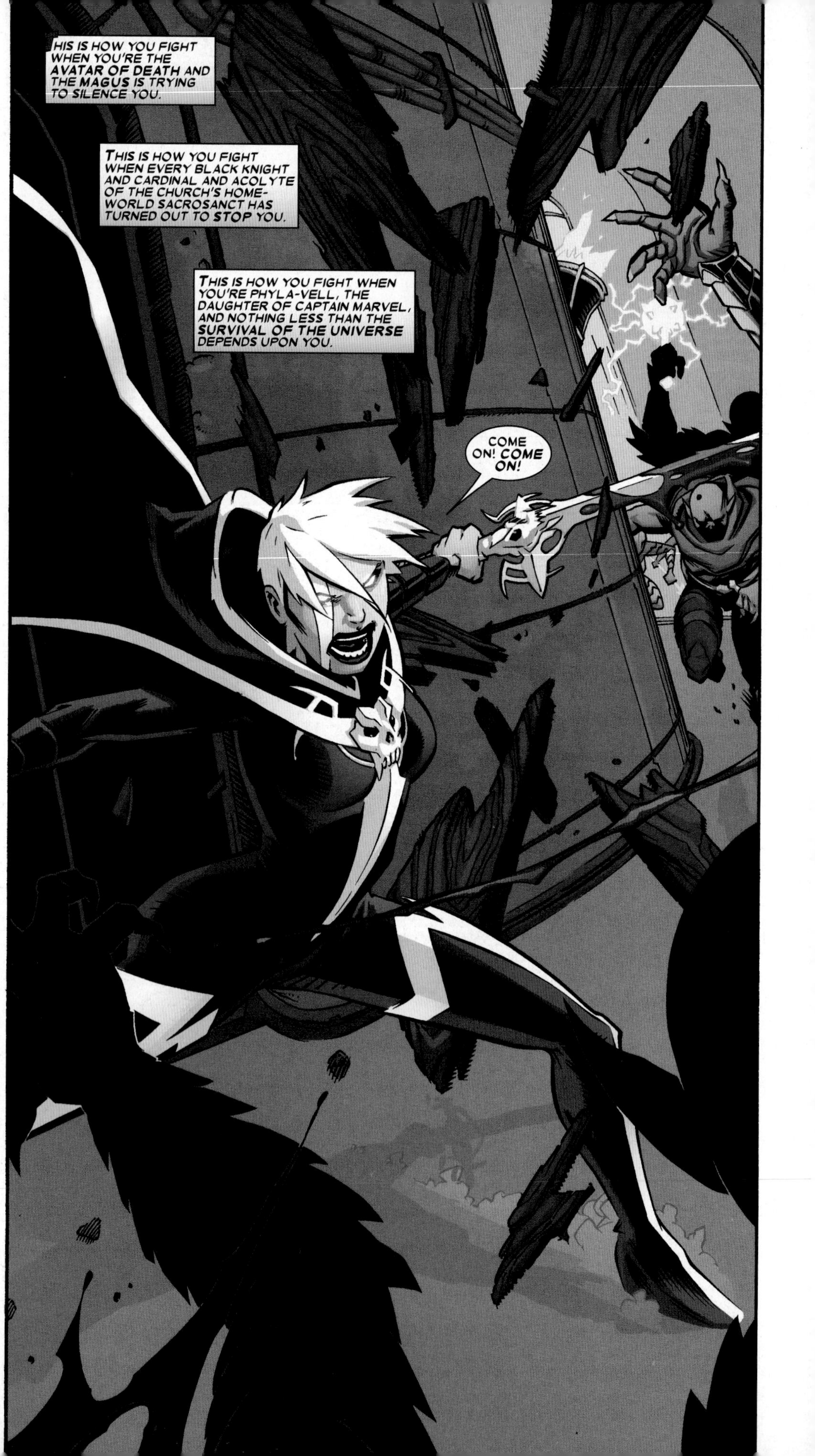
HIS IS HOW YOU FIGHT WHEN YOU'RE THE AVATAR OF DEATH AND THE MAGUS IS TRYING TO SILENCE YOU.
THIS IS HOW YOU FIGHT WHEN EVERY BLACK KNIGHT AND CARDINAL AND ACOLYTE OF THE CHURCH'S HOME-WORLD SACROSANCT HAS TURNED OUT TO STOP YOU.
THIS IS HOW YOU FIGHT WHEN YOU'RE PHYLA-VELL, THE DAUGHTER OF CAPTAIN MARVEL, AND NOTHING LESS THAN THE SURVIVAL OF THE UNIVERSE DEPENDS UPON YOU.
COME ON! COME ON!

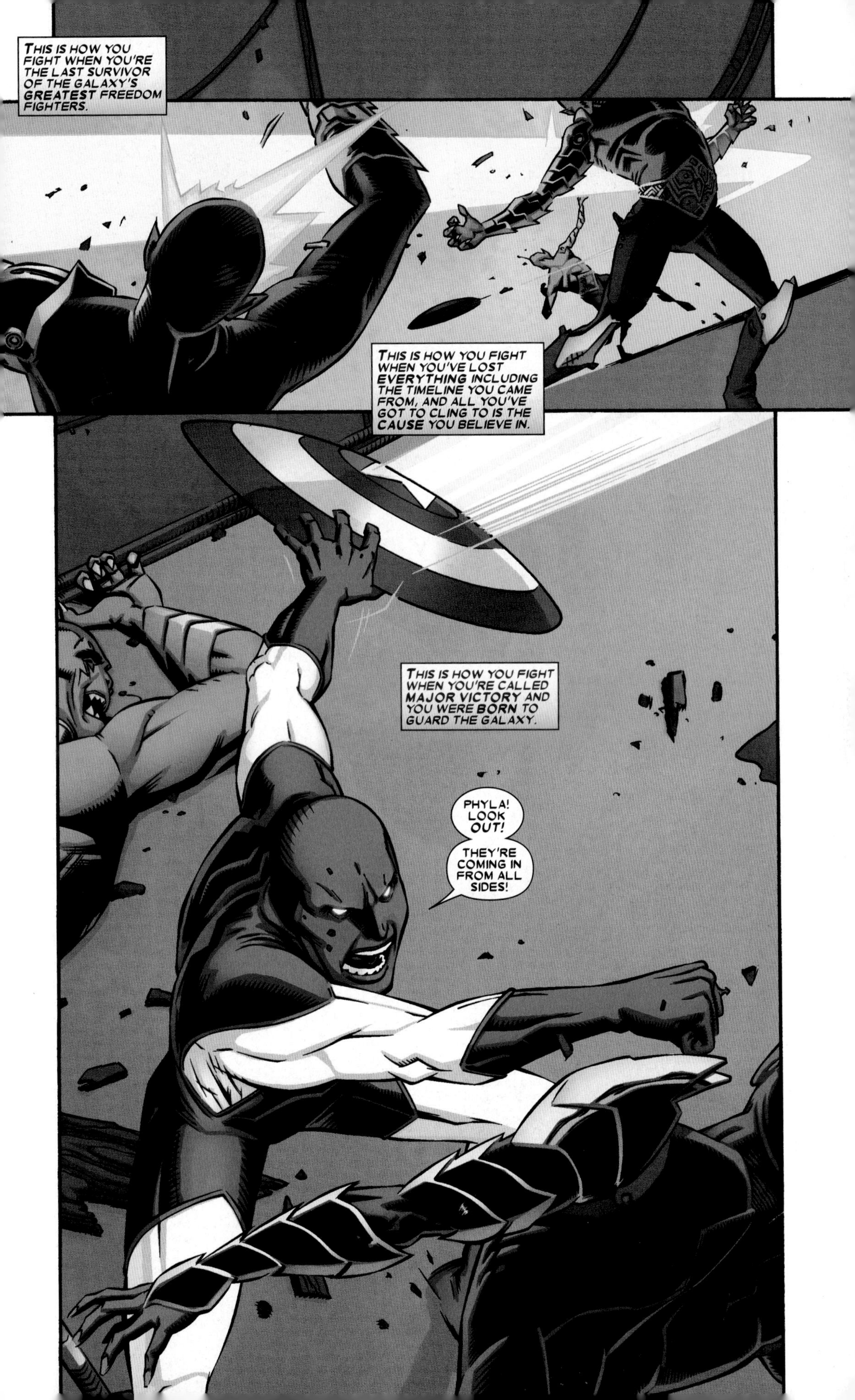
THIS IS HOW YOU FIGHT WHEN YOU'RE THE LAST SURVIVOR OF THE GALAXY'S GREATEST FREEDOM FIGHTERS.
THIS IS HOW YOU FIGHT WHEN YOU'VE LOST EVERYTHING INCLUDING THE TIMELINE YOU CAME FROM, AND ALL YOU'VE GOT TO CLING TO IS THE CAUSE YOU BELIEVE IN.
THIS IS HOW YOU FIGHT WHEN YOU'RE CALLED MAJOR VICTORY AND YOU WERE BORN TO GUARD THE GALAXY.
PHYLA! LOOK OUT!
THEY'RE COMING IN FROM ALL SIDES!

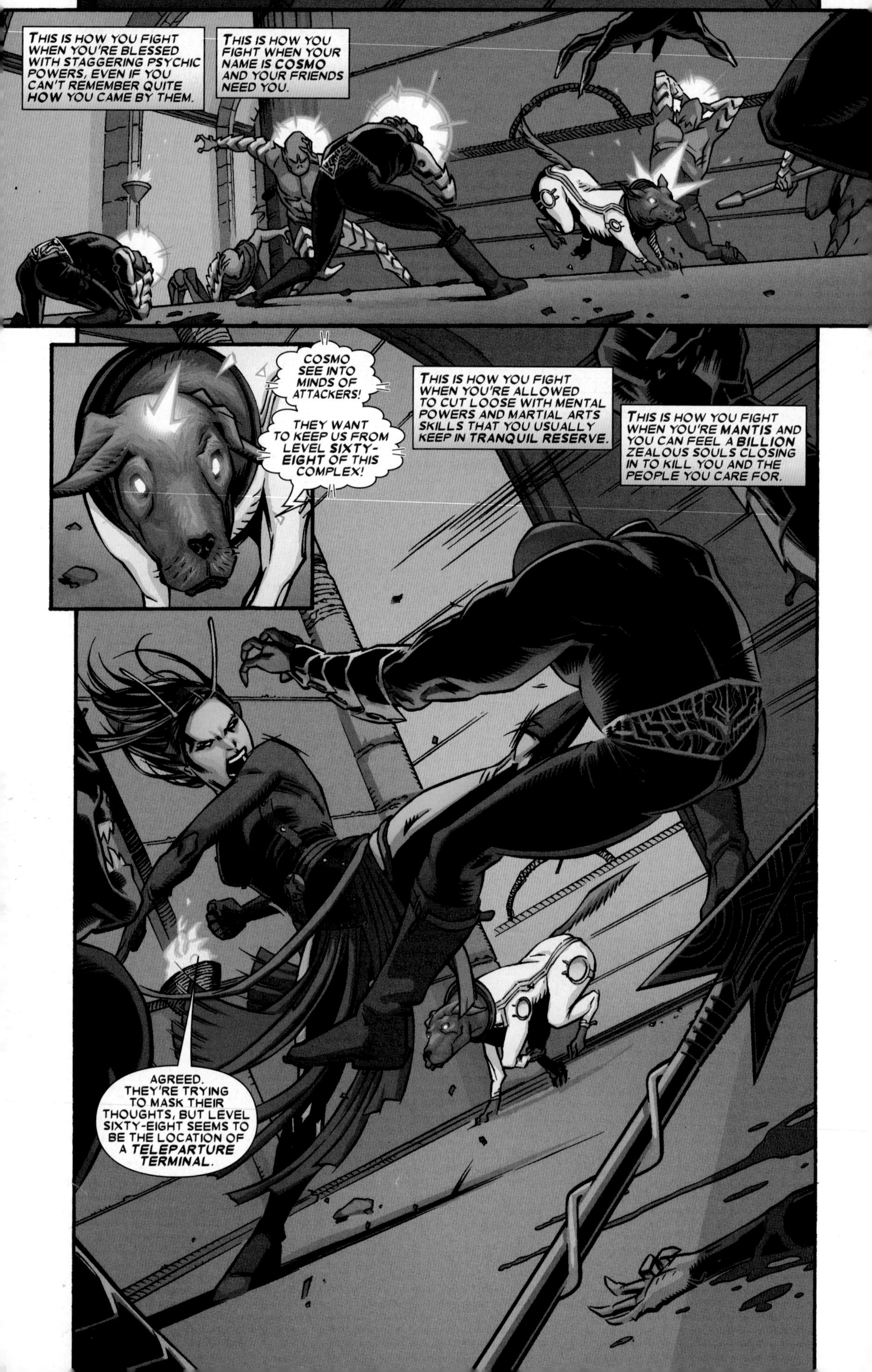
THIS IS HOW YOU FIGHT WHEN YOU'RE BLESSED WITH STAGGERING PSYCHIC POWERS, EVEN IF YOU CAN'T REMEMBER QUITE HOW YOU CAME BY THEM.
THIS IS HOW YOU FIGHT WHEN YOUR NAME IS COSMO AND YOUR FRIENDS NEED YOU.
COSMO SEE INTO MINDS OF ATTACKERS!
THEY WANT TO KEEP US FROM LEVEL SIXTY-EIGHT OF THIS COMPLEX!
THIS IS HOW YOU FIGHT WHEN YOU'RE ALLOWED TO CUT LOOSE WITH MENTAL POWERS AND MARTIAL ARTS SKILLS THAT YOU USUALLY KEEP IN TRANQUIL RESERVE.
THIS IS HOW YOU FIGHT WHEN YOU'RE MANTIS AND YOU CAN FEEL A BILLION ZEALOUS SOULS CLOSING IN TO KILL YOU AND THE PEOPLE YOU CARE FOR.
AGREED. THEY'RE TRYING TO MASK THEIR THOUGHTS, BUT LEVEL SIXTY-EIGHT SEEMS TO BE THE LOCATION OF A TELEPARTURE TERMINAL.

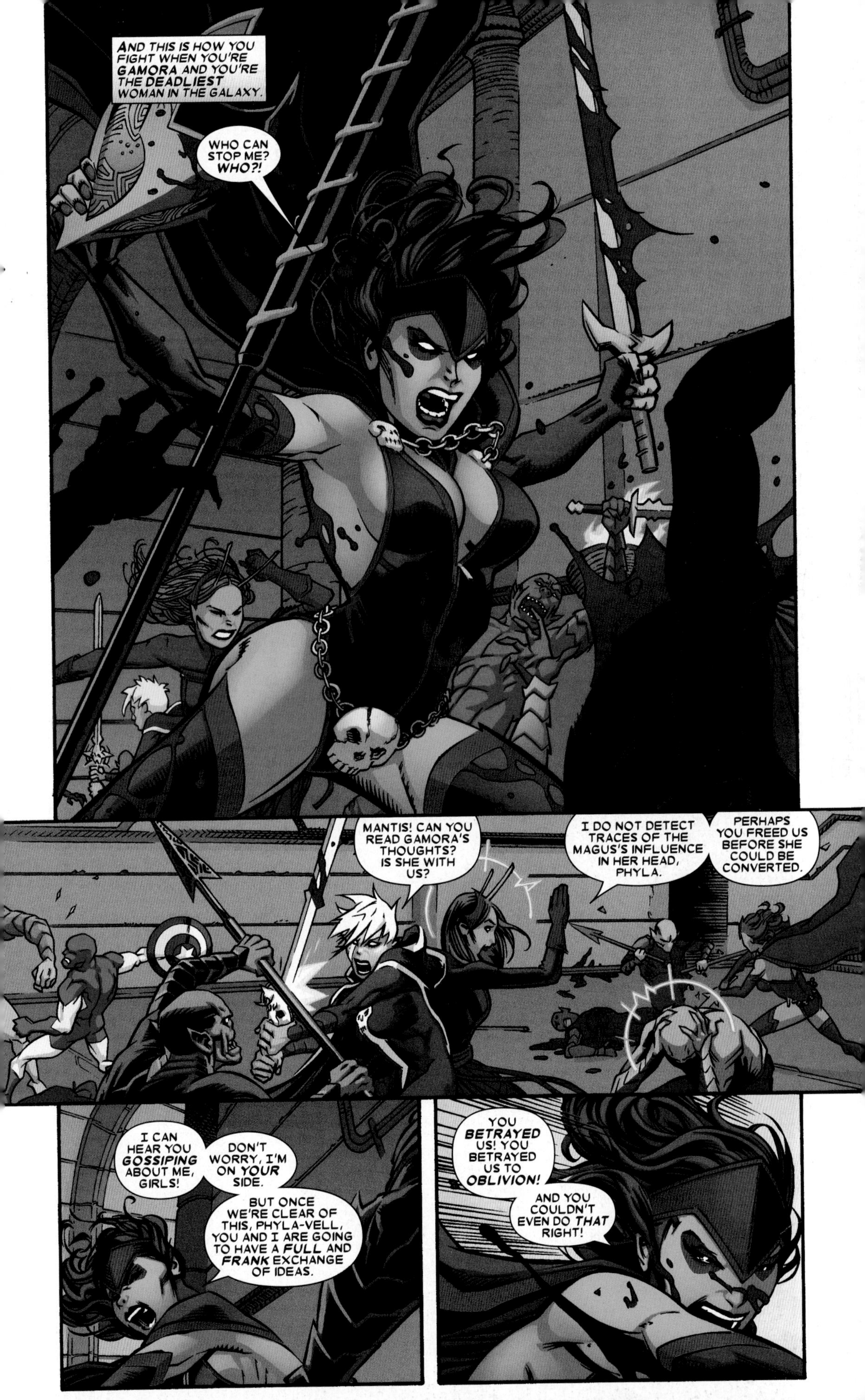
AND THIS IS HOW YOU FIGHT WHEN YOU'RE GAMORA AND YOU'RE THE DEADLIEST WOMAN IN THE GALAXY.
WHO CAN STOP ME? WHO?!
MANTIS! CAN YOU READ GAMORA'S THOUGHTS? IS SHE WITH US?
I DO NOT DETECT TRACES OF THE MAGUS'S INFLUENCE IN HER HEAD, PHYLA.
PERHAPS YOU FREED US BEFORE SHE COULD BE CONVERTED.
I CAN HEAR YOU GOSSIPING ABOUT ME, GIRLS!
DON'T WORRY, I'M ON YOUR SIDE.
BUT ONCE WE'RE CLEAR OF THIS, PHYLA-VELL, YOU AND I ARE GOING TO HAVE A FULL AND FRANK EXCHANGE OF IDEAS.
YOU BETRAYED US! YOU BETRAYED US TO OBLIVION!
AND YOU COULDN'T EVEN DO THAT RIGHT!

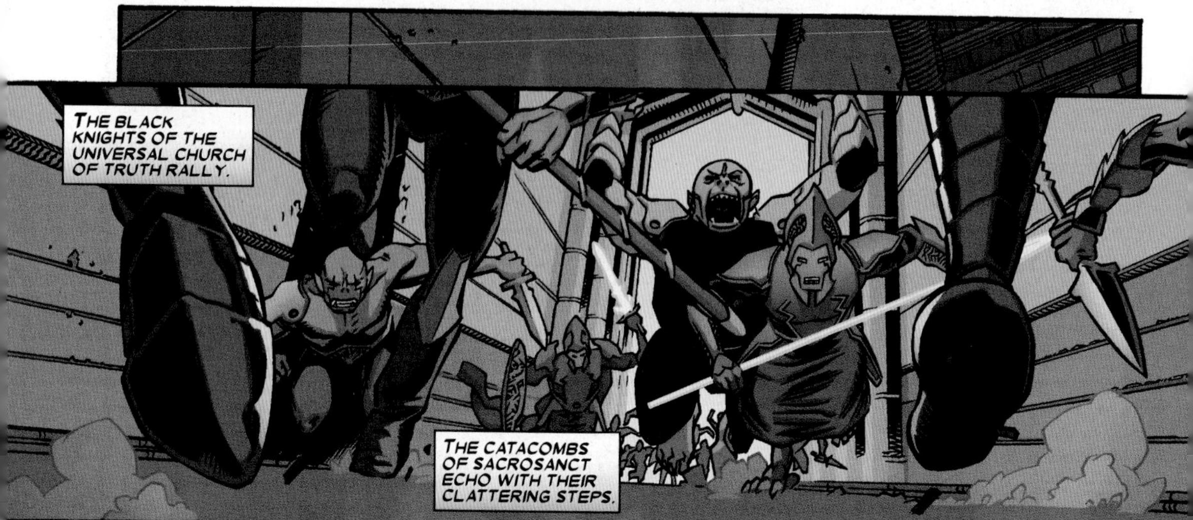
THE BLACK KNIGHTS OF THE UNIVERSAL CHURCH OF TRUTH RALLY.
THE CATACOMBS OF SACROSANCT ECHO WITH THEIR CLATTERING STEPS.

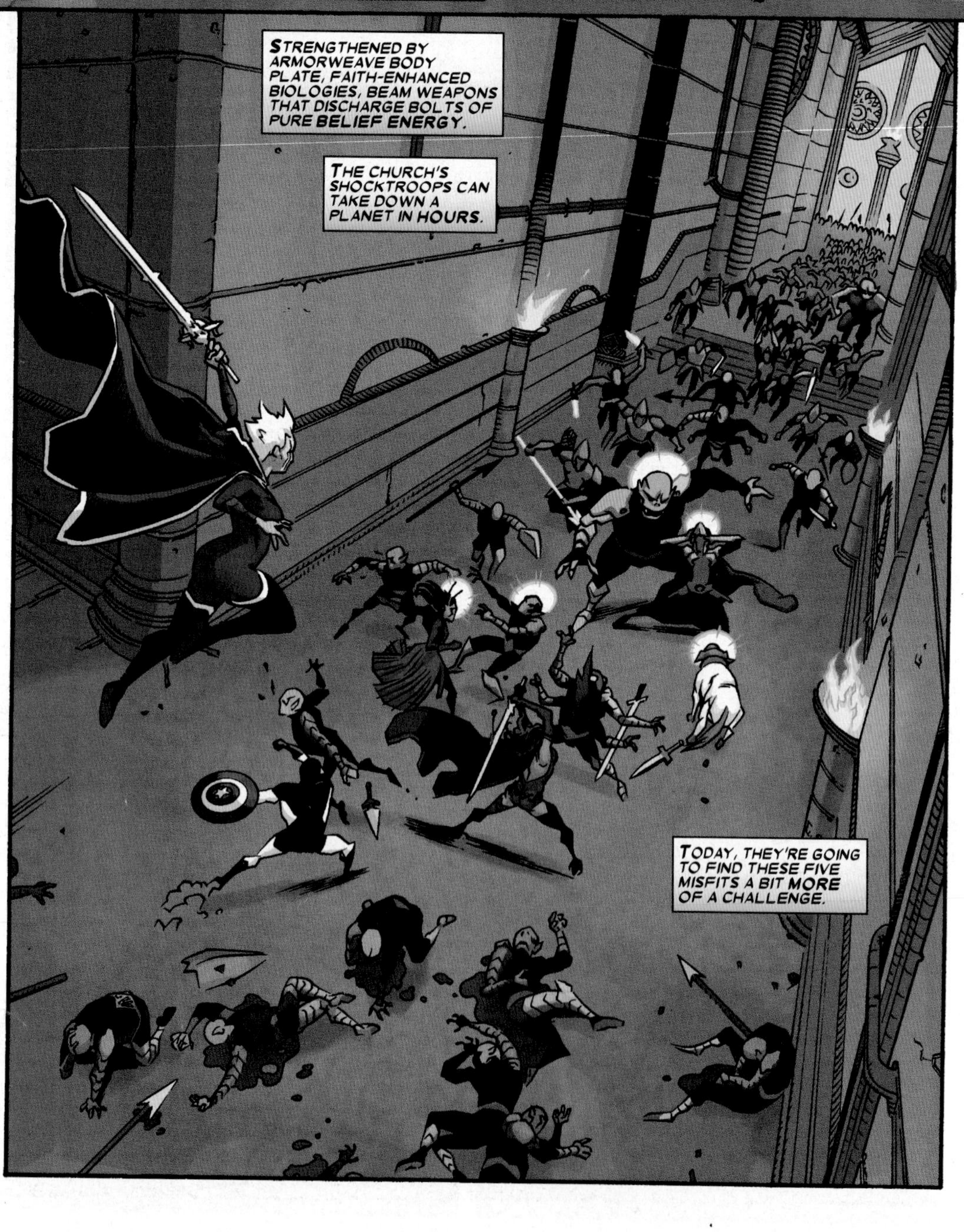
STRENGTHENED BY ARMORWEAVE BODY PLATE, FAITH-ENHANCED BIOLOGIES, BEAM WEAPONS THAT DISCHARGE BOLTS OF PURE BELIEF ENERGY.
THE CHURCH'S SHOCKTROOPS CAN TAKE DOWN A PLANET IN HOURS.
TODAY, THEY'RE GOING TO FIND THESE FIVE MISFITS A BIT MORE OF A CHALLENGE.

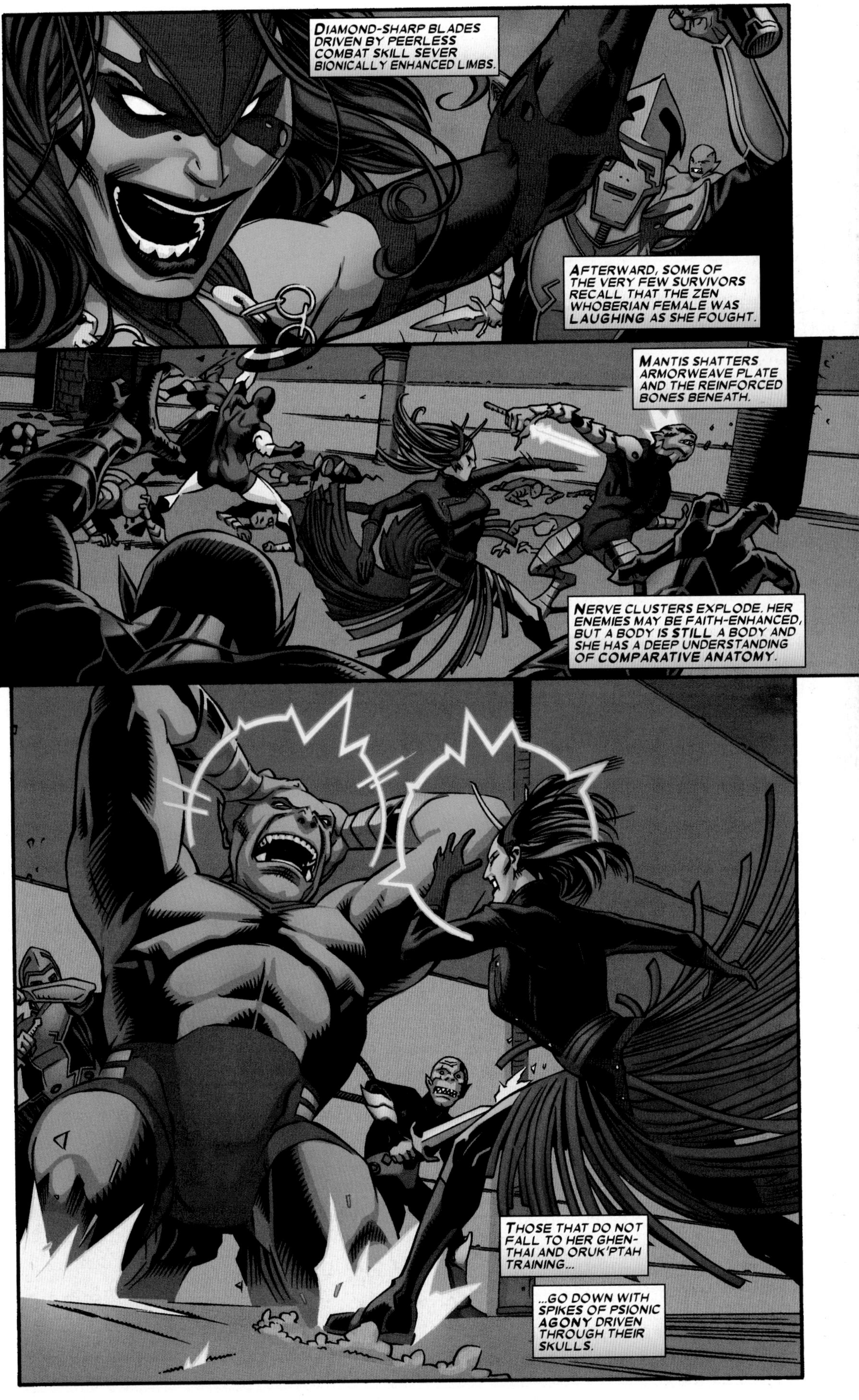
DIAMOND-SHARP BLADES DRIVEN BY PEERLESS COMBAT SKILL SEVER BIONICALLY ENHANCED LIMBS.
AFTERWARD, SOME OF THE VERY FEW SURVIVORS RECALL THAT THE ZEN WHOBERIAN FEMALE WAS LAUGHING AS SHE FOUGHT.
MANTIS SHATTERS ARMORWEAVE PLATE AND THE REINFORCED BONES BENEATH.
NERVE CLUSTERS EXPLODE. HER ENEMIES MAY BE FAITH-ENHANCED, BUT A BODY IS STILL A BODY AND SHE HAS A DEEP UNDERSTANDING OF COMPARATIVE ANATOMY.
THOSE THAT DO NOT FALL TO HER GHEN-THAI AND ORUK'PTAH TRAINING...
...GO DOWN WITH SPIKES OF PSIONIC AGONY DRIVEN THROUGH THEIR SKULLS.

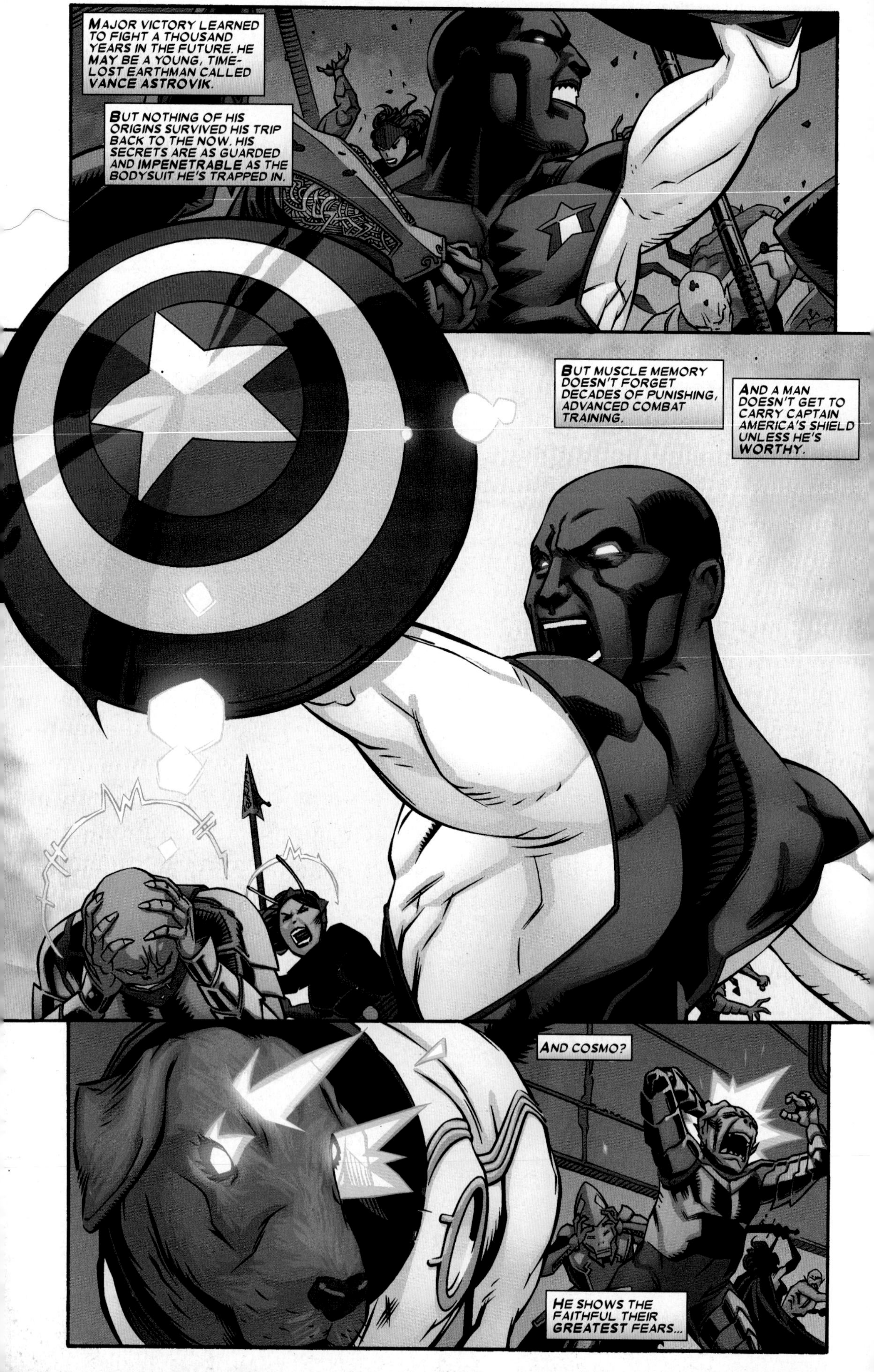
MAJOR VICTORY LEARNED TO FIGHT A THOUSAND YEARS IN THE FUTURE. HE MAY BE A YOUNG, TIME-LOST EARTHMAN CALLED VANCE ASTROVIK.
BUT NOTHING OF HIS ORIGINS SURVIVED HIS TRIP BACK TO THE NOW. HIS SECRETS ARE AS GUARDED AND IMPENETRABLE AS THE BODYSUIT HE'S TRAPPED IN.
BUT MUSCLE MEMORY DOESN'T FORGET DECADES OF PUNISHING, ADVANCED COMBAT TRAINING.
AND A MAN DOESN'T GET TO CARRY CAPTAIN AMERICA'S SHIELD UNLESS HE'S WORTHY.
AND COSMO?
HE SHOWS THE FAITHFUL THEIR GREATEST FEARS...

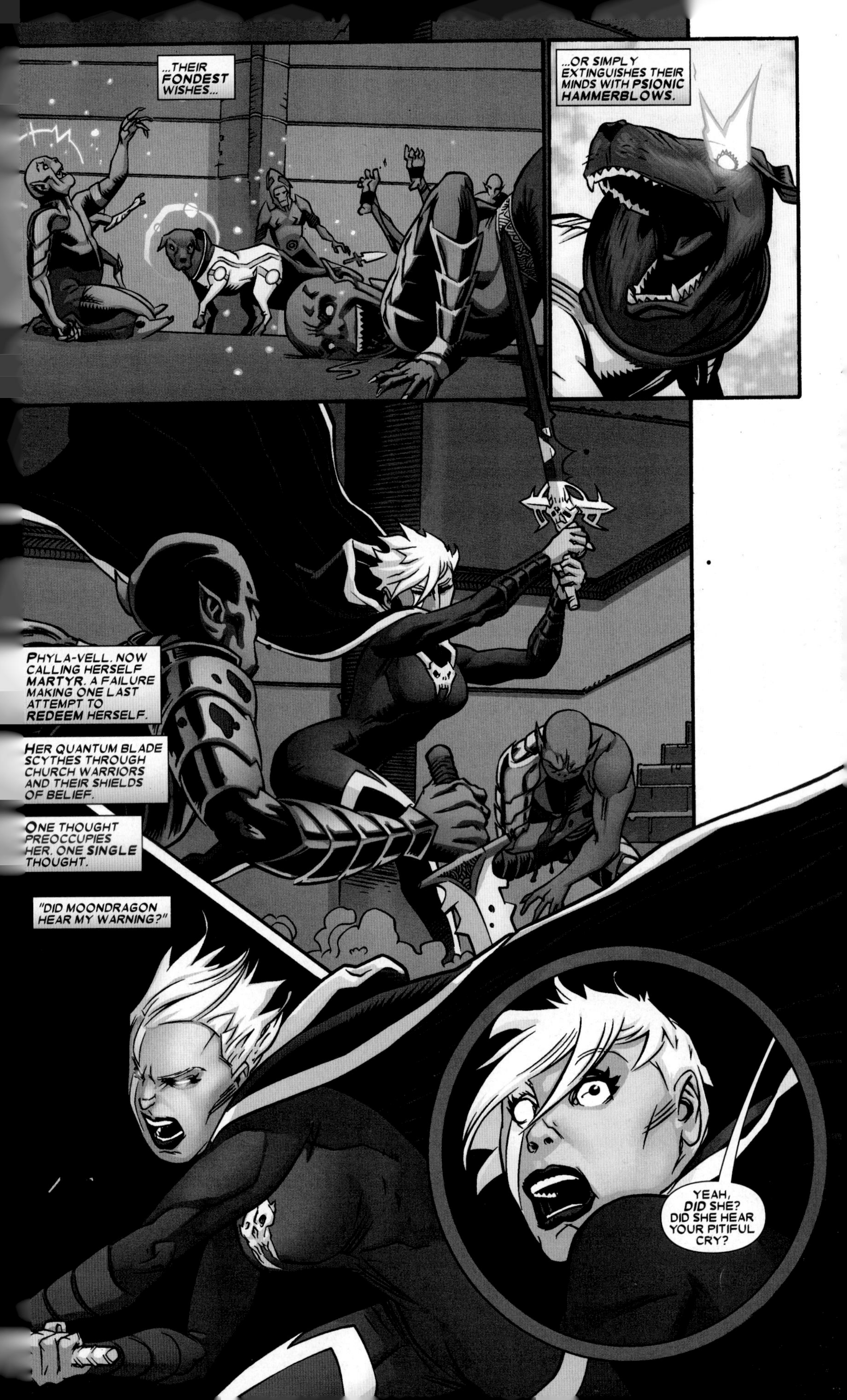

...THEIR FONDEST WISHES...
...OR SIMPLY EXTINGUISHES THEIR MINDS WITH PSIONIC HAMMERBLOWS.
PHYLA-VELL. NOW CALLING HERSELF MARTYR. A FAILURE MAKING ONE LAST ATTEMPT TO REDEEM HERSELF.
HER QUANTUM BLADE SCYTHES THROUGH CHURCH WARRIORS AND THEIR SHIELDS OF BELIEF.
ONE THOUGHT PREOCCUPIES HER. ONE SINGLE THOUGHT.
"DID MOONDRAGON HEAR MY WARNING?"
YEAH, DID SHE? DID SHE HEAR YOUR PITIFUL CRY?

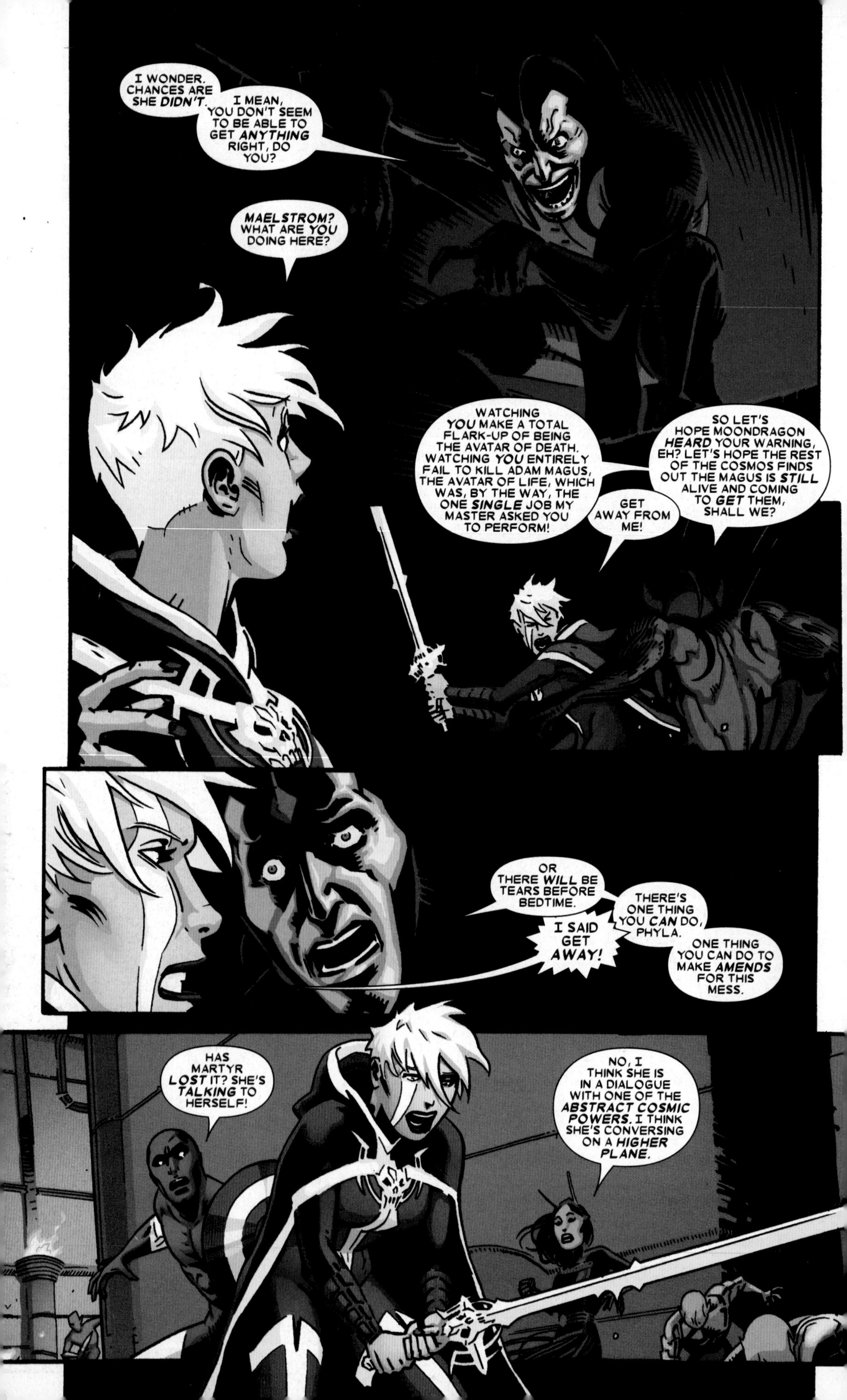
I WONDER. CHANCES ARE SHE DIDN'T.
I MEAN, YOU DON'T SEEM TO BE ABLE TO GET ANYTHING RIGHT, DO YOU?
MAELSTROM? WHAT ARE YOU DOING HERE?
WATCHING YOU MAKE A TOTAL FLARK-UP OF BEING THE AVATAR OF DEATH. WATCHING YOU ENTIRELY FAIL TO KILL ADAM MAGUS, THE AVATAR OF LIFE, WHICH WAS, BY THE WAY, THE ONE SINGLE JOB MY MASTER ASKED YOU TO PERFORM!
SO LET'S HOPE MOONDRAGON HEARD YOUR WARNING, EH? LET'S HOPE THE REST OF THE COSMOS FINDS OUT THE MAGUS IS STILL ALIVE AND COMING TO GET THEM, SHALL WE?
GET AWAY FROM ME!
OR THERE WILL BE TEARS BEFORE BEDTIME.
I SAID GET AWAY!
THERE'S ONE THING YOU CAN DO, PHYLA.
ONE THING YOU CAN DO TO MAKE AMENDS FOR THIS MESS.
HAS MARTYR LOST IT? SHE'S TALKING TO HERSELF!
NO, I THINK SHE IS IN A DIALOGUE WITH ONE OF THE ABSTRACT COSMIC POWERS. I THINK SHE'S CONVERSING ON A HIGHER PLANE.

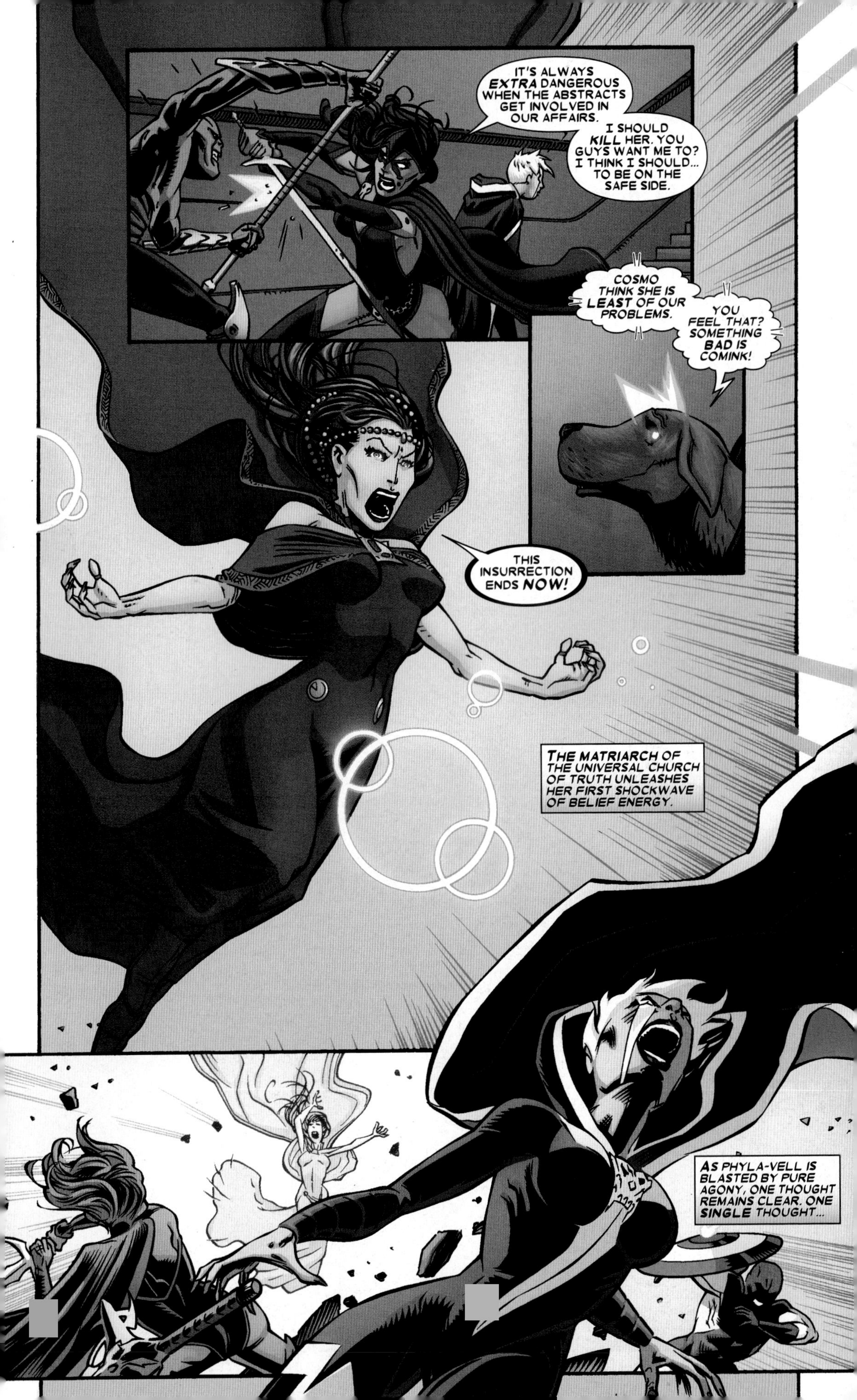
IT'S ALWAYS EXTRA DANGEROUS WHEN THE ABSTRACTS GET INVOLVED IN OUR AFFAIRS.
I SHOULD KILL HER. YOU GUYS WANT ME TO? I THINK I SHOULD... TO BE ON THE SAFE SIDE.
COSMO THINK SHE IS LEAST OF OUR PROBLEMS.
YOU FEEL THAT? SOMETHING BAD IS COMINK!
THIS INSURRECTION ENDS NOW!
THE MATRIARCH OF THE UNIVERSAL CHURCH OF TRUTH UNLEASHES HER FIRST SHOCKWAVE OF BELIEF ENERGY.
AS PHYLA-VELL IS BLASTED BY PURE AGONY, ONE THOUGHT REMAINS CLEAR. ONE SINGLE THOUGHT...

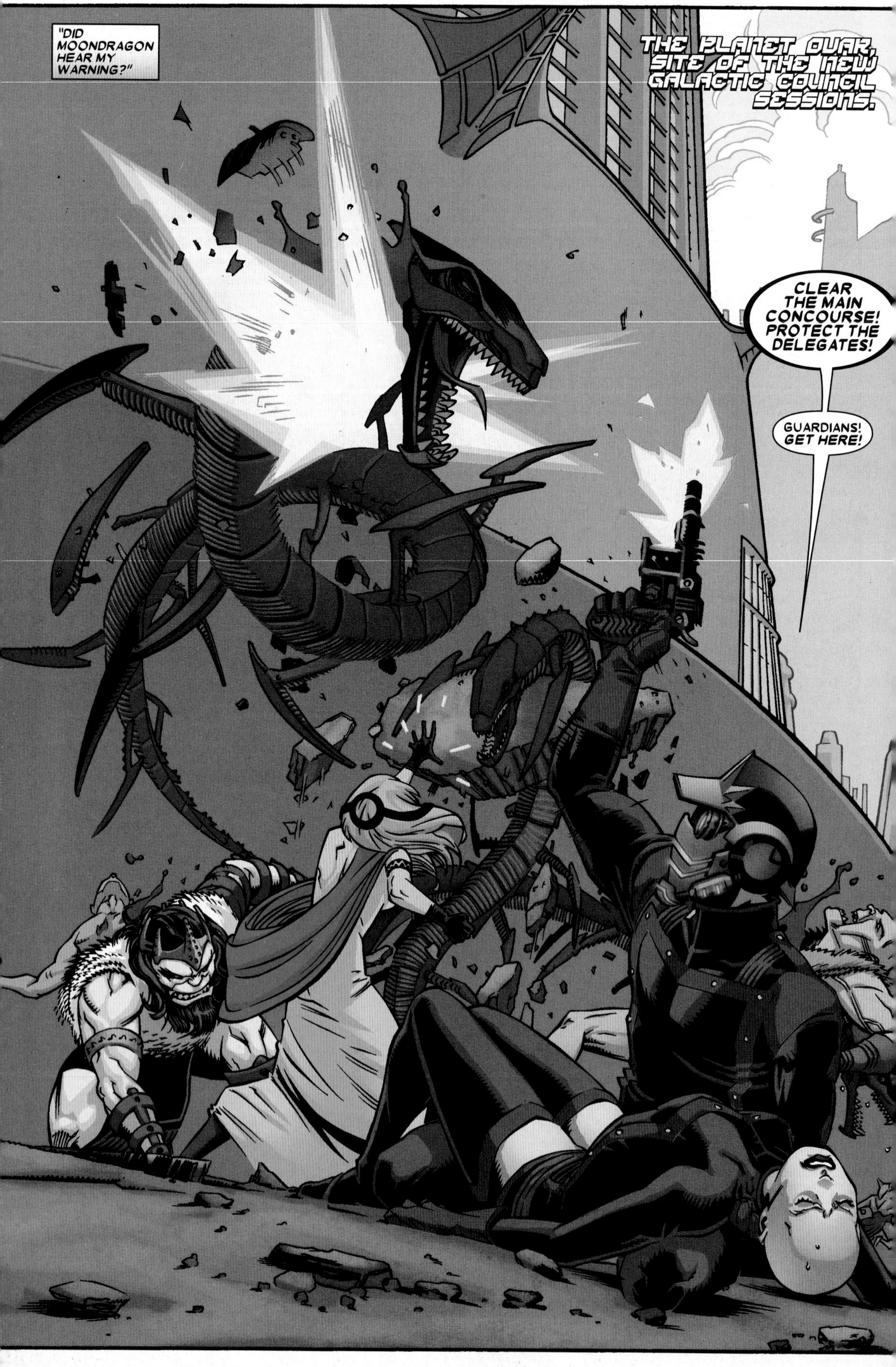
"DID MOONDRAGON HEAR MY WARNING?"
THE PLANET QUAR, SITE OF THE NEW GALACTIC COUNCIL SESSIONS.
CLEAR THE MAIN CONCOURSE! PROTECT THE DELEGATES!
GUARDIANS! GET HERE!

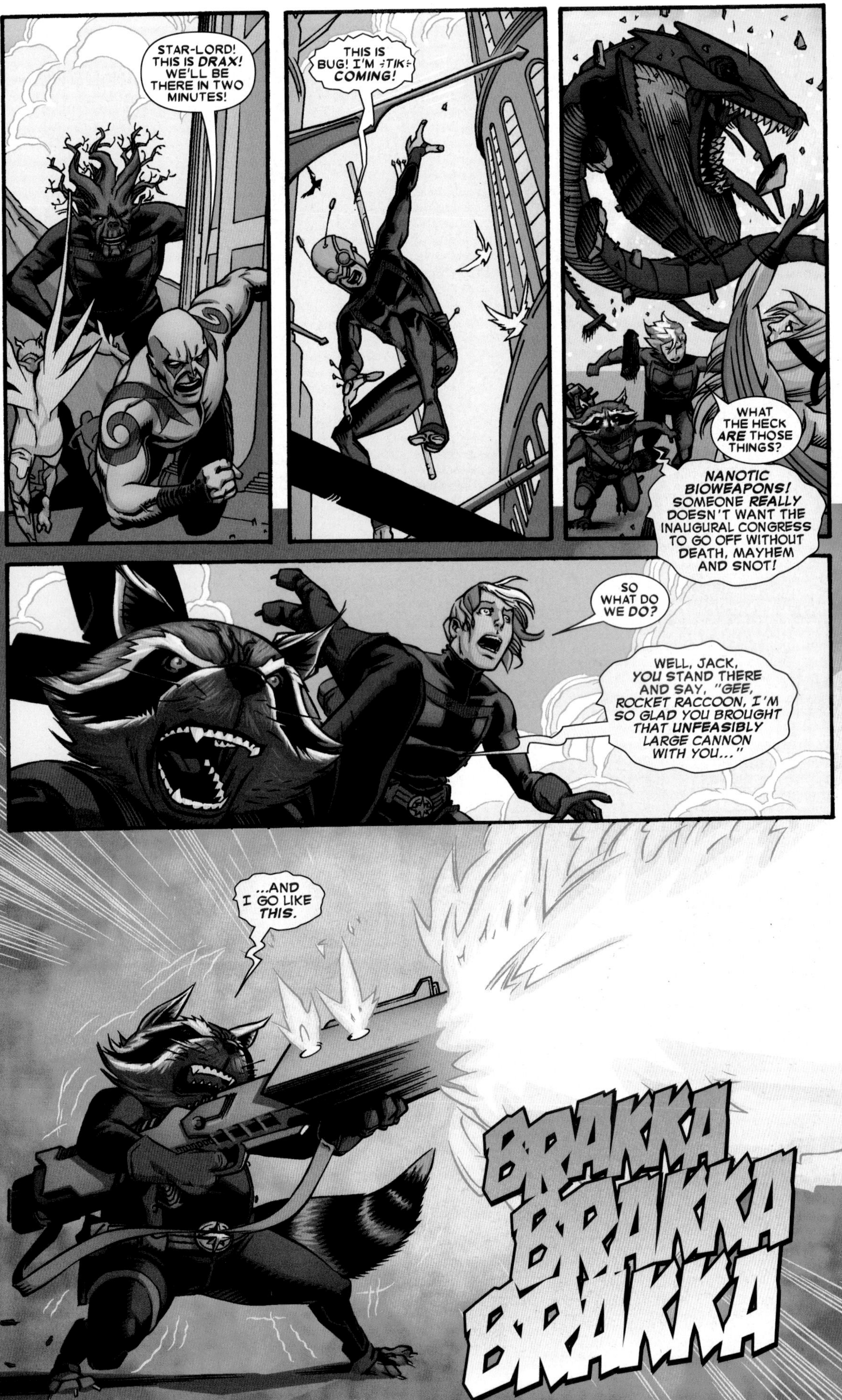
STAR-LORD! THIS IS DRAX! WE'LL BE THERE IN TWO MINUTES!
THIS IS BUG! I'M ÷TIK÷ COMING!
WHAT THE HECK ARE THOSE THINGS?
NANOTIC BIOWEAPONS! SOMEONE REALLY DOESN'T WANT THE INAUGURAL CONGRESS TO GO OFF WITHOUT DEATH, MAYHEM AND SNOT!
SO WHAT DO WE DO?
WELL, JACK, YOU STAND THERE AND SAY, "GEE, ROCKET RACCOON, I'M SO GLAD YOU BROUGHT THAT UNFEASIBLY LARGE CANNON WITH YOU..."
...AND I GO LIKE THIS.
BRAKKA
BRAKKA
BRAKKA

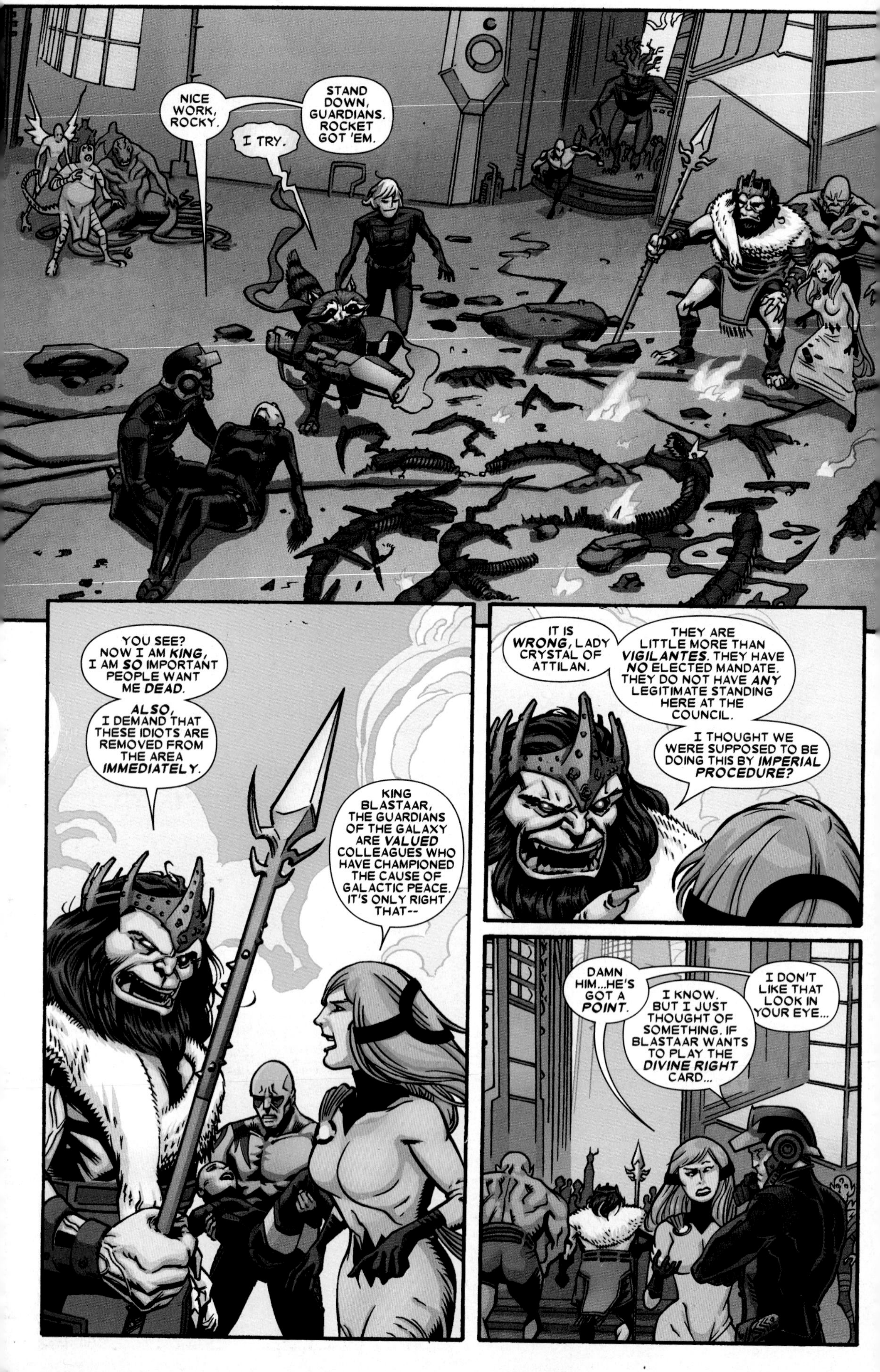
NICE WORK, ROCKY.
I TRY.
STAND DOWN, GUARDIANS. ROCKET GOT 'EM.
YOU SEE? NOW I AM KING, I AM SO IMPORTANT PEOPLE WANT ME DEAD.
ALSO, I DEMAND THAT THESE IDIOTS ARE REMOVED FROM THE AREA IMMEDIATELY.
KING BLASTAAR, THE GUARDIANS OF THE GALAXY ARE VALUED COLLEAGUES WHO HAVE CHAMPIONED THE CAUSE OF GALACTIC PEACE. IT'S ONLY RIGHT THAT--
IT IS WRONG, LADY CRYSTAL OF ATTILAN.
THEY ARE LITTLE MORE THAN VIGILANTES. THEY HAVE NO ELECTED MANDATE. THEY DO NOT HAVE ANY LEGITIMATE STANDING HERE AT THE COUNCIL.
I THOUGHT WE WERE SUPPOSED TO BE DOING THIS BY IMPERIAL PROCEDURE?
DAMN HIM...HE'S GOT A POINT.
I KNOW. BUT I JUST THOUGHT OF SOMETHING. IF BLASTAAR WANTS TO PLAY THE DIVINE RIGHT CARD...
I DON'T LIKE THAT LOOK IN YOUR EYE...

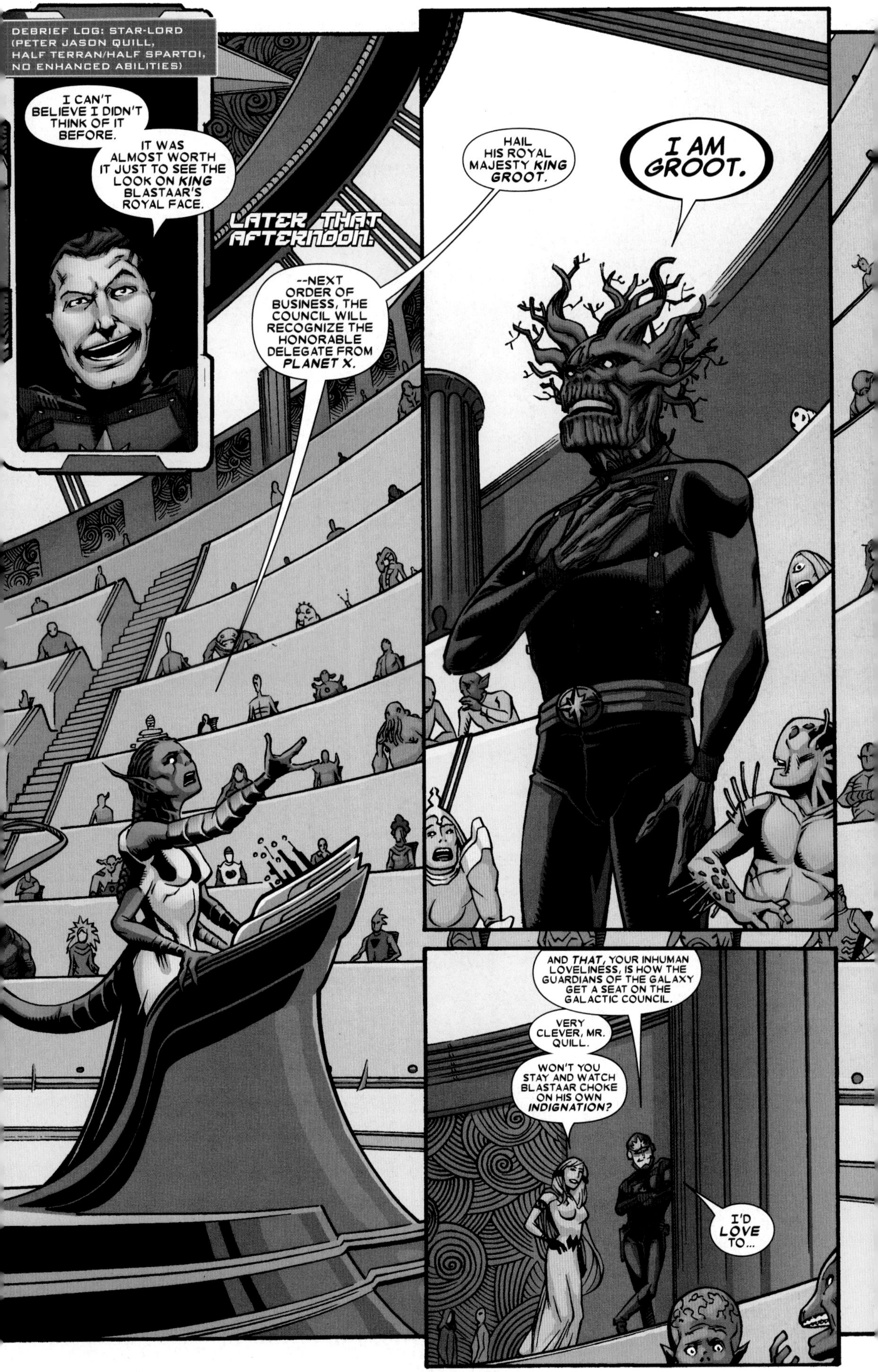
DEBRIEF LOG: STAR-LORD (PETER JASON QUILL, HALF TERRAN/HALF SPARTOI, NO ENHANCED ABILITIES)
I CAN'T BELIEVE I DIDN'T THINK OF IT BEFORE.
IT WAS ALMOST WORTH IT JUST TO SEE THE LOOK ON KING BLASTAAR'S ROYAL FACE.
LATER THAT AFTERNOON.
--NEXT ORDER OF BUSINESS, THE COUNCIL WILL RECOGNIZE THE HONORABLE DELEGATE FROM PLANET X.
HAIL HIS ROYAL MAJESTY KING GROOT.
I AM GROOT.
AND THAT, YOUR INHUMAN LOVELINESS, IS HOW THE GUARDIANS OF THE GALAXY GET A SEAT ON THE GALACTIC COUNCIL.
VERY CLEVER, MR. QUILL.
WON'T YOU STAY AND WATCH BLASTAAR CHOKE ON HIS OWN INDIGNATION?
I'D LOVE TO...

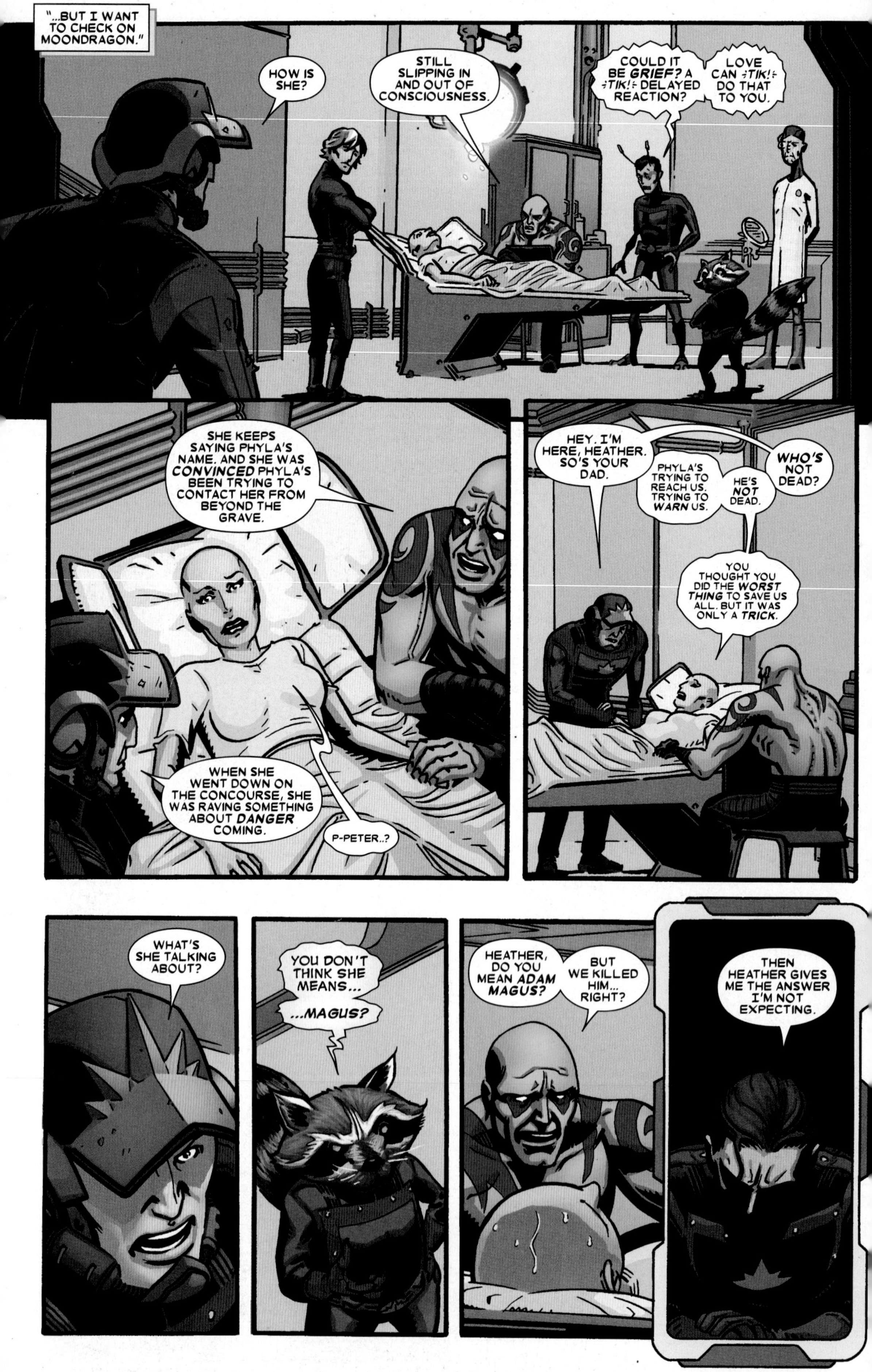

"...BUT I WANT TO CHECK ON MOONDRAGON."
HOW IS SHE?
STILL SLIPPING IN AND OUT OF CONSCIOUSNESS.
COULD IT BE GRIEF? A -TIK!- DELAYED REACTION?
LOVE CAN -TIK!- DO THAT TO YOU.
SHE KEEPS SAYING PHYLA'S NAME. AND SHE WAS CONVINCED PHYLA'S BEEN TRYING TO CONTACT HER FROM BEYOND THE GRAVE.
WHEN SHE WENT DOWN ON THE CONCOURSE, SHE WAS RAVING SOMETHING ABOUT DANGER COMING.
P-PETER..?
HEY. I'M HERE, HEATHER. SO'S YOUR DAD.
PHYLA'S TRYING TO REACH US. TRYING TO WARN US.
HE'S NOT DEAD.
WHO'S NOT DEAD?
YOU THOUGHT YOU DID THE WORST THING TO SAVE US ALL. BUT IT WAS ONLY A TRICK.
WHAT'S SHE TALKING ABOUT?
YOU DON'T THINK SHE MEANS...
...MAGUS?
HEATHER, DO YOU MEAN ADAM MAGUS?
BUT WE KILLED HIM... RIGHT?
THEN HEATHER GIVES ME THE ANSWER I'M NOT EXPECTING.

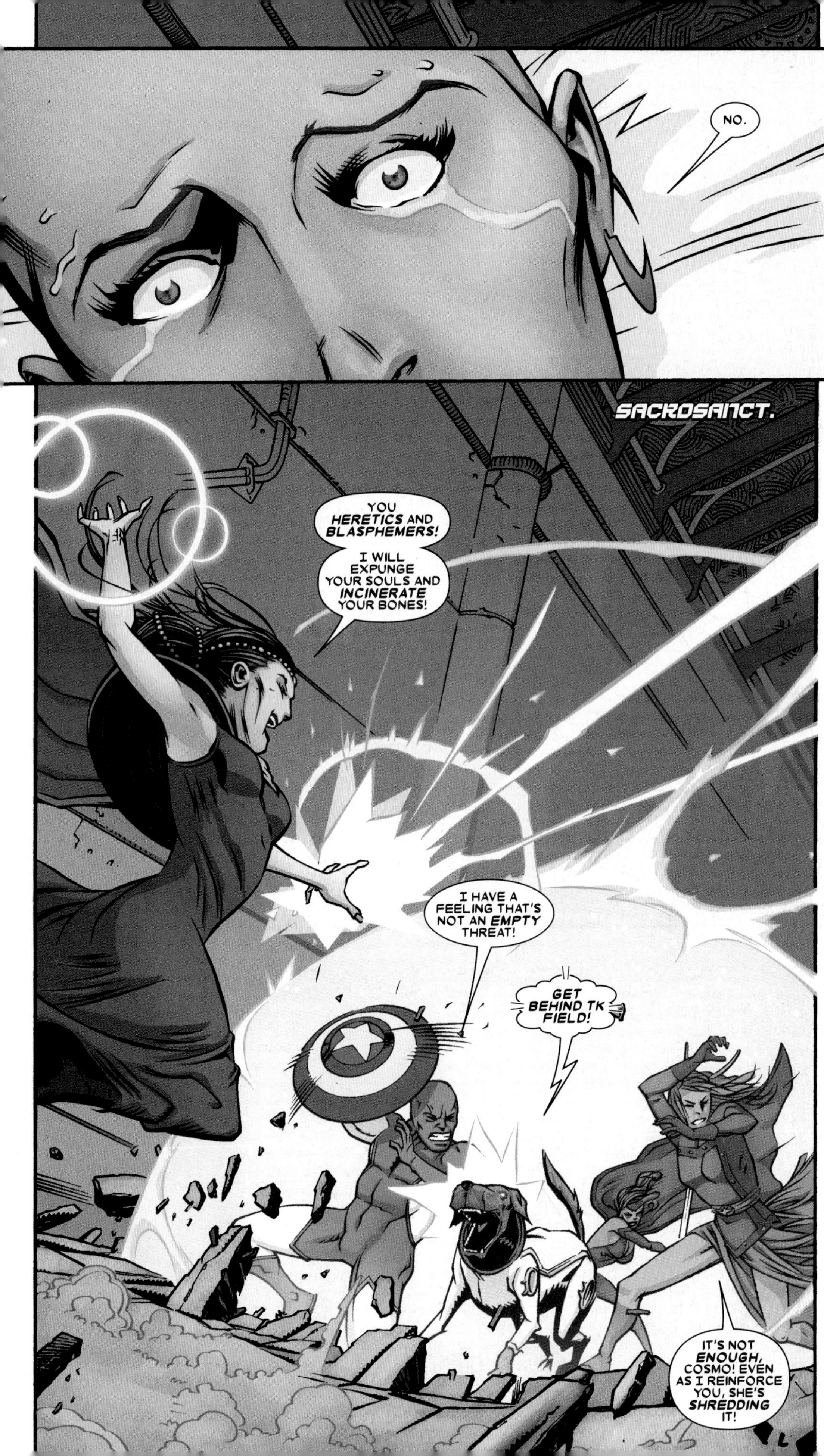
NO.
SACROSANCT.
YOU HERETICS AND BLASPHEMERS!
I WILL EXPUNGE YOUR SOULS AND INCINERATE YOUR BONES!
I HAVE A FEELING THAT'S NOT AN EMPTY THREAT!
GET BEHIND TK FIELD!
IT'S NOT ENOUGH, COSMO! EVEN AS I REINFORCE YOU, SHE'S SHREDDING IT!

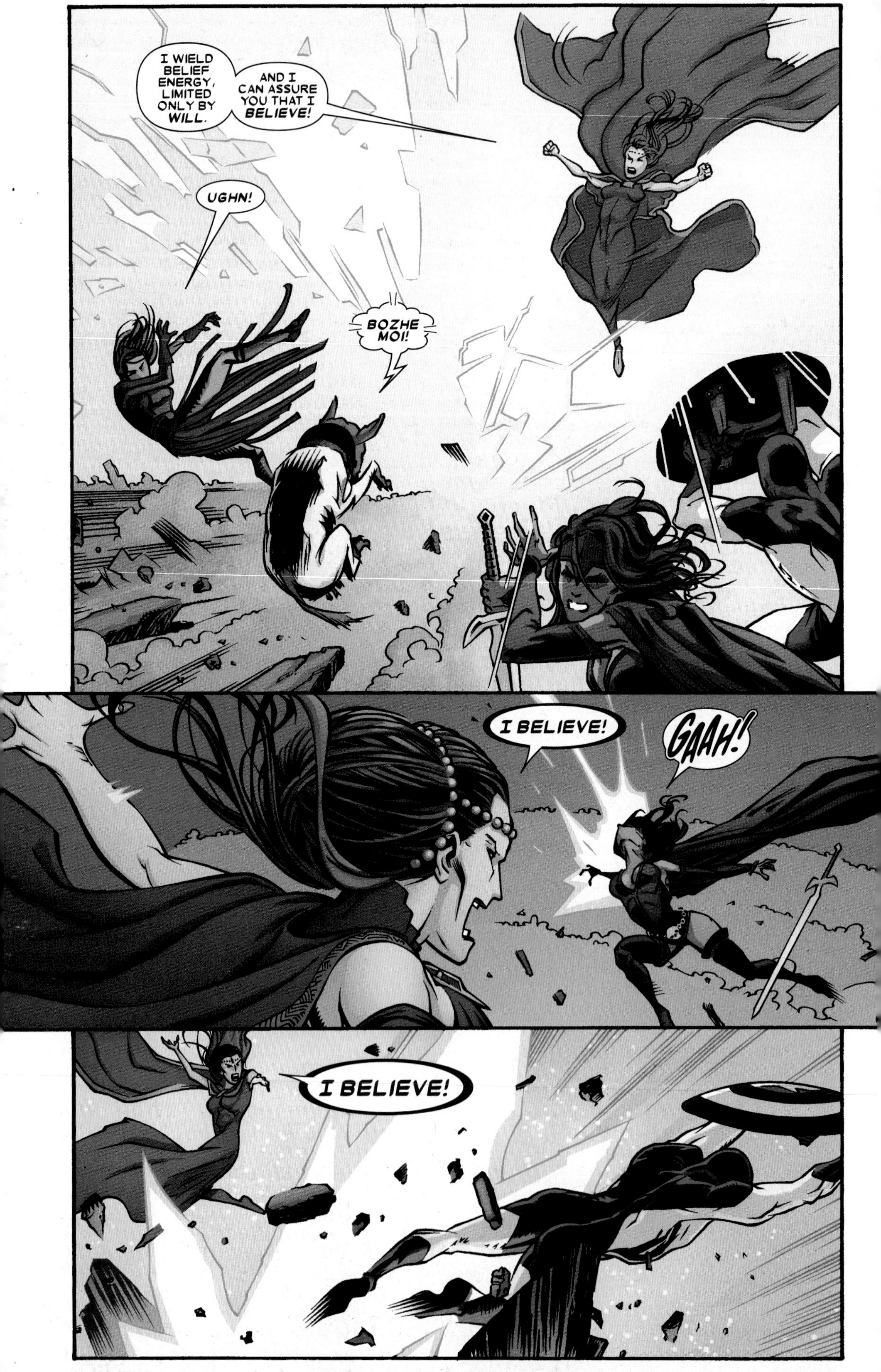
I WIELD BELIEF ENERGY, LIMITED ONLY BY WILL.
AND I CAN ASSURE YOU THAT I BELIEVE!
UGHN!
BOZHE MOI!
I BELIEVE!
GAAH!
I BELIEVE!

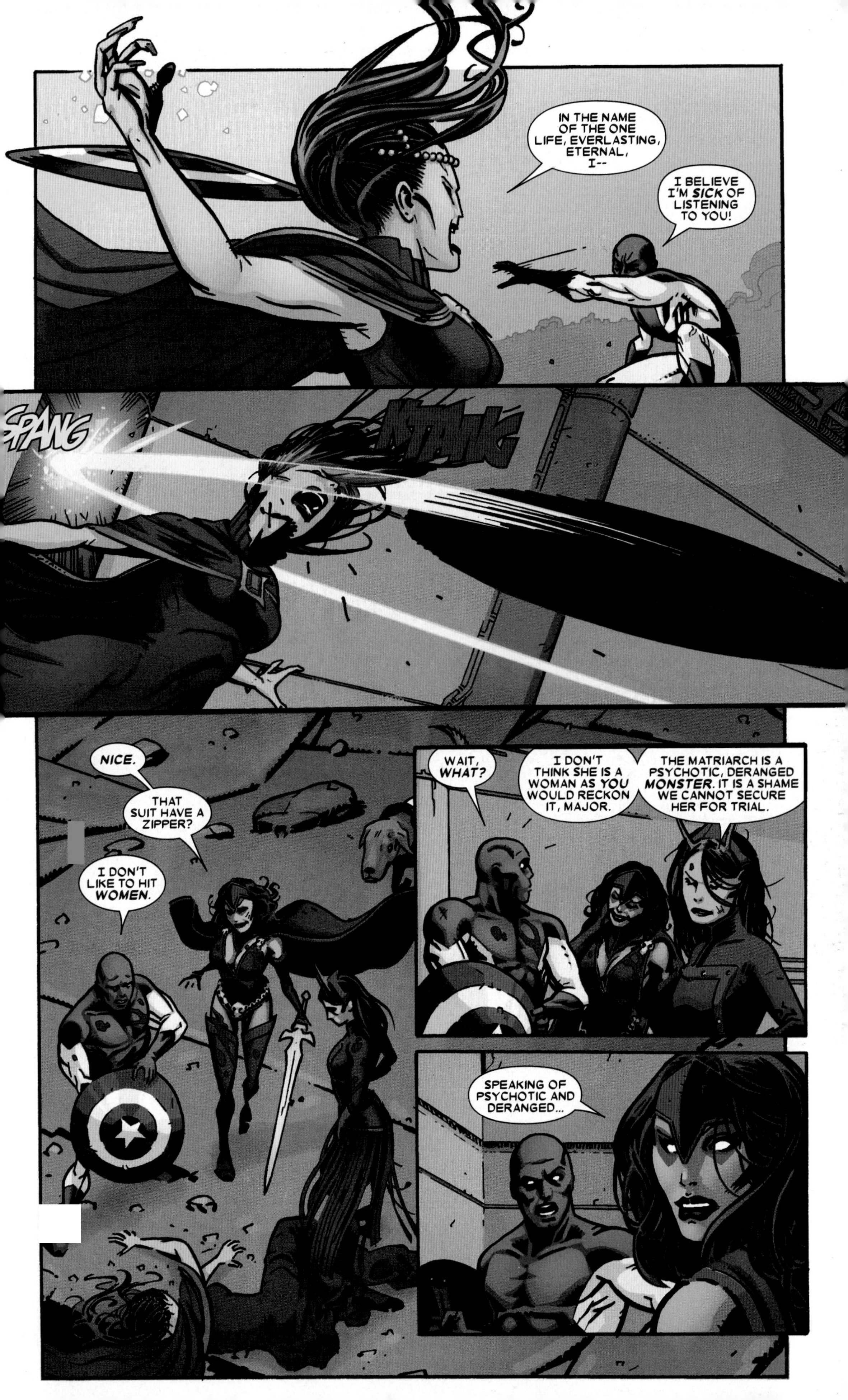
IN THE NAME OF THE ONE LIFE, EVERLASTING, ETERNAL, I--
I BELIEVE I'M SICK OF LISTENING TO YOU!
SPANG
NICE.
THAT SUIT HAVE A ZIPPER?
I DON'T LIKE TO HIT WOMEN.
WAIT, WHAT?
I DON'T THINK SHE IS A WOMAN AS YOU WOULD RECKON IT, MAJOR.
THE MATRIARCH IS A PSYCHOTIC, DERANGED MONSTER. IT IS A SHAME WE CANNOT SECURE HER FOR TRIAL.
SPEAKING OF PSYCHOTIC AND DERANGED...

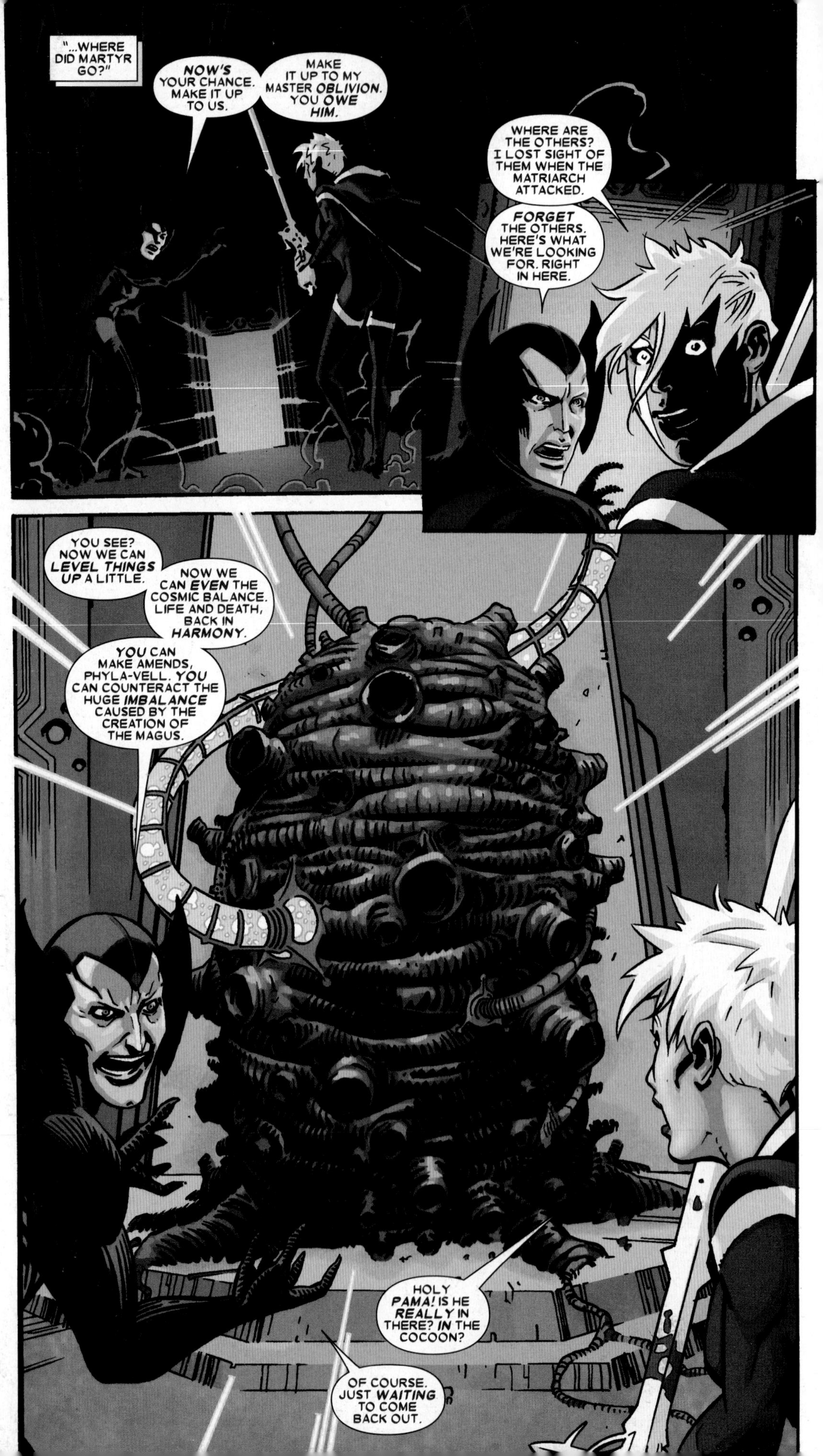

"...WHERE DID MARTYR GO?"
NOW'S YOUR CHANCE. MAKE IT UP TO US.
MAKE IT UP TO MY MASTER OBLIVION. YOU OWE HIM.
WHERE ARE THE OTHERS? I LOST SIGHT OF THEM WHEN THE MATRIARCH ATTACKED.
FORGET THE OTHERS. HERE'S WHAT WE'RE LOOKING FOR. RIGHT IN HERE.
YOU SEE? NOW WE CAN LEVEL THINGS UP A LITTLE.
NOW WE CAN EVEN THE COSMIC BALANCE. LIFE AND DEATH, BACK IN HARMONY.
YOU CAN MAKE AMENDS, PHYLA-VELL. YOU CAN COUNTERACT THE HUGE IMBALANCE CAUSED BY THE CREATION OF THE MAGUS.
HOLY PAMA! IS HE REALLY IN THERE? IN THE COCOON?
OF COURSE. JUST WAITING TO COME BACK OUT.

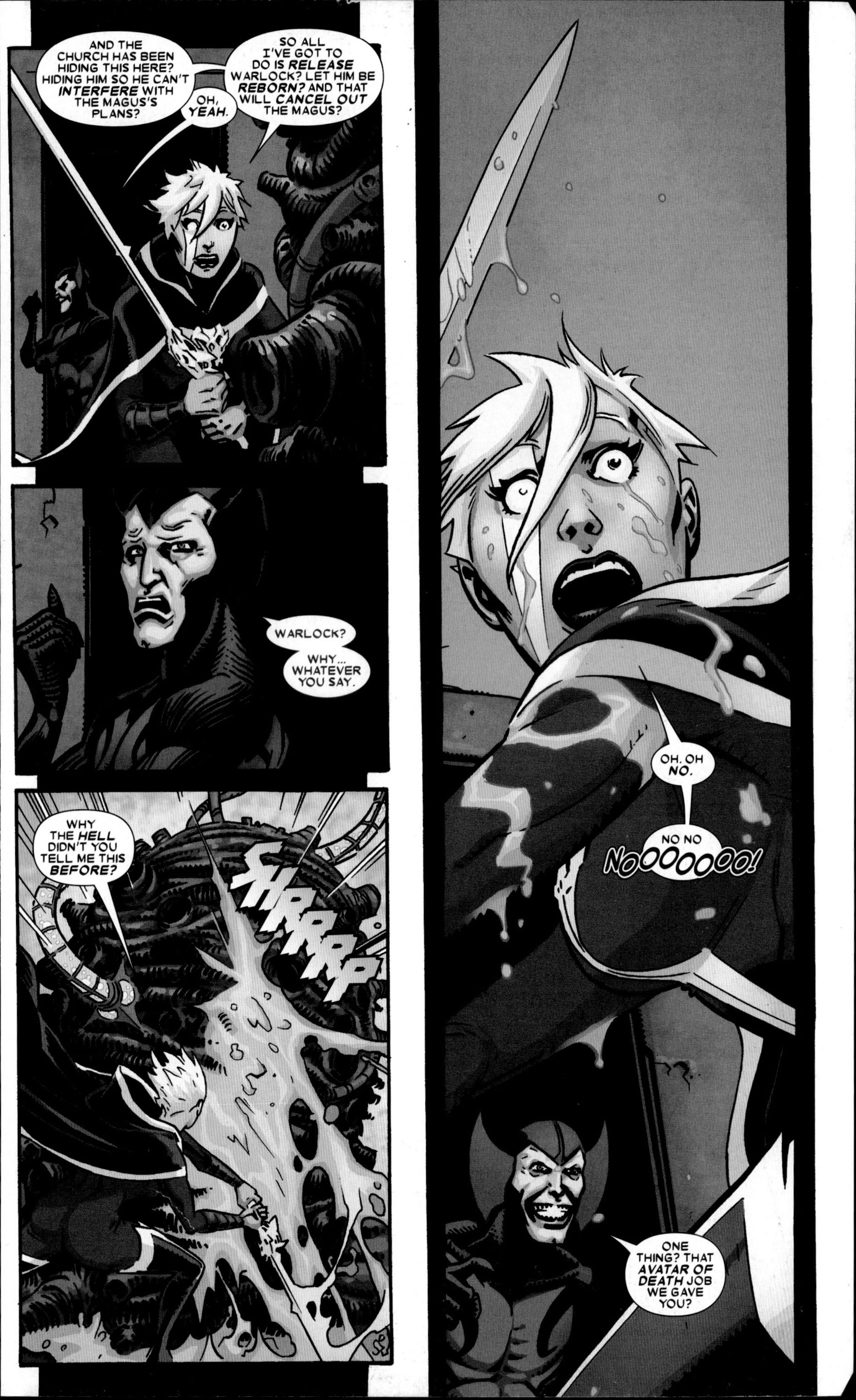
AND THE CHURCH HAS BEEN HIDING THIS HERE? HIDING HIM SO HE CAN'T INTERFERE WITH THE MAGUS'S PLANS?
OH, YEAH.
SO ALL I'VE GOT TO DO IS RELEASE WARLOCK? LET HIM BE REBORN? AND THAT WILL CANCEL OUT THE MAGUS?
WARLOCK?
WHY... WHATEVER YOU SAY.
WHY THE HELL DIDN'T YOU TELL ME THIS BEFORE?
SHRRRP
OH. OH NO.
NO NO NOOOOOOO!
ONE THING? THAT AVATAR OF DEATH JOB WE GAVE YOU?

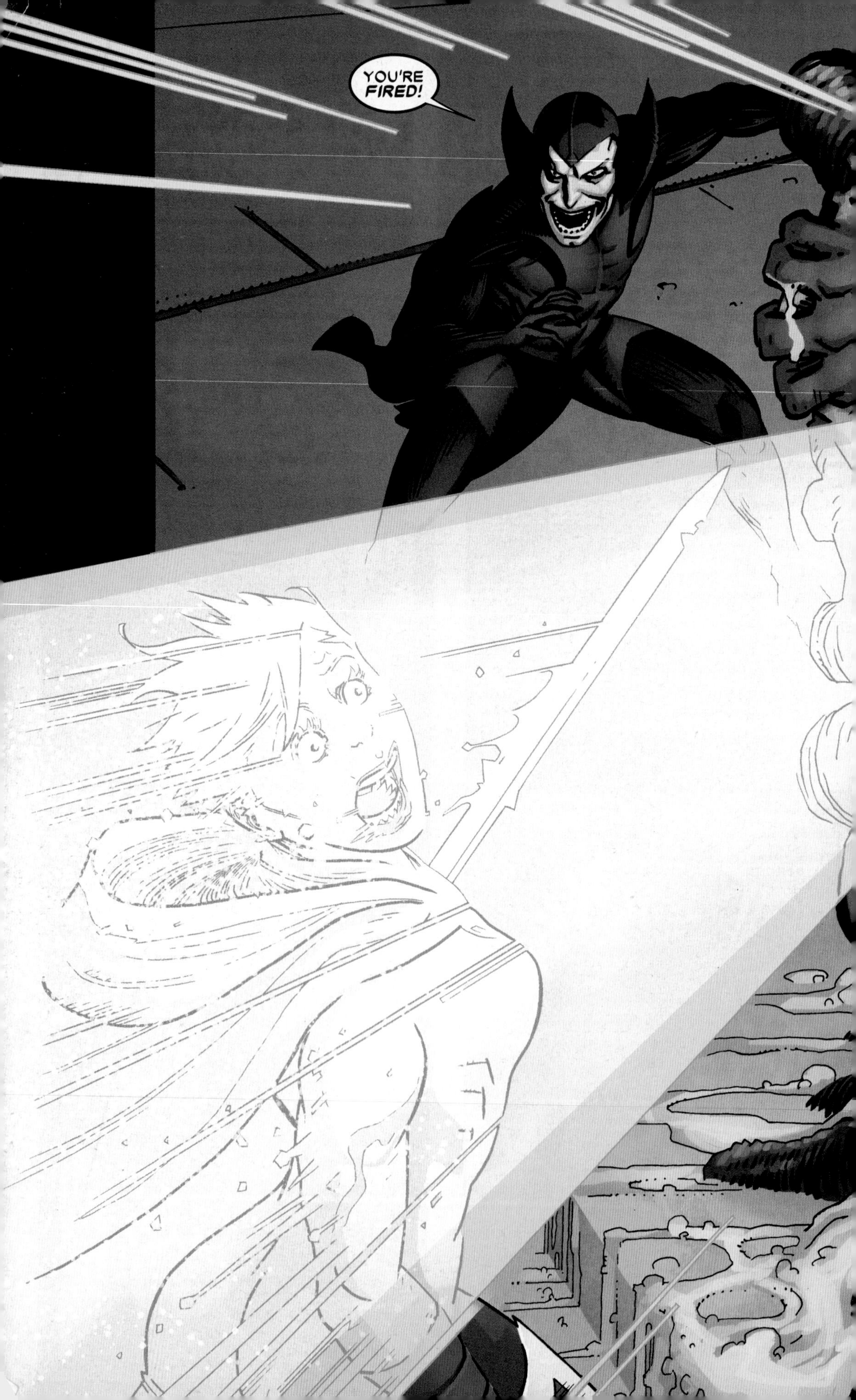
YOU'RE FIRED!

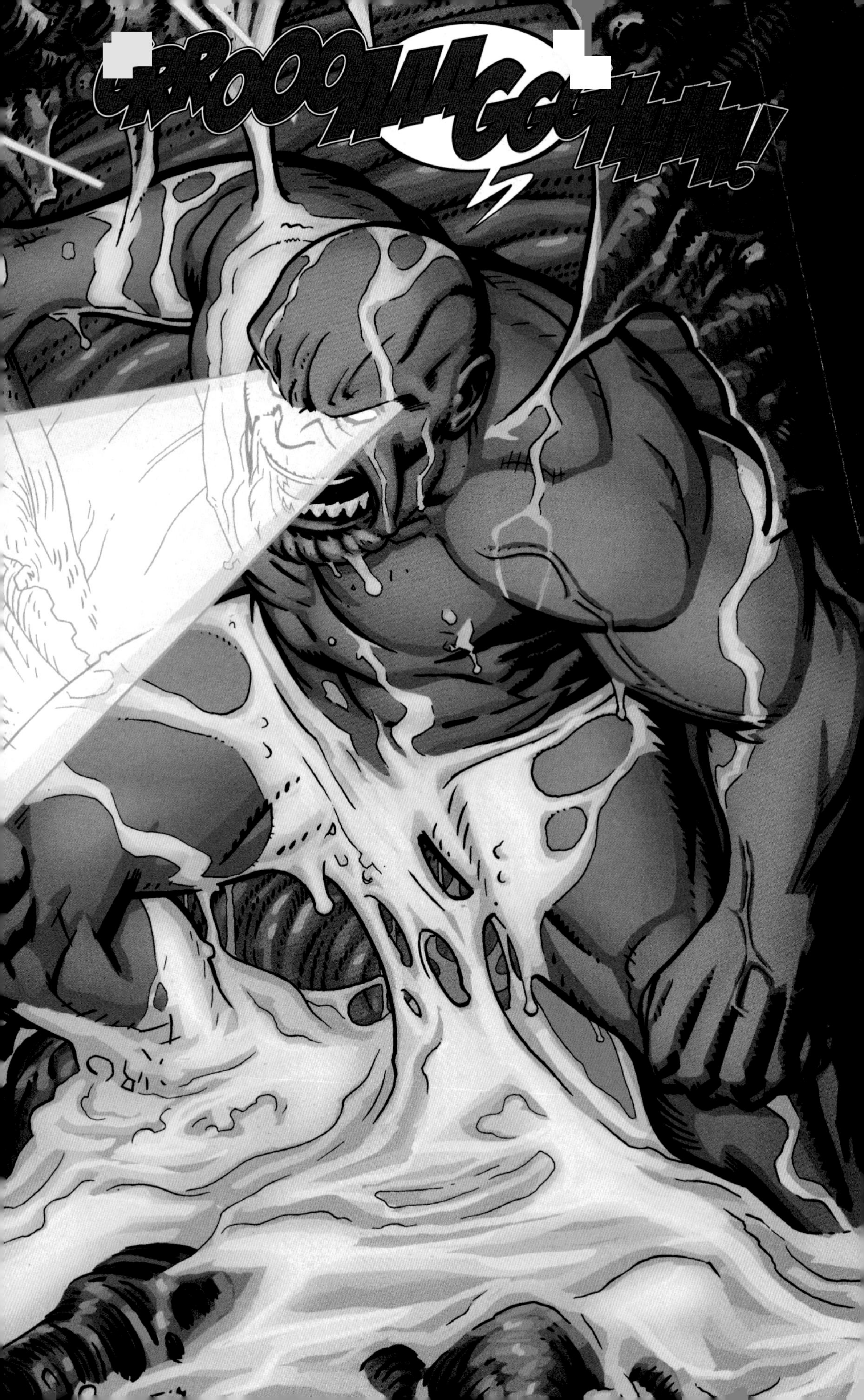
GRROOOHHHGGHHHH!

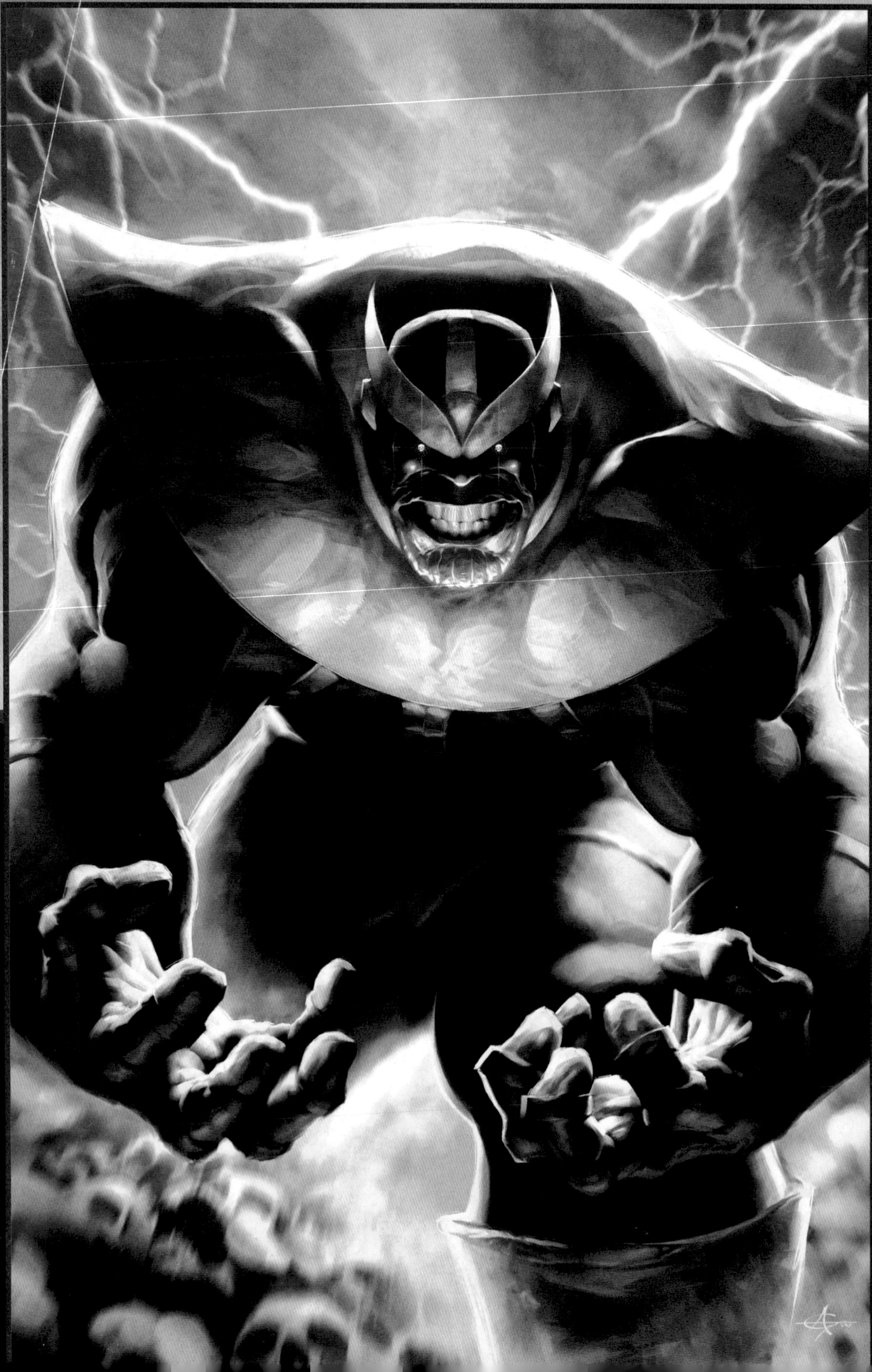

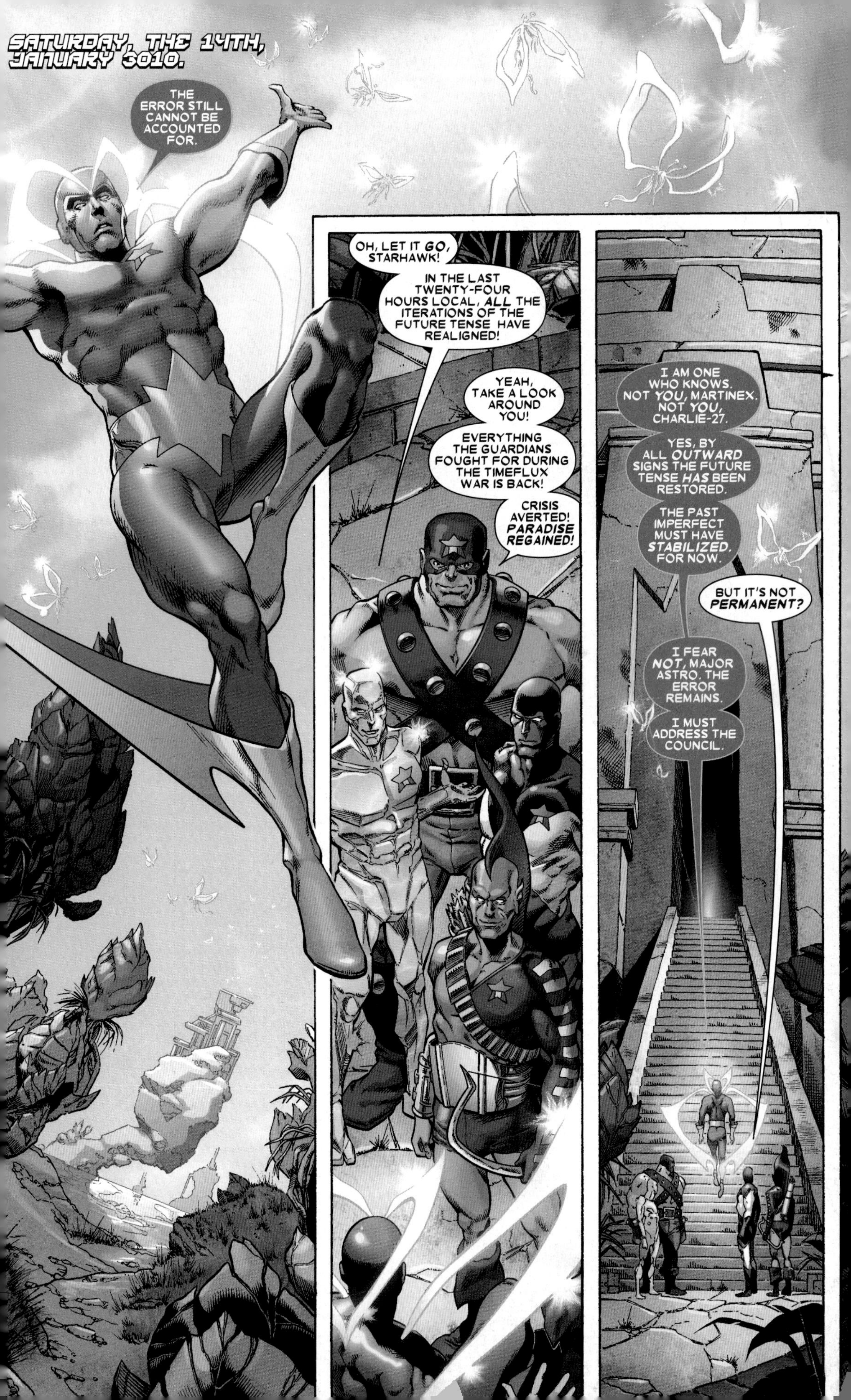
SATURDAY, THE 14TH, JANUARY 3010.
THE ERROR STILL CANNOT BE ACCOUNTED FOR.
OH, LET IT GO, STARHAWK!
IN THE LAST TWENTY-FOUR HOURS LOCAL, ALL THE ITERATIONS OF THE FUTURE TENSE HAVE REALIGNED!
YEAH, TAKE A LOOK AROUND YOU!
EVERYTHING THE GUARDIANS FOUGHT FOR DURING THE TIMEFLUX WAR IS BACK!
CRISIS AVERTED! PARADISE REGAINED!
I AM ONE WHO KNOWS. NOT YOU, MARTINEX. NOT YOU, CHARLIE-27.
YES, BY ALL OUTWARD SIGNS THE FUTURE TENSE HAS BEEN RESTORED.
THE PAST IMPERFECT MUST HAVE STABILIZED. FOR NOW.
BUT IT'S NOT PERMANENT?
I FEAR NOT, MAJOR ASTRO. THE ERROR REMAINS.
I MUST ADDRESS THE COUNCIL.

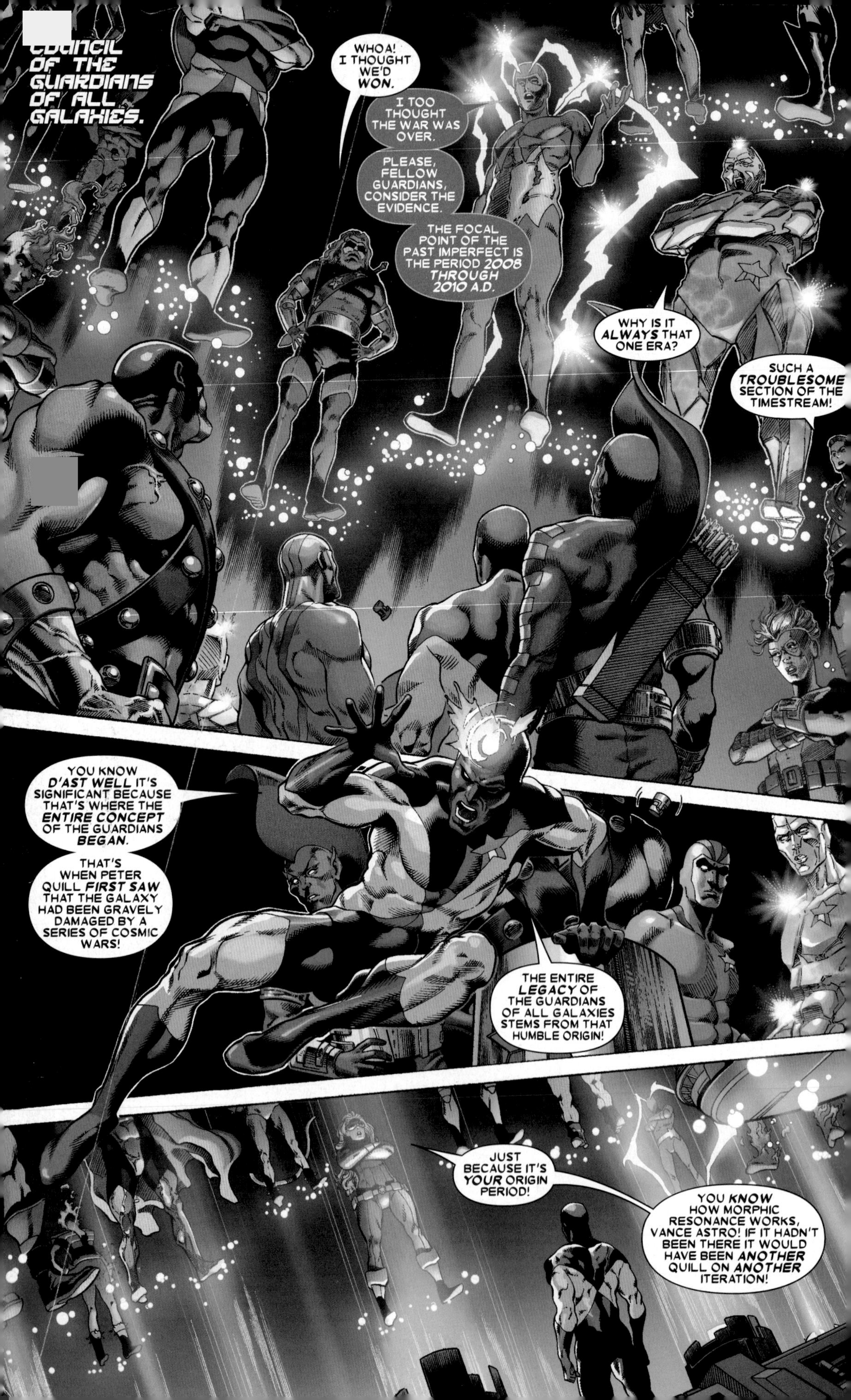
COUNCIL OF THE GUARDIANS OF ALL GALAXIES.
WHOA! I THOUGHT WE'D WON.
I TOO THOUGHT THE WAR WAS OVER.
PLEASE, FELLOW GUARDIANS, CONSIDER THE EVIDENCE.
THE FOCAL POINT OF THE PAST IMPERFECT IS THE PERIOD 2008 THROUGH 2010 A.D.
WHY IS IT ALWAYS THAT ONE ERA?
SUCH A TROUBLESOME SECTION OF THE TIMESTREAM!
YOU KNOW D'AST WELL IT'S SIGNIFICANT BECAUSE THAT'S WHERE THE ENTIRE CONCEPT OF THE GUARDIANS BEGAN.
THAT'S WHEN PETER QUILL FIRST SAW THAT THE GALAXY HAD BEEN GRAVELY DAMAGED BY A SERIES OF COSMIC WARS!
THE ENTIRE LEGACY OF THE GUARDIANS OF ALL GALAXIES STEMS FROM THAT HUMBLE ORIGIN!
JUST BECAUSE IT'S YOUR ORIGIN PERIOD!
YOU KNOW HOW MORPHIC RESONANCE WORKS, VANCE ASTRO! IF IT HADN'T BEEN THERE IT WOULD HAVE BEEN ANOTHER QUILL ON ANOTHER ITERATION!

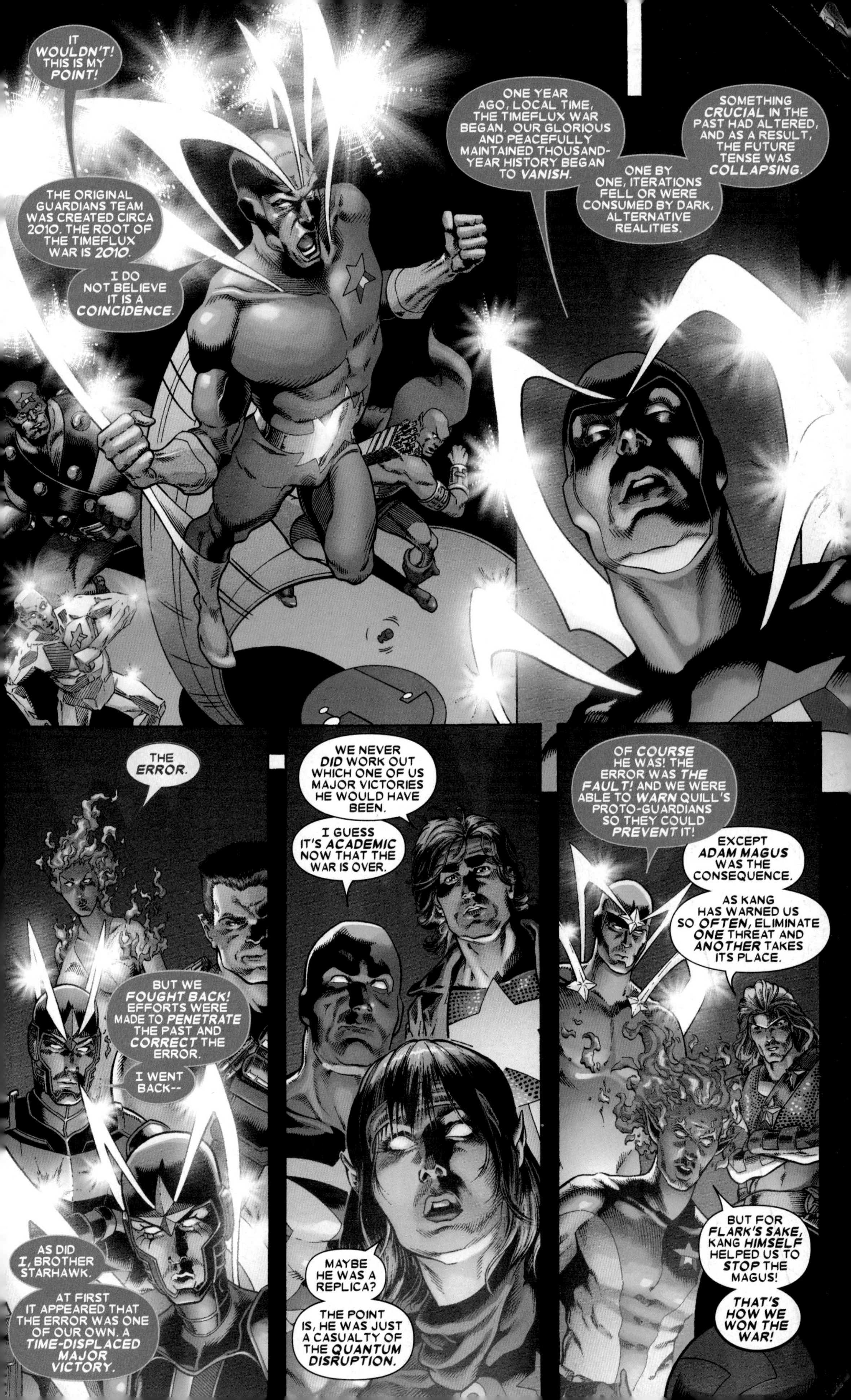
IT WOULDN'T! THIS IS MY POINT!
THE ORIGINAL GUARDIANS TEAM WAS CREATED CIRCA 2010. THE ROOT OF THE TIMEFLUX WAR IS 2010.
I DO NOT BELIEVE IT IS A COINCIDENCE.
ONE YEAR AGO, LOCAL TIME, THE TIMEFLUX WAR BEGAN. OUR GLORIOUS AND PEACEFULLY MAINTAINED THOUSAND-YEAR HISTORY BEGAN TO VANISH.
ONE BY ONE, ITERATIONS FELL OR WERE CONSUMED BY DARK, ALTERNATIVE REALITIES.
SOMETHING CRUCIAL IN THE PAST HAD ALTERED, AND AS A RESULT, THE FUTURE TENSE WAS COLLAPSING.
THE ERROR.
BUT WE FOUGHT BACK! EFFORTS WERE MADE TO PENETRATE THE PAST AND CORRECT THE ERROR.
I WENT BACK--
AS DID I, BROTHER STARHAWK.
AT FIRST IT APPEARED THAT THE ERROR WAS ONE OF OUR OWN. A TIME-DISPLACED MAJOR VICTORY.
WE NEVER DID WORK OUT WHICH ONE OF US MAJOR VICTORIES HE WOULD HAVE BEEN.
I GUESS IT'S ACADEMIC NOW THAT THE WAR IS OVER.
MAYBE HE WAS A REPLICA?
THE POINT IS, HE WAS JUST A CASUALTY OF THE QUANTUM DISRUPTION.
OF COURSE HE WAS! THE ERROR WAS THE FAULT! AND WE WERE ABLE TO WARN QUILL'S PROTO-GUARDIANS SO THEY COULD PREVENT IT!
EXCEPT ADAM MAGUS WAS THE CONSEQUENCE.
AS KANG HAS WARNED US SO OFTEN, ELIMINATE ONE THREAT AND ANOTHER TAKES ITS PLACE.
BUT FOR FLARK'S SAKE, KANG HIMSELF HELPED US TO STOP THE MAGUS!
THAT'S HOW WE WON THE WAR!

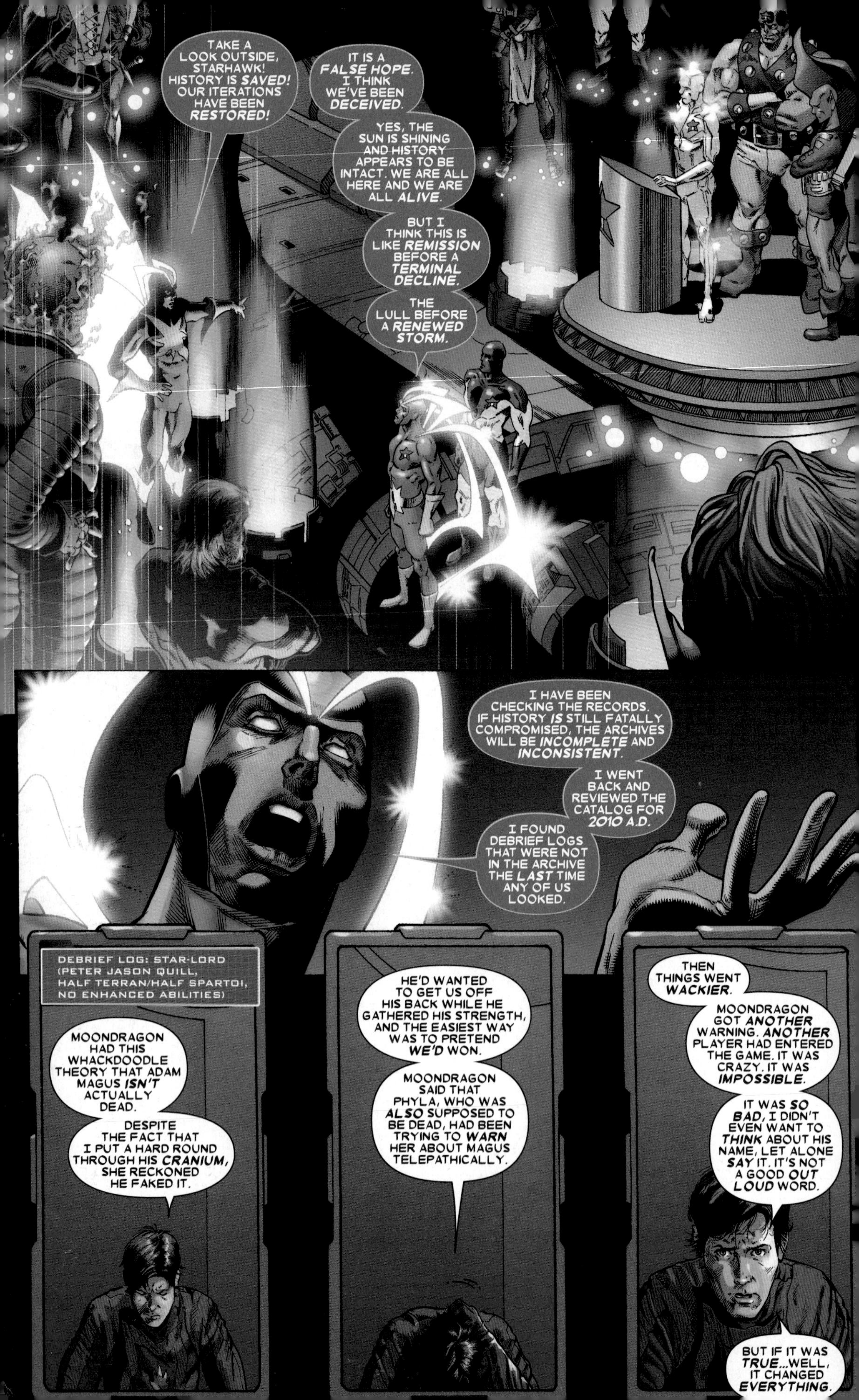
TAKE A LOOK OUTSIDE, STARHAWK! HISTORY IS SAVED! OUR ITERATIONS HAVE BEEN RESTORED!
IT IS A FALSE HOPE. I THINK WE'VE BEEN DECEIVED.
YES, THE SUN IS SHINING AND HISTORY APPEARS TO BE INTACT. WE ARE ALL HERE AND WE ARE ALL ALIVE.
BUT I THINK THIS IS LIKE REMISSION BEFORE A TERMINAL DECLINE.
THE LULL BEFORE A RENEWED STORM.
I HAVE BEEN CHECKING THE RECORDS. IF HISTORY IS STILL FATALLY COMPROMISED, THE ARCHIVES WILL BE INCOMPLETE AND INCONSISTENT.
I WENT BACK AND REVIEWED THE CATALOG FOR 2010 A.D.
I FOUND DEBRIEF LOGS THAT WERE NOT IN THE ARCHIVE THE LAST TIME ANY OF US LOOKED.
DEBRIEF LOG: STAR-LORD (PETER JASON QUILL, HALF TERRAN/HALF SPARTOI, NO ENHANCED ABILITIES)
MOONDRAGON HAD THIS WHACKDOODLE THEORY THAT ADAM MAGUS ISN'T ACTUALLY DEAD.
DESPITE THE FACT THAT I PUT A HARD ROUND THROUGH HIS CRANIUM, SHE RECKONED HE FAKED IT.
HE'D WANTED TO GET US OFF HIS BACK WHILE HE GATHERED HIS STRENGTH, AND THE EASIEST WAY WAS TO PRETEND WE'D WON.
MOONDRAGON SAID THAT PHYLA, WHO WAS ALSO SUPPOSED TO BE DEAD, HAD BEEN TRYING TO WARN HER ABOUT MAGUS TELEPATHICALLY.
THEN THINGS WENT WACKIER.
MOONDRAGON GOT ANOTHER WARNING. ANOTHER PLAYER HAD ENTERED THE GAME. IT WAS CRAZY. IT WAS IMPOSSIBLE.
IT WAS SO BAD, I DIDN'T EVEN WANT TO THINK ABOUT HIS NAME, LET ALONE SAY IT. IT'S NOT A GOOD OUT LOUD WORD.
BUT IF IT WAS TRUE...WELL, IT CHANGED EVERYTHING.

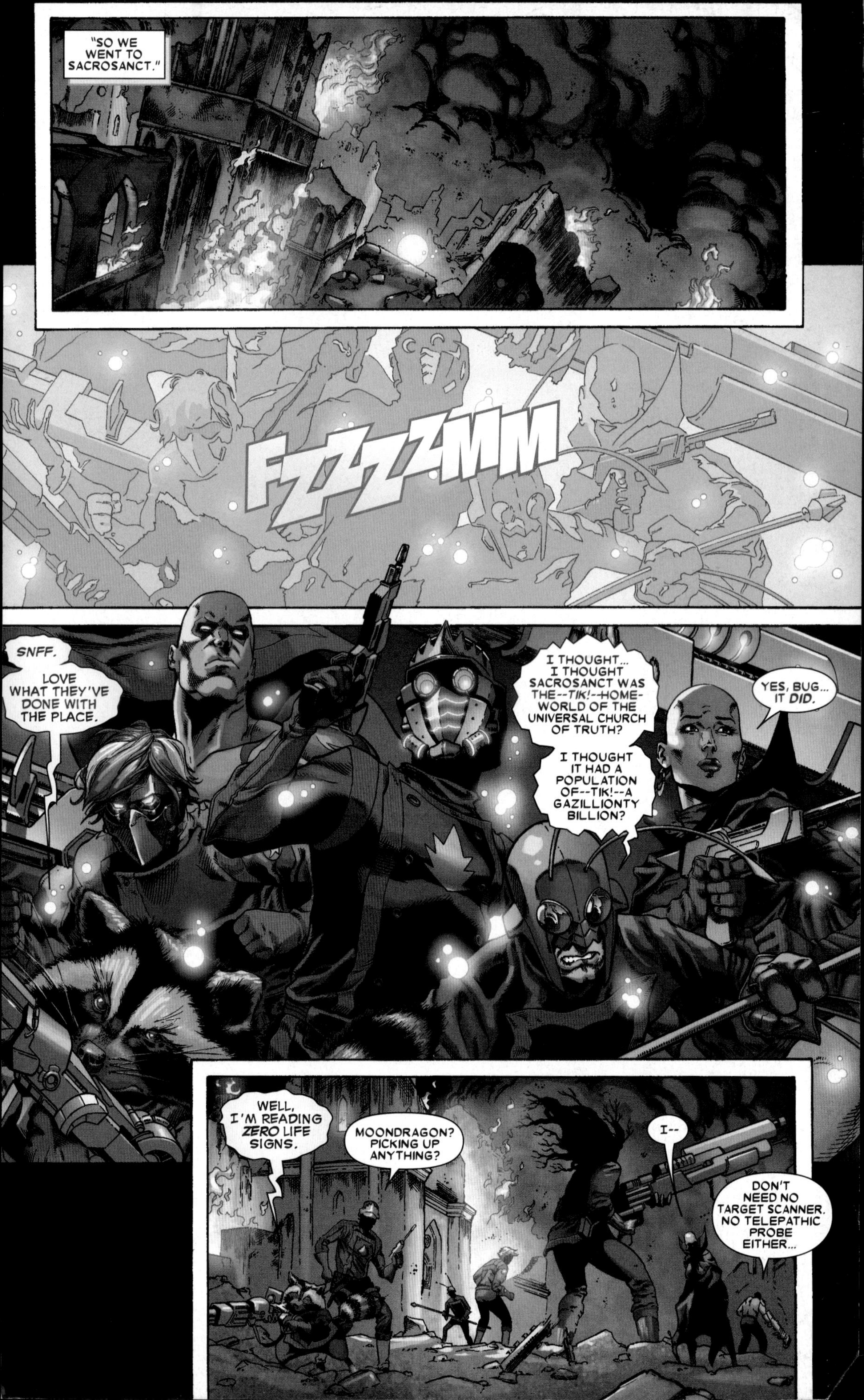
"SO WE WENT TO SACROSANCT."
FZZZZMM
SNFF.
LOVE WHAT THEY'VE DONE WITH THE PLACE.
I THOUGHT... I THOUGHT SACROSANCT WAS THE--TIK!--HOME-WORLD OF THE UNIVERSAL CHURCH OF TRUTH?
I THOUGHT IT HAD A POPULATION OF--TIK!--A GAZILLIONTY BILLION?
YES, BUG... IT DID.
WELL, I'M READING ZERO LIFE SIGNS.
MOONDRAGON? PICKING UP ANYTHING?
I--
DON'T NEED NO TARGET SCANNER. NO TELEPATHIC PROBE EITHER...

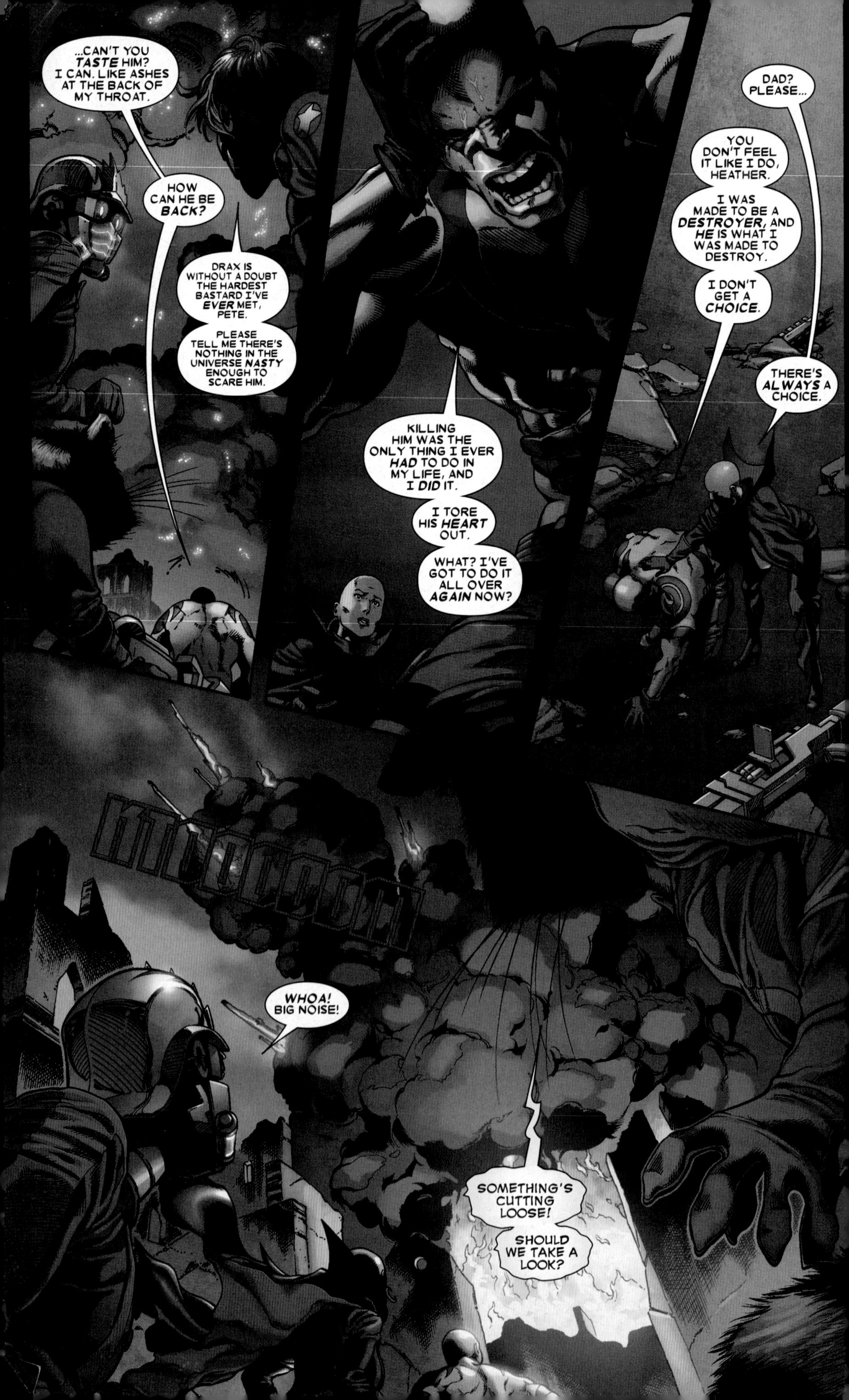

...CAN'T YOU TASTE HIM? I CAN. LIKE ASHES AT THE BACK OF MY THROAT.
HOW CAN HE BE BACK?
DRAX IS WITHOUT A DOUBT THE HARDEST BASTARD I'VE EVER MET, PETE.
PLEASE TELL ME THERE'S NOTHING IN THE UNIVERSE NASTY ENOUGH TO SCARE HIM.
KILLING HIM WAS THE ONLY THING I EVER HAD TO DO IN MY LIFE, AND I DID IT.
I TORE HIS HEART OUT.
WHAT? I'VE GOT TO DO IT ALL OVER AGAIN NOW?
DAD? PLEASE...
YOU DON'T FEEL IT LIKE I DO, HEATHER.
I WAS MADE TO BE A DESTROYER, AND HE IS WHAT I WAS MADE TO DESTROY.
I DON'T GET A CHOICE.
THERE'S ALWAYS A CHOICE.
WHOA! BIG NOISE!
SOMETHING'S CUTTING LOOSE!
SHOULD WE TAKE A LOOK?

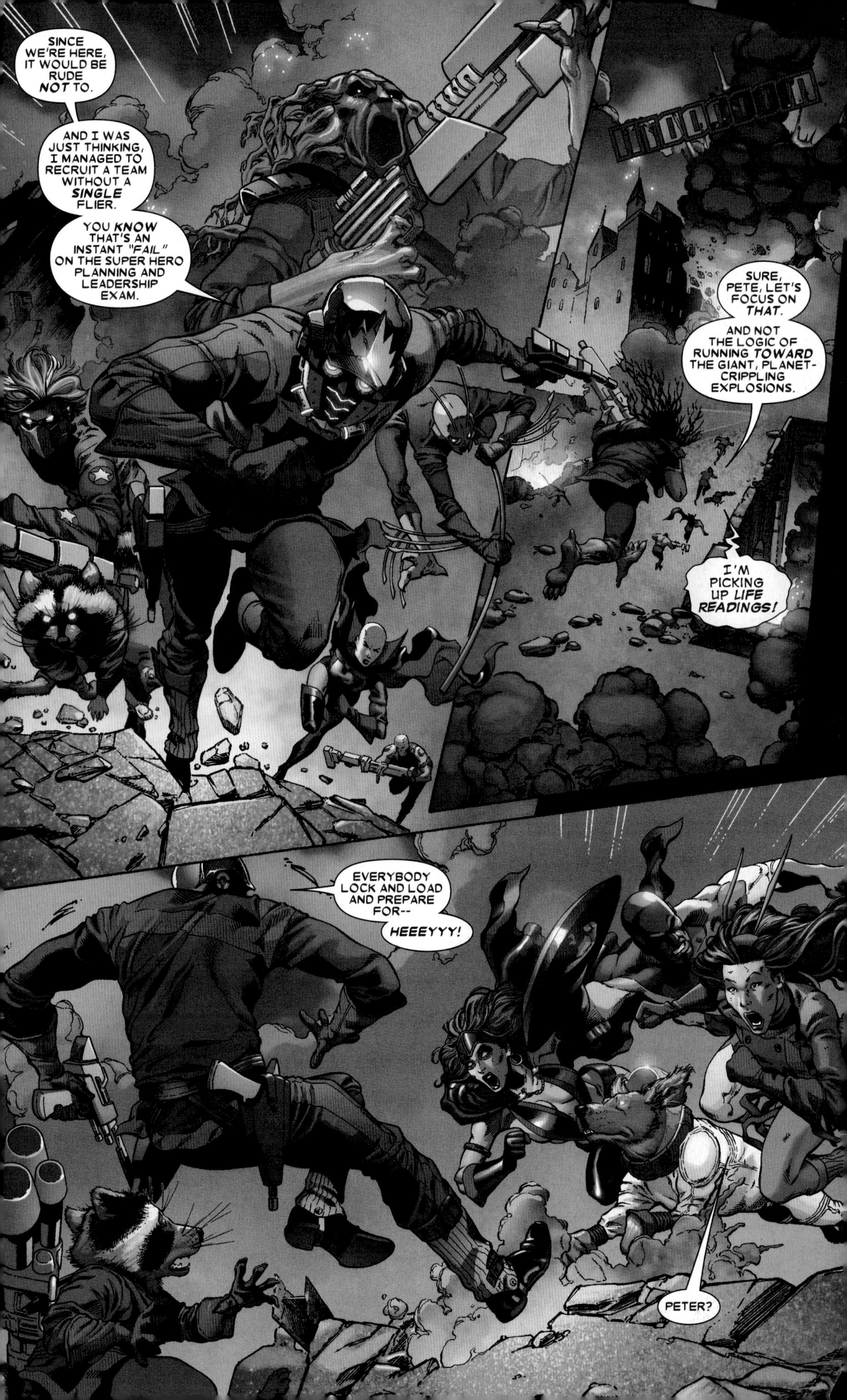
SINCE WE'RE HERE, IT WOULD BE RUDE *NOT* TO.
AND I WAS JUST THINKING, I MANAGED TO RECRUIT A TEAM WITHOUT A *SINGLE* FLIER.
YOU *KNOW* THAT'S AN INSTANT *"FAIL"* ON THE SUPER HERO PLANNING AND LEADERSHIP EXAM.
SURE, PETE, LET'S FOCUS ON *THAT*.
AND NOT THE LOGIC OF RUNNING *TOWARD* THE GIANT, PLANET-CRIPPLING EXPLOSIONS.
I'M PICKING UP *LIFE READINGS!*
EVERYBODY LOCK AND LOAD AND PREPARE FOR--
HEEEYYY!
PETER?

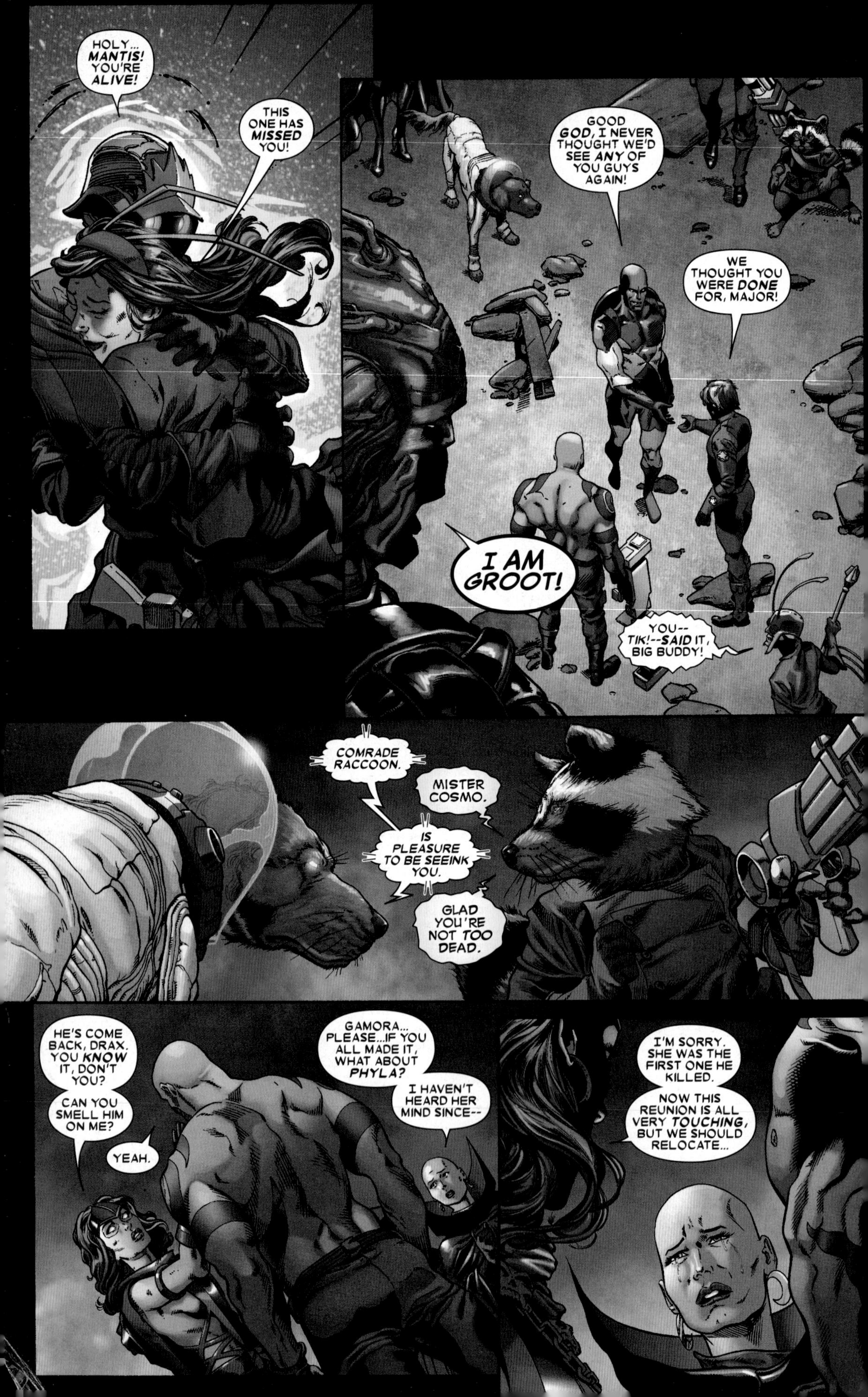
HOLY... MANTIS! YOU'RE ALIVE!
THIS ONE HAS MISSED YOU!
GOOD GOD, I NEVER THOUGHT WE'D SEE ANY OF YOU GUYS AGAIN!
WE THOUGHT YOU WERE DONE FOR, MAJOR!
I AM GROOT!
YOU--TIK!--SAID IT, BIG BUDDY!
COMRADE RACCOON.
MISTER COSMO.
IS PLEASURE TO BE SEEINK YOU.
GLAD YOU'RE NOT TOO DEAD.
HE'S COME BACK, DRAX. YOU KNOW IT, DON'T YOU?
CAN YOU SMELL HIM ON ME?
YEAH.
GAMORA... PLEASE...IF YOU ALL MADE IT, WHAT ABOUT PHYLA?
I HAVEN'T HEARD HER MIND SINCE--
I'M SORRY. SHE WAS THE FIRST ONE HE KILLED.
NOW THIS REUNION IS ALL VERY TOUCHING, BUT WE SHOULD RELOCATE...

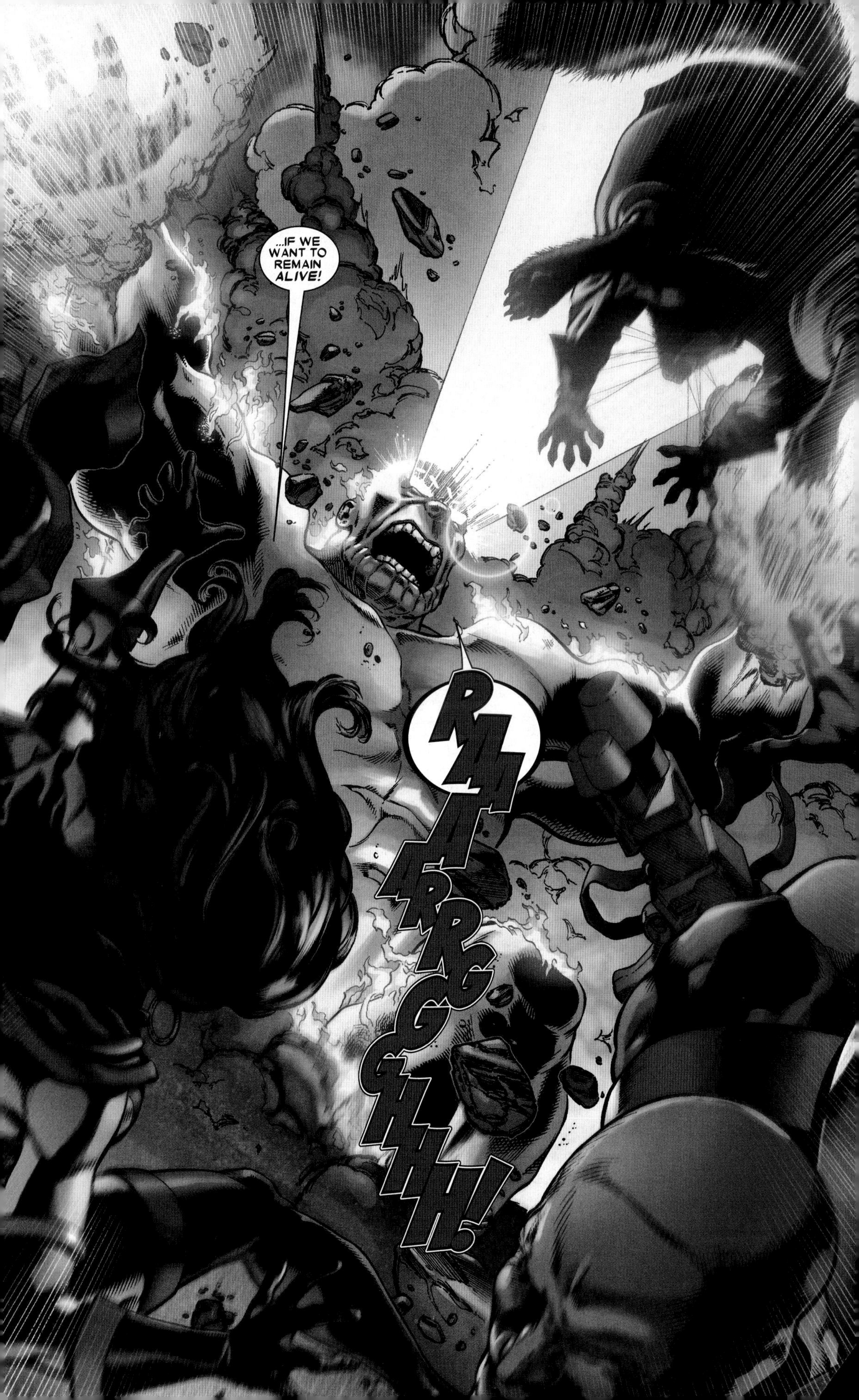
...IF WE WANT TO REMAIN ALIVE!
RAAARRGGHHH!

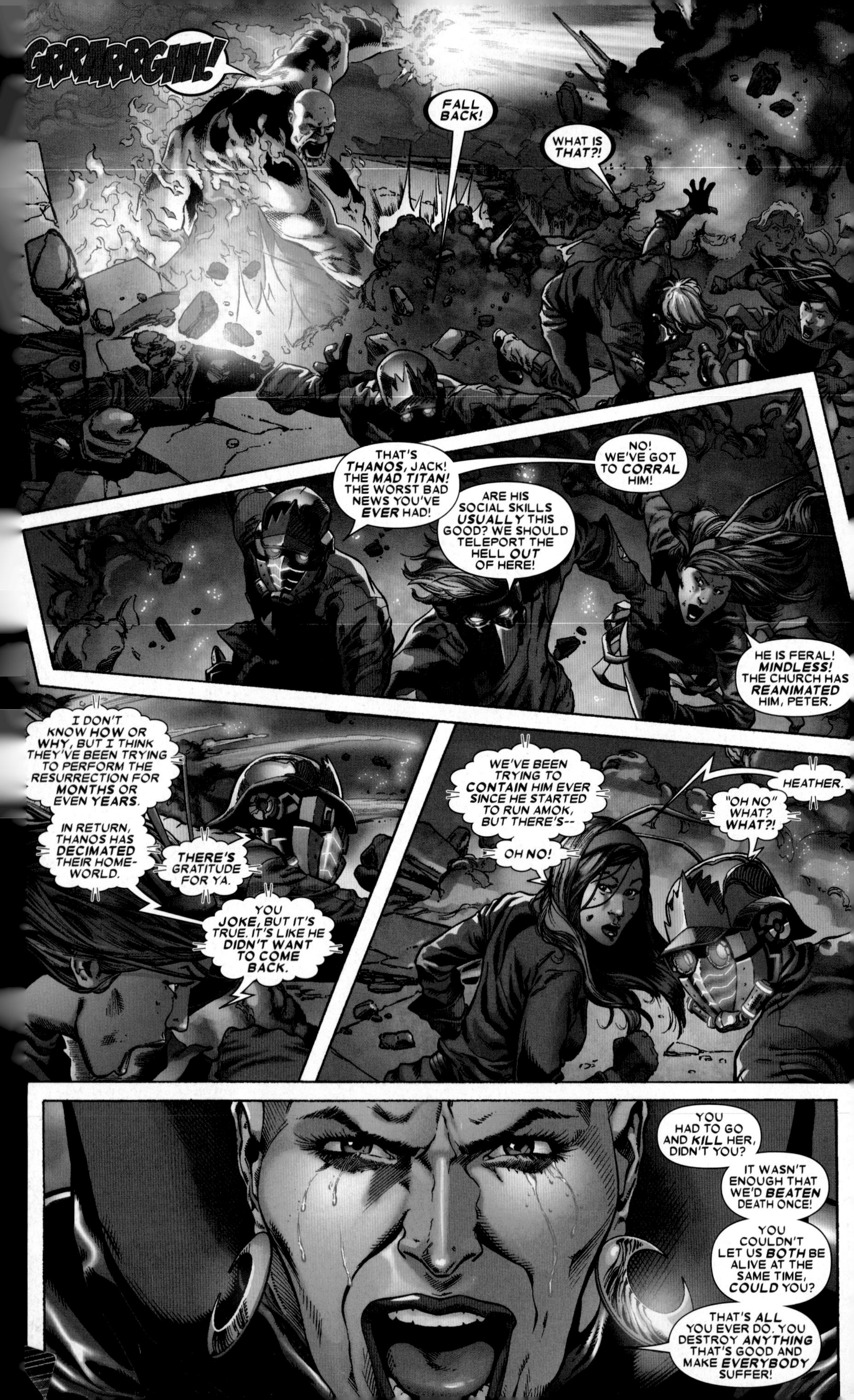
GRRAARRGHH!
FALL BACK!
WHAT IS THAT?!
THAT'S THANOS, JACK! THE MAD TITAN! THE WORST BAD NEWS YOU'VE EVER HAD!
ARE HIS SOCIAL SKILLS USUALLY THIS GOOD? WE SHOULD TELEPORT THE HELL OUT OF HERE!
NO! WE'VE GOT TO CORRAL HIM!
HE IS FERAL! MINDLESS! THE CHURCH HAS REANIMATED HIM, PETER.
I DON'T KNOW HOW OR WHY, BUT I THINK THEY'VE BEEN TRYING TO PERFORM THE RESURRECTION FOR MONTHS OR EVEN YEARS.
IN RETURN, THANOS HAS DECIMATED THEIR HOME-WORLD.
THERE'S GRATITUDE FOR YA.
YOU JOKE, BUT IT'S TRUE. IT'S LIKE HE DIDN'T WANT TO COME BACK.
WE'VE BEEN TRYING TO CONTAIN HIM EVER SINCE HE STARTED TO RUN AMOK, BUT THERE'S--
OH NO!
HEATHER.
"OH NO" WHAT? WHAT?!
YOU HAD TO GO AND KILL HER, DIDN'T YOU?
IT WASN'T ENOUGH THAT WE'D BEATEN DEATH ONCE!
YOU COULDN'T LET US BOTH BE ALIVE AT THE SAME TIME, COULD YOU?
THAT'S ALL YOU EVER DO. YOU DESTROY ANYTHING THAT'S GOOD AND MAKE EVERYBODY SUFFER!

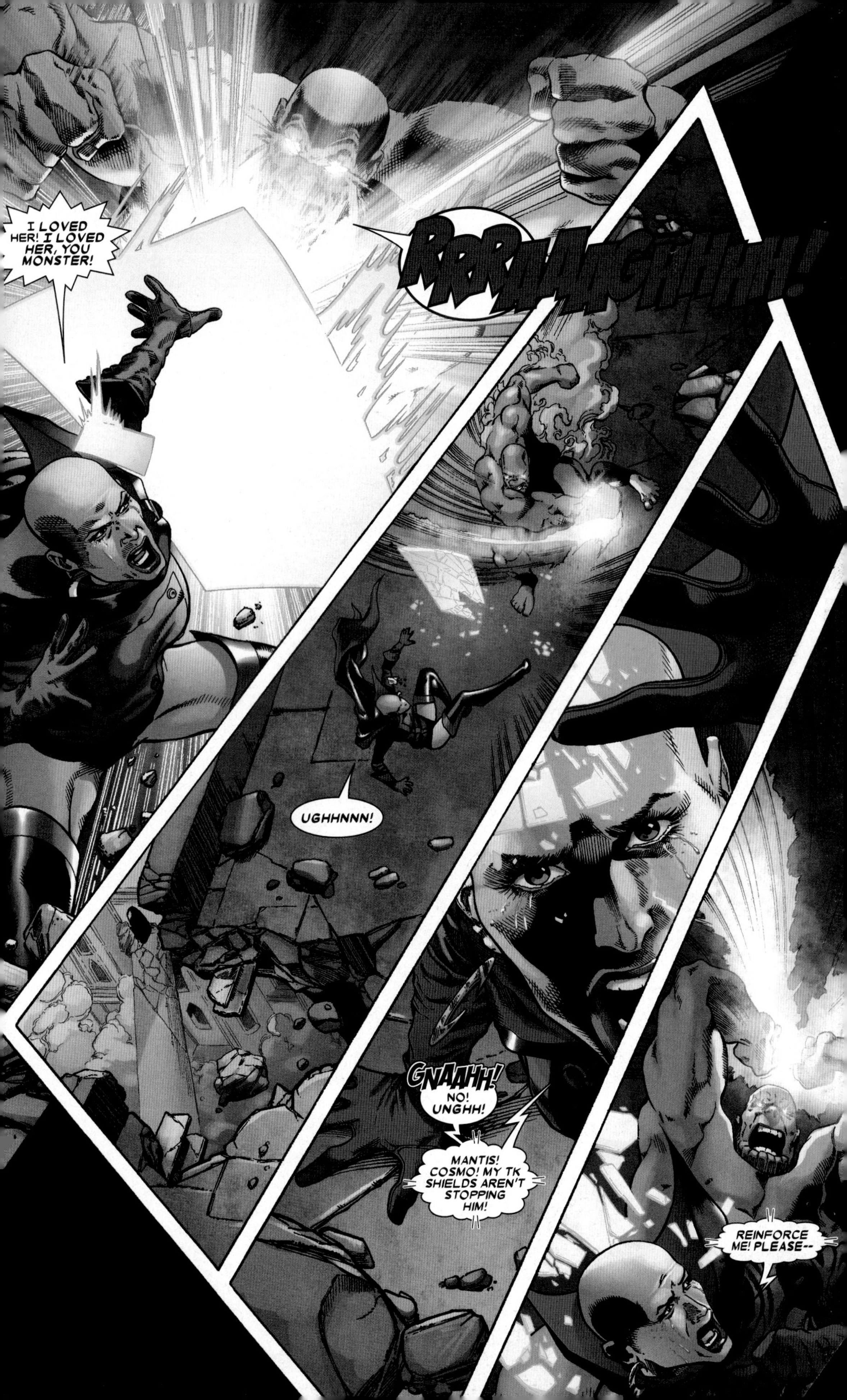

I LOVED HER! I LOVED HER, YOU MONSTER!
RRRUUAAGHHHH!
UGHHNNN!
GNAAHH!
NO! UNGHH!
MANTIS! COSMO! MY TK SHIELDS AREN'T STOPPING HIM!
REINFORCE ME! PLEASE--

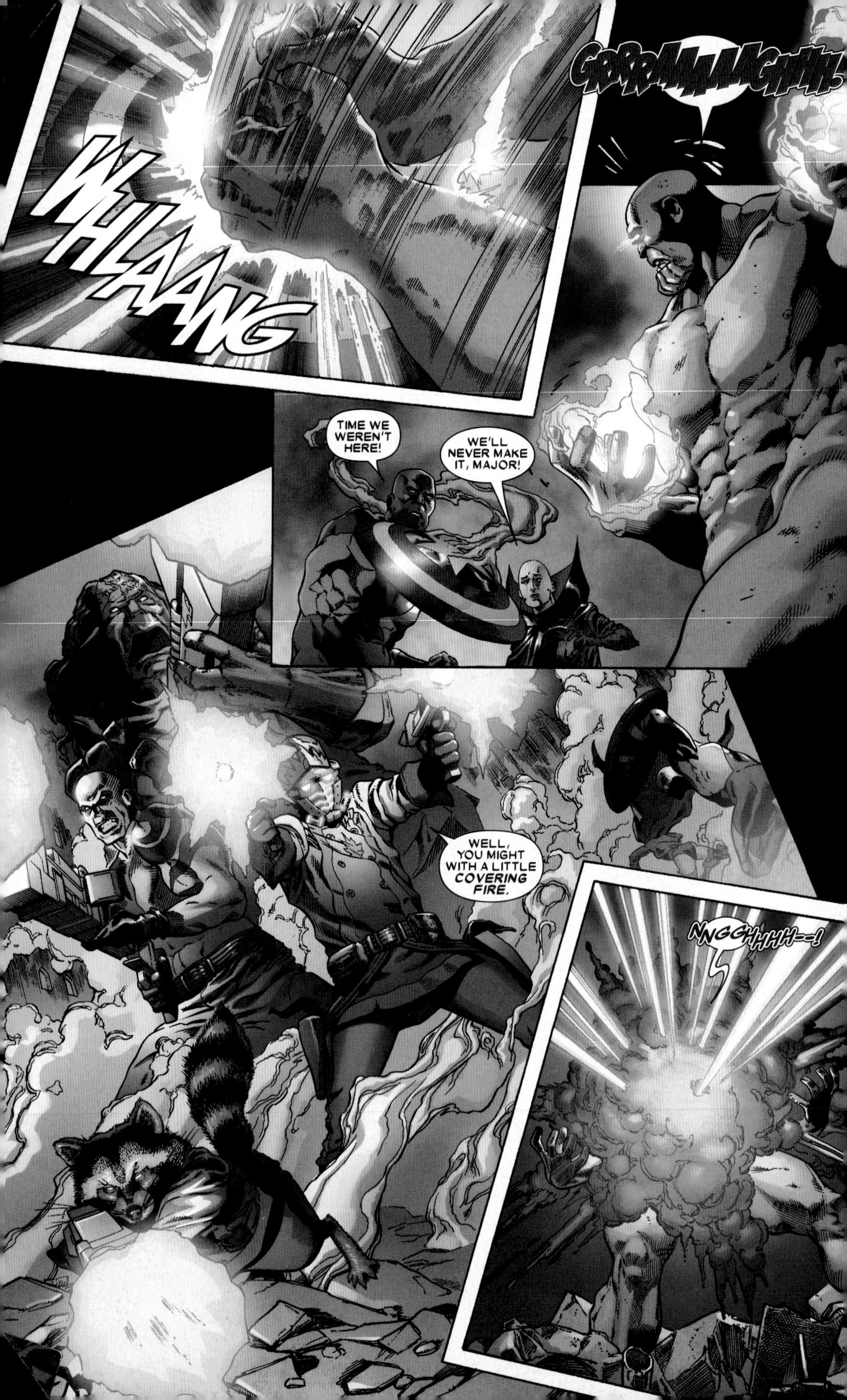
WHLAANG
GRRRAAAAAGHHH
TIME WE WEREN'T HERE!
WE'LL NEVER MAKE IT, MAJOR!
WELL, YOU MIGHT WITH A LITTLE COVERING FIRE.
NNGGHHHH--!

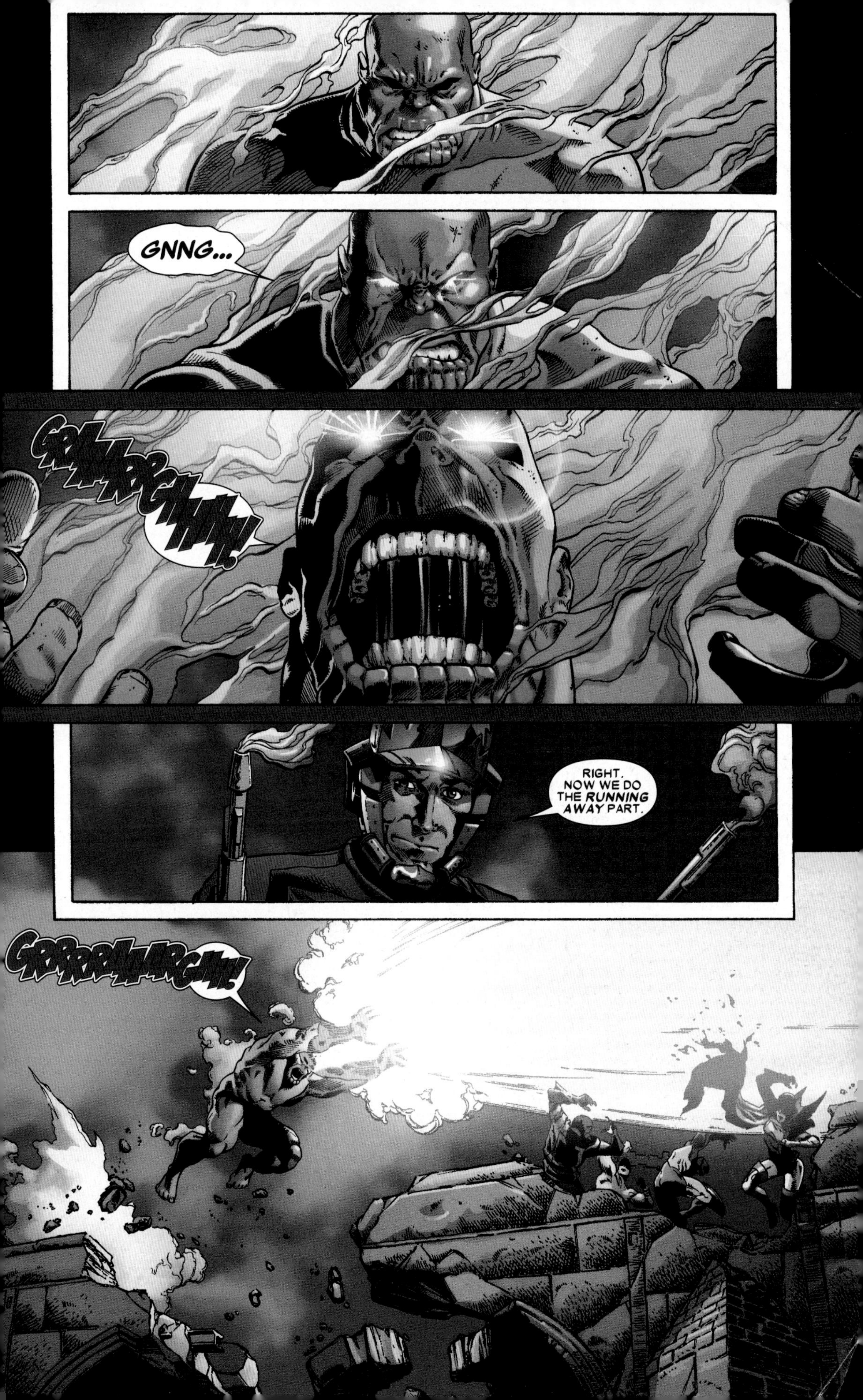
GNNG...
GRAAARGHHHH!
RIGHT. NOW WE DO THE *RUNNING AWAY* PART.
GRRRAAARGHH!

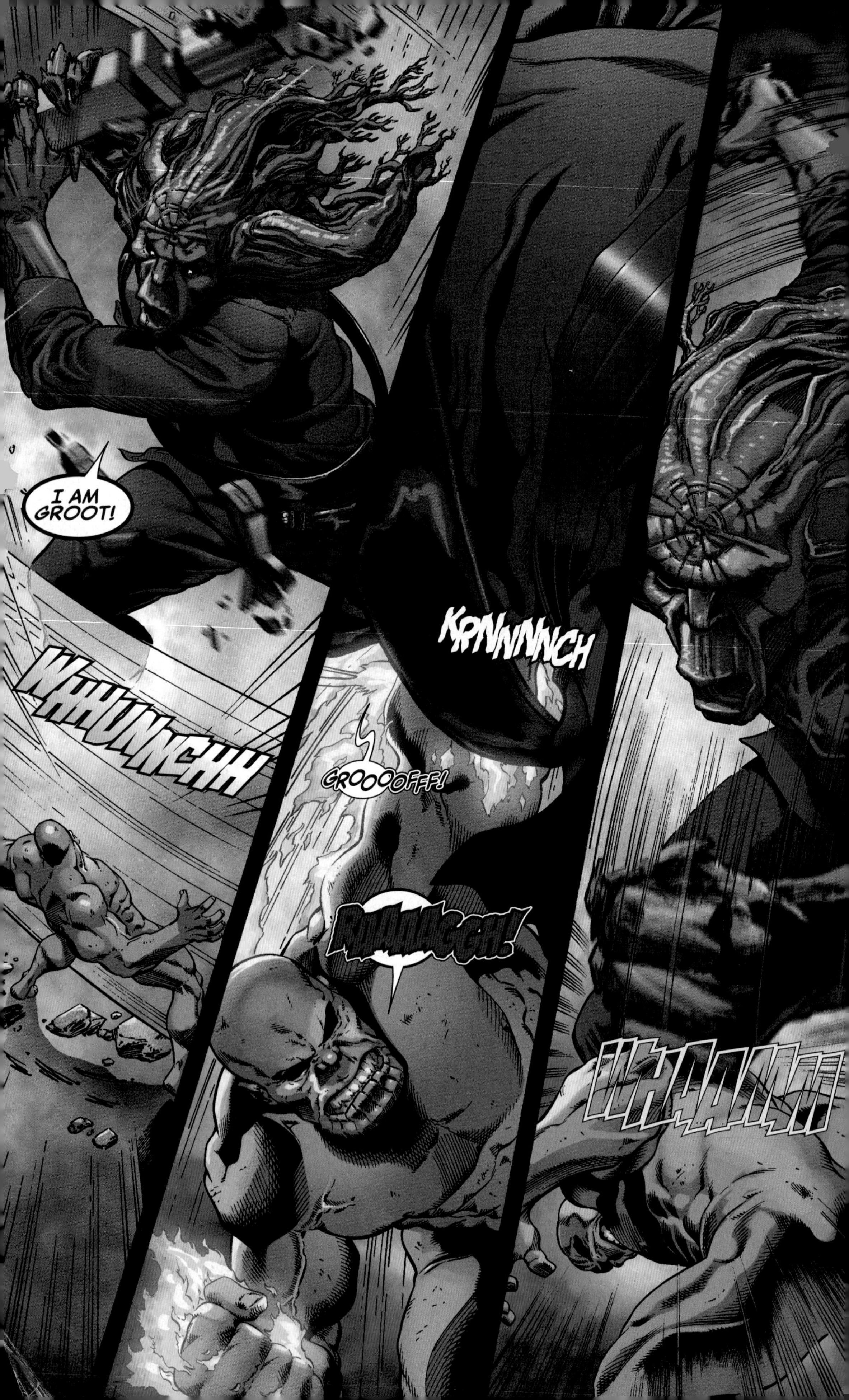
I AM GROOT!
WHHUNNCHH
KRNNNNCH
GROOOOFFF!

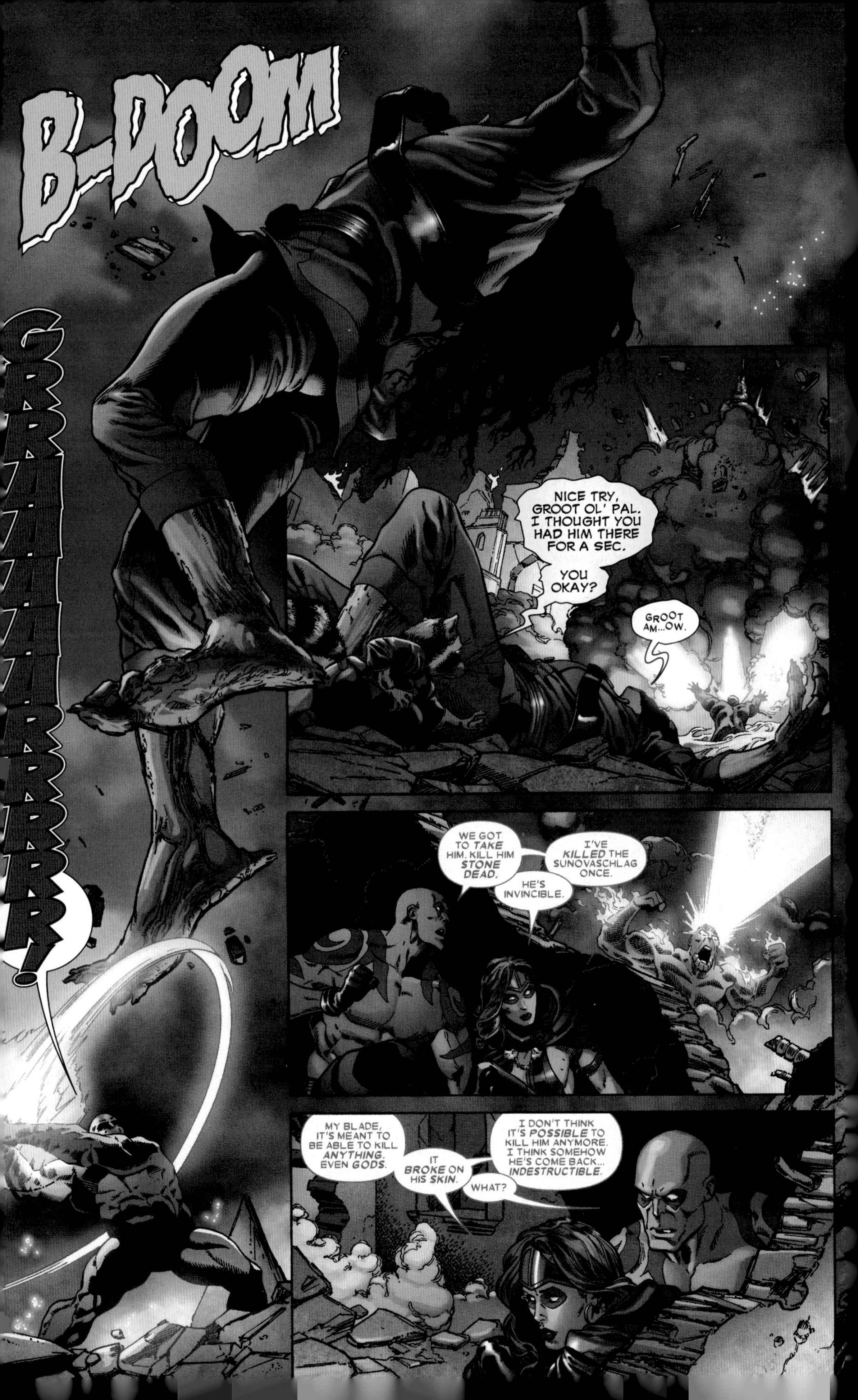
B-DOOM
GRRRAAAAAAARRRRRR!
NICE TRY, GROOT OL' PAL. I THOUGHT YOU HAD HIM THERE FOR A SEC.
YOU OKAY?
GROOT AM...OW.
WE GOT TO TAKE HIM. KILL HIM STONE DEAD.
I'VE KILLED THE SUNOVASCHLAG ONCE.
HE'S INVINCIBLE.
MY BLADE, IT'S MEANT TO BE ABLE TO KILL ANYTHING. EVEN GODS.
IT BROKE ON HIS SKIN.
I DON'T THINK IT'S POSSIBLE TO KILL HIM ANYMORE. I THINK SOMEHOW HE'S COME BACK... INDESTRUCTIBLE.
WHAT?

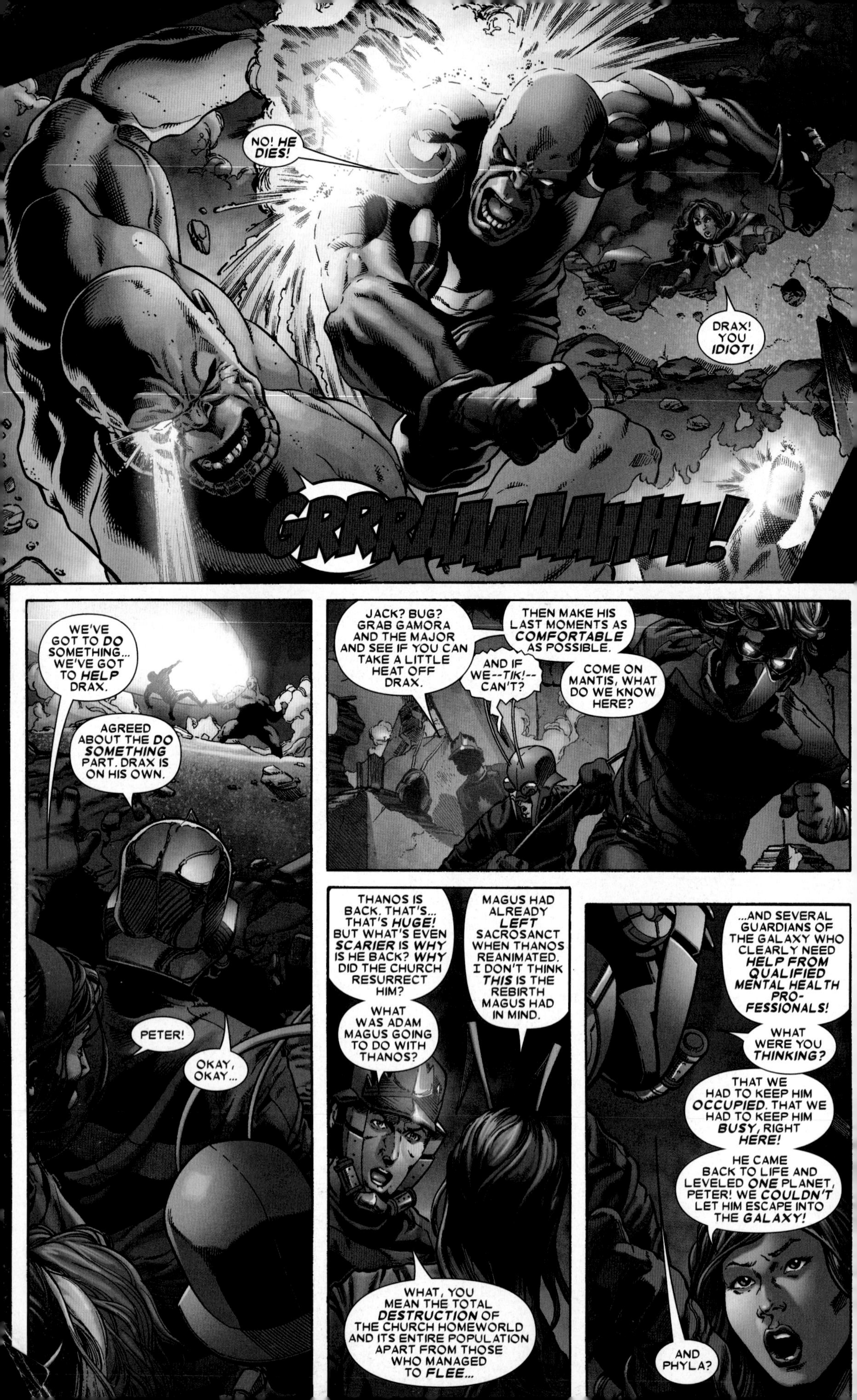

NO! HE DIES!
DRAX! YOU IDIOT!
GRRRAAAAAAHHH!
WE'VE GOT TO DO SOMETHING... WE'VE GOT TO HELP DRAX.
AGREED ABOUT THE DO SOMETHING PART. DRAX IS ON HIS OWN.
PETER!
OKAY, OKAY...
JACK? BUG? GRAB GAMORA AND THE MAJOR AND SEE IF YOU CAN TAKE A LITTLE HEAT OFF DRAX.
AND IF WE--TIK!--CAN'T?
THEN MAKE HIS LAST MOMENTS AS COMFORTABLE AS POSSIBLE.
COME ON MANTIS, WHAT DO WE KNOW HERE?
THANOS IS BACK. THAT'S... THAT'S HUGE! BUT WHAT'S EVEN SCARIER IS WHY IS HE BACK? WHY DID THE CHURCH RESURRECT HIM?
WHAT WAS ADAM MAGUS GOING TO DO WITH THANOS?
MAGUS HAD ALREADY LEFT SACROSANCT WHEN THANOS REANIMATED. I DON'T THINK THIS IS THE REBIRTH MAGUS HAD IN MIND.
WHAT, YOU MEAN THE TOTAL DESTRUCTION OF THE CHURCH HOMEWORLD AND ITS ENTIRE POPULATION APART FROM THOSE WHO MANAGED TO FLEE...
...AND SEVERAL GUARDIANS OF THE GALAXY WHO CLEARLY NEED HELP FROM QUALIFIED MENTAL HEALTH PRO-FESSIONALS!
WHAT WERE YOU THINKING?
THAT WE HAD TO KEEP HIM OCCUPIED. THAT WE HAD TO KEEP HIM BUSY, RIGHT HERE!
HE CAME BACK TO LIFE AND LEVELED ONE PLANET, PETER! WE COULDN'T LET HIM ESCAPE INTO THE GALAXY!
AND PHYLA?

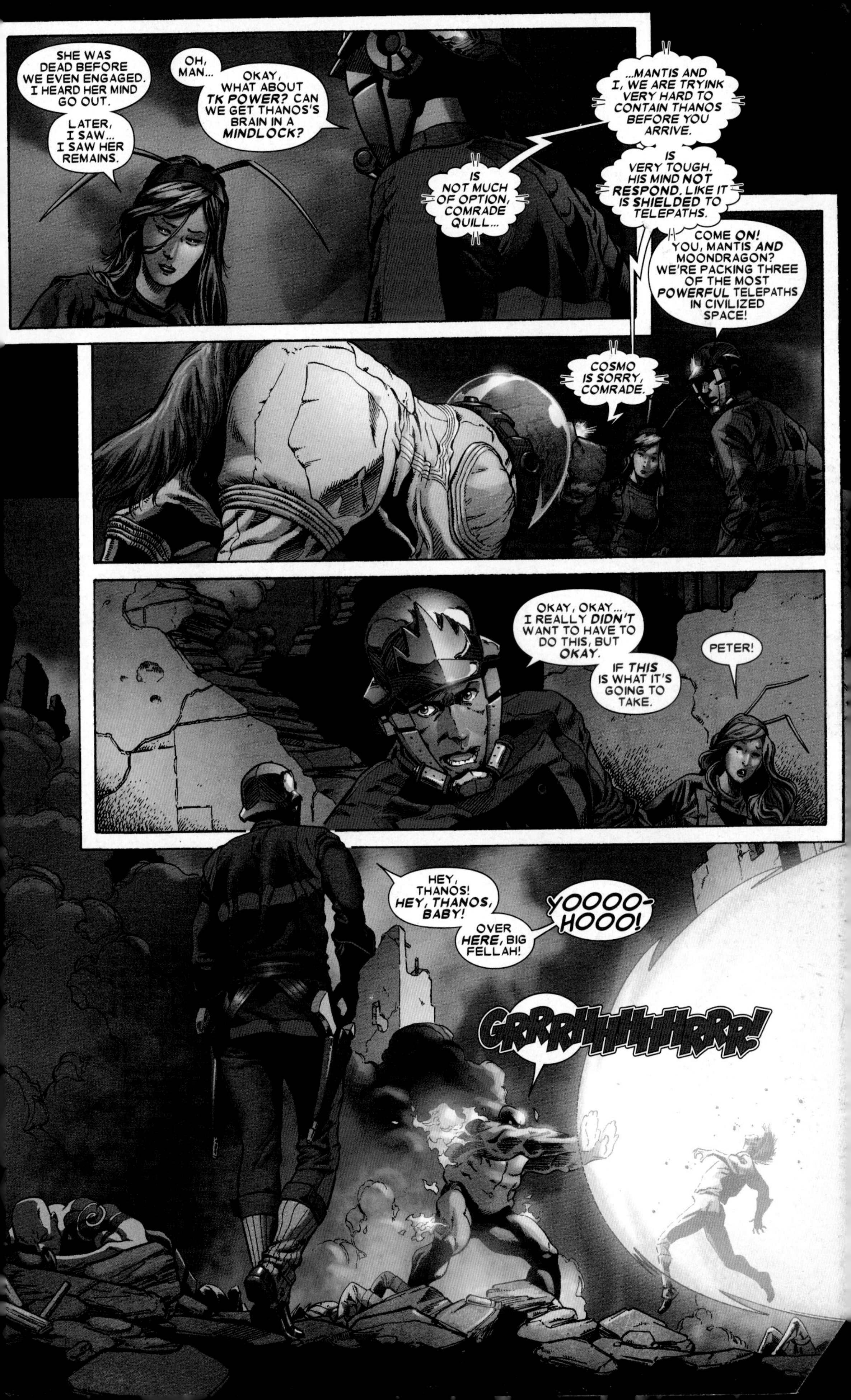
SHE WAS DEAD BEFORE WE EVEN ENGAGED. I HEARD HER MIND GO OUT.
LATER, I SAW... I SAW HER REMAINS.
OH, MAN...
OKAY, WHAT ABOUT TK POWER? CAN WE GET THANOS'S BRAIN IN A MINDLOCK?
IS NOT MUCH OF OPTION, COMRADE QUILL...
...MANTIS AND I, WE ARE TRYINK VERY HARD TO CONTAIN THANOS BEFORE YOU ARRIVE.
IS VERY TOUGH. HIS MIND NOT RESPOND. LIKE IT IS SHIELDED TO TELEPATHS.
COME ON! YOU, MANTIS AND MOONDRAGON? WE'RE PACKING THREE OF THE MOST POWERFUL TELEPATHS IN CIVILIZED SPACE!
COSMO IS SORRY, COMRADE.
OKAY, OKAY... I REALLY DIDN'T WANT TO HAVE TO DO THIS, BUT OKAY.
IF THIS IS WHAT IT'S GOING TO TAKE.
PETER!
HEY, THANOS! HEY, THANOS, BABY!
OVER HERE, BIG FELLAH!
YOOOO-HOOO!
GRRRHHHHHHRRR!

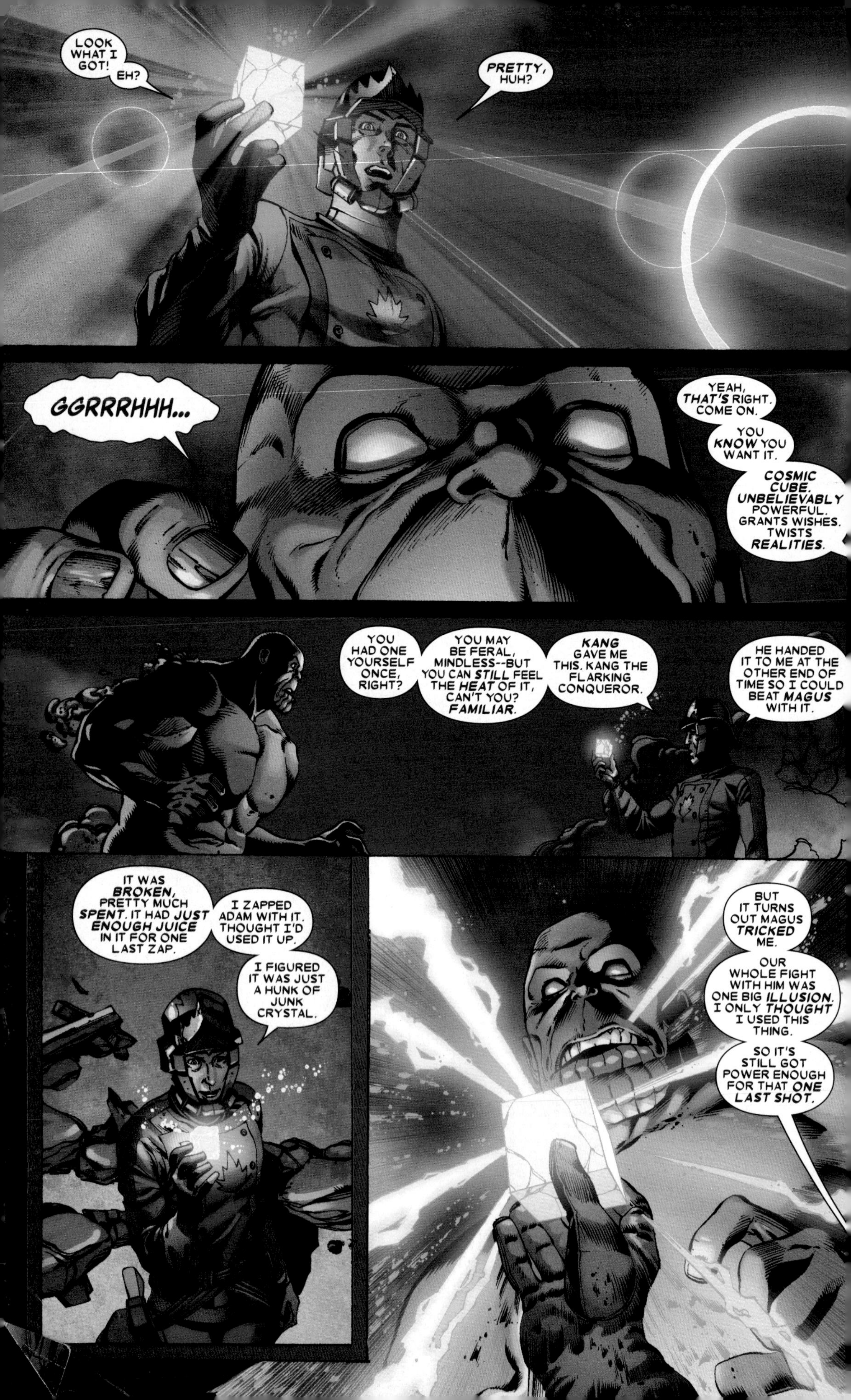
LOOK WHAT I GOT! EH?
PRETTY, HUH?
GGRRRHHH...
YEAH, THAT'S RIGHT. COME ON.
YOU KNOW YOU WANT IT.
COSMIC CUBE. UNBELIEVABLY POWERFUL. GRANTS WISHES. TWISTS REALITIES.
YOU HAD ONE YOURSELF ONCE, RIGHT?
YOU MAY BE FERAL, MINDLESS--BUT YOU CAN STILL FEEL THE HEAT OF IT, CAN'T YOU? FAMILIAR.
KANG GAVE ME THIS. KANG THE FLARKING CONQUEROR.
HE HANDED IT TO ME AT THE OTHER END OF TIME SO I COULD BEAT MAGUS WITH IT.
IT WAS BROKEN, PRETTY MUCH SPENT. IT HAD JUST ENOUGH JUICE IN IT FOR ONE LAST ZAP.
I ZAPPED ADAM WITH IT. THOUGHT I'D USED IT UP.
I FIGURED IT WAS JUST A HUNK OF JUNK CRYSTAL.
BUT IT TURNS OUT MAGUS TRICKED ME.
OUR WHOLE FIGHT WITH HIM WAS ONE BIG ILLUSION. I ONLY THOUGHT I USED THIS THING.
SO IT'S STILL GOT POWER ENOUGH FOR THAT ONE LAST SHOT.

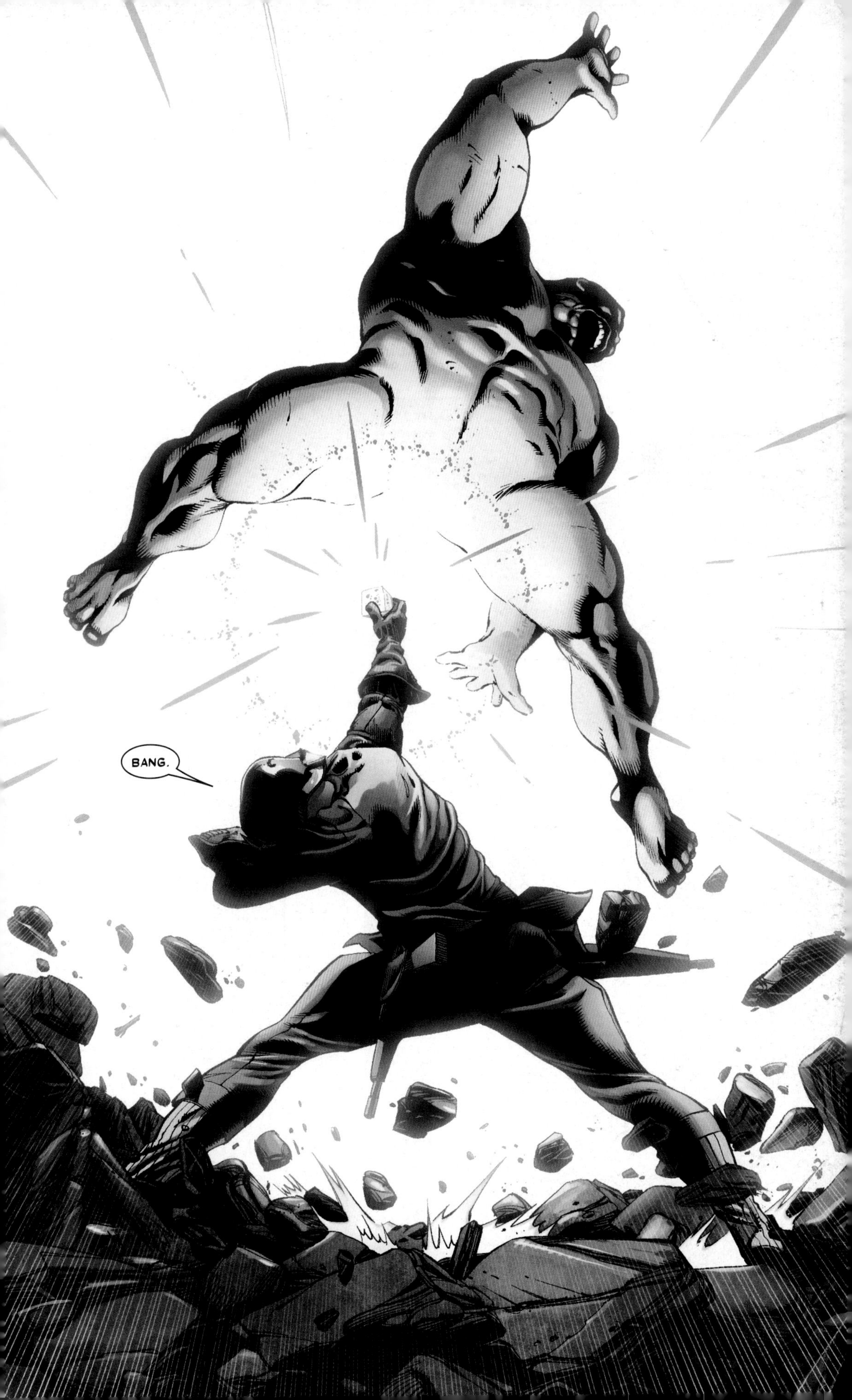
BANG.

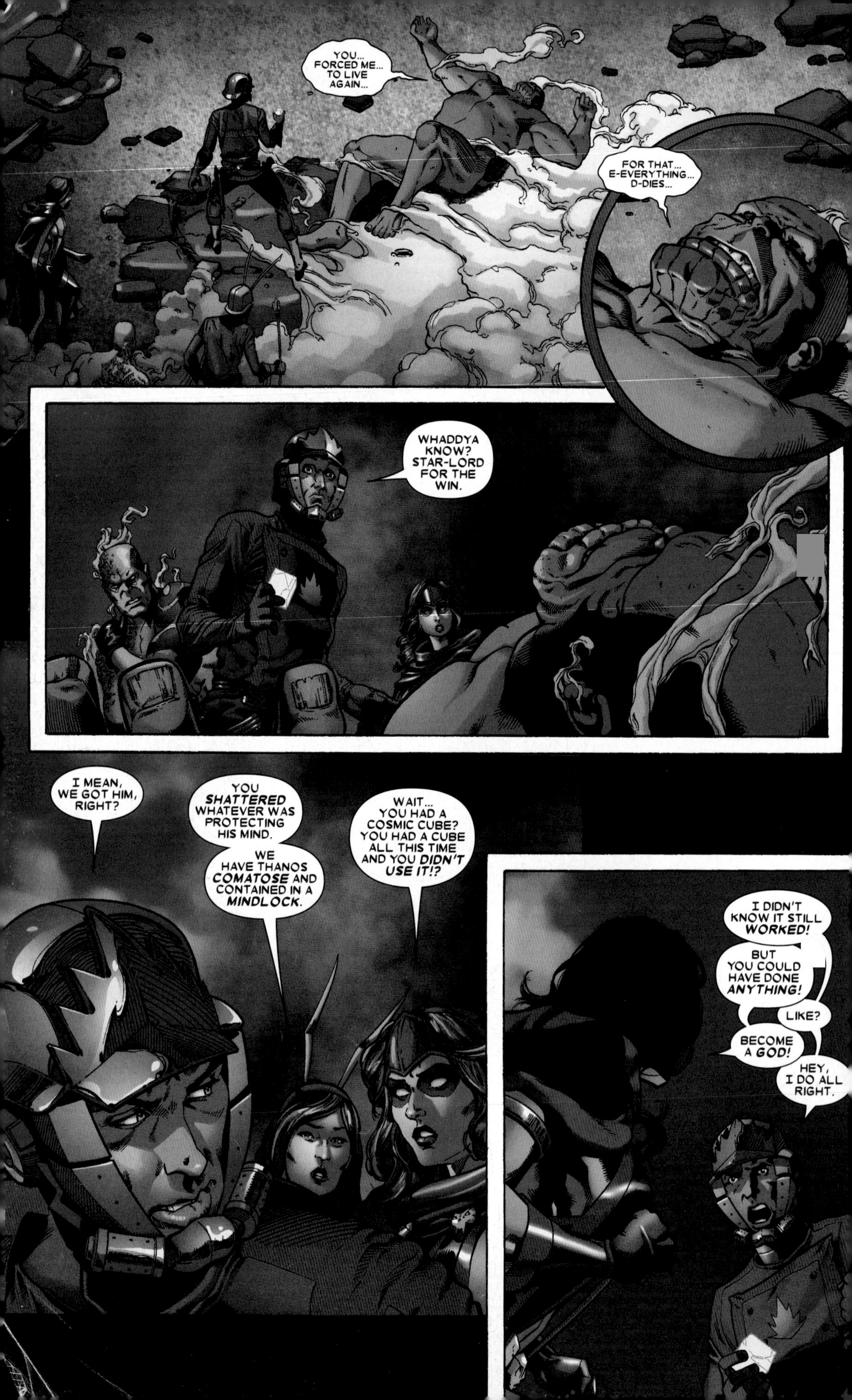
YOU... FORCED ME... TO LIVE AGAIN...
FOR THAT... E-EVERYTHING... D-DIES...
WHADDYA KNOW? STAR-LORD FOR THE WIN.
I MEAN, WE GOT HIM, RIGHT?
YOU *SHATTERED* WHATEVER WAS PROTECTING HIS MIND.
WE HAVE THANOS *COMATOSE* AND CONTAINED IN A *MINDLOCK*.
WAIT... YOU HAD A COSMIC CUBE? YOU HAD A CUBE ALL THIS TIME AND YOU *DIDN'T USE IT!?*
I DIDN'T KNOW IT STILL *WORKED!*
BUT YOU COULD HAVE DONE *ANYTHING!*
LIKE?
BECOME A *GOD!*
HEY, I DO ALL RIGHT.

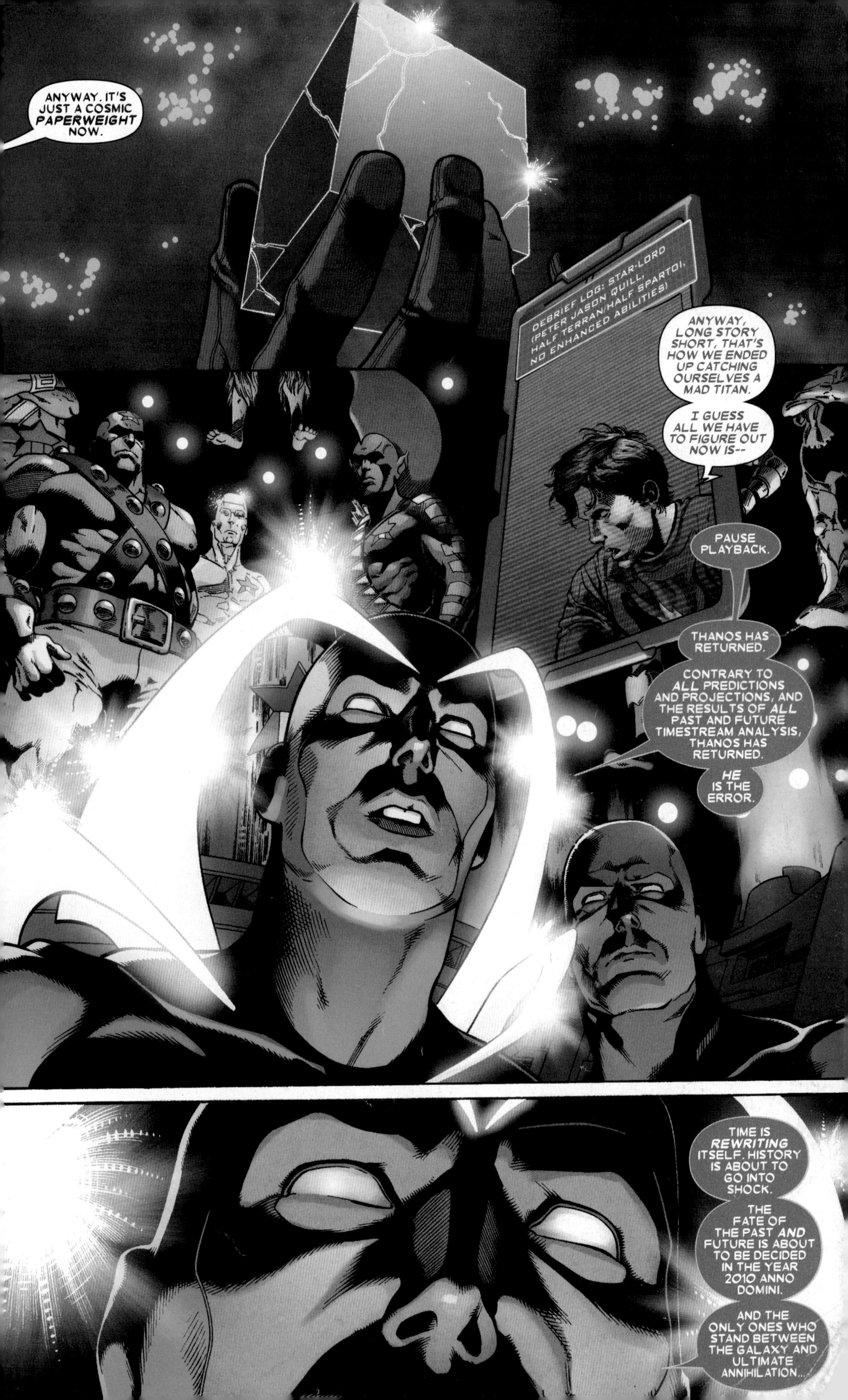
ANYWAY. IT'S JUST A COSMIC PAPERWEIGHT NOW.
DEBRIEF LOG: STAR-LORD (PETER JASON QUILL, HALF TERRAN/HALF SPARTOI, NO ENHANCED ABILITIES)
ANYWAY, LONG STORY SHORT, THAT'S HOW WE ENDED UP CATCHING OURSELVES A MAD TITAN.
I GUESS ALL WE HAVE TO FIGURE OUT NOW IS--
PAUSE PLAYBACK.
THANOS HAS RETURNED.
CONTRARY TO ALL PREDICTIONS AND PROJECTIONS, AND THE RESULTS OF ALL PAST AND FUTURE TIMESTREAM ANALYSIS, THANOS HAS RETURNED.
HE IS THE ERROR.
TIME IS REWRITING ITSELF. HISTORY IS ABOUT TO GO INTO SHOCK.
THE FATE OF THE PAST AND FUTURE IS ABOUT TO BE DECIDED IN THE YEAR 2010 ANNO DOMINI.
AND THE ONLY ONES WHO STAND BETWEEN THE GALAXY AND ULTIMATE ANNIHILATION...

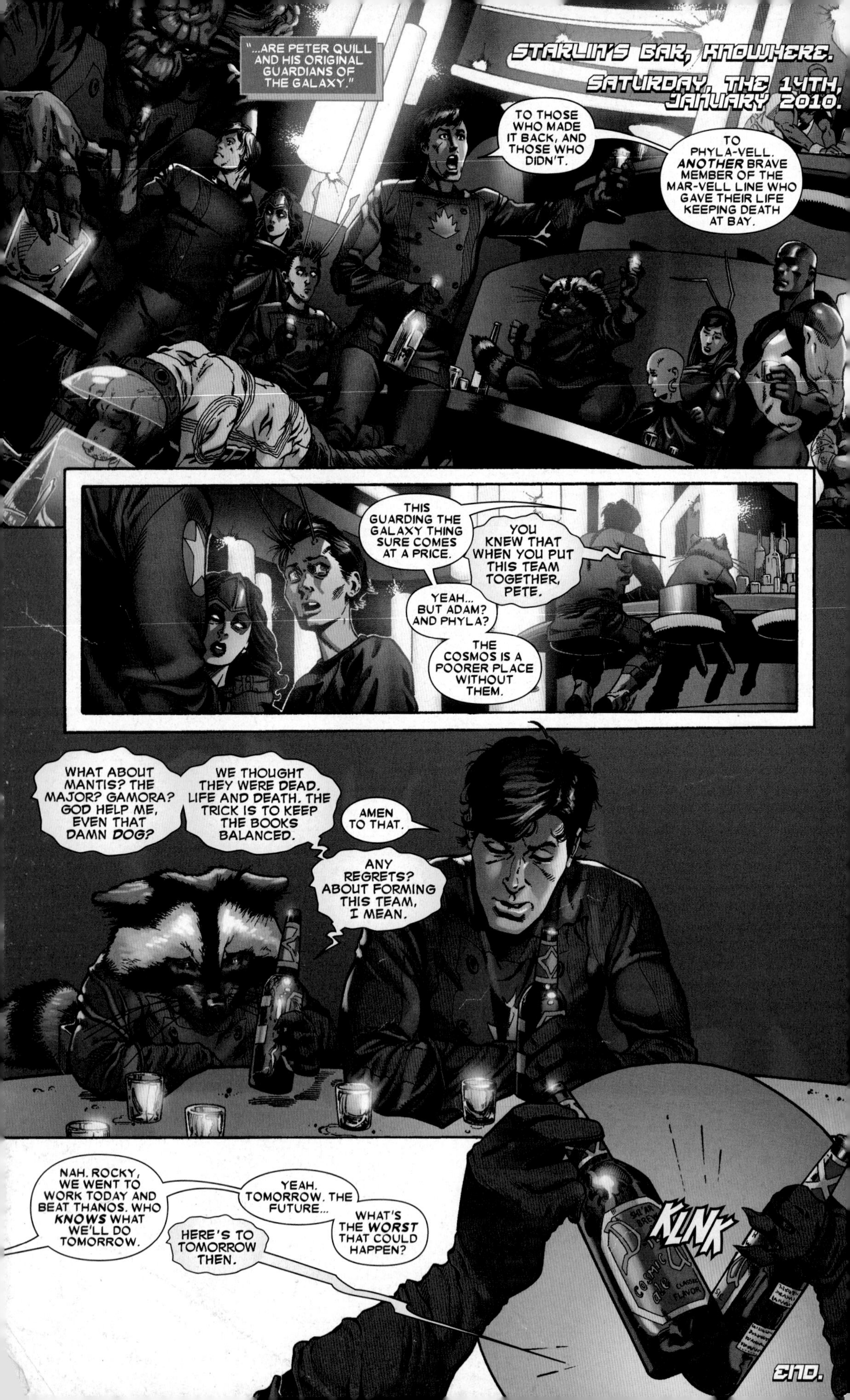
"...ARE PETER QUILL AND HIS ORIGINAL GUARDIANS OF THE GALAXY."
STARLIN'S BAR, KNOWHERE.
SATURDAY, THE 14TH, JANUARY 2010.
TO THOSE WHO MADE IT BACK, AND THOSE WHO DIDN'T.
TO PHYLA-VELL. ANOTHER BRAVE MEMBER OF THE MAR-VELL LINE WHO GAVE THEIR LIFE KEEPING DEATH AT BAY.
THIS GUARDING THE GALAXY THING SURE COMES AT A PRICE.
YOU KNEW THAT WHEN YOU PUT THIS TEAM TOGETHER, PETE.
YEAH... BUT ADAM? AND PHYLA?
THE COSMOS IS A POORER PLACE WITHOUT THEM.
WHAT ABOUT MANTIS? THE MAJOR? GAMORA? GOD HELP ME, EVEN THAT DAMN DOG?
WE THOUGHT THEY WERE DEAD. LIFE AND DEATH. THE TRICK IS TO KEEP THE BOOKS BALANCED.
AMEN TO THAT.
ANY REGRETS? ABOUT FORMING THIS TEAM, I MEAN.
NAH, ROCKY, WE WENT TO WORK TODAY AND BEAT THANOS. WHO KNOWS WHAT WE'LL DO TOMORROW.
YEAH. TOMORROW. THE FUTURE...
WHAT'S THE WORST THAT COULD HAPPEN?
HERE'S TO TOMORROW THEN.
KLINK
END.

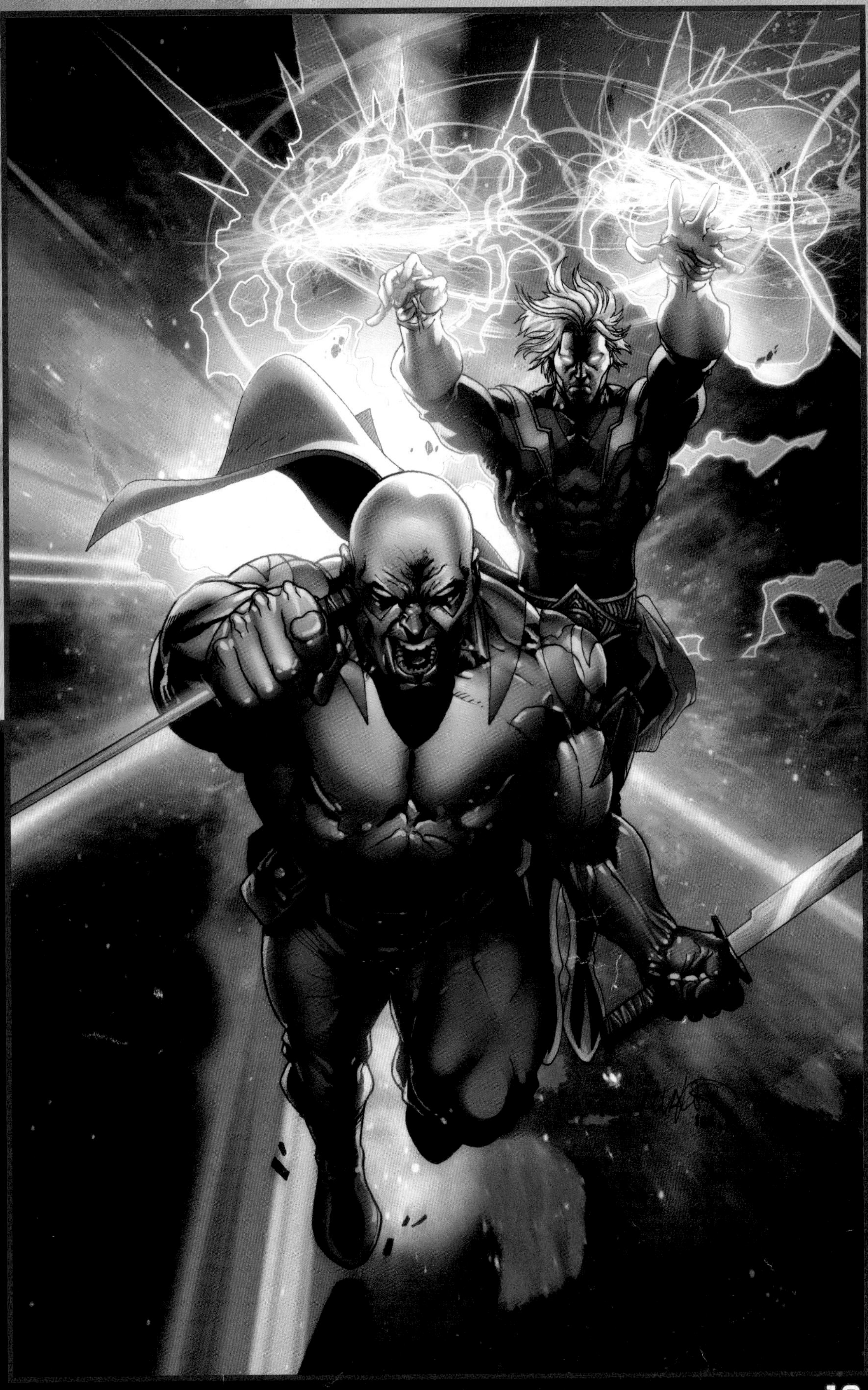

UNUSED COVER BY SALVADOR LARROCA & FRANK D'ARMATA

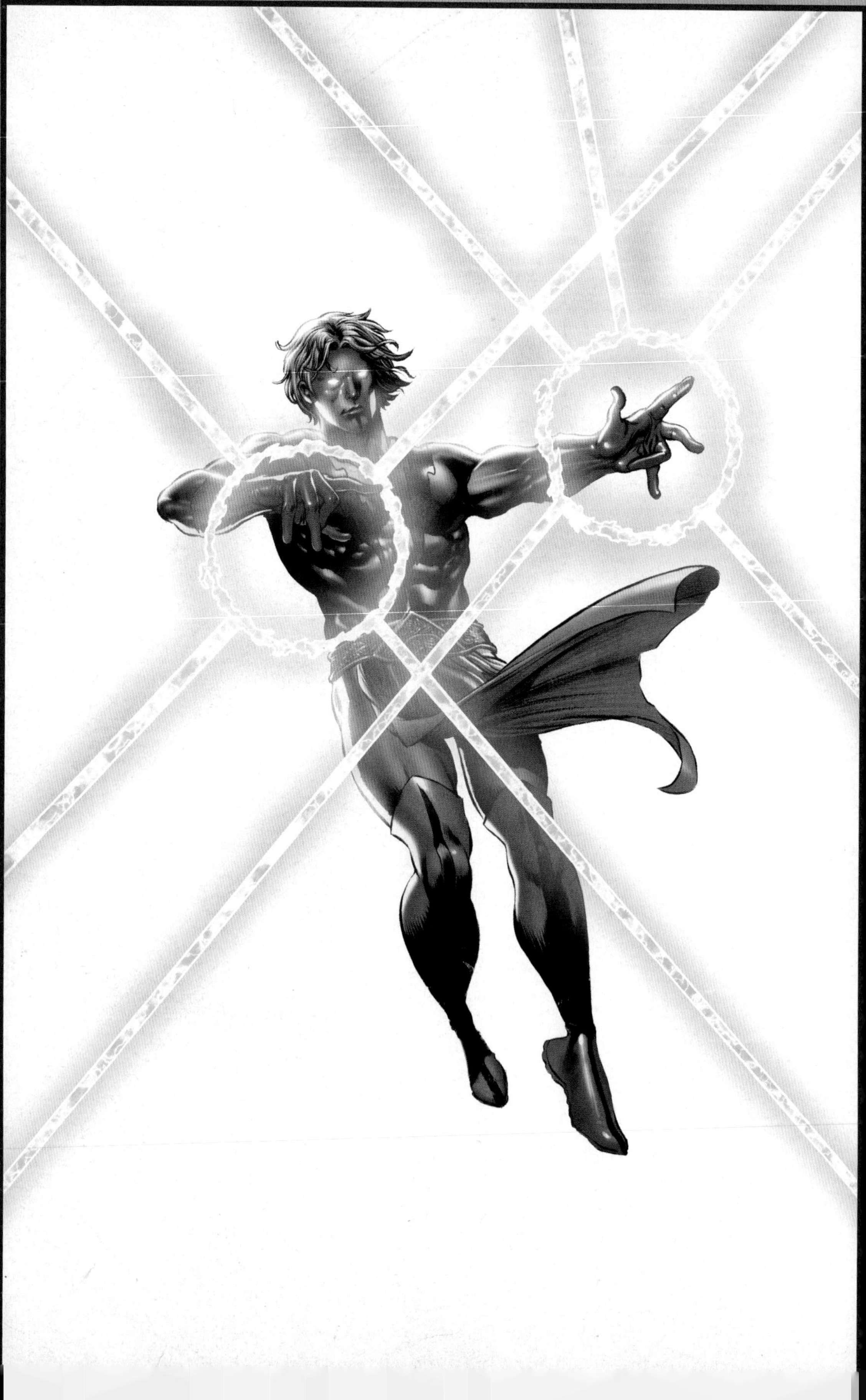

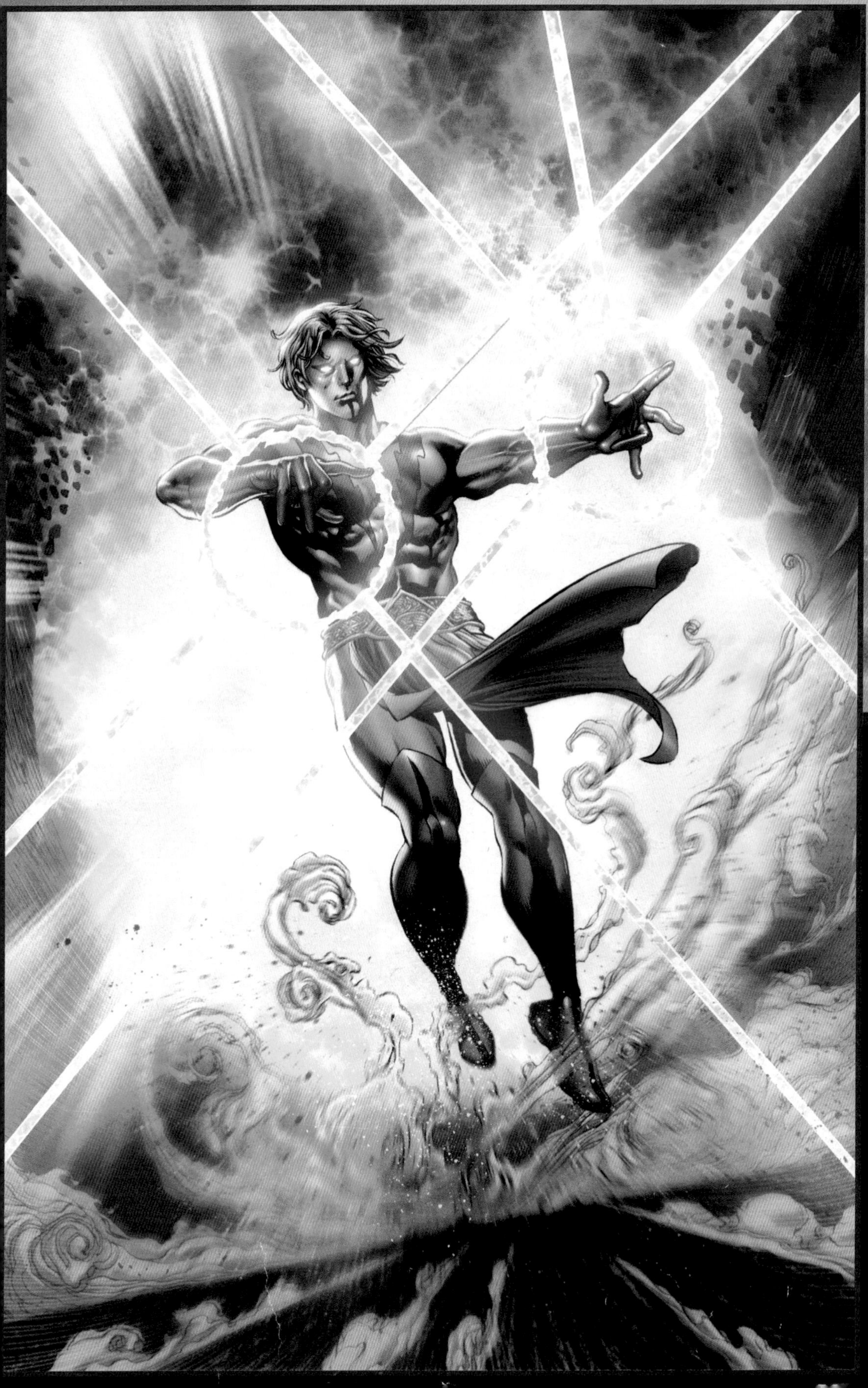

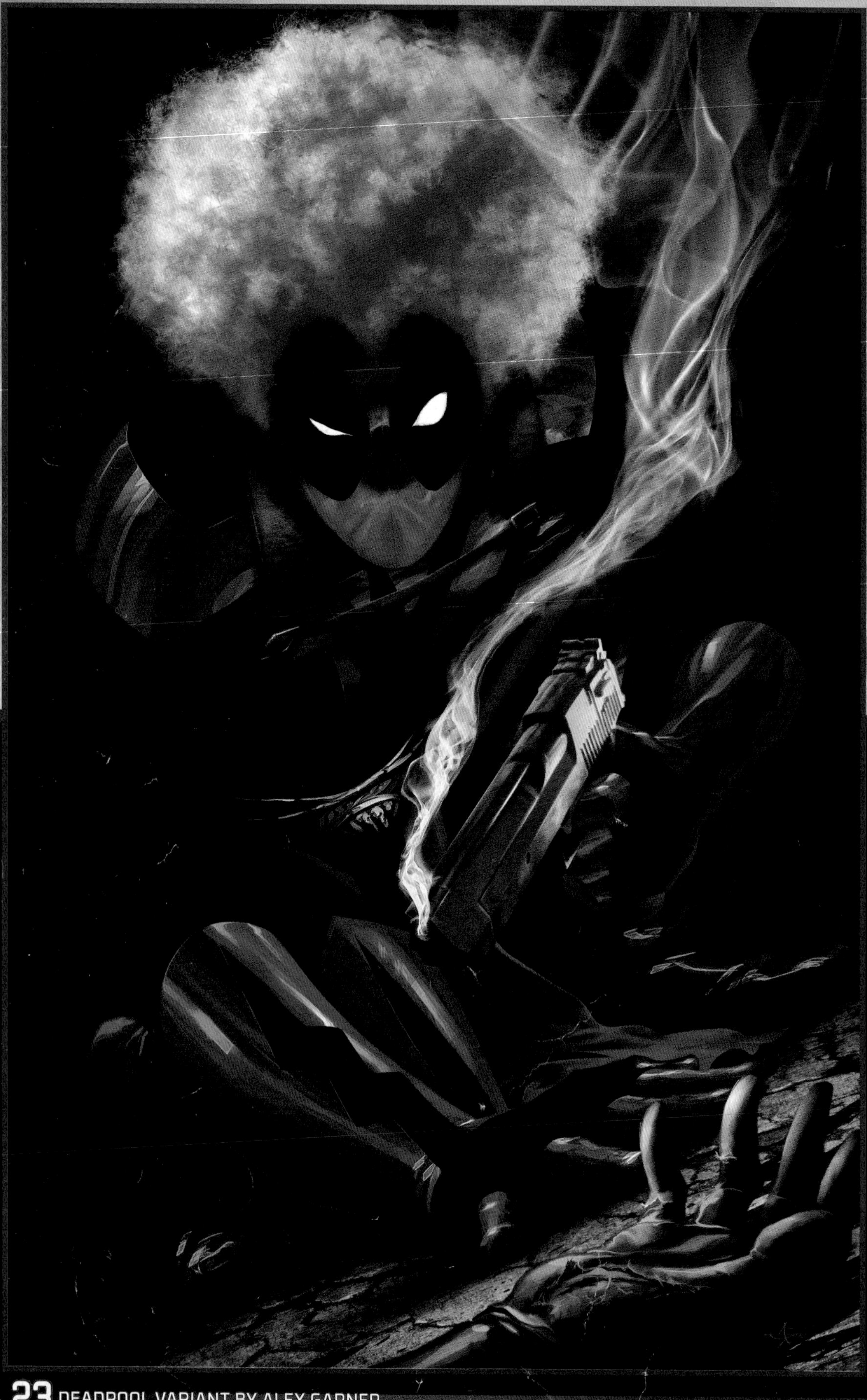

23 DEADPOOL VARIANT BY ALEX GARNER

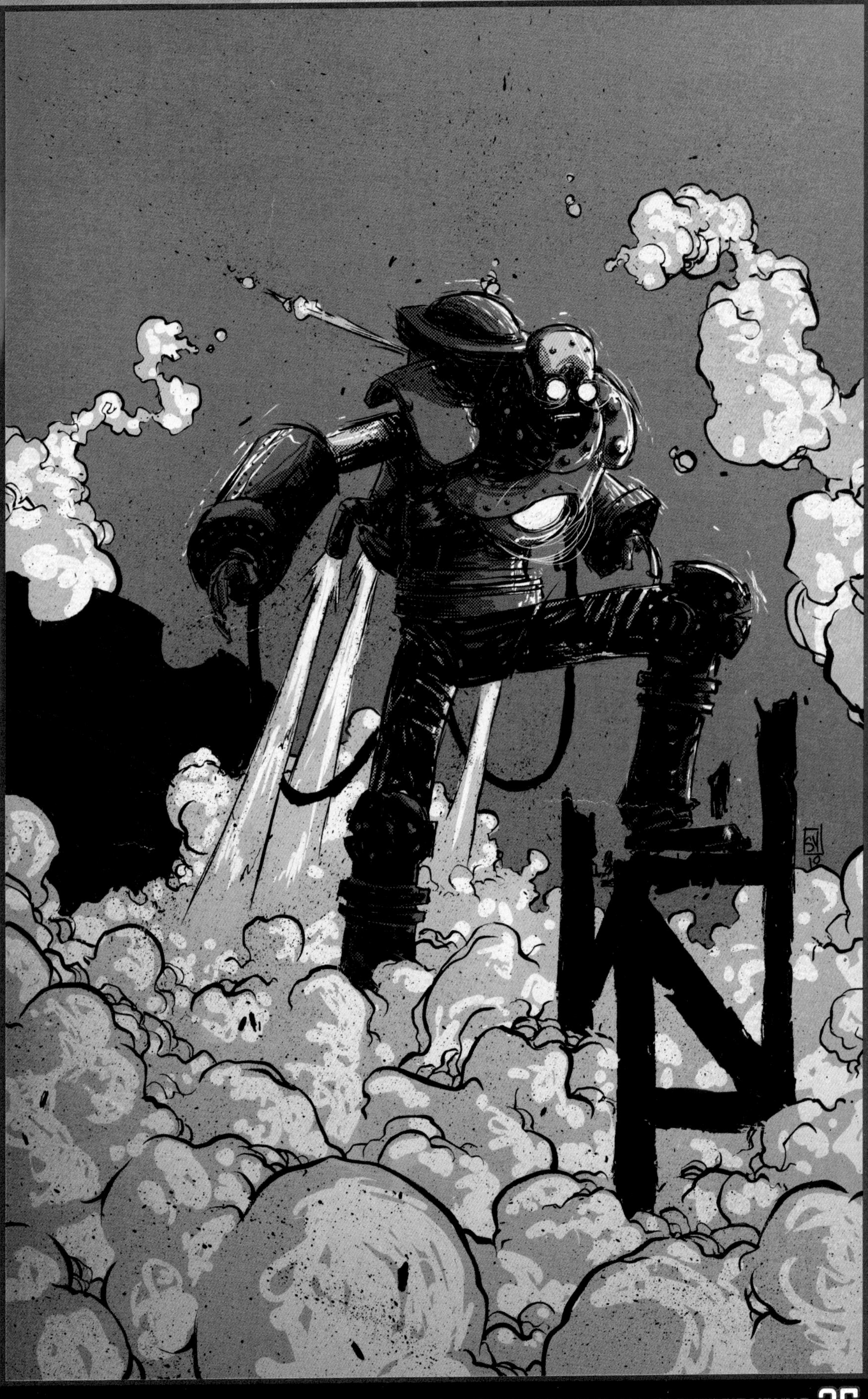

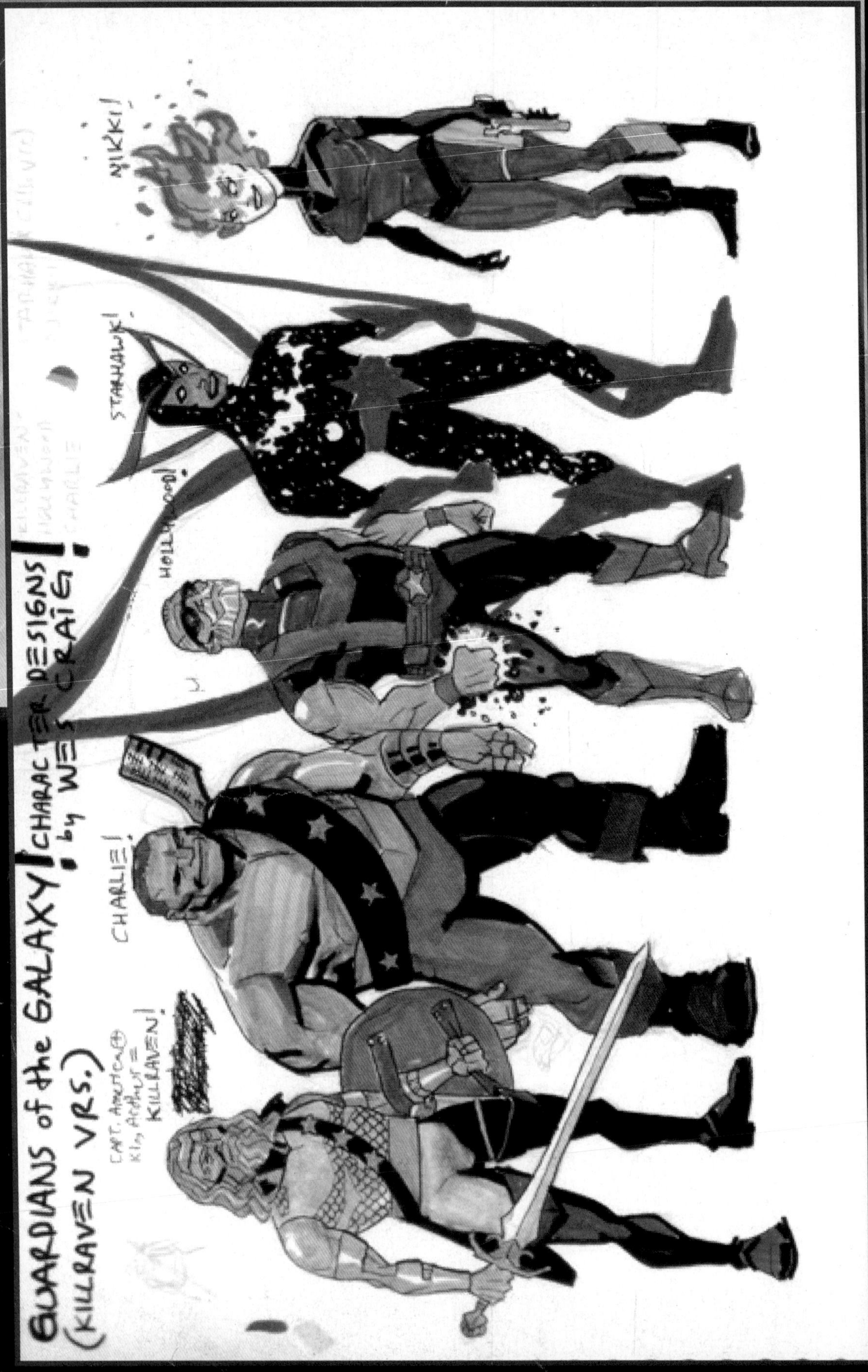
GUARDIANS of the GALAXY! CHARACTER DESIGNS!
(KILLRAVEN VRS.)
by WES CRAIG!
CAPT. AMERICA + KING ARTHUR = KILLRAVEN!
CHARLIE!
HOLLYWOOD!
STARHAWK!
NIKKI!

CHARACTER DESIGNS BY WES CRAIG

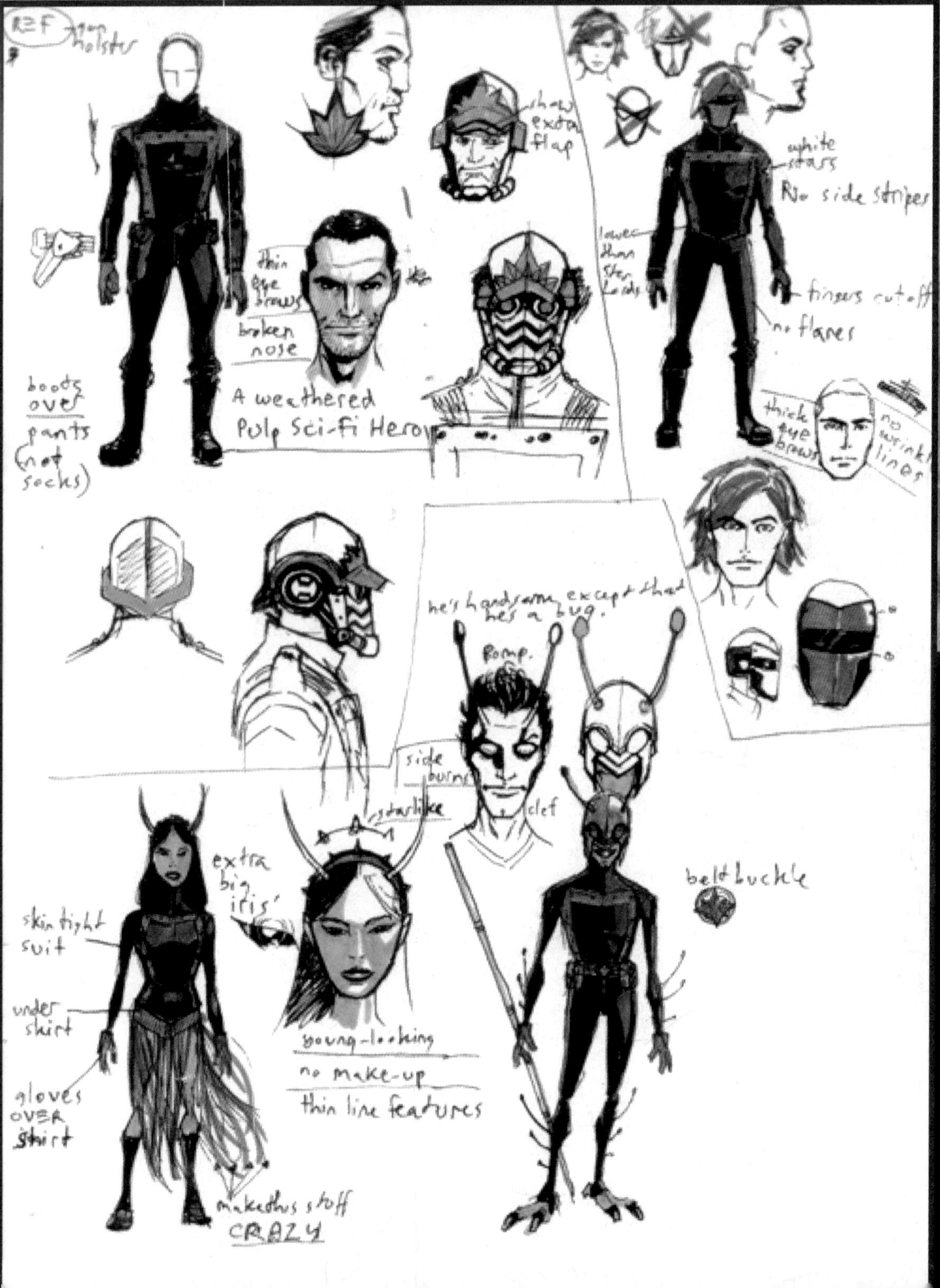
REF
gun holster
boots over pants (not socks)
thin eye brows
broken nose
A weathered Pulp Sci-Fi Hero
show extra flap
white stars
No side stripes
lower than Star Lords
fingers cut off
no flares
thick eye brows
no wrinkle lines
he's handsome, except that he's a bug.
Pomp.
side burns
starlike
clef
belt buckle
extra big iris'
skin tight suit
under skirt
gloves over skirt
make this stuff CRAZY
young-looking
no make-up
thin line features

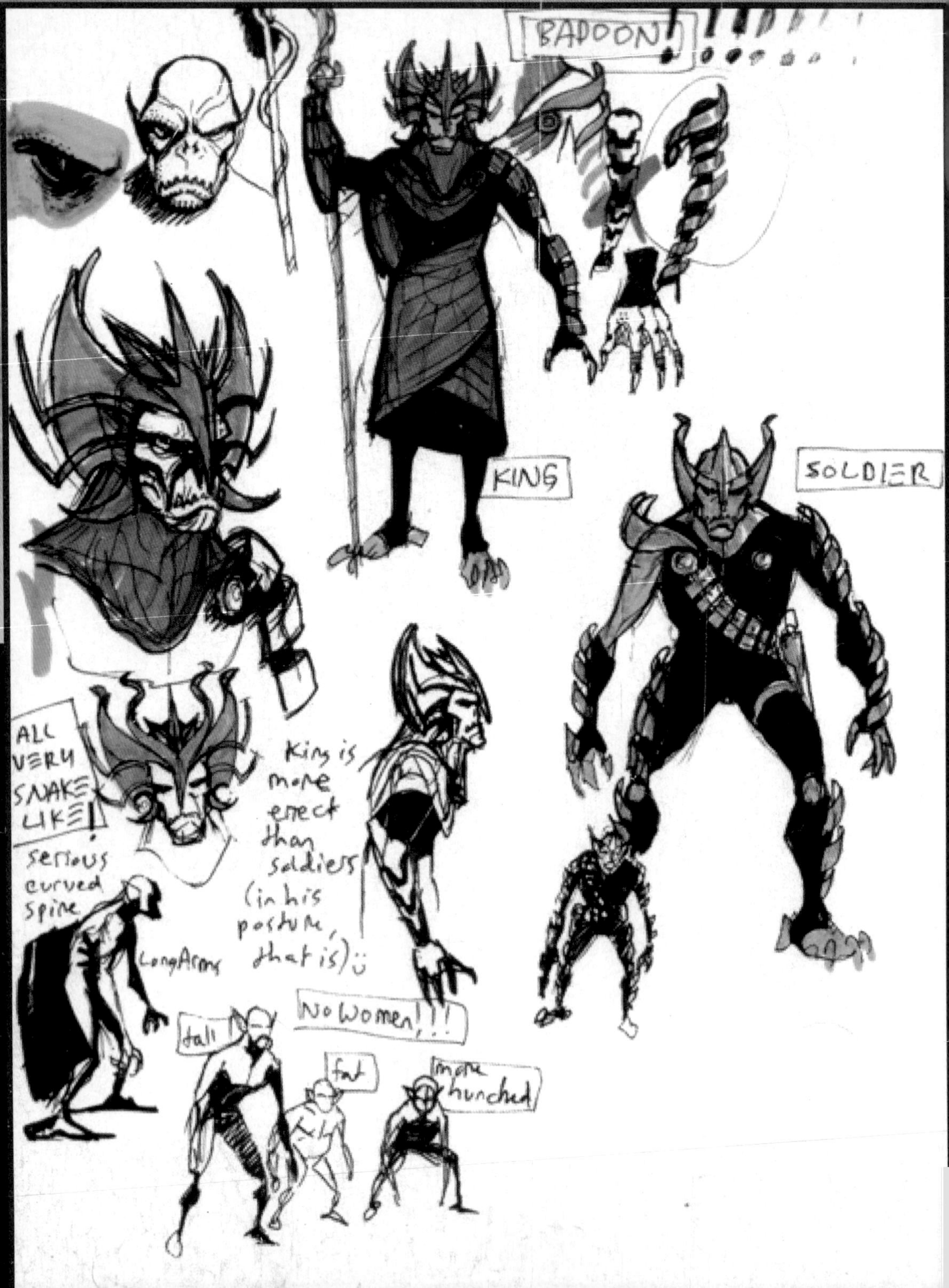
BADOON!
KING
SOLDIER
ALL VERY SNAKE LIKE!
King is more erect than soldiers (in his posture, that is)
serious curved spine
Long Arms
No Women!!!
tall!
fat
more hunched